POSTSCRIPT

to

YESTERDAY

American Life and Thought

1896 - 1946

POSTSCRIPT

to

YESTERDAY

American Life and Thought

1896 - 1946

By LLOYD MORRIS

HARPER COLOPHON BOOKS

Harper & Row, Publishers, New York

This book was originally published by Random House, Inc., under the title *Postscript to Yesterday—America: The Last Fifty Years,* and is here reprinted by arrangement.

First Harper Colophon edition published 1965 by Harper & Row, Publishers, Incorporated, New York.

LIBRARY OF CONGRESS CATALOG CARD NUMBER: 47-11260

TO
MARY JO DANGERFIELD
AND
FRANCIS SPENCER
BECAUSE THEY ARE VERY YOUNG
AMERICANS

Table of Contents

PREFACE   xi

INTRODUCTION: *The Look of Life*   xv

Part One: THE SOCIAL SCENE

CHAPTER I: *The Lady Vanishes*   3

    1. An Old Lady and a New Day   3
    2. Pleasures and Palaces   7
    3. The Restlessness of the Elect   11
    4. Career in the Drawing Room   21
    5. Lady Into Fox   26

CHAPTER II: *The Woman Takes Over*   32

    1. The Volcano of Unrest   32
    2. Deputy for Conscience   35
    3. Rebels   42
    4. Anonymous Transformers   47
    5. The Dictators and the Folkways   52
    6. Puritan Crusader   56

CHAPTER III: *The Fingers in the Pie*   64

    1. Old Plot, New Trappings   64
    2. The Manners of Normalcy   68

3. "Decay's Effacing Finger"   74
4. The Day Before Tomorrow   83

Part Two: THE INTERPRETERS' HOUSE

CHAPTER IV: *The Melancholy of the Masters*   89

1. The Return of the Native   89
2. The Morals of Mammon   96
3. The Will to Believe   102

CHAPTER V: *The Skepticism of the Young*   107

1. A Gospel of Doubt   107
2. The Frightened Optimist   110
3. A Lost Leader   115
4. Puzzled Iconoclast   121
5. Mirage   130

CHAPTER VI: *Seven Pillars of Wisdom*   134

1. The National Gadfly   134
2. Babbitt Strikes Out   145
3. The Great Liquidation   148
4. Salvage   154
5. Sphinx in the South   157
6. Thunder on the Left   162
7. Fiery Gospel   166

CHAPTER VII: *Across the Footlights*   172

1. Man-Milliner, Plus   172
2. "All Man's Blundering Unhappiness"   177
3. The Imp in Doctor Pangloss   184
4. A "New Realism"   189
5. Protest and Prophecy   199
6. Gay, but Wistful   204

Part Three: A MATTER OF RECORD

CHAPTER VIII: *The Uses of News*   217

    1. Tribune of the People   217
    2. Problem in Yellow   227
    3. Bluestocking in Babylon   246
    4. The Conscience of Main Street   252
    5. Savior of the Simple-Minded   259

CHAPTER IX: *"Raising the Tone of Democracy"*   267

    1. Grand Lama of the Matrons   267
    2. The Mirror of the Muckrakers   278
    3. Evangelists and Entertainers   310

Part Four: THE FEAST OF REASON AND THE FLOW OF SOUL

CHAPTER X: *All Life is an Experiment*   321

    1. Yankee Socrates   321
    2. The Great Dissenter   339
    3. Savonarola in Silk   356
    4. A Pragmatist Looks at Tomorrow   368

CHAPTER XI: *The Mourners Go About the Streets*   378

    1. The Pensive Trinity   378
    2. The Horizons of Despair   401

CHAPTER XII: *The Mysticism of the Middle Classes*   422

    1. The Unity of Good   422
    2. Hope for a Miracle   431

CONCLUSION: *At the End of an Era*   444

Bibliography   451

Index   467

Preface

THIS BOOK is not a formal history.

It is the first of two in which I hope to sketch the principal social changes that took place in American life between 1896 and 1946, and consider what their effect has been on our minds and hearts. The attitude of a people to the society in which they live is important. It modifies the climate of their experience, the moral weather of their time. In the past fifty years, the attitude of Americans has undergone a spectacular reversal. Their moral weather has shifted from fair to overcast.

The half century from 1896 to 1946 was an extraordinary era. It completely transformed our physical and social environment. Unprecedented advances in science, invention and technology radically altered the American way of life. The era brought us the most characteristic features of our present civilization: the automobile and airplane; the modern newspaper and magazine; the movie and radio; the skyscraper; mass production; a developed finance capitalism; nationwide labor organization—to mention only a few. Customs, manners and morals were revolutionized. The democratic process effected numerous, far-reaching reforms on many fronts. The American woman achieved an entirely new status. The American standard of living steadily rose, surpassing that of every other country in the world.

To the citizens of less fortunate nations it seemed that Americans, almost miraculously, were being granted conditions which should insure a good life for everyone. In 1896, most Americans believed it. Confidence in the future, and faith in their collective ability to make things come right, prevailed. Of course there were dark areas in the national life; and many grave problems were still to be solved. Time would do away with both; conscience required it, and intelligence would find a way. The American people knew that they were moving along the highroad of progress, and moving fast. They were convinced that just beyond the horizon lay the promised land. The sense of certainty came as naturally to them as the vision of a splendid destiny. To be a pessimist was to be a very queer fish. Even the discontented were optimistic, and the reformers who pleaded their cause admitted no doubts of eventual success. Who could deny that a more abundant life was within the nation's grasp? Americans differed chiefly about the best means of reaching what was so obviously attainable.

Their mood, in 1946, was very different. During the interval they had advanced, as no other nation in history, toward power, wealth and material possessions. In the common view these were what made existence more secure and more satisfying. But few Americans considered life as secure and satisfying as it had been fifty years earlier. Those who looked to the future displayed no serenity. Visitors from abroad noted with astonishment an atmosphere of tension and apprehensiveness more extreme than that prevailing in war-wrecked Europe. Confidence and faith had evaporated. Skepticism was commonplace. Pessimism was not eccentric. But this reversal of attitude, this shift in moral weather, had not come about suddenly. The American outlook had been gradually changing for many years.

In this there is an astonishing paradox. The past fifty years were not only an era of unexampled progress and remarkable social gains. They were also an era of deepening spiritual disillusion: Those writers and thinkers who spoke most authoritatively for the American people, and who most influenced their attitude to life, expressed it. In their interpretations of American life, there is the record of an increasing disenchantment with the social order; a growing conviction that existence, for the average American, was deteriorating. As the years passed, the old American dream took on the quality of a mirage. Faith gave way to disbelief in the possibility of achieving that more abundant life for all which—however defined—had been the dominant national ideal. We began the period with a sense of security and an assumption of orderly progress. We end it apparently bereft of both—a people whose freedom, power, material advantages and way of life are widely envied throughout the world; but whose confidence, and faith in their future, have signally diminished.

The parallel developments of progress and disillusion are the subject of this book, and of the one with which I hope to follow it. The next volume will deal with what may be described as the tangible features of our civilization: industrial change under expanding finance capitalism; the relations of capital and labor; science, invention and technology; politics; the evolution of our characteristic architecture; the effect of the movie and radio on our culture.

The present book deals with factors notably less tangible. It surveys radical changes that occurred in our way of life. These, in the aggregate, amounted to a revolution in customs, manners, morals and experience. While American life was thus being transformed, the attitude of the American people was being influenced by newspapers and magazines; by writers of fiction and writers for the theater; by philosophers and social theorists; by proponents of various gospels which attracted large followings. In so far as they interpreted the nature and probable consequences of social change, all these forces were shaping our contemporary culture. I have tried to deal with them as makers of the moral weather in which we are living today.

In a sense, this book attempts to tell the story of the American mind and heart during the past fifty years. Because it is a story I have used the narrative method. Because the story involves many people not all of whom will be equally familiar to all readers, I have sought to make them as vivid and vital as they seemed in their own day. Throughout the book, I have used phrases taken directly from the writings of authors; from correspondence and books of memoirs; from articles in magazines and newspapers. I have used quotation marks only to identify a quotation of several connected sentences. Readers who may be interested in consulting the sources will find a complete bibliography for their use.

A number of people have contributed generously to the making of this book. I am greatly indebted to Robert N. Linscott of Random House, whose enthusiasm for the project led me to undertake it. During the long period of research and writing, I drew heavily on his guidance, always wise; and on his patience, apparently inexhaustible. He read and discussed with me every draft of every chapter as it was completed. He constantly opened fresh perspectives, and always furnished incentive and encouragement. His contribution was a collaborative effort. My gratitude is the greater because, in time, I learned that he did not consider it an effort. It was natural to him to give what he gave, and he would be the last to realize—as I do very profoundly— that the gift was unique and, to any writer, beyond price.

Miss Nannine Joseph, my good friend as well as my agent, also tire- lessly read many versions of a long manuscript. She was devoted in her solicitude, and very helpful in her criticism, and I record my lasting appreciation. For information about various matters within their per- sonal experience, I am deeply grateful to Mrs. Yvette B. Andrews; Mr. and Mrs. Will Irwin; Dr. Frank A. Manny; Miss Sarah Warder Mac- Connell; and the late Richard W. G. Welling. For an unselfish kind- ness which advanced my work, I warmly thank Dean Robert G. Ram- say, of Olivet College, Olivet, Michigan.

The research for this book owes much to the exceptional resources of The New York Society Library. For their courteous assistance, and many useful suggestions, I am grateful to Miss Edith Crowell, Mrs. Frederick G. King, Miss Helen Ruskell, and Miss Marjorie Watkins of the Library's staff. My friend George Freedley, Curator of the Theater Collection of the New York Public Library, placed at my service all of the Collection's valuable material. To him, and to Paul Myers of his staff, I offer my thanks. For some bibliographical assistance, I thank Richard McLaughlin; and for assistance in preparing the manuscript for the press, Kendall Smith.

INTRODUCTION

The Look of Life

SOME RECALLED the tinkle of bells on bright winter mornings, after snow, when the sleighs came out. Some thought fondly of drives homeward, through the summer dusk, in the family surrey, everyone happily weary after a picnic. Others—and in 1946 they were quite elderly—saw themselves among a band of youths and girls, swiftly pedalling along quiet streets: the "bicycle craze" had been at its height. To those old enough to remember it, the America of 1896 returned in quaint images. In fifty years it had become almost as remote, very nearly as idyllic, as the America of the founding fathers.

Across the land, in tree-shaded cities and towns, existence was unhurried and seemed tranquil. For many people, it was also gracious. Looking at their own communities, most Americans took pride in what William Dean Howells called the large cheerful average of health and success and happy life. One noticed this in the residential quarters. The houses wore an air of solid comfort; they had been built to endure, to pass from one generation to another. Set back from the street on lawns or grass plots guarded by a metal stag, they were embellished with fretwork and fancy glass, and many had wide verandahs. On warm nights, after the lamplighter had made his rounds, the young people gathered there. One heard the strumming of mandolins and guitars, and voices singing "Only a Bird in a Gilded Cage," or something from *Robin Hood* or *The Geisha*.

From the windows of these houses, behind two layers of lace curtains, the upper middle class surveyed its world and found it good. Did not the future lie with them? And was it not inexhaustibly promising? Indeed, a kind of renaissance had begun, a flowering of the middle-class individualist spirit that was not confined to the prosperous. This spirit was purposeful and expansive. It was certain that the abundant life in America was not a frail plant. The old physical frontiers had closed; but there would always be new frontiers of opportunity. No matter how humble one's immediate circumstances, one could scarcely help, in time, rising above them. The traditional American faith in progress projected itself upon personal life, and hope ran high. Had not the nation's "big men"—Andrew Carnegie, John D. Rockefeller, George F. Baker, for example—come up the hard way, from modest beginnings as clerks or laborers? What they could do, others could also. On every social level the general experience afforded ample warrant for confidence. Today was good. But tomorrow would be still better.

The social aspects of life were pleasant. Even in the great cities there was much neighboring and casual dropping in. It originated in a simple errand, or no errand at all, and was often prolonged into a leisurely visit. People also paid calls, but these were of a more ritual nature. One always called on a bride soon after her marriage, and, accompanied by her mother, she promptly returned the courtesy. When anyone had died, one called on the bereaved, bringing a delicate but nourishing token of affection: a jar of calf's-foot jelly flavored with wine, a light cake or meringue, a bottle of Tokay, to tempt the reluctant appetite of sorrow. Church people—and who were not?—called on newcomers to the parish as soon as they were properly settled. These were visits of ceremony, obligatory to the well bred, like the party call with which one acknowledged hospitality, even from one's closest friends—calls with cards and kid gloves, as the womenfolk said.

In the larger cities, matrons who were sensitive to fashion had begun to receive on stated "days at home." The gas-lit parlor was thronged, and so was the adjacent dining room, where honored friends of the hostess presided over a coffee urn and chocolate pot, for tea was not considered appropriate to a "collation." The long dining-room table was spread with a snowy damask cloth that touched the floor, and it gleamed with silver and cut glass. There were salads of chicken and lobster; dainty sandwiches; trays of pastry; dishes of mints and chocolates; and sometimes a fancy ice from the caterer's, a rococo structure of spun sugar, lace-paper frills and satin ribbon bows. On New Year's Day, ladies remained at home to receive, and gentlemen went from house to house paying their respects. And in the dining room there would be a great bowl of creamy eggnog, flanked by a ham and a turkey, a dish of scalloped oysters, massive cheeses and a majestic plum pudding.

For Americans liked to eat heartily. They relished good, solid breakfasts: eggs, with pork chops and fried potatoes, hot bread with jam, buckwheat cakes or waffles with maple syrup, coffee with heavy cream. A meal was "not right" without meat, so for dinner there would always be a large roast, and for luncheon or supper a thick beefsteak or a fowl. The family table was loaded with homemade pickles and preserves, and midday and evening meals ended with several kinds of cake or pie. In many communities, prosperous folk never thought of having fresh fruit or green vegetables during the winter, and could not have procured them had they wished to. When spring came, they laid away their heavy underwear and thick outer garments, and underwent a course of sulphur and molasses, or rhubarb and soda, or sarsaparilla, which were reputed to relieve the ailments resulting from a rich winter diet.

Within the home, an established routine strengthened the sense of permanence which nearly everyone took for granted. The same rhythm, inflexibly regular as that of a metronome, governed those who "kept help" and those who did not. Monday was washday; it was a matter of pride to have everything sunning on the line as early as possible. Tuesday was given over to ironing; Wednesday, to sewing and mending. On Thursdays, the womenfolk usually enjoyed a respite; attired in their best, they went shopping or paid a round of calls. On Fridays, there was house cleaning to be done, and every week a different room was thoroughly "turned out." Saturday brought the week's baking, for good housekeepers took a dim view of the newfangled "baker's bread." After church on Sunday there was always company for dinner: this meant extra cooking, a display of the best napery and china, and a sherbet served with the roast.

Notwithstanding these recurrent physical disciplines, the popular "doctor books" had begun to warn women of the dangers attending a sedentary, indoor existence. It would hurt their figures and complexion, relax their solids, weaken their minds. Could they then vie with Miss Lillian Russell, the reigning cynosure of masculine admiration? Miss

Russell's figure and complexion were exquisite, her solids notably un-relaxed; it was obviously not the strength of her mind that fluttered male hearts. Indeed, strength of mind appeared to be a dubious at-tribute. As exemplified by the members of women's clubs, it was arousing some concern. The clubs were a source of special anxiety to Edward Bok, who had succeeded in making *The Ladies' Home Journal* a final authority on all amenities. Presently, in the pages of the maga-zine, ex-President Grover Cleveland would condemn them: the best and safest of clubs for a woman to patronize was her home. American wives and mothers, he declared, should be happy and contented in following the Divinely appointed paths of true womanhood, though all others, he said, might grope in the darkness of their own devices. The ex-President's admonition summed up a familiar uxorious text.

The vogue of the bicycle was taking the younger women outdoors. But, however healthful, it was not universally approved. It required the wearing of shorter—alas, one might say short—skirts, and fur-nished an incentive to impulsive ramblings. Old-fashioned folk doubted that it promoted feminine virtue. Mrs. Marion Harland Terhune—author of a widely esteemed volume of *Talks Upon Practical Subjects*—reserved her decision, but indicated little enthusiasm. The *fin-de-siècle* girl and her bicycle, Mrs. Terhune remarked, had not been acquainted long enough for the passage of correct judgment upon the consequence of the intimacy. However, the Boston Woman's Rescue League, experienced with intimacies unquestionably deplorable, based censure upon statistics. Of the frail and fallen to whom the League ministered, thirty percent, at one time or another, had been bicycle riders. Was further proof necessary that wheeling had a demoralizing influence on feminine character? Nevertheless the vogue persisted, a symptom of declining gentility, of the new, rude, free ways unaccount-ably attractive to the young. Clergymen in their sermons, newspapers in their editorials reiterated alarm in a searching question: "Where will this freedom end?"

In "Society"—that playground of the elect so exhaustively reported by the press—an old guard was making its last stand in the defense of decorum. Its rule was being contested, but its prestige had scarcely suffered. So, on the whole, manners and customs reflected a conven-tional elegance. And, even behind its invisible Chinese wall, the

American woman's capacity for enjoyment flourished. Existence was a round of dinner parties and balls. At formal dinners for the young set, there were half a dozen wine glasses at every plate. One was served sherry, hock, champagne and either claret or port. The girls might inadvertently permit their glasses to be filled, but they drank nothing unless a little champagne. When, at a signal from their hostess, they retired to the drawing room, a tray of liqueurs, generally six or more, was brought to the men in the smoking room, with their coffee. Ball dresses swept the floor, and the waltz often jeopardized their future, but to have carried the train over her arm for economical reasons would have queered a girl's career.

The whole country was still discussing the recent foreign alliances of three of its wealthiest heiresses. The daughter of William C. Whitney had been given in marriage to Sir Almeric Paget, and the daughter of Jay Gould had been won by Comte Boni de Castellane, an impecunious aristocrat whose candid avowal of financial ambition displeased a large segment of the public. But the wedding of Miss Consuelo Vanderbilt to the ninth Duke of Marlborough—the most magnificent in American social annals—had provided a vicarious esthetic experience, as well as an occasion for the moral interpretation of economics. Presently, European economic realism was to disenchant even the most senti-mentally nostalgic of Americans. For publication of correspondence between the estranged King and Queen of Serbia revealed that the royal pair had determined to rehabilitate the fortunes of the dynasty by marrying their heir to any available American girl possessed of a suf-ficient fortune. Meanwhile, the American moral sense was being stim-ulated by the recreations of a native aristocracy. In one of New York's costliest restaurants, a bachelor dinner terminated with the ap-pearance of an immense pie from which there emerged, not an inno-cent four-and-twenty blackbirds, but too many young women too scantily clad. And, at the new Waldorf Hotel, a costume ball of un-precedented extravagance thrilled "Society," but produced a nation-wide storm of disapprobation.

Americans who did not live in the metropolitan centers read of these diversions, but continued to indulge a predilection for church suppers and picnics. The church supper was not only an ethical op-portunity, but a competitive ritual, since every family provided a share of the refreshments, and there was great rivalry among the women to contribute the largest amount of the richest, most palatable and irresistible food. As the spring advanced, families were seized by a nostalgia for the simple life. A special equipment of stout market baskets, tin plates, cups and spoons, steel knives and forks, and worn napkins was exhumed; appropriate fare was prepared and packed; and behind a patient horse the household set out to spend a day communing with nature. City folk, on warm summer evenings, often rode out to the new "trolley parks"—miniature Coney Islands developed by the streetcar companies to increase their revenue—where the pleasures to be enjoyed included dancing and boating, as well as excellent concerts by famous bands, such as John Philip Sousa's, which played the most popular marches and melodious operatic selections. Some of the trolley parks even boasted a "Midway" remotely patterned upon the celebrated attraction of the Chicago World's Fair, but destitute of the notorious "hoochy-koochy" introduced there by a buxom cultural missionary named Little Egypt.

There were, already, indications of more sophisticated amusements to come, though few took them seriously. At Koster and Bial's Music Hall, in New York City, there had been an exhibition of Thomas A. Edison's "kinetoscope," and audiences strained their eyes at a perplexing novelty—pictures that flickered on an enormous screen, in which human beings appeared to be in motion. In Chicago, an endurance run had been held for the new, preposterous horseless carriage. The son of a Michigan farmer, employed in a Detroit machine shop, had built himself one of these contraptions, and had never wanted anything so much as to get to the Chicago race. But Henry Ford was unable to borrow enough money to make the trip. In 1896, astute old P. T. Barnum was featuring, in the foreground of his spectacular circus posters, a horseless carriage to be seen every day in the new street parade—"the famous Duryea Motorwagon or Motorcycle"—moving under its own power among the elephants, camels, clowns and freaks.

In the nation's capital Professor Samuel P. Langley of the Smithsonian Institution had built large models of a steam-driven "aerodrome"—and the strange-looking things had managed to fly through the air for distances of from one half mile to one mile. Professor Langley was seeking to interest the War and Navy Departments in the further development of this device. He was a taciturn man, proud, dignified, always awesome, but the initial success of his experiments so delighted him that he offered a young woman the greatest treat he could give his friends. He took her, after hours, to the Rock Creek Zoo, and made the kangaroo jump and the hyena laugh. Meanwhile, in Dayton, Ohio, two brothers named Wright—they were bicycle mechanics, and had received no professional training as engineers—read of the death of Otto Lilienthal, a German pioneer in experiments with gliding machines. And the Wrights, in their spare time, began to build one.

Who would have anticipated more than momentary interest in pictures that flickered, or horseless locomotion? And certainly there seemed to be little possibility that men would fly until they became angels. As for diversions, city folk already had an embarrassing choice. There were the "variety" or vaudeville shows, and the old-fashioned minstrel shows still put on by Lew Dockstader and "Honey-boy" Evans. There was the theater, and there was grand opera. Those who had been enchanted by Edwin Booth and Lawrence Barrett, by Mme. Ristori and Mme. Modjeska and the Italian Salvini, sometimes complained that the stage was falling upon evil days. Younger folk did not agree. Could not one still see Joseph Jefferson in *Rip Van Winkle*, and James O'Neill in *Virginius* and *The Count of Monte Cristo*? Did not Ada Rehan tour the country in Shakespere? The elegant John Drew furnished a model to gilded youth. Which was the more beautiful, blonde Lillian Russell or brunette Maxine Elliott? One bought cigarettes because their pictures were in the boxes. The girls quarreled over the merits of their "matinée-idols," James K. Hackett and William Faversham. Everyone admired the talent of William Gillette—but was Julia Marlowe or Maude Adams the finer actress?

One saw these celebrated players on tour. And one could attend grand opera on tour likewise. But it was even better to visit the Metropolitan Opera House in New York. The "diamond horseshoe" furnished a spectacle of fashion and wealth superior to the display visible, during the after-theater-supper hour, at Delmonico's and Rector's. One could hear *Tristan und Isolde* with Mme. Lillian Nordica and the famous de Reszke brothers—what feminine heart did not beat the faster for Jean de Reszke? One could hear *Faust*, and have one's choice of Marguerites among Mme. Nellie Melba, Mme. Emma Calvé, and regally lovely Mme. Emma Eames. One could hear Melba in any of a half dozen great coloratura roles, and Calvé in her sultry, coquettish *Carmen*. There were other pleasures for music lovers, also. Throughout the country they flocked to the piano recitals of handsome, romantic Ignace Paderewski, who played the music of Chopin as only

Chopin himself may have played it to George Sand. And, for the really earnest, there were the great symphony orchestras of New York, Boston, Chicago, Cincinnati and Pittsburgh.

A trip to Chicago or New York was an event; except to the very wealthy and those in delicate health, winter holidays were little known. Summer was holiday time, and for July and August city dwellers of moderate means sent their wives and children off to boardinghouses and hotels at the shore, the lakes, or in the mountains. For weeks beforehand, the womenfolk were busy with seamstresses and with house cleaning. There was a continuous sloshing of water, a pervasive noxious odor of ammonia, strong soap, tarpaper and camphor. Carpets were removed, beaten, rolled, wrapped. The furniture lost its identity under drab gray covers as shapeless as a nun's habit. Intricately scrolled chandeliers were sheathed in tin foil. Every picture, sculpture and clock was shrouded in varnished mosquito netting. Awnings were lowered and shutters drawn against the sun. Familiar objects disappeared, and comfortable rooms were suddenly bleak and beggared. Then a big "carry-all" would drive up to the door, and the annual expedition was under way.

Old Orchard, Magnolia, Narragansett Beach, the resorts of the Jersey shore, Saratoga Springs, Great Barrington in the Berkshires, the Adirondacks, Mackinac—all had the same vast, wooden hotels with long, wide piazzas where the married women embroidered and gossiped, and the girls, always "pretty as a picture," idled away the time awaiting the attentions of any eligible youth whom providence might, but until the week end probably would not, send. The clerks were likely to be college boys earning their way—and this made the girls' mothers unusually vigilant from Mondays to Fridays. On Saturdays things looked up, with the arrival from town of brothers and beaux, and in the evening there was always a "hop"—usually followed by a late supper served with the compliments of the management. During the week, the older women rested or wrote letters in their rooms every afternoon, and the girls played croquet, or went for strolls. After the evening meal, a group would gather about the piano in one of the gaslit parlors, and sometimes there was a concert by the hotel "orchestra." In the long afternoons and longer evenings, many novels were read and discussed.

In 1896, they were reading *The Red Badge of Courage*, a curiously unsentimental tale of the War between the States by Stephen Crane, a twenty-five-year-old writer about whom everyone was talking. Another new writer, F. Hopkinson Smith, had won a large audience with *Tom Grogan*; and there was *A Lady of Quality*, by Mrs. Burnett. Old-fashioned readers were being disturbed by two religious novels: Elizabeth Stuart Phelps' *A Singular Life*, and Harold Frederic's *The Damnation of Theron Ware*. But everyone adored J. M. Barrie's *Sentimental Tommy*, and hoped for a sequel. Scarcely anyone had heard of a book destined to have a far more profound effect on American life than any of these. This was the work of a red-haired, strong-willed Boston spinster, in frail health as the result of a paralytic stroke suffered in girlhood. She had taken her manuscript to a firm of Boston publishers who agreed to print, at her expense, a few thousand copies for which she would be repaid if the demand warranted it. For who would have supposed that Miss Fannie Merritt Farmer's *The Boston Cooking School Cook Book* was to become a national domestic bible? Miss Farmer supervised a cooking school, but she did not enjoy even local fame as a born cook. And, in a day of seven-course dinners, when to be prosperous was also to be a gourmet, there seemed to be scant promise of delight in her puritanical doctrine that "food is anything which nourishes the body."

As the summer waned, Americans were being divided by a bitter political contest which aligned section against section, and class against class. Yet they were united in respect to the kind of future they wanted—whether they chose to secure it by casting their votes for "Morgan, McKinley and the Trusts," or for William Jennings Bryan, the boy orator of the Platte, whom conservative folk condemned for appealing to a roaring mob of inflammatory and reckless men on a platform of revolution. Governor McKinley announced himself as the implacable foe of a sudden, dangerous and revolutionary assault upon law and order. His opponent declared that the Democratic party was fighting in defense of American homes, families and posterity. By radically different means, McKinley and Bryan promised to bring about what everyone wanted: an enrichment of the abundant life in America. Apart from this, their purposes were as unlike as their platforms. They agreed only in believing the abundant life and the national destiny to be identical.

This was the belief of most Americans. Skeptics like Henry Adams were few, and even he asserted only privately that a materialistic society had no life except in materialistic success. A majority of his countrymen would have reckoned this conclusion false. Even to the most critical, the national scene presented a fairer picture. William Dean Howells, for example, was deeply troubled by many of the new forces in American life. He had become a socialist, and hardly liked to trust pen and ink with all the audacity of his social ideas. To his old friend, Henry James, he confessed that after fifty years of optimistic contact with "civilization," and its imputed ability to come out all right in the end, he was convinced that it would come out all wrong unless it based itself anew on a real equality. Yet he acknowledged that, in the main, the more smiling aspects of life were the more truly American. Could anyone, he wondered, not feel affection for the everyday world of America? Could anyone fail to catch the charm of its work-worn, care-worn, brave, kindly face?

Life, in that everyday world, still moved in a fixed orbit, and few questioned the permanence of its centers of attraction. This tacit assumption yielded a sense of security which later generations could scarcely understand. To Americans who reached maturity in the nine-teen-thirties, for example, it seemed as if something warm and wonder-ful had vanished from the world before their birth, leaving the look of life utterly changed. That Howells had once been considered a realist bewildered them. If they dipped into his novels, they found a world all dimity and innocence. Its fundamental axioms struck them as imma-ture, as irrelevant to reality as those of a fairy tale. Could anyone, ever, have believed them true? If life had approximated his picture of it, why did Howells become a socialist? Inclined themselves to radicalism, they wondered at the inconsistency of his art and the social ideas which he considered so audacious. Were not these, in the circumstances, a rather shocking perversity?

On the whole, later generations felt far more at home with sad, skep-tical Henry Adams. His view of Howells' America was distinctly jaun-diced. The young were likely to assume that it was therefore more "ob-jective" and "realistic." They understood what he meant by saying that he should have been a Marxist, and regretted that a narrow trait of the New-England nature seemed to blight Socialism for him as, apparently, it had blighted nearly everything else. Many things had been blighted for them, likewise, and the experience tended to confirm Adams' dark premonitions. No longer, they were certain, could anyone take for granted a large cheerful average of health and success and happy life in the United States!

Sometimes, arguing with their elders, they referred to *Middletown* and *Middletown in Transition*, books in which Robert S. Lynd and Helen Merrell Lynd, distinguished sociologists, made an appraisal of American civilization. These authorities subjected the culture of a typical Mid-Western city to the kind of scrutiny which anthropologists direct upon the life of aboriginal tribes. To good Americans of 1896, the project would have seemed impertinent. Many of the conclusions which it inspired would have struck them as preposterous. Could anyone have dreamed that, within thirty years, scientists would question the validity of American culture's exuberant boast of a classless society? That they would deny the soundness of Andrew Carnegie's advice to enterprising youth to begin at the bottom, and point to the helpless commitment of a growing share of the population to working for others, with a diminished chance of "getting ahead"? That a man might face the prospect of doing, day after day, fortuitously assigned things, chiefly at the behest of other people, would have been considered as wildly improbable as that getting a living should become an instrumental, rather than an inherently satisfying, activity!

And, in 1896, could anyone foresee that the antics of America's most beloved entertainers would be interpreted, in all seriousness, as a bitterly tragic commentary on the nature of American life? Yet this was the interpretation advanced, in 1946, by Professor Abram Kardiner of Columbia University, an eminent social psychologist. The films of Charlie Chaplin, he asserted, afforded every American the satisfaction of feeling that the ultimate flight from social goals to loneliness is an act of choice, and not a symptom of his defeat. And in Charlie McCarthy, he suggested, Americans could find a "Mr. Everyman"—a wooden dummy who is the puppet of powerful forces, and whose behavior epitomizes the polarities of abasement and cruelty. Americans of 1896 would have shaken their head sadly, and wondered—if these things were true—why their descendants were making a joke of them, and why millions were laughing at the joke.

For, in that distant day, it seemed that there would always be new frontiers of opportunity. And the most sensitive of spirits might have agreed with Howells that, "in America, life is not yet a joke with us, even when it is grotesque and shameful, as it so often is, for we think we can make it right when we choose." At the very heart of American life, hope could scarcely be distinguished from certainty. The look of life was the look of confidence, the look of faith.

Why, in fifty years of progress such as no nation in the world had ever known, did disillusion overtake the American mind and heart?

Part One

THE SOCIAL SCENE

CHAPTER I

The Lady Vanishes

[1] AN OLD LADY AND A NEW DAY

In 1896 a small, shapeless old lady was, as usual, passing the summer at Newport. Though her clothes always looked uncared for, and her bonnets never sat quite straight on her head, she had an air of distinction. Sometimes her face wrinkled in laughter, and a naughty imp mocked in her eyes. For Julia Ward Howe enjoyed the comic aspects of life, and had a talent for fooling. Young folk liked this, and wondered why their elders spoke of her as if she were a national institution. In effect, she was. Her presence seemed to be requisite to the success of public meetings. So she would appear, in lace hood and flowered silk cloak and lilac satin gown, to recite the "Battle Hymn of the Republic."

During the winter, she had lectured at the New England Women's Club of Boston. Her topic was the question, "Is Polite Society Polite?" She was mildly skeptical. "I do not think that the manners of so-called polite society today are quite so polite as they were in my youth," she told the ladies. There was a perceptible shiver. Surely Mrs. Howe couldn't doubt the existence of a genuinely polite society? "On the other hand," she went on, "outside this charmed circle of fashion, I find the tone of taste and culture much higher than I remember it to have been in my youth. . . . So the community gains, although one class loses—and that, remember, the class which assumes to give to the rest a standard of taste."

On this topic, Mrs. Howe could speak with authority, even in Boston, where she suffered disadvantages. For one thing, she had been born in

New York. But her people were bankers and, in a way, patricians; at least, they had harps and marble statues in their salons. They considered her marriage to the romantic Dr. Howe of Boston little less than a misalliance. Her brother had behaved more correctly in marrying the daughter of William Astor.

Polite society in Boston looked askance at Mrs. Howe. Had not her husband attached himself to those social outcasts, the Abolitionists? Nowadays, everybody in Boston knew her. One couldn't help knowing her. She was not only famous, she was a kind of living memorial, like Edward Everett Hale. This had not resulted in making her acceptable —to polite society. She resided in Beacon Street. Individual Beacon Street knew her by sight and reputatioń; collective Beacon Street ignored her.

The nature of her social talents and the character of her following displeased it. Her house was always full of writers, reformers, Persians, Armenians and the professors of strange new faiths. She collected all manner of people around her, and most of them were people who should not be received by anyone. It was of a piece with the preposterous tilt of her bonnets, about which she could not be persuaded to care. How was Beacon Street to know that their rakish angle was natural to a poet who never forgot the laurels on her brow?

Year after year, at Newport, Mrs. Howe had an opportunity to observe the manners of so-called polite society, the charmed circle of fashion. Newport had become the unrivalled playground of American fashion, and the newspapers treated it as the national social citadel. Newport had changed. Only the old town, remote from fashion, where the fine mansions of eighteenth-century merchants were slowly moldering, identified it with the past.

It was a sleepy watering place when Mrs. Howe first went there, with a barrack-like hotel where, year after year, one saw the same dignified families from Boston and New York. Then, it seemed almost overnight, Newport became fashionable. Cottages festooned with scrollwork, adorned with turrets and balconies and crenellation, rose along Bellevue Avenue, inhabited, during the "season," by people of wealth. For there was a season, and Mrs. August Belmont, the daughter of Commodore Perry, who had opened Japan to the world, and niece of Oliver Hazard Perry, the hero of Lake Erie, set its tone. Her husband, a protégé of the Rothschilds, had little taste for simple ways. So Mrs. Belmont, a woman of singular sweetness and grace, startled the summer visitors with her archery parties, her *grand daumont de visite*, drawn by four magnificent horses and attended by two postillions in livery. It had been the talk of the eighteen-seventies.

But now, in 1896, most of the wooden cottages of Mrs. Belmont's era had disappeared. Her successor, the wife of one of her sons, dwelt in a huge marble palace with pilasters as large as those of the Temple of the Sun at Baalbek. During the interval, Mrs. Howe's friend, the architect Richard Morris Hunt, had changed the look of Newport, transforming its wood to marble. An architect had to fall in with the spirit of the times, and if his wealthy clients demanded palaces, palaces he must give them. So Hunt designed palaces reminiscent of Touraine, or of the Ile-de-France. They were extraordinary, colossal French chateaux, sometimes in the high Rothschild manner; but Hunt had a lively sense of humor, and for new wealth that exacted "something mediaeval" he was capable of turning out a replica of the Bourges mansion of Jacques Coeur, the greatest upstart of the Middle Ages. As a result of his vogue, Newport positively bristled with chateaux that were all cry and no wool, all house and no garden.

To one who recalled the old days, it seemed that the face of nature was now as much obliterated as possible, and the original shy sweetness of Newport as much as possible bedizened and bedevilled. What were Hunt's spectacular creations, if not white elephants, monuments merely to pecuniary power, that spoke only of distressful, inevitable waste? This was the question Henry James asked, a little later, returning after long absence to the Newport of his youth. The thing had been done, he felt, with the best faith in the world; but scarcely with the best light. All that remained of his Newport were the tiny, sunny, empty vistas, perspectives that came to a sudden stop, like the very short walks of very old ladies.

By 1896, Mrs. Howe's friend, old George Bancroft, the historian, had died, and Hunt, too, was in his grave. The earlier Newport had been proud of the rare specimen roses which filled Bancroft's gardens, but it was not long before Mrs. Howe was to see these wantonly destroyed, and his comfortable old villa replaced by still another marble palace, likewise called "Roseclyffe," though its garden contained no roses. This mansion, with its fifty rooms and vast Louis XV ballroom, was designed by Stanford White, Hunt's successor in the architecture of grandeur; the Moses and Aaron and Mohamet of the *impayable* new rich, who sometimes put life-size crucifixions in the grand stair-case hall of his patrons' residences. "Roseclyffe" he created, at a cost of nearly three million dollars, for Tessie Oelrichs, daughter of Senator James Graham Fair, a poor Irish immigrant who had gone to California in the gold rush, and had found his fortune in the Comstock Lode. Mrs. Howe lived long enough to witness its major social triumphs, among them a celebrated "white ball" said to have cost thirty thousand dollars. But she did not live long enough to see the withered age of fashionable Newport, when most of the palaces were boarded up and deserted, looking weary and overpainted and too spectacular, like their absent chatelaines. It was in those latter days that "Roseclyffe," put up at auction, was bought for a few thousand dollars by Miss Gertrude Niesen, a lusty, gusty torch singer who thereby confirmed the opinion of Henry James, of whom she may never have heard. Mrs. Howe, whose zest for life was insatiable, and whose acquaintance was almost universal, never met a torch singer. It was one of the few social opportunities of which death cheated her.

The cycle of "Roseclyffe" implied the history of that charmed circle of fashion which Mrs. Howe described as so-called polite society. She liked, now and again, to make brief forays into it, if only to observe its follies and gently rebuke them, or rebuke herself for enjoying them. She was leading—for her—an unusually quiet life, content with her books and her papers, busy writing her memoirs, and listening, every morning after breakfast, while one of her daughters read aloud from Green's *History of the English People*, and her young, active grandsons protested their dislike of being edified.

West of Narragansett Bay, that summer of 1896, the country was in a turmoil. A grim mood was rising in the land. The plain people considered themselves oppressed. They believed that they were in danger of becoming economic serfs; the old, wide, free American opportunity had seemingly disappeared. They wanted a crusade against the power of big business and the corrupt political bosses who served it. Business was at a standstill. Industries had shut down. Millions of workers were unemployed. The debt-ridden farmers of the Middle West were raising less corn and more hell. A financial crisis was paralyzing the nation.

The unrest came to a head at the convention of the Democratic party in Chicago, one sweltering July day. For young William Jennings Bryan won the presidential nomination by shouting the defiance of the underprivileged, their scorn of bankers, corporations, trusts: "You shall not press down upon the brow of labor this crown of thorns—you shall not crucify mankind upon a cross of gold!" To Brooks Adams, lawyer, scholar and descendant of two presidents, it was an exciting moment. "If I ever saw revolution it was in that meeting," he wrote to his brother Henry in Paris. A young reporter on a Chicago daily saw Bryan, the "peerless one," in his hotel bedroom after the nomination; handsome, tall, clear-eyed, his face still glowing under his mane of black hair. Ray Stannard Baker was to remember him always as an admirable man, who believed, sincerely, tenaciously, powerfully, in things that were not so. But his speech had sounded like a revolutionary tocsin. And the most savage and bitter campaign that the United States had yet witnessed was about to divide the American people.

[2] PLEASURES AND PALACES

Of all this turmoil, Newport showed no reflection. On sunny afternoons, Bellevue Avenue was filled with smart turnouts. For "Society" was in residence. Its customary afternoon diversion, in intervals from calling and leaving cards, was the carriage parade, along the Avenue and out on the new Ocean Drive. On this circuit between wilderness and waves, one saw all the elderly ladies and the young ones, leaning back in victorias or barouches, or the newfangled vis-à-vis, a four-seated affair with a rumble for the footman. The young ladies sat in their carriages as in a showcase, prepared to be looked at, wanting to be admired in their lacy dresses and feathery hats. The dowagers were stiffly elegant in brocaded or satin-striped gowns, rigidly whaleboned, and flowered bonnets tied under the chin with large tulle bows. Young and old alike flirted fringed silk or velvet sunshades, usually with jointed handles of intricately carved ivory, to protect delicate complexions from the effects of sunlight, should it chance to penetrate their dotted-tulle veils. A ceremonious etiquette governed their promenade. One young matron, whose new coachman did not recognize her mother's carriage, found that she had inadvertently passed it. Early next morning, she hastened to apologize, explaining that her coachman could not have known the offense he was committing. Her mother's only comment was an icy, "You might have told him!" It summed up the axioms of a social code. One was polite, considerate of others, careful of the accepted formulas—because such were the principles of the well bred.

Newport represented the pride of life, with all its great houses open, and the grounds around them petted and pampered and sleekly groomed. There was no end to the fashionable gatherings: dinners, with gold plate and orchids, and a footman behind every chair; luncheons, small dances and elaborate balls with jeweled favors for the cotillion; bright mornings at Bailey's Beach, and tennis at the Casino— the natives no longer asked whether the net was a new device for catching birds; indolent hours on white yachts as spacious and richly decorated as ocean liners. Monsieur Paul Bourget, the eminent French novelist, had said that Newport reminded him of Cannes: in the sumptuousness of its villas, the costliness of its entertainments and the notable absence of any *petite bourgeoisie.* Yet there was a slight difference. Cannes was cosmopolitan; but about Newport there was something genuinely American. It struck Monsieur Bourget when he noticed that the interiors, like the exteriors, of its palaces lacked proportion. There were too many precious Persian rugs, too many priceless tapestries, paintings and antiques. Europe had been rifled of too much bric-a-brac. Possibly too much money had been spent merely to insure that enough would be.

Visitors from Europe were apt to be surprised by a condition which Americans were beginning to take for granted. "Society," whether in Newport or New York, was a picture poor in the male presence. The gentleman of leisure was not yet extinct, but in 1896 he represented a small and diminishing species. The old aristocracy had begun to yield to the importunate big money-makers from the West, soon to be followed by the lords of Pittsburgh. It was becoming increasingly difficult to resist the pressure of these new men—masters of railroads and mines, steel and ships and banks, who had made their incredible millions since the end of the War between the States. The acquisition of wealth had ceased to interest the old aristocracy. The new men were of a tougher breed; their goal was not money, but power. To suppose that they worshiped money was a delusion. They respected money less than Europeans did, wasted it more recklessly, endured its loss more easily. Like social position, it was merely a symbol, an index of power. In terms of money, their stakes were fantastically high; higher than any ever before played for. The pursuit of power absorbed them completely. The game exacted unremitting vigilance. They had little or no time for leisure; when they spared the time, leisure was apt to make them restless. One could spend money, but how did one kill time? So leisure, as an end in itself, as a way of life, was going out of fashion. It was coming to seem discreditable, effete, almost decadent.

In these circumstances, the conduct of social life had become—to a degree unknown in any other country—the responsibility and obligation of women. "Society" was ruled by women, though supported, more and more invisibly, by men. The lady, the female of the favored social class, was touching her spectacular zenith. Within a very few years, the gentleman of leisure became almost as extinct as the dinosaur, perhaps equally involuntarily. The lady survived him briefly. But her exit was voluntary. It was a gesture of protest against boredom. Perhaps, too, against a meaningless existence. The civilization which produced her also deprived her of a *raison d'être*. Her significance was merely ritual. Like an ornamentally wrought weapon or a splendid offering to the gods, she was an emblem of some man's power to waste —a measure of his competitive superiority over other men.

This situation was already evident to one privileged inhabitant of the citadel, and her subsequent comment on it was to interest the American public for three decades. Why, her elders wondered, should so handsome a young matron choose to spend her time in scribbling? She had developed the dubious habit in childhood, at an age when she might better have been playing with her dolls. The staid blood of Rhinelanders, Schermerhorns and Stevenses had not restrained her. Nor had her marriage to Edward Wharton, one of Boston's most eligible bachelors. To New York, a degree of eccentricity was quite acceptable. Among Mrs. Wharton's remote cousins there had been one, immensely wealthy, who spent his last years sitting on a marble shelf, in the happy illusion that he was a bust of Napoleon. But an aspiration to authorship was a very different matter. Any friend could have told her that authorship was a disreputable median between a black art and a form of manual labor. Sometimes she had a conviction of social failure. In Boston they thought her too fashionable to be intelligent. But in New York they were certain that she was too intelligent to be fashionable.

Young Mrs. Wharton thought that the group in which she grew up was like an empty vessel into which no new wine would ever again be poured. Nearly half a century was to pass before memory invested it with a pathetic picturesqueness. Then she concluded that one of its uses lay in preserving a few drops of an old vintage too rare to be savored by a youthful palate. Her instinctive social assurance was threatened by morbid shyness. She adopted the armor of formality, and gave an impression of cool, detached appraisal. In time, this armor came to seem more real—perhaps even to herself—than the woman whom it insulated from disturbing intimacies and the bruising touch of vulgar things. After she had taken up residence in France, where society was patterned like one of the formal gardens she admired, and where culture was an eminently social quality, distinguished residents of the Faubourg St. Germain who frequented her salon remarked that, "*On est trop organisé chez elle.*" By then, this criticism was literary as well as personal. It attested her skill in observing, arranging and perfecting—perhaps too fastidiously—the elements of situations in which she was unable to participate. For to life, whether in her stories or her salon, Mrs. Wharton's hospitality was always civil, never affectionate.

At Newport she continued to add to the hoard of manuscript that had accumulated since her childhood. Poems, stories, tragedies begun and abandoned, novels in which her sober judgment detected no promise. With whom could she share her intense pleasure in the art of literature? To whom did she dare confide her ambition to master it? Though she might—and would—write of other times and places, the result could stand only as practice. Her predestined subject, as she knew, lay at hand in the existence and scene that confronted her. Already she had begun to detect an underlying note of irony. Why was it that the people who regarded "Society" as an end in itself were precisely those who belonged to it? Was not its proper use that of an escape from work? When it became the thing worked for, did it not distort all the relations of life? The surface of Newport, as of fashionable New York, reflected the glitter of lost opportunities. Underneath, there was to be found only a poverty of achievement. Did not the significance of a frivolous society lie in what its frivolity destroyed? Did not its tragic implication lie in its power to debase both people and ideals?

These questions were the burden of her faintly astringent reflection. A number of years were to pass before, in *The House of Mirth*, she gave them the status of a literary theme. She was then to learn that her literary success puzzled and embarrassed her old friends far more than it impressed them. In her family, it created a constraint that increased as the years went on, and her celebrity widened. Her relatives did not mention her books; they ignored them. The subject of her work was avoided as though it were a kind of family disgrace, which might be condoned but could not be forgotten.

[3] THE RESTLESSNESS OF THE ELECT

That "Society" was a fixed constellation to which one either did, or did not, belong, was known to readers of newspapers throughout the country. For, by the highest authority, the press had been given the names of the fortunate elect. To make matters clearer, a diagram of the hierarchy had been supplied, not unlike Dante's description of Paradise, with the greater and lesser saints circling in their appointed places about the Mystic Rose.

The central figure in the complex system was a cold, autocratic old woman who became, in her lifetime, the subject of a national legend, and eventually took her place in the pantheon of American folklore, with Daniel Boone and Davy Crockett and Jesse James, among the fierce individualists whose exploits were genuinely remarkable. Cowboys, millhands, clerks, shopkeepers, snowbound farmers whose lives her activities would never touch, eagerly followed them. Though she professed a contempt for the press, and appeared to resent any mention of her name in its columns, even the smallest local papers throughout the country recorded her regal progress. For, in a way, Mrs. Astor, too, was a national institution.

When Mrs. Astor accepted an invitation, it was understood that she took precedence over all other guests. Thus, when she dined out, she was invariably placed at the right of her host. Her manners were pleasant and cordial, and there was a touching element of naïveté in her enjoyment of her unique position, but she presented a formidable appearance. An immense dignity invested her. In decorous *décolletage*, her withered body blazed with diamonds, which she wore with the most effective prodigality, and an ornate tiara glittered from the high-piled pompadour of her black wig. In Newport, she held court at "Beechwood." Richard Hunt had designed her New York mansion, on Fifth Avenue, a noble establishment in the style of the French Renaissance. She moved from one to the other, with occasional rustic interludes at the earlier Astor place on the Hudson, and less frequent visits to Paris, where she sometimes went to confer with that other great autocrat, Monsieur Worth. The windows of her New York home framed a charming view of Central Park, but it could be said of Mrs. Astor, as Henry James said of a character in one of his novels, that her imagination was all bounded on the east by Madison Avenue.

An invitation to Mrs. Astor's annual ball—the very acme of New York's social season—was an accolade. It conferred membership in "Society," the hierarchy of the Four Hundred. Was not so large a congregation necessarily somewhat indiscriminate? To Mrs. Ogden Mills, a descendant of the landed Livingstons, the defect was apparent; she proposed to limit the elect to the members of only twenty families. But Mrs. Astor, whose Schermerhorn ancestors had derived their wealth from commerce, applied a more flexible standard. To restrict the number of the ultrafashionable was, in the nature of things, essential; she conceded the principle without sacrificing the Christian virtue of charity. One hundred and fifty people would include everyone genuinely worthy. These she was able to certify by invitation to one of her dinner parties. And so, as the Reverend Charles Wilbur de Lyon Nichols informed a curious world, not to have dined at Mrs. Astor's virtually debarred one. Nobody asked from what.

At Mrs. Astor's dinner parties, as at nearly all others, little was done for the entertainment of guests beyond providing them with a large amount of elaborate food. There were seldom fewer than seven courses, accompanied by many varieties of wine, with a Roman punch in the middle of the meal to stimulate flagging courage. One was rarely amused by one's table-companion. New York did not run to good talk. "Society" was given to a deplorable habit of tête-à-tête prattling. People felt that saying anything to their neighbor was more polite than listening to anyone else. Under a convention that no pauses must occur, the art of conversation had been lost. The general effect was flat and arid. "Society" was a Sahara without oases, without lions, and certainly without lion hunters. The Four Hundred would have fled in a body from a poet, a painter, a musician, or a clever Frenchman.

Yet who would have declined an invitation to dine with Mrs. Astor? Hunt had provided her with a chateau, and she had made it a social Montserrat, a republican Versailles. Its splendors evoked national pride: the celebrated ballroom, reputedly planned to hold comfortably only four hundred guests, where dowagers of impeccable ancestry had been observed to weep when denied a place on the dais; the white and gold art gallery, where hung a collection of masterpieces whose authenticity nobody questioned, and whose esthetic merits nobody dared discuss; the vast oak-panelled dining hall, with its French tapestries, its ceiling of painted flowers and fruits, among which the Astor monogram was traced in bright gold; the series of enfiladed drawing-rooms—in one of which, standing beneath her life-sized portrait by Carolus Duran, Mrs. Astor received her guests. There she was still to stand, before her death in 1908, when her weary mind had, at last, clouded. Still erect, still bravely gowned and jewelled, she stood quite alone, greeting imaginary guests long dead, exchanging pleasantries with ghosts of the utmost social distinction.

In "Society" there were symptoms of restlessness. The nature of its diversions was, perhaps, ineffable; but a suspicion that they were tedious could not be suppressed. Was not the star of Mrs. Astor perceptibly dimmer? Had it, indeed, begun to wane? The star of Ward McAllister, long her accredited chamberlain, had lately set in a storm of laughter. This paunchy, pompous cousin of Mrs. Howe had established himself as the autocrat of drawing-rooms. He had found his inspiration at the court of the Grand Duke of Tuscany, and he returned from Europe as the prophet of a religion of amenity. He preached the dogma of social predestination: "Fashion selects its own votaries. . . . The talent for and of Society develops itself as does the talent for art." An attenuated Castiglione, McAllister was indifferent to the substance of manners, the cultivated attitudes of mind and spirit for which they furnish a language. He was concerned with externals for their own sake; he applied to social life the decorative exuberance of a Victorian upholsterer. He was an anxious student of genealogy and the problems of etiquette and form. He became a connoisseur of food and wine. These branches of scholarship were essential to his mission: to form the smallest of circles and teach it to give the largest of parties. Unfortunately he lacked the wit, intelligence and taste of his gifted relatives, the Wards. He was merely dull; never more so than when giving interviews to the press, which, literally reported, invited ridicule. In the end, he found himself repudiated by his disciples. "McAllister is a discharged servant," Stuyvesant Fish informed the press when asked whether, as usual, the social arbiter was assuming the direction of a great ball. Yet, fifty years after his death, his prestige survived in a meaningless phrase. One of his pleasures was to compile lists of the socially eligible. His major invention was the Four Hundred.

Even Mrs. Astor seemed to sense the increasing ennui of her little world. Had the old forms of entertainment been exhausted? Had repetition made them stale? Unprecedently, she issued invitations to a garden party with a performance by professional talent. On the lawn at "Beechwood" a young girl danced for the pleasure of Mrs. Astor's guests. She was unknown, and arrestingly beautiful. Her nude body gleamed through a flowing, diaphanous tunic, moving with astonishing fleetness and magnificent freedom, so that it seemed effortlessly lifted and supported by the air. For this was dancing of a kind that had never been seen before. She performed once again at Newport, for the guests of a philanthropic Miss Mason, of Boston. As an old lady, Mrs. Wharton was to recall, with regret, that a prejudice had prevented her from seeing Isadora Duncan in the radiance of youth. Newport failed to appreciate her, and Isadora confided to her journal her disappointment in it. It was so wrapped up in the glory of being rich, she felt, that it had no art sense whatever. To Newport, an artist was an inferior, a sort of upper servant. Shortly thereafter, disenchanted with the culture of her native land, she set out for Europe—to become, within a very few years, one of the most widely known of Americans.

The old dignity had become fusty. The old ceremonious formality was merely old-fashioned, outdated. In their eclipse, few noticed the lapsing of standards that they had expressed. These standards were narrow and limited, but they represented a republican version of an aristocratic ideal. They summed up a conscious effort to establish a true polite society responsive to traditions of honor and conduct, of education and manners. These traditions had been cherished and, in the main, lived up to. Now they were being discarded, and those who observed this attributed it to the climate of materialism, of moral cynicism, that had settled on the country after the War between the States. Was this deterioration, or was it progress?

By the turn of the century, the "lady" found herself in a paradoxical situation. Never before had she enjoyed more unrestricted power or greater affluence. Never were the instruments for realizing her aspirations more various or more completely at her command. But seldom, in her long history, had the lady received less collaboration from men. The conditions necessary to her function were withheld by her environment. She required a society of men and women keenly interested in the same subjects; the complexities of social life, and the relation therein of the sexes to each other. The existence of such a society was implied by the later novels of Henry James—but where, in the United States, was the lady to find men devoted to the pursuit of happiness under the forms of art? The novels of James' friend and disciple, Mrs. Wharton —who he felt *must* be tethered in native pastures, even if it reduced her to a back yard in New York—indicated that the lady's hope was quite vain. The American man was prepared to lavish his fortune on his wife, perhaps because he didn't know what else to do with it—or her. But he was prepared neither to share her interests nor admit her to his own. Absorbed by his pursuit of power, he asked only that she remain in her own sphere, creating for herself whatever kind of world she chose, provided that others found it enviable. Its architecture and organization were her responsibility. On the whole, he was indifferent to them.

Possessing the instruments, but denied the conditions for making social life an art, it was almost inevitable that the lady should make it a competition for prestige and power. There was a curious parallel between her game and the man's. The stakes were equally high; the play was extravagant, obsessive and exhausting. When Lady Paget, who had been Miss Stevens of New York, made a visit to Newport after long absence, she asked in bewilderment, "Just what is it that you are all after, anyway?" Nobody could explain. "You don't give parties to enjoy yourselves," a young bachelor shrewdly remarked, "but to advance yourselves." What else was to be said of a situation which the lady conceived as a kind of private warfare? Did not everyone know that Mrs. Belmont—a valiant warrior to whom opposition was as the breath of life—had undertaken to "launch" a socially ineligible tin-plate king and his beautiful wife merely for the satisfaction of compelling her rivals to bend to her will, to have them follow her in the end, meek, sheeplike?

The world which the lady created for herself had, to a later age, the look of pure fantasy. For a decade and more, Newport—which, like Versailles, was isolated from the common people and the practical exigencies of life—resembled a rococo theater where a continuous spectacle was in performance; the décor and costumes constantly changing, but the same actors being displayed in a single, static situation. At most spectacles, the audience may be under an illusion, but the actors know that real life lies on the other side of the footlights. It was the peculiar characteristic of this one that all the illusion was confined to the actors. "The immensity of the native accommodation, socially speaking, for the childish life, is not that exactly the key to much of the spectacle?" So it seemed to Henry James.

In elaborating her world, the lady proved herself both ingenious and exorbitant. She demanded an immediate materialization of the improbable; for the impossible she was willing to wait, briefly. Several

Newport establishments were equipped to serve banquets for one hundred and fifty guests upon an hour's notice. One hostess whose residence, as originally planned, was not large enough for a ball, resolved to give one. She appealed to the resourceful architect: in a magically brief time there arose a fine ballroom, with vaulted roof splendidly decorated with mural paintings. Among her neighbors was a bachelor, uniquely distinguished for a whim that was the reverse of hers. He owned a beautiful villa whose Nile-green ballroom and panelled dining room ornamented with the delicate Gothic scrolls of Walter Crane were considered the last word in elegance. Possessing a ballroom, he could afford to indulge his prejudice against giving balls, which he considered too destructive of his tranquil surroundings.

In somewhat similar spirit, Mrs. Stuyvesant Fish commanded the creation of a fine Gothic bedroom. After it had been completed, she refused to sleep in it, but had her bed put in the adjoining dressing-room; it was too perfect as a period room. Mrs. Belmont imported Chinese artisans to construct a red-and-gold lacquer tea house on the cliffs at Marble House. The structure was gorgeous and authentic, but contained no provision for making tea. A miniature railroad was therefore laid from the pantry of the mansion to the cliffs, its course masked by elaborate planting, and footmen with trays were thereby whisked down to the lacquered toy. The stables of Mrs. John Drexel were reputed to contain twenty-six different types of carriage; all were necessary if an appropriate one was to be available for every probable social occasion. It was said that, at the beginning of each Newport season, Mrs. Pembroke Jones set aside three hundred thousand dollars for entertainment. This budget was not considered excessive. Other hostesses were believed to spend more. To have one's power acknowledged, vast wealth was a requisite. "Not to have wealth would have been to have only a straw crown in a madhouse. Diamond tiaras were not empty symbols."

There was a vogue for costume balls. They afforded an escape for the members of a group who knew each other almost too well to find continuous pleasure in meeting. For them, the *grands couturiers* of Paris were commissioned to design costly period gowns, to be worn but once and discarded. Two of these balls had repercussions in circles far removed from "Society."

One winter morning in 1896, Mrs. Bradley Martin, reading of the

deep financial depression in which the country was submerged, and
the consequent acute misery of the poor, was moved to take remedial
action. Would not a great ball furnish an impetus to trade? She
resolved to give one. The festivity was held at the new Waldorf
Hotel in New York, in February, 1897. It represented an expenditure
of more than a quarter of a million dollars. For a fortnight, the
press of the United States and Europe reported it as a prodigy—which
indeed it was. The result was a storm of popular protest at the heartless extravagance of the rich, which drove Mrs. Martin and her husband into permanent exile in England.

In 1905, James Hazen Hyde, who had just come into the fortune
amassed by his father as president of the Equitable Life Assurance
Society, determined to give a costume ball which would eclipse in
splendor any entertainment that had ever been given in New York.
Educated in France and at Harvard, he was perhaps remarkable for
his eagerness to assist in the creation of a highly artificial society. A
bibliophile, an excellent whip, a gourmet, a devoted patron of opera
and theater, Hyde professed to be a man of taste who made a cult of
perfection. He therefore enlisted the talents of Stanford White to
create his splendid fantasy.

White chose to reproduce a court ball of Louis XVI. The guests
were requested to observe historical accuracy; the waiters and other
attendants were clothed in the livery and peruques of royal lackeys.
The state suite of Sherry's restaurant, in Fifth Avenue, was transformed to resemble the salons of the Grand Trianon. Thousands of
orchids were massed in clusters on every wall. In niches garlanded
with flowers there were marble statues brought from France. The
floor of the supper room was thickly covered with rose petals. The
great actress Gabrielle Réjane was engaged to cross the Atlantic
and recite some verse. All in all, Mr. Hyde could scarcely doubt that
White had achieved the desired effect.

But the costly fantasy was widely reported by the press, with an
undertone of extreme disapproval. The journalism of exposure—
Theodore Roosevelt called it "muckraking"—was then at its height,
and the American public was deeply shocked by the conditions which
it revealed. Confidence in insurance companies was seriously threatened by the newspaper accounts of the Hyde ball. Indirectly, they
led to a legislative investigation of insurance affairs, conducted by
Charles Evans Hughes, and the consequent opening of his public

career. For Mr. Hyde, the result was less agreeable. With unforeseen haste, he found it convenient to transfer his residence to Paris.

Meanwhile, the inner circle of fashion was being convulsed by a palace revolution. Two precursors of the the still distant Jazz Age took it upon themselves to bring "Society" up to date. Their view of the calendar, as of many other things, was highly original. The result was a glimpse into an unimaginable future—a vision which, to a later age, seemed to anticipate the amusements of Hollywood, the manners of Alexander Woollcott and the social talents of Miss Elsa Maxwell. For, during the bloodless reign of terror instituted by Mrs. Stuyvesant Fish and her protégé, Harry Lehr, the cult of the cockeyed was born full grown.

Mrs. Fish loathed dullness as Jonathan Edwards loathed sin. Quick-tempered, malicious, easily bored and incapable of enduring monotony, she determined to puncture the complacency of "Society" by compelling it to make itself ridiculous. At a moment when the stinging verbal flippancies of Whistler and Oscar Wilde passed for wit, Mrs. Fish was reputed to be witty. The surviving examples of her talent point to a remarkable virtuosity in insult. She established imaginative rudeness as a form of decorum.

In Harry Lehr, Mrs. Fish found a predestined court jester. It was his ambition to live for his wit and his elegance, and his good fortune to live by his wits and his vulgarity. Lacking wealth and social position, abhorring work and craving luxury, he made a profession of prankishness. He was a shrewd and cynical judge of his environment; he saw that it would succumb to insolence, spite, and savage ways. These he did not need to master, and their exercise brought him celebrity. Until he condescended to marry an heiress, his wants were supplied without cost by fashionable tailors, jewelers, florists, restaurants, hotels. The prestige of his patronage was profitable. He invented the commission as a source of revenue for the socially elect.

For "Society" there was piquant novelty in the techniques devised by Mrs. Fish and Harry Lehr. At the beginning of a Newport season, she was able to electrify her dinner guests with the remark, "Well, here you all are, older faces and younger clothes." He was able to furnish a thrill by despatching a bruised flower to a hospital in an ambulance. Together, they developed a formula for sophisticated silliness. Eventually, it fell into disrepute, only to be revived, and exploited as a new discovery, by the Jazz Age. Mrs. Fish and Harry Lehr arranged a banquet to honor a Corsican prince. To everyone's delight, this distinguished visitor turned out to be someone's pet monkey, seated at a table in the place usually accorded Mrs. Astor. They sponsored formal dinners for dolls and dogs, and parties where guests masqueraded as their favorite enemies or their servants. They made personal abuse a social art, and malicious practical jokes a favorite diversion.

Informed by the press that these innovations represented the accepted manners of polite society, the plain people of the United States were plainly bewildered. What invisible line distinguished the mores of aristocratic Newport from those of vulgar Long Branch? At the New Jersey resort, abandoned by fashion, Diamond Jim Brady, with the beautiful Lillian Russell at his side, rolled along the Ocean Drive at twilight in one of the new electric broughams. It had been built to meet Brady's specifications. It had a semicircular glass front, and its interior was illuminated by one hundred concealed lights which shed their radiance on Miss Russell's blonde loveliness, and Mr. Brady's gaudy jewels. The standards of Newport excluded Miss Russell and Mr. Brady. They were socially ineligible.

The final commentary on Newport's palace revolution came from Mrs. Fish herself. After the outbreak of the first World War, long after her court jester had married his heiress and become a resident of Paris, the rumor reached New York that Harry Lehr had lost his mind. His old friend wrote to him. Affectionately, she urged him to return to the United States, and resume his place in "Society." His condition was by no means a disadvantage. "You know quite well that you won't need any mind to go with the people in our set," Mrs. Fish assured him. Mrs. Astor, quite correctly, had considered her a disintegrating force. Mrs. Fish was singularly free of illusions.

Though "Society" was indifferent to public opinion, it was nervously susceptible to blackmail. This discovery was made by Colonel William Mann, an elderly, debonair veteran of the Union Army with an addiction to experiment. Having invented a cannon and a pioneer sleeping car, he embarked upon a career in journalism. He published a society weekly, *Town Topics*, and a handsome annual, *Fads and Fancies of Representative Americans*, which was available to subscribers for a mere fifteen hundred dollars.

Colonel Mann was a self-taught psychologist, and a resourceful publisher. He devised methods of securing information which a later generation of gossip columnists were to find exceedingly useful. His Newport correspondent gained access to fashionable homes as a musician; his news of Fifth Avenue was acquired by discreet payment to servants; he cultivated the favor of the more mischievous gossips among the socially elect. These methods brought him a large harvest of unsavory anecdotes. It was his boast that his safe contained the reputations of the Four Hundred. When finally opened, it held only a few bottles of brandy. But fear had filled it with dubious ghosts and skeletons.

Much of the information that Colonel Mann gathered did not find its way into print. His purpose was merely to control it. His income was derived from an intangible, and very valuable product: silence. Colonel Mann sold nothing. But he was usually willing to accept munificent loans from prominent gentlemen whose dismal secrets had come to his attention. These loans were freely made, and no vulgar revelations followed. Those who were not cowardly enough to pay for silence found their peccadilloes reported in *Town Topics* with an embarrassing spiciness of allusion. In this subtle commerce, Colonel Mann had the legal and moral support of a well-known jurist, Justice Joseph M. Deuel of New York City.

At length, after more than a decade of prosperity, a public attack was made upon this estimable partnership by *Collier's Weekly*. Justice Deuel promptly brought suit for libel, and the case came to trial in 1906. The evidence produced, and the facts elicited in court, proved to be sensational. Twelve of the most respected gentlemen of "Society"—among them, several astute financiers—had been snared by the Colonel and his partner, and had willingly made loans aggregating nearly two hundred thousand dollars; a great insurance company had paid out a sum almost as large. On the charge of libel, the jury returned a verdict of acquittal. Colonel Mann and his associate were thus publicly discredited, and their power was destroyed. But the implications of the case were reassuring to nobody. A way had been opened for a type of journalism which, under the guise of moral reform or social criticism, might cater to a prurient interest in the private affairs of those whom the public had lifted to prominence. In time, the element of blackmail having been eliminated, this activity was to become a routine, respectable and remunerative province of journalism. The public, inured to sensational disclosures, would cease to distinguish between scandal and news.

[4] CAREER IN THE DRAWING ROOM

In the first decade of the new century, the lady became dissatisfied with her lonely, ritual eminence. The skepticism of Mrs. Fish was a symptom. It indicated a state of ennui, and suggested a conviction of futility. For experienced players, the game was losing its savor. The attractions of wilfulness and war had begun to pall. Her environment had prevented the lady from creating a way of life. Her situation was static. It could be maintained; it could not be developed. Newport could never be made to resemble the court of Margaret of Navarre. The most luxurious of Hunt's or Stanford White's palaces would never foster those forms of experience which had flourished in the mansion of Madame de Rambouillet. Disillusioned with her exalted position, the lady—when intelligent—began to assess the opportunities actually open to her. If intelligent, she wanted to be judged on her merits; not on her charms, her caprice and her costliness. This was a new desire. It implied a rejection of the traditional social pattern. It involved the possibility of a free development irrespective of its bearing on the other sex. It could be satisfied only by an independent career.

The first practical consequence of this radical notion was the appearance of oases in the social Sahara. In them, the casual talk was likely to be exciting. One met painters and poets and politicians, singers, actresses; all the clever brood from whom the Four Hundred would have fled in a body. Their note was informality. Their tone was dynamic and lively. They existed to produce the friction of ideas, and anybody who could contribute was welcomed, be it President Theodore Roosevelt, Paderewski, or the ravishing Maxine Elliott.

One of these centers was to be found in Washington Irving's old New York home, on Seventeenth Street. It was presided over by jolly Elisabeth Marbury and Elsie De Wolfe. Miss Marbury had professional relations with the theater, and Miss De Wolfe, long a familiar figure at Ward McAllister's Patriarch Balls, had ventured on the stage and become a star. She was soon to desert the theater for the new profession of interior decoration, and make her mark in that, too. As Lady Mendl, after the first World War, she would become the guiding spirit of an international set in Paris; and during the second World War she was still indefatigably playing hostess, in Hollywood, to whatever talent came her way.

The little house in Seventeenth Street was usually filled by a mad cyclone of people, but Henry Adams thought the hostesses grand and universal, and was struck blind by the brilliancy of their world. This was a major tribute. For Adams considered the American woman a failure; she had held nothing together, neither State nor Church, nor Society, nor Family. She was a worse failure than the American man, who was surely failure enough. Adams thought her more a failure when she tried a "mission" than when she didn't. The mission of Miss Marbury and Miss De Wolfe—if they had one—was to provide a climate congenial to the mind. Watching them, in the crowded, cyclonic laboratory where they functioned so expertly, Adams judged them to be the only men of the lot.

In Boston, as was to be expected, the most conspicuous oases were even more elevated. They were conducted by two remarkable women. Mrs. Henry Whitman and Mrs. John L. Gardner were ladies, but they wished to be something more, and they succeeded. Boston first heard of Mrs. Whitman as an unknown from some savage town— Baltimore, perhaps—who had married into its sacred circle. She soon became a center of social influence; that peculiar kind of social influence in which there were strands of art, idealism, intellect. One associated her with ostrich feathers, beaver bonnets, marvellous fans and arresting shades of silk or satin capriciously but unerringly chosen, and her adjectives were no less precious than her costumes. For her most salient quality was an extreme intensity of spirit, almost mystic in its enthusiasms.

Like her friend William James, Mrs. Whitman had impetuous perceptions and emotions. She was conscientious and troubled: she shared James's unrest, and his desire to penetrate to—and champion— the hidden facts, the submerged classes, the disquieting ideas which polite Boston preferred to ignore. She was not content merely to appreciate the fine arts; she studied to become an artist, and then designed stained-glass windows. Her chief interest lay with young people; she attempted to communicate the meaning and value of the arts to working-girls' clubs and to collegians. Intellectual Boston said that she had rediscovered the importance of conversation, and brilliant men, as well as artists, flocked to her home. She offered them, too, on the altar of youth—asking old James Russell Lowell to dine with a dozen young people; stimulating Justice Holmes and the philosopher Josiah Royce to debate the Infinite in her drawing room; spending semifestive evenings with James and his colleague George Santayana, and their students in philosophy. There was about her a grace of heart, a faith and joy in life, which cancelled any vanity that may have attached to those interests. She added something pleasant and pure to the world, and such was the effect of her influence that when she died, a whole society seemed to be suddenly extinguished.

The personality of Mrs. John L. Gardner was quite different, and it was only in her old age that Boston fully accepted her, much as Margaret Fuller accepted the universe, not with entire approval, but out of respect for the accomplished fact. In earlier years she had charmed and scandalized the city with her flirtations, her extravagance, her Lenten, repentant pieties. She had had Paderewski play for her alone, before arranging concerts to which she invited all of the city's students of piano. She had romped with a lion in the corridor of the zoo, and supported the Boston Red Sox, and maintained a chamber orchestra to delight her musical friends. Far from beautiful, she dressed magnificently and boldly; but, during Holy Week, robed in black, she knelt and scrubbed the altar steps of the Church of the Advent. Always, she stood out vividly, in full relief, completely individual; she set you to thinking of other times and places in which passions burned brighter, pleasures were more sumptuous, and repentances more dramatic. Ladies in New York, to whom Henry James had described her with a few exquisite touches, sighed and wished that they knew how to be like that. It required no divination to be certain that they did not know. Sturgis Bigelow, an eccentric Brahmin who was also a Buddhist, thought her the champion all-round Samaritan, unrivalled as a gloom dispeller, corpse reviver, and general chirker-up. Henry Adams said that the effect of an hour with her was that of the Absolute. William James reported that she had a very extraordinary and wonderful moral influence. But it was Henry James who found the *mot juste*: his dear wild and wandering friend reminded him of a figure on a wondrous cinquecento tapestry. For, as Isabella Gardner sometimes liked to believe, she resembled Isabella d'Este. She was as erudite as she was frivolous, as witty as she was unscrupulous—and her court attracted scholars, philosophers, men-of-letters, artists, musicians, lovers of the humanities.

They continued to surround her, in her old age, at the Venetian palace which she had built in the Fenway, as Egyptian monarchs built their tombs and went to live in them. For the palace, with all its treasures, had been designed as a museum, to be left to the city which she had defied and startled in her youth, and which so long had tried to hold aloof from her. As George Santayana remarked, her palace and her pictures had become the last audacity by which she would vanquish old Boston.

There was something touching in this old lady who, as time went on, came to deny herself all forms of luxury in order to perfect her bequest to the people. As a young woman, it was said that at the end of every season she had ordered all her ball dresses burned in the furnace. Now she was thought equally pretentious for living in modest rooms on the third story of her palace, and keeping no cook. When her girlhood friend, Mrs. Schuyler Van Rensselaer of New York, passed through Boston, Mrs. Gardner invited her to dinner. Dinner was announced, and oysters awaited the ladies on a beautifully appointed table. When these had been consumed, Mrs. Gardner took her guest to a nearby hotel for the rest of the meal; she had felt obliged to offer the traditional bread and salt at her own board. Her Boston friends sometimes teased her about her purposeful deprivations, saying that they expected to find her one day on a street corner, wearing all her pearls, playing her Stradivarius and begging alms.

But Fenway Court had been conceived and planned as a gift to the people; only incidentally as the residence of its mistress. This initial dedication was to serve as a kind of beacon for other collectors —the Morgans, Huntingtons, Fricks and Mellons whose paintings and manuscripts and varied objects of art, acquired for their personal satisfaction, were eventually to enrich the culture of the American people. Mrs. Gardner, who never followed fashions but undertook to set them, in this instance created a tradition of responsibility and obligation to future generations which wealth could not lightly disregard. It was to be followed throughout the country: in the Morgan Library and Frick Museum of New York, the National Gallery and Folger Library at Washington, the Huntington Library in California, and many more.

Fenway Court, in every least detail, was a personal creation. It bore the unmistakable stamp of Mrs. Gardner's masterful character, her taste, her knowledge and her unbridled prodigality. She made large drafts on the specialized scholarship of her friends, but she bought nothing by which she was not herself profoundly moved. Charles Eliot Norton advised her for a time; Henry Adams secured for her an early thirteenth-century stained-glass window from Saint Denis, the finest example in the United States; Bernhard Berenson, the critic and expert whom she had discovered as a brilliant student at Harvard, and whose early career she had financed, served as her technical authority. But the large, noble design was purely her own; and its execution was her absorbing passion, her creative activity. What wonder, then, that she decreed that, after her death, nothing be moved from where she had placed it, and nothing be added to what she had chosen? As time went on, the very inviolability of Fenway Court, its few errors and strongly contemporary judgments, were to become a major interest. For what would today's lovers of art not give to see the Mantuan Isabella's palace just as she had arranged it?

The exterior of Fenway Court was massively plain, but the interior was a fairyland. A large central court, glassed over at the top, formed a garden where mimosas bloomed and fountains tinkled and nightingales sang. Its façade was that of the Ca'd'Oro in Venice, with the original carved arches and balustrades, marble pillars, galleries, and double-arched windows. There was a mediaeval Spanish chapel and cloister. The furnishings of the great, stately rooms were individual works of art, and on the walls one saw the superb Tintorettos, Rembrandts, Titians and Giorgiones, as they might have been displayed in Venice or Florence during the High Renaissance. In other, smaller rooms, were the works of modern painters whom Mrs. Gardner admired: her friend John Singer Sargent, whose portraits of her in middle age, and as a venerable sybil, white-swathed and white-hooded, were among his finest; the Swedish painter and etcher, Andreas Zorn, of whom she was the earliest American patron; various young Americans whose fortunes she tried to advance. For, unlike most other great American collectors of the period, who thought of art only as a relic of past greatness, Mrs. Gardner had a lively interest in the contemporary. And although a later age might deprecate her judgment, her taste was vital for its time.

Vitality was her dominant attribute. She was still taking courses at Harvard in her eightieth year, when paralysis finally confined her to a couch spread with silver sable or finest ermine. It did not impair her vivacity, or the bright malice of her green eyes, as Sargent's water color showed. Two years later, she wrote to a friend whom she had not seen in nearly fifty years, a hermit in darkest Africa. She said that she had a rather jolly house filled with really good things, and that she still led an interesting life, with young and old friends. "The appropriately old are too old—they seem to have given up the world. Not so I, and I really shove some of the young ones rather close. I really have energy."

This quality of energy—the Amazonian trait which seems specifically characteristic of American women—goes far to explain the lady's decision to vanish. It was a trait for which "Society" furnished no appropriate outlet; and, in due time, even the creation of social oases ceased to offer an absorbing vocation. At that point, an independent career was to become synonymous with the practice of a profession or an art; and, later still, with the alternative of an entry into the world of business. To the ladies of the older generation these opportunities seldom occurred.

But before the lady—seeking to be judged on her merits alone, and trying to find an opportunity for independent, free development— turned to the arts, the professions and business, she discovered a field of activity that was both interesting and genuinely social. This was the field of public service, of "reform," and the force of her example had a significant effect upon American culture. In devoting herself to a cause, the lady learned how to become a woman. The woman learned something more. She learned how to become an individual, and take her place as a citizen.

[5] LADY INTO FOX

The long, arduous struggle for the political emancipation of American women was the most important, as it was the most educative, cause through which both lady and woman were to break down the Chinese wall of convention that restricted them to decorative futility. In this struggle, the credit for final victory belongs to the American woman, not the lady; but the fortunes of the lady were deeply involved. For a number of prominent and socially powerful ladies chose to identify themselves with the suffrage movement, and perhaps becoming more engrossed than they had anticipated, established new values and new patterns of activity for others of their kind.

Of these, the most widely publicized was Mrs. O. H. P. Belmont. Her metamorphosis—as it were from lady into fox—signalized the disappearance of the lady, as a social type, from the social scene. Plump, pugnacious and intrepid, Mrs. Belmont had begun her conquest of "Society" by outmaneuvering Mrs. Astor, who had not wished to admit her to the sacred citadel. She was able, in the end, to wrest the scepter of dictatorship from Mrs. Astor's failing grasp. She liked to think of herself as a pioneer. "I always do everything first," she boasted; "I blaze the trail for the rest to walk in." She had married a Vanderbilt when Vanderbilts were considered socially ineligible; she had been the first society woman to ask for a divorce. She had been the earliest patron of Richard Morris Hunt, and her lifelong passion for building led to her election as the first woman member of the American Institute of Architecture. After the death of her second husband, in 1908, having exhausted the possibilities of the world of fashion, she was apparently eager for new fields of battle. She was both an Amazon and, in a way, a puritan; contest was, for her, the whole moral content of life, and victory was therefore a kind of disaster.

In England, the militant suffragists had begun their spectacular struggle to win the franchise. Their example gave added impetus to the American movement, launched many years earlier by Susan B. Anthony, Elizabeth Cady Stanton, Lucretia Mott and other pioneer feminists. To this movement, and especially to the branch which promised to adopt the new tactic of militancy, Mrs. Belmont determined to contribute her wealth, her energy and her considerable talent for strategy. She went to England to confer with Christabel Pankhurst. She founded the Political Equality League, and built, in Washington, a home for the National Woman's Party. Then she joined Mrs. Stanton's daughter, Harriott Stanton Blatch, and two young, aggressively militant leaders, Alice Paul and Lucy Burns, in planning the campaigns and demonstrations sponsored by the Congressional Union. Before the cause was won, these were to lead to hunger strikes in jail, to picket lines around the White House, and to various other forms of effective dramatization previously untried.

Meanwhile, Marble House, Mrs. Belmont's residence at Newport, became the scene of mass meetings for the cause; at one of them Mrs.

Howe, who since the days of Miss Anthony and Mrs. Stanton had preached the gospel that "women are people" wherever she roamed, made a stirring appeal. By 1912, Mrs. Belmont had become one of the dominant figures in the movement. In that year, she led her forces in a monster parade down Fifth Avenue, in New York, which, to the country at large, demonstrated the insurgent spirit of the feminists. Two years later, with characteristic swift decision, she closed and dismantled Marble House. The largest and most sumptuous of the palaces which Hunt had designed for Newport's fabulous era stood vacant, boarded up like a cenotaph of departed glories. It seemed a monument to the death of "Society," the desuetude of Newport and its way of life. It was a portent, and certainly a symbol, of the disappearance of the lady as a social type. When another thirty years had passed, the way of life, the culture and mores of the era of magnificence were to seem as remote as those of the court of the Grand Monarque, and some of its relics as worthy of preservation, for their historical interest, as Versailles. In the nineteen-forties, at the instigation of President Franklin Roosevelt, the palatial home of Frederick Vanderbilt, in the Hudson Valley, with all its furnishings and works of art, was given to the nation as a museum—a representative example of a single, almost forgotten, aspect of the national past.

For the younger generation of women of the favored social class, the empty privileges of the lady exercised a rapidly diminishing appeal. It was not enough, as Eleanor Roosevelt asserted, to be kind to the poor, to assume limited obligations of philanthropy, to dine and to dance with the right people only, and live where you would be in their midst. A social conscience had begun to make itself felt in other spheres, and its influence spread. Miss Mary Harriman, daughter of the railroad magnate, made a serious study of sociology, became actively involved in the work of a settlement house in New York City, and, with a talent for organization that resembled her father's, worked out a program of welfare service which, taking form as the Junior League, was adopted in many other cities. Miss Anne Morgan, equally active in social welfare, devoted herself especially to advancing the status of women engaged in the professions.

Such efforts indicated a widening horizon of aspiration. At their best, the wealthy and advantaged had felt an almost feudal sense of obligation toward the less fortunate. This operated to alleviate distress, but seldom attempted to remedy the causes which produced it. It was not incompatible with ignorance, or with a repudiation of responsibility for enlightened leadership. It was humanitarian, but it was inadequate, and the younger generation began to suspect that it was socially unproductive. When the United States entered the first World War, Eleanor Roosevelt's younger brother promptly enlisted in the army. Her grandmother inquired why he didn't buy a substitute, as many gentlemen did during the Civil War. The question moved Mrs. Roosevelt to her first really outspoken declaration against the accepted standards of the surroundings in which she had spent her childhood. Like others of her generation, she had begun to think for herself—and neither the standards nor the education which she had received appeared to have any genuine validity. This critical attitude had long been evident among American women who enjoyed none of the advantages of inherited wealth or social position. The lady, insulated as she was from the stresses and tensions of common experience, was the last to adopt it. But the results, as the example of Mrs. Roosevelt and many others were to show, led to an expanded horizon. A new prospect opened. The opportunity which it offered had the force of an obligation. It was the prospect of more thorough self-mastery, more complete function, more significant participation in the creative life of the nation.

For Mrs. Roosevelt—who, as the years passed, was to devote her energy to every worthy social cause—the field of politics provided the threshold to a career. It afforded one to her cousin, Theodore Roosevelt's daughter, Alice Longworth, who became an able and witty political journalist. It led Mrs. Borden Harriman to a position in the high councils of the Democratic party. Appointed by President Wilson as a member of the Federal Industrial Relations Commission set up to investigate the causes of widespread conflict between capital and labor, the minority report upon which she collaborated at the end of three years' study established her as an authority on one of the most important issues confronting the nation. The effect of this experience upon the psychology of the lady was revealed by the striking tribute which Mrs. Harriman paid to "Mother" Jones, the old labor agitator who, for more than half a century, had kept alive the worker's hunger for freedom. Mother Jones had been a firebrand, foul-mouthed and partisan, but Mrs. Harriman thought her the most significant woman in America, though her life had been alien to everything comfortable American womanhood is supposed to stand for. The gulf between the worlds of Mrs. Astor and Mother Jones had been bridged; and this was in many ways more remarkable than that Mrs. Harriman, appointed Minister to Norway by President Franklin Roosevelt, should render distinguished service as a diplomat.

Mrs. Wharton, who had been one of the first to question the values of the traditional social pattern, thought herself, like Theodore Roosevelt, a self-made man. In her old age, she came to question the value of emancipation; though, to a limited degree, she had sought emancipation for herself. Considering the grandchildren of her contemporaries, young women taught by their elders to despise the kitchen and the linen room, and to substitute the acquiring of University degrees for the more complex art of civilized living, she was inclined to think the higher education of women a social danger. Brooks Adams, whose studies in history led him to anticipate the decline and collapse of modern civilization, took an equally pessimistic view. The effect of woman's emancipation, he felt, was to make her ashamed of her sex, and compel her to imitate the man. As the cement of society, the head of the family, the center of cohesion, the woman had virtually ceased to exist. She had become a wandering isolated unit, rather a dispersive than a collective force. These opinions, whatever their merit, registered the phenomenal swiftness with which social change had taken place. Even as a subject for fiction and drama, the world of "Society"—the world of Henry James' novels, and Mrs. Wharton's, of Clyde Fitch's comedies, and Langdon Mitchell's—had ceased to have any relevance. In letter after letter, James lamented that his later novels were unread. In the nineteen-twenties, writing to Scott Fitzgerald, Mrs. Wharton ruefully suggested that, to his generation, her work must seem the literary equivalent of tufted furniture and gas chandeliers.

If the world about which she wrote had diminished in significance, she was, so to speak, the victim of her personal example. For it had been quickly followed, even by her former neighbors at Newport. Elsie Clews Parsons, daughter of the banker Henry Clews, went to study the Zuni Indians of the Southwest, pushed her explorations into Mexico, and wrote a series of books which awakened the nation to the necessity of preserving a heritage of art, folklore and culture in danger of extinction. She wrote other books as well, admirable studies in history, ethnology and anthropology; she wandered to the Cape Verde Islands, and the Sea Islands off Georgia to prosecute her studies; she helped to edit the *American Journal of Folklore*. Another Newport neighbor, Gertrude Vanderbilt Whitney, seriously practiced the art of sculpture. Young American artists knew her as a modest, generous benefactor; and the public was to profit by her foundation of the Whitney Museum in New York, and its constantly expanding collection of the works of contemporary American painters and sculptors. And there was young Miss Alice Duer, who profoundly shocked Mrs. Astor by proposing to work her way through college after her family's fortune had been lost. She carried out her intention, specializing in advanced mathematics and astronomy; only the spur of financial necessity led her to develop, professionally, a natural aptitude for writing. As Alice Duer Miller, she was to have a long career, to win wealth and popular success through her fiction, journalism and verse, and to work in the theater, the movies and radio.

Such diverse careers were symptomatic of the nature of social change. The world of Newport and Fifth Avenue had little in common with the learned society of scientists. It was remote from the studios of painters and sculptors, for it understood art only as a relic of the past. And what could it make of the roisterous group of sophisticates who, in the Jazz Age, foregathered at a round table in the dining room of the Hotel Algonquin in New York, won journalistic celebrity as the "Thanatopsis Literary and Inside Straight Club," and invited a Duer to charter membership?

By then many of the great establishments of Newport were vacant; those on Fifth Avenue were falling to the wreckers, and being replaced by towering blocks of apartments. As an influence on fashion, on manners, on the complex art of civilized living, the vanished lady had been superseded. Her successor, for the American public, was the movie star—who often exceeded her in audacity, capriciousness and extravagance. The lady's daughter, or granddaughter, was usually being taught some means of earning her livelihood. She was to be found, in increasing numbers, making a career for herself; in the offices of women's magazines, in Hollywood and the theater, among entertainers in nightclubs, among professional models, in fashionable shops; occasionally in the practice of law or medicine, or teaching in a college. Whatever she was doing, it seemed clear that she was seeking that free development irrespective of its bearing on the other sex which announced her final emancipation and declared her refusal to be—as the lady often had been—a ready-made garment, designed to fit the average man.

CHAPTER II
The Woman Takes Over

[I] THE VOLCANO OF UNREST

As the new century dawned, America's most popular poetess discussed one of its emergent problems in *The Cosmopolitan*. A stately figure, Mrs. Ella Wheeler Wilcox was softly enveloped by plumes, chiffons and Oriental metaphysics. Her life was blameless, but her imagination simmered. Day after day she boiled gently, always with a singing sound. Over the land, millions of women throbbed to her verses, little suspecting that her psychic temperature, like their own, was induced by daydreams. Many of them wrote to her. The mountain of mail that reached her, she said, was often a seething volcano of unrest. Was it not time that something be done about the restlessness of the modern woman? Mrs. Wilcox thought it was.

Others, equally aware of the condition, shared her anxiety. Charlotte Perkins Gilman, a feminist and the author of many excellent books, expressed concern about the new type of home that had begun to appear in American cities. What would be the effect of a dwelling lifted clean off the ground—yardless, cellarless, stairless, even kitchenless? Did the American woman know how to make wise use of her new leisure? Mrs. Gilman doubted it. She described her as relieved of much household drudgery, but too ignorant, too timid, too self-indulgent to do other work, wasting her time, laboring at amusement, and salving her conscience with charity.

This description provoked soul searching among leaders of the General Federation of Women's Clubs, founded in 1889 as the channel of a new force in progressive womanhood. Were its more than fifty thousand members actually ignoring the new life for women, the startling fact that "women now form a new social group, separate, and to a degree homogeneous"? Surely the earnestness of the clubs could not be doubted! Was not each of them a "mutual improvement society," leading its members "out into better hopes, nobler aspirations, and larger life"?

There were clubs organized for the study of the art of the Renaissance, Chinese religions before Confucius, or the mystery of Browning. In cities, towns and even remote villages, women were meeting every second Wednesday to read papers on Plato and Dante, on the language of the Iroquois, or the trail of the Saracens in Spain. They bravely embarked on a series of programs devoted to Goethe's *Faust*—first debating the question, "Can we best attain to a true appreciation of the poet and his work by viewing him as a man like other men, or as one touched by the Divine fire?" Could it be true, as a prominent member charged, that such effort came to precisely nothing? For Mrs. Rheta Childe Dorr, a successful journalist, tartly suggested that the effect of club papers was merely to prove whether the writer was a skimmer, a wader, or a deep-sea diver in standard editions of the encyclopedias! Clearly, Mrs. Dorr lacked respect for the "Middle-aged Woman's University."

But so did others. In 1904, the Federation installed a new president. Brisk, buxom Mrs. Sarah Platt Decker was a resident of Denver, accustomed to high altitudes but given to an impish humor. In Colorado women were full citizens, familiar with the ballot for more than a decade, and Mrs. Decker had worked actively among politicians in behalf of reform. She had a hearty contempt for little bodies of congenial spirits who gathered in musty study clubs. To the delegates assembled in convention, she issued a challenge. "Dante is dead," she told them. "He died several centuries ago, and a great many things have happened since his time. Let us drop the study of his *Inferno* and proceed in earnest to contemplate our own social order!"

The immediate results were surprising. Six years later, another president was able to announce that the Federation had no platform except "the care of women and children, and the home, the latter meaning the four walls of the city, as well as the four walls of brick

and mortar." Even Mrs. Dorr marveled at the rapidity of change, recording with pride that the great majority of the women's clubs were
organized for social service.

Leaders developed who could foresee the immense power that an organized womanhood might some time wield, and who had courage to
direct the forces under them towards vital objects. The old programs
had been laughed out of existence. Instead, the clubs were grappling
with child welfare, public health, the protection of women in industry,
pure food legislation, extension of educational facilities, civil service
reform, the elimination of commercialized vice. "What are you eating
with today, garbage or the social evil?" Miss Jane Addams was asked by
an elevator boy in the Chicago City Club, as she hastened to a luncheon.
For the interest of the clubs in self-culture had given way to a militant
effort for social reform. Even the exclusive Colony Club of New York,
which appeared to be nothing more than a beautiful toy for its
wealthy and aristocratic members, inaugurated a course in industrial
economics given by John Mitchell and lesser lights of the labor world.
In many communities, the women's clubs were the only agencies
actively working for civic improvement. Miss Addams, herself deeply
involved in their projects, found them ready to investigate any situation
which seemed to call for vigorous action.

With more than a million members by 1912, the federated clubs
represented a vast social and civic movement. Their assistance was invited by the Federal government when social discontent among workers
on the Panama Canal threatened to postpone its completion; a representative was sent to the Isthmus, and organized the wives and
daughters of government employees into clubs. The Federal government recognized the power of women's organizations, and approved
their interest in public questions. But vested interests were beginning
to fear it. The president of the National Association of Manufacturers
warned his colleagues against the club activities of their wives and
daughters; they were becoming too friendly toward reforms inimical to
industrial profits.

The mood of the women was as earnest as ever. But hadn't it become
disquietingly belligerent? They professed to repudiate the view—
held by man in the aggregate—that strife is not only inevitable but desirable; that material gain and visible reward are alone worth coveting.
They boldly asserted that they were weary of wars and hatreds, impatient of greed and privilege, sickened of poverty, disease and social

injustice. They had evolved a group opinion and a group ideal. They were learning how to exert mass pressure on politicians and industrialists. They were becoming adept in the tricky business of shaping public opinion. They declared themselves ready to display, in their new-found enthusiasm, a singularly obstinate spirit. Conservative folk sighed for the good old times when a woman knew her place.

The lady had wanted to transform her personal life. But the woman was proposing to transform her environment—and this was quite another matter. It was not altogether her own idea; the notion had, as it were, a history. A current of discontent had been rising over the land, and powerful voices were calling into question certain aspects of the established social order. Rapid industrial expansion, together with increasing concentration of financial control, were creating great depressed areas in the national scene. Was it true that a condition had arisen which enabled a wealthy minority to exploit the masses? Was it true that the avenues of opportunity were closed? That large segments of the population were permanently condemned to a degraded existence?

The woman could not have avoided these questions, had she wanted to. They were being debated, bitterly and passionately, in nearly every quarter. By politicians like William Jennings Bryan and Theodore Roosevelt. By labor leaders like John Mitchell and Eugene V. Debs. By a little band of writers in the popular muckraking magazines. By Christian Socialists and other liberal clergymen from their pulpits. And, in the colleges, by such scholars as Richard T. Ely, John R. Commons, Vida D. Scudder, Simon N. Patton and Thorstein Veblen, who often reached nonacademic audiences by means of popular lectures and articles. A quest for social justice was under way. The women's organizations were quickly drawn into it. On all levels of this general movement women soon began to assume the responsibility of leadership.

[2] DEPUTY FOR CONSCIENCE

Miss Jane Addams exemplified their new outlook on life. Already, she was the most famous woman in the country, and Europeans sometimes called her its first citizen. This was a tribute to her idealism, which they liked to think was genuinely American, though in America perhaps almost extinct. But Americans, who knew her to be an innovator, were aware that she was no exception. The women of her day recognized her ideals as their own. They felt that she had anticipated their experience, and was undertaking to express it for them. She was, in a sense, the deputy of their consciences, speaking and acting for them on the grand scale and the national scene.

In part, this was an effect of her personality. For, to the women of the time, she reflected their favorite image of themselves. There was no accent on youth in those days. Maturity was a badge of honor, proudly displayed. And it almost seemed as if Miss Addams had always been middle-aged. She was conventional, well bred, well dressed. She was serious, public spirited and efficient in action. She led a crowded, busy life. As she aged and grew stout, and her hair whitened, she came to resemble a wise, kindly maiden aunt; the person to whom a family would turn in time of trouble, confessing all its shameful secrets, somewhat dreading her rebuke, but sure of comfort and shrewd advice.

Miss Addams' family was the nation. She exercised the prerogatives of a universal maiden aunt, and one of them was to speak her mind plainly. Though she was a consistent champion of unpopular causes, her personal popularity seldom suffered by it. Even when she gave her support to Henry Ford's peace ship and opposed American participation in the first World War, she was eventually forgiven. In her role of maiden aunt she could scarcely help resembling a moral porcupine. Her prickly independence was often inconvenient, but there was something admirable about it. Wasn't it almost her duty to go poking about in queer places which everyone else agreed to ignore, and blandly prod the family into tidying them up? Where after all would one expect to find her, if not in the forefront of every movement to improve the world—international peace, woman suffrage, child welfare, or whatever? The more "advanced" the movement, the likelier it was to appeal to her. But all this did not curtail her right to censure. Miss Addams made the most of it.

In her make-up there was a strong element of Middle-Western, middle-class common sense. This gave even her most advanced ideas the color of respectability. When people called her an idealist, the term implied no reproach. She was the kind of idealist whom Americans liked and understood even if they disagreed with her, for her ideals always furnished a program for action; they were practical. She saw every social problem as a moral issue. But wasn't this the characteristic

American way of stating a problem, in order to get it solved? Stated in any other terms, nothing might be done about it. An intellectual, social, or economic problem might leave the public cold. An appeal to conscience was certain to rouse the American people. Miss Addams knew their habits of thought. She shared them.

The fact that she was an idealist led her, one summer, to journey to Russia in order to spend a day with Leo Tolstoy. The visit was to prove how little radical she was, and how impatient of eccentricity, even in the realm of ideals. Tolstoy was living as a peasant on his ancestral estate, abstaining from all comforts, despite his advanced age; laboring in the fields; practising an extremely literal Christianity. Miss Addams was known to him as one who had long shared the lives of the poor. When they met, she noticed that he glanced distrustfully at the sleeves of her dress. The leg-of-mutton sleeve was fashionable; hers were monstrously large. He took hold of a sleeve, pulled it out to its fullest breadth, and reproachfully observed that there was enough stuff on one arm to make a frock for a little girl. Did she not find such a dress a barrier to the people? For women, he approved a cotton blouse following the simple lines of the human form. Though she did not argue the point, Miss Addams thought the "people" of Chicago might find it peculiar. Presently, he inquired about the domestic economy of Hull House. Where did the food come from? She admitted that it came from a farm which she owned, but did not herself cultivate. Tolstoy was profoundly shocked. Was she, then, only a social parasite, an exploiter of the suffering masses? Brooding on this afterwards, Miss Addams concluded that Tolstoy was more logical than life warrants. Such excess of logic, even in respect to moral principle, was a form of eccentricity. And wasn't eccentricity only a way of evading, instead of meeting, the real problems of life?

It was like her to brood over such questions. She had always been serious minded. At college she was an excellent student, rather proud of her erudition. There was talk of her becoming a missionary; the predestined spinster may already have been detected. When women of her generation remained single from choice, vanity usually urged them to explain their motives. Thus, Miss Ida M. Tarbell told that when only fourteen she was praying to God on her knees to keep her from marriage. Her prayer, she said, was an echo of the strident feminist cry filling the air at that moment, the cry that woman was a slave in a man-made world. Miss Addams, however, had not sought divine intercession. In her day, she said, women were unable to combine a career with marriage. Men did not want to marry women of the new type. Public opinion did not tolerate the double role of profession and homemaking. And modern inventions had not yet made a new type of housekeeping practicable. Did she cherish a grievance for having predated the washing machine, vacuum cleaner and kitchenette? Probably not. The real point was that, while still at college, she made up her mind to study medicine and live with the poor.

A breakdown in health compelled her to abandon this project. So, like the heroines of Henry James' novels, she set out for Europe, in search of culture. As a sightseer in London she was taken, late one night, on a tour of the East End slums. The misery and wretchedness she saw haunted her. On her travels, she became aware of social maladjustment everywhere, gibing at her with a sense of her uselessness. Soon, she was suffering a moral revulsion against her feverish search after culture—as American clubwomen were subsequently to do. Was she not completely out of touch with reality? Was not life, with all the difficulties removed, too much like eating a sweet dessert the first thing in the morning?

She visited the great European museums, and came away with an admiration for Dürer, who had been unwilling to lend himself to a smooth and cultivated view of life. Her faith in the moral worth of "culture" had been rudely shaken. Was it not merely a kind of ornament, a costly superfluity? She recognized the futility of all artistic and intellectual effort when disconnected from the ultimate test of the conduct it inspired. What about her own scholarship, her own conduct? How could she justify her pleasant, self-centered existence? She had been lulling her conscience with a dreamer's scheme.

This conclusion was natural to one who, in youth, had worshiped Emerson. Her enthusiasm for Emerson led her, when his friend Bronson Alcott lectured at Rockford College, to clean the old philosopher's heavy cloth overshoes in a state of ecstatic energy. In those days she heard the clear summons of an "inner voice," and had resolved to share the lives of the poor; for Emerson urged absolute compliance with the dictates of one's inner voice. Had it not spoken again, that night in London?

In London, a group of university graduates had lately established Toynbee Hall, a social settlement in the East End, the first of its kind. Miss Addams joined them as a resident worker. Her vocation, her duty, could no longer be ignored. She would work for social adjustment by seeking to break down the existing barriers between classes. So, during the winter of 1889, with her friend Miss Ellen Gates Starr, she opened Hull House in the heart of a Chicago slum.

Something resembling Miss Addams' crisis of conscience occurred in the lives of many other American women. Their discovery of widespread social maladjustment came as a challenge to which culture furnished no adequate answer. It produced a mood of moral earnestness. It incited them to action, even when they weren't very certain about what kind of action to take. Any action was better than none; and one could learn as one went along. Shortly after Miss Addams opened Hull House, another Middle-Western woman went to New York City to study trained nursing. Miss Lillian D. Wald knew nothing about the awakening of a social conscience or the existence of a settlement movement. She had little more than an inspiration to be of use in some way or somehow. An errand of mercy took her into the slums of the lower East Side. She was distressed by the misery of the underprivileged masses who dwelt there. Presently she went to live among them as a volunteer nurse. In time, Miss Wald established the Henry Street Settlement, and a district-nursing service. Because of her experience in all forms of social welfare—gained by the experimental, trial-and-error method of meeting problems as they arose—she, like Miss Addams, soon became a national figure.

Hull House and Henry Street, and similar institutions in cities throughout the country, developed social services which later became public functions. They initiated progressive social legislation. They provided opportunities for representatives of labor, management and government to meet and discuss controversial issues. They co-operated with agencies of the Federal government, and gradually brought about an expansion of its responsibility to dependent social groups. From the ranks of their residents they furnished specialists in many varieties of public welfare work, originators of reforms like Mrs. Florence Kelley, Miss Julia C. Lathrop, Miss Josephine Lowell and Miss Gertrude Barnum. Even on poets like Edgar Lee Masters and Vachel Lindsay the experience of residence at Hull House left a decisive impression which affected their future writing.

Indeed, as the years passed, Miss Addams' sentimental decision to share the lives of the poor produced some very extraordinary results. From its modest start, Hull House developed into a complex organization which acquired the prestige of a national social laboratory. It served as a model, not only in the United States, but in many foreign countries. Visitors came from all over the world to study its varied operations, which were as extensive as those of a university or a municipal government. But its true importance did not lie in its practical achievements, notable as these were. Hull House was more significant for what it represented than for what it did. For it expressed a new social attitude, as it were a new philosophy, to which the plain American people, in increasing numbers, were pledging their allegiance.

This was why Theodore Roosevelt asked Miss Addams to help prepare the platform adopted by the Progressive party in the campaign of 1912—when the demands for social justice, so long discussed by small groups, were at last thrust into the stern arena of political action. Who, better than Miss Addams, could state the principles in which the new point of view was grounded? She had already analyzed them in a series of provocative books. Again and again, on lecture tours that took her into the smallest towns served by the Chautauqua circuits, she had discussed them with all types of audiences. She had served as missionary, apostle, propagandist. And—most improbably— she had succeeded. The new doctrine was like a rising wind, sweeping over the country. Theodore Roosevelt, challenging privilege in the name of decent government and fair play, knew that Miss Addams had opened the way to Armageddon.

For the moment, the battle was taking place in the arena of political action. The issues were being defined in economic terms. But to Miss Addams, and to many like-minded Americans, the heart of the matter was neither political nor economic. It was purely moral. The long-range solution would therefore have to be an ethical one.

In their view, the economic structure of society, like its political structure, existed to serve a purpose. That purpose was to make possible, for all, a particular way of life. The American economic system, with its trusts and tycoons, its concentration of power and wealth, no longer facilitated that way of life; it obstructed it. Americans had assumed that evolution was synonymous with progress. But in economic as in biological development, evolution was a blind force. It resulted in the reign of jungle law; only the ruthless and powerful survived—by treading down their fellows. If the American way of life was to be preserved, the process must be halted. Economic operations must be controlled by ethical principle. They must be made responsive to a truly social ideal. They must be directed, not so much to the survival of the fittest, as to the fitting of as many as possible to survive. In a broad sense, property rights must yield to human rights. Americans would have to add the social function to democracy.

This doctrine clashed with that of the powerful high priests of the "bitch-goddess Success." Had not William Graham Sumner laid down the principle that the social order is fixed by laws of nature precisely analagous to those of the physical order? That the most that man can do is by his ignorance and conceit to mar the operation of social laws? By man's ignorance and conceit, Sumner meant humanitarian effort; the absurd attempt to make the world over. And George Baer, president of a Morgan railroad, speaking for the tycoons, had expressed Sumner's doctrine in warning the workers that their rights and interests must be confided to the Christian gentlemen to whom God in his infinite wisdom had given the control of the property interests of the country.

But Miss Addams, with certain other Americans, was confident that the world *could* be made over, and was hopeful that it would be. The immediate, urgent problem was to make the plain people believe in this possibility, and persuade them to care. Philosophers like William James and John Dewey insisted that society is a plastic organism; that social environment is only material to be shaped, by intelligence, to accord with men's desire; that the world is wild and young and subject to change. To simple folk throughout the country, who perhaps had never heard of James and Dewey, who were ignorant of all social theory but aware that the "American dream" had somehow been lost, she carried the hopeful new gospel. Nature will care for progress if men will care for reform, Professor Simon N. Patton declared, attempting to reduce the creed of liberalism to a phrase. Miss Addams made reform seem an exciting adventure as well as an ethical obligation.

Reform demanded patience and faith. Not all liberals had these qualities in the ample measure of Jane Addams. The eminent lawyer Clarence Darrow, one of her earlier associates at Hull House, concluded that "it's no use putting cold packs on the brow of a feverish man; find the source of the fever and rout it out of the body." Was Hull House, were all unselfish efforts dedicated to reform, no more than a cold pack, a mere palliative? As an old lady, well past her seventieth year, Miss Addams sometimes wondered. She had seen a postwar generation cynically desert the quest for social justice, and make a gospel of individual freedom—especially in sex relations—perhaps because their predecessors had been too exclusively concerned with the masses. Now, she saw the country sunk in an abysmal economic depression, the people in a mood of despair. After nearly fifty years of valiant effort, Hull House was still surrounded by fetid slums, still only an island in a vast sea of human misery. An old, intimate friend said that Miss Addams's accumulated honors in no way consoled her for her utter failure to lessen poverty even in her own settlement neighborhood.

Social maladjustment was greater than ever. Miss Addams thought she knew why. Was not its real cause the failure of our ideas and conventions, not to mention our prejudices, to keep up with the pace of material change? The American mind had not kept abreast of its own inventions. Culture still lagged behind civilization. Culture, which had provoked a revolt of conscience in her youth, returned to plague her at the end. Yet she, herself, would be remembered by what she had added to it. For—as much as any American of her time—she had awakened the nation to the gravity of social issues, and equipped it with a social conscience. If, in the great mass of the American people, there existed a resolute will to bring about change, that will had been fostered by a maiden aunt who never failed to speak her mind.

[3] REBELS

Before women of the prosperous classes had begun in earnest to contemplate their own social order, women leaders had arisen among the underprivileged. In 1877 there occurred a nationwide railroad strike which paralyzed nearly every city. Violence, disorder and destruction broke out everywhere, but in Chicago they precipitated a reign of terror. Watching the unequal struggle between workers and United States troops sent in to put down "the ragged commune wretches," Mary Harris Jones resolved to join the forces of the workers. She was the middle-aged widow of an iron molder, who earned a good living as dressmaker to the rich. She closed her shop, joined the Knights of Labor and became an organizer. Later she identified herself with the coal miners of Pennsylvania and fought their battles until past her ninetieth year.

Mother Jones, as she came to be known, was tough, sentimental, impatient of all social theories and most reforms. A benign little old woman in a tidy bonnet, she was incendiary. It was her pride that she had always raised hell to keep alive the hunger for freedom among her boys, the miners. Her aim was to make labor a religion with labor, and to do this she would use any means that offered. She could out-talk and outswear any man. Once, in order to dramatize the plight of the miners, she led an army of ragged, starving children through a dozen Eastern cities. She lived in an atmosphere of violence, at the very center of bitter industrial warfare. She was often homeless, sometimes penniless, usually in danger of arrest and imprisonment. Her fiery spirit never subsided; she was incapable of understanding defeat or despair. It was this spirit which led Clarence Darrow to describe her as the Wendell Phillips of the labor movement. Her own verdict on her life was nearer the mark. "I have made the nation know that I am alive and on the ground," she once told an audience of clubwomen. She had.

Two women of similar caliber were among the leaders of the agrarian revolt that surged up in the Middle West during the decade of the eighteen-nineties. Mrs. Anna L. Diggs and Mrs. Mary E. Lease came from farms that for, ten years, had been parched by drought and seared by hot winds. They knew the plight of the debt-ridden farmers of the Great Plains. Simple women, without much education, they had a bitter sense of grievance and injustice which flared into the eloquence learned at revival meetings. Throughout the Middle West, great crowds poured into the little towns to hear them speak in churches, schoolhouses, public squares—and, for a season, Mrs. Lease made the country ring with her battle cry: "What you farmers need to do is raise less corn and more Hell!"

But it was in the ranks of organized labor that the new leadership of women became most rapidly effective. With few exceptions, the younger generation of leaders bore no resemblance to pioneers like Mother Jones. They made little use of invective or spellbinding oratory. They became experts in practical strategy, makers of policy; and, in order to meet on their own ground men like Samuel Gompers who were "labor statesmen," they proceeded to acquire a thorough grounding in economics, general social theory and the laws affecting labor. Women like Rose Schneiderman, Agnes Nestor and Fannia M. Cohn, emerging from the cap-makers', glove-makers' and garment-makers' unions, made themselves powerfully felt in the crusade against sweat-shops, and soon rose to positions of influence in the national movement, spokesmen for women in industry, but likewise representatives of labor as a social group.

The fiery example of Mother Jones had one conspicuous follower. Elizabeth Gurley Flynn had been brought up in the extreme radical wing of the labor movement. Her father was an early "wobbly"—a member of the revolutionary, roistering, reckless Industrial Workers of the World. This organization represented workers excluded from the conservative craft-unions—migratory and unskilled labor; the "bums" and "bindle-stiffs" and "hall-cats" who, by leaders like Sam Gompers, were considered a proletarian rabble. A handsome, vivacious girl of nineteen, Miss Flynn received nationwide publicity during a spectacular conflict between the I. W. W. and the authorities of the city of Spokane. As the "wobbly Joan of Arc," she was among the leaders of a series of violent mass strikes conducted by the I. W. W., using her Irish gift of eloquence both to incite the workers and to plead their cause with the public. In the opinion of Emma Goldman, she was one of the first American women revolutionists of proletarian background.

Of such women, Emma Goldman herself was the most notorious. Short, stocky, exceedingly plain, she looked like a strong-minded, respectable housewife. She was strong-minded, no housewife, and anything but respectable. Her prim white shirtwaist and black skirt disguised a proletarian Aspasia whose tempestuous love affairs, whatever their private passion, were always public demonstrations of a theory. Emma Goldman loved theories with an indiscriminate ardor. The violence of her affection for ideas was equalled only by the violence of her antipathy to capitalists and reformers. As she was convinced that every attractive idea ought to be adopted, her life—except for intervals spent in prison—held few vacant moments. In the phrase of the day, she "believed in experience." So her path was littered with abandoned lovers and discarded philosophies. To all of them she had been faithful, in her fashion. Each had seemed irresistible—for a while.

Like Miss Addams, Emma Goldman was a sentimentalist with a swollen conscience. This combination can produce a domestic nuisance, or a woman with a mission, who applies the same tactics to a larger group. Miss Goldman never doubted her mission. Indeed, she was incapable of any doubt. Humor was not her strong point. She displayed that exasperating consistency about minor matters characteristic of the genuine zealot; and, running true to form, she ignored consistency in the large. Thus, the refusal of life to be bound by the logic of the moment reduced her to permanent perplexity. There was something childlike about her persistent efforts to make it submit, to bring off the trick; and about her aggrieved surprise at having failed. It was her only perplexity. The problems raised by her industrious conscience were seldom more than rhetorical questions. She was ready with the answers even before the questions were uttered.

She had two careers, and her talent for dogmatic affirmation was serviceable to both. She was a political revolutionary. She was also, during the second decade of the century, a very popular lecturer. Liberalism was then at flood tide, and "new" ideas were exercising a powerful attraction. There was a "new school" in every field—social theory, fiction, poetry, drama, painting, philosophy—and everyone was eager to be brought up to date. Even the women's clubs, suspicious as they were of "culture," succumbed to the cult of the contemporary. The male lecturer—who sometimes felt like a species of eunuch admitted to circles where no normal male, whatever his motives, would dream of intruding—was already provoking an agreeable confusion in the minds of women bent upon improving the world. The situation was an ideal one for Emma Goldman. Who was better equipped to offer the plump and pretty pupils of extravagance, as H. G. Wells described them, a repertory of new ideas? Had she not dallied with all of them—free love; birth control; psychoanalysis; syndicalism; the social novel and the social drama; Russian literature; Karl Marx and his errors; Peter Kropotkin and the true gospel? Like Margaret Fuller, she felt competent to speak with authority on any subject. And she did. Women who pursued culture in bands, as if fearing to meet it alone, emerged from her lectures slightly dazed, somewhat exalted, with a pleasant sense of vicarious peril. Sometimes their peril was very real. She had a way of starting them thinking.

Her mission, however, was to help bring about the proletarian revolution. It had been disclosed to her as an immigrant girl, newly arrived from Russia and sewing garments in a factory for seventy hours every week at a wage of two dollars and fifty cents. She became a convert to the theory of anarchism—and what wonder? Presently, she went to live in the slums of the lower East Side in New York City. Touring these slums many years later, Henry James concluded that, in the United States, there was such a thing as the freedom to grow up to be blighted, which might be the only freedom in store for the smaller fry of future generations. Emma Goldman anticipated his conclusion. It was the only freedom she knew in her youth. It made her a friend of the people. It also made her an implacable foe of the state.

She received her education in East Side cafés where foreign intellectuals debated how to save the American workers whose language they seldom understood. There was much talk of the class struggle and the social revolution. How could it best be expedited? By terrorism, as in Russia? Why not dynamite a factory? Why not bomb a prominent millionaire, no less an oppressor of the masses than any Russian grand duke? Grim Johan Most, a political exile from Europe, had published a pamphlet on the science of revolutionary warfare. He was Emma Goldman's mentor. This kind of talk went to the head of Alexander Berkman, an intense young philosophical radical. He was Emma Goldman's lover. One day, during a strike at the Homestead works of the Carnegie Steel Company in which several workers had been shot, Berkman made an unsuccessful attempt on the life of Carnegie's partner, Henry C. Frick. Overnight, Emma Goldman became notorious. Thenceforward she was known as "Red Emma" and was seldom free from surveillance by the police. She achieved further notoriety when a demented youth, Leon Czolgosz, assassinated President McKinley, and it developed that, under an assumed name, he had talked with her several times before setting out on his murderous errand. She was ignorant of his intention, and innocent of complicity in his act.

In point of fact, she had a deeply bourgeois abhorrence of such crimes. Isolated instances of political terrorism served no useful purpose; cruelty could not be defeated by cruelty. The revolution was another story. It was the inevitable prelude to utopia. It would usher in a condition of affairs that would replace ruthless competition by voluntary co-operation. Coercion would be unknown. Poverty, war and crime would cease to exist. The need for government would disappear. The state would wither away. For the first time, the individual would know absolute freedom. This was the revolutionary utopia which she foresaw. Her anarchism was a doctrine of individualism carried to its extreme conclusions. In 1920, after serving a year in prison for obstructing wartime military conscription—like Miss Addams, she was a conscientious pacifist—Emma Goldman was deported to Russia as a dangerous radical. She expected to find her vision of utopia realized in the revolutionary fatherland. Her disillusion in Communist Russia was the major tragedy of her life.

No less than Miss Addams, Emma Goldman represented the earnest, social-minded, restless mood common to many American women in the early years of the twentieth century. Conscience, sentimentality and the new culture often conspired to make them muddleheaded, however well meaning. Emma Goldman never understood that the individualism which she professed as an ideal had produced the economic order which she hoped to see destroyed. She was contemptuous of reformers and liberals because they were not logical; and not revolutionists. She thought the settlement people—like Miss Addams—sincere but misguided idealists whose efforts, being merely palliative, only served to obstruct social change. Yet, disbelieving in reforms, she gave herself indiscriminately to all radical causes, and defended with impartial zeal all efforts to bring about the improvement of a society which she wanted to overturn. This meant only that her heart and her head did not always march in step. Her heart attached itself to all liberal— and liberating—projects. Her mind demanded the extreme, uncompromising solution. Even had she been aware of this major inconsistency, she would not have acknowledged it. Vanity would have compelled her to declare herself, as she did, a revolutionary to the very end.

Whatever their differences in outlook, the clubwomen, the social reformers, the labor leaders and the spokesmen for the proletariat all had a common objective. If only as women, they were acutely sensitive to social injustice, and hoped to eliminate it. Their purpose was to transform their environment, to bring about a "better life." But, ironically, the most radical change produced in the social scene was in no way due to their efforts. This change was not deliberate, but its effects touched nearly every area of American life. It was produced by women destined to remain anonymous.

[4] ANONYMOUS TRANSFORMERS

By the middle eighteen-nineties, women had begun to invade the field of economic activity. The foray soon became a mass movement. In 1900, almost one-fifth of all American women over the age of ten were reported to be breadwinners. Ten years later, the proportion had reached nearly one-quarter. The greatest relative increase occurred in office and store employment. New instruments of business efficiency were coming into general use. Women were virtually swept into office work by the typewriter, cash register, addressograph and filing system. Miss Tarbell noted that by 1900 there existed in Wall Street the phenomenon of a private secretary drawing a salary of ten thousand dollars a year. It was not long before women gained a monopoly of the stenographic field, occupying ninety-seven percent of all available positions. But although it was only a step from the confidential position where a woman had made herself essential into the ranks of the directorate, the step required time.

The spectacular conquest of the stenographic field was paralleled in others. The rapid movement of women into business appeared to involve a widespread, dramatic break with tradition. But, to many women who participated, the break was more apparent than real. They had been trained, in the home, for an older form of the same service. As unmarried daughters at home they had "helped Father with his letters," the novelist Dorothy Canfield pointed out; as wives they had attended to a thousand tiresome small details so that their husbands could be free for real business. The transition to professional service in office and factory was easy and natural, though it required a more subtle adaptation than the earlier transition from sewing at home to making garments in a factory.

Yet the expanding share of women in economic activity sometimes exacted a heavy cost. In the eighteen-eighties, as a young, aspiring journalist from Kansas, Mrs. Florence Finch Kelly attempted to breach the stone walls of Boston, then still the literary center of the country. It was only after months of futile search that she obtained a job on a newspaper at a weekly salary of ten dollars; its proprietor wanted the feminine touch but disapproved of women in journalism. In 1894, when S. S. McClure invited Miss Tarbell to join his editorial staff, he offered her a weekly salary of forty dollars. Miss Tarbell had to her credit fifteen years of professional experience, and an established reputation. But forty dollars represented more money than she had ever expected to earn.

The Bureau of Labor undertook a comprehensive investigation of the position of women in four major industries during the years between 1907 and 1909. It reported that the large proportion of women wage earners were paid very low wages—wages in many cases inadequate to supply a reasonable standard of living for those dependent upon their own earnings for support. The immediate effect of a vast increase in the labor pool was to depress wages for women. Low pay was for a long time their only economic merit in competition with men. In 1914, nearly half the nonprofessional working women over sixteen years of age were earning less than six dollars a week. Nearly three-quarters were earning less than eight. Economists reported that seven dollars was necessary for bare subsistence, while more than eight dollars was required to provide a living wage.

In these circumstances, it became increasingly clear that mere equality of opportunity for women did not prevent their exploitation. By 1910, Mrs. Emily James Putnam was asserting that the working woman must have a special situation created for her if society is to get the utmost from her that she can do. It was obvious, even then, that in unrestricted competition with men she comes to grief and the race is injured. Under existing conditions she was bound to go to the wall. Though the interests of the working woman and the lady were essentially conflicting, they agreed in shrinking from the naïve law of force.

Women began taking steps to create a special situation for themselves. The National Woman's Trade Union League had been founded in 1903. Its immediate object was to raise compensation, for even in skilled work women were being paid only one-third as much as union men. The movement for labor organization spread rapidly. So did the attempt to force enactment of social legislation protecting women and children in industry. In this, the women's clubs co-operated with social workers like Miss Addams, Miss Wald and Mrs. Kelley, and with union leaders like Miss Schneiderman, Miss Nestor and Miss Cohn. The effort demonstrated the concerted power of an organized womanhood when directed towards vital objects. A beginning was made with the passage of laws restricting working hours and prescribing sanitary and safe standards for industrial plants. And by 1912, state laws were being enacted providing for minimum wage standards to eliminate unrestricted competition.

Yet not all women were convinced that legislation of this kind was desirable. Opposition to it developed among the organized suffragists. They resented regulation in behalf of women as a weaker sex requiring social protection. They wanted no special situation. They argued—with a show of realistic logic—that unless minimum wages were made equally applicable to women and men, they would merely become maximum wages for women, and might have the effect of excluding women from many types of employment. The controversy over this issue was to continue into the nineteen-forties, with opponents of the special-situation theory agitating for an equal-rights amendment to the Constitution as the only acceptable solution.

The movement of women into industry, the professions and public life was enormously speeded by the First World War. President Wilson did not exempt them from his call to service: "It is not as an army that we must shape and train for war, it is as a nation." The Woman's Committee of the Council of National Defence was set up to mobilize them. Among its members were such prominent representatives of feminine leadership as Dr. Anna Howard Shaw, Mrs. Carrie Chapman Catt, Miss Tarbell and Miss Agnes Nestor. The emergency demands of war opened opportunities for women on a scale never before conceived possible. Reviewing their activities a decade later, the historian Charles A. Beard asserted that they had worked in every capacity save that of the soldier at the battlefront, foreshadowing, perhaps, the day when equal opportunity would have no limitations or exceptions even there.

During the war, millions of women replaced absent men in manufacturing industries, business offices, financial institutions, transportation and communications services, and government bureaus. As the novelist Inez Haynes Irwin reported, "the executive secretary came into full power. Banks and department stores put women into executive positions with hundreds of subordinates. Women invented and established the tearooms which stretch from coast to coast." By the war's end, women were firmly entrenched in occupations that had previously been open only to men. Five hundred and seventy-two occupations were listed in the census of 1920. Of these, women were actively engaged in five hundred and thirty-seven.

Because of this condition, their long-belated enfranchisement, in 1920, failed to yield any very spectacular results. It did not usher in the millennium confidently predicted by the pioneer feminists. Nor did it confirm gloomy oracles like Brooks Adams who expected the vote to destroy the influence of woman in modern civilization, save in so far as her enfranchisement tended to degrade the democratic level of intelligence. It increased the political power of women to force the enactment of social legislation, and they used it for that purpose. In less than a decade, their political effort produced more than four hundred national, state and local laws promoting social welfare.

Partly in consequence of their enfranchisement, women began entering public service in increasingly responsible posts. A woman was elected to the bench of the Supreme Court of Ohio. During the administration of President Franklin D. Roosevelt, Mrs. Ruth Bryan Rohde and Mrs. Borden Harriman were appointed ministers to Scandinavian countries, and Mrs. Frances Perkins entered the Cabinet as Secretary of Labor. In many of the states, women presided over juvenile courts, and courts of domestic relations. Women had served in the Senate, and were frequently elected to the House of Representatives. They were as much at ease in Wall Street and political party conventions, Mrs. Mary R. Beard asserted, as they were by the fireside or in their beauty salons.

By the opening of the decade of the nineteen-forties it was possible for Mrs. Margaret Culkin Banning, a popular novelist, to say that work which was once begged by women as a right, and later chosen as a privilege, was then approaching an obligation. In the competitive arena, they had levelled all barriers. They operated railroads, public utilities, department stores, chains of hotels and restaurants. They controlled international enterprises in cosmetics. They were retained by great corporations as foreign trade consultants and public relations counsellors. They helped shape the policies of some of the nation's largest newspapers and magazines. They were successful in all branches of engineering. On the radio, and in the columns of the press, women— Miss Dorothy Thompson and Mrs. Eleanor Roosevelt were outstanding examples—told the people of the nation what they ought to think, and few any longer considered it remarkable. Theirs seemed a boundless horizon, Mrs. Beard declared. And Mrs. Banning noted that the American girl could now direct her ambition toward almost any kind of job without either losing face or being extravagant in hope for her future.

This was a social change as drastic, as pervasive in its effects, as any that had occurred in the nation's history. Nothing revealed it more clearly than the complete reversal of public opinion about the "woman question." At the turn of the century, the restlessness of the modern woman had been under attack: her disposition to question the social order; her reforming proclivities; her wistful desire for a career. Who, asked Mrs. Marion Harland, would banish from our midst the matronly figures so suggestive of home, comfort and motherly love? And a public official, reporting the drift of women into industry, called

it a sad comment on our civilization, since it would inevitably bring
about the loss of all maidenly modesty and those qualities which are
so highly prized by the true man.

But by the decade of the nineteen-forties, criticism had long been
directed against the woman of leisure; the women supported by men,
or economically independent, who were neither homemakers nor
wage earners, nor otherwise socially productive. The fiction of leading American novelists furnished a crowded gallery of satirical
portraits of the type—selfish, superficial, materialistic, predatory. Her
complacent egotism was the medium for boundless aspirations, and
whether she was called Undine Spragg or Fran Dodsworth made little
difference, for she was always the same. She was recognizably true to
the American scene, and the public, like the novelists, considered her
nothing to be proud of.

[5] THE DICTATORS AND THE FOLKWAYS

Even before the turn of the century, American writers were discussing
the peculiar power enjoyed by American women. Henry James believed, for many years, that the young girl was the one frail carrier of
culture in American civilization. Later, after long absence, he visited
the United States and revised his opinion: the young girl appeared to
be a pathetically broken reed. Henry Adams considered the American
man a negligible quantity, and felt that if a *dix-neuvième* was to be
built up for America, it must be for—and by—the women. But the
most revealing comment of all came from William Dean Howells, a
deeply sympathetic portrayer of the sex. Howells complained, somewhat ruefully, that the fate of every serious American writer was in
the hands of the women, for he had to go for their taste and their
sensibilities and their sex-piety along the whole line. However benevolent, they were absolute dictators.

Forty years later, it became evident that American women, in the
mass, commanded a power probably unique in history. Its effect upon
the character of American civilization was not meeting universal approval. Howells' complaint was frequently revived as an indictment,
furnishing a controversial theme for novelists, dramatists and critics.
Thus, for example, the witty and intellectual novelist John Erskine—
a former university professor—discussed *The Influence of Women and
Its Cure*. Americans, he charged, were now living in what was es-

sentially a woman's world—in a set of ideas which were qualified by woman's point of view rather than by man's. Analyzing that set of ideas as they operated in various fields of activity, Mr. Erskine found them, on the whole, defective and stultifying. This view was shared by another novelist, for the moment turned critic. In *Generation of Vipers*, Philip Wylie examined the nature of current American civilization and culture. These, he contended, were no longer being shaped by men, but by women. Women constituted the American audience for all art and all ideas. They were the ultimate consumers of most of the goods produced. They were the final arbiters of the "way of life" cultivated by the nation. The results of this condition were, in Mr. Wylie's opinion, scarcely to be commended. His judgment of the American woman was no more complimentary than that passed by the Adams brothers in their more candid moments.

If Americans were actually living in a woman's world, was not the situation due to the social inertia of American men? Woman's power to produce or obstruct changes in the mores had long been acknowledged by everyone. In these matters, the American woman habitually took her stand on moral principle, justifying the results—whatever their nature—on the highest ethical grounds. To men, the process was sometimes confusing.

For example, the American woman gave her allegiance, from its inception in the early eighteen-nineties, to the temperance movement. Men might ridicule the saloon-wrecking raids of that humorless crusader, Miss Carrie Nation; women applauded them. Lacking their support, the movement might never have resulted in nationwide prohibition. Like President Hoover, they thought it—for a time—a great social and economic experiment, noble in motive and far-reaching in purpose. As late as 1930, the predominantly dry sentiment among the women of the country was regarded as a guarantee of its permanence. "Repeal of the Eighteenth Amendment is almost an impossibility," declared Mrs. Mabel Walker Willebrandt, lately Assistant Attorney General in charge of enforcement. And Senator Sheppard, author of the amendment, felt that there was no more chance for its repeal than there was "for a hummingbird to fly to the planet Mars with the Washington Monument tied to its tail." But presently women —nearly a million and a half, organized as a pressure group—were striving to reverse the law of the land. Their argument was not based on the practical consequences of such action. They advocated repeal of prohibition, as women had previously advocated its enactment, in be-half of an abstract moral ideal. In the attempt to make the world over did it matter if intelligence faltered, so long as conscience remained versatile?

Over the years, as her public conscience applied itself to her private life, the American woman produced a remarkable change in the mores. That Howells, of all men, protested against the tyranny of her sex-piety was extremely significant. For Howells, whose art was "as natural as the toothache," was by temperament finicking and squeamish. But in those days Anthony Comstock—bearded, silk-hatted, frock-coated, as befitted a Victorian Savonarola—kept a virtuous, uneasy vigil over the arts. Respectable folk were outraged by novels like Stephen Crane's *Maggie* and Theodore Dreiser's *Sister Carrie*. The English actress Olga Nethersole, playing Daudet's *Sapho*, was beset by the attentions of the police. The city of Boston, having commissioned from Frederick Mac-Monnies a statue for its Public Library, rejected with horror his lovely nude Bacchante. To her old friend and admirer, Professor Charles Eliot Norton, Mrs. Wharton sent a copy of her new novel, *The House of Mirth*. The distinguished translator of Dante, forgetting Paolo and Francesca in his anxiety, urgently cautioned her that no great work of the imagination had ever been based on illicit passion.

Illicit passion, excluded from art, met with stern punishment when-ever it blemished the smooth and cultivated surface of life. One ex-ample of this punishment deeply impressed the English novelist H. G. Wells on his first visit to the United States. After the Russian revolution of 1905 Maxim Gorki came, out of a terrific confusion of bloodshed, squalor and injustice, to tell America, the land of light and achieved freedom, of all these evil things. Gorki was accompanied by a lady, presumably his legal wife. For a brief period they basked in an im-mense sunshine of public honors. Then it was discovered that his companion of many years was not, in fact, Mme. Gorki, but Mme. Andreieva; their union had not been sanctified. Denounced by the press, ejected by hotels and deserted by their friends, they found them-selves at last, after midnight, in the streets of New York City with every door closed against them.

But was it not precisely to guard against the improbable contingency of illicit passion that convention imposed a nice decorum? The power of convention to destroy those reckless enough to ignore it was absolute. Everyone knew this, and the knowledge made *The House of Mirth* an exciting book to read. Was not the inevitable doom of its heroine implicit in the first chapter? Lacking a chaperon, she refused to have tea with a young man in a public restaurant. But—oh, imprudent girl! —she consented to have tea in his bachelor apartment. On this point, the official arbiters of etiquette were explicit. Even an "elderly girl" of thirty-five must not visit an artist's studio alone—although there was in art an ennobling and purifying influence which should be a protection. So ruled Mrs. John Sherwood. And Mrs. Burton Harrison— although she was a professional author, she had been born a Cary of Virginia—also made chaperonage mandatory: a girl would not venture to combat it without the risk of sharp criticism from alien tongues. Mrs. Frank Learned expressed serious concern because, in many parts of the West and South, young girls had the privilege of visiting places of public refreshment and amusement alone with a young man. There was no telling what derelictions might not be condoned, once the delicate precautions were relaxed!

Yet, within the sacred citadel of matrimony, drastic changes were already taking place. Divorce was increasing. The birth rate was suddenly falling. And these changes were occurring chiefly among families on the higher social and economic levels. President Theodore Roosevelt, who shared the American woman's propensity to make every social problem a moral issue, scathingly denounced the modern woman's selfishness in bringing about race suicide. Was not contraception illegal, as well as immoral?

A mild-mannered, serious-minded, quixotic social worker vigorously dissented. Mrs. Margaret Sanger had served as a district nurse in the slums of New York City. She knew the law. But she was impressed by the social need for family limitation among the underprivileged, in the interest of child welfare and maternal health. In 1914, she brought out the first issue of a magazine, *The Woman Rebel*, devoted to birth control. It was promptly banned by the Post Office. Subsequently, she was sentenced to a term in prison for circulating a pamphlet on the same subject. Released, she continued her crusade. Quite apart from the social results to be achieved, was not this, likewise, a problem for conscience? Justice was deeply involved. For how could one speak of equal justice under the law, when the law itself deprived the poor of information readily accessible to the prosperous? Over the years, by sheer moral zeal, another victory was won.

Where did conscience stand with respect to the old sex-piety? In little more than two decades, women had achieved emancipation. The suspicious conventions and fussy decorum of yesteryear were obsolete. Illicit passion had become a commonplace subject for fiction and the drama. The nude had been admitted to respectable art. The theories of Freud were a favorite topic of conversation. In the realm of ideas, sexual freedom was no longer a disturbing novelty. In the realm of practice, conscience wavered. As the nineteen-twenties dawned, a new generation came on the scene and a new era opened. Scott Fitzgerald, the brilliant unfortunate symbol of the jazz age, afterwards characterized it as a whole race going hedonistic, deciding on pleasure. It was an age of miracles, it was an age of art, it was an age of excess, and it was an age of satire. The earnest older generation chiefly noticed its excess. Miss Addams was not alone in deploring the new gospel of individual freedom, especially in sex relations.

Remarkably, it was a representative of the older generation who stated the case for conscience. Judge Ben B. Lindsey was almost as closely associated with reform as Miss Addams herself. He had founded the children's court in Denver, thereby launching a movement that spread over the entire nation. The author of several widely read books, he had long been a favorite lecturer with the women's clubs, and his ideas always commanded respectful attention. He, too, was alarmed by the sexual laxity of the rising generation. Under the existing mores, could it result in anything but social disaster—divorce, illegitimacy, wrecked homes and ruined lives? Pondering the probable consequences, he held to the philosophy of reform, the theory of experimental social change. Better revise the mores than attempt to turn back the tide of nonconformity. Should not the mores be fitted to life, rather than life to the mores? He proposed that society legalize a prenuptial trial period, a companionate marriage. A bitter controversy developed. Yet Judge Lindsey knew the conscience of the American woman as well as any man in public life. His willingness to risk his reputation on a daring formula implied a belief that the outlook of conscience had shifted, that the old sex-piety had been—at least tacitly—discarded. His faith proved to be premature. But the next twenty years were to show that it had not been altogether misguided. By the nineteen-forties, public conscience no longer made an issue of sexual freedom.

[6] PURITAN CRUSADER

There was a characteristically American irony in the fact that the most notable exponent of sexual freedom was, like Miss Addams, a puritan

—though unaware of being one. Yet it was not as a puritan that the American public saw Isadora Duncan when, fresh from European triumphs, she first toured the United States. Her small lovely head laurel-crowned, her nude body scarcely veiled, her feet bare, she danced her way across the continent. This was in the era of muffling fabrics, whaleboned morality. The mantelpiece had not yet shed its lambrequin, or the piano its pall. The female form had been invisible for nearly a century—a biological convenience designed, like the clothes tree, to support layered deposits of stuffs. Famous, beautiful and utterly fearless, Isadora challenged prudery. Wearing only a tunic, she restored to the living flesh its ancient authority.

She danced to the accompaniment of an orchestra conducted by Walter Damrosch. Parting the blue draperies of an empty stage, she entered like a figure from Greek sculpture, animated by the music of Gluck or Beethoven. Her dancing evoked chaste memories of classical antiquity. The purity of Greek art was obvious, especially to Americans who had never read their Plato. Isadora, returning to her native land as an evangelist of culture, inspired it to adopt her as a cult.

She had become a cult in Europe, also. There she was among the most widely known of all Americans, identified, like royalty, by her first name alone. Her beauty captivated and distracted great artists. Rodin made countless drawings of her body; so did Maillol and Bourdelle. She moved in a world of celebrities: actresses, writers, Russian princes, German philosophers, the leaders of society in London and Paris. Rumor was busy with her spendthrift extravagance, her successive infatuations. The legend which would long survive her was already in the making. The legend was false. Isadora was genuinely—and ingenuously—American, at heart a puritan bent upon improving the world. It was this simplicity which, to Europeans, made her seem so exceptionally complex.

She had a gipsylike childhood in San Francisco, where her mother, a divorced woman, supported a family in precarious respectability by teaching the piano. She wheedled credit from skeptical tradesmen, and taught dancing to neighborhood children to add to the family income. Sent to a master of ballet, she took three lessons and refused to continue: the exercises were ugly, and against nature. She escaped from school, as quickly as possible, in the same way. All during her life she was to resent any discipline, and dislike making any difficult intellectual effort. Like the heroine of "The Siege of London," she might have protested that these things didn't matter: "If I once get there, I shall be perfect." It was the common faith of the women of her day, and in her case it was justified.

As a girl, she read indiscriminately. Books afforded an escape from unlovely fact. From all her haphazard fluttering of pages she emerged with a distaste for reality, a tendency to mistake the obscure for the profound, and a cluster of wistful preferences. She had already decided that she would live to fight against marriage, and for the emancipation of women. She felt a constant spirit of revolt against the narrowness of the society in which she lived, against the limitations of life, and a growing desire to fly eastward, to a life which might be broader. Two generations of American artists, under the spur of the same discontent, were to follow her, reversing the tide of migration. Meanwhile, she had acquired some local reputation as a teacher: she called hers a new system of dancing, but in reality there was no system. Yet it was enough to give her a sense of vocation.

At eighteen, she set out eastward, to conquer the world. Untrained, uneducated, with nothing more than a strong conviction of her own talent, her purpose was quite clear. She would not study and master an art. She had invented one for herself; she would practice and teach it. Had she not "discovered the dance"? This was in the pioneer tradition of her forefathers, who had crossed the continent in a covered wagon. But it also expressed the puritan spirit: contemptuous of the accumulated experience of the past; concerned with the new and untried; intent only upon the future—upon what may be and ought to be. Isadora's way led her, briefly, through Chicago and New York, where no welcome detained her. Then, on a cattleboat, to Europe.

Like James' Isabel Archer she brought to Europe little more than her meager knowledge, her inflated ideals, her confidence at once innocent and dogmatic, her temper at once exacting and indulgent. It was with these slender resources that, in her day, women were trying to make the world over. What wonder that they made a virtue of fumbling, or that they thought experience a continuous experiment? Isadora was no exception. She was unique only in carrying the prevailing attitude to its extreme consequences.

After five years of privation—sometimes she spent her days in museums, her nights in a public park—success came, as she had always known that it must. For had she not crossed the Atlantic, as she told a bewildered impresario, to bring about a renaissance of religion by means of the dance? Was she not a real American? The real

American, she was certain, was not a gold chaser, or a money lover, as the legend classed him, but an idealist and a mystic. One needed only to listen to one's "inner voice," follow the gleam of one's "inner light"— and share the resulting revelation. For experiment was, or should be, the most eloquent evangelism.

No less a reformer than Jane Addams and the others, she aspired to produce change over a wide realm of human affairs. "I was never able to understand," she said, "why, if one wanted to do a thing, one should not do it." She wanted to revolutionize the art of the dance, and she did. She wanted to reform the early education of children; her schools had some effect upon later "progressive" methods. She wanted to make women cultivate their bodies, and adopt a new freedom in clothes. But, above all, she hoped to make the world accept a new gospel of sexual freedom, and a new ideal of maternity.

Her love affairs were numerous, and many were spectacular. Though they sprang from passion, Isadora conducted them on principle; they furnished a medium for her personal evangel. Every new development in her life seemed to promise the beginning of an absolutely new life. So she embarked on every love as if it were destined to be perfect and permanent. She was less promiscuous than psychically virginal. None of the major loves to which she gave herself brought her more than a transient happiness. Men failed her with a tedious unanimity. She asked nothing of them—except perfection. That passion was so often accompanied by a torrent of capitalized, abstract nouns did not, on the whole, make it easier for men to understand her. Most of them, captivated by her beauty, her fame, or her art, were soon disconcerted by her ideals, which they were expected to share but seldom even grasped. They wanted an adventure, and were offered an education. She was the victim of her conscience. Over love, the inner light burned perpetually. It was a prodigal contriver of mirages.

Isadora was always attracted by genius—or what she took to be genius. Sometimes, she was just attracted, and then the discovery of genius followed automatically. In either case, it led to trouble. There was, for example, Gordon Craig, the son of her friend, the great actress Ellen Terry. They met in Russia, where Isadora, already famous, was having a sensational success. Craig was on the threshold of his career as a designer of scenery for the theater. Young and extravagantly handsome, he was—like Isadora—supremely confident of his ability to revolutionize theatrical art. He, too, was deeply aware of a messianic vocation.

There were some months of wild, impassioned lovemaking, during which she made an effort to advance his career, while he endured, and tried to fulfill, her exorbitant ambitions for him. Then there began the fiercest battle ever known, between the genius of Gordon Craig and the inspiration of her art.

There was at a later stage, Paris Singer—she called him "Lohengrin" —the expatriate heir to a great American fortune. He entered her life when the expenses of her fabulous school in Paris were draining her equally fabulous earnings. It had always been her hope to have her school, and her art, subsidized by the state; the insecurity of her childhood inclined her to a vague kind of socialism. Failing this, "I must find a millionaire," she had said in jest. When Lohengrin offered to finance the school and provide her with her own theater, Isadora could think him nothing less than a modern Lorenzo de Medici. And had not Lorenzo been a genius too? Soon, they became lovers. There opened the period of her legendary, expansive splendor. But Lohengrin had never been disciplined to the responsibilities of a Renaissance prince. He enjoyed the luxurious, selfish, meaningless existence of the modern rich. He was improbably generous, but did he, did he *really*, understand her art, share her ideals? He professed to, but—could she be certain? In endowing the artist, was he not merely indulging the mistress? Was this to be endured? Not by the inner light. Not by Isadora.

In her attraction to "genius" there was a large element of principle. Disbelieving in marriage from childhood, she had an exalted concept of maternity. She believed sexual freedom to be an inalienable right, and felt herself obliged to make society acknowledge it as such. Free unions opened new possibilities in maternity; above all, the exercise of eugenic selection in the choice of the father. Through such selection, society might deliberately produce great artists, philosophers, scientists. The dedicated moral will of women might bring about another golden age. In these circumstances, was it not also her obligation to illustrate the noblest use to which sex freedom could be put? On this theory she bore, and tragically lost, three children by different fathers. Two were accidentally drowned; one was born dead. She had conceived them as her hostages to faith. They were to have been her most eloquent argument for the need to make the world over. She never recovered from their loss. "A part of me," she said long afterward, "died with them."

In middle age, when her fortunes touched their lowest ebb and her public career appeared to be finished, there came to Isadora the opportunity for which she had always hoped. The government of the Soviet Union invited her to Moscow. She was to establish, and direct, a school to be maintained by the state. Her knowledge of the doctrines of Marx and Lenin was superficial. But the Russian experiment made claims upon her diffuse idealism, and it was easy for her to see in it the architecture of a future world order. She accepted the invitation enthusiastically. She would devote the rest of her life to creating a new proletarian art. The venture was to prove the most disastrous of her many projects.

Among other disillusions, it led to the last of her major love affairs; the only one which, in the end, left her baffled and humiliated. Her lover was Sergei Alexandreivitch Essenine, one of the literary discoveries hailed by the new Russia. He was a poet of doubtful merit. A blond peasant youth, still in his early twenties, he had been a violent partisan of the revolution, and had turned to writing verse about the life of the proletariat. The subject matter of his poems made their popularity inevitable. His work went through many editions. He was, officially, proclaimed to be a genius.

This valuation Essenine was not disposed to question. Nor was Isadora, though their first meeting should have forecast what was in store for her. He came to her studio with a group of drunken comrades. She danced for him. When she had finished, he made a remark which provoked coarse laughter. Puzzled, Isadora asked for an explanation. Someone translated, in obvious embarrassment, "He says it was—awful. . . . and that he can do better than that himself." Whereupon Essenine stumbled to his feet and began dancing about the studio like a crazy man.

He was an alcoholic, given to uncontrollable rages; perhaps in the early stages of an insanity which later led to his suicide. His brawling and his quarrels were among the favorite legends of Moscow's bohemia. But whatever tales rumor brought to Isadora she chose to ignore. She knew no Russian, and could not read his work. He knew no other language, and could not translate it for her. Could she doubt his genius? Apparently she detected in Essenine, awkwardly striving to invent an art of poetry, some spiritual affinity to the girl who, in a distant past, had determined to invent a new art of the dance. By this time, the Soviet government had withdrawn its promised financial support from her school. Characteristically, she decided to carry it on unaided. In order to raise money, she secured official permission to make a foreign tour. Arrangements were made for her to appear in Germany and the United States, and there were plans for engagements in France. She proposed to take Essenine with her, to show him all that Europe had of beauty, and all that America had of wonder. Under Soviet law, this was impossible unless he became her husband. Despite her lifelong prejudice against marriage, she married him.

The private misery of her tour was equalled only by its professional failure. In a letter to his coterie, Essenine outlined a poetic creed. "Let us be Asiatics. Let us smell evilly. Let us shamelessly scratch our backsides in front of everybody." This, he proceeded to apply to life with single-minded devotion. There were drunken rages, and much smashing of furniture in palace hotels. There were constant visits from the police, who always reduced him to meekness. There was a day when, finding Isadora weeping over the photographs of her drowned children, he tore them away from her and flung them into the fire. There was the discovery that he had stolen most of her clothing, which he destined as a gift to his mother and sister in Russia. There were daily scenes; there was daily public humiliation.

When they arrived in the United States, anti-Soviet sentiment was running high. They were detained at Ellis Island on the suspicion of being political agents. Isadora's indignation vented itself in an ill-advised speech at her first performance in New York. The press raised a hue and cry. In Boston, she used a red scarf in one dance; when complaint was made, she berated the audience from the stage. By this time, the charge of revolutionary activity had become a public sensation. In Indianapolis the police refused to permit Isadora's appearance, but were persuaded to remain in the wings, ready to interrupt any seditious exhibition. The American portion of her tour collapsed in disaster.

After further scandals in France, Isadora returned to Russia, and was persuaded to divorce Essenine. Her belief in his genius was unshaken. She was able to forgive all the indignity to which he had subjected her. She could not forgive her failure to save him from himself. This cut deeply, as the sequel demonstrated. Some years later, Essenine committed suicide. Isadora was then in France, and completely destitute. The Soviet government proposed to transfer to her Essenine's funds, amounting to more than a quarter of a million francs. She refused to accept the money.

For two more years she existed in poverty and obscurity. Of her beauty, there remained only a melancholy ruin. Of her art, there remained only a memory. She continued to look hopefully to the future, She wrote her memoirs and, in a studio at Nice, worked at an art of mime which, she believed, would liberate her from dependence upon physical grace and the lost loveliness of youth. One day word was brought to her that Lohengrin, from whom she had long been estranged, had determined to come to her assistance.

At a nearby garage, there was a handsome youth who owned a small, low-slung car which he drove for tourists who made excursions in the vicinity. To celebrate her good fortune, Isadora sent him word to bring his car: she would make an expedition to a nearby hill town. She wound a bright scarf over her head and about her throat. She waited with a friend at her door, the long scarf trailing on the ground. The car came, and she took her seat. Jestingly, she said to her friend, *"Je vais à la gloire."*

The car sped forward. Her scarf flew out in the breeze like a banner. Then it dropped, tangled in a wheel, and her neck was broken. The youth, returning with her body, became hysterical. "I have killed the Madonna," he kept repeating.

The Madonna? In its paradoxical truth, the image might have pleased Isadora. But did it not have a wider application? The Madonna concentrated in herself the whole rebellion of man against fate, and the whole unutterable fury of human nature beating itself against the walls of its prison house. She was above law; she took feminine pleasure in turning hell into an ornament; she delighted in trampling on every social distinction in this world and the next.

And had not they, too, shared this emotion—all the grave, troubled ones who, in the American "paradise of women," devotedly interceded to procure remission of the sins of men?

CHAPTER III

The Fingers in the Pie

The famous English novelist was impressed. He was fascinated. Having conquered America with his books, he came over to see for himself what America was like. In every way it exceeded his anticipations. The impact brought on an eruption of adjectives. Arnold Bennett enjoyed nothing more, in 1912, than his own continuous surprise.

Friends in New York City took him on a tour of the Bronx. Still an outlying borough, although penetrated by the new subway, it was engaged in a frenzy of building. Where could one more clearly discern the shape of the future? Even a stranger, like Bennett, saw at once that the Bronx was different. It was beginning again, at a stage earlier than art, and beginning better. It was a place to which the fit would be attracted, and where the fit would survive. It had, he felt, a rather harsh quality. Indeed, the Bronx struck Bennett as a place where the right of the inefficient to die would be cheerfully recognized.

Less than two decades later, this conjecture was being verified—abundantly, though perhaps not quite as Mr. Bennett had expected.

At the time of his tour, a ten-year-old boy was consorting with a tough gang in the streets and open lots of the Bronx. The boy grew to manhood. He was a disappointment to his patient, pious hard-working mother. Deserted by her husband, she had taken in washing to support her boy and girl. She did her utmost to train her son for some respectable trade. But Mrs. Flegenheimer failed. In his own peculiar fashion, Arthur was an uncompromising realist. Though a master of realism and a prophet of efficiency, Arnold Bennett could have taught him little about how to live on twenty-four hours a day. Arthur despised inefficiency. He cheerfully recognized the right of the inefficient to die. He actively promoted it, in ways that were sometimes imaginative but always unlovely. His willingness thus to advance the evolutionary process had far-reaching consequences. Temporarily, it brought him a fortune estimated at many millions, and a notoriety which—to some Americans of his time—seemed very like true prestige. By the late nineteen-twenties "Dutch Schultz," as he was known in many circles, was commonly regarded as a portent, or as the representative of a new dispensation in American life.

In point of fact, however, the most remarkable feature of this new dispensation was that it contained few genuinely novel elements. The scenery, costumes, properties and dialogue were brought up to date; the plot and theme of the play were old, even historical. During the era of the gangsters and racketeers, which extended from 1920 to 1940, Americans witnessed the creation, within the body politic, of an allegedly new society based upon lawlessness; enforcing its own code by means of a private police system; corrupting public authority for its own ends; setting up its own industrial combinations, bankers and legal staff; efficiently organizing its own distributive outlets; finally appointing its own "impartial arbiters" to regulate its internal conflicts of competition, when methods of violence had become too costly.

To Americans with some knowledge of their country's history, all this had a familiar look. Did it not bear a close resemblance to the era of the robber barons and the trusts—the period of railroad construction, industrial expansion, erection of monopolies and ultimate financial concentration which began after the War between the States? For the underworld, during two decades of spectacular power and gaudy affluence, adapted to its economic purposes the tactics, strategy and techniques developed, far earlier, by a generation of ambitious plutocrats equally greedy for power. There was, indeed, a deadly parallel in nearly all aspects of the two periods.

At first sight, the outbreak of gang wars and wholesale murders seemed a disagreeable novelty. In 1926, the O'Banion gang of Chicago, with a score to settle, sent a convoy of eight automobiles into surburban Cicero in broad daylight, to rake with machine guns the headquarters of Al Capone. Had Americans forgotten that, in 1869, rival armed gangs controlled by J. P. Morgan and Jim Fisk had terrorized a large part of New York state in a sanguinary war for physical possession of a railroad? Americans professed to be astonished by rumors that Capone owned the municipal administration of Chicago; that the operations of Schultz, in New York City, were protected by the political power of Jimmy Hines, a Tammany boss. Had they forgotten the railroad Congressmen of the eighteen-seventies; the curious dealings of Mrs. Howe's brother, Sam Ward the "king of the lobby"; the cynical bribing of state legislatures undertaken by Jay Gould and Commodore Vanderbilt? When they heard that "Uncle" Goldberg—a racketeer apparently universally trusted by his fellows—had been appointed arbiter and sort of impartial chairman of the crime industry, did they find ironical prototypes in Mr. Will H. Hays, who performed similar service for the movie industry, and Judge Kenesaw Mountain Landis, the czar of baseball?

When the robber barons had amassed their fortunes, they built palaces at Newport, and mansions in Fifth Avenue. They collected paintings, patronized the opera and theater, entertained with spectacular magnificence. The plutocrats of the underworld followed this pattern of conspicuous waste. James Stillman of the National City Bank had collected Rembrandts; Arnold Rothstein, leading banker of the underworld, went in for Whistler etchings and Oriental rugs. Al Capone became the seigneur of a luxurious Florida estate, with a marble swimming pool unrivalled at Newport. He was an inveterate first-nighter, and no robber baron had ever achieved the imaginative touch of being accompanied to the theater by eighteen gentlemen in waiting in faultless evening clothes. The Vanderbilts and Astors had maintained costly yachts. But Capone rode about Chicago in a custom-built limousine with armor-plated body and bullet-proof windows, preceded and followed by the cars of his retainers, as in a regal procession.

In the days when Mrs. Astor ruled Society, she had appeared at the opera proudly wearing her fabulous diamonds. Miss Texas Guinan, the Queen of the night clubs, was buried wearing diamonds almost equally fabulous. When Joe Masseria, boss of the Unione Siciliane, was killed, he lived in a penthouse overlooking Central Park, and entertained the mobsters, when his wife was away, at opium smoking parties. As against bachelor dinner parties on horseback, the aristocrats of the underworld enjoyed "kicking the gong around." Weddings and balls had afforded the old plutocracy opportunities for costly display. One Newport ball was said to have cost thirty thousand dollars. Perhaps as a result of the hazards of their life, the new plutocrats exalted a different social ceremony. The great public funeral of Frankie Yale, who met a violent end, cost fifty-two thousand dollars. There was a silver casket. Thirty-eight cars heaped with floral offerings followed the hearse. Ten thousand mourners either attended the requiem mass, or assembled at the cemetery.

In the cult of ostentation, there was little significant difference between the old tycoons and the new. But there was a marked difference in their formal relations with the public. At a crisis in his career, William H. Vanderbilt had been goaded into exclaiming, "The public be damned!" At the time of the Northern Pacific panic the elder J. P. Morgan, when asked by a reporter whether some statement were not due the public, testily replied, "I owe the public nothing!" For the most part, the new tycoons were seldom guilty of such barefaced arrogance.

Many of the most prominent acknowledged a wistful yearning to be accepted as respectable. Al Capone wondered why he met with opprobrium. "All I ever did was to sell beer and whiskey to our best people," he asserted, claiming that he had merely supplied "a demand that was pretty popular." It irked him that "the very guys who make my trade good are the ones that yell loudest about me." And wasn't he, perhaps, the unfortunate victim of moral inconsistency—since some of the leading judges used the stuff? In his later years, Arnold Rothstein boasted of friendships with people listed in the Social Register. He declared that he had never been connected with a crooked deal, and was heartily sick and tired of having his name dragged in on the slightest provocation whenever a scandal came up.

The very word "racketeer," pained Larry Fay, who ran his many enterprises from elaborate offices in a New York skyscraper. "I'm a businessman," he would say; "just a regular businessman like any broker or merchant." At one period in his career Dutch Schultz, as proprietor of the fashionable Embassy Club, became acquainted with some Park Avenue people. He called at their homes, at their invitation, began perfecting his wardrobe and polishing his grammar, and was heartbroken when he became convinced that they were merely exploiting him for their amusement. The episode made him, socially, a cynic; Jay Gould, universally snubbed by Society, could scarcely have felt more aggrieved.

Nearly all the new tycoons felt, with Al Capone—or with Mrs. Astor, who had often expressed the same sentiment, but less pungently—that "there's a lot of grief attached to this limelight." And most of them could have protested, with as much truth as Jay Gould: "I began life in a lowly way, and by industry, temperance, and attention to my own business have been successful, perhaps beyond the measure of my deserts."

Their own business was widely diversified, and touched the life of the nation at many salient points. By the early nineteen-twenties, crime had become "big business"—and it appeared to be as necessary to the national economy as oil, steel, electric power; or the other, lawful, slaughtering industry. It was illegal. But, sanctioned by custom, it wore the guise of legitimacy; for it accorded with the requirements of logic, if not of law. It was nefarious. But it was abetted by the people, protected by their chosen officials. It was morally proscribed. But the patronage of millions, otherwise ethically upright and devout, made its efficient services profitable. The nature of crime had not changed. The mood of the American people had. So had their folkways.

[2] THE MANNERS OF "NORMALCY"

The eighteenth amendment to the Constitution aroused no organized opposition. The Senate debated it for thirteen hours; the House, for only seven. The prospect of national sobriety infatuated the American conscience, pitched to the highest idealism by a great crusade—a war to end all wars forever, to make the world safe for democracy. Then, after hostilities ceased and the last parades disbanded, idealism suddenly collapsed. When the prohibition amendment became effective, in 1920, Americans were tired of causes, surfeited with conscience. Did they care to follow Woodrow Wilson to those heights upon which there rests nothing but the pure light of the justice of God? They did not. Presently Wilson, broken and embittered, made way for genial, handsome Senator Harding. "Normalcy," the familiar dead level, was preferable to lonely, inaccessible heights. In the emotional reaction which that choice represented, a new dispensation began.

All at once, America was going on the greatest, gaudiest spree in history. The older generation was merely weary of idealism. The young generation was truculently cynical. Heroism, and the sweetness of dying for exalted principles? Let John Dos Passos answer for them, in *Three Soldiers*, or E. E. Cummings, in *The Enormous Room*; both had been "over there." F. Scott Fitzgerald, recently of Princeton and the army, spoke for them too. The note was one of utter disenchantment; pride alone modulated tears into a febrile, heartbreaking laughter. *This Side of Paradise* announced the jazz age—the reign of the beautiful who thought themselves damned, the lost generation whose casual couplings were casually reported by Ernest Hemingway in *The Sun Also Rises*.

Gentlemen might prefer blondes, but youth declared its extreme disillusion: the older generation had pretty well ruined this world before passing it on to them. It had grown up to find all Gods dead, all wars fought, all faiths in man shaken. What remained—except, perhaps, the mystical gospel of the wisdom of the flesh expounded by D. H. Lawrence? Wasn't it worth a trial? In one's stride. Without pledges. If possible, burdened by no hope but the hope of a momentary oblivion. So, disappointment would be cheated of its opportunity. The new vocabulary of passion excluded sentiment: Edna St. Vincent Millay—her shining palace built upon the sand—wrote the bittersweet, skeptical love songs of a frightened generation.

Over the land, youth was convinced that life was lousy, but that sex might be swell. The word "neck" ceased to be a noun; abruptly became a verb; immediately lost all anatomical precision. Closed automobiles swiftly replaced the familiar old open car. In Muncie, Indiana, a judge of the juvenile court told the investigating Lynds that the family bus had become a house of prostitution on wheels. This new use was expedient, and prevalent. After a little, older folk picked up the trick from their juniors. Sheiks and their shebas flocked to the movies to see *Women Who Give*, and *The Queen of Sin*. They sang and danced to, "Hot Lips" and "Baby, I Need Lovin'." Two and one half million literates emptied the newsstands of Bernarr McFadden's *True Stories*. In New York City's austere temple of classical music, Paul Whiteman offered the first performance of George Gershwin's "A Rhapsody in Blue." With *Black Oxen* Mrs. Gertrude Atherton, a novelist no longer young, aroused wistful hopes in her feminine contemporaries. The story revealed how, by means of a glandular operation, grandmothers might be rejuvenated, and thereafter raise the temperature of youthful sophisticates.

"Normalcy" was being ushered in by the ubiquitous wail of the saxophone. By petting parties and gate crashing. By drunken brawls in exclusive country clubs. By bootleggers and speak-easies; rumrunners, hijacking, bank robberies. By a procession of weeping women eleven blocks long which filed past the mortal remains of Rudolph Valentino. By the cosy extermination of new enterprisers whose disgruntled competitors took them "for a ride" or buried them alive in barrels filled with cement. The Federal government fostered a boom in padlocks. Jewelers did a brisk trade in hip flasks. These new accessories were usually made of silver; but one could likewise procure them in gold, sometimes encrusted with gems. For this was the coprosperity era of Harding, Coolidge and the luckless Hoover—who foresaw a national destiny of two automobiles in every garage, a fat chicken in every pot. Cooks, bootblacks, clerks, housewives, teachers, errand boys were plunging into the maelstrom of a runaway bull market in Wall Street.

An outstandingly successful advertising agent became the nation's favorite theologian. Were not the gospels obsolete? Bruce Barton unveiled *The Man Nobody Knows*. Barton knew, and told the world. In the new gospel according to Bruce, Jesus was an efficient executive who picked twelve men from the bottom ranks of business and forged them into an organization that conquered the world. His parables were the most successful advertisements of all time. He was, in short, the founder of modern business. There was another man whom nobody knew who, by the efforts of Barton's professional colleagues, achieved an almost equivalent celebrity. This was "Mr. Addison Sims of Seattle." He was the American whom everyone had met and promptly forgotten. But it was important to remember him; to be able to greet him by name, after years of oblivion. It was important if one wanted to be, like Jesus, an efficient executive—as who did not? Why it was important, except as a minor matter of courtesy, was a mystery understood only by copy writers for a memory course; but the mystery became an article of faith. When Dr. Charles W. Eliot, president-emeritus of Harvard, sternly rebuked America's "best people" for setting an example of lawlessness, few heeded him. The age of ballyhoo had invented its retort to all old-fashioned moralists: "Aw, you're nuts!"

At luncheon, at the cocktail hour—a freshly-minted social occasion —at dinner and long into the night, Dr. Eliot's best people were to be found in their favorite "speaks." In New York City, the number of these establishments was reputed to stand at thirty-two thousand. This was the official estimate of the commissioner of police, Grover Whalen, whose urbanity presently elevated him to the function of metropolitan greeter aboard a municipal yacht. His estimate was, however, disputed by another, equally affable, public servant. Izzy Einstein, a fellow of infinite jest, was "prohibition agent number one" for the New York area. He intended no humor in asserting that the city contained one hundred thousand speak-easies. He was professionally acquainted with most of them. In four years, he raided many—disguised as a waiter, drummer, visiting buyer, grave digger, football player, iceman, musician, automobile cleaner, or mere Sunday stroller. Then he retired, to write his memoirs—touchingly dedicated to the four thousand nine hundred and thirty-two persons he arrested—and predict that "the day when Prohibition is repealed will not be in our lifetime." This prediction had an ominous note of probability. For, by then, the Federal government was causing lethal poisons to be added to legal alcohol. Conscience was taking the form of a sinister chemistry.

The speak-easies of midtown New York were domiciled in old brownstone houses formerly inhabited by Mrs. Wharton's world. Some were operated in the guise of clubs, under titles like "The Bombay Bicycle Club." These issued membership cards to trustworthy patrons. But, whether club or not, all had their lookouts posted at the entrance. The best people descended the basement steps of a decaying residence, stood patiently at a metal-reinforced door, waited until a grille snapped open and the hard eye of Tony or Leon or Charlie had appraised them —and hoped not to be denied admission. For, once inside, they could drink at a bar. The Scotch was poured from bottles seemingly authentic, on which the historic labels had been artfully reproduced. So was the gin. A polite fiction had it that both were imported. Usually, they were the product of stills tended by Sicilian alky-cookers. Beyond the bar, there was a restaurant. The fare, Italian or allegedly French, was likely to be good and almost certain to be costly.

Toward midnight, revelers could move on to the night clubs. These opened and closed and reopened with startling rapidity, confusing changes of name and location: their peripatetic and protean nature derived from the attentions of patrons like Izzy Einstein. The most celebrated were, in sequence, presided over by Miss Texas Guinan. Miss Guinan claimed that she had turned New York's night life into an essential and basic industry. The sedate New York *Times*, apparently recognizing that her contribution to social history was equivalent to those of Mrs. Astor and Mrs. Fish, whom in many ways she resembled, attributed to her a "national vogue." In ten months of her heyday she converted an inconsiderable investment into a fortune of nearly one million dollars. Over the years, she added to both the gaiety and vocabulary of the nation, introduced many nuances of etiquette, and greatly spurred the purchase of padlocks.

Her career was largely accidental. She was born in Waco, Texas, and christened Mary Louise Cecilia. At the age of four, she won a scholarship in music endowed by Marshall Field. She became, in turn, a broncho rider in a circus, a chorus girl, a vaudeville trouper, and the gun-girl heroine of early Western movies. In 1923, buxom, blonde, and middle-aged, she was to be seen playing a minor role on the stage of the Winter Garden, in New York. One night, friends took her to a restaurant for after-theater supper. "But it was dull," as she recalled, long afterwards. "Someone suggested that I sing. I didn't need much coaxing, so I sang all I knew; my entire repertoire. First thing you know we were all doing things. Everybody had a great time." The inspiration to improve the world, to make it more agreeable if not better, had visited her. As in the case of her earnest predecessors, it provided a philosophy and led to a career.

It led, first of all, to Larry Fay. He was a long-jawed, cordial person, with a weakness for indigo-blue shirts, declamatory neckties, and a high polish on the fingernails. He was among the most prosperous of the new tycoons. Three years earlier, he had been a taxi driver earning twenty-five dollars a week. He got into rumrunning. With his profits he bought a fleet of gaudy taxis, and by strong-arm methods gained control of the stands at the city's two railroad terminals. He then persuaded a large company to buy out these stands; in addition, to pay him an income of ten thousand dollars a year in return for his promise to abstain from the taxi business. Though he was to be arrested forty-nine times in his forty-four years of life, Fay had a yen for respectability and wanted to associate with people of importance. Ownership of a smart night club promised to realize these desires, at a profit. Fay went to Europe to gather ideas. He returned with a knowledge of the latest nocturnal refinements, and twelve trunks of English clothes, to form a partnership with Miss Guinan.

They launched the first of a series of *boîtes-de-nuit* which, as the *Times* recorded in its obituary of Miss Guinan, attracted out-of-town buyers, theatrical celebrities, and a sprinkling of the social and underworld elite. It was the conjunction of the last two elements that constituted Miss Guinan's major social innovation, for this gave the age its peculiar tone—and, in time, resulted in the emergence of a Society as beguiling to the American imagination as that of Newport in the days of its splendor. Had there existed, ever before, an "underworld elite" capable of being so described by the chaste, austere *Times*? And, if there had, would the social elite have chosen to mingle with it?

Like Mrs. Stuyvesant Fish, Miss Guinan wished to redeem her world from the cardinal sin of dullness. Like Mrs. Fish, she was singularly free of illusions and possessed a notable talent for imaginative insult. Seated in the center of a nightly bedlam, her diamonds blazing and her gown shining with sequins, armed with a clapper and police whistle to ward off any intolerable momentary silence, she would welcome patrons with a loud, cheerful, full-throated "Hello, sucker!"—and an amused world, ignoring her jovially contemptuous meaning, responded delightedly to her flippancy. Her high spirits were infectious. Who could take offense at her salty, good-humored abuse; at her cynical bonhomie? She laid about her with wisecracks and nifties and made them like it. And when one of her girls came out to perform—at one time she had a mob of seventy-eight—who could resist her command to "give this little girl a great big hand"? One night an unknown "live one" made his appearance, and received as a title her most celebrated phrase. He paid the couvert charge for everyone present, distributed fifty-dollar bills to the entertainers, and when asked to identify himself refused his name, remarking only that he was in the dairy-produce business. Miss Guinan promptly christened him the "big butter-and-egg man." This phrase became part of the vernacular. Like Sinclair Lewis' Babbitt, it crystallized an American type.

Indeed, Miss Guinan's view of the national life was not unlike Lewis'. She, too, was a disillusioned sentimentalist, and there was a strong tincture of puritan moralism in her contempt for her public. Her jocular wisecracking was seldom far from explicit censure. It was as if, elevated to fame by a world suddenly gone cockeyed, she had taken her fortune as a measure of the world's moral aberration. The spectacle invited shame and scorn; and she had no illusions about herself. Life, as she saw it from her table, had the look of madness, and she took a malicious pleasure in abusing it, making it more whacky, stepping up its frenzy. For, by nature, she was a small-town woman inclined to simple decencies; devoted to a family whom she kept from public view, fiercely solicitous for the welfare of her girls, loyal to old friends who had never emerged from obscurity. The rest was livelihood. She dealt with it shrewdly, realistically. But—was there not something more than shrewdness and high spirits behind

the retort discourteous which was her habit, her trademark? A
commentary or a verdict? Or, perhaps, a deep distaste; an almost
forgotten integrity which included herself among the objects of her
derisive cynicism?

After a time, Miss Guinan broke with Larry Fay. In addition to his
luxurious nightspots, Fay went on to develop an industrial racket
which served as a model to the new tycoons who gradually began
extending their operations from illegal liquor to fields of legitimate
enterprise. Fay chose the milk industry, dominated in New York
City by two great corporations, but likewise served by many independent producers among whom a disastrous competition prevailed. Taking advantage of their disorganization and his own army of mobsters,
he combined them into a "trade association" for which he established
a code of "fair practice." For this, he received a royalty of five cents
on every forty-quart-can of milk which the "members" shipped into
the city. This pattern was soon applied to many other lines of business.
By creating a so-called trade association, dominating a labor union,
and making ruthless use of a "goon squad," the new tycoons were
able to terrorize businessmen into paying costly tribute; the cost
was passed on to the public in advanced prices. The practice came to
be accepted as almost inevitable. Did it not reflect the historic tendency
of all American business toward some sort of monopolistic agreement
that would file the rougher edges off competition? Nineteenth-century
America had tolerated approximately similar methods in the heyday
of the robber barons. But, although twentieth-century America appeared to have lost its conscience, it had developed a kind of squeam-
ishness. There came a time when murder, mutilation, terrorism and
miscellaneous violence no longer seemed normal components of a
system of free enterprise.

[3] "DECAY'S EFFACING FINGER"

Meanwhile, tabloid readers, absorbing the stories of gangster kill-
ings, found in them adventure and splendor and romance; to be
followed, presently, by movie audiences. And behind the gaudy,
glittering façade of New York's night life a network of corruption
spread over the city—later to be exposed, in a series of sensational
trials, by the brilliant young district attorney, Thomas E. Dewey. It
had its duplicates in nearly every other American city of large popu-

lation; and thoughtful Americans, remembering the sordid scandals of President Harding's administration, found cause to study the social ethics of "normalcy." The new tycoons, the elite of the underworld—products of that great social and economic experiment which was so noble in motive, so far-reaching in purpose—required a number of services necessary to large-scale business enterprise. Among others, they needed banking facilities for credit, legal talent, and useful political connections. It was in order to secure these that they set up their complex network.

As became clear after his murder in 1928, Arnold Rothstein was the Morgan of the underworld; its banker and its master of economic strategy. He came of a well-to-do, respectable family. Early in life he chose the career of a professional gambler. As his fortune mounted, this career served chiefly to conceal his major, less admissible, activities. His fist, rather than his finger, sank deep in the pie. He owned gambling houses; financed a worldwide trade in narcotics; had a share in the illegal liquor traffic; controlled a number of industrial rackets; disposed of stolen jewels and stolen bonds; directed the operations of Wall Street "bucket-shops"; was a silent partner in several fashionable night spots run by gangsters. Undoubtedly, these did not exhaust his interests.

Rothstein was a Broadway figure, the friend and companion of well-known journalists, theatrical and sporting folk, reputable businessmen and their wives, influential politicians. Rumor connected him with unsavory episodes such as the bribing of the Chicago White Sox to "throw" a World's Series of baseball games; the theft of Liberty Bonds valued at five million dollars. But, although many believed these rumors, no factual proof of them was established during his lifetime. His fortune was variously estimated at from two to ten million dollars. He owned valuable real estate, maintained large accounts in excellent banks, kept an expensive Fifth Avenue apartment. He was a man of position; he had the influence which flows to wealth and prestige. Why spurn so advantageous an acquaintance? Few did. Then, too, he did not lack social grace. He owned a stable of horses. He had some reputation as a collector of art, furniture, rugs. He entertained in a quiet way; his guests spoke favorably of his wit; women seemed to find his flashing black eyes, his pale skin, chin dimple and courtly manners irresistible. One of his mistresses considered him a sentimental and tender lover, a genial and humorous companion. Everyone agreed that his confidence in his own intelligence was unbounded. He was apt to be impatient with those who "dubbed along." He was well mannered, soft of speech, but his associates were chary of trifling with him. It was his opinion that the majority of the human race were dubs and dumbells, and he was always ready to turn to profit the fact that they had rotten judgment and no brains. Therefore, they thought him crooked. Only because he had learned how to do things and how to size people up and dope out methods for himself!

The mystery of Rothstein's murder was never solved. He went to his grave, like many another of the new tycoons, faithful to the common code: he refused to name his assailant. The range of his activities, the part that he played in elevating crime to the status of big business, were quickly established. His private files were seized, after his death, by the authorities. It appeared that certain of their contents had already been removed. But the fact that they remained so full of dynamite for the community at large that one responsible custodian after another came to the conclusion they were better suppressed—this offered a theme for moral reflection. Rothstein's ruling passion was money. His attorney, William J. Fallon, once described him as "a man who dwells in doorways . . . a mouse standing in a doorway, waiting for his cheese." The thresholds across which his sinister shadow fell evidently included those of the "best people."

Fallon, his attorney, represented the kind of legal talent which the new tycoons found useful. As counsel for the major figures of the underworld, he was called the "great mouthpiece." Because of his peculiar ability to secure jury disagreements which freed his clients— the vote usually stood at eleven to one—he was also known as the "jail robber." Auburn-haired, and handsome in a flamboyant way, Fallon was an eloquent pleader. His theatrical sense was so pronounced that David Belasco tried to persuade him to become an actor. He was a legendary figure in the weird society invented by Miss Guinan, almost the first of a line of notorious playboys. The surface was spectacular, and many found it likeable. Underneath, there flickered an intermittent ray of genius. For Fallon's intelligence was exceptional. His mastery of criminal law, his startling grasp of technicalities, his knowledge of medical and psychological theory—these evoked the reluctant admiration of eminent jurists and honorable members of the profession. Like Rothstein, Fallon came of a respectable, well-to-do family. He had had what are called advantages. Yet such was the moral climate of the roaring twenties, the age of normalcy, that he regarded the bribing of jurors as a proper professional function; that he and his legal associate were willing to become the payroll employes of a crime machine.

In distinction to Fallon, "Dixie" Davis was called "the kid mouthpiece." Davis was the attorney for Dutch Schultz, and the inventor of his most brilliant business exploit. He was a tailor's son who went from comparative rags to considerable riches the easy way. As a young lawyer, he practiced in the magistrates' court in Harlem—the political bailiwick of the Tammany leader James J. Hines. The district included a large Negro and Latin-American population and, by virtue of certain night clubs where the best jazz bands were to be found, it had become the Montmartre of New York. A peculiar form of illicit gambling, the so-called "numbers" or "policy" game based upon a daily lottery, flourished among the indigenous population. Davis specialized in defending the operators of this game, at cut rates. He was suave, a master of the fascinating idiom of the lower depths, well tailored with dark-hued suits and white starched collars. Experience convinced him that the setup of the policy game involved a conspicuous economic waste. There were too many operators. Too much money was being spent on "ice"—political protection. What the game needed was monopoly; an efficient organization under an impartial chairman who would impose, and enforce, a code of fair practice. Davis took this program of economic reform to Dutch Schultz. Schultz took action. Under his efficient administration, the policy game soon yielded an annual take estimated at one hundred million dollars.

Schultz was small of stature, given to swift, dangerous rages; an expert with the "typewriter" or submachine gun, reputedly likely to shoot and kill on the slightest provocation. When he died, at the age of thirty-three, he had been arrested thirteen times, in several instances on charges of homicide; and he was known to have been guilty of a number of murders. But he served only one sentence in prison, for a robbery committed in his adolescence, when he was a Bronx hoodlum. Though he died a fugitive from justice, he had been forced to "go on the lam" only because he was under indictment for evasion of income tax. At one time, he was appointed a deputy sheriff of Bronx County by Edward J. Flynn, the Democratic boss. This appointment was subsequently canceled, and Schultz's badge of office was withdrawn, But, nominally, he had served as an officer of the law while also acting as "trigger man" for two notorious gangsters, "Legs" Diamond and Owney Madden.

Dutch Schultz performed a traditionally approved economic function. By effecting the consolidation of independent units he eliminated waste, promoted efficiency, and replaced the disorder of an obsolete individualism with rigorous discipline. His economic thinking was not unlike that of John D. Rockefeller who, when building the Standard Oil trust, declared that he wanted in his organization only competitors who had proved their ability to do a big business, remarking that "as for the others, unfortunately they will have to die." Death solved the problem of competition.

Schultz was not as conspicuously devout as Rockefeller, yet he held religion in deferential regard. He sought its comfort in times of crisis, and after he had become wealthy was a soft touch for representatives of any religious denomination seeking small contributions. During his first trial for income-tax evasion he accepted with equal courtesy and apparent gratitude a rosary from a woman who wished him well, and the Yiddish wish for good luck uttered by some of his henchmen. "I guess I'm going to need all the good luck I can get," he told a reporter. "I ain't passing anything up." At various times during his career, he declared himself a member of the Jewish, Protestant, and Roman Catholic communions. He was buried as a Roman Catholic, but his mother—to whom, on his deathbed, he cried for the comfort and protection of childhood—was an orthodox Jewess, and at her insistence a praying shawl mantled his body in its last resting place.

Rockefeller was once described as having the soul of a bookkeeper, and the phrase is likewise applicable to Schultz. He was humdrum, money loving, abstemious. He cared nothing for gambling, luxury, or the diversions of a playboy. His only picturesque quality was a faculty of coining underworld slang, a gift for quick, cryptic phrases to describe persons and things. For the rest, he was a model of industry with a remarkable talent for business organization. Death found him hard at work. He was murdered, late one night, while in conference with his lieutenants, the fabulous figures of his enterprises spread out before him.

In 1928, Schultz was a bartender in a Bronx speak-easy. He became a partner. The murder of his former employer, which he later avenged, set him up as an independent enterpriser. Soon, he owned three more speak-easies. He ran his beer into the Bronx from New Jersey, across the Hudson, and had to hire gangsters to protect it from hijacking; thus, he acquired a mob of his own. Presently, he entered the field of wholesale distribution; became the dominant partner in eleven speaks; gradually extended his operations from the Bronx to Harlem. One of his offices was in a warehouse having a masked elevator on which trucks could be lowered into a cellar and loaded. Another, like a fortress, had walls armored with steel. Less than five years after he ceased being a bartender, his annual income from beer sales alone exceeded two million dollars, and he had accounts in eighteen banks. It was at this point in his fortunes that Davis proposed that he take over the Harlem policy games.

There were some forty "bankers" conducting policy games in Harlem when Schultz entered the field. Within six months, Schultz consolidated the six most important into a monopoly; the others found it discreet to discontinue operations. He financed his bankers when luck ran against them and they had to pay off. The odds against this contingency were a thousand to one, but since the pay-off was at a rate of six hundred to one, Schultz—always cautious about money matters—soon found a method of rigging the game. For his services as monopolist, the muscular protection afforded by his mob, and the political fix which ensured freedom from interference by the police and courteous dismissal in the courts of justice, Schultz took sixty per cent of the revenues received by his bankers.

Like the early builders of railroad systems and industrial trusts, Schultz found that the law obstructed this evolutionary economic process. Like them, he hoped to purchase immunity, and succeeded in acquiring protection. Like them, he bought a politician—one with unquestioned ability to deliver the requisite services and accomplish the necessary results.

James J. Hines was not on the public payroll. But in New York City he controlled many who were, and his political power was sufficient to give him influence throughout the state, and with the Federal administration in Washington. He had clashed with Charles F. Murphy, the old-line boss of Tammany Hall and, after Murphy's death, his insurgency brought him into a position of dominance. For Tammany Hall was wracked by criticism and reform.

It had been disavowed by Franklin D. Roosevelt in his first campaign for the presidency. But Hines, the opponent of the organization, enjoyed the friendship of James A. Farley. When Mr. Roosevelt assumed office, Mr. Farley became Postmaster General; as such, he was responsible for the distribution of Federal patronage. Tammany Hall was ignored, and Hines won preference in suggestions for Federal appointments. It was therefore possible for his lawyer to declare, at the time of his arrest on charges relating to his connection with Dutch Schultz and Dixie Davis, that "a few years ago the President of the United States praised Mr. Hines for humanitarian activities. Even today people crowd into his office in such droves that he can't take care of them."

Hines' humanitarian activities were indisputable, and followed a traditional pattern. As district leader, the supreme boss of a local machine, it was his function to get out the vote. To this end, it was necessary that he be prepared always to help people in trouble; that he see to it that turkeys were distributed among the deserving poor at Thanksgiving and Christmas; that he have funds at his disposal to advance to the needy; that he have access to jobs for the jobless. Under the American political system the district leader is both a philanthropist and a social-welfare agency—the most reliable source of direct, immediate relief. "In politics the thing to do is to build yourself an army," Hines once said. "Whenever a man comes to me, no matter whether or not I can do what he wants, I begin to think what else I can do for him. By the time he's through telling his story, I'm giving him maybe what he's asking for or maybe something he didn't know he could get. I see hundreds of people every day. It's a lot of work but I keep it up." As his lawyer remarked, Hines "has been a father to thousands. He's an angel." What wonder that, if his bail were to be set at one million dollars, it would be "supplied by thousands of citizens"?

To deliver the vote, Hines needed money and an army; Schultz possessed both, and required the use of such political power as, in New York, Hines alone commanded. Already, Hines had tested Schultz's political usefulness: his mob had proved to be an excellent resource in elections; and only an innocent could doubt the value of his money in future municipal campaigns. Hines was no innocent. He was the man who, although merely a private citizen, held in his grasp the police, the courts, and the public prosecutors of the world's second largest city—the man who, for all practical purposes, controlled the law.

He was rugged, blue eyed, square faced. His white hair was cropped short, and his skin was very ruddy. One noticed his flinty stare but, on the whole, he had the look of a prosperous farmer. He had come up the hard way, leaving school at the age of fifteen to work in his father's smithy; following his grandfather and father as a Tammany election captain. He had operated a successful trucking business. He lived modestly with his wife and family, spending his mornings on his political affairs, his afternoons playing golf or at the races. It was assumed that he had private means; at his political head-quarters he frequently gave away as much as a thousand dollars a day.

When, ultimately, it was proved that he had been the paid hireling of a thug named Arthur Flegenheimer, also known as Dutch Schultz, many were disposed to condone his lapse from grace. Had he not, in his lifetime, done a lot of good? It could be said that of the enormous financial return that came into his hands through crime, relatively little stayed with him. It could be said, apparently with truth, that a large percentage of this blood-stained money was scattered by him in service of the poor. But that he left his people to be preyed upon by those who operated the rackets was a fact he never looked in the eye. Nor did the importunates whom he served. During the two long, sensa-tional trials which preceded Hines' conviction and sentence to prison, thoughtful Americans had an opportunity to study the operations of a political system for which, as citizens presumably discharging their civic duties, they were themselves in large part responsible. They might have been moved to wonder whether Hines' attorney was not accurate, after all, in declaring that "his name is legion."

Hines was not indicted until more than two years after the death of his associate, benefactor, and employer—the man whom he had set up as one of the overlords of New York City, able to subvert its civil government to his own ends. Death came to Dutch Schultz late one autumn night in 1935. Under indictment in New York, he had transferred his headquarters to New Jersey. That night, he was sitting with three of his lieutenants in the back room of an obscure tavern in Newark, poring over a sheaf of papers which appeared to be a monthly financial report of his enterprises. Two armed men entered. There was a sudden fusillade of shots. The three lieutenants were

killed. Somewhat later Schultz, mortally wounded, was removed to
a hospital by the police. For two hours, he was closely questioned by
a police official, and a stenographer sat at his bedside taking down
every word that he uttered. His wife was sent for, to bid him farewell.
A priest of the Roman Catholic Church administered the last rites for
the dying. The questioning continued.

In the gathering twilight of his pain and fear, Schultz's mind
struggled with its hallucinations. Determined not to reveal the identity
of his assailant, he denied knowing him, then mumbled that he had
been shot by "the boss himself"—one John—in a dispute involving
over a million, five million dollars. He gave instructions to his
lieutenants—"George, don't make no bull moves." He spoke of old
enemies: the "cowboy in one of the seven days a week fights" who had
"no business, no hangout, no friends, nothing; just what you pick up
and what you need." He realized that he might be dying, and expressed concern for the future welfare of his wife: "Oh, sir, get the
doll a roofing." And from his rambling discourse there strangely
emerged one meaningless metrical sentence: "A boy has never wept,
nor dashed a thousand kim."

Among the letters of the poet Baudelaire, there is one written in
extreme despair, under a compulsion to suicide. It is addressed to the
mother whom, again and again, he had disappointed and betrayed; it
is an appeal that she come to him at once. "I supplicate you, come," he
entreated her; "I am at the end of my nervous powers, at the end of my
courage, at the end of hope." In his anguish, his memory revived the
passionate love for her that he had felt in childhood, and he wrote
heartbrokenly of his awareness that she had always sacrificed herself
to him.

As life ebbed, Dutch Schultz, too, recalled his childhood and sank
back into its helplessness. He kept crying out for his mother, the
pious, hardworking woman who had tried to make a good man of
him, and whom he had failed. "Oh, mama, mama, mama," he moaned.
He pleaded with her not to judge him too sternly: "Please, mother,
don't tear. Don't rip. That is something that shouldn't be spoken
about. . . . Please, mother, you pick me up now. Do you know me?"
She was not there, but to him she was visibly present and, very near
the end, as if in judgment on his life, he said, quite clearly, "Mother
is the best bet and don't let Satan draw you too fast." His last words
were, "I want to pay. Let them leave me alone." Four days later,

with elaborate secrecy, he was buried close to his contemporary, Larry Fay, and near Anna Held, a beautiful actress who, at the turn of the century, had come from France to enchant the American public with a song which protested her inability to make her eyes behave.

[4] THE DAY BEFORE TOMORROW

In 1945, Schultz had been in his grave for a decade. Hines had served a prison sentence, and had been paroled, all political activity forbidden to him. An angry wave of reform had swept the country. The nation had survived the longest, most hideous economic depression in its history. It had emerged victoriously from a second World War. It was faced either by a magnificent destiny or an ignoble fate. These were the alternatives posed by the abrupt incidence of the atomic age. For now, at last, civilization had developed the means to commit suicide at will.

Newport was a mausoleum, and the lady was supposedly extinct. But, in Newport, a debutante "came out" at a party for which her parents paid forty thousand dollars. In the autumn, the opening of the Metropolitan Opera was one of the most brilliant in many years. Mrs. Cornelius Vanderbilt arrived five minutes before her usual time, in a five-year-old red-lamé dress; Mrs. George Washington Kavanaugh, never seen at an opening without her diamond tiara, paused to smile and pose for cameramen. Richness and variety of furs dominated the scene and diamond necklaces were worn in their own splendor, or decorated with one or two clips. As usual, many of the audience sweated out the opera at the bar. Some weeks later, in time for the Christmas season, a New York department store advertised its stock of mink coats for dogs.

The rackets, it was widely believed, had been broken up. But the new social organism invented by Miss Guinan had persisted, and come of age. Even the *Times* had adopted the established term for that fusion of the social and underworld elite. It was universally referred to as "café society." The gossip columnists of the tabloids and the radio chronicled the exploits of its members in meticulous detail, to the apparent satisfaction of millions of Americans. It was, in one respect at least, socially conservative; it displayed a certain reverence for its principal tradition. It continued to cultivate murder as a fine art. Miss Guinan herself had been immortalized, with appropriate splendors, by Hollywood biographers. And now Hollywood was glorifying the world's most exclusive nightspot, the glittering rendezvous where every night was New Year's Eve. Even in Plainville, U.S.A., the plain people no longer languished for the amenity of New York's Stork Club.

Women had long been emancipated. No woman sat on the bench of the nation's Supreme Court. None now held a Cabinet portfolio. But Mrs. Eleanor Roosevelt had been appointed a delegate to the United Nations. Many women were returning to domestic life after wartime employment; many did not wish to. Senator Myers of Pennsylvania urged American manufacturers not to discharge women workers and replace them with men during the period of reconversion to peacetime production. In Plainville, U.S.A., a Middle-Western agricultural community, girls knew that women were supposed to be the equals of men. But few occupations other than teaching were locally open to them and, except as wives, they were seldom able to migrate. In Plainville, when a girl became a "hasher" (waitress) or hotel maid she was generally assumed to have become also a prostitute.

The climate of public opinion was no clearer than usual. The editor of *Life* oscillated between a conviction that the nation might make this an "American century" and a fear that it was morally incapable of facing the most portentous decisions in its history. The editor of *The Saturday Review of Literature* declared that modern man was obsolete. The editor of *The Atlantic Monthly* rejected such counsels of despair; modern man, he suggested, was merely passing through a crucial period of readaptation and social growth.

Modern man himself, perhaps seeking relief from their disagreement and his own confusion, was turning to a "better class" of pulp magazines devoted to detective, mystery, and crime stories. One of these illustrated its fictions with posed photographs, thus equipping the characters with an illusion of reality; would not readers receive an incremental thrill from the inference of an authentic fact case? Neither the carnage of war nor the ominous implications of the atomic bomb had dispelled the American preoccupation with violent death. Murder continued to find a rising literary market. J. Edgar Hoover, director of the Federal Bureau of Investigation, deplored widespread juvenile delinquency, our national shame, and warned that, in glaring red for all to see, there were unmistakable portents of a new era of gangsterism.

As the year 1945 drew to an end, it became increasingly certain that the nation was about to be plunged into industrial strife, probably on a scale unprecedented in its history. The relations of labor and management had never been worse. The President of the United States, expounding his personal faith in the nation's future, exhorted all his fellow-citizens to get in and push, reminding them that the achievement of a benign destiny did not require anything in the world but a plain understanding among ourselves. Though this might be all that was needed, it appeared to be lacking.

In New York City's Times Square, one million frenzied hornblowers, cow-bell swingers and clapper manipulators hailed the advent of a new year, a new age. Elsewhere, as the old year died, one might have found other Americans of all faiths, in their houses of worship. Their hearts neither empty of fear nor full of hope, they were praying —perhaps for light with which to meet the equivocal future.

As the new year, the new age, opened, an American soldier established communication with the moon. A radar signal, launched into celestial space, touched the moon and bounced back to earth in approximately two and one-half seconds. For the perplexed world of men, the goddess Diana had no counsel.

Part Two

THE INTERPRETERS' HOUSE

CHAPTER IV

The Melancholy of the Masters

One summer day in 1904, a long-time resident of England disembarked in Hoboken, for New York City. He was a bulky figure, of rolling and voluminous outline. His head was massive, sculptural. His bold features and big, dramatic mouth resembled those of a noble Roman mask. There was about him an air of ceremonious, diffident formality, of snobbishness both insecure and arrogant, but as faint as the scent of cologne on a handkerchief. It had been said that he lived hidden in the midst of his strange, heavy, alien manners and customs. These served him as an armor, which, just then, he may have needed. For, months before, he foresaw, as an absolute certainty, that he would alight on the dock in abject and craven terror.

A very distinguished author, he enjoyed an immense prestige and suffered from a paucity of readers. Was he—as his brother candidly asserted—becoming a mere curiosity of literature, destined to remain unread and neglected? Moments of doubt afflicted even those ardent champions who considered him the brightest ornament of American letters. For, after all, was not Henry James in a fair way to achieve the exquisitely unintelligible?

Within a few months there would be published his most recent novel, *The Golden Bowl*. The enthusiasts would be dampened, if not utterly daunted. And among them, some would liken the author to one of his own characters, would ruefully suspect that Henry James, "betraying, extraordinarily, no wasted year, had been inscrutably monotonous behind an iridescent cloud."

He had left the United States of President Grant to take up permanent residence in Europe. He had not seen his native land in nearly twenty-five years. Now, he was returning to the United States of President Theodore Roosevelt—in quest of exotic experience, hopefully anticipating a romance of belated and elderly discovery. This venture had been affectionately discouraged. William James predicted inevitable shocks. Henry would be certain to find American vocalization ignobly awful, and must surely be repelled by the peculiarly horrid way in which his compatriots dealt with soft-boiled eggs. William Dean Howells, was no less apprehensive. But Henry James could not be shaken. Surprises and disconcertments were precisely what he desired; they would be grist to his intellectual and "artistic" mill. Besides, he could learn from Howells to be shocked and charmed in the right places.

His program was ambitious. In youth he had lived in New York, Newport, Boston and Cambridge. In these places, he would revive old friendships and early memories. But he wanted, also, to explore the rest of the land, which he had never seen. There was the South, the Middle West, the Far West. There was the whole vast, queer, wonderful country where, in presence of the native phenomena, and in his quality of restored absentee, he might—he *just* might, luck being with him—find everything very interesting and quite unexpectedly and almost uncannily delightful and sympathetic. He was still sufficiently American to grasp a relation between probable pleasure and possible profit. He intended to write a book of impressions.

His first one awaited him on the wharf of disembarkation, with an embodied intensity which no subsequent experience was to diminish. It was produced by that most significant of all native phenomena, the monstrous form of Democracy. The strange, frightening thing tormented his curiosity, shattered his peace, provoked endless speculation, and left him permanently bewildered but rich in dogmatic conclusions.

At the very outset, he realized that, in the new United States, the "common man" and the common woman had their appointed paradise and sphere, and that the sign of it was the abeyance, on many a scene, of any wants, any tastes, any habits, any traditions but theirs. The condition, he conceded, might represent an immense boon. But what did enjoyment of the boon represent? In this vast crude democracy of trade, he sought the answer in what was usual. Alas, the usual was always the new, the simple, the cheap, the common, the commercial, the immediate, and, all too often, the ugly.

The "will to grow"—at no matter what or whose expense—continually betrayed itself; anything might be done that any sufficient number of subscribers to any sufficient number of sufficiently noisy newspapers might want. The process that was taking place was a perpetual repudiation of the past, so far as there had been a past to repudiate, so far as the past was a positive rather than a negative quantity. Everywhere, he felt the breath of an interested passion that, restless beyond all passions, was forever seeking more pliable forms. And, if he could not fail to note the ubiquity of the unmitigated businessman face, he also could not escape an impression of the surrounding scene as a huge Rappacini-garden, rank with each variety of the poison plant of the money-passion.

The most remarkable consequence of this universal pursuit of wealth, he felt, was a social one. For, over the land, the women appeared to be of a markedly finer texture than the men, and there existed, between the sexes, a queer deep split or chasm which, to him, seemed *the* feature of the social scene. What could be more characteristic than this apparent privation, for the man, of his right kind of woman, and this apparent privation, for the woman, of her right kind of man? As civilization was tending in the United States, the right kind of woman for the American man might turn out to be one who would require him only to support her and bear with her. Equally, the right kind of man for the American woman might really be the man who intervened in her life only by occult, by barely divinable, by practically disavowed courses. So far as he could see, American life was a society of women located in a world of men—so different a matter from a collection of men of the world!—the men supplying, as it were, all the canvas, and the women all the embroidery.

Yet pecuniary power, when achieved, appeared condemned to beat its wings in the void. The new, shining skyscrapers of downtown New York—supposed temples of the dominant American passion—did not have the authority of things of permanence or even of things of long duration. They were expensively provisional, merely the last word of economic ingenuity only till another word be written. The very mission of New York, Henry James surmised, was to gild the temporary with its gold and then, in its splendid cynicism, abandon its exorbitant work as the merest of stop-gaps. The truth was, he suspected, that New York did not believe in itself; it failed to succeed, even at a cost of millions, in persuading you that it did.

He noted, too, that wealth beat its wings in the void in its social flight—in that vivid show of a society trying to build itself, with every elaboration, into some coherent sense *of* itself, that appealing, touching vision of waste. The effort of Society struck him as no less tentative and temporary than its domestic architecture. For the pompous palaces of upper Fifth Avenue, in their florid majesty, sat only in the lurid light of business between an absent future and an absent past. They enjoyed no security whatever; they were built but to be torn down. The whole costly uptown demonstration, he thought, was only a record of individual loneliness. Customs, forms, functions, the assurance of perpetuity were lacking, and these lavish experiments—bristling with friezes and pinnacles, but discernibly deficient in reasons—could anticipate no magnificent compensatory future.

In one of these palaces, Henry James attended a dinner party, and he came away amazed by a social organism floundering in its own splendor, but betrayed by its paucity of real resource. The ladies, beautiful, gracious and glittering with gems, were in tiaras and a semblance of court trains, a sort of prescribed official magnificence. To what, in the wide American frame, could such magnificence relate? In Europe, a great court function would alone have met the strain. But in New York, there was nothing to do at eleven o'clock—for the ladies at least —but to scatter and go to bed. Had there been a court function, the ladies must have gone on to it alone, for all the exalted reference of the occasion was to them—and not to the gentlemen in whose so often quaint presence, yet without whose immediate aid, the effort of American society to arrive at the "best" consciousness still went forward.

Certainly, the implications of completeness, that is, of a sustaining social order, were conspicuously absent. Was not the deficiency attributable to that oddest of native phenomena—the failure of the sexes to keep step socially? This failure met him at every turn, and he came to believe—as he privately told the young playwright Langdon Mitchell, offering it as his reason for refusing to live in his native land—that, in a democracy, there could be no opportunity for subtlety of sex relationship.

For what, then, was there opportunity in America? As he traveled about, Henry James pondered this question. There was, he concluded, only one basis for any successful accommodation to the prices, the manners, the other inconveniences of existence: the basis of active pecuniary gain, and of active pecuniary gain only. The whole theory of life was to make so much money that you would not, that you did not, "mind," did not mind anything. The faculty of making money was, he realized, the commonest of all; even in the slums of the great cities there was a new style of poverty which indicated an immense rise in the living unit's paying property in himself. Yet would not this rise shrink and dwindle under the icy breath of the Trusts and the weight of the new remorseless monopolies? Would not the living unit's property in himself soon be diminished by those great aggregations of capital that allow the asking of no questions and the making, for co-existence with them, of no conditions? Sometimes it seemed to him that there was such a thing as freedom to grow up to be blighted, and that it might be the only freedom in store for the smaller fry of future generations.

But, however dark the future prospect, Henry James observed that the immense majority of people who were condemned to live under the effect of American pressure seemed perfectly satisfied with the existing order. There were, however, scattered individuals—a modest body —who "minded" on a scale beyond any scale of making. The relation of these unfortunates to their country was baffled and blighted. The prevailing wash of gold failed to reconcile them; what hope was there for them? Perhaps they might, like himself, withdraw to Europe. Or they might even find refuge in the universities, which, in the American scene, impressed him as being stamped with the character and func- tion of the life-saving monasteries of the dark ages.

The more he saw of the United States, the more Henry James was struck by the fact that it was a happy land for every sort of person rather than the middle sort. Those of the upper sort—in the scale of wealth, the only scale now—could to their hearts' content build their own castles and move by their own motors. People of the lower sort— who were masters of gain in *their* degree—could profit, as nowhere else in the world, by an enormous extension of those material facilities which could be gregariously enjoyed. He saw them able to rush about in promiscuous packs and hustled herds, while to the act of so rushing about all felicity and prosperity appeared for them to have been com- fortably reduced. The frustrated American, as James saw him, was the one who "made" too little for the castle and yet "minded" too much for the hustled herd, who could neither detach himself from the society around him, nor happily surrender to it. The pathetic sacrificial victim on the altar of the new United States was, he intimated, the old-fashioned survivor of the obsolete upper middle class.

Indeed, during almost the whole of his year's visit, Henry James was transcendently homesick—and not only for his tight anchorage in England. In the perpetual presence of the impudence of private greed, he suffered an acute nostalgia for the old distinguished life, the common intelligence that had flowered formerly, for attesting fame, from so strong a sap and into so thick and rich a cluster. Had the old formula, that of Puritanism educated, anything more to communicate, except for "business"? He could find scant indication of any capacity for the uplifting *idea* or aptitude for the finer curiosity. The whole tenor of life spoke more of the power of the purse and of the higher turn for business than of the old intellectual, or even of the old moral, sensibility. Of the new material and political power so eloquently and abundantly exhibited by an imperialistic America, he could report only that it was almost cruelly charmless.

As specimens of the probable flower of the new order, Henry James was deeply and disagreeably impressed by the commercial travelers who filled the trains and the hotels everywhere. The lusty drummer, the brawny peddler more or less gorged by the fruits of misrepresentation and blatant and brazen in the key of his "special line of goods," was an ominous figure. He was, as to facial character, vocal tone, primal rawness of speech, general accent and attitude, extraordinarily base and vulgar. The type was in completely unchallenged possession and it treated Henry James to so lurid a vision of its triumph as to make him brood, heavily, on its significance for civilization. He wondered what specific human process of any sort it was possible to impute to them; what women, living with them, could yet leave them as they were—how, in short, when people were like that, did any one trust any one enough to begin, or understand any one enough to go on, or keep the peace with anyone enough to survive?

For once intimidated, his imagination refused any answer. It could only suggest the potential innocence of these peculiar people. Rather than makers of the new order, were they not among its victims and martyrs, creatures touchingly, tragically doomed? For, surely, they had not elected to be almost the only figures in the social landscape. They had not proposed to carry on life without aid of any sort from other *kinds* of persons, other types, presences, classes. If such was their present situation, did not the blame lie with the American moral outlook, which denied other possibilities in man than the mere possibility of getting the better of his fellow-man over a "trade"? Confronted by what a later generation was to call Babbittry, Henry James was shocked and dismayed. The pages that he consecrated to the ambassadors of business were among his most pessimistic. As if anticipating Sinclair Lewis, he could only lament the sterility of aspect and blight of vulgarity, humanly speaking, where a single type has had the game, as one may say, all in its hands.

He found—he so desperately *tried* to find—mitigations. Making acquaintance with that new institution, the "country club," he had the misguided notion that it applied, in the most delicate conditions, the democratic theory of universal eligibility. It impressed him as being one of the great garden lamps in which the flame of Democracy burns whitest and steadiest—an image no doubt as exasperating to the socially elect as to the rigorously excluded. He was awed by the gorgeous golden blur, the wondrous complexity of great new hotels like the Waldorf-Astoria, which seemed to express a social, indeed positively an esthetic ideal—the ideal of a gregarious life led wholly in public—and he speculated as to whether the hotel spirit may not just *be* the American spirit most seeking and most finding itself. Did it not completely satisfy the restless ambition of most Americans to unlearn as many as possible of their old social canons, and in especial their old discrimination in favor of the private life?

Again and again he was forced to reckon with the perpetual repudiation of the past. It was not only the native-born who eagerly jettisoned their tradition and inheritance; the principle likewise held true for all the myriad immigrants from foreign shores. He was appalled by the scale of foreign infusion. A visit to Ellis Island, giving him an intimate view of the inconceivable alien, put a new chill in his heart. He suffered a sense of dispossession under the affirmed claim of the alien, however immeasurably alien, to share in an American's supreme relation—his relation to his country. The old American homogeneity had broken down before the monstrous, presumptuous interest and claims of the foreign-born—and he doubted whether Americans would ever again know a close and sweet and *whole* national consciousness. But he wondered, studying the process of assimilation, what became of the good manners which it had taken long ages of history, in the other world, to produce. In his new environment, the immigrant accounted them only a great mistake. Like the native-born, he wished only to surrender to the great equalizing pressure, in order the more success-fully to cultivate the "will to grow."

So far as Henry James could see, this will to grow was accompanied, with respect to every serious ideal, by a vast general unconsciousness and indifference. The Americans of 1905 struck him as being so in-tensely bent upon becoming something other than they had been, or than they actually were, as to ignore utterly the question of what it was they wished to be. Change, expansion, growth for their own sake were all that the nation cared about; and, to Henry James, this blind de-sire succeeded only in piling up enormous arrears of the undone—a pathetic accumulation of the unretrieved and the irretrievable. "Is the germ of anything finely human," he questioned at the last, "of anything agreeably or successfully social, supposably planted in conditions of such endless stretching and such boundless spreading as shall appear finally to minister but to the triumph of the superficial and the apothe-osis of the raw?"

Terror had, indeed, met him on the wharf of disembarkation, and had been the companion of his travels. And in the novel of the new America which, back in England, he began but did not live to finish, it became almost a living presence. What other god could he invoke, aware as he was of the black and merciless things that are behind the great possessions? For his native land filled the heart of Henry James with dread—the dread which he ascribed to the hero of his unfinished novel, who, looking at the Newport house he had inherited, likened it to some monstrous modern machine, one of those his generation was going to be expected to master, to fly in, to fight in, to take the terrible women of the future out for airings in. . . .

[2] THE MORALS OF MAMMON

During the Christmas Holidays of 1907, an English visitor left the Plaza Hotel in New York City to make an afternoon call. In a few days, she was to be guest of honor at a dinner party to which her hosts had likewise invited the handsomest and most attractive young man in America. But her mind was not on Jack Barrymore, though romance was her hobby as well as her livelihood. Driving down Fifth Avenue, to the plain red-brick house at Ninth Street once occupied by Washington Irving, she was busily plotting strategy. She was calling on America's most eminent man of letters and most famous private citizen. And her purpose was not merely to pay a compliment.

She had already learned that Americans were primitive in many ways, but wonderfully kind hearted. Shortly after her arrival, for example, she had been invited to spend a week end at a celebrated marble palace on the Hudson. The very "democratic" behavior of porters in Grand Central Station astonished her, and she was dismayed by having to travel in a railway coach with all sorts of weird people. The palace proved to be splendid beyond all the dreams of avarice. In the bedrooms, embellished with Louis XV furniture and real Venetian lace, even the humblest porcelain accessories were decorated with blue satin bows. At tea, the hostess wore fifty-thousand-pounds' worth of pearls round her neck, and long white kid gloves. On the whole, the visitor was not pleased. But later week ends on Long Island reassured her. There were men who looked exactly like English hunting squires. It was odd, indeed, to find that there was a side of American society that was not so different from English life after all!

It was even more odd that she, who so well understood America and the Americans, should be grossly misjudged by a people most of whom had a faint look of the Red Indian. Her present notoriety was—or perhaps merely ought to be—distasteful. She had lately published a novel: it meant everything to her; it was the outpouring of her whole nature, romantic, proud, passionate. It celebrated the joys of earthly love, alas so absent from her personal life, and it had been condemned as highly immoral. She was the victim of a storm of abuse. And there were unkind folk who asserted that her motive in writing the book was purely mercenary!

How, then, could she help despising the materialism of Americans, who genuinely believed that the amassing of money was the be-all and end-all of their existence? Condemnation and abuse had multiplied the sales of her book, but this quaintly lucrative result was significant only as a tribute to her literary Muse. Her notoriety had caused the press to solicit her views on a variety of topics, and she furnished them, however reluctantly, for was it not her mission to plant and foster the growth of the ideal in America? In the interest of that mission, so urgently required, the controversy over her book must not be permitted to die down. Quite unselfishly, and impelled only by her profound concern for American culture, Mrs. Elinor Glyn was calling on

Mark Twain. She wanted him to issue a statement attesting the elevated moral idealism of a novel entitled *Three Weeks*.

Mark Twain thought her incontestably beautiful, but made the shrewd reservation that she *acted* charm, and did it well, but it did not convince. He surmised that the hero of *Three Weeks*, a susceptible young man, would have prodigiously admired her, but if he chose would have been able to get away with his purity in good repair. Indeed, Mark Twain was less impressed by Mrs. Glyn's beauty and her book than by the distinctly unusual character of their long talk. He himself spoke with daring frankness, frequently calling a spade a spade. It was one of the damndest conversations he had ever had with a beautiful stranger of her sex. Though he praised her book, and agreed with her unconventional theories about sexual relations, he refused her request for support and defense. For he was convinced that no wise, intelligent, and experienced person should suddenly throw down the walls that protect and conceal his *real* opinions. As for himself, he exposed to the world only his trimmed and perfumed and carefully barbered public opinions and concealed carefully, cautiously, wisely, his private ones.

Seventy-two years old, Mark Twain was enjoying the inconsistency of a double life. Occasionally he made one of his whimsical, witty speeches at a public banquet, an arresting figure in his white suit; his dense crest of hair, thick eyebrows and heavy moustache resembling a white plumage. He had become a kind of joint Aristides, Solon, and Themistocles, an accredited spokesman for the nation. The world, loving him as a humorist, honored him as a moralist and reformer. But privately, Mark Twain held that civilization was a shabby poor thing and cherished a profound contempt for the "damned human race." Long before, he had arrived at the conclusion that the universe was a blind mechanism, and man but a useless thought. He believed, or professed to believe, that only dead men could tell the truth in this world. "The human race," he recorded, "is a race of cowards; and I am not only marching in that procession but carrying a banner."

So, every morning, Mark Twain was dictating his autobiography. Propped up in bed, smoking one cigar after another, he dealt with both the present and the past, unburdening his mind of those *real* opinions which he found so many excuses for concealing. It was his intention to reveal himself fully and with absolute candor in relation to his times. The book, he thought, might safely be published at the expiration of one hundred years. He anticipated that it would make a stir when it came out.

His own life story, as he was vividly aware, furnished a spectacular illustration of the fulfillment of the old democratic faith of America. More Alger-like than any tale by Horatio Alger, it proved the truth of the concept of individual opportunity. It demonstrated the old theory that, with talent, enterprise, sagacity, hard work, any man might achieve success, might attain the "good life." For it was a tale of swift rise from rags to riches, from obscurity to fame. The backwoods boy who had been a tramp printer, river pilot, miner, roistering frontier journalist, professional humorist, businessman and reckless speculator, had won worldwide fame as an author. Now, with an income of ninety thousand dollars a year, he walked as an equal among the great of the world. The President of the United States eagerly sought his approval. Millionaires like Carnegie and Rockefeller were proud to claim his friendship. Washington politicians, British aristocrats, sprigs of European royalty were honored by his society. And he had risen from the grimy sons of labor, the real builders of empires and civilization, the stevedores!

Yet Mark Twain, who knew beyond any doubt that his life had been an American success, took as dark and hopeless a view of his country as did his contemporary Henry Adams, who considered his own life an American failure. Looking at the United States of the dawning twentieth century, both were filled with abhorrence. Neither retained the slightest faith that the future could hold anything good.

To Mark Twain, ranging from the eighteen-forties to the probable state of the nation a century later, history suggested an ominous parallel. Clearly, the United States was going the way Rome had gone. During his own lifetime he had witnessed the emergence of deadly gifts which looked like benefits and were welcomed, and promptly thereafter had observed the beginning of a process of decay and destruction. In his childhood, the country, like Rome, had briefly exemplified stern virtue, incorruptibility, love of liberty, and all-sacrificing patriotism— this when she was young and poor. Then, there had come sunbursts of material prosperity and spreading dominion. In these, the people had exulted, never suspecting that they were not fortunate glories, happy benefits, but were a disease and freighted with death.

As always before, vast material prosperity had produced conditions which debased the morals and enervated the manhood of a nation. The country's liberties were coming into the market and would be sold or squandered. Had not two plutocrats, Clark of Montana and Guggenheim of Colorado, allegedly bought the legislatures of their respective states in order to secure for themselves, and the interests which they represented, seats in the United States Senate? Had not President Theodore Roosevelt, under an executive order issued in an election year, considerably enlarged the pension list—"the sole purpose back of the additions being the purchase of votes"? It was obvious, too, that irresistible circumstances would gradually take away the powers of the states, and concentrate them in the central government. The ultimate result was perfectly clear—"for we have not ceased to be human beings by becoming Americans." In the end, a popular idol would be permanently enthroned by a debauched and worshiping people. The United States, Mark Twain believed, must inevitably become a monarchy—or, as a later generation would describe it, a dictatorship. The necessary condition of this change had already arrived: vast power and wealth, which breed commercial and political corruption and incite public favorites to dangerous ambitions. By 1908, Mark Twain saw the monarchy already present and the republic a thing of the past. The republic, in name, remained. The republic, in fact, was gone. The retiring monarch, Theodore Roosevelt, had appointed his own successor, William Howard Taft, and Mark Twain himself would vote for the continuance of the monarchy, since nothing could ever unseat it.

He tried to analyze the causes of the transformation which had taken place in American life. First among them, he was inclined to place material prosperity. In the region of the Mississippi Valley, during his own youth, there had been nothing resembling a worship of money or its possessor. The people had desired money, and had respected men of means, but they had likewise respected the character and industry which formed the moral basis of success. Jay Gould—the mightiest disaster which had ever befallen the country—had taught the entire nation to worship money, to make a god of the money and the man, no matter how the money might have been acquired. And, in the twentieth century, Jay Gould's gospel was continuing to do giant work— the gospel which exhorted men to get money quickly, in prodigious abundance: "dishonestly if you can, honestly if you must." The gospel had become almost universal, and every member of the robber gang who had amassed millions by shady methods could think himself a fine and great and noble being, and a proper model for the emulation of the rising generation of young men. For had not such a man been worshiped because of his wealth, and particularly because of his shady methods of acquiring it, these many years?

Looking at the life of his country in his old age, Mark Twain poured an acid contempt on its universal passion for wealth; on its subordination of every value to that single value—a value diseased, and freighted with death. Jay Gould had subverted the American people. Not Carnegie, or Rockefeller, or Henry H. Rogers. These men were his friends. Like himself, they had come up the hard way, by practicing the old American virtues. Carnegie and Rockefeller were the greatest philanthropists known to history, and their wealth was doing incalculable good. And who but Rogers, the financial wizard of Standard Oil, had retrieved Mark Twain's fortunes when disaster overtook him and he was forced into bankruptcy?

These men, his friends, were not devils, as the politicians and the newspapers alleged. They were not dishonest, though their fortunes were derived from monopolistic corporations. For such corporations had been created by an iniquitously high tariff. They could have been curbed by reducing the "robber tariffs" to a figure which would allow the rest of the nation to prosper, instead of conferring the bulk of the prosperity upon a few dozen multimillionaire producers. But the people, already subverted, had not insisted that this be done. And the politicians, with an eye to the vast election contributions of the money of stockholders, had not done it. Instead, they had persisted in attacking the symptoms and in letting the disease carefully alone, meanwhile convincing the multitudinous and grateful unrich that the tariffs were instituted in *their* interest. And there was much to be said for the great corporations. They gave employment to millions. They spread progress everywhere. Yet Mark Twain, whose career proved the essential soundness of the old American, democratic doctrine, felt that something had gone profoundly amiss. The American dream had not been realized. It had been betrayed.

Of these things, however, he would not speak during his lifetime. He would content himself with writing from the grave. It made no difference that William Dean Howells had assured him that his foundations were struck so deep that he would catch the sunshine of immortal years, and bask in the same light as Cervantes and Shakespeare. He could not tell the whole truth. The moralist he detected in himself was thoroughly aroused. But was the man in a position to commit himself to the side of the angels? In youth, he had declared his ambition to become a rich man, had spoken of the fortune "which I shall make, as surely as Fate itself." He had devoted himself unremittingly to the making of money. So perhaps he felt, as he said humorously in another connection, that "it is but common prudence for those of us who got in on the ground floor to refrain from boring holes in it." But, talking for posterity, he could not refrain from expressing an embittered sense of the failure of American society, and of the collapse of the American dream.

[3] THE WILL TO BELIEVE

For the evening of March 2nd, 1912, Colonel George Harvey had arranged a banquet at Sherry's, in New York City. The editor of *The North American Review* and *Harper's Weekly* was an expert in affairs of this kind, and he did not lack assurance. Within a few months he would be deeply involved in the political destiny of Woodrow Wilson, the Democratic "reform" governor of New Jersey. But for this occasion he had angled for a larger, and a Republican, fish: William Howard Taft, President of the United States.

"I have traveled here from Washington," the President told the assembled company, "to do honor to the greatest living American writer and novelist. Easily at the head of living literary men of the nation, Mr. Howells is entitled, on this celebration of his seventy-fifth birthday, to this tribute of respect."

A stout man, with twinkling eyes and a friendly smile playing under his clipped white moustache, William Dean Howells was deeply moved. For the President's tribute, made in behalf of the nation, was but one of many. Eminent Americans, rising to speak, praised his long service to the country's literature, and there were read messages of homage from distinguished men in other lands. Fame had been his for many years, but, in the twilight of a career that had opened more than a half century earlier, the world's affection warmed his heart.

In acknowledgment, he talked as one who had known the great American writers of the past: Hawthorne, Emerson, Thoreau, Longfellow, Whitman. Yet he felt that the era of greatness had not closed. Though literature had become more and more of the forum and incidentally of the market place, this signified no decline. It was still actuated by as high and noble motives as ever it was in the history of the world. For his evidence, Howells appealed, not to literature, but to life, and what he said sounded like a profession of faith: "all of human life has turned more and more to the light of democracy, of equality, if you please."

In respect to the life of the United States, this turn, this trend toward democracy and equality, had always been his hope, nourished by what his old friend Henry James described as Howells' incurable optimism. But from his middle age onwards, it had been only a hope; never a certainty. For Howells was a realist—one who felt in every nerve the equality of things and the unity of men—and he had been compelled to acknowledge that the drift of American life was in the opposite direction. Thus, over the years, he had been unable to reconcile his sunny temperament and his troubled conscience.

He profoundly desired to believe the true American gospel that "it will all come right in time." But the harsh actualities of the new America had brought him to doubt it. At first, he had seen the new industrial age opening before the country as an age of promise. He had taken the view of the scientists; it was a new phase of evolutionary progress. It would advance democratic opportunity, extend prosperity to all, fulfill the old American vision of a socially good life. But observation of its results convinced him that the new age had betrayed that vision, not fulfilled it. Industrial strife spread over the land. The gulf between rich and poor was rapidly increasing. Wealth accumulated in a few hands, and vast areas of desolation appeared, to which the masses were relegated. The field of individual opportunity was narrowing; for a majority of Americans the outlook no longer was bright with hope. Howells sadly pondered the life of the men who hopelessly and cheerlessly made the wealth that enriched the alien and the idler, and impoverished the producers. He sympathized with their blind groping for fairer conditions. He fully shared their attitude— "they feel that something is wrong, and they know that the wrong is not theirs."

Like Mark Twain, but much earlier, Howells came to feel that there was no longer an American republic, but an aristocracy-loving oligarchy in place of it. The American people, who once had taken their ideals of character and conduct from their statesmen, and later from their philosophers and men of letters, had entered a phase of material expansion and sudden towering fortunes—and there was no doubt but that the millionaire was now the American ideal of greatness. He described the new morality, in its dubious materialism, as founded on the creed that "you pay, or you don't pay, just as it happens." As for the American of the new age, Howells saw that the acceptance of the moral fact as it was, without the unconscious effort to better it, or to hold himself strictly to account for it, was the secret of the power in the man which would bring about the material results he desired. The old Puritan moral sense had given way to a calculating view of affairs in which ethical principle played no part.

This view was one which Howells himself could not share and, under the influence of Tolstoy, he turned to the doctrines of Christian Socialism. His conscience persuaded him that his optimism had been misguided. He now abhorred "civilization," and was convinced that it was coming out all wrong in the end, unless it based itself anew on a real equality. His indignation was aroused by the moneybags who had a hole where their souls ought to be. For himself, he wished only to be settled somewhere very humbly and simply, where he could be socially identified with the principles of progress and sympathy for the struggling mass. In the actual conditions of American society and American business, he considered his own position, as an artist, anomalous and perhaps even a little ridiculous. For the artist could never feel at home as long as there were masses whom he ought to consort with, and classes whom he could not consort with. In the United States, the prospect was not brilliant for any artist then living. But Howells retained enough faith in his countrymen to believe that the artist of the future would see in the flesh the accomplishment of that human equality of which the instinct had been divinely planted in the human soul. Meanwhile, he felt that the American writer could serve a useful function, since it was good to be confronted with the ugly realities, the surviving savageries, that the smug hypocrisy of civilization denied; for till we recognized them we would not abate them, or even try to do so.

This conviction that it was the office of the American writer to make the world better and kinder—Howells believed that since morality penetrated all things, it was the soul of all things—lay at the heart of much of his later writing. In one way or another, many of his books were concerned with the dawning movement for social justice, and he rejoiced in the work of a younger school of writers whose books furnished pictures of certain sides of American life, usually blinked. The evils of big business, of expanding finance capitalism and wage slavery, "the slavery implicated in our liberty," gave his conscience no peace. In two fantasies—*A Traveller From Altruria* and *Through the Eye of the Needle*—he examined, from the standpoint of a citizen of a Socialist co-operative commonwealth, the sincerity of American democratic professions as they were illustrated by the civilization of the most advanced country of its time. In these books, Howells' Altrurian visitor impressed the Americans with whom he came in contact as being a sort of bad conscience; and it was this impression of himself that, as a social critic, working from and through the truth, Howells wished to leave with his readers. The disparity of democratic principles and plutocratic practice was, in his view, the gravest issue confronting Americans of the twentieth century.

But Howells, concerned as he was for social justice, could not bring himself to rely on mere external change to achieve it. During an outbreak of savage industrial warfare, he recorded his conviction that strife was only a symptom, not a remedy; the troubles had to go on as long as competition went on; they were themselves an essential part of competition. He tried to forecast the ultimate replacement of competition by co-operation, of unbridled individualism by social altruism. He saw that, for this, "reform" was totally inadequate. Nothing less than a spiritual reorientation could bring it about.

He learned, in time, to live with his troubled conscience, and perhaps did so more easily because, unlike Mark Twain, he had given no personal hostages to the forces which his conscience accused. Believing that social change depended upon the state of men's souls, he could, in his old age, look at American life and find areas in which the state of the soul was good. He had always cared most deeply about those aims which unite men in a family, "as private property never does," and he returned to the province that he had made his own in youth— the broad sphere of American middle-class existence—in order to study the loyalty, affection, and unity which, to him, gave American family relations a large cheerful average of health and success and happy life. In *The Kentons*, he reaffirmed his faith in one segment of the American scene, the small Middle-Western city which, two decades later, Sinclair Lewis was to portray so caustically. But Howells felt that wherever life is simplest and purest and kindest, that is the highest civilization, and his Kenton family, drawn from what he called the fruitful fields of our common life, illustrated this thesis. Henry James, quite rightly, hailed the book as a "perfectly classic illustration of your spirit and your form." But other critics were not so kindly. The learned reviewer of *The Atlantic Monthly*—Harriet Waters Preston, herself a novelist, translator, and scholar—considered Howells' simple Americans "the monstrous offspring of barbarous and illicit social relations" and protested that "to approach their sad case with paraphernalia of literary preparation" was like "riding in pink, and with winding of horns, to a hunt of cockroaches!"

Howells ruefully confessed that he was disheartened by the stupid and stupefying cry of "commonplace people." Did American readers want only novels about the false and impossible? "I had hoped I was helping my people to know themselves in the delicate beauty of their everyday lives," he told Brander Matthews, "and to find cause for pride in the loveliness of an apparently homely average, but they don't want it." But he persisted in believing that common, crude material was the right American stuff, and thought that, long after his death, he might be likened to an insect, scraping about on the surface of American life and trying to get into its meaning for the sake of the other insects larger or smaller. He had been the precursor, and to a degree the master, of a new generation of American writers who developed a realism far more drastic than any he had practiced. In a measure, his leadership had prepared for the withering of his own laurels; for, in time, his work came to be accounted old-fashioned. In 1915, he was writing sadly to Henry James: "I am comparatively a dead cult with my statues cut down and the grass growing over them in the pale moonlight." He did not protest, but quietly accepted the verdict of the day, acknowledging that "my sort of fiction is no longer desired." Perhaps it made little difference, for he was nearly eighty years old, and tired, tired. And perhaps that "late phase," of which the novelist Henry B. Fuller had written to him so admiringly, "must find its fullness in some other air than this."

CHAPTER V

The Skepticism of the Young

[I] A GOSPEL OF DOUBT

As the new century opened, an American named Stephen Crane died of tuberculosis in a small German resort. He was not yet twenty-nine, a writer, and already famous. Hamlin Garland had "discovered" him. William Dean Howells and Henry James had pronounced his talent to be magnificent, unique. The English critic Edward Garnett, whose opinions were influential with American readers, had declared him the one indisputable genius of the young school.

Crane's meteoric success was inspiring to other young Americans who wanted to write. One of them, Ray Stannard Baker, a junior editor on *McClure's Magazine*, was to remember him, nearly fifty years later, sitting on top of a desk with his knees drawn up to his chin and his long arms clasping his legs—a pale, slim, tired-looking young fellow, full of half-cynical, half-pessimistic talk.

It was this streak of skepticism in Crane that made his work so important, so exciting to his contemporaries. He was unsettled, and so were they. Looking at the life around them, they could not agree that the more smiling aspects of existence were the more American. Society showed great splotches of misery and squalor. For millions of Americans, the promise of life appeared to have been reduced to permanent hopelessness. The individual could no longer control his own destiny; he was at the mercy of immense, impersonal forces. Was this what progress came to?

But literature had nothing to say of these things. With few and notable exceptions, American writers still clung timidly to a kind of official version of American life: sunny, kindly, illimitably rich in opportunity. There appeared to be a vast conspiracy of silence, a deliberate intention to deny the truth by ignoring it. The young people wanted to break it wide open. That was why Stephen Crane meant so much to them. He had written stories that told the truth about life, that uttered an angry protest—the wail of a whole section, a class, a people. And since, in spite of this, he had succeeded, might not they succeed likewise? His fame hardened the will of young unknowns. Jack London, out in California. Theodore Dreiser, working as a reporter in Pittsburgh. Frank Norris, on *McClure's*. And many another. To all of them he seemed not only a precursor but a beacon.

Crane had drifted into New York City at the age of twenty. He wanted to write, and had done some free-lance reporting. His father, long dead, had been a Methodist minister. But he had lost the family faith, and his views on all subjects were wildly unconventional. In New York, he spent his time on the Bowery, a tough street, and in the adjacent slums. He came to know the folk who inhabited squalid back courts, the garish saloons, the filthy lodging houses. He would sit and talk by the hour with the beaten men and forlorn painted women who haunted Union Square by night. Elbert Hubbard, an early friend, protested that he had no sense of propriety. The fact was that the human wreckage of the great city appalled and fascinated him. What caused their degradation? Were they the victims of a cruel, callous society? Were they doomed by "a sort of cowardice," a disposition "to willingly be knocked flat and accept the licking"? If so, wasn't it because they were the product of their environment? He was "not very friendly to Christianity as seen around town." The world he knew best had little virtue in it, but it was dominated by the myths and taboos of smug respectability. He did not have any personal theories of social justice. He only wanted to write books that would "show people to people as they seem to me."

By the time he was twenty-one, he was writing *Maggie: A Girl of the Streets*, a short novel about a girl of the slums driven by her environment into prostitution. It was a cool picture of a human cesspool, and no publisher would have anything to do with it. Where was the kindliness, the sentiment, with which authors habitually portrayed the lives of the poor? Here was only brutality. Drunkenness, ignorance, vice were taken for granted. Richard Watson Gilder, of *The Century*, to whom Crane submitted it, called it cruel, and acknowledged that it was too honest for his readers. Crane borrowed money from a brother, had a paper-bound edition printed under a pseudonym, and tried to dispose of it through bookshops. Some copies went to light a fire in his lodgings, most of the rest were finally stored. Eventually, a copy came into the hands of Hamlin Garland. He invited the young writer to dinner, found him penniless and hungry, and was shocked to learn that he would give away his literary future for thirty dollars.

Garland's literary career had been launched by William Dean Howells, and he was now fairly established. A son of the middle border, the valley of democracy, he had taken part in the Populist movement, and had campaigned among the farmers with Mary E. Lease. His gaunt, embittered stories dealt with the conditions that had provoked their sullen rebellion against government and against God. He thought he understood what Crane was trying to do, and sympathized with him. For was not Crane, like himself, demanding justice for the toiling poor wherever found? Was he not speaking for all those who, through no fault of their own, were destroyed by a society based on industrial slavery? Whether or not this was his intention, Garland thought it the effect of his work. Who would be more responsive to it than Howells, the dean of American letters, the champion of realism, the convert to socialism? He sent a copy of his book to his old friend, whose critical articles in *Harper's Magazine* were followed by all intelligent readers.

Crane, dining at Howells' home in a borrowed suit, was surprised to hear his eminent host introduce him as a writer who had sprung into life fully armed. The talk turned on Mark Twain, and Howells asserted that "Mr. Crane can do things that Clemens can't." After dinner, the older man took down a copy of the lately published poems of Emily Dickinson, and read some aloud. The new, strange music fired Crane —and he produced two slim volumes of verse inspired by Emily's poems which a later generation of American poets were to regard as transmitting a sacred, almost extinguished flame. Meanwhile, Howells, deeply stirred by Crane's story of the slums, tried to place it. In vain. Even the celebrated Dr. Parkhurst, engaged in a dramatic crusade against vice, failed to acknowledge the copy sent to him. Years afterward, Howells still could not understand what was found offensive in the little tragedy. But Crane, exuberant because of his praise and Garland's, went off to the home of a brother in the country, and set to work on another novel. It dealt with a recruit in the War between the States. Once published, *The Red Badge of Courage* became a best seller overnight. At twenty-five Crane was free from want, and assured of fame.

Suddenly, anything he chose to write was acceptable, and eagerly bought. Because he had written a novel about war, William Randolph Hearst sent him off to report the war between the Turks and the Greeks, and later, when the Spanish-American War broke out, he went to report the campaign in Cuba. Yet his novel about war contributed nothing to the legend that war is noble and heroic. His soldier, like his slum girl, was a helpless victim of blind chance, a mere molecule whirled about by irrational forces, the prey of fear—fear of fear; fear of death; fear of the opinion of others, with its power to degrade and destroy. What he saw of actual war on the beaches and in the brush of Cuba did not produce any change in the conclusions which his imagination had projected. "I was a mere corpse," he confessed. "My limbs were of dough and my spinal cord burned within me as if it were a red hot wire." There was, he thought, an excellence of human conduct independent of culture, but the mob had no courage. "What were we doing there at all? There was no definition." War was meaningless, ridiculous. So was life. But men went on engaging in both. It was preposterous to ask why.

This, in sum, was all that Crane had to say. Let others apportion social responsibility and social guilt, if they chose. In one of his stories, a drunken Swede was murdered by a mild little man in a Nebraska saloon. His corpse, "alone in the saloon, had its eyes fixed upon a dreadful legend that dwelt atop the cash machine: 'This registers the amount of your purchase. . . .'" Such grim irony was incompatible with the official American view of life. But to youth, at the turn of the century, it seemed to blow away the pious cant of popular myth. And Crane, untimely dead, was their leader. Like him, they hoped to be among those who tried to write honestly about things.

[2] FRIGHTENED OPTIMIST

In the summer of 1896, when the fame of Stephen Crane was spreading across the United States, a tramp steamer anchored off a Honduran port. The steamer was smuggling brandy, and it was obvious that the passenger who came ashore had been tampering with the cargo. He wore a full-dress suit lacking one of its tails; his uncombed mat of red hair stuck through the crownless brim of a silk hat. He made for the squat bungalow that housed the American consulate. On the verandah, an ample, dignified figure in immaculate white ducks looked at him without laughter. When addressed, this gentleman inquired what had caused the new arrival to leave the United States in the haste indicated by his attire. The question was scarcely correct, for extradition did not obtain in Honduras. So the reply was equivocal: "Perhaps the same reason as routed yourself." Presently the two men set off for the nearest bar.

The red-headed disreputable was Al Jennings, a bandit and outlaw. He and a brother, after a daring bank robbery, had fled from New Orleans with thirty thousand dollars. They hoped to settle in Central America, perhaps as ranchers. The dignified gentleman in white ducks was William Sydney Porter, formerly a journalist and a bank teller in Texas. After his resignation from the bank, errors had been found in its accounts. He had been charged, probably erroneously, with small embezzlements. On his way to face a grand jury, he was overcome by fear, made his way to New Orleans, and took ship for Honduras.

Porter's antecedents and environments were respectably middle class. He was married and the father of an infant daughter. His young wife was tubercular; a frail, proud, highly sensitive girl. He foresaw the social punishment which respectable society would visit on the family of a convict—and it was fear of this that had put him to flight. Arriving in Honduras, he developed the intention of settling there permanently, establishing a home for his family, and rehabilitating himself among strangers. But, back home, his wife's health worsened rapidly, and the plan came to nothing.

A year after his flight, Porter learned that his wife was dying. He returned to the United States. Arrangements were somehow made for him to remain at liberty until after her death. Then he voluntarily stood trial. One of the thefts with which he was charged had occurred when, having resigned from the bank, he was working as a journalist in another city. There were indications that his responsibility for the earlier ones was merely technical; they had taken place during his employment as teller. He would not allow his attorney to raise these issues. In one of his few subsequent references to his misfortunes, he compared himself to Joseph Conrad's Lord Jim: "We both made one fateful mistake at the supreme crisis of our lives, a mistake from which we could not recover." To the jury considering the case against him, his flight was damning. They returned a verdict of guilty. He was sentenced to five years in the Federal Penitentiary at Columbus, Ohio.

There, presently, Al Jennings also came as a prisoner. According to Jennings, whose imagination was vividly romantic, Porter had teamed up with his brother and himself in Honduras, and the trio had traveled widely until the brothers' loot was exhausted. Then the Jenningses had returned to their trade of bank robbing, in which Porter had refused to join them. When Jennings arrived at the penitentiary, he found Porter working on night duty in the prison pharmacy, and writing short stories during the quiet hours. These Porter signed with pseudonyms and despatched to someone in New Orleans who circulated them among the magazines. Several were accepted, paid for, and published. He thought that, after his discharge, he might be able to earn his living by writing. In this case, he would adopt the name "O. Henry." Good behavior reduced his term by nearly two years. He was liberated in the summer of 1901. By spring of the following year, his stories were attracting favorable attention, and the editors of *Ainslee's Magazine* invited him to come to New York City.

O. Henry was then forty years old, and was to live only eight more years. In that time, he became the most popular writer of fiction in the United States, reaching an audience that included all levels of readers from the most intellectual to the nearly illiterate. Lodged in a cheap furnished room on Irving Place, or a shabby little hotel off Madison Square, he ground out story after story, sometimes as many as fifty in a year, until the gathered output filled twelve volumes. This incessant industry was essential. He was always behind schedule with editors from whom he constantly extracted large advances. But they were glad to meet his drain on their good nature and their budgets. For his stories justified it by their popularity with readers.

In a sense, O. Henry was the creator of a new and acceptable American myth. He turned away from the prosperous levels of society, so popular at the time as a subject for fiction. He ignored the Four Hundred to deal with the four million. This choice was more the result of his previous misfortunes than of any interest in social reform, but its net effect was to produce an optimistic social myth. His stories mainly turned on the fortunes of humble folk, shop girls and clerks and mechanics; a group that, on the whole, had been anonymous and inarticulate in American life, and absent from American fiction. They formed the group that a later generation was to describe as "the little people," and that politicians would aggregate as the "forgotten man" and "common man." In the rapid urbanization and industrialization of American life, their numbers were constantly increasing. They were the vast, hard-pressed, hard-working, lower middle class of the great cities, to whom the present was usually precarious and the future equivocal.

It was O. Henry's special gift to portray them as they saw themselves. They did not consider themselves proletarians, victims of an exploiting social order, tragic subjects for rescue or salvage. Although this interpretation of their condition might be made by political radicals like Emma Goldman and social reformers like Jane Addams, by the muckraking journalists and the young school of writers, it was not acceptable to them. Did not the old tradition of American life hold out the assurance that they might rise in the social scale? Did not the American Federation of Labor teach that every skilled worker might, in time, become a member of the bourgeoisie? However hard pressed, they were still abundantly hopeful. "It ain't the road we take; it's what's inside us that makes us turn out the way we do," said one of O. Henry's characters—and spoke for all the little people.

O. Henry might, and often did, excoriate the capitalists who were sweating their workers in factories and shops. In this he had behind him the approval of public opinion, for these harsh conditions had been widely exposed, and a crusade against them was already making headway. But his indictment, though it indicated generous social sympathies which recommended him to the reformers, implied no such social skepticism as other young writers were beginning to express. The workers of his stories were seldom defeated by their environment. They had confidence in their future, and he appeared to share it. He gave the old dogmas a new sanction in terms of the commonplace. His myth was the one which most Americans lived by, and wanted to believe. In an age of wealth for the few and poverty for the many, it asserted that all things were still possible to the common man, and that most of them would turn out to be good.

Thus, his stories pleased every type of reader. Social reformers counted him sympathetic to their aims. Apologists for an expanding capitalism found their complacency reinforced by his optimism; and, because he seemed to be a conservative, they were quite willing to praise him for being a democrat. The class about whom he wrote liked him for shedding on their existence a light of romance. The range of his appeal was curiously attested by a single incident. One day, looking at a display of his books in a Cambridge shop, a Harvard freshman and an elderly, bearded gentleman, strangers to each other, fell into excited discussion of his work, and it developed that he was the favorite American writer of both. The freshman was John Reed, soon to become a celebrated political radical. The other enthusiast was William James.

Ironically, this prophet of optimism was, himself, a frightened and hopeless man. The physician under whom he served in the penitentiary had never known a man who was so deeply humiliated by his prison experience. Al Jennings, pardoned and restored to citizenship by President Theodore Roosevelt, soon achieved success by publicizing as picturesquely as he could his career in banditry. But O. Henry felt constrained to an almost impenetrable reticence about his past. If he wrote about the lower middle class it was, chiefly, because among them he could remain anonymous and feel secure.

Editors who came to know him noticed that he would glance quickly around him as if expecting an attack whenever he entered a restaurant or other public place. To Jennings he confessed his continual terror of being recognized, and addressed, by some former prison mate. In time, his secret became known to a few of his associates. But his own attitude forced them to keep up a polite pretense of ignorance which made true intimacy impossible. They were patient with his eccentricities. After fame came to him, he refused to be either interviewed or photographed. He would not meet the literary lights of the day who admired his work so extravagantly. He rejected all opportunities to enter prosperous, conventional social circles. Solitary, lonely, secretive, he made casual acquaintances in low bars and cheap eating places. He liked to play the king in disguise, tipping waiters twice the amount of his bill, and handing out goldpieces to tramps. His fashionable raiment, his expensive gloves and gold-headed cane, seemed to those who knew him best in themselves a kind of armor against intrusion. He wanted only to be anonymous.

O. Henry was neither a social reformer nor a social theorist. He was a middle-class American to whom respectability was precious. He thought he had forfeited it and accounted the loss a personal tragedy. The values which his stories celebrated were those from which he felt himself to be forever excluded. The decent respectability, the honorable ambition, the instinctive self-respect and sense of equality which he extolled as characteristic of common American life—these were the things about which he cared most. Sophisticated critics of a later generation, to whom his secret became known after his death, were inclined to consider him a sentimentalist, whistling in the dark to keep up his courage. Reformers of a radical cast, contemptuous of his social optimism, were to declare him a reactionary. But, nearly forty years after his death, the "common man" about whom he wrote, having survived two great wars and a decade of extreme economic misery, showed little indication of being persuaded that O. Henry's view of American life was false.

[3] A LOST LEADER

In the early nineteen-hundreds an earnest, unhappy woman writer was staying in the pleasant town of Carmel, on the California coast. Long isolated in a remote desert valley, she had become friendly with the Indians who were settled there. Having studied their religious myths and rituals, Mrs. Mary Austin was now an ardent mystic. This inclined her to dislike the young literary celebrity who was visiting her neighbor. His spiritual nature was not noticeably in evidence.

He was exceptionally handsome. Women flung themselves at him, lay in wait for him. He told Mrs. Austin that they preferred the tenth share in a man of distinction to the whole of an average man; men of genius must therefore be prepared for their assault. She thought certain of his ideas very odd. Never before had she met a man who could get drunk joyously in the presence of women whom he respected. She was suspicious of the constantly dissolving and re-forming ring of his admirers who resented the fact that she was unimpressed by his recent discovery of Darwinian evolution. All in all—though strictly on an intellectual plane—Mrs. Austin and Jack London had to shake down a bit before they became friends. Then, she was quite ready to take him seriously, with respect to the Social Revolution.

So, for a few years, were many other Americans, especially those allied with the more radical branches of organized labor. Among them, he enjoyed a unique prestige as spokesman and teacher. Had he not risen from the ranks of the exploited and underprivileged? Had he not proudly declared his proletarian origin and reported, in book after book, his personal experience of the pit, the abyss, the human cesspool, the shambles and the charnel house of our civilization? Did he not preach the doctrine of the class war, the stern necessity for a mili-

tant socialism? He hated the rotten and irrational system which capi
talism had fastened upon American life, and many of his books were
undisguised propaganda for its overthrow. Yet, so skillful a storyteller
was he, that they were eagerly read by the great middle class which
he professed to despise. For a time it seemed likely that Jack London,
an avowed revolutionary, might exercise a powerful influence upon
the social outlook of the American people, might actually hasten the
success of that crusade for social justice which seemed to be beginning
on so wide a front. But this possibility soon faded.

Jack London was an illegitimate child, offspring of a casual alliance
between an eccentric woman and a professional astrologer who deserted
her in her pregnancy. He never knew his father, but accepted as his
own the kindly, inefficient man whom his mother presently married.
His childhood was spent in deepest poverty along the waterfront of
Oakland, on San Francisco Bay. He sold newspapers in saloons, drove
an ice wagon, worked in a bowling alley. He got through grade school,
then worked long hours in a cannery. At fifteen, he was an oyster
pirate on the bay, a hard-drinking, worldly-wise hoodlum; member of
a gang, and a juvenile delinquent. At seventeen, he signed on a sealer
for a long voyage in Siberian and Japanese waters. A year later, he
joined the western division of "General" Coxey's army of protest, organized to march on Washington. He deserted the marchers midway
across the continent, and roamed the eastern states as a hobo. He was
jailed for vagrancy; the experience gave him a contempt for the
sanctity of the law, and a respect for its absolute power and its injustice. He made his way back to the Pacific coast, spent one year in
high school, and then one unhappy year at Stanford University. He
joined the radical wing of the Socialist party, read voraciously, and determined to become a writer. After leaving the university, he went to
the Klondike during the height of the gold rush there. He found no
gold, but the adventure, as literary material, was presently to bring
him fame and financial success beyond his dreams.

He took up writing rather as a livelihood than as a means of self-
expression. This was the attitude of a member of the working class.
None of the odd jobs he had held after leaving the road paid him more
than ten cents an hour; precisely the wage he had earned in the cannery as a child. He concluded that mere brawn would never give him
a decent livelihood; but brains were marketable, and he would apply

his mind to making money. He never disguised the purely materialistic basis of this decision; in time, his genuine talent tended to obscure
it, and the circle of radical intellectuals in which he chose to move
blamed him for selling out, both as a social reformer and as an artist.

In his two years of high school and university, he came into contact
with what, to him, seemed the ease and grace and security of middle-
class life. As a convinced socialist, he despised the middle class. But as
an individual who had lived only in the cellar of society, down in the
subterranean depths of misery about which it is neither nice nor proper
to speak, he wanted the comforts and luxuries which they enjoyed. And
he likewise suffered from a resentful sense of social inferiority. Could
he make the middle class respect his proletarian contempt for them
unless he achieved success in terms of the only standard they recognized—the standard of money? There occurred a conflict between
social ideals and personal ambition which he was never able to resolve.
It left a deep fissure in his moral nature, and produced a startling inconsistency in his life and his writing.

His reputation as a writer was quickly won with stories based upon
his experiences in the Klondike—a subject which in time he came to
hate, but from which he could never quite work free. For the public,
these stories formed the last chapter in the epic of the frontier; and an
industrialized, fiercely competitive America looked back at the vanished frontier with a feeling of romantic nostalgia—it was a refuge, a
vicarious escape from the complexity and drabness of existence. Into
these stories, Jack London wove two doctrines which he had absorbed
in the public library—the survival of the fittest and the will to power
of the Nietzschean superman. His "abysmal brutes" and violent strong
men became heroes in a romantic version of the typical success story.
The formula was not so different from that of Horatio Alger, and the
triumph of rugged individualism delighted a vast audience most of
whom, in their personal lives, could exercise very little. The success of
the formula persuaded Jack London to continue with it, and among his
later novels were many which celebrated the ruthless will to power,
the strong man, the man on horseback who, indifferent to the fate of
the dumb and stupid masses, would redeem society from its rotten
futility. These books shocked his socialist friends, and in time alienated
the great audience which he had won among the industrial workers
of the United States. They were persuaded that he had betrayed their

cause, had become a renegade, had sold out to the capitalists for wealth
and ease and luxury. For, as he made more and more money, he chose
to live in circumstances of well-publicized extravagance.

When he began his writing career, he hoped to achieve financial independence and, after he had won it, make his writing serve his social
ideals. His intention was to produce books which would advance the
war of the classes, and hasten the social revolution in the United States.
But even before the publication of his first book, he was acknowledging
that "it's money I want, or rather, the things that money will buy, and
I could never possibly have too much." He was, he said, in pursuit of
dollars, dollars, dollars—and his motto was, "If cash comes with fame,
come fame; if cash comes without fame, come cash."

In spite of this materialistic ambition, he wrote a series of books
which uttered a ringing call to the crusade for social justice. These included both fiction and factual social studies. Among the prosperous
classes of the United States they added forcibly to that awakening of
the social conscience which was so rapidly progressing between the
turn of the century and the outbreak of the first World War. Liberalism and reform were in the air. The journalism of exposure had
aroused the public to the conflict between human rights and property
rights brought about by an expanding industrialism. The need for
curbing the power of big business was coming to be widely recognized.
The Socialist party was steadily growing in strength. In these circumstances, Jack London's revolutionary novels and tracts were read by
the prosperous classes who, however shocking they found his ideas,
could still regard these works as being either romances or mere discussion of abstract theory, and therefore not too seriously unsettling.
Their greatest influence was among the more militant groups of the
underprivileged: the radical factions of organized labor, the "intellectuals" in the slums and social settlements of the great cities, and other
discontented folk who were beginning to consider their situation hopeless. To all of these, Jack London's vigorous summons to war seemed
to offer both a gospel and a program of action.

For he wrote, not as a reformer, but as a political and social revolutionary. One of his novels, *The Iron Heel*, projected into the future the
outbreak of class warfare in the United States. It dealt with an abortive
revolution of the workers, put down by the nation's armed forces, maintained to protect the power and property of organized capital. The inevitable development of capitalist society, as London described it, was a

regime almost identical with the then unknown Fascist state. His "Oligarchs"—the great capitalists—as a class believed that they alone maintained civilization. They had a high sense of ethical righteousness and this moral conviction accounted for their great driving force. To keep the masses in subjection, they created a favored labor class—which London described as resembling the American Federation of Labor, already committed to co-operation with the employers. The Oligarchs increased the disunity of labor by subsidizing the great unions. It was such disunity, according to London, that kept the workers of his day from making their power effective. Like Eugene V. Debs, he saw hope only in the formation of a single, all-inclusive organization of workers, banding together the skilled and the unskilled, and making progress on a common front. In his novel, London dramatized a situation with which Americans were to become increasingly familiar as the years passed. It was to be interminably repeated in all major industrial disputes. It developed from the fatal willingness of union leaders to act independently for the advantage of their own organizations—to effect settlements which obtain concessions for a single group, without reference to what is best for the rest of labor. To do this, as London tried to show, is only to play into the hands of the employers.

The issue, as Jack London presented it in his revolutionary books, was a simple one. The major problem confronting American society was to wrest the control of government and industry from the bourgeoisie. He agreed with Debs that "the capitalists have stolen our country, debauched our politics, defiled our judiciary and ridden over us roughshod," and that "the issue is the Workers versus the Plutocracy." He felt that the proletariat of the twentieth century wanted democracy applied to industry and summoned it to possess itself of the government, abolish wages, which were merely legalized robbery, and run the business of the country in its own interest. The twentieth century, he declared, was "the common man's day, or, rather, the dawning of the common man's day."

This theory was predicated upon a belief—not uncommon among social reformers—that the gateway of opportunity had been closed, and closed for all time in the United States. "These doors will not open again, and before them pause thousands of ambitious young men to read the placard: NO THOROUGHFARE." Had he been born fifty years later, London asserted, Andrew Carnegie, the poor Scotch boy, might have risen to be president of his union, or of a federation of unions, but he would have had no opportunity to become the builder of Homestead and the founder of multitudinous libraries. For, as London continually emphasized, the old myths which were the heritage of the American boy in his own boyhood had ceased to be valid. Though Jack London's novels were, for the most part, unblushing transcripts of his personal experience and adventures, he seems never to have recognized that his own career illustrated the continued validity, in American life, of the "old myths" which he sought to discredit. The rise to wealth and fame of a wharf rat and hobo was no less impressive than that of the poor Scotch boy—and London himself exemplified the persistence of an opportunity in which he professed to disbelieve.

As the years passed, and his income approximated that of a successful capitalist, Jack London's taste for luxury increased, his self-indulgence expanded; and his faith in the common man, the high destiny of the proletariat, dwindled away. Like others of his generation, he had come under the spell of the mechanistic philosophy current at the time. He began to feel that man faced a universe brazen with indifference toward him and his dreams, that it was good for him to accept at face value the cheats of sense and snares of flesh, since, in any case, all lives lost the game in the end. "Sometimes I wish I had never opened the books," he confessed to a friend. The ideas derived from his youthful reading still haunted him; his own existence began to seem futile; he could not be at peace with himself.

Always the most industrious of writers, he came to hate the drudgery of creative work, to which he was chained by a mounting burden of debt which his extravagance piled up. He announced, publicly, that he had been trying hard to get out of the writing game for many years, that he wanted to quit pen-scratching for good. At length, he resigned from the Socialist party, to which his adherence had added considerable prestige. He gave as his reason its lack of fire and fight, its loss of emphasis on the class struggle. He had always believed that the working class, by fighting, by never fusing, by never making terms with the enemy, could emancipate itself. But the whole trend of Socialism in the United States during recent years had been one of peaceableness and compromise, and he asserted that his mind refused a further sanction of this policy. But, in the nineteen-thirties, Austin Lewis, the early friend who had drawn him into the Socialist movement as a boy, declared that, from the very outset, Jack London had stood with one foot in social democracy and the other in the philosophical teachings from which have sprung Fascism.

When Jack London died, probably a suicide, at the age of forty, he was the proprietor of a baronial estate where, in a projected mansion resembling a mediaeval castle, he hoped to lead the existence of a millionaire country gentleman. Though he had gratified every material ambition, he confessed that he had never enjoyed a sense of fulfillment. "The things that I had fought for and burned my midnight oil for, had failed me"—and he instanced, among them, success, recognition, social prestige, art, and culture. In fourteen brief years, he had produced forty-one books. With these, too, he was utterly disillusioned. Thirty years after his death, all but a very few had been forgotten by American readers. But in Russia, where a social revolution occurred which he did not live to see, his revolutionary tracts and novels were still widely read. His fame, there, endured—as a precursor and a prophet; a genius compromised and blighted by the capitalist society in which it had been his misfortune to live.

[4] PUZZLED ICONOCLAST

One summer afternoon in the eighteen-nineties, Paul Dresser was showing the sights of New York City to his young brother. It was Theodore's first visit. He was a lanky, earnest youth who held a reporter's job on a Pittsburgh paper. Paul felt that he was wasting his time there. New York was the only place to carve out a career for one's self. All really ambitious people gravitated to New York. It was *the* city, no less.

His own was a case in point. Years earlier, he had run away from the seminary in which he had been placed to study for the priesthood. Dropping the family name of Dreiser, he joined a medicine show, then a minstrel show, finally wound up as an entertainer on the Bowery. Now, he ranked high in the world of the theater. Droll, genial, excessively fat, he was a popular star in farce on the road. He also composed music of a tender, sometimes sad, sometimes gay, kind, and his songs had caught on. They were, indeed, heard everywhere in the land.

The brothers strolled along the Gay White Way. This stretch of Broadway, from Madison Square to Forty-second Street, was a legend to all provincial Americans. It had the hard, bright glamour of a chromo. At the lower end were the Fifth Avenue Hotel, the Hoffman House with its celebrated bar, Delmonico's. At the upper, there was the new Metropole, with a vast restaurant open to three streets where stage folk congregated. Between, the broad avenue was lined with theaters, expensive shops, luxurious hotels. Lacquered carriages passed in a continuous procession. The sidewalks were a promenade for pretty women and prosperous looking men.

To Theodore Dreiser, this scene was eloquent of wealth and power. It impressed him as pruned of almost every trace of poverty or care. The hand organs were grinding out Paul's ballads—"My Gal Sal," "On the Bowery," "Just Tell Them That You Saw Me"—and passers-by constantly hailed or stopped him. Everyone recognized him. He knew everyone of importance. Theodore Dreiser observed this admiringly, with a touch of envy. He was poor, unknown, still seeking. An outsider, hungrily looking in on a bright world. When had he not been on the outside, looking in?

Paul told him about the banquets and balls of the wealthy, at Delmonico's and the fabulous new Waldorf. Theodore, he said, ought to write about these things some day. Out in the Middle West, people didn't know what was happening. The rich were gaining control of the country, and presently would own it. Theodore ought to show up what was going on, make people aware of it. Theodore listened, felt the challenge. Some day, perhaps . . . But, just now, how could he secure a foothold in New York?

The city awed him, fascinated him. He explored the shuttered splendors of Fifth Avenue. Wall Street, which raised images of millions made in stocks overnight, of yachts, orgies, travels. Printing House Square, where the great dailies were located. He stared at their buildings with the eye of one who seeks to take a fortress. City Hall Park, its benches filled by those whom the huge, terrible city had broken. Bums, loafers, tramps hoping for a handout, waiting for the bread lines to form. There were zest and security and ease for some, cheek by jowl with poverty and longing and sacrifice. Wherever he turned, he felt a sense of power that had found itself and was not easily to be dislodged. There was an indifference to ideals, however low or high. And there were huge dreams and lusts and vanities being gratified hourly. Everywhere, he was aware of a terrifying desire for pleasure or wealth, accompanied by a heartlessness which was freezing to the soul, or a dogged resignation to deprivation and misery. Could anything other than chance lift the average man out of his rut? Yet he wanted to live in New York, Theodore Dreiser realized, once he was back in Pittsburgh. He soon returned. He had a little money, a vague hope that he might succeed at something, a vague resentment of his circumstances.

The hope and the resentment were what he knew best in life. He had seen them working, always: in himself, his parents, his brothers and sisters. He was the twelfth of thirteen children born to German immigrants settled in Indiana. The father was an embittered failure; stern, puritanical, devoutly religious. Much of the time he was separated from the family. The mother tried to hold it together, with scant success. They moved from town to town, always poor, always made to feel inferior, always seeking to become acceptable. The older children drifted away to the cities. The younger knew what it was like to be famished for want of food, to steal coal from the railroad yards for fuel, to be kept out of school for lack of clothes and shoes. At times, when Paul sent money home, things were better. Theodore managed to get through school. Later, he had a year at Indiana University, paid for by a teacher who detected promise in him. In one town where the family became almost respectable, a sister was seduced and jilted by a sprig of the local aristocracy. The family moved on, joining the great migration to Chicago. There, another sister, craving the luxuries and excitements which poverty denied her, had eloped with a married man much older than herself, who deserted his family for her. What, if not the hope of a "better life," resolved his sisters on these desperate ventures? Were they sinful? Religion, morals, social convention condemned them. Could anyone, caught in the enormous grip of chance, and so swerved from the established customs of men, be guilty of that depth of vileness which the attitude of society implied? Theodore Dreiser thought not.

The point was to live, grow, rise in the world, become somebody. "Anyone could legitimately aspire to be anything in America, and nearly all aspired. Not to want to be rich or to be willing and able to work for riches was to write yourself down a nobody. Material possessions were already the goal as well as the sum of most American life, and so one could not help feeling the state of isolation and indifference which accompanied a lack of means." Money. Success. Power. Social recognition. Were not these the very stuff of the better life, the fabric of the American dream?

In Chicago, Theodore Dreiser was shunted from job to job. Order boy in a wholesale hardware firm. Driver of a laundry wagon. Clerk in a real-estate office. Canvasser and collector for a company selling cheap furniture on the installment plan. This job he lost because, needing an overcoat and having no money to buy one, he falsified his collections. The dreary search for work began again. Finally, after many failures, he was taken on the staff of a newspaper.

Long afterward, he was to write of Chicago, by its shimmering lake, as a king of shreds and patches, a maundering yokel with an epic in its mouth, a tramp, a hobo among cities. The city that he knew was crude, primitive, vicious—but it sang of high deeds and higher hopes, and its fame already girdled the world. It was a city of violent, bewildering contrasts. The fetid slums, where Miss Addams hoped to inaugurate the reign of social justice. The arrogant new palaces of the new rich, whose foresight and ruthlessness had captured railroads, gas works, stockyards, streetcar systems. The flat monotony of jerry-built middle-class neighborhoods. When the titans of finance clashed over a franchise, or the possession of a public utility, the issue was decided by politicians who controlled the ballot boxes and sold them to the highest bidder. In these contests the people—both the middle class and the enslaved poor—were mere pawns, disposed of by forces which they could scarcely identify, still less expect to control. This was democracy at work. Where was the place of virtue, either private or public—that quality of generosity which offers itself willingly for another's service? Everyone professed to believe in it. But, so far as Theodore Dreiser could see, existence in an American city like Chicago resembled the brute struggle for survival in a jungle. And this was complicated by a wild desire to get out of the ranks of the commonplace, to seize and enjoy some shred of imagined luxury or beauty. The test of success in American society had no room for virtue. The test was self-preservation.

He moved on to St. Louis, and then to Pittsburgh. There, the profits of the steel magnates were tumbling in so fast that they scarcely knew what to do with them. They were building immense mansions crowded with art and historic furniture, endowing vast libraries and universities. They were also refusing to increase the wages of the toilers in their metal infernos and forbidding them to organize in unions. As a reporter, Theodore Dreiser interviewed the magnates, who talked eloquently of the American equality of opportunity which had enabled them to rise in the world. Off duty, he prowled in the squalid, congested quarters where the mill workers were herded, and the dismal back streets where prostitutes hung about at night. Never before had he had so vivid a sense of the vast gap which divides the rich from the poor in America. How did this square with equality of opportunity, with the official American idealism which professed a profound faith in God, in goodness, in virtue, and in duty? In the Public Library, he read the works of Herbert Spencer and other evolutionists. Years later, he reported that they "quite blew me, intellectually, to bits." They verified a dawning conjecture as to the unsolvable disorder and brutality of life.

He moved on to New York. There, he turned again to the newspapers, failed as a reporter, worked at manual labor for a railroad, tried his luck as a free-lance writer, and took editorial jobs with various magazines. He remained desperately poor, and became despondent. For five years he worked at his first novel, then peddled it from publisher to publisher without luck. Frank Norris, in the first flush of his repute as a novelist, finally secured its acceptance. *Sister Carrie* was a revolutionary book, and Norris persuaded the publishers to send advance copies to prominent critics who, he felt, would recognize its merits. They were outraged by it, and the publishers stored the rest of the edition in their cellar. Eleven more years were to pass before Dreiser's second novel was put into general circulation. That book, and most of its successors, were denounced as immoral and corrupting. Not until more than a quarter of a century after the acceptance of *Sister Carrie* would a nationwide audience acknowledge the power and truth of his picture of the American scene.

What were respectable Americans to make of his novels? He dealt with their universal quest for a more abundant life, but in terms which, at best, made it seem morally dubious. These terms did not derive from traditional American culture but from recent American social practice, and his books demonstrated that the two had no relation. American culture, with its puritanical assertion of the supremacy of moral law, and its optimistic belief that social environment is always subject to change for the better—this, according to Dreiser, might have some meaning as the expression of an idealistic hope. But it had little relevance to the way in which American life was being lived. To show that the culture was obsolete and the practice savage was to invite the hatred of those whose interest it is to support the one in order to profit by the other.

He had not learned the elementary literary lesson that so successful a writer as Mrs. Wharton, at the age of eleven, had been taught by her mother. She had shown her first story, which began, "If only I had known you were going to call, I should have tidied up the drawing room." Said her mother, icily, reading no further: "Drawing rooms are always tidy." Americans preferred fiction which portrayed life as it was displayed in the parlor—where, along with the piano, the bric-a-brac, the jar of pampas grass and the copy of Dr. Conwell's heartening *Acres of Diamonds*, they kept their ornamental Sabbath faiths.

Dreiser's novels had the effect of shattering these pious convictions. For they compelled the conscience of middle-class Americans to face the actual stuff of American existence in the raw. Here was the common enterprise of getting on in the world. Had it not given birth, in some fifty years, to a unique civilization—an age of vast industrial combinations, enormous concentrations of capital, more and better things for everybody, limitless progress? Here was the potent religion of success which made the progress possible. To keep the whole incredible mechanism running smoothly, Americans had had to find an ethical sanction for their materialism. So they had invented the dogma that to accumulate or manage money in order to achieve good, or needed services, was a worthy moral principle. Of course, everything depended upon your definitions of good, and of needed services. Culture proposed one set, which you used for ceremonial occasions. Social practice taught you another, and if you hoped to get on you adopted them. One of Dreiser's characters, gazing at a bank building, thought of it as almost partaking of the nature of a church. This was not a comment on architecture. It was a profession of faith. For Americans were queerly ruled by conscience. Had the American conscience been duped?

The evidence that Dreiser accumulated indicated that it had. True, he presented American civilization from odd angles of vision—or so they seemed to readers in the first decades of the new century. A simple-minded country girl, like his own sister; the city lured her; she became a kept woman, and wound up as a musical-comedy star. The son of a poor bank clerk who rose to be a great tycoon. A small-town youth who, like Dreiser himself, became an artist. A boy from the city slums who got his start as a bellhop in a luxury hotel. However odd they seemed, they were truly representative of American society, on many of its levels. An identical hope of rising in the world, of somehow achieving a more abundant life, was the mainspring of their dissimilar careers. The goad of a restless heart—wasn't that the compulsion from which all Americans suffered? So far as Dreiser could see, it led to no ultimate peace, no real understanding, but only hunger and thirst and wonder. Conditions were such that "whole masses suffer who have no cause to suffer, and, on the other hand, whole masses joy who have no cause to joy." Even the successful seldom achieved a stable satisfaction. They got what they wanted, but there was always something beyond more alluring still of which they were likely to be defrauded. As for the others, the great masses of people, they were doomed from the outset. Their existence was led under a damnable scheme of things.

The readers whom Dreiser outraged seldom realized that, like themselves, he was a product of American culture and society and, as a result, that he was quite as conscience ridden as they were. So they did not see that he was often making a plea for social justice, as eminent Americans like Miss Addams and Theodore Roosevelt were likewise doing. The reformers held to the old cultural ideals, thought they would work if given a chance, preached that society could be improved. Dreiser, looking at the way society actually operated, took a dim view. In practice, it discounted all ideals; taught hypocrisy, rapacity and accumulation; encouraged men to undertake whatever they thought they could get away with. Those who succeeded under this amoral education became, by virtue of their success, the real models for others to imitate.

The most obvious current model was the millionaire. Americans might inveigh against monopoly and protest against the tribute extorted by the trusts, but Dreiser saw, as Howells had seen before him, that the millionaire was their genuine ideal of greatness. He was what most Americans secretly wanted to become. So Dreiser gave them a full-length portrait of a representative example. Unlike Howells and Henry James, Dreiser did not draw his hero from imagination and hearsay. He went into the arena for an actual figure—Charles T. Yerkes, the traction magnate—and, using the technique of a trained reporter, thoroughly documented his subject's public and private career at every step. The two long novels that resulted, *The Financier* and

The Titan, were more social history than fiction; a study of the operation of the new finance capitalism, in the form of a biography of one of its outstanding exponents.

Yerkes, or as Dreiser called him, Frank Cowperwood, was a true product of the American divorce between social conviction and social practice which, as William Graham Sumner said, led to moral anarchy. "So far as he could see, force governed this world—hard, cold force and quickness of brain. If one had force, plenty of it, quickness of wit and subtlety, there was no need for anything else." Some might pretend to be guided by other principles, ethical or religious, but if they were, they were following false or silly standards—for in those directions lay failure. "To get what you could and hold it fast . . . that was the thing to do; and he genially ignored or secretly pitied those who believed otherwise." From one point of view, as Dreiser saw, it might have been said of him that he was seeking the realization of an ideal—and the same could have been said of Gould, or Morgan, or Rockefeller, who also sought a better life according to the only terms proposed by their environment. In the career of Yerkes-Cowperwood—a born fighter and leader, strong, resourceful, intelligent, inspiring to men and fascinating to women—Dreiser traced the working out in life of the unofficial American gospel of success. This man, in the course of his rise to power, disrupted the economy and debauched the politics of two great American cities. He fleeced the public again and again. He wrecked nearly every enterprise that he touched. He brought tragedy to the life of every human being with whom he came into intimate contact. Such, seen in the raw, was the perfect flower of the American system. Naturally, the cohorts of Dr. Conwell and Orison Swett Marden, the charmed audience that had delighted in O. Henry, were aghast.

But Dreiser always made them furious. Long before the theories of Dr. Sigmund Freud had become generally acceptable, he was busy showing up the hypocrisy in which were grounded all conventional taboos concerning sex. His characters, men and women, succumbed to lust—and he merely remarked that we suffer for our temperaments, which we did not make, and for our weaknesses and lacks which are no part of our willing and doing. Respectable folk said that his characters were "amoral." Perhaps they were, but if so, the unacknowledged social practice which they were following was amoral, too. Dreiser only pointed out that the practice had no relation to the official social code. This was precisely what made him seem dangerous. For many years, societies for the suppression of vice sought to forbid the circulation of his books. It took nearly forty years for Americans to realize that Dreiser was a stern moralist, deeply disturbed by the fatal inconsistency of culture and conduct in American life. And the eventual acceptance of his books may have been more reliably the index of a change in taste, than of a change in moral outlook.

Like many Americans of his generation, Dreiser was bewildered by the civilization that had developed during his lifetime. Like them, he was bent upon discovering its meaning; he was engaged in a perpetual search for a theory that would explain it. As a thinker, he was in no way superior to the average man, and his many books thus recorded the changing course of popular philosophy. In his youth, Herbert Spencer and the evolutionists were the last word in radical speculation. From their books he patched up a theory of mechanism not unlike the one at which Mark Twain had arrived in his old age. It comforted his conscience, as it had Mark Twain's. It made life a tragic business, but it absolved the individual of all moral responsibility.

As the years passed, his bleak theory failed to satisfy Dreiser. He could not help feeling that life was a problem in social justice. If this were true, it followed that there must be a Creative Divinity, and so a purpose, behind all of this variety and beauty and tragedy of life. His final attitudes betrayed his muddled thinking, and demonstrated his passionate sincerity. Just before his death, he joined the Communist Party as a protest against the injustices suffered by the masses under capitalism; the gesture was, he said, the logical conclusion of his lifework and experience. He likewise left, for posthumous publication, a novel, *The Bulwark*, upon which he had been working for some thirty years. It dealt with the religious life, and emphasized the human need for an "inner light"—nothing could be accomplished without love toward all created things. Like many other Americans in the nineteen-forties, Dreiser was persuaded that society must be reorganized upon some more equitable basis. But, in the end, he was likewise persuaded that the shape of society is a product of the spiritual life of men. The change had to begin within.

In the thirty years before his death, Theodore Dreiser had published but one novel. To the generation that grew to maturity in the interval, he seemed less a living contemporary than an Olympian of the remote past. How could they be aware of the derision, persecution, and bitter disappointment which, for nearly a lifetime, had been endured by this tall, grey, lonely man whose appearance was as awkward and anxious and earnest as his cumbersome novels? Honors came to him late, among them, with a kind of irony, a medal of merit from the American Academy of Arts and Letters, custodian of the official insignia of respectability. The official arbiters had long subjected him to detraction. But, as the critic Howard Mumford Jones put it, when he died it was as if something primary had disappeared from the American scene; as if a headland crumbled and slid into the sea.

[5] MIRAGE

Shortly after Theodore Dreiser left Pittsburgh to seek a reporter's job in New York, a young woman joined the staff of a Pittsburgh newspaper. Miss Willa Cather had just graduated from the University of Nebraska. She was not seeking a career in journalism. Though but twenty years old, she had long since chosen a profession. She was determined to become a writer of fiction.

For some ten years, Miss Cather worked as a journalist, and subsequently a teacher of English, in Pittsburgh. She spent holidays in Europe, in Nebraska, Colorado and Wyoming. She tried her hand at verse, and published some short stories. One of these attracted the attention of S. S. McClure and when, in 1906, most of the brilliant original staff of his magazine resigned to launch their own publication, he invited Miss Cather to an editorial post on *McClure's*. Six years later, having meanwhile become its managing editor, she retired from the magazine, and from journalism. She was ready to undertake her chosen career.

Later, she explained this long delay. "It is always hard to write about the things that are near your heart. From a kind of instinct of self-protection you disguise and distort them." She had won the friendship of Miss Sarah Orne Jewett, the distinguished writer of New England stories, who gave her one of the few really helpful words she was ever to receive from an older craftsman. Said Miss Jewett: "Of course, one day you will write about your own country. In the meantime, get all you can. One must know the world *so well* before one can know the parish." But Miss Jewett did not live to see the fulfillment of her prediction. It was not until 1913, when she was approaching her fortieth year, that Miss Cather began her long record of a changing aspect of American life. By then, the principal writers of her own generation—

except for Theodore Dreiser—had already produced their best work. Her major books were to be published contemporaneously with those of a new generation of American writers, and this was to make her seem a solitary figure, a writer whose view of American life was as remote from that of her juniors as it was from that of her true contemporaries.

Miss Cather's family, for several generations settled behind the Blue Ridge in Virginia, migrated to a Nebraska ranch when she was nine years old. Their new home was near a small town on the Burlington Railroad, still in course of construction, in a thinly populated part of the state. In Virginia, life was ordered and settled, the people in good families were born good, and the poor mountain people were not expected to amount to much, and there had been no element of struggle since the War between the States. But in the new country, life seemed to be full of adventure.

Nebraska then was largely unbroken prairie, open grazing land for the great herds of cattle driven up from Texas. But the economic interests of the advancing railroads required settlement, and their foreign agents were already luring to the great plains immigrants from Scandinavia, Russia, Bohemia, France. "No child with a spark of generosity," Miss Cather wrote, "could have been kept from throwing herself heart and soul into the fight these people were making to master the language, to master the soil, to hold their land and to get ahead in the world." Even in childhood, she thought them underrated, and wanted to explain them to their neighbors. In a sense, the best of her work was to do precisely this. It was to be founded upon the recollection of some childhood experience, of something that touched her while a youngster —for, as she acknowledged, she had never found any intellectual excitement more intense than that produced in her by the stories of the pioneers.

With but few exceptions, therefore, her books dealt with the American past, and the most significant recorded that swift, dramatic process of historical change which, in less than two decades, transformed the great plains. This change began when grazing gave way to agriculture, and the open prairie was mastered by European immigrants suffering privation and loneliness in a raw new land. Then the pioneers and the builders of towns and railroads—dreamers, enthusiasts and visionaries led on by the prophecies of their own boundless hopes—gave way to a second generation which undertook the industrial exploitation of the soil. The heroic age was over. Prosperity was achieved; civilization had come; the pioneer was replaced by the successful farmer, the small-town businessman and banker; the culture of Main Street had been established; and a brief, inarticulate dream had been forever overwhelmed by the gospel of materialism.

Looking back over this process of change after it had run its course, Miss Cather found it no matter for rejoicing. Had not the inexorable needs of an economic system destroyed much that might have been fruitful for culture and society? Natures that resembled a rich mine of life like the founders of early races were vulgarized, or forced into dull, conventional molds—and the result was held to be "Americanization." The morality of the new order amounted to little more than the compromise of cowardice, apologetic and sneaking—to it, any righteousness, alive and burning, was dangerous, and so must be extinguished. Vast, impersonal economic forces had shaped a society appropriate to their ends. To the achievement of those ends, standardization and conformity were essential. The free play of individuality had become reprehensible. The only incentive which society recognized as meritorious was the making of money. Such was the final term in a process which had begun with the vision of the pioneers—whose dream it was to achieve—in the very midst of insecurity—dignity, social life, art, a humane culture!

This verdict, implied by Miss Cather's novels about the past, was made explicit by the few novels in which she undertook to deal directly with the United States of her own time. In them, she studied the fortunes of characters who inherited the pioneer vision, and found themselves in conflict with an environment that no longer afforded it genuine opportunity. They were those in whom the old belief flashed up with an intense kind of hope, an intense kind of pain—the conviction that there was something splendid about life, could they but find it. They were idealists, out of harmony with a materialistic society, and rebels against it. Of them, the hero of *One of Ours*, her story of the First World War, was typical—a farm boy, born in a coarse and prosperous environment, tormented by the discrepancy between his own vague vision of a superior form of life, and the surrounding unlovely reality. In the culture and art and life with which he became familiar in France, he found expressed all that the United States had denied him. And its moral was simple: "Men could still die for an idea; would burn all they had made to keep their dreams. . . . Ideals were not archaic things, beautiful and impotent; they were the real sources of power among men." But it was a moral which he had never found exemplified at home.

In Miss Cather's books, skepticism about the American present took the form of an elegy on the American past. Her vision of life was not prospective, but nostalgic. She spoke, not for some better future, but for the hopes of vanished yesterdays. And, because of this, she seemed the most melancholy of the major novelists of her generation. For in her work America contemplated the victory of industrial civilization and material prosperity, and the defeat of a dream.

CHAPTER VI

Seven Pillars of Wisdom

[1] THE NATIONAL GADFLY

William Dean Howells, born in the America of Andrew Jackson, was still writing in the America of Henry Ford. No longer widely read, he was widely honored—an historic figure, surviving from an era that seemed great because it was so distant. And was he not also the last of a distinguished line? Since the days of Irving and Cooper, the country had never lacked a man of letters who, speaking for the whole nation, interpreted it to the whole world. When Howells died, in the spring of 1920, this high succession became vacant.

That it was filled almost immediately was not obvious at the time. In the autumn of 1920, Sinclair Lewis' *Main Street* swept across the continent on a whirlwind of controversy, which soon carried it around the globe. Ten years later, having meanwhile produced four other major novels, Lewis was the first American to be awarded the Nobel Prize in Literature. By 1930, therefore, world opinion accounted him not only the most eminent of living American writers, but the most authoritative interpreter of American life and culture. As to the correctness of these appraisals, the sanction of his countrymen was not unanimous.

Nevertheless, it was as a spokesman that Lewis, in accepting the award, discussed some aspects of the life of his greatly beloved native land. The United States, he declared, was as strange as Russia and as complex as China. It had passed through the revolutionary change from rustic colony to world empire. Possessing billions of money and

134

tons of faith, it was undeniably vital and experimental. But, speaking with complete and unguarded frankness, Lewis questioned whether the American mind had kept pace with material progress. Most Americans—not only readers but even writers—still feared any literature which did not glorify the national faults as well as the national virtues. Serious writers and artists were condemned to work alone, in confusion, supported only by their integrity, oppressed by a sense that their work did not matter, and that they did not count, in a land that produced eighty-story buildings, motors by the million, and wheat by the billions of bushels. Lewis deplored the divorce in America of intellectual life from all authentic standards of importance and reality. Though for the future of American literature he had every hope and every eager belief, he considered his country the most contradictory, the most depressing, the most stirring in the world.

This statement accurately defined the impression of America conveyed by Lewis' novels. What wonder that, in some quarters, he was condemned as a literary delinquent who had consistently killed sacred cows, washed native linen before the eyes of the world, fouled his own nest, discredited a fatherland?

Main Street established Lewis, at thirty-five, as a major novelist. Tall, lean, angular, red haired, he was a prodigious talker, a talented mimic and, in society, "as noticeable as a bashful cyclone." The son of a country doctor, he grew up in a Minnesota village for which his later affection was not conspicuous. He went to Yale, at a time when the movement for political and social reform—the tide of liberalism—was rising to its crest. Attracted by socialism, he made a brief stay at a communistic colony organized by Upton Sinclair, serving as janitor with as great discomfort as Hawthorne had felt when tending the manure pile at Brook Farm. He lived, for a while, in the slums of New York City, like a conscious, intelligent proletarian. Later, he became a charity worker there. Thereafter, he was a reporter in California, worked on a magazine in Washington, and held various jobs with publishers in New York.

He had begun writing while at college—the first study for *Main Street* dated from that period—and he continued, during his years of itinerant job holding. As a means of purchasing his freedom, he sold a number of story plots to Jack London. The intention was not realized, but the plots were probably good of their kind, for London used nine of them. Gradually, Lewis' short stories began to appear in magazines.

By 1915, his work was being accepted by *The Saturday Evening Post,* and he felt able to strike out as a free lance. When he began writing *Main Street,* he was the author of six previous books, the best of which indicated his discipleship to H. G. Wells, whom, he said, his generation had adopted as master and teacher.

Lewis submitted the manuscript of *Main Street* to James Branch Cabell for criticism. Cabell was in the limelight, for the postal authorities had attempted to suppress his *Jurgen,* but he was not a practitioner of realism. He ranked realistic fiction with dancing and *The Literary Digest* and golf, as aberrancies of dullness. Nevertheless, he suggested changes in the novel, and persuaded Lewis to delete from it "an avalanche of constructive criticism." For Lewis, a liberal and a humanitarian socialist, was at heart a reformer, bent upon improving society by instructing it.

Indeed, Lewis had already published a constructive criticism of one facet of American society, perhaps the most significant. In it, he expressed the boundless confidence with which liberal thinkers of his generation—such men as Herbert Croly, Walter Lippmann, George Soule—faced the future, before American entry into the First World War. Whatever their reservations about the actual state of things, they saw change at hand, and they identified it with progress. The election of Woodrow Wilson had given liberalism an official status, and widespread social reform appeared to be guaranteed by his promised "New Freedom." Seldom had the true American gospel of optimism seemed more warranted by the immediate outlook.

Sinclair Lewis, pondering the new America of Henry Ford, was unperturbed by the fact that it was dominated by business. He reckoned it an advantage that business was being recognized—and was recognizing itself—as ruler of the world, and was reducing to the role of its servants the egotistic arts and sciences and theologies. In its new consciousness of power, it was reforming its old, petty, half-hearted ways. The vision of an altruistic efficiency was already discernible in the scientific businessman and the courageous labor leader. Indeed, business could be described as a valiant effort to unify the labor of the world!

He foresaw a complete change in the fundamental purpose of organized business from the increased production of soap—or books or munitions—to the increased production of happiness. How was this utopian change to be brought about? By nothing less than a socializing that would crawl slowly through practical education and the preaching of kinship, through profit sharing and old-age pensions, through scientific mosquito slaying and cancer curing and food reform and the abolition of anarchistic business competition, to a goal of tolerable and beautiful life.

A tolerable and beautiful life for everyone was the old American dream—and liberal reformers thought it could be realized. To adopt it as a practical objective was, in their view, neither utopian nor visionary. And, being their goal, it also became their criterion for judging the immediate state and prospect of American society. Beginning with *Main Street*, Sinclair Lewis' most important novels were to expose, with savage humor, those facets of American society which contradicted this ideal. But his moral scorn often obscured for readers the fact that their pitiless indictment of failure was dictated by passionate faith. He believed in the genuine possibility of a personal kinghood, an education in brotherhood and responsible nobility. The basis of his indignation remained constant. He became, as it were, a nostalgic gadfly tormenting the nation—himself tormented by its repudiation of his exalted youthful ideals.

For, even as Lewis was writing *Main Street*, the mood of the American people underwent a drastic change. With the end of the war, idealism collapsed. A cynical view of life prevailed. The aims of liberalism looked foolish. Social reforms went out of fashion; the people wanted not nostrums but "normalcy." This was the America of gangsterism, political corruption, the big business boom, Billy Sunday and the Fundamentalists, the Ku Klux Klan. The gospel of democracy and the democratic way of life were under heavy attack. H. L. Mencken, the most influential critic of the day, pilloried the American masses as a "booboisie." The War Department, in a training manual, defined democracy as a government of the masses, asserted that its attitude toward property is communistic, and warned that it resulted in license, agitation, discontent, anarchy. At the best universities, scholars like Paul Elmer More and Irving Babbitt were calling for an intellectual elite to assume leadership, since the democratic order, in their view, had thoroughly debased all civilized standards. Among the plain people, mass conversions were made to a new religion of prosperity and free spending. Its gospels were "service" and "efficiency" and the ethical duty of keeping up with the Joneses. Bigger-and-betterism would issue in genuine success. Earnest Elmo Calkins, a specialist in public relations undertaking the role of seer, announced—in words not very unlike those previously used by Sinclair Lewis—that the work that religion, government, and war have failed in must be done by business. As Calvin Coolidge was later to declare, the business of America is business. Most Americans agreed with him. Disillusioned, but remaining a liberal, Sinclair Lewis found himself a counter-revolutionary.

Lewis staked out as his province that bewildered empire called the American Middle West. This was the old "Valley of Democracy," now become the nation's center of agricultural and industrial production. With few exceptions, American novelists had described its villages as the domicile of a pure, simple, kindly life; its cities as pleasant, friendly places. Lewis saw it as a land of dairy herds and exquisite lakes, of new automobiles and tar-paper shanties and silos like red towers; a land where cities thrust shining shafts into the air, and ringed them with smut and slums. "What is its future?" he inquired. "The ancient stale inequalities, or something different in history, unlike the tedious maturity of other empires?" Would it breed courage to sift the sanctified lies? Would it justify a hope that is boundless? His novels, examining the present by which its future would be determined, furnished an answer.

His study of the small town—"Main Street is the climax of civilization"—exploded a cherished legend, added a pejorative to the national vocabulary, and exasperated many a patriot. Gopher Prairie was complacently satisfied with its unsparing unapologetic ugliness, and its physical appearance reflected the state of its soul. It was an economic parasite in a region of fertile farms. It was a citadel of philistinism, hypocrisy, and intolerance. Its people thought not in terms of hoss-swapping but in cheap motorcars, telephones, ready-made clothes, silos, alfalfa, kodaks, phonographs, leather-upholstered Morris chairs, bridge prizes, oil stocks, motion pictures, land deals, unread sets of Mark Twain, and a chaste version of national politics. Its intellectual arbiter —a spinster schoolteacher—stood out for sweetness and a cautious use of the uncomfortable properties of light. It worshipped the Tribal God Mediocrity. This committed it to an unimaginatively standardized background, a sluggishness of speech and manners, a rigid ruling of the spirit by the desire to appear respectable.

The goal of life in Gopher Prairie, Lewis reported, "is contentment . . . The contentment of the quiet dead, who are scornful of the living for their restless walking. It is negation canonized as the one positive virtue. It is the prohibition of happiness. It is slavery self-sought and self-defended. It is dullness made God." The root of Main Street's trouble, Lewis declared, was spiritual, and no League or Party could enact a preference for gardens rather than dumping grounds. Still a reformer, he wondered what could be done about it, and concluded that only one attack could be made: "you can keep on looking at one thing after another in your home and church and bank, and ask why it is, and who first laid down the law that it had to be that way."

The danger of Main Street, in Lewis' view, was the tremendous energy of its inertia, which gave it power to impose its own ideals on American culture and civilization. In a sense, it was a force seeking to dominate the earth. "Sure of itself, it bullies other civilizations. . . . Such a society functions admirably in the large production of cheap automobiles, dollar watches, and safety razors. But it is not satisfied until the entire world also admits that the end and joyous purpose of living is to die in flivvers, to make advertising pictures of dollar watches, and in the twilight to sit talking not of love and courage but of the convenience of safety razors." In a later novel, Lewis pungently summed up the American creed to which Main Street, as missionary, was seeking to convert the world. It was a theological belief that it was more important to have your purchases tidily rung up on a cash register than to purchase what you wanted.

Having touched off a nationwide controversy by his report on the village, Lewis went on to investigate the nature of life in a Middle Western city. In sequence, he explored the careers of four representative citizens: a Rotarian booster, a scientist, a spellbinding clergyman, a millionaire manufacturer of automobiles. Though Babbitt, the first of these, was to enter American folklore and provide the language with a new descriptive term, the city which Lewis created was more important than any of its inhabitants, for it illustrated all the forces which were shaping American society.

Said a foreign visitor, of Zenith: "I hate your city. It has standardized all the beauty out of life. It is one big railroad station—with all the people taking tickets for the best cemeteries." The radical lawyer to whom he was speaking attributed this effect not to standardized commercial products, but to standardization of thought, and, of course, the tradition of competition. The true villains, he declared, were the clean, kind, industrious family men. Constituting an effective majority, they were socially menacing precisely because they were so good and, in their work at least, so intelligent. This made it difficult to hate them properly, and yet their standardized minds were the enemy. But—had not the vast efficient mechanisms of mass production itself produced the human type which it required in order to function smoothly? In relation to the great machine, this type was a willing cog and a ready consumer. Was not the surface of his life, what he believed to be his individuality, determined by the great national advertisers? Their wares —toothpastes, socks, tires, cameras, instantaneous hot-water heaters— were his symbols and proofs of excellence: at first the signs, then the substitutes, for joy and passion and wisdom.

In Zenith, forever hustling for hustling's sake, this emergent new American, the child, servant, and beneficiary of technological progress and industrial concentration, could dwell at peace—provided that he neither thought nor questioned. But sometimes, incautiously, he was led to explore the meaning and values of his own existence. Certainly he had done all the things which his environment required and approved. He had supported his family, acquired a good home and six-cylinder car, built up a nice business, joined the church and the country club, associated only with good, decent fellows. Why, then, did he find himself dissatisfied? Why was he forced to confess that "I've never done a single thing I've wanted to in my whole life"?

Could it be true that "we hustlers, that think we're so all-fired successful, aren't getting much out of it"? In a flash of rebellious insight, the new American might see his way of life as incredibly mechanical. What were its elements? "Mechanical business—a brisk selling of badly-built houses. Mechanical religion—a dry, hard church, shut off from the real life of the streets, inhumanly respectable as a top hat. Mechanical golf and dinner-parties and bridge and conversation." This was rank heresy, and Zenith—American society—could not afford to tolerate it. For, if it spread, the great machine which supported existence might be seriously crippled, perhaps even wrecked. It was balanced, precariously, upon universal acceptance; upon the axiom of its ethical rightness. So skepticism must be policed, and the rebellious desire for personal freedom must be chastised into conformity. Punitive social pressure could be exercised. Was there not a Good Citizen's League— dedicated to enforcement of the patriotic thesis that American Democracy did not imply any equality of wealth, but did demand a wholesome sameness of thought, dress, painting, morals and vocabulary?

Was the life of the captain of industry in any way more fruitful than that of the hustler? He, if anybody, might be expected to profit by the efficient functioning of the great machine. He was poised at the apex of the social and financial pyramid. He might, indeed, dream of motors like thunderbolts, as poets less modern than himself might dream of stars and roses and nymphs by a pool. He might have a large house in a fashionable street, a taste in etchings, an acquaintanceship with the works of Marcel Proust, an occasional susceptibility to the music of Beethoven. Financial power and social prestige permitted him the luxury of these deviations. But what about the content of his life?

He was forced to acknowledge that none of his industrialized friends in Zenith were very much interested in anything. They had cultivated caution until they had lost the power to be interested. As for himself, he was "chained by every friend who had made life agreeable—bound not to shock or lose them. He was chained by every dollar he had made, every automobile he had manufactured—they meant a duty to his caste. He was chained by every hour he had worked—they had left him stiff, spiritually rheumatic." He, too, was in bondage to the great machine. Pondering his existence, he was able to discover almost no reason for thinking it worthwhile. Although he was common sense apotheosized, he suddenly found himself at odds with the society of which he was a pillar.

Was Sinclair Lewis suggesting that, judged by the standard of common sense, American society made no sense whatever? Many Americans so understood him, and this was why, as a bishop of the Episcopal Church acknowledged, his novels caused a good deal of foreboding among the older men of the country. For his novels reported that the fruit of material success was spiritual frustration. The American people had set out to subdue a continent in order to achieve a better life. They had accomplished the conquest of their physical environment. Were they to become the victims, rather than the masters, of their unique civilization?

This was the question at which Lewis kept hammering in his novels. As his picture of American life expanded, it became obvious that he had anticipated many of the conclusions later stated by social scientists in such studies as *Middletown* and *Middletown in Transition*. Though never professing to be a social historian, his books recorded the results of a swift, dramatic change in the life of his region. During Lewis' boyhood and youth, the people of the Middle West—still in the main pioneers—had been progressive in their thinking, had furnished leadership as well as support to all movements for political, social, and economic reform. But, in less than the span of a generation, they had become the country's most obdurate conservatives. In the new bewildered empire, Middle-Western farmers, experimenting with advanced technological methods, steadfastly opposed the political and social changes made necessary by scientific progress. Middle-Western businessmen, applying experimental methods to industry, bitterly contested their application to the national economy and social situation. Lewis' picture of Middle-Western life made clear the effects of this repudiation of the liberal tradition.

A moralist and a reformer, he could not rest his case on a mere picture. He kept reminding his countrymen of the grim choice that confronted them. They could submit to the sacred institutions imposed by their industrialized society. They could purchase the peaceful enjoyment of prosperity at the cost of their souls. Or they could resist the group pressures which threatened to reduce most of them to the condition of a machine for digestion and propagation and obedience. Zenith "will always try to bully you, and tame you down." Did Americans have courage enough to tell Zenith to go to the devil? Lewis' most appealing characters were quite average Americans who became rebels against their environment.

His meaning was explicit. He was old-fashioned enough to believe in the efficacy of a will to liberty. It could be trusted to strike a balance between necessary social constraints and desirable personal independence. If Americans could revive it, they might recover their country and reclaim their own lives. They might even, he hinted, once again become aware that "it is an adventure that we have here—the greatest in the world—and not a certainty of manners in an uncertainty of the future, like all of Europe."

This, however, was not the notion of the accredited intellectual arbiter of the nineteen-twenties. So pervasive was his influence, so immense his authority, that the gay and gaudy decade came to be called by his name. It was the age of H. L. Mencken, whose celebrity exceeded that of any previous critic of the national culture. Mencken was the pontiff of the rebellious younger generation of writers. He was the prophet of raccoon-coated collegians, to whom the latest issue of *The American Mercury* was as indispensable as their hip-flasks. And he was the favorite dispenser of scorn to the prosperous urban middle class, whose appetite for disesteem from high quarters dated back to the days of Cotton Mather. Mencken, the archenemy of all puritanism, was himself more puritanical than the puritans whom he derided. He was, so to speak, the satanic Mather of a cockeyed era which, seeing nearly everything topsy-turvy, understood his gospel of the old salvation as the new damnation.

With his colleague George Jean Nathan, a critic of the theater, Mencken made the *Mercury* the liveliest and most turbulent of current magazines: a monthly national insult as withering in its effect as the sub-machine guns of gangsters; a periodic jeremiad delivered in tones of sardonic glee. Editorially, it held that progress was an illusion and democracy a poor joke, so for an intellectual elite there remained only the sophisticated pleasure of amusement at the antics of the common herd. Its pages formed a treasury of the absurd mores of the "boobus Americanus"—whose intelligence roughly approximated that of a mentally retarded child, and whose sorry capers identified him as a member of the "mob," or the "bible-belt Fundamentalists." For Mencken, a native of Baltimore, and Nathan, a native of Indiana, defined provincialism as original sin; and, like Jonathan Edwards, they felt that the torments of the wicked in hell should be no occasion of grief to the saints in heaven. Hell, for them, was the vague region west of the Hudson, south of the Battery, north of the Harlem. But heaven lay eastward, across the Atlantic. They were as ardently spiritual expatriates as Henry James, whom they resembled in being persistently obsessed by a defective homeland.

Mencken confessed himself a bitter and incurable scoffer at democracy in all its forms. The besetting sin of the United States, he asserted, was the national habit of turning intellectual concepts into emotional concepts; the vice of orgiastic and inflammatory thinking. As a result, there was no orderly and thorough working out of the fundamental problems of American society. There was only an eternal combat of crazes. For this situation, Mencken blamed the American lack of an intellectual aristocracy—sound in its information, skeptical in its habit of mind and, above all, secure in its position and authority. Such an aristocracy, possessed by all civilized countries, would furnish, he thought, a natural corrective of "enthusiasms from below." But in the United States he saw only two forces, equally to be despised. There was the populace, more powerful than in any other land; more capable of putting into execution its "idiotic ideas," more eager to follow "platitudinous messiahs." And there was the ruling plutocracy; ignorant, hostile to inquiry, tyrannical in the exercise of its power, suspicious of all ideas. Between them, in a kind of middle ground, Mencken could distinguish only an indistinct herd of "intellectual eunuchs," chiefly professors, who were often quite as stupid as the plutocracy and always afraid of it.

Mencken's assertion that the American people had a pathological susceptibility to messiahs was corroborated by his own vogue. Never sweetening his contempt for their stupidity, he insisted on the necessity for an intellectual elite, an aristocratic leadership, to redeem them from the damnation of their contented barbarism. The ironical result was that his readers invariably supposed themselves members of his Nietzschean superior order. His effect, like that of Sinclair Lewis, was to fortify the complacency of the upper middle class. For, although they acknowledged that America was a wilderness of the booboisie, some divine grace, operating upon them as individuals, had unmistakably designated them as among the elect. The membership of every club might be Babbittry—but what man recognized the Babbitt in his own mirror?

However akin in method and effect, Lewis and Mencken were radically unlike in social outlook. Lewis never relinquished his faith in democracy, though he unmercifully castigated its current failures. He retained his earliest vision of America as an adventure, possibly the greatest the world had ever known. But Mencken saw, in America, only a ludicrous, hopeless experiment in imbecility. Like Lewis a moralist at heart, Mencken genuinely wished to preach to his countrymen, convert them, perhaps even save them—though he was skeptical of salvation. But he succeeded best in entertaining them. With the onset of the Great Depression, the cult of an intellectual elite lost much of its appeal, even for the very young. And the Nietzschean doctrine of an aristocratic leadership—illustrated by Fascist Italy and Nazi Germany—exercised a diminishing attraction. So Mencken's influence, as a social critic, abruptly dwindled. Meanwhile, his frustrated, indignant love of his country—so seldom distinguishable from hatred—had found another outlet. His preoccupation with the American scene had early led him to explore the American language, and his continued masterly researches in this field seemed likely to become his most enduring contribution to the national culture. But, as a retired messiah, certain satisfactions were not denied him. In the confused nineteen-forties, his gospel was enjoying a revival. It may have pleased him to find, in the columns of *Life*, all his old doctrines in a refurbished form. Apparently Americans would always be willing to heed those who told them—with sufficient dogmatic assurance—that what they required most was to be saved from themselves by the self-sacrificing leadership of a self-consciously superior class.

[2] BABBITT STRIKES OUT

In 1919 the intelligentsia, as they were called, were celebrating the advent of a great, new American writer. Less sophisticated readers, attracted by the commotion, received a nasty shock. Sherwood Anderson's *Winesburg, Ohio* inflamed their moral sense, bruised their good taste. These tales of a Midwestern village in the eighteen-eighties stripped the veils of decency from community life. Here were only thwarted, lonely, warped people; shame ridden, and driven at last to a catastrophe of sexual abnormality. Old-fashioned readers recoiled in disgust—this was decadent stuff, morbid, clinical, and certainly false to common American experience. They could scarcely be expected to forsee that the book would become one of the most important of all influences on American realistic writing—or that, twenty-five years later, a conservative magazine would fix upon Anderson's village as a classic symbol of the American small town!

The Winesburg stories were Anderson's fourth book. He had published his first, three years earlier, at the age of forty. A large, florid man, he had an air of permanent perplexity, and seemed always to be groping toward some meaning that—to his anxiety and exasperation—eluded him. He resembled one of his own characters of whom he reported that never did he succeed in getting what he wanted out of life and he did not know what he wanted. Late in life, he spoke of himself as an eternal amateur. He had begun to write, he said, only because he wanted to clear up certain traits in himself. Practically all his books recorded his incessant effort to deduce some general and final truth from his personal experience—the experience of a Babbitt at odds with his environment.

The son of a hard-drinking harness maker and sign painter, Anderson knew only bitter poverty during his childhood in the village of Clyde, Ohio. He received little schooling, and his mother's death set him adrift at the age of fourteen. For some years he wandered about as a tramp, a casual laborer and factory hand, a stable boy at race tracks. He enlisted for the Spanish-American War, and returned with an ambition to make money. Long afterwards, he said that he had always been a rather foxy man, with a foxiness which at times approached slickness. When he entered business, this native shrewdness served him well. Presently, married and the father of a family, he was the owner of a prosperous paint factory in Elyria, Ohio. He was conforming to an unstated and but dimly understood American dream by making himself a successful man in the material world.

But, though about to become rich, he had become dissatisfied with the tenor of his existence. He turned to books, finding in them a kind of refuge from the tangle of things in daily life. In secret, he likewise commenced to write. Was it not possible that a great many of the writers of books had been visited by just such thoughts as he was having now? The nature of those thoughts was, for a businessman, peculiar. For Anderson had an overwhelming feeling of uncleanness; his thoughts got fixed upon prostitution; he was seized by the conviction that he must quit buying and selling. One day, when dictating a business letter, he calmly walked out of his factory, never to return either to his family or his business. It was, he confessed later, melodramatic and even silly enough. But it expressed his repugnance to a society in which the attempt to sell goods had become a sort of madness. He went to Chicago. There, he supported himself by writing copy for an advertising agency until, after some years, his books furnished a livelihood.

Anderson's act of personal rebellion was his most explicit criticism of his environment. In his books, he tried to rationalize and justify it, and to set forth a standard of values persuasive enough to prevail over the standard of the society he had fled. He spoke of himself as a confused child in a confused world, and he succeeded notably in stating both his perplexities and his failure to solve them. In doing so he spoke, perhaps, for many Americans who, having accepted without question the social values of the majority, came to disbelieve in them, yet found no others to which they could pin their faith. For them, as for Anderson, the religion of bigger-and-betterism proved inadequate, but a plausible substitute was lacking.

There was, Anderson believed, something wrong with modern American life, and Americans did not want to look at it. That every one had come here for gain, to grow rich, to achieve, impressed him as having brought a curse upon the land. Everywhere, throughout the country, things were in a good deal of a muddle. "Everywhere lives are lived without purpose. Men and women either spend their lives going in and out of the doors of houses and factories or they own houses and factories and they live their lives and find themselves at last facing death and the end of life without having lived at all."

What had caused individual life to become so futile and empty? Anderson blamed the great industrial expansion that had occurred during his own youth. This replaced the craftsman by the machine tender, and Anderson, having won his freedom by painfully learning the craft of using words, was disposed to take a romantic view of the displaced handworkers he remembered from childhood. He concluded that when you took from man the cunning of the hand, the opportunity to constantly create new forms in materials, you made him impotent. Industrial standardization he saw as necessarily a standardization in impotence—and since Henry Ford had carried it to its logical end, Anderson denounced him as the great killer of the age. He foresaw a future in which we would have a great machine moving slowly down a street and depositing cement houses to the right and left as it went, like a diarrheic elephant, with all the best minds properly employed making car wheels out of waste newspapers and synthetic wines out of crude oils.

He protested against an America of speed, hurried workmanship, cheap automobiles for cheap men, cheap chairs in cheap houses, city apartment houses with shining bathroom floors, the Ford, the Twentieth Century Limited, the World War, jazz, the movies. What he wanted was an America conscious of itself as a living homemaking folk, that had at last given up the notion that anything worth while could be got by being in a hurry, by being dollar rich, by being merely big. But he saw no way to bring it into being except by reaching down through all the broken surface distractions of modern life to that of old love of craft out of which culture springs. His gospel, in the end, reduced to turning the clock back.

But, as he pondered the present and the past, Anderson saw that its hands would have to be pushed further and further backward. For, in America, something went wrong in the beginning. Americans had really intended building a land to the glory of Man, had been as earnest in their intention as the medieval French who built the cathedral of Chartres to the glory of God. Could it be that the affair only blew up in the process, or got perverted, because Man, even the brave and free Man, is somewhat a less worthy object of glorification than God? During his boyhood, Anderson recalled, "there had been a great and glowing faith in Americans. It has weakened since. That is the obvious reason for the puzzled uncertainty about life in America."

To the young intellectuals of the years after the First World War, Anderson seemed an authentic master. Though few of them shared his cult of the past, most of them understood that it expressed nothing but his despair of the future—and this, they shared fully. Like Anderson, they were adrift, and knew with certainty only what they did not want. They, too, were in revolt against materialism, mechanics, business, bigness and prudery. They agreed with him that it is only at rare moments that we live, and they were no more clear than was he about the nature of such moments. But, most of all, they responded to his resentment against all social dogmas or, as he called them, manmade truths. For they felt, as he did, that the moment one of the people took one of the truths to himself, called it his truth, and tried to live his life by it the truth he embraced became a falsehood.

[3] THE GREAT LIQUIDATION

In one respect, the young writers of the nineteen-twenties were very unlike Sherwood Anderson. Though his radicalism of feeling made him seem contemporary, his point of view was actually that of an older generation. He spoke for those Americans who, dubious about the social effects of industrialization, still wished to think their life worth living when, to look at what it contained, it might not have seemed so. His books were significant chiefly because they recorded an average American's bewildered effort to find some meaning in his life. The meaning eluded Anderson, yet he never doubted that one existed. But this problem seldom occurred to his juniors. Most of them started from the premise that life has no meaning whatever.

At the conclusion of the decade, Walter Lippmann summed up its principal achievement in a single phrase. It had brought about the dissolution of the ancestral order. An intellectual revolution took place between the end of the Great War and the onset of the Great Depression. When it had run its course, many things were changed. Manners and morals were different. The American cultural heritage was in disrepute. The authority of the past had been broken. The example of precedent was heavily discounted. A structure of values, slowly built and long established, had swiftly collapsed. Familiar ideals had the look of "old illusions that are dead forever." The new generation was thinking about American life in a new way.

One of its leading exponents, later reviewing his own career, described the attitude of the war generation. Life, said F. Scott Fitzgerald, was largely a personal matter. The main problem was to hold in balance the sense of the futility of effort and the sense of the necessity to struggle; the conviction of the inevitability of failure and still the determination to "succeed"—and, more than these, the contradiction between the dead hand of the past and the high intentions of the future.

For young Americans, this was a novel way of facing their futures. Had any previous generation set out upon life assuming effort to be futile and failure inevitable? Had any, ever before, gone into battle completely disarmed—deprived of such inherited weapons as strong political or religious convictions, a sound culture applicable to experience, a standard of values that could be approximated in living? This generation claimed that they had been handed broken weapons. The old ideals no longer had any relation to reality. The truths they had been taught were false to life, and wouldn't work. The sanctified values had become sheer nonsense. Their education had been worthless. The culture they had inherited was bankrupt. This was the dead hand of the past—and it had cheated them.

Feeling cheated, the war generation was cynical rather than revolutionary. It was tired of Great Causes. It was capable of no more than a short outbreak of moral indignation. So it had no interest in politics at all and refused to be exercised about the social and economic problems confronting the country. Alienated by the prevailing order, its cynicism extended to all programs looking to a better one. The whole generation was in a state of nervous stimulation, not unlike that of big cities behind the lines of a war. It wanted slices of the national cake. There resulted the general decision to be amused.

As he noted afterwards, ruefully, Scott Fitzgerald was pushed into the position not only of spokesman for the time but of its typical product. He reached celebrity overnight with a novel which made him the apologist for the most expensive orgy in history—the "jazz age" whose name he coined. But later it became clear that he was not so much the apologist as the social historian of the period. He was twenty-four when he produced *This Side of Paradise*, the book which, in the phrase of his contemporary Glenway Wescott, haunted the decade like a song, popular but perfect. It expressed the revolt of "flaming youth" against the dead hand of the past—against tribal mores and ancestral faiths. It expressed that resentful cynicism which found outlets in the new insolence of flappers and collegiate slickers, in necking parties, booze fights, casual sex. And its popularity obscured the genuine significance of Fitzgerald's subsequent work. For, as the years passed, his writing matured and deepened. In the best of his books he was a vigorous, forthright, and damaging critic of adult American society.

A native of St. Paul, Minnesota, Fitzgerald came of a prosperous Roman Catholic family among whose forebears was the author of "The Star Spangled Banner." The war found him at Princeton. He enlisted, became a staff officer, failed to be sent overseas. He began his first novel while in service, finished it after his demobilization, found himself famous a week after its publication, comparatively wealthy within a year. Thereafter, for fifteen years, his life resembled one of his novels. Perennially youthful, he was blond, green eyed, pale, handsome. His time was passed between Europe and the United States; he was perpetually in movement before an unchanging background of Ritz hotels, where the same barmen and head waiters had different names so that guests might identify the city they happened to be in. Fitzgerald knew the odd expatriate circles that flourished in Paris and along the French Riviera. He dipped into the equally strange society of Hollywood. He frequented the fashionable and literary worlds of New York, the smart suburbs of Long Island, the equine colonies near Washington. His existence—prodigal, footloose, often rowdy and drunken, usually spectacular—exemplified success as the times defined it. It was, to many, enviable.

It furnished Fitzgerald with all the material of his fiction. But in the end he condemned it, and himself, unsparingly. When the Great Depression came, his books lapsed from popularity, and presently his health gave way. For a time, his creative ability deserted him. Exploring the reasons for his misfortunes—those inherent to his character, those produced by the character of society and the nature of the times—he was dismayed by one simple fact: "I had become identified with the objects of my horror or compassion." This was indeed a grave mistake for a writer who also knew that "I am too much a moralist at heart, and really want to preach at people in some acceptable form, rather than to entertain them."

Horror and compassion were what Fitzgerald quickly came to feel for the segments of American society he chose to explore. These segments were as narrow as those claimed by Henry James and Mrs. Wharton, but they were equally representative. They exhibited the way of life deliberately adopted by those who were absolutely free to choose. And, while they represented the reality of only a very few, they also represented the aspiration of the many. Almost from the first, Fitzgerald had been pretty aware that living wasn't the reckless, careless business these people thought. And, in even his earliest tales, unnoticed by most readers, there was always a touch of disaster—"the lovely young creatures in my novels went to ruin, the diamond mountains of my short stories blew up, my millionaires were as beautiful and damned as Thomas Hardy's peasants."

Damned, certainly. Not only because effort was futile and failure inevitable. Not only because life was meaningless so what the hell. Almost without exception, the hereditary members of Fitzgerald's smart world exhibited a singular callousness of heart. There was in them a streak of brutishness. It seemed to result from the absence of something which enabled the normal human to distinguish between those actions which will nourish life, and those which will destroy it. Was it conscience, moral sense, good taste? These people were supported, and insulated, by vast accumulations of power, apparently inexhaustible wealth. Aware that they could always buy their way out of any situation, the kind of situation they got into was of no consequence whatever. Again and again Fitzgerald insisted that this was their attitude. For him, it did more than characterize the privileged products of American success. It expressed the national frame of mind during a period when the maximum of national prosperity coincided with the extreme of national corruption.

It was the coincidence of these two factors which, in the nineteen-twenties, gave a peculiar tone to American life. In Fitzgerald, it produced what he said was an abiding distrust, an animosity, toward the leisure class—not the conviction of a revolutionist but the smoldering hatred of a peasant. More accurately, his hatred was intellectual and moral. It was the resentment which any intelligent American might have felt after exposure to, and disillusion by, the world he had been bred to revere. Like most middle-class Americans, Fitzgerald had been shaped by an environment in which the acquisition of wealth was the sole test of worth, and the ways of those who possessed it the sole criterion of excellence. Two of his novels showed the disastrous results of these standards, when deliberately applied or successfully imposed. His hapless bootlegger, Gatsby—a poor, highly imaginative farm boy—was led to his doom by single-minded pursuit of the stereotyped American dream. Making quick millions by alliance with racketeers, he succeeded at last in entering the American world of presumptive excellence and worth, only to be destroyed by its degraded ethics. Equally destroyed, in a society of decadent expatriates, was the brilliant psychologist Richard Diver upon whom these same standards were arbitrarily imposed by marriage to a woman of wealth.

In Fitzgerald's view, there was something inherently evil in a society which elevated as models those who were so demonstrably rotten at the core. Was not the average American being deceived and ruined by what his environment proposed for his emulation? For, like Gatsby, did he not, in utter innocence, account himself a son of God who perforce must be about His Father's business? And did not that business, so imaginatively conceived in grandeur, turn out to be, at best, the service of a vast, vulgar, and meretricious beauty; and, at worst, the service of cynical, powerful corruption? Like the "little people" of his friend Ring Lardner's stories, Fitzgerald's "outsiders" were pathetic victims of a myth. The function of the myth was to keep prosperity going.

To this society, traditional standards and ideals were absurdly irrelevant. Like most of his generation, Fitzgerald discarded them. Unlike most, he did so regretfully and reluctantly; for though his mind rejected them as false, his heart clung to them as noble. He was therefore morally adrift, and his dissatisfied awareness of this condition sharpened his moral vehemence. In his last, and most significant novel, left unfinished at his death, he was attempting to fuse in a single picture all the most characteristic elements of the American society of his time. He saw that, almost without exception, they converged in Hollywood.

Hollywood exercised a curious attraction for Fitzgerald. As a man of letters, he believed that the talkies were rapidly making literature archaic. He was convinced that they were providing for Americans, and perhaps for the whole world, whatever culture would supplant the traditional one that had suddenly become obsolete. Hollywood, itself big industry, was in the business of inventing and merchandising the attitudes to life, the official values, which would enable big industry to perpetuate its dominion over American society. It was, in Fitzgerald's view, a more glittering, a grosser power than had ever before existed to seduce and enslave the mass mind. He proposed, therefore, to portray it as typical industry, as cultural source, and as social phenomenon—a society whose fantastic ways of life determined the romantic social aspirations of the American people as, in an earlier day, these had been shaped by the mores of Newport and Fifth Avenue. His novel centered on the fortunes of the last tycoon—youngest and most brilliant of the film industry's pioneers. Of lowly birth, uneducated, untouched by traditional culture or the influence of contemporary ideas, this man had a spark of genius and indomitable faith in the rightness of his own judgments. Old-fashioned both in his rugged individualism and his paternalistic attitude toward his great enterprise, he was exposed to attack by three powerful forces in the American economy. He was vulnerable to the masters of capital in Wall Street, bent upon acquiring control of the films, as of other industry; to the power of organized labor, determined to eliminate industrial paternalism; to the sinister pressure of the racketeers, operating collusively with the other two. In the struggle for mastery which Fitzgerald projected, he saw the probable development of Hollywood foreshadowed by the fate of his tycoon.

What came to be called "defeatism" was implicit in Fitzgerald's mature work. America had somehow missed its great opportunity. A present that was tawdry and evil must lead, inevitably, to a future even more corrupt. Things might have been different, for America had once been "the last and greatest of human dreams; for a transitory enchanted moment man must have held his breath in the presence of this continent, compelled into an aesthetic contemplation he neither understood nor desired, face to face for the last time in history with something commensurate to his capacity for wonder." But the past was irretrievable. And although in his youthful first novel Fitzgerald had found hope in a vague kind of socialism, in middle age he had no faith in the success of any high intentions toward the future. From his station in an unlovely present, all that he could affirm as spiritually useful was the wise and tragic sense of life.

[4] SALVAGE

In Paris, during the nineteen-twenties, that majestic sybil, Miss Gertrude Stein, observed the young American writers who were congregating there. "You are all a lost generation," she told Ernest Hemingway. His first novel, carrying this verdict as its motto, translated it into a slogan. To readers in President Coolidge's America, remote from the adolescent tempests of the Boulevard Montparnasse, the compensations of being lost appeared greatly to outweigh the disadvantages. The effect, though gratifying, was not quite what Hemingway intended.

A big, dark, square-featured young man, Hemingway was on the staff of the Paris edition of an American newspaper. A native of Oak Park, Illinois, he had graduated from high school but had not gone on to college. Instead, he worked as a reporter in Kansas City, and before the United States entered the Great War was driving an ambulance on the Italian front. Presently he enlisted in the Italian infantry, was severely wounded, returned home with a platinum kneecap. After the war, he spent a year in the Near East for a newspaper, then settled in Paris. An inveterate sportsman, he passed his holidays in Spain with a troupe of itinerant bullfighters. Meanwhile, under the tutelage of Miss Stein and the poet Ezra Pound, he was producing his first short stories.

The characters of Hemingway's early books struck a new note. They made a virtue of being hard-boiled. They tried to maintain an attitude of defiant indifference. They boozed and brawled and wenched with a truculent heartiness—but, in the cold clarity of solitude, they often wept. Distrusting all mental processes, they could not entirely suppress them. Though they strove to live only by instinct and feeling, they could not extinguish their minds. When the mind asserted itself, they were miserable. It showed up the fallacy of the doctrine that enjoying living was learning to get your money's worth and knowing when you had it. For they weren't enjoying themselves as much as they pretended; and, except when they bought the oblivion of liquor, sex, or extreme danger, they hadn't got their money's worth. "I did not care what it was all about," one of them acknowledged, recording his attitude to life. "All I wanted to know was how to live in it. Maybe if you found out how to live in it you learned from that what it was all about."

This character was a young American. But he wasn't taking life experimentally. To the contrary, he was taking it desperately, with an oddly belligerent resignation. It wasn't a good, or even an opportunity. It was something to be endured, a kind of penalty. You salvaged whatever you could, paying for the things you got by learning about them, or by experience, or by taking chances, or by money. What you got was usually not worth the outlay. Hemingway's characters were happiest when they were closest to death, or what resembled death: in battle, or the bull ring, or the prize ring, or in a drunken stupor. The critic Edmund Wilson noted that Hemingway's vision of life was one of perpetual annihilation.

From one point of view, this was logical. The cause which Hemingway represented was an old American article of faith: the worth and dignity of the individual. He saw modern society, quite simply, as a vast conspiracy to deny it. Twentieth-century civilization had merely emasculated the individual. In any effort to assert his will, to impose himself on his environment, he was foredoomed to defeat. Forces which he had scarcely learned to identify had already reduced him to impotence. Though free to incur danger, he could never achieve victory. What price life, liberty, and the pursuit of happiness?

Hemingway indicated his view of American life in a story which was also a parable. Two gangsters come to a suburban town to kill a man they have never seen; the victim, warned, knows that "there ain't anything to do"; he will presently rise from bed, walk down the dark street, and yield to the invisible sawed-off shotguns. Though expressed at its maximum of violence, this was what existence came to for the individual—a brief, anguishing reprieve from destruction by a hostile environment. Hemingway cherished a conviction that it ought to be otherwise. In a decent society the individual would get an even break.

Up to the nineteen-thirties, though he had written eight books and had acquired a substantial reputation, this was all that Hemingway had to say. But two events of the decade altered his view of life. Like many another literary expatriate, he was brought back to the United States by the Great Depression. He settled in Key West, formerly the center of a prosperous tobacco industry, normally a center for the fishing expeditions of wealthy sportsmen. It was a town suddenly dying for lack of livelihood, most of its population on government relief, a microcosm of the universal social sickness of the nation. For Hemingway, it provided an eloquent demonstration of capitalist irresponsibility. The novel that he wrote about what he saw was not only a blistering indictment of free enterprise, but an oblique statement of the necessity for some form of social collectivism. In both respects the novel gained force because Hemingway used, as his protagonist, a member of the middle class; a small businessman by conviction thoroughly conservative and an old-fashioned individualist. "I don't know who made the laws but I know there ain't no law that you got to go hungry," Captain Morgan reflects, amidst the wreckage of his economic order. And it is only his determination that "my kids ain't going to have their bellies hurt and I ain't going to dig sewers for the government for less money than will feed them" which launches him on the desperate lawlessness and crime that eventually destroys him. Morgan's final conviction, bursting through his delirious death agony, is that "one man alone" stands no chance.

The outbreak of the Spanish Civil War inevitably took Hemingway back to Spain. Some of his earliest stories about Italy after the Great War had expressed his hatred for Mussolini's brand of fascism, and he was one of the first American writers to grasp the implications of what was happening in Spain. Sinclair Lewis had produced a prophecy of the advent of fascism in the United States, as a result of prolonged economic depression; Hemingway, in his superb novel of the Spanish Civil War, used that conflict to project what he conceived to be the major issue of the century—the issue of a society dedicated to human rights, or dedicated to the perpetuation of the dominance of privilege.

Hemingway once again used an American for his central character, thus focusing upon American society the import of a conflict occurring in a foreign land. And, for the first time in his work, this character was mentally mature—a man who neither distrusted intelligence nor sought to evade experience in one of the various forms of perpetual annihilation. Robert Jordan, an instructor in Spanish at a Western college and a volunteer with the Loyalists, is aware that he is taking part in a crusade. He feels—in spite of all bureaucracy and inefficiency and party strife—a sense of consecration to a duty toward all the oppressed of the world. It is a feeling that he has never known before, and the reasons for it are so supremely cogent that his own probable death becomes completely unimportant. "But the best thing was that there was something you could do about this feeling and this necessity too. You could fight." An American in his belief in a republican form of government, in his conviction that all people should be left alone and you should interfere with no one, he submits to the discipline of the Communists because he respects it—and he lives out the martyrdom which it imposes on him. As he is awaiting death, he realizes that you can do nothing for yourself but perhaps you can do something for another; one thing well done can make all the difference, even in so vast a conflict. The world is a fine place and worth the fighting for, and he regrets leaving it. "I have fought for what I believed in for a year now," he reflects. "If we win here we will win everywhere."

That the "lost generation" had salvaged a social faith, a principle worth fighting and dying for, was noteworthy. Even more noteworthy, however, was the fact that its bellwether envisaged, as the sole hope for individual liberty, the establishment of a collective form of society.

[5] SPHINX IN THE SOUTH

In the mid-nineteen-thirties, President Franklin D. Roosevelt declared that the South was the nation's "economic problem number one." To millions of Americans, natives of other parts of the country, this statement was only incidentally clarifying. The South, for them, was a perpetual enigma. It existed, as it were, behind a wall of incomprehensibility, apart from the main stream of national life.

In fourteen states—apparently physically, socially, and psychologically depleted—thirty-five million people lived in sullen tension and rancor. They were divided by a barrier of race. Nine million Negroes were subject to complex restrictions. Twenty-six million whites, internally split by class hatreds, seemed nevertheless to be firmly unified against the rest of the nation. They were on the political, economic and moral defensive, hypersensitive to outside criticism, suspicious of new ideas—particularly if these impinged upon their racial attitudes—and resentful of governmental and individual interference with their inherited processes. A vast retrograde area, fitfully illuminated by fiery crosses, echoed with the rhetoric of political demagogues, religious bigots, racial persecutors, educational fanatics, apostles of various forms of malevolence. This was the South as the rest of the nation saw it. They were inclined to consider it a grim challenge to the public conscience.

Meanwhile, the conscience of the South was itself troubled. "By almost every gauge by which a culture or civilization can be measured, the South is still at the bottom—in literacy, in crimes of violence, in productivity except for children, in social legislation, in per capita income, in public health, in working conditions, in housing." This was not the verdict of a "damyankee" investigator. It was the sober conclusion, in 1946, of Hodding Carter, Southern-born editor of a Mississippi newspaper, one of an increasing number of spokesmen for a new attitude and a new direction. Over two decades a quickened conscience had found outlet through a substantial literature produced by Southern writers. Fiction, especially, had been rescued from the nostalgic sentimentality of the Lost Cause, the standard regional props of crinolines, camellias and chivalry. If Southern novelists were, in the main, facing the life of their region in a spirit of criticism, events in the South, highlighted by national publicity, were partly responsible.

For some of these events, equally shameful equivalents had been found elsewhere in the land, but to the troubled Southern conscience this offered no mitigation. The brutal excesses of the Ku Klux Klan, revived after the First World War, were matched in spirit, if not in degree, by the cruelties visited upon labor in Northern and Midwestern industrial centers, as exposed in Congress. The travesty of justice in the Scottsboro trials in Alabama was scarcely less than that of the Sacco-Vanzetti case in Massachusetts. But for other social symptoms, there appeared to be no adequate parallel.

There was, for example, the tragi-comedy of the celebrated "monkey trial" which, in 1925, drew national attention to the State of Tennessee. This was a planned case, to test the validity of a state law prohibiting the teaching, in public schools, of the Darwinian theory of evolution. A teacher named John Thomas Scopes offered himself as the victim. The Fundamentalists, sponsors of the law, accepted the services of William Jennings Bryan—old, embittered, and fanatical—as prosecutor. Clarence Darrow, the great agnostic, liberal lawyer who had made a lifetime career of defending unpopular causes, served as chief counsel for the defense. The issue on trial was modern scientific thought. It was overwhelmingly defeated. Twenty years later, two spectacular scientific developments had taken place in Tennessee which might have been expected to change the cultural situation of its people. The greatest American experiment in socialization—the Tennessee Valley power development—was being successfully operated; and the atomic bomb had been produced at Oak Ridge. In 1946, a journalist who had reported the Scopes trial returned to learn whether these developments had produced the anticipated changes. Had the cultural situation improved? The conclusion of Russell Owen was that, basically, it had not. Such was the South.

Equally symptomatic of the South was the career of Huey P. Long, the "Kingfish" who, during the nineteen-thirties, achieved national prominence as senator from Louisiana. At his death, Long stood revealed as a dictator in the fascist pattern. He was a "poor white," meagerly educated and enduringly embittered. As a young lawyer, he ran afoul of the Standard Oil Company. Its ruthlessness, he afterwards declared, had prevented him from gaining wealth and achieving his social ambitions. He entered politics as the implacable foe of all "corporate interests," and in time became governor. He eliminated from the legislature all representatives of the rich and well born, replacing them by an obedient and corrupt machine. His power was founded upon the ignorance, prejudices and economic misery of a large segment of the rural population—and in their behalf he undertook a magnificent program of education and public works. These were financed by heavy taxation of corporations, utilities, and private wealth. Long's objective appeared to be a socialized economy. But his program was so devised as to yield enormous financial profits to himself and his henchmen. Translating himself to the United States Senate, Long proceeded to launch a share-the-wealth movement during the Great Depression. Raging furiously about underprivilege and unendurable poverty, he was regarded by many as a champion of the masses. He attempted, he said, to make the battle for a distribution of wealth among all the people a national issue. An assassin's bullet terminated his activities. Thereafter, it was seen that, in the South, economic degradation could persuade free Americans to seek social salvation under a fascist system.

The acute despair on which Huey Long rode to power was vividly illustrated by the militancy of the Southern Tenant Farmers' Union during the nineteenth-thirties. This organization, in which white and Negro sharecroppers subordinated their racial animosity to their common plight, dramatically exposed the existence of a widespread system of peonage. Its activities had been preceded, and prepared for, by the startling books of a Southern writer. Erskine Caldwell, a native of Georgia, had intensively studied the poor whites. In *You Have Seen Their Faces*; in his stories, *Tobacco Road*—soon dramatized, and played for thirteen years—and *God's Little Acre*, he focused a lurid light on a form of existence bereft of hope. His characters were sunk in squalor, degeneracy, misery, imbecile shiftlessness. They were the product of a social situation in which ignorance and incompetence sought to cope with exhausted soil, peonage, and an attitude that valued the welfare of animals more highly than that of the human beings whom it exploited. Apart from his proposal that the sharecroppers organize in an agricultural union, Caldwell offered no program of action. But, in his books, the troubled conscience of the South became articulate.

Meanwhile, in the Capitol at Washington, Southern legislators were opposing enactment of an anti-lynching law, a minimum-wage law, legislation to prevent racial or religious discrimination in employment, and to abolish the poll taxes which, in certain Southern states, prevented both Negroes and poor whites from exercising the suffrage. When resistance to the passage of progressive social legislation did not avail, its purposes were frequently defeated by the historic expedient of local nullification. These things, too, colored the picture of the South formed by the rest of the nation. How much were they offset by the efforts of a growing minority committed to the necessity for social change? Was there any solution to the enigma of the South?

This question, in its broadest sense, underlay the novels and stories of William Faulkner. A native of Mississippi, Faulkner grew up in Oxford, a small town interchangeable with and duplicate of ten thousand little dead clottings of human life about the land. He attended public school, but did not graduate from high school. He served with the Royal Flying Corps during the first World War, returned to Oxford, for a while took classes at the state university. He spent a winter in New Orleans, and another working as a clerk in a New York City bookshop. One year he took a long walking trip in Europe; he made several sojourns in Hollywood as a writer for the films. But, for the most part, he remained at Oxford, writing in isolation, a shy, solitary man with a taste for what he described as undirected and uncorrelated reading.

Certain features of Faulkner's work suggested that it originated in a profound need to account, to himself, for the retarded condition of culture and civilization in the South. To some extent, therefore, his books recorded an exploration, a sustained and consistent effort to arrive at a coherent explanation of the nature of his environment in his own time. His exploration was imaginative rather than purely historical. His purpose was to understand events in terms of the human experiences which had produced them; the ambitions, the needs, the attitudes of mind and heart that had shaped destiny. The result was a series of volumes which, collectively, formed a single saga.

In them, Faulkner created a microcosm of the South, a fictitious but representative county in northern Mississippi, and portrayed its life over the century from early settlement to the present. This saga of the life of an area wove together the developing fortunes of the major social groups which composed its population—the owners of plantations and their descendants; the merchants and professional class in the county seat; the poor whites of the marginal lands, by-passed by civilization; the Negroes.

Faulkner's picture of contemporary life afforded no comfort to complacency. His little world was nightmarish in its violence, degeneracy, fear and madness. It was the product of a ruinous social change, and the portent of another. The War between the States had destroyed an established order. For the old ruling class, there had followed long years of increasing deterioration. In them, power—economic, social, political—had gradually passed to the poor whites who, mean spirited but ruthlessly ambitious, became horse traders, owners of cotton gins, merchants, finally bankers and politicians. In the process, they consolidated a dynastic control over the life of the region surpassing that of their predecessors. They had risen to wealth and had seized leadership, but had scarcely advanced beyond their original cultural level. Their ambitions were fostered by ancient social hatreds; and, if their course ran to a form of fascism, it was because of their grievance against both the old aristocracy and the Negroes who, traditionally, despised them. So they formed a natural alliance with the industrial order that had arisen outside the South, that had already invaded the South and intended to conquer and exploit it.

In Faulkner's view, this new conquest by a mechanical civilization prefigured a disaster even greater than the destruction of the old order. The descendants of the old ruling class, though wishing to avert it, were powerless to resist. As Faulkner portrayed them, they had neither strength nor courage nor faith. They were decadent: victims of inertia, eccentric or mentally defective, obsessed by an ancestral guilt which reduced them to helplessness or drove them to some violent and meaningless self-destruction. Moral leadership had fallen into the hands of those who lacked all moral principle. Those who had inherited a tradi-

tion were incapable of applying it to their new circumstances. So
Faulkner, as the critic Malcolm Cowley pointed out, saw the present
only as a period of moral confusion and social decay.

Behind the enigma of the South, as Faulkner implied, there was not
only a tragic social history and a profound guilt. There was also the
land that had made these inevitable, a land where everything hangs on
too long—"the rich black land, imponderable and vast, fecund up to
the very doorsteps of the Negroes who worked it and the whites who
owned it; which exhausted the hunting life of a dog in one year, the
working life of a mule in five and of a man in twenty—the land in
which neon flashed past them from the little countless towns, and
countless shining this-year's automobiles sped past them on the broad
plumb-ruled highways, yet in which the only permanent mark of man's
occupation seemed to be the tremendous gins. . . ." To this Southerner,
the social destiny of his region was still implicit in the land—opaque,
slow, violent, shaping and creating the life of man in its implacable
and brooding image.

[6] THUNDER ON THE LEFT

During the decade of the nineteen-thirties, a new school of writers arose
—barometers of the immediate social situation, weather vanes for the
stormy winds of doctrine. Like the President, they addressed the
American people as a stricken nation in a stricken world. Like him,
they were convinced that only a foolish optimist could deny the dark
realities of the moment. But they were far from sharing his confidence
that "plenty is at our doorstep." Their appeal was to social consciousness, and because most of them studied the causes of failure at the level
where suffering was most widespread and acute, they came to be known
as the "proletarian school."

Of this school, the most industrious, and in some ways the most
powerful, was James T. Farrell. He was a short, stocky, owlish-looking
man whose dark hair was usually rumpled, whose expression was
habitually serious, whose scholarly air, accented by thick-lensed spectacles, scarcely suggested that his boyhood ambition had been to become
a baseball star. He was a native of Chicago—the city where John Peter
Altgeld had gone down to lonely martyrdom as a champion of social
justice; where Miss Addams, after nearly fifty years at Hull House, had
lamented the failure of her effort to make it prevail; where Clarence

Darrow, after a lifetime devoted to defending the oppressed, had confessed the uselessness of all reform. The Chicago about which Farrell wrote was the city which had fired the indignation of these reformers. It was the same city of dreadful night, of social wastage. Farrell was no reformer.

His parents had lived in extreme poverty from which, in childhood, Farrell was rescued by more fortunate relatives. He was brought up, on the city's South Side, in an environment which he described as lower middle class, Irish-American, Catholic. Educated in parochial grammar schools and high school, he worked for a time in an express office, then developed an ambition to become a lawyer and entered Chicago University. Presently, the law ceased to attract; he had determined to be a writer. Leaving the university he bummed his way to New York City, lived in a Mills hotel, worked as a clerk, an advertising solicitor, a salesman. Finally he returned to the university to take courses in writing. Then he began his first novel, which eventually became a trilogy. This he followed up with a tetralogy—he had planned a total of twenty-five books, all interrelated. The first seven dealt with a homogeneous social group and its environment—the people among whom he had been brought up. In the most general sense, their subject was a culture and an education, the social factors which determined the responses to life of his own generation.

Even while studying at the university, Farrell wrote chiefly about death, disintegration, human indignity, poverty, ignorance, human cruelty. These were familiar phenomena during his childhood and youth; if the environment recognized some of them as evils, it accepted them as inevitable. Long after he had achieved reputation as a novelist, Farrell declared that "if there is any hatred in my books . . . it is not directed against people, but against conditions which brutalize human beings and produce spiritual and material poverty." There was, in his books, little explicit hatred or indignation. Unlike most writers of his school, he maintained a dispassionate tone. He preferred to confine himself to the strictest possible objectivity, to let a clinical demonstration of pathological processes speak for itself. He differed from the other writers of his school in another significant respect. He did not attribute the conditions he exposed to the single cause of dire economic want.

He began his attack on the American social system with a study of life among the American petty bourgeoisie and the American labor aristocracy. His trilogy of *Studs Lonigan* exhaustively analyzed one of its typical and normal products. Studs was the end-product of Americanization, two generations removed from Irish immigrants who had come to the United States as to a new world, whose lives were dedicated to work, to advancing themselves, to saving and thrift, to raising their families. They and their descendants rose in the social and economic scale. The second generation became owners of real estate, ward politicians, small businessmen, boss craftsmen, and the like. Because they exemplified it, they believed in the American myth of success and advancement. They believed in the dogmas of their faith, but their church was a sanctified institution; it had little real connection with their daily experience. They sought to educate their children with homilies, platitudes about faith and work, and little fables about good example—to the end that the children might advance so many more rungs on the economic and social ladder.

For Studs Lonigan, as for most of the boys in his neighborhood, the important institutions of education—the home and the family, the church, the school and the playground—quickly break down. Home is a humdrum boredom of nagging correction and acrimonious bickering; even affection is tainted by moralizing; intellectual exchange takes the form of reiterated prejudices or platitudes: it is a place to be escaped from whenever possible. School is tedious drudgery, to be resisted. Church is irrelevant ritual; a form of punishment. The playground is supervised by feminine or effeminate do-gooders. What replaces these institutions as educative agents? The streets, the gang, the poolroom, the bar, the house of prostitution, the deserted parks at night, the gambling joint. The mental life which these produce is as barren as a bald rock—and discouragingly recognizable!—but there are a few lichens: group hatreds of infiltrating "kikes" and "dinges"; a cult of sexual prowess; a group itch for money, and those material goods which represent social status. The moral life which this education yields is not even rudimentary. The outcome for Studs Lonigan is defeat and frustration by a total situation which is characterized by spiritual poverty. His impulses are essentially good, but his values are the values of his environment, and they furnish no positive or compelling focus for his capacity for allegiance. He is crippled by paralysis of function; he has no genuine relationship to society, no object for his loyalties, no valid incentives. He is, as Farrell claimed, a social manifestation—a clinical specimen of preventable social wastage. "Given scope as a boy, given a pattern of values bearing some adequate relation to the life around him," the critic John Chamberlain declared, "Studs might have been a fine citizen." But what Farrell describes as the making and the education of an ordinary American boy is a preparation for atrophy.

If the inward decay of the lower middle class is obvious on the level of relative prosperity, what can be said of the level more exposed to economic want? Farrell answered this question in his tetralogy about Danny O'Neill—who, like Farrell himself, driven by an exceptional personal endowment, escapes from his environment. The family, here, slips rapidly down into a fusty existence of incessant toil, privation, squalor, and squabbling. The flat has "junk all over, the dresser in the corner piled with it, rags, clothes, junk, and the table on the left with a slab of grocery box in place of one leg; it, too, was piled and littered with every damn thing in the house." Danny, like Farrell, is rescued by relatives whose income, though small, is larger than that of the O'Neills, who regard as a windfall the damages received when one of their children is run over.

The tribal doctrines are familiar. "The possibilities in this country are endless. America is going to be the richest nation in all history. Why, we've got everything here. . . . Resources? They are beyond calculation. We are coming into an age that is bound to be the wealthiest the human race has ever known." Can it be doubted that everybody in America who's worth his salt ought to be rich? How? One way is through salesmanship—it doesn't make any difference what the product is. The cardinal principle is "the irradiation of confidence." People want to have faith, they'll pay the person who'll give them confidence, especially when times are bad and they think they're licked. After all, good salesmanship—and all good business—is based upon the power of wishing and concentration. This is indefeasible, for isn't it the true kernel of wisdom in the teaching of Jesus? Anyone who votes for the Republicans is a damn fool; if the Democrats get in, maybe they'll give the people some things; the Socialists will never get anywhere—they're lunatics. Of course, any decent soul will believe in God, the Holy Trinity, the Pope—who is too far off to matter—the parish priest, sometimes too inconveniently at hand; will hate all Jews and Negroes; will take as gospel whatever the newspaper tells him to, will grouse that he isn't getting enough, and be sure that he is going to get more. Among those who were later to be described as ill-housed, ill-clad, ill-nourished—if one could believe Mr. Farrell's portentous accumulation of evidence—the American dream had become a tawdry and meaningless myth.

In Farrell's view, the people of his stories—whether of the exploiting or exploited class—were the natural products of a competitive social order in which material acquisition represented the highest good. Their human failure, to the degree that they were brutalized and rendered both spiritually and socially sterile, flowed inevitably from the culture which an acquisitive society had imposed on them. As a novelist, Farrell reported the mores of an economic jungle. Only those who read his critical essays realized that what he assailed was the "folklore of capitalism"—the body of creeds which, as Thurman Arnold argued, men do not consciously choose, or intelligently appraise, but automatically absorb through the loyalties and enthusiasms which bind them to existing organizations. Farrell was no reformer. He was an intellectual convert to Marxism. His solution was seldom more than implied in his novels, though he developed it in his criticism. For him, the "dark realities" and the "pervasive spiritual poverty" of American society could not be eliminated within the present social order. For regeneration, for restoration of genuine social function, only the Marxian revolution would suffice.

[7] FIERY GOSPEL

As the Great Depression settled over the nation, calamity fell on the central prairie lands. This region, extending from the Dakotas southward, through Kansas and Oklahoma, to the Texas panhandle, formed the national granary. For decades, intensive agriculture had systematically depleted its soil. Droughts and dust storms had further eroded it. In 1933 there came the "black blizzard." When it was over, houses, trees, farm machinery were buried under dust and the topsoil had blown away. Ruin had arrived, at last.

Fewer than one third of the farmers owned their land. Another, and larger, group were so heavily mortgaged that, in effect, they had become tenants. Still lower in the economic scale were the nomad sharecroppers. All three groups were deep in debt, and the end of the black blizzard found them virtually bankrupt. Foreclosures and wholesale evictions resulted. The absentee owners—banks and corporations—took over the land, to apply large-scale methods and mechanization. And a whole population was suddenly homeless.

Presently, there began a mass migration such as had not been seen since the days of the pioneer settlers. Hundreds of thousands of families, many of them almost penniless, took to the roads in their jalopies. Word had been spread that there was work to be had in California; work for everyone who wanted it, in the orange groves, the vast orchards, on the ranches. And so the great trek commenced, setting a people adrift on the highways, toward the promised land.

Out in California a young writer, following the progress of this migration to its tragic, terrible end, determined to tell its story in a novel. After a long apprenticeship to fiction, John Steinbeck had already won a wide audience with two novels, and the play which he had made from one of them. He was a native of California, born and brought up in the town of Salinas, where his father had been county treasurer and his mother had taught school. After graduating from high school, he had attended Leland Stanford University for one year as a special student, developing an interest in marine biology. Thereafter, he had worked as a reporter, and had begun writing fiction. His first three books attracted little attention and failed to sell. Married, and settled in Monterrey, he managed to live on a monthly income of twenty-five dollars, and to continue writing until, in his middle thirties, he met with success.

Like most intelligent Americans of his generation, Steinbeck realized that the Great Depression brought into question all the basic assumptions of American society. The single issue with which it confronted the nation was one of primary purpose. Which should have absolute precedence—the social welfare of all the people, or the maintenance of a social situation in which, under normal circumstances, the greatest possible profit was assured to private enterprise? Most Americans had always assumed that social welfare was contingent upon the prosperity of private enterprise. But the Great Depression generated a widespread suspicion—despite the oracular pronouncements of statesmen, bankers, and industrialists—that this equation was not an axiom handed down by God.

In the two novels which first won him an audience, Steinbeck studied a local situation which brought the issue into vivid relief. The great fruit industry of California was dominated by a few powerful corporations, which imposed their will upon all independent producers through a system of trade associations. The industry required the existence of a large pool of migratory workers, available for the brief harvest periods but not employable at other times. In prosperous times, when this pool contracted, wages would advance. But when bad times swelled the pool, wages would be reduced, often to a level that did not support life. Since the workers, as migratory and casual labor, were not unionized, they were entirely at the mercy of the producers whose interests were best served by the most rigid economy of costs. And since the workers were not citizens of the state, nor voters or taxpayers, their plight was a matter of small concern to the public authorities. It was to the advantage of the producers, and the local authorities, that these workers be regarded as social outcasts—bums and hoboes by choice, parasites on the economy—and that any protest on their part immediately brand them as dangerous, subversive radicals to be summarily dealt with by groups of vigilantes.

It was the signal merit of Steinbeck's two novels that they exposed, not only the wretched situation of the migratory workers, but the falsity of the social legend which had been fastened on them. The people about whom he wrote could be accused of nothing more criminal than failure under the prevailing economic system. They were derelicts, lonely, wandering, cut off from all stability—the marginal human wreckage of an industrialized society. Was the fault theirs, or that of the society which had permitted them to sink into an abyss of wretchedness? Their most extravagant dream was identical with the universal hope of little people throughout the United States—a basic security, an assurance of opportunity, a sense of attachment to some community. They dreamed of having a little land of their own, a rabbit and a few fowl, things to live for and to cherish. Was there not something inherently wrong with a social situation that made such simple ambitions impossible? These people were not conspirators against the established order. They were the more pathetic for having faith in it, when the cards were so obviously stacked against them. One of Steinbeck's novels dealt with a strike, promoted by communist organizers. The strike failed, not only because of the superior power of the organized employers: so profound was the antipathy of the workers to communist doctrine, so instinctive their faith in the traditional system, that they could not bring themselves to subordinate their individual advantage to the collective purpose.

Steinbeck's two novels about the agricultural workers prepared him to deal with the epic subject of the mass migration of the "Okies"— the dispossessed families who trekked to California in search of a future on the land. In *The Grapes of Wrath* he produced a twentieth-century equivalent of *Uncle Tom's Cabin*. For this story so poignantly challenged the conscience of the nation that there arose an insistent demand for swift remedial action. To this demand, the Federal government responded with legislation in behalf of dispossessed farmers. The state of California made a belated effort to adopt a humane attitude—to cease harrying the migrants, like dangerous beasts, from one dreadful "Hooverville" to another; to curb the blood frenzy of its vigilantes. These results were important. Possibly there was an additional one, even more important, though it could not be estimated. How many Americans, having read *The Grapes of Wrath*, were pondering the soundness of the social system under which they lived? For this was the question that thundered through the book. This was what it was about.

In this sense, it was a kind of allegory, and the trek and tragedy of the Okies represented a general social process of deterioration of which the Great Depression was a spectacular symptom. Was the fabled American "ladder of progress" merely an illusion? A committee of experts, appointed by President Franklin D. Roosevelt to investigate the condition of America's agricultural population, reported some disturbing facts about the ladder. It had become a one-way passage—movement from rung to rung had been predominantly in the direction of descent rather than ascent. Furthermore, there was an increasing tendency for the rungs of the ladder to become bars—forcing imprisonment in a fixed social status from which it was increasingly difficult to escape. And that these facts were equally binding upon the industrial workers of American cities, was also evident. It had been made clear by such sociological surveys as those conducted by the Lynds. Steinbeck's Joad family—whose ancestors had fought in the American Revolution, and on both sides in the War between the States—were not merely victims of a major but an isolated catastrophe: they were symbols. Their fortunes implied the probable fate of a large segment of the American people.

What had made this fate inevitable? In Steinbeck's view, the perversion of the American social system. Initially dedicated to the welfare of all, it had been warped to serve the interests of a capitalist economy—controlled by a few, and devised for purely exploitative production, without reference to social consequences. His book piled up a massive picture of the human toll which it exacted. Nearly half a million dispossessed Americans, homeless and hungry, looking at the fallow fields which might produce food but not profit and knowing that a fallow field was a sin and the unused land a crime against the thin children. Carloads of oranges dumped on the ground—a million people hungry, needing the fruit—and kerosene sprayed over the golden mountains to maintain the price level. "Burn coffee for fuel in the ships. Burn corn to keep warm, it makes a hot fire. Dump potatoes in the rivers and place guards along the banks to keep the hungry people from fishing them out. Slaughter the pigs and bury them, and let the putrescence drip down into the earth." Said Steinbeck, flatly, "there is a crime here that goes beyond denunciation." The crime of production for private profit, accruing to a socially irresponsible minority. The social consequences were even blacker than starvation. "The great owners formed associations for protection and they met to discuss ways to intimidate, to kill, to gas." What did democracy amount to when, countenanced and often aided by the forces of the law, the private police of the great capitalists could bludgeon, gas, machine-gun in cold blood masses of Americans whose only crime was their poverty and their protest? For, under the American social sytsem the great capitalists could do these things with impunity. Theirs was the power and the glory.

Steinbeck asserted that he subscribed to no solution of social and economic problems so far propounded. But *The Grapes of Wrath* made explicit the direction that his social thinking had taken, and this direction was significant if only because it was then shared by an increasing number of Americans of liberal outlook. The direction was toward communism. If the established social system inevitably resulted in the conditions exposed by his book, better that it be destroyed. Better the overthrow of society than the eventual degradation of millions, their reduction to a form of slavery more hideous than that which once had provoked a war. On page after page that blazed with indignation, Steinbeck sounded an ominous warning. Let those who now control society take heed: "When property accumulates in too few hands it is taken away"—"when a majority of the people are hungry and cold they will take by force what they need"—"repression works only to strengthen and knit the repressed." The patience and docility of Americans were not inexhaustible. They would become hardened, intent, and dangerous: "if ever they move under a leader—the end"—

"the land will be theirs, and all the gas, all the rifles in the world won't stop them."

Steinbeck's fiery gospel did not preach communism as a political principle. It preached communism as a form of religion, a *mystique*. This was the only form in which it was acceptable to the American conscience, and that it could be so preached made it genuinely ominous. In a country commanding the greatest wealth and productive capacity in the world, yet failing to provide for the material welfare of a majority of its population, it was perhaps natural that the most materialistic of philosophies should come to seem the only alternative for a spiritual faith that no longer succored the helpless. In Steinbeck's novel, the first convert was—symbolically—a preacher who had lost his faith, and who had "been a-goin' into the wilderness like Jesus to try find out somepin'." He had gone to find his soul. He learned that he had only a "little piece of a great big soul," and that it was useless unless united with the rest and made whole: "a fella ain't no good alone." It was this principle of unity as a promise of social salvation that appealed to the American conscience, it was a mystical concept, and Steinbeck reminded his readers that man always grows beyond his work, walks up the stairs of his concepts, emerges ahead of his accomplishments. The time would never come, Steinbeck asserted, "when Manself will not suffer and die for a concept"—and "when the bombs plummet out of the black planes on the market place, when prisoners are stuck like pigs, when the crushed bodies drain filthily in the dust" every bomb would serve as proof that the spirit had not died. The day of wrath might not be imminent, but under the present social system, it was inescapable—for "in the souls of the people the grapes of wrath are filling and growing heavy, growing heavy for the vintage." That, in essence, was the import of Steinbeck's epic novel.

"You got to have patience," Ma Joad told her son. "Why, Tom—us people will go on livin' when all them people is gone. Why, Tom, we're the people that live. They ain't gonna wipe us out. Why, we're the people—we go on."

CHAPTER VII

Across the Footlights

[I] MAN-MILLINER, PLUS

At the turn of the century, a new residence picturesquely invaded the brownstone decorum of Fortieth Street, east of Park Avenue, in New York City. Newspapers over the land were soon lavishing pages on one of the most unique homes in the country, a building distinctive in its façade and in its furnishing. Its five stories of severe brick, chastely trimmed with limestone, were enclosed by a grill of Venetian ironwork; a small terrace was embellished by two radiant figures of Cupid standing in nonchalant attitudes, giving an air of defiant sentiment to a bachelor's house. Like every other detail of the establishment, the Cupids were delightfully appropriate. This was the home of Clyde Fitch.

Fitch, at the age of thirty-five, was the most successful and celebrated of American playwrights. His annual income was said to exceed a quarter of a million dollars. Four of his plays were running simultaneously in New York, and others were touring the country. His prestige had already traversed the Atlantic. Some American critics of the drama hailed him as a deliverer: no longer need the American theater rely, for artistically worthy fare, upon the output of British, French and German dramatists. To actors and actresses of talent he seemed little less than a god. There was scarcely one whose career he had not, or would not, signally advance. Maude Adams and John Drew. Effie Shannon and Herbert Kelcey. Viola Allen, Henry Miller and William Faversham. Beautiful Maxine Elliott, and her husband,

Nat Goodwin. The radiant Julia Marlowe. Amelia Bingham. Elsie De Wolfe, the best-gowned actress in New York. Exquisite young Ethel Barrymore. Mary Mannering, who had been brought over from England. Clara Bloodgood, a recruit from New York Society. Even the fading Victorian beauty Lily Langtry, the aging Helena Modjeska . . .

Charles Frohman, the tycoon of the American theater, the star maker, had first call on all of Fitch's plays. This was the true accolade; it elevated Fitch to the exalted level occupied by the English dramatists Pinero and Henry Arthur Jones, the Frenchmen Donnay and Bataille. The young American had come a long way since, a mere decade earlier, the actor Richard Mansfield hired him, for a weekly stipend of thirty dollars, to confect a vehicle in which Mansfield would appear in the role of Beau Brummel. Could anyone doubt the permanence of his fame? Presently his plays would be produced in theaters of Germany and Italy. Presently his boyhood friend, Professor William Lyon Phelps of Yale, the amiable young Solon of the women's clubs, would pronounce Fitch's *The Girl With the Green Eyes* the finest exposition of jealousy since *Othello*. What wonder that Americans, proud of this unexpected swan, should find him a subject of inexhaustible interest?

So the journalists ambushed him at the pier, on his annual return from Europe; they trooped to his town house, to "Quiet Corner," his Italianate country place in Connecticut. As a subject, he richly rewarded these forays. He had a vivid personality. He was "different," and always had been: in childhood unlike the normal boy in clothes, gait, manners, tastes, language, and voice; as a collegian at Amherst composing verse, decorating his room with a frieze of pink apple blossoms against a Pompeian background, participating in dramatics as designer, scene painter, producer, player of female roles. His puzzled, puritanical father hoped to make him an architect, but the boy knew his vocation. And success came quickly.

In a period convinced that it aspired to elegance, Fitch's plays seemed to illustrate it, Fitch himself to exemplify it. Figuratively, as well as literally, the esthete in him demanded tapestries and crystal. He complained bitterly that his actresses and actors knew nothing of the manners of good society—had he not been compelled to teach certain eminent stars the delicate use of a dinner service; was he not always under the necessity of supervising the actresses' gowns, perfecting their diction, laboring to civilize their posture and movement? Had he not, when rehearsing a scene which required a profusion of flowers, forced a horrified producer to send to the nearest florist for a thousand dollars' worth of fresh roses? He was, as his friend the playwright Marguerite Merington said, like a glowing patch of color on a somber day—small, slender, nervous, fine textured as to dark hair and white skin; warmly lustrous as to eye, and fastidiously appointed with a foreign accent on the decorative note.

Even more than his public personality or his plays, Fitch's home expressed those qualities which the times were seeking, and which he sought to translate to the stage. Immediately upon entering it, one became aware of an indefinable atmosphere which made it different from other houses. Men servants in blue and white livery performed the domestic functions with clockwork regularity and precision. One entered a dimly lit white hall. From one wall there looked down a Madonna and Child by Della Robbia. A marble mantel was garnished with five Wedgwood urns. A fountain sent up a tiny shaft of water that fell with a tinkle into a creamy marble basin edged with fresh roses— or violets, or lilies. Ascending the stairs, one passed a marble statue of the adolescent Adonis. Above was the drawing room, with its old gilt ceiling and crystal chandelier; its wall hung with Gobelins tapestries; its Louis XIV desk lined with old paintings of Watteau shepherds and shepherdesses; its grand piano of blond mahogany, which the painter Everett Shinn had decorated in eighteenth-century style, standing between two yellow marble columns at the window end, against old crimson draperies. A fire blazed on the hearth. Above the Louis XIV chimney piece, a French Salome ignored the old gilt and needle-point chairs, grouped in pairs, the vases of short-stemmed roses, colored china figures and jeweled and enameled boxes scattered about on tables.

In the dining room, of California redwood, with red brocade hangings, tapestries and soft-shaded, old gilt candelabra, the table settings were beautiful: sometimes a gold service would be used, with Italian china and bunches of violets and red roses; sometimes it would be English glass with old silver. The English critic Clement Scott, on a visit to the wilds of America, reported home—with ill-concealed astonishment—that Fitch's "artistic breakfasts are a joy to the soul. . . . He collects together the most intellectual men and, to his credit be it said, the most beautiful and brightest of women. . . . your cutlet, cooked by a Parisian chef, reposes on a plate of the rarest Delft or Spode or Lowestoft ware, and you quaff Tokay or the rarest Chateau-Yquem from the oldest of spiral Venetian glasses."

Yet Fitch was never quite content. He worked industriously in his green study above the drawing room, its book-lined walls holding only three favorite paintings: a Gainsborough, a Corot, and a Meissonier. As the years passed, depression settled on him at night, in his oaken bedroom hung with crimson brocade; and the three Watteaus from Malmaison, the tall silver crucifix once owned by the Empress Josephine that stood beside the great four-posted bed, could not dispel it. Had he fulfilled his promise? The critic James Huneker, reproaching him for the triviality of his plays, called upon him to accomplish what he set out to do—write a real, sterling American play. Better than Huneker, he knew that he possessed *technique*—not alone the piffling deftness of a man-milliner. But, beyond this, was not something lacking? Sometimes he wondered.

"I live my life in a mist of shams," Fitch told William Dean Howells, who wrote an article warmly praising one of his failures. Maude Adams, commiserating him on that failure, had hinted at his weakness. "You are just at that age when a man has two dangers to face—a substitution of an emotional enthusiasm for a real one and his resentment of criticism. . . . I wish you could do some things that you'd hate to do. I wish you could give over for a while your beloved Italy and your admired France and go to some place where the art is dead and life is uppermost—common life. We live so much among people of morbid tendencies, neurasthenics . . . and the like—that we begin to think they are real, and they are real of their kind but it isn't a red-blood kind." In 1909, when he died, Fitch had been writing for twenty years. He had turned out thirty-six original plays, twenty-one adaptations, and five dramatizations of novels. But he had scarcely ever come within sight of the common life, or reality of a red-blood kind.

There was, in Fitch, a *grand couturier* of genius. He could, with equal success, either invent a mode or perfect an established one; the result was always certain to become the actress for whom he designed it. When historical romances and costume plays were in vogue, he produced the best. When taste shifted to drawing-room drama, he was quick to excel in that fashion also. Howells complained that the American novelist was subject to the dictates of the American women who composed his sole audience; but the tyranny which American women exercised as a playgoing public stood greatly to Fitch's advantage. Women of leisure—the rich, the new rich, and those who hoped to become rich—were the audience for whom he wrote. They wanted plays about the world of fashion, and he provided them. They relished an occasional flick of the lash, and sometimes he used a silken, perfumed whip. They had a prejudice against unhappy endings; he spoiled a play by forestalling an inevitable suicide with an implausible coincidence. "The sensitive predominates in his work," James Huneker remarked, "delicacy, tact, and a feminine manner of apprehending the meanings of life." One of his most characteristic and intuitive scenes showed two women bargaining with a just-bereaved widow for the new Paris frocks made useless by her enforced assumption of black. In some ways, Fitch understood women almost better than they understood themselves. This insight accounted for much of his success.

His best comedies framed a series of portraits of the American woman of fashion at the opening of the twentieth century. Their effect strikingly resembled that of the portraits then being painted by John Singer Sargent. In Fitch, as in Sargent, there was a puritan who, all too cruelly, passed silent judgment on his sitters—the artist rendering with marvelous fidelity the shimmer of fabrics, the glitter of jewels, the opulent background; and the moralist betraying him into exposing triviality and meanness of spirit. Fitch's most memorable heroines, for all their presumptive elegance and fastidiousness, were apt to be deeply tainted. Possessive, acquisitive, exploitative, they were snobs, meanly admiring mean things; unscrupulous liars, monsters of jealousy, climbers ruthlessly pursuing social advancement; extravagant wasters demanding more and more money, ever greater luxury, who drove their menfolk to bankruptcy, disgrace, and suicide. The flower of native "good society," they were, fundamentally, what a later generation would describe as vulgar bitches.

All this, the moralist in Fitch perceived and implied. The artist in him—fashionable painter of a fashionable world—sought to disguise it by sheer bravura, so that the "mist of shams" might seem to represent the solid substance of life. That his audience accepted it as such proves how closely Fitch observed, and how truthfully he interpreted, his world. For, forty years afterwards, Fitch could still be reckoned a master of scenic illusion whose drawing rooms were peopled by women idly chattering, displaying their vacuous souls and their delightful gowns, whose "society" queerly resembled a wilderness of apes and wantons. A very few critics, like Huneker, detected this at the time and, assuming that Fitch himself was not aware of it, charged him with accepting the moral values of a decadent society. They were mistaken. This was as close as Fitch dared come to expressing his sober verdict on his social environment. Why did he not dare more? His predicament was precisely that of a painter like Sargent, living in a commercial society which looked on art with an economic eye, and forced to earn his living by the sale of his wares. As Brooks Adams asserted, a portrait is a commercial article, sold for a price, and manufactured to suit a patron's taste; were it made to please the artist, it might not find a buyer. And Fitch, the collector of antiques, the esthete who demanded tapestries and crystal, the master of two fabulous homes, produced portraits that flattered the vanity of his patrons. It was not remarkable that he did not dare more, though his conscience troubled him because he did not. The wonder was, rather, that he dared so much.

[2] "ALL MAN'S BLUNDERING UNHAPPINESS"

In 1915 a group of writers, winter dwellers in the Greenwich Village quarter of New York City, were passing the summer at Provincetown on Cape Cod. They had a lively interest in the drama, and despised the thin fare being provided by the commercial Broadway producers. Some of them had written one-act plays, and they tried these out on a porch in Provincetown. The experiment fired their ambitions. In 1916, they improvised a theater and announced a "season."

Word reached them that a young man had arrived in the village with a trunk full of plays. Said Miss Susan Glaspell, "Well, tell him we don't need a trunk full, but ask him to bring one." The young man came round—tall, lean, dark . . . with burning eyes—and read his play aloud. It was accepted immediately. Two of his plays were produced during the summer. In the autumn, on their return to New York, the group rented a ramshackle stable in Macdougal Street, converted it into The Playwrights' Theater and, as The Provincetown Players, dedicated themselves to the experimental drama. Thus was launched the career of Eugene O'Neill—to whom, two decades later, a Nobel Prize would be awarded.

At twenty-eight, O'Neill had led a varied and unconventional life. His father was the romantic actor James O'Neill, who for two generations had toured the country in *The Count of Monte Cristo*. The son's early childhood was largely spent on the road. Educated at New England boarding schools, he entered Princeton and was suspended, during his freshman year, as the result of a prank. He never returned. He worked, for a while, in a mail-order business; made a gold-prospecting trip to Honduras; toured briefly with his father as assistant company manager; then shipped as a seaman. His first voyage—sixty-five days on a Norwegian barque—landed him in Buenos Aires. He worked at various jobs, but passed most of his time among the sailors, stevedores, and outcasts of the waterfront, himself an outcast. He made a voyage to South Africa, tending mules on a cattle steamer, returned to Buenos Aires, where there followed a lengthy period of complete destitution "on the beach," and finally shipped back to New York.

There he lived in a waterfront dive, with a back room where you could sleep with your head on a table if you bought a schooner of beer. He shipped out for England, returned, joined his father in New Orleans, and with him played an abbreviated version of *Monte Cristo* in vaudeville theaters—appearing twice a day between a trained-horse act and a group of flying acrobats. At the family summer home in Connecticut, he found work as a reporter. Then his health broke down, and there followed a year in a sanitarium. Here, his mind got the chance to establish itself, to digest and evaluate the impressions of many past years in which one experience had crowded on another with never a second's reflection. When he was discharged, he had found his vocation. James O'Neill did not understand why his son should want to write the kind of plays he did, because there was no market for them, but he must have thought there was something to them—for Eugene O'Neill was sent to Harvard for a year's course in playwriting with Professor George Pierce Baker. There followed a winter of residence in Greenwich Village; then the first productions in Provincetown and New York. Ten years later, O'Neill's plays were being performed in England, in the principal theaters of Europe, in Japan. And, in the interval, they had even become acceptable to Broadway.

This was noteworthy. For O'Neill's plays did not fall within the prevailing pattern of Broadway entertainment. They discarded all established conventions of the "well-made play." They experimented with a bewildering series of technical innovations—expressionism; masks; stylized movement; the soliloquy, used to reveal the stream of a character's consciousness. But these were not mere theatrical tricks, employed for their novelty alone. They were means—sometimes successful, sometimes not—to a difficult end.

For O'Neill seemed confident that, if audiences were sufficiently moved, they might also be persuaded to think. Was there not room in the theater for the work of a confirmed mystic whose aim it was to interpret Life in terms of lives, never just lives in terms of character? Why should not modern Americans be as responsive as ancient Greeks to the transfiguring nobility of tragedy—even, where the Greeks would not have found it, in seemingly the most ignoble, debased lives? Were not Americans, who rejoiced in their mastery over forces more powerful than themselves, spiritually adrift? Were they not the victims of a singular modern sickness?

The symptoms of that sickness were obvious at every level of American life: social unrest, skepticism, lawlessness and despair, the innumerable neuroses which were sending more and more people to the psychoanalysts. It almost seemed that the deepest desires of men were being frustrated by the society in which they lived. O'Neill thought that the heart of the matter involved something more than individual economic success or failure. He said that he was always acutely conscious of the Force behind—(Fate, God, our biological past creating our present, whatever one calls it—Mystery certainly)—and of the one eternal tragedy of Man in his glorious, self-destructive struggle to make the Force express him instead of being, as an animal is, an infinitesimal incident in the expression. But, for the modern American, this inescapable tragedy had become more profoundly tragic. Needing a relationship to the Force behind, he lived in a society which had lost its faith in the existence of any such Force—except as physical or mechanical forces already subjected to human control.

For O'Neill, the "sickness of today" which he conceived as the only possible big subject, resulted from the death of the old God and the failure of science and materialism to give any satisfactory new one for the surviving primitive religious instinct to find a meaning for life in, and to comfort its fear of death with. Was not this the primary source of all man's blundering unhappiness? This sickness—the disorientation of the individual—became O'Neill's major theme. The unhappiness, in an extraordinary variety of illustrations, furnished him with the stories of his plays. In general, O'Neill's characters were of two kinds: those who regarded themselves as "belonging," as identified with something that transcended their personal lives; and those who, having lost any conviction of such relationship, were desperately seeking an equivalent for it. For both kinds of character, O'Neill's plays showed that life was apt to be tragically frustrating. Those who believed that they belonged usually discovered that what possessed them was an illusion, or a reality that turned out to be worthless, or of a nature quite different from what they supposed. Those who sought something to belong to, found nothing transcendent to which they could attach themselves—and their chosen substitutes were insignificant.

O'Neill was to acknowledge, ultimately, that he was not interested in the relation of men to men but only in the relation of men to God. Like the characters of his plays, he lived in a society less godless than deprived of God—was this why he achieved, in his finest plays, a poignancy and power unique in the modern theater? Did he not speak for all those Americans who, requiring a meaning for life, could not rest content with personal satisfactions, material achievements, or even social causes—for those Americans who, acknowledging the scientific mastery upon which their society rested, yet felt a profound need "to be saved from ourselves, so that we can be free of the past and inherit the future and not perish by it"?

Writing for those deeply aware of the absence of God, O'Neill repeatedly stated their pathetic need of an assurance that man's fleeting life in time and space can be noble; of a new ideal to measure the value of our days by—only to suggest that all merely mortal dedications must, in the end, prove inadequate. If men were to have an intensified feeling of the significant worth of man's being and becoming, it would be achieved only through identification with something larger than and superior to themselves. Thus, for example, the hard-bitten men of the forecastle in O'Neill's earliest plays no longer belong to the sea, as did their predecessors who shipped under sail. Yank, the "hairy ape" stoker of a luxury liner, expressed O'Neill's argument; served as its symbol. Yank is satisfied with his lot so long as he can believe himself indispensable to the great mechanism. Sure, he's "at de bottom" and "dere ain't nothin' foither," but "I'm de start! I start somep'n and de woild moves!" But a chance encounter with a member of the effete, privileged class destroys this confidence. Thereafter, Yank is shattered by discovering the ignobility of his true status. For the metropolitan world of luxury and sophistication, he scarcely exists. The world of radical labor —the dispossessed proletariat of which, unconsciously, he has always been a part, and to which, in his new resentment of his lot, he now wishes to belong—will have none of him. And the great hairy ape in the zoo, resembling him enough to be a brother, does not welcome him—but crushes and kills him.

Sometimes the thing to which O'Neill's characters genuinely belong is what they most despise and resent. They seek to escape it, only to find that it possesses and defeats them—as in *The Emperor Jones* and *Anna Christie*. Or, loving it like the two brothers of *Beyond the Horizon*, they may relinquish it in favor of some less cogent satisfaction, and their lives are thereby stultified. But, in O'Neill's "sickness of today," the abyss of misery is reached only by the contemporary intellectual, such a character as the artist Dion Anthony of *The Great God Brown*. Anthony has lost all sense of relationship to anything that transcends himself; and reason persuades him that the universe is empty of anything to which he can attach himself: the old God to whom his heart turns spontaneously has become the "Old Graybeard" of a sterile myth. For him, there is nothing left to belong to—and he illustrates the plight of the modern mind. In the perspective of eternity, it is not enough to have merely loved, lusted, won and lost, sung and wept.

Never directly concerned with social criticism, O'Neill nevertheless furnished an oblique commentary on the America of his day. In studying the various substitutes for a relation to God through which men seek satisfaction, he frequently dealt with two which, in effect, were the normal, prevalent ones in the United States: material success, and personal achievement, or "self-expression." In his plays, these appear as the most fruitless of dedications. When the rich brother of *Beyond the Horizon* returns home, the dying failure tells him: "your gambling with the thing you used to love to create proves how far astray you've gotten from the truth. So you'll be punished." Dion Anthony, in *The Great God Brown*, bitterly forces upon Brown the realization that, although society accounts him a success, life has actually passed him by. For O'Neill, Brown, the respectable man of business, is "the visionless demi-god of our new materialistic myth—a Success—building his life of exterior things, inwardly empty and resourceless, an uncreative creature of superficial pre-ordained social grooves."

He carried this criticism further in *Marco Millions*, using the past as a medium for ironical commentary on the present. Marco Polo is Babbitt, the spirit of American business enterprise. Willing to incur great risks in order to acquire great profits, he is blind to all beauty and mystery. Wherever he trades, he corrupts life by his efficient, blighting materialism. Yet he is courageous, single-minded, resourceful in emergencies, and dedicated to the ideal of "progress." Was it for this, Kublai Kaan pensively speculates, that the word was made flesh? Through such as Marco, can the flesh ever again become the word? In Marco's colloquies about the soul, with the Pope and with Kublai Kaan, each of whom represents a form of spiritual wisdom, O'Neill phrased the characteristic modern spiritual profession which, since it expresses nothing more than a hypocritical assent, constitutes the most devastating of negations.

The modern American dedication to self-expression or personal achievement O'Neill projected most fully in *Strange Interlude*—a play which, because of its extraordinary length, its use of the soliloquy to reveal the secret thoughts of the characters, and its intentionally disagreeable tonal coloring, bewildered the audiences who nevertheless made it a sensational success. Its central character was a typical American woman of the middle class in the twentieth century; educated, already emancipated, intelligent according to the standards of the time, and deeply ambitious for personal fulfillment. O'Neill traced her career over a period of some two decades, from girlhood to middle age, largely in terms of her effect upon the five men who stand in closest relation to her: her father, her two lovers, her husband, her son. She is a monster of unconscious selfishness and, except for the son who finally escapes from her, she succeeds in destroying, with the amiable inevitability of a praying mantis, all of them.

Was it true, as O'Neill appeared to suggest, that the American woman of the protected and advantaged class regarded the men in her life as her legitimate prey; to be dominated, to be used, to be favored or discarded, merely in the interest of her own selfish purposes? Was it true that, in the United States, woman's unquestioned authority over social life had resulted in a sexual relationship within which women were morally irresponsible, and men their accredited servants? Was it true that in women, as wives and mothers, as conservators of the race, the dedication to personal achievement could lead only to social disaster? O'Neill did not answer these questions explicitly, but the effect of his play was scarcely to glorify American womanhood. Clyde Fitch had intimated that his flowers of "good society" were other than they seemed, but he had portrayed them as they looked, not as they were. O'Neill achieved a portrait, not in the spirit of Sargent, but in that of Hogarth. Nina Leeds was presented as a neurotic bitch—and her disastrous social effect was minimized neither by her ultimate frustration, nor by the fact that her neuroses and her bitchery resulted from her lack of a relation to God.

O'Neill's two finest plays—*Desire Under the Elms* and *Mourning Becomes Electra*—dealt with the relation of men to God at a time when this relation, as he conceived it, still retained a genuine reality. Both plays were placed in the American past, in the New England of the mid-nineteenth century, when the Yankee conscience, beginning to lose its authority over the external world, was likewise beginning to turn inward, to become repressed, sinister, poisoned by doubt and suspicion, morally sick. The old Puritan God was sinking into twilight; and no longer permitted to be divine, was becoming diabolic. The warped, perverse life which O'Neill portrayed in *Desire*, and in the trilogy of *Electra*, could have obtained only when a sick conscience confronted a dying god. Both were doomed, but both still lived, so a vital relationship existed. And—since, in it, men, however sinister, identified themselves with a transcendent moral force, however malign —this relationship was also potent; though potent only for evil, for destruction, for catastrophe. Thus, O'Neill was able to make both plays true tragedies; and the *Electra* trilogy a tragedy in the Greek sense, in modern psychological terms with Fate and the Furies working from within the individual soul.

This was why, in these plays, O'Neill achieved a moral elevation lacking to any of his plays about contemporary life. Was there not grandeur in Ephraim Cabot's final surrender to his Puritan God?— "God's hard, not easy! Mebbe they's easy gold in the West but it hain't God's gold. It hain't for me. I kin hear his voice warnin' me agen t'be hard and stay on my farm. . . . I kin feel I be in the palm o' His hand, His fingers guidin' me. It's a-goin t'be lonesomer now than ever it was afore—an' I'm gittin' old, Lord—ripe on the bow—Waal—what d'ye want? God's lonesome, hain't he? God's hard and lonesome." And was there not grandeur, likewise, in Lavinia Mannon's decision to immolate herself, within the family home, on the altars of her quite different gods?—"I'll live alone with the dead, and keep their secrets, and let them hound me, until the curse is paid out and the last Mannon is let die! I know they will see to it that I live a long time! It takes the Mannons to punish themselves for being born!"

The effect of these plays, in the theater, was eloquent proof that O'Neill's thesis, seemingly so remote from contemporary American life, remained a living issue to many more people than might have been anticipated. They were, presumably, those Americans who had failed to find "a meaning for life" in any of the currently offered substitutes for God—in the worship of success, the cult of personal happiness, the religion of a communist society; in any of the discordant, broken, faithless rhythms of our time.

[3] THE IMP IN DOCTOR PANGLOSS

In the gay, gaudy 'twenties, a coterie habitually met for luncheon over a round table at the Hotel Algonquin, in New York City. Most of them were, for one or another reason, "celebrities"; and, as word got around, the anonymous public, and those who liked to receive a nod of recognition from the great, came to gape. Presently, there arose a legend of the power exercised by "The Thanatopsis Literary and Inside Straight Club." Was not the round table a kind of stock market, establishing the daily values of professional reputations? The author of tonight's play, or tomorrow's book, studied them anxiously. Several members were popular newspaper columnists whose verdicts could make or break.

The members of this coterie had some traits in common. None of them, for example, was what a former mayor of New York had irritably described as an "art-artist." The authors had undertaken authorship as a livelihood; the profit motive was scarcely unknown to the journalists. They had been highly successful, they were highly paid, they relished the freedom and luxury which their incomes permitted. They were exceedingly competent craftsmen whose wares suited the public taste, who expressed what large numbers of Americans were thinking and feeling today, or would think and feel tomorrow: and this was no mean achievement. It indicated a certain soundness of instinct, a certain knowingness.

They preferred, on the whole, to be thought knowing than to be thought literary. For scholarship and literature were in disrepute. Seriousness was a liability, not an asset. When the vogue was clearly for flippancy and cynicism, who would choose to seem pompous—a highbrow, a sourpuss? If you were erudite you concealed it, and you played down your intellectual interests; if you were forced to admit them, you did so deprecatingly, turning the joke on yourself. Mrs. Alice Duer Miller, author of best-selling light fiction, seldom acknowledged her private passion for higher mathematics and the more abstruse forms of philosophy, or revealed her secret ambition to achieve fame as a poet. In her historical novels, Miss Edna Ferber painstakingly diluted with romance her considerable scholarship in American history. Franklin P. Adams—later to become a human encyclopaedia of the air waves —dealt only lightly with books and ideas. Heywood Broun wrote of grave issues in the irrelevant idiom of sports. And there was Alexander Woollcott. . . .

Woollcott, their darling and dearest enemy, flaunted without shame one trait which they all shared. It was held absolutely damning to any "sophisticate": sentimentality. The rest of them disclaimed it, tried to disguise it. But Woollcott dripped it with the relentlessness of Chinese water-torture. Posing as a man-about-town, a supersophisticate, he was too naïve to be aware how naïve he was. He had the tongue of a viper, but the temperament of a schoolgirl; he wisecracked cruelly, or he gushed. Forests were laid waste in Finland, Canada, the remote American Northwest—and Woollcott spilled onto paper his peculiar brew of poison, treacle, and tears. He exemplified one phase of the times; for in any night club you could watch killers weeping whenever a torch singer broke out with a number about "Mammy."

All these distinguished folk had, or were soon to have, a connection with the theater. At one or another time, several of them took a whirl at playwriting. But one of their number was to win outstanding success as a dramatist. Over the next two decades, the name of George S. Kaufman was to become as familiar to Americans as that of any member of the coterie. The way of thinking, the attitude to life which, in general, prevailed in the work of the others likewise found expression in his plays. Although, as time passed, each year's Kaufman play was as up-to-date as the latest model automobile, with few exceptions they all reflected the spirit of the nineteen-twenties. Even their air of strenuous up-to-dateness recorded the mood of that day, when people felt obliged to cut loose from the past, and become contemporary no matter how; when prestige seemed to depend upon being "on the inside" and "in the know."

In all but one instance, Kaufman's plays were collaborations. Some of his collaborators, later writing independently, tried to exploit his manner and vein. Many other young playwrights, made ambitious by his success, deliberately imitated his work. And frequently his expert knowledge of the stage was drafted to rewrite, to "doctor," and to direct the plays of less skillful authors. So, from the 'twenties into the 'forties, he was one of the most important influences on the American theater.

He soon became the accredited spokesman of Broadway. Broadway was "show business," and Kaufman was a brilliant showman. He disclaimed any serious intentions as a writer, asserted that his plays were meant only to amuse. One of his most memorable wisecracks—quoted by the critic Joseph Wood Krutch—disposed of the contention that, with his remarkable talents, he ought to aim higher. Why did he not attempt genuine satire? Said Kaufman: "Satire is what closes Saturday night." But it was largely due to him that Broadway came to stand for more than show business. When he began writing plays, it was merely a street in New York, a congested thoroughfare. Kaufman soon made it a national state of mind. Not until the onset of the sober, earnest 'thirties did unkind critics protest that its traffic of ideas seemed to be all fouled up—if not, indeed, permanently stalled.

The nineteen-twenties, which set a premium on sophistication, taught middle-class Americans—who, just then, were touching new heights of material prosperity—a new attitude. They could look at the odd, the more fabulous, aspects of American society and find these funny; they could look at their neighbors and laugh. But their laughter, made urbane by easy money, swollen profits and general optimism, was not inconsistent with a high degree of complacency. Perhaps lots of things were wrong—like gangsters and crime, political corruption, the nefarious doings of great capitalists—but these had their funny aspects, too; in any case one ought to be hard-boiled about them—only silly idealists would get morally overwrought; besides, all of them would come right with time. Who could doubt that all was going to be for the best in what was surely going to be the best of all possible societies? Only some despicable, subversive radical, bent upon upsetting the national apple cart. Not Babbitt! Babbitt didn't object to cynicism and flippancy, so long as they kept to the surface of things. But let no one seriously question the soundness of fundamentals! His opinions were safely middle-of-the-road, which were what all opinions ought to be. Sure, he was as up-to-date and sophisticated as anyone. But, at heart, he was an old-fashioned sentimentalist—and proud of it.

Kaufman's major talent—it amounted very nearly to genius—consisted in being hard-boiled about whatever, at any given moment, was a safe topic, and, simultaneously, in being sentimental about all fundamentals. His plays projected the funniness of things-as-they-are, and sometimes the ugliness also. But they seldom intimated that anything was seriously amiss; they intruded no searching, disturbing question; usually they proceeded to a happy ending, often highly improbable;

and the opinions that they expressed were likely to be safely neutral. They surveyed contemporary American life from the slightly detached, slightly cynical standpoint of those who had managed to play the game successfully and had come out on top; who could well afford to laugh, but would never really be moved to doubt.

Thus, in the 'twenties, after Sinclair Lewis had made provincialism, the dullness of dull women, and the materialism of businessmen safe for laughter, Kaufman ridiculed them heartily. In *Dulcy*, he extracted fun from the dullness of a moron. In *To the Ladies*, he satirized Rotary banqueteers, and came to the comforting conclusion that a dumbbell husband could always be saved from disaster by the native shrewdness of the little woman who loved and believed in him. In *Beggar on Horseback*, he lampooned the more obvious absurdities of efficient big business, took a sideswipe at its shoddy materialism, its cult of power, and its ignoble tyranny—but the play was a dream-play, a fantasy, and despite the masterly irony of certain scenes, all came right in the end. When the Great Depression began, and popular clamor arose against the failure of the Hoover administration to formulate a constructive policy, Kaufman once again rose to irony with certain scenes in *Of Thee I Sing*. This musical, with a score by George Gershwin, was a trenchant satire on politics, directed impartially at the shady practices of party manipulation, and the political inertia of the electorate. Its effect was to make democracy seem cuckoo without giving offense to anyone.

As the Great Depression deepened—the national apple cart had upset, and Babbitts had been reduced to selling the apples on every street corner—Kaufman produced *You Can't Take It With You*, the moral of which was obvious in its title. In this play, the mad family of Grandpa Vanderhof did as it pleased, instead of doing what society assumed to be reasonable. It lived by whim, for Grandpa, who had retired from business on a dependable income, cherished a faith that "life's pretty simple if you just relax," and was convinced that if people relaxed, there "wouldn't *be* times like these." Life, he asserted, would be "simple and kind of beautiful if you just let it come to you. But the trouble is, people forget that." Surely the creed of Doctor Pangloss had seldom been more touchingly expressed!

When the Second World War broke out in Europe, and the possible rise of an American fascism was troubling many serious American writers, Kaufman dealt with the subject in *The American Way*. This traced the fortunes of an immigrant German family from their arrival in 1896 to the year 1939. The father, a cabinetmaker, with the assistance of a kindly local banker rises, over the years, to proprietorship of a great furniture industry, and a position of eminence in his town. The depression wipes out his fortune, but fails to destroy his faith in his adopted land. There is a use for freedom even if, as his embittered grandson asserts, "it doesn't get you anywhere." Freedom, he declares, "still is, and that is what *does* matter." Few Americans could fail to agree. But few appeared to notice that Kaufman's defender of freedom rested his argument exclusively on the fact that the American way had enabled him to achieve material success and social prestige. The patriotism of the play was admirable, but the reasoning that supported its thesis might have been derived from the propaganda put forth by the National Association of Manufacturers. And, as an historical saga of American life over a period of nearly fifty years, the play might have been adapted—as it was not—from a confident, romantic, sentimental novel by Miss Edna Ferber.

Yet, as time passed, there were occasional indications of another facet of Kaufman's mind. In him, along with Doctor Pangloss, there appeared to coexist an imp. The imp mocked at the rightness of things-as-they-are; it insinuated that to jibe at obvious oddity was merely to dodge the serious issues of life; it protested that, although you could always get a laugh with a wisecrack, to do so wasn't to get away with much. The imp got out of hand when Kaufman was writing *Dinner at Eight*. This play exposed the social decadence of so-called good society —and although it expressed no deep sense of outrage at the corruption of the people whom it portrayed, it did not imply any hope for their regeneration. The imp took an even larger share of *The Man Who Came to Dinner*. In this play, Kaufman surprisingly attempted to puncture all the comfortable assumptions of his erstwhile coterie. For its central character, he used Alexander Woollcott; and Woollcott, despite some misgivings, was finally persuaded to act the role. His misgivings were justified, for the portrait was savagely cruel. But, in the theater, the spectacular coincidence of character and actor monopolized the audience's attention, to the detriment of Kaufman's real theme: the indictment of a way of thinking, an attitude to life, which the character exemplified, and which the American public presumably approved.

Once, and only once, did Kaufman's skeptical imp achieve absolute freedom of expression. Significantly, it did so in a play about a successful playwright; *Merrily We Roll Along* had the tone of personal confession. It traced the rebuking story of how proud youth debased itself into shoddy middle age. It dealt with a dramatist who, by catering to popular taste at the sacrifice of his personal and intellectual integrity, achieves wealth, celebrity, social prestige. An old friend upbraids him for the compromises he has made to gratify his desire for these things, reminding him that in youth he had written a fine play. Says the dramatist: "All right, and what happened to it? Two weeks at the Provincetown Playhouse." And he goes on to argue that it isn't wrong to be successful, that despite success, he can still write fine plays—the finest that ever closed in a week—and will, indeed, do so when he has all the money he now requires. But his friend, who speaks for conscience, is implacable: "You're getting away from the guts of things into a whole mess of polite *nothing*. . . . Besides, the trouble with the plays you're doing is you don't dare stop. You've got to write one a year, or they'll forget you ever wrote a line. But you write one good play and they'll always know who you are."

Ten years earlier, in the fantasy *Beggar on Horseback*, Kaufman had shown an idealistic young artist captive to big business, imprisoned in the "Cady Consolidated Art Factory." He is serving a life sentence, and prefers to escape it by suicide. He rattles the door of his cell. It opens freely. It was never locked. The artist may imagine himself the prisoner or the slave of an economic system. But he is not. The surrender of his integrity is a matter of personal choice. Doctor Pangloss had no reason to know this; but the imp never doubted it. Nor, perhaps, did George S. Kaufman.

[4] A "NEW REALISM"

It was during the decade of the 'twenties that dramatic critics began speaking hopefully of a "renascence" in the American theater. The drama had never kept pace with the advancing maturity of native fiction. The courage, force, and honesty with which American novelists had portrayed American life were seldom equalled by American playwrights. But now a change was setting in, and there were signs that the drama was at last becoming adult. A new generation of writers had stormed Broadway, and were achieving conspicuous success. Such playwrights as Sidney Howard, George Kelly, and Maxwell Anderson

were portraying the American scene with an exciting vitality and fresh-
ness of outlook.

Sidney Howard, a native of California and a graduate of its university, spent a year studying his craft with Professor Baker at Harvard. He volunteered as an ambulance driver in the First World War,
later saw service as a captain of aviation. Returning, he collaborated on
a book about labor espionage, adapted some European plays, experimented with the poetic drama, and won immediate recognition with
his first play about contemporary American life.

The qualities which made *They Knew What They Wanted* so remarkable continued to dominate all of Howard's subsequent work.
Unlike many of his contemporaries, he was neither a moralist, a sentimentalist, or a propagandist for some theory of social reform. Whatever his private philosophy may have been, it found no outlet in his
plays. They offered no facile conclusions about life, either comforting
or grim, though sometimes they posed questions about it. Fascinated
by the American life of his time—by its variety, its hazardousness, its
perpetual solicitation to adventure—Howard wanted only to portray
it as he saw it. He saw it from a point of view peculiarly American:
that of sound common sense, unprejudiced by commitment to any
doctrine. Thus, he spoke for the fundamental sanity of the average
man, who can take theories or leave them, who finds them useful only
so long as they "work," who is too absorbed in the experience of living
to become intellectually obsessed by any rules for life, and who trusts
to good sense to solve his major problems.

It was about people who felt as he did that Howard wrote most
successfully—old Tony, the owner of a California vineyard made prosperous by prohibition; the gentle, lonely waitress whom he has wooed
by mail; Carrie McCobb, confronted by the wreck of her marriage and
the probable frustration of her hopes in the little lunchroom she has set
up in the old McCobb home in Maine. What attracted Howard was
their raciness, their integrity, their self-reliant independence. What he
expressed was their quiet confidence, their inexhaustible courage, and
their instinctive unstudied goodness. Like the American pioneers, he
knew that life is something which must inevitably go forward, whatever the obstacles—and he so portrayed it in his plays. His most heroic
characters were not, in the dramatic sense, heroic or tragic figures.
They were essentially simple Americans, often bewildered and har-
assed by circumstance, but usually tough minded, who genuinely

knew what they wanted. Such people, he implied, however balked, are seldom defeated; they are, so to speak, on the side of life; they continue, and survive. Howard was intelligent enough to perceive that the cost of survival is great—that it may involve the disappointment of the individual's most profound desires; that it may entail compromises which he would prefer not to endure: yet the effect of Howard's plays was to show that the individual can find, short of utter surrender, a solution that will reconcile his spirit to a world he did not make. "Doin' right," says Carrie McCobb, "kills fewer 'n doin' wrong does. Bein' strong's mebbe harder 'n bein' weak but its a sight safer."

Though Howard advanced no social claims for the "common man," he succeeded in expressing the American's conviction of the genuine worth and dignity of his existence. Even the cagey, unscrupulous racketeer, Babe Callahan, the vulgar prohibition-made "success" Sam McCarver, the reckless labor-radical Joe, share it—and gain moral stature because of it. And in *Yellow Jack*—which dramatized the victory of American scientists over yellow fever at the end of the Spanish-American War—Howard again spoke for the common man in the characters of the four Army privates who volunteered as guinea pigs for experimentation.

But Howard did not always restrict his plays to the fortunes of people in modest circumstances. In three plays, he dealt with the lives of the wealthy. A hater of war, he tried to project what might happen should the United States resolve to remain neutral in a second World War, and he placed this issue in the realm of wealth and power where it would logically occur. In many ways, *The Ghost of Yankee Doodle*, produced a year before Munich, proved prophetic. Howard showed the dilemma of liberals, taking as examples a family of wealthy manufacturers—democrats and pacifists of puritanical integrity—who, refusing to make armaments, close their factory. The result is widespread unemployment and misery for the workers whom they are seeking to protect; and the irony is pointed up in the revival of prosperity that occurs when, the nation having been launched into war, the factory gets into high-speed production and provides jobs for everyone by turning out the instruments of death.

In *Lucky Sam McCarver*, Howard dealt with the world of fashion, the embryonic Park-Avenue café society of prohibition days. Here he opposed Carlotta Ashe, a fastidious sophisticate, and McCarver, the naïve, vulgar, successful proprietor of a night club, an opportunist and careerist. McCarver's disgust at the social corruption of Carlotta's world, his awareness that its vulgarity and immorality far exceed those which he takes for granted in his own, expressed the only comment required. In *The Silver Cord*—Howard's most popular play—he approached, but did not quite touch, explicit social criticism. This dealt with the familiar American female parasite of the wealthy class; the woman bred by our society to dominance without responsibility. At a moment when the theories of Freud were first becoming a conversational topic with the general public, *The Silver Cord* achieved wide notoriety as a vivid illustration of one of them. Howard pitilessly exposed a "son-devouring tigress"—a woman whose perverted, fiercely possessive "love" for her children will wreck their lives unless they escape her. Popular interest in the play centered on this character, as a Freudian "case," and audiences tended to ignore other aspects of the relationship. But Howard, with his usual common-sense realism, did not. He implied that the two sons were equally responsible—at least to the degree that they manifested the sentimental adoration, the unquestioning adolescent dependence which, among American men of so-called gentle breeding, passes for filial virtue and has the look of a singularly unpleasant and prevalent neurosis. In two senses, therefore, the play furnished a homily for Mother's Day.

Unlike Howard, who was seldom concerned with social criticism, his contemporary George Kelly soon showed that he was a powerful and caustic critic of at least one aspect of American society. His older brother, Walter Kelly, had long been a vaudeville headliner, a humorous monologuist billed as "the Virginia Judge." George Kelly served an apprenticeship as an actor, then followed his brother into vaudeville, learning his future craft by writing the one-act plays and sketches in which he toured the country. He turned to playwriting for the legitimate theater only when the great postwar expansion of the movie industry indicated the swift doom awaiting vaudeville.

Kelly's first full-length play, *The Torchbearers*, was an amusing satire on the amateur "little theater" movement then sweeping the country. He gently ridiculed the cultural pretensions of a typical group; the pompous silliness of the professional lady "coach" who exploited them; the intellectual naïveté of the audiences to whom, as missionaries, they were carrying the enlightenment of "Art." But, implicitly, Kelly satirized upper-middle-class society in an American city.

He showed it as a rude form of female warfare in which personal vanity is the incentive and group envy the only possible prize.

Kelly went on, however, to more ambitious projects and more penetrating conclusions. In *The Show-Off*, he considered the mores of "normalcy" in terms of their moral effect upon the middle class. He touched on all the principal gospels of the era: the obligation to get rich by quick and easy methods; the duty to keep up a front, even when no money is available for the purpose; the axiom that it is socially sound to mortgage the future for immediate material satisfactions; the dogmas of "service" and "efficiency" and bigger-and-betterism. Kelly showed the collective impact of these urgent admonitions upon a typically receptive American—a bluffing, back-slapping, breezy opportunist who, equipped by his environment with no other moral or social values, assumes that they represent ultimate wisdom, and that their persistent application will eventually make him a tycoon and an acknowledged "leader of men."

As Kelly gained in confidence, he discarded the medium of satire, and he began to concentrate upon the role played by women in the American social scene. Presently it became clear that, although his social criticism took account of the significance of economic factors in shaping the prevailing mores, his standard of judgment expressed an austere, uncompromising, even puritanical moral sense. In *Craig's Wife* he studied one attitude to middle-class marriage which, though seldom explicitly acknowledged, is neither exceptional nor socially condemned. This portrait of a woman of the leisure class—Kelly drew her with cold fury and savage contempt—furnished an illustration admittedly extreme; but it represented a type so generally sanctioned by the social code that most Americans had ceased thinking of it as being singular or questionable.

As Kelly presented her, Harriet Craig differed from the average of her class only in being more intelligent, more consciously aware of her motives, and more obviously ruthless in her determination to achieve them. She has been bred to expensive tastes, but she has no private fortune. She is without special equipment for earning her living, and she has no desire to work. She is superior to petty economies, and has no liking for a meager, shabby-genteel existence. In her situation, marriage must provide a way toward emancipation.

So she has married—and with shrewd worldly wisdom—for "the

only road to independence for *me* that *I* could see, was through the
man I married. It isn't financial independence that I speak of particularly. I knew that would come—as the result of *another* kind of independence; and that is the independence of authority—over the man
I married. . . . I have a full appreciation of Mr. Craig—he's a very
good man; but he's my husband—a lord and master—my master. And
I married to be independent." What she wants, of course, is economic
security, personal freedom, social prestige, and domestic power. She
sets about acquiring them at the lowest possible cost to herself. She
has no reason to believe her methods morally reprehensible; in the
circumstances, they are merely intelligent. They involve perpetual
chicanery, an inflexible domestic tyranny, and an occasional calculated
prostitution when she finds it advantageous to submit to her husband's
sexual desires.

Kelly showed Craig as typical of his class, and, in his attitude, typical
of American husbands in general. Intelligent about his business, successful, respected, and likable, he is blind to what takes place under his
roof. He loves his wife, indulges her, sentimentally idealizes her, is
content to invest her with full authority over his home, his social and
family relations, his leisure and his pocketbook. Are not all these the
woman's province? He does what he is told to do, and although sometimes it occurs to him that his marriage is not fulfilling all his anticipations, he assumes that the fault is exclusively his. Being without suspicion it requires a major crisis to open his eyes. When the crisis arrives,
he suddenly realizes that his wife is capable of sacrificing him, without
even a momentary scruple, to her peculiar gods. He turns on her, more
in astonishment than in rage: "You've been *exploiting me,* consistently,
in your shifty little business of personal safety," he remarks. "What
have you ever done, or a million others like you, that would warrant
the assumption of such superiority over the men you're married to?"

That question Kelly did not answer, either in *Craig's Wife,* or in any
of his subsequent plays. But the object of his criticism was obvious: the
masculine surrender to feminine authority so characteristic of American social life which, if it has made the United States a "paradise of
women" has done so, in Kelly's view, only at a heavy loss of moral
and spiritual values. Again and again, Kelly showed American middle-
class life pervaded by a blighting spiritual vulgarity, a moral callousness; and these he despised. Had women—elevated now to a power of

exploitation unprecedented in history—actually cheapened the quality of American life?

Kelly's plays suggested that they had. In *Daisy Mayme*, he showed the household of a prosperous middle-aged bachelor, whose decency compels him to assume, as he thinks, moral responsibility for the lives of his sisters and nieces. They have long since reduced him to a bondage which he accepts as his obligatory destiny in the nature of things. He meets a shrewd, breezy businesswoman who cleverly puts the parasites to rout. Not herself a parasite, she is perfectly ready to become one. She will replace the others, and substitute her own form of tyranny for theirs. In *Behold the Bridegroom*, Kelly made an excursion into the realm of wealth and so-called elegance, to study another aspect of the American woman's emancipation. What were the moral consequences of her recent exemption from traditional sexual taboos? Kelly's answer was the portait of a "sophisticate"—smart, intelligent, charming—whose casual, well-mannered love affairs are merely symptoms of the irresponsible use she makes of her power, and whose futile, sated life exposes her total lack of any genuine moral values.

The career of Maxwell Anderson, contemporary of Howard and Kelly, was to show a greater diversity and a more restless experimentation than theirs. After a youth in North Dakota, Anderson spent some years as a teacher, notably at Stanford University, then became an editorial writer on various publications. He had already written and produced one play when, with Lawrence Stallings, a colleague on *The New York World*, he collaborated in the writing of *What Price Glory?*, which met with sensational success. Dealing with the life and psychology of professional soldiers in the first World War, the play stunned audiences with its hard-boiled cynicism of attitude, feeling, and language, and was usually credited with having inaugurated the "new" realism which presently made headway in the American theater.

Subsequently, Anderson was to rebel against both the mood and the mode which he had done much to establish. He was to become convinced that "the theater is a religious institution devoted entirely to the exaltation of the spirit of man. It is an attempt to justify, not the ways of God to man, but the ways of man to himself. It is an attempt to prove that man has a dignity and a destiny, that his life is worth living, that he is not purely animal and without a purpose." In the light of this ideal, Anderson made a long, valiant, and often successful attempt to revive the poetic drama, usually drawing his subjects from the historical past, but in two instances seeking to express poetically aspects of the contemporary American scene.

As a result of his preoccupation with poetry, and with the past, some critics accused Anderson of retreating from reality, and possibly it expressed, obliquely, an adverse verdict on contemporary American life and society. Those plays in which he dealt directly with his own times certainly supported this conclusion. For all Anderson's professed faith in the dignity and destiny of man, in the worth of life, his view of the immediate present seldom reflected any exuberant joy in it. Indeed, the tone of his plays about the present, rising from wistful melancholy to passionate indignation, suggested a degree of disillusion and despair that made his profession of faith sound very like a frightened whistling in the dark.

Melancholy was the note struck by *Saturday's Children*, a gentle comedy about young married life on a shoestring. Anderson lightly sketched the lives of an urban middle-class family of modest means. The elder daughter, by approved feminine wiles, has caught a husband —and the hope of economic security. The younger daughter, a romantic dreamer, disapproves both of the method and its objective. Nevertheless she is secretly terrified by the bleak future to which she will be condemned should she act on her idealistic theory of conduct— for, failing to trap herself a husband, she will either remain a stenographer all her life, or become a dependent on her family. So she compromises and catches her man. Having married, she finds herself tricked by the mores. Matrimony, which society insists is the primary purpose in a girl's life, turns out to be no less a tedious servitude than stenography. "What we wanted," she tells her husband bitterly, "was a love affair—just to be together and let the rest go hang—and what we got was a house and bills and general hell. . . . I don't want a house. I don't want a husband. I want a lover." Behind this play, as in a spectral mist, there lurked the principle of economic determinism. Indeed, no Marxian would have taken issue with the view of society which it logically presumed. But this view Anderson scarcely even implied. The play stated no more than a conviction that, as society is now organized, Saturday's children get little chance for any but a meager, drab, defrauded existence.

But the principle of economic determinism became a factor in *Gods of the Lightning,* which Anderson wrote in collaboration with Harold Hickerson, and in which he turned to forthright social criticism of the American scene. Written shortly after the celebrated trial of Sacco and Vanzetti, it dealt with their case and their execution. This had unleashed a storm of protest, not only in the United States, but throughout the world. That the two men were condemned to death on inadequate and possibly falsified evidence seemed probable. That they were punished rather for their political opinions than for the crime with which they were charged seemed certain. To Marxians especially, though to other social radicals as well, the fate of Sacco and Vanzetti was a spectacular illustration of the perversion of justice in behalf of vested economic interests. According to the principle of economic determinism, such perversion of justice is inevitable in a developed capitalist society.

It is not only inevitable, however, but "historically necessary"—being one phase of the process whereby society will progress toward the socialist state. But its historic necessity creates a dilemma for all radicals having a tender conscience. Since they will hasten the advent of the socialist utopia, are not such social evils to be welcomed on strategic grounds? Yet, since they inflict hideous suffering on the helpless masses, are they not to be condemned on ethical grounds? Here, logic and conscience are at odds. Social radicals are notoriously respectful of logic, and usually fiercely committed to the principle of economic determinism. But they are seldom persuaded to acquiesce in such social evils as "class justice." Though these evils may advance progress toward a better life; though they may be "historically necessary" and, from the standpoint of their ultimate consequences, seem good—social radicals, like other men, persist in denouncing them. Conscience continues to protest that they are not good, continues to declare them morally evil.

It was, perhaps, this dilemma that accounted for one curious effect in *Gods of the Lightning.* The play was a powerful, embittered, indignant study of "class justice"—the justice that, acting as the agent of vested economic interests, extirpates men who preach doctrines inimical to those interests. Anderson's sympathy was profoundly stirred by the fate of Sacco and Vanzetti. Altering their personalities as characters in the play, he portrayed them as innocent victims; as martyrs whose death was exacted by American capitalist society. Though he may not have shared their political opinions, he presented them fairly and forcefully. But there was little doubt that he shared, with social radicals of all persuasions, a conviction of the necessity for drastic changes in the form of society. He made a grimly eloquent plea for social, as well as legal, justice. He spoke for an aroused conscience, to such good effect that the critic of the conservative New York *Times* found the play cruelly disturbing in the theater. Yet, having presented the two "social rebels" as martyrs, he likewise suggested that their labors were futile and their martyrdom useless.

Was his conscience nauseated by the doctrine of historic necessity? Or was this curious recantation the effect of his disillusion with the contemporary scene, his despair at the American society of his time? "Uplifters you are, dreamers, reformers, thinking to make over the earth," says a character in *Gods of the Lightning*. "I know you all and you are fools. The earth is old. You will not make it over. Man is old. You will not make him over. You are anarchists, maybe, some of you socialists, some of you wobblies, all of you believers in pap. The world is old and it is owned by men who are hard. Do you think that you can win against them by a strike? Let us change the government, you say. Bah! They own this government, they will buy any government you have. I tell you there is no government—only brigands in power who fight always for more power! It has always been so. It will always be so. Till you die! Till we all die! Till there is no earth!" Pessimism could hardly go further than this. Is there no hope for a better society, for social justice? If conscience makes us hate oppression, shall skepticism make us think futile those who dedicate their lives to the long, disheartening struggle against it?

Seven years after *Gods of the Lightning*, Anderson returned to the case of Sacco and Vanzetti in his poetic tragedy, *Winterset*. In it, he carried the story into the next generation, using as his central character the son of a man condemned and executed under similar circumstances. The son lives only to clear his father's name. He learns that a sociologist has discovered the existence of a witness to the crime who, mysteriously, was not called to give evidence at the trial. He comes to interrogate this witness. So, also, does the trial judge, now conscience ridden and half crazed by having, as a hireling of vested interests, secured the execution of a man whom he knew to be innocent. So, finally, does the gangster who was actually guilty of the murder. The tragedy springs from this situation. But Anderson added little to the social criticism made explicit in the earlier play. The judge defends his conduct with a specious argument. Justice was rendered, in a clear burst of anger, righteously upon a common laborer, a confessed anarchist; furor would have rocked the state had the decision been reversed because the truth was discovered; the record had to stand, since justice holds the common good to be worth more than small injustice, and justice, in the main, is governed by opinion. Finally, our civic rights can be maintained only while we are held to be the peers of those who live about us, and a vendor of fish is not protected as a man might be who kept a market. Beyond this, there is only the assertion that the glory of men is never to yield, to take defeat, to die unsubmitting: a man's mind is his own, and his heart a cry towards something dim in distance superior to himself.

Two days after the first inauguration of President Franklin D. Roosevelt, Anderson produced *Both Your Houses*, a play written to express his contempt for political corruption, and savagely arraigning the methods of lobbyists and legislators. It opposed a young progressive reformer who comes to Washington to serve the people with the hard-headed old party wheel horses who control such vital matters as appropriations, and who succeed in tricking him. Though the play spared neither big business nor practical politicians, its effect was to suggest that the conditions which it exposed were, in fact, inseparable from a democratic form of government. Here, too, Anderson's genuine indignation was tempered by a kind of disillusion or despair which made him infer that reform, being almost impossible, may be dismissed as futile. Four years later, in *High Tor*, a poetic fantasy, Anderson set forth what was probably his most personal comment on the American society of his time. The play dealt with a romantic young man who, hating the modern world and all its works, has found an isolated refuge from it, only to be dispossessed by the industrialists who are buying up the region. All that lies before him, therefore, is a further flight from the encroaching reality that he despises. It is folly to resist the incursion of the new and hateful; his forefathers displaced men of another race, and these, far earlier, displaced the Indians—and, as a surviving Indian explains, all that man builds makes, in the end, good ruins!

[5] PROTEST AND PROPHECY

In the mid-nineteen-thirties, as the Great Depression wore on, a one-act play by a youthful, previously unknown writer had a sensational success. It was being played in some sixty towns which had never before witnessed a theatrical performance. Simultaneously, in conjunction with another play by the same author, it was being performed in thirty-two cities. The social consciousness that had produced a new school of novelists was now invading the drama. And, quite literally overnight, Clifford Odets had emerged from obscurity as a vigorous, passionate spokesman for the social dissidence of American youth.

Odets was the son of a printer who rose to ownership of an advertising agency. In childhood, living in Philadelphia and in the Bronx quarter of New York City, he was brought up among the lower middle class, the little people who led a modest existence, sometimes prosperous, sometimes extremely straitened, but never far removed from anxiety. Early attracted to the stage, Odets was acting minor roles for the Theater Guild in New York when, as the decade opened, the Group Theater was projected. He joined this new organization. Announcing exalted ideals and an ambitious policy, it managed to realize both, and during its ten-year lifetime became a vitalizing force. Odets joined the venture as an actor, but one of its purposes was to develop young playwrights of talent. So he began writing plays. And, although his efforts met with little encouragement, he continued to write.

Presently, another organization opened a competition for one-act plays suitable for presentation by labor unions, and other groups of workers, in their meeting halls. Odets, it is said, wanted comradeship; he wanted to belong to the largest possible group of humble, struggling men prepared to make a great common effort to build a better world. In three evenings, he wrote a play which forcefully dramatized this desire. It won the competition, and its production in New York was a theatrical sensation.

In *Waiting for Lefty*, Odets showed a union meeting in progress. He projected the conflict between a militant membership and its reactionary, corrupt leaders. Brief episodes illustrated the typical social factors which had made the workers class conscious, rebellious, determined to strike. The play closed with a strike vote put to the audience. In performance, it proved to be a ringing summons to join the good fight for a greater measure of life in a world free of economic fear, falsehood, and craven servitude to stupidity and greed. To many people, it seemed to give a voice to inarticulate American youth, at a standstill in the Great Depression. It dramatized their plight. It declared their resentment, and their impatient demand for constructive social action. Above all, it expressed their faith in the possibility of a better social order and their determination to bring one into being.

Odets went on to develop these elements in a series of full-length plays produced by the Group Theater. As a result, he soon became the subject of an explosive controversy. Conservative critics denounced his plays as propaganda for communism. (It was the time when, according to the Lynds, prosperous folk in Middletown began hoarding foodstuffs, and preparing to defend their homes against a dreaded revolutionary outbreak by the disgruntled masses.) Communism was a bugbear—but party members found little to praise in Odets's plays. The communist press regarded them dubiously; they were tainted with "bourgeois sentimentality." Both points of view were, in the immediate circumstances, entirely natural.

In nearly all his plays, Odets asserted youth's faith in the possibility of a better social order. Most of them began on a note of protest, and rose to eloquent prophecy. But the prophecy was a form of *mystique*. The faith that Odets expressed was a poetic intuition rather than a political formula; it was a fervent, quasi-religious emotion, not a program for revolution. Thus, for example, in *Awake and Sing*, an old, contemplative, ineffectual Marxian exhorts his vacillating grandson to "do what is in your heart and you carry in yourself a revolution." But, characteristically, the import of this radical counsel is general, not specific: "Be something! Make your life something good. For the love of an old man who sees in your young days his new life, for such love take the world in your two hands and make it like new. Go out and fight so life shouldn't be printed on dollar bills." This sounds more like Ralph Waldo Emerson than Karl Marx.

The vision, or prophecy, expressed in Odets's plays was abstract. The protest was not. What aroused his indignation and compassion was the effect of the immediate social situation on youth. Youth, because of the Great Depression, was being defrauded of its opportunity to seek a good life after its own fashion; its presumably inalienable right to "the pursuit of happiness." His protest was directed against all obstructive factors, whatever their nature. But the times insistently suggested that social paralysis had been produced by an economic cause. In a prostrate society, all obstructions to a good life reduced to one— the grim problem of money and livelihood. The existence of people who had never heard of economic determinism was apparently being determined by relentless economic forces. Odets spoke for his own generation in condemning a social order so indifferent to human welfare as to permit life to be printed on dollar bills.

Few critics noticed that his plays did not deal with proletarian life.

But that they did not, probably increased their cogency. The people of Odets' plays belonged to the lower middle class. In *Awake and Sing*, the Berger family, living in the Bronx on the wages paid to minor employees. A similar family in *Paradise Lost*. In *Golden Boy*, the household of an Italian fruit vendor. An office clerk and a small-part actress in *Night Music*. In *Rocket to the Moon*, an unsuccessful dentist, the girl who keeps his books and cleans his instruments, his prosperous father-in-law. These characters were the "little people" of American cities. Unlike class-conscious members of the proletariat, they had never questioned the existing social order, or their own place in it, or the truth of its official myths. They were the people who had always cherished the American dream. They would somehow rise in the social and economic scale. They would surely attain—some time in the indefinite future—their individual ambitions, their personal visions of fulfillment. The Great Depression, prolonging itself year after year, confronted them with the collapse of the social order they had taken for granted, and the only philosophy or culture with which it had equipped them.

In his plays, Odets exposed the pathos of their situation. He showed the bewilderment, the disquiet, the frequent terror in which a large segment of the American people, abruptly deprived of all their in-herited certainties, were striving to adjust themselves to an environment which they no longer understood, and which—for the first time—they realized that they could not control. Essentially, Odets had but one subject: the death of an illusion. Like many of his generation, he believed the old order to be literally dead, and he was convinced that its reputed excellence had never been more than an illusion in any case. His people therefore existed in a kind of purgatory between two worlds, one prostrate and finished, the other as yet unborn. The older generation, in his plays, pathetically cling to the past. The young people turn to a future about which they know little except that it must not, shall not, resemble the past. Neither the old nor the young have many ideas. What they do have is dreams, ambitions, and allegiances.

For Odets' "little people" the bottom had dropped out. He showed their state of mind as it really was—"with all its vacillation, dual allegiances, fears, groping, self-distrust, dejection, spurts of energy, hosannas, vows of conversion, and prayers for release." The obstinate, struggling family of *Awake and Sing*, typical of the people about whom Odets chose to write, also represented a vast, anxious, restive population grimly determined to survive, though it no longer had an official faith to sustain it, and had no goal except somehow to endure.

As Odets portrayed them, no one member of the Berger family understands what any of the others want from life. But it is clear that each of them—except, perhaps, the Marxian grandfather who serves as commentator—might have realized his modest hopes, were it not for the desperate need of money which compels them to remain together so that, individually thwarted, they may collectively survive. The family is dominated, and held together, by a shrewd, efficient mother who clings, pathetically, to the vestiges of respectability, and whose protective instinct, developed by years of stubborn effort to keep her household alive, and her children decent, produces tragedy for everyone. She coerces her daughter into a safe, loveless marriage, never suspecting that the girl asks something more of life. She compels her son to give up the girl with whom he believes himself in love; these are no times for marrying—and, besides, the household needs his weekly contribution. She taunts her father—his Marxian ideas constitute a threat to everything for which she stands; she has long anticipated his bitter quotation from Marx, "Abolish such families!" Yet she, too, would have life other than it is; and to the welfare of the family she has unhesitatingly sacrificed the pitiful little dreams of her girlhood. In such circumstances of abject frustration, youth can see that existence amounts to little more than sitting around "with the blues and mud in your mouth," that "a chance to get to first base" will never come. And, resentfully, it feels that life must not continue being "printed on dollar bills."

So, in Odets' plays, youth inevitably rebels. But Odets felt the need of showing that purely personal rebellion—the determination to achieve material satisfaction—is useless; that it is one of the illusions of the dead world of the past, and has no relevance to the new world that must be created. Usually, he stated this thesis in the form of a contrast. In *Awake and Sing*, the married daughter deserts her husband to run off with another man who offers her excitement, money, comfort: but it is clear that this union, too, will break up. The son, however, sublimates his private unhappiness and his personal battle against poverty in a decision to take his appropriate place as a militant in the class struggle. Some form of collective action, some unified front of the underprivileged was all that Odets postulated as a solution.

He restated this contrast in *Golden Boy*, his most popular play. In it, a young musician, led astray by the old social myth that made money the measure of all things, makes the wrong choice. He gives up the violin that promises him only a meager livelihood—"you can't pay people back with music." He enters the prize ring, which lures him with the possibility of easy wealth and swift celebrity. He achieves both. Then he realizes that he has lost his human identity; he has become a kind of commodity, the property of other men who care only for a quick return on their investment in him. His rebellion, being purely materalistic, is merely a form of surrender. But his brother, an organizer for the C.I.O., represents the alternative for which Odets always pleaded—action, necessarily collective, in behalf of a better social order, dedicated not to wealth and power but to the well-being and happiness of all men.

There was nothing radically new about Odets' vision or prophecy, except, perhaps the symbols through which he expressed it; these were furnished by the moment, and reflected it. His faith in the possibility of a better world was as old as America, and had seldom been absent from its literature. One heard not the voice of Marx but the challenge of all American history in the words with which his philosophical detective, in the poetic fantasy *Night Music*, bids farewell to a confused, frightened, truculent boy and girl: "You had the wisdom and foresight to born in the twentieth century. Go, go with love and health—your wonderful country never needed you more. . . ."

[6] GAY, BUT WISTFUL

From the dramatic "renascence" of the 'twenties, there emerged several writers of high comedy. Surprisingly enough, they produced some of their best work during the terror-stricken 'thirties and the confused 'forties, when conditions favorable to this particular form of art seemed conspicuously lacking. The intellectual maturity of the American people could be inferred from the fact that, in literature and the drama, social protest and high comedy flourished simultaneously. The reading public acclaimed James T. Farrell and John Steinbeck. But it also accorded to the novels of Henry James a popularity which they had never previously enjoyed. Audiences in the theater were receptive to the indictment of society made by Clifford Odets and more explicitly "proletarian" writers. But they likewise responded appreciatively to the plays of Philip Barry, S. N. Behrman, and John van Druten, who looked at life from a very different standpoint.

The sharp difference in attitudes sometimes trapped unwary or partisan critics into foolish charges. One was that of snobbery, made by both sides. Was it true, as Lionel Trilling asserted, that writers moved to social protest by the dire plight of the underprivileged were guilty of "inverted condescension"; that their "democratic piousness" was founded on a conviction "that the less a man is established the greater is his personal glory"? A character in one of S. N. Behrman's plays echoed that charge with a flippant question: "Why is a book about unhappy dirty people better than one about gay and comfortable ones?"

To critics in the proletarian camp, high comedy seemed the very acme of obsolete snobbery. What could be more callous, more futile, in an era of extreme social tension, than to write about gay and comfortable people—as if to exalt the mission and superior merit of the dominant social class? To do so was to indulge in irresponsible frivolity; and such socially radical critics of the theater as Miss Eleanor Flexner considered it a kind of betrayal. For did it not merely cater to an exploiting class eager to escape from certain menacing aspects of life that threatened its hitherto unchallenged immunities?

Fortunately, the American playgoing public saw the strong element of prejudice in both arguments. If the theater was to become a social forum, the public would listen to all contenders. They would hear from writers convinced that the principle of economic determinism furnishes an explanation of all human conduct. But they would likewise hear from writers who were convinced that it does not. Was there not some truth in a theory advanced by Miss Rachel Crothers in one of her plays: "The vital things of character don't belong to anybody's day—they're eternal and fundamental"?

This theory reflected the attitude common to writers of high comedy—which, as Joseph Wood Krutch stated, often haunts the drawing room because it is in the drawing room that human nature in the abstract can best be studied. High comedy, fixing on the presumably permanent elements of human nature, likes to study them in relation to the most evolved mores of its time. This explains its preference for characters who are cultivated, who enjoy a relative freedom from material anxieties, who command abundant leisure. Such characters are immediately credible as intelligent people who can devote themselves to the cultivation of their intelligence, and who find the intellectual and emotional solution of their problems all-sufficient. Without people of this kind, high comedy is seldom possible; its special province is the play of intelligence on social life.

To earnest-minded folk, the characters of high comedy may always seem frivolous. To passionate reformers armed with some universal panacea for the evils of society, they may seem highly irrelevant. Being intelligent, they are very likely to be skeptical also. They seldom surrender to prejudices, whether moral, political, or economic; they distrust facile formulas. They are enviably free from the pressures which warp the judgment of people less fortunate. Their virtue is to see all sides of any complex problem, even if the problem involves their personal fate. Their frequent vice—and also their constant peril— is to do nothing whatever about it. Unlike most members of the audience, they exist in a climate of perpetual debate. It is precisely this unnatural atmosphere which makes them such admirable instruments of social criticism. In the 'thirties and 'forties, the plays of Barry, Behrman, and van Druten were as genuinely examples of social criticism as those of Odets or the proletarian dramatists.

Philip Barry was born to the social and cultural advantages of wealth, received his early education from priests and nuns, went on to Yale University and, after graduating, studied playwriting under Professor Baker at Harvard. His first play, written while still a student in Baker's course, won him a prize and a production on Broadway. For a brief period, he served the State Department in Washington and London, but thereafter devoted himself exclusively to writing.

Barry exploited a talent for comedy in plays which, for the most part, disguised a grave, reflective judgment of the social scene with a sparkling, sometimes brittle surface. Himself a "sophisticate" and a cosmopolitan, he wrote about people who, as the critic H. T. Parker said, "need take no thought of the financial morrow, since their balances in bank are renewed like the widow's cruse in Scripture. It is their privilege to rise up and depart, to sit down and linger, the world around, as impulse without obligation may prompt." But this very freedom—as critics often failed to notice—was precisely the condition that set their problems. For there is no such thing as absolute freedom from obligation, and the conflicts in Barry's plays usually occurred between "modern" impulse and plain, old-fashioned sense of duty. This fact might have been more obvious had Barry not been a writer of high comedy—had he not, as was said of an earlier American playwright, considered it merely ill bred to be solemn as well as serious about human affairs, since this imputes to the human animal a dignity which he does not possess.

In *Paris Bound*, Barry's theme was the "fundamental," or ethical, concept of marriage—which reflects human nature in one of its permanent aspects—in conflict with the current mores, which favor individual "liberty," casual love affairs, and easy divorce. Barry drew a peculiarly subtle, and modern, distinction between sex and love: "I don't mean to belittle sex. It holds a high and dishonored place among other forms of intoxication. But love is something else again, and marriage is still another thing. . . ." He returned to this theme in *Tomorrow and Tomorrow*, and again in *The Animal Kingdom*. In the first, there was a kind of paradox. Barry's definition of marriage posed a spiritual and intellectual union, with all the shared values to which such a condition may give birth in time. But, in *Tomorrow and Tomorrow*, the actual marriage does not fulfill the definition; it is the love affair that does; and this paradox sets the problem, which Barry, concerned here more with ethics than individual happiness, resolved in favor of intelligence and duty, rather than that "freedom" which the mores approve.

In *The Animal Kingdom*, so far as marriage is concerned, the situation resembled that of *Tomorrow and Tomorrow*. But the problem, complicated by another theme, is solved—legitimately, according to Barry—by rebellion and freedom. The second theme makes the difference: it is the pressure of a materialistic, industrialized society upon the spiritual integrity of the individual, a pressure which, if he is tempted by the lure of "success" to compromise his ideals, is likely to destroy him. Barry's resentment of big business as a force in American society was scarcely exceeded by that of any playwright of social protest, though his arraignment of it was made on quite other grounds. He despised it chiefly as a vulgarizing influence; as a tyranny whose gospel was the mean worship of mean things, always seeking to dragoon the individual into a cheap conformity. In this guise, he indicted it in *Holiday*, in *The Animal Kingdom*, in *The Joyous Season*, and to some extent in *Hotel Universe*. To its sterility as a way of life, Barry offered the alternative of a rational ethics, to the intelligent ideals of which the individual, if he chooses, can approximate his conduct—though not, in contemporary American society, without paying a heavy price. As a critic of that society, Barry was scarcely less pessimistic than Howells or Henry James; if the tone of his comedy was gay, its implications were none the less wistful.

That Barry's view of life was essentially serious, that his interest was rather in permanent than in immediate issues, was indicated by two plays in which he abandoned the mood of high comedy. In *Hotel Universe*, he dealt with the power, for good or evil, of the basic illusion which so frequently shapes the individual's life. The play—actually a symposium on philosophy, complicated by some excursions into the "new" psychology, and some novel speculations about the nature of time—puzzled its audiences rather more than it illuminated them. In *Here Come the Clowns*, he dealt reverently and movingly with the contemporary American's search for God. As if to answer critics of the proletarian school who might allege his lack of interest in the "common man," Barry set this play in the world of the little people of the theater. Clancy, its protagonist, is a stage hand. Barry intended him as one man ready and willing to go down in the battle with evil which continues to be fought throughout the world. In the end, he finds God in the will of man. Clancy's expressed hope is that there may come a day when they, or their like, will be able to look with more approval upon an earth which they may have at last inherited. With this hope, even the Marxian playwrights would probably not have quarreled. Nor, since their gospel, too, was a form of *mystique*, could they have logically disputed Barry's fundamental mysticism: that it is infinitely better to die in this struggle than to continue to live in fear or in the questionable security which follows any compromise with all those things in government and human society that we know in our hearts to be wrong.

The early environment of S. N. Behrman, unlike that of Philip Barry, appears to have been shadowed by some degree of economic poverty. He grew up in Worcester, Massachusetts, and developed an early passion for the theater, collecting autographed photographs of the leading players at the Worcester stock company. He decided then to write for the stage, and also to act. He fulfilled both ambitions by writing a vaudeville sketch, and acting in it. Subsequently, he went to Clark University, transferred to Harvard and the drama courses of

Professor Baker, went on to postgraduate study at Columbia. He began his writing career as a book reviewer, served as a theatrical press agent, and wrote several plays in collaboration with an established playwright before undertaking his first independent venture. This first play, *The Second Man*, won him instant celebrity.

The society represented in Behrman's plays—so far as it corresponded with an existing reality—had its prototype in that super sophisticated, cosmopolitan "set" which, according to the fashion magazines and other competent authorities, originate all standards of elegance, and inaugurate the absolutely latest modes in art and literature. If Behrman, in his plays, attributed to them a greater degree of intelligence than they seemed to possess, he probably did not exaggerate either their influence or their often diverting irresponsibility. Like Henry James, he wished to deal with the "best" society of his time, in which the human spirit might be supposed to flower most liberally, and with the greatest graciousness. But the favor of an aristocracy involves a peril which even Henry James—born in the best society of the United States of his day—did not fully escape. And that staunch democrat, Mark Twain—born on the wrong side of the tracks—also succumbed to it during his residence in Europe.

To a French writer, and perhaps even to an English one, there would be nothing surprising in the spectacle of a duchess climbing five stories to visit his attic; his position in society is established by the distinction of his art, not by his financial success. But writers in the United States do not—until popular success makes them lions—associate in casual intimacy with leaders of Society. And such intimacy, should it come, is likely to leave them bedazzled. There was always, to Henry James, something titillatingly glamorous about a duchess; and Mark Twain, at the very height of his worldwide fame, wrote ecstatic letters in his astonished delight at the afternoon call of an Austrian princess. Behrman's plays frequently suggested that he had never recovered from exposure to his first duchess, or his first Newport hostess.

The standard of values implied in all his plays was that of the little Society which he transferred to the stage; unlike Philip Barry, who dealt with much the same world, Behrman never viewed its conduct in the light of any morality, or ethical principle, external to it. As social criticism, therefore, his plays made an oblique indictment of that not inconsiderable portion of the social order excluded from the best society; the ideal which he proposed for imitation was the mores and morals of the privileged beings who peopled his plays. "What this country needs," the hero of *The Second Man* remarks, "is a dilettante class, interested in art, with no desire to make money out of it. Why shouldn't there be an amateur class in art, as there is in sports?" The people of Behrman's plays were, in perhaps the best sense, magnificent dilettantes—amateurs not only of art, but of morals, philosophy, politics; highly intelligent, fastidiously discriminating; who fulfilled their function by making wise appraisals, but who need not translate their wisdom into action. Their virtue, as Behrman saw it, was to cultivate intelligence, but not necessarily to practice it. All of them could have echoed the desire of the young girl in *The Second Man*: "I wish I could do that. . . . Escape from the dreary exile of the actual world." Or that of the hero: "I'd like to be Henry James and live with you in England on a private income."

But, as time passed, and the "actual world" began to look as if it were going to pot, it broke destructively into the charmed and insulated never-never land inhabited by Behrman's characters, facing them with issues not to be solved by exquisite cultivation. Was it any wonder that one was driven to acknowledge: "Dear darling, life is sad. I know it's sad. But I think it's gallant—to pretend that it isn't"? In *Meteor*, written just before the onset of the Great Depression, Behrman portrayed the havoc wrought by a rebellious and disorganized genius who puts his intelligence to the service of an obsessive lust for power. Behrman attributed the responsibility to the American social order, which rewards its financiers, when successful, more abundantly than its scholars or artists, and hence offers young genius no worthy example to emulate. He did not, however, conceal his repugnance to the achievements of finance capitalism commonly glorified. His genius' major enterprise was the exploitation of a Central American republic—dominated in its politics and social order by his wealth—which is to be converted into a Utopia run by expert accountants, on the model of the American "company towns" to which a paternalistic capitalism points with pride.

In *Biography*, his most popular play, Behrman, through his heroine, made articulate his ideal of the discriminating amateur: a woman who, required to choose between an opportunist conservative politician and a fanatical radical, refuses both, defending the inherent wisdom of cultivating the greatest possible tolerance for all points of view, while committing herself to none. But in *Rain from Heaven*, Behrman confronted a woman of the same type with issues less personal and far more insistent. In this play the conflict was between the representative of an American fascist-capitalist movement, and a liberal, driven from Germany by the Nazi persecution bent not only upon destroying his race but the culture to which he has given his best years. The heroine, once again, stands aloof. Whatever the outcome of the battle, liberals like herself will not disappear from the earth; when the cataclysm has passed, they will be at hand, and help to produce a society in which existence is exquisitely gracious, and intelligence always tolerant. Yet it was obvious that Behrman himself had some misgivings about his quietist liberals—inhibited by scruple and emasculated by charm. They might be indispensable to what he conceived to be the good life, but they seemed scarcely capable of underwriting it. A character in one of his earlier plays had exploded, petulantly: "The trouble is, the masses bore me, democracy bores me." Could one continue to feel so, with civilization threatened? The refugee in *Rain from Heaven*, about to return to Germany and join the underground, furnished Behrman's reluctant comment upon his favorite world: "I see now that goodness is not enough, that liberalism is not enough. I'm sick of evasions. They've done us in. Civilization, charity, tolerance, progress—all catchwords. We'll have to redefine our terms."

Intellectually honest, and himself an exemplar of that discriminating intelligence which he valued as the highest of virtues, Behrman confronted his own predicament in *No Time for Comedy*, a play about a playwright. Like his own, the playwright's talent is for high comedy; but the age forces upon him conflicts and issues which the comic spirit is incapable of meeting. Shall he relinquish his medium, which compels him to seem irrelevant to all the profound concerns of his time, or shall he attempt to deal with those concerns—which, alas, do not vitally enlist his sympathies? As perhaps was inevitable, Behrman failed to solve the problem. In an ideal world, in which discriminating intelligence and tolerant liberalism would be sufficient principles, one might anticipate the emergence of a spirit and an understanding transcending the clamors and ferocities of the marching lustful mobs. In such a world, of course, the problem simply wouldn't arise.

John van Druten was born in England, and was teaching law in Wales when—because of the whimsical censorship of the Lord Chamberlain—his first play made a success, not in his native land, but in the United States. He promptly came to the United States, fell in love with it because, as he said, it was "a puritan land," for many years spent most of his time there, and eventually became an American citizen.

It was not, however, until comparatively late in his career that he began writing plays about contemporary American life. Conceived in the vein of high comedy, his plays moved out of the drawing room, and out of the narrow confines of the "best society." In *Old Acquaintance*, he dealt wittily with literary circles in New York City. In *The Damask Cheek*, working with a collaborator, he achieved an amusing picture of Mrs. Wharton's brownstone, upper middle-class New York in the first decade of the twentieth century, showing the impact upon its elaborate conventions of a character who not only embodies intelligence, but practices it in conduct. In his most successful play, *The Voice of the Turtle*, he balanced the mores of sexual freedom, which permit two young people to drift into what is to be no more than a casual love affair, against the eternal human hope for a permanent union founded on love.

But, unlike the gay and carefree pair of van Druten's earlier, charming *There's Always Juliet*, the girl and man of *The Voice of the Turtle* have no courage for love. They are, in a sense, prejudiced against it; they are afraid of "being hurt." Says the man, "I gave up looking forward to anything seven years ago, and I've got along all right that way." And, to the girl, "it can go on being fun" only if the man doesn't "spoil it"—by changing the key of emotion. Though the playwright never made it explicit, there was in this fear of experience, this frightened retreat from life itself, a pertinent criticism of contemporary society.

But, in another way, *The Voice of the Turtle* was a perfect barometer of the mores of the time. That the playwright should have been able—without offense to the American public—to have carried the physical drama of a love affair to a bed, the extinguishing of a light, and a passage of evocative dialogue: this perhaps declared the moral emancipation of the American stage. If the ghost of Charles Eliot Norton visited the playhouse, it was not heard to murmur his dictum of forty years earlier: "no great work of the imagination has ever been based upon illicit passion." Times had, indeed, changed; and van Druten, in more than one sense, had perhaps represented only "what every woman knows."

It was in *I Remember Mama,* founded upon a sequence of stories by Kathryn Forbes, that van Druten offered his most genial picture of American life. In this saga of a family of Norwegian immigrants, living in San Francisco, meeting with gallantry and wisdom the tribulations of lower middle-class existence, the playwright expressed a profound faith in the common life. At a time when the established social order was subjected to attack from many quarters, van Druten suggested, with considerable force, that the good life probably depends less upon the nature of the prevailing economic system than it does upon the wise exercise of freedom, possible alone to the pure in heart. The suggestion, as the twentieth century neared its midpoint, was one that Americans could ponder.

Part Three

A MATTER OF RECORD

CHAPTER VIII

The Uses of News

In 1896, ruthless war broke out on Newspaper Row, in New York City. This was a battle of titans, for the supremacy of Joseph Pulitzer, owner of the *World*, had been challenged, was in peril. Young William Randolph Hearst, coming on from San Francisco with nearly eight million dollars, had bought the *Journal*, a moribund sheet, and was prepared to pour his wealth into the attack. He intended to outdo the *World*, to capture its mass circulation, to defeat it, and if possible to wreck it.

Fascinated, the nation watched a long, costly, spectacular contest. It was destined to leave enduring effects on the American press. One of its by-products was a new and scandalous sensationalism, soon described as "yellow journalism." This raised a whirlwind of denunciation from conservative papers, the clergy, and outraged segments of the respectable public. Nevertheless, it continued to flourish. Yellow journalism prospered and survived. Fifty years later, its style had changed, but not its formula; it was still being sold to the American people as a staple commodity. The clash of titans produced another journalistic legacy, equally permanent. This, too, was a by-product. It was the embryo of the modern mass newspaper: shrieking headlines, multiple "features," comic supplements and strips, "magazine sections," bulky Sunday editions. All these issued from a struggle for power by two fabulous characters who recognized their effectiveness as weapons of war.

When taking up Hearst's challenge Pulitzer announced, in a editorial, that he preferred power to profits. Probably a flamboyant declaration seemed requisite. This one happened to be true. For Pulitzer, whose happiest boast was his total independence, was the slave of pride. So exorbitant was his pride that nothing short of absolute power could gratify it. Consequently, all his exactions were extreme. He acknowledged no limits whatever. He had, as it were, an instinct for infinity, and his visions were no less grandiose than those of the elder J. P. Morgan. Every triumph, therefore, brought him a fresh agony; there was always a greater victory beyond, and another beyond that, and they tormented him like a perpetual itch. Brilliant, neurotic, incapable of satisfaction or tranquillity, Pulitzer drove his subordinates as remorselessly as he drove his own mind and body. In little more than a decade, he had made the *World*, in actual influence, the foremost newspaper in America. But he was already a tragic figure when Hearst threatened its supremacy.

After one of the exposures of municipal corruption for which the paper was celebrated, Pulitzer was overtaken by a nervous breakdown. His vision, always defective, began to fail. In 1890, assured that permanent blindness was inevitable, he announced that he had relinquished personal editorship of the paper. Thereafter, the *World* would continue to be guided by the ideas of the man who made it what it was, but by remote control. From his yacht, his town house in New York, his summer residence at Bar Harbor, his winter establishments—at Jekyl Island, and Cap Martin on the French Riviera—Pulitzer lashed at his editors, reporters, business managers. He paid but one visit to the massive, golden-domed building on Park Row that dominated the New York skyline. It had been erected to house his paper, and he intended it to be his monument; but he never saw it. Sightless, he went on working far into the night, racking his sleepless brain for new and better ideas, crowding long journeys into days that knew no rest.

As a youth of seventeen, tall, gangling, myopic, Joseph Pulitzer slipped over the side of a ship in Boston harbor and swam to shore. Born in Hungary, he wanted to be a soldier, and had wandered across Europe vainly seeking enlistment. The War between the States was in progress and, in Hamburg, a Union recruiting agent shipped Pulitzer to America. Penniless, he needed to collect his own bounty, so he jumped ship, made his way to New York, and enlisted. He knew no English when he joined the army, and had learned little when he was mustered out at the end of the war. Finding no work in New York, he made his way to St. Louis, more or less as a vagrant. He worked as a ferry hand, a hostler, a stevedore, waiter in a restaurant. He spent all his spare time in the Mercantile Library, reading avidly, and so mastering English. Finally, he secured a job traveling from county to county, recording provisions of the charter of the new transcontinental railroad.

This turned his ambition to the law, for which he began to prepare himself. But chance brought him an opportunity to work as a reporter for a German-language newspaper. Carl Schurz was one of the owners. Schurz and the Scottish philosopher Thomas Davidson, then in St. Louis and later to become the friend of William James, recognized Pulitzer's genius, took him in hand, and trained his mind. At twenty-two, he was elected to the Missouri legislature; served one term as a foe of legislative corruption; achieved local notoriety by shooting a politician whom he had denounced. At twenty-five, he acquired a proprietary interest in the paper for which he worked. Presently, he sold it for thirty thousand dollars. Thereafter, he traveled widely, campaigned for Samuel J. Tilden as Democratic candidate for the presidency, reported political news from Washington. At thirty-one, having meanwhile married, he bought a failing St. Louis paper for a song. Soon he combined it with another, as the *Post-Dispatch*. Within two years, the new paper was an assured success.

Pulitzer made it a crusading organ, continuously exposing political corruption and demanding reform. One of its exposures involved a lawyer of great local repute. While Pulitzer was absent from the city, Pulitzer's assistant and the lawyer had a furious altercation; guns were drawn; the lawyer was killed. Popular feeling ran high, and the paper was widely denounced for its policy of personal attack. Convinced that he was no longer welcome in the city, Pulitzer put his paper in the hands of a former associate, and went to New York. There, in 1883, he bought the *World* from Jay Gould. In less than seven years he increased its circulation from under twenty thousand to nearly two hundred thousand; paid Gould three hundred and forty-six thousand dollars; erected the *World* building at a cost of two and one-half millions, all without recourse to any loans. When Hearst entered the field, Pulitzer was not yet fifty, and many times a millionaire. The circulation of his morning paper was the largest in the country. Its Sunday edition—

edited by Morrill Goddard, and afterwards by the bizarre Arthur Brisbane, both of whom Hearst quickly lured away—sold six hundred thousand copies. An evening *World* had been launched, and was prospering.

This astonishing success rested on Pulitzer's basic policy. This he announced in his first editorials for the *World*. During his lifetime he never permitted his papers to deviate from it. His newspaper would be not only cheap, but bright, not only bright but large, not only large but truly democratic—dedicated to the cause of the people rather than that of purse potentates. The *World* was to be an organ that would expose all fraud and sham, fight all public evils and abuses—that would serve and battle for the people with earnest sincerity. His method of achieving this object became clear two days after he took control of the paper. He wanted to demonstrate that it was to be the organ of a true aristocracy—the aristocracy of labor. So he published an editorial on "Our Aristocracy" which excoriated the upper ranks of Society. The *World*, he said, believed that it ought to have no place in the republic —that the word ought to be expunged from an American vocabulary. Here, fully revealed, was Pulitzer's cardinal principle: to create by destroying; to affirm by attacking.

He never allowed his staff to forget it for an instant. Just before his death, nearly thirty years later, he was still urging a managing editor always to remember the difference between a paper made for the million, the masses, and a paper made for the classes. Every day, he insisted, the *World* should play up one distinctive feature, fight, crusade, public service, or big exclusive. And why not? This recipe, over the years, had brought him an immense power over the mass mind. It had enabled him to indulge his passion to be felt in the strife of public forces and to be heard in the consideration of national concerns. And, quite incidentally, it had piled up for him the modest reward of some nineteen millions of dollars.

Pulitzer's policy may have had its original source in the grim poverty and hardship from which he suffered after his discharge from the army, and which began the gradual breakdown of his health. He saw that American democracy had produced both masses and classes. He judged their interests to be irreconcilable. He seems to have suspected that strife between them was inevitable. Certainly it was not mere cupidity that enlisted him on the side of the masses, where profits to a newspaper were almost certain. There was in him a genuine reformer, a very real idealist. There was also an extremely shrewd man of business, who realized that the strategy of attack and exposure would inflate circulation as a crusade for a worthy cause might not. His policy reconciled these two elements of his character. The tycoon played up profitable scandals. The idealist tied them to a moral principle—whenever possible.

He insisted, always, upon accuracy of facts. But he saw no objection whatever to the most sensational presentation of them. He asserted that there is only one way to get a democracy on its feet in the matter of its individual, its municipal, its State, its National conduct, and that is by keeping the public informed about what is going on. And he had a retort for those who accused him of debasing the press by cheap and vulgar sensationalism: "There is not a crime, there is not a dodge, there is not a trick, there is not a swindle, there is not a vice which does not live by secrecy. Get these things out into the open, describe them, attack them, ridicule them in the press, and sooner or later public opinion will sweep them away." This should be done, of course, with "good taste"—"the kind of good taste which demands that frankness should be linked with decency, the kind of moral tone which is braced and not relaxed when it is brought face to face with vice." The formula of the moralist left the door wide open for the products of the tycoon. Some of Pulitzer's scandals—particularly during his long, arduous contest with Hearst—were juicy, sulphurous, nauseating. When public clamor arose over this aspect of yellow journalism, and circulation began to suffer, Pulitzer himself decided that they were degrading. When, having spent most of his seven million dollars and established himself in New York, Hearst proposed that the contest be called off, Pulitzer relinquished to him the more disreputable provinces of yellow journalism with evident relief. His pride was embarrassed by having been placed in a position of indignity.

Over the years, his most spectacular achievements were exposures of corruption in the realms of politics and high finance. The effect on circulation was always prodigious. The effect on the public mores was seldom what Pulitzer professed that he intended. His debut was an exposure of the "boodle aldermen" of New York City, who had been bribed to vote a street-railroad franchise. He made this scandal a great occasion for cleaning up New York politically—but its effect was to throw the corrupt franchise into the hands of William C. Whitney and Thomas Fortune Ryan, thus enabling them to make themselves multimillionaires by building up the colossal pyramid of high finance that went to smash with the Metropolitan Street Railroad. Whitney, incidentally, was one of Pulitzer's few intimate friends. Later, he exposed the ice-trust scandals, involving the mayor of New York, Charles F. Murphy of Tammany Hall, and several prominent millionaires; the issue presently was forgotten.

In the presidential campaign of 1904, Pulitzer charged President Theodore Roosevelt with securing campaign contributions from the great trusts, and from those financiers whom he was soon to arraign as "malefactors of great wealth." This charge Pulitzer was able to substantiate, three years later, by printing, on the first page of his paper, a letter from E. H. Harriman to his lawyer, filched from the financier's files, in which Harriman revealed the President's appeal to him for financial assistance. The moral effect upon Roosevelt was nil—for the public seemed to feel that having trimmed a magnate the honors were his. Realizing this, Pulitzer made no further attack on the President, but concentrated on a campaign keyed to the slogan that "Harriman must go." The financier's reorganization of the Chicago and Alton Railroad—Pulitzer denounced it as a swindle—provided a suitable springboard, and public sentiment was behind Pulitzer. But Harriman was too powerfully entrenched to be dislodged. Such ventures as this led the historian Harvey Wish to assert, long afterwards, that trial by newspaper became an increasing threat to judicial processes; the invasion of private rights was often without redress for the injured.

Yet in one instance, Pulitzer performed a notable public service, and was directly responsible for a permanent and thoroughgoing reform. This originated in the *World's* masterly exposure of the corrupt practices of the gigantic insurance corporations centering in New York City, which led to an investigation by Charles Evans Hughes that launched him upon his distinguished public career. The *World* delved into the affairs of the Equitable, the Mutual, and the New York Life, large advertisers, and institutions generally held to be above suspicion. It came up with a mess of financial chicanery and political corruption that shocked the whole nation. The public learned that George W. Perkins, a vice-president of the New York Life and a Morgan partner —he was to be campaign manager for Theodore Roosevelt in the Progressive revolt of 1912—had handled corruption funds in the common interest of the insurance companies, employed to buy or suppress laws. It learned that E. H. Harriman, through improper access to the funds of the Equitable, had been able to acquire control of the Southern Pacific system, and build a personal fortune of seventy-five million dollars. Besides Harriman, and the heads of the insurance companies, the scandal eventually involved the elder J. P. Morgan and Thomas F. Ryan, and touched the reputation of ex-President Grover Cleveland. New York state was in the hands of the Republican party; no malefactor was sent to prison. But Hughes drew, and secured the passage of, two laws which thoroughly reformed insurance practices, broke up interlocking relationships with high finance, took the corporations out of politics and protected the policy holders.

The last sensational exposure made by the *World* during Pulitzer's lifetime once more brought him into conflict with Theodore Roosevelt, and threatened him with a criminal indictment on the novel charge of libeling the United States. This was the so-called "Panama scandal." It related to the circumstances in which President Theodore Roosevelt, in 1903, had acquired the right to build the Panama Canal. Pulitzer had, at the time, protested Roosevelt's action as an outrage. A revolution had been engineered in the Colombian province of Panama. A defunct French canal company had received, from the United States government, forty million dollars for its "rights." The new republic of Panama had been paid ten million dollars for cession of the Canal Zone.

In all these arrangements there had figured, somewhat mysteriously, William Nelson Cromwell, a New York lawyer well known for successful corporate "reorganizations." During the unsuccessful negotiations with Colombia that had preceded the Panamanian revolution, Cromwell had acquired control of the Panama Railroad. After the revolution he, with the elder J. P. Morgan, was appointed fiscal agent of the new Panamanian government. In 1908, on the eve of the presidential election, a startling story came to the *World*. It alleged that Cromwell had formed an American syndicate which had grossly profited on both the forty-million-dollar and ten-million-dollar payments. Among the members of this syndicate, the story asserted, were Douglas Robinson, brother-in-law of President Theodore Roosevelt, and Charles P. Taft, brother of the Republican nominee for the presidency.

The *World* broke the story. Subsequent developments led to the publication of a long article implying that Roosevelt had been guilty of collusion with Cromwell's alleged syndicate. Roosevelt, about to retire from office, countered with a threat to have the United States government send Pulitzer to prison for defaming his country. The case reached the Supreme Court in 1911, just before Pulitzer's death, and the indictment was quashed. Meanwhile, it had given the *World* a prominence that no other occasion ever supplied and placed it definitely out of comparison with the Hearst newspapers; for this was something they could not imitate or follow. But the public never learned the answer to Pulitzer's question—"who got the money?"

How much, indeed, was Pulitzer a defender of popular rights, regardless of party interests or relationships? How far did he genuinely represent "the people," the "aristocracy of labor"? His personality was enigmatic, complex, and even he may not always have known the true motives of his actions. A public champion of international peace, he once confessed, with respect to the Spanish-American War, that he had rather liked the idea of a war—not a big one—but one that would arouse interest and give him a chance to gauge the reflex in his circulation figures! In the Populist uprising, and in William Jennings Bryan's platform of 1896, Pulitzer saw nothing but a dangerous revolutionary tendency. Later, he was privately to deplore anything that bred discontent and socialism among the masses of the poor. He approved the principle of the founding fathers that a President should not be elected by the masses, and would have had the chief executive chosen by electors specially selected for their superior coolness and eminence, and actually forbidden to meet together. He came to think that the republic was safe despite its wealth, however in need of progress and reform, and that the power of financiers was only financial, and not political. He was inflexibly opposed to every phase of populism and socialism and believed in true democratic ideas as the hope of the republic. And he thought President Taft quite radical enough! Yet, in a letter to his managing editor written just before his death, and commenting on the *World's* treatment of a labor dispute, he said: "Generally speaking my sympathies are with the people, and with the strikers even in a just cause. But it is not necessary to show such interest nor such treatment." Contradiction could scarcely go further.

In private life, Pulitzer's blindness and his neuroses made him a fabulous eccentric. Tortured by insomnia, the slightest noise drove him frantic, and he became obsessed with a determination to achieve absolute quiet. It led to some peculiar results. When traveling, on steamers and in hotels, the rooms above, below, and adjoining his suite were retained in his name, to be left unoccupied. His yacht, the *Liberty*, was specially designed to provide undisturbed silence. At "Chatwold," his Bar Harbor residence, there was a huge granite pile called, by the unfortunate secretaries who shared it with him, the "Tower of Silence." To the vast Italianate palace on Seventy-third Street, New York, built for him by McKim, Mead and White at the turn of the century, he added a single-story annex, double walled and ventilated through the chimney: it was so still as to be uncanny. He hoped to pass his few remaining years in that palace—which contained, among other splendors, a great library; a ballroom that was not used; a swimming pool allowed to go permanently dry; an octagonal dining room completely surrounded by other rooms and ventilated by a glass dome supported on pale green columns of Irish marble. But although so magnificently quartered he spent, at most, only a few weeks of the spring or autumn in his palace. Wherever he settled, a demon of restlessness always evicted him.

So he spent his later years ceaselessly moving, from one home to another, or aboard his yacht, accompanied by a major-domo and six secretaries, two of whom were always on duty. One of them remarked that Pulitzer saw as much of his wife and children as he could; but the intensity of his family emotions was such that they could only be given rein at the price of sleepless nights, savage pain, and desperate weariness. Tall, broad-shouldered, emaciated, with a reddish-grey beard and dark hair flecked with white, it was his eyes that people always remembered: one was dull and half closed, the other was of a deep, brilliant blue which, so far from suggesting blindness, created the instant effect of a searching, eagle-like glance. His personal entourage and his editors had constantly to exercise caution to avoid offending his prejudices and wounding his susceptibilities. In personal intercourse, he was always interesting, seldom companionable, taking all he could from the minds of others, but rarely giving much back, his method being to dispute and to reap the benefits of an aroused defense.

His secretaries were required, during their leisure hours, to read, digest, sometimes to commit to memory, enormous quantities of printed matter with which to keep Pulitzer occupied during their tours of duty. One of them—Alleyne Ireland—recorded that his personal experiences and observations were no longer his own—"they belonged to some one else, to the blind man in whose service I was pledged to a vicarious absorption of 'material.'" On one occasion Pulitzer complained of feeling utterly tired out mentally. Ireland inquired whether he should stop talking. Pulitzer's reply was an emphatic negative: "Never stop talking or reading, I must have something to occupy my mind all the time, however exhausted I am." Could any condition of mind be worse than that in which the constant flogging of a tired brain was the only anodyne for its morbid irritability?

Pulitzer delighted in refashioning the habits of thought of the men closely associated with him—and for this tyrannical purpose no form of duplicity was too cruel. At the *World*, it was his habit always to require two men on the same job and to then let them fight it out. The policy, according to his associate and official biographer, Don C. Seitz, never worked. But, thought it often led to his discomfiture and despair, Pulitzer could never be persuaded to abandon it. Theodore Dreiser, who for a period worked as a space writer on the *World*, later recalled the atmosphere of suspicion, jealousy, and intrigue that Pulitzer's policy generated in the city room. There was, Dreiser thought, "something disillusioning in the sharp contrast between the professed ideals and preachments of such a constantly moralizing journal as the *World* and the heartless and savage aspect of its internal economy. There was no time off for the space men, unless it was for all time. One was expected to achieve the results desired or get out; and if one did achieve them the reward was nothing." Another novelist, David Graham Phillips, after personal association with Pulitzer as an editorial writer, produced a portrait of him in *The Great God Success* which was far from affectionate, and which keenly hurt the sitter. Had he not been very fond of Phillips, and striven hard to develop in him a fitness for first place on the paper? But to develop a personal affection for Pulitzer one needed a godlike compassion. The only road he knew to the human heart passed through rough territory.

The posthumous fate of Pulitzer's enterprises was ironical. All his fierce attachment was given to the morning *World*; he cared little for its evening counterpart, and scarcely even kept in touch with the St. Louis *Post-Dispatch*. The morning *World* he wanted to be more powerful than the President. It was to go on, through the years, free to tell the truth and perform every service that should be performed in the public interest. After his death, it met with vicissitude. Eventually, it ceased publication. The evening *World* survived—but only as the New York organ of the Scripps-Howard chain. But the *Post-Dispatch* continued to prosper under his heirs, and remained a power in its territory. Pulitzer's proud architectural monument in Newspaper Row was soon dwarfed by towers far more pretentious, and passed to other uses than that for which it was built. The noble palace where he so seldom resided was converted into luxury apartments. It was as if all traces of his personality were condemned to be erased.

But his fame was preserved by the School of Journalism which he endowed at Columbia University. And the public, every year, was reminded of his name by the award of annual prizes provided for in his will. These rewarded newspapers for disinterested and meritorious public service; reporters for the accomplishment of some public good; cartoonists for excellence of a similar kind. They were bestowed upon novelists whose work presented the wholesome atmosphere of American life, and the highest standard of American manners and manhood; and upon playwrights whose efforts met this condition; upon authors of the best American biography, teaching patriotic and unselfish service to the people illustrated by an eminent example; upon historians, for the best book of the year on the history of the United States; upon poets who were required merely to produce the best book of verse without reference to patriotism or morals. Annual announcement of the Pulitzer awards was always eagerly awaited, and from some heaven of benevolent tyrants, an implacable spirit may have chuckled in satisfaction—naturally, far from complete.

[2] PROBLEM IN YELLOW

As the twentieth century aged, splendor deserted the American social scene. The palaces at Newport stood shuttered and vacant. Fifth Avenue was a palisade of clustered towers. Those few ornate mansions which had survived their era seemed patiently to await the wreckers. Change sometimes struck the note of irony. On Long Island, it was a mission of Russian proletarians that occupied the former home of Pierpont Morgan.

But, in the plebeian dusk, one altar to magnificence was raised and tended. Lest Americans forget the nature of a princely life, they were furnished an illustration. Since it was likely to be final, ought it not also be supreme? Was not exorbitance a duty? So it appeared, as the memorial to grandeur took form through two decades—realizing the architecture of fantasy, absorbing the pillage of centuries long past. Was this a residence, a museum, a monument, or a tomb? Beyond his eightieth year, William Randolph Hearst continued to perfect San

Simeon, continued to hold court there. Almost unanimously, visitors described it as "out of this world." It was.

The domain of San Simeon was about half the size of the State of Rhode Island, and stretched for fifty miles along the California coast, midway between San Francisco and Los Angeles. At its center, on an "enchanted hill," a fabulous congeries of white buildings dazzled the eye; the master's great house, twin towered, like a Spanish mission; the three guest houses that were as large as palaces; the various play houses. Thirty guests might be in residence, or fifty, or even a hundred. The master liked to surround himself with ambassadors and ministers, with frivolous royalties and pampered courtiers. Such they ought to have been, to be worthy of the background created for them, the way of life to which they were admitted. Only the times were at fault; not the host. Could he be blamed because the plenipotentiaries were no more than prosaic executives, administrators of his far-flung empire? Because the charming prodigals were only Hollywood folk, gay youths and pretty ladies? Had plebeian America yielded an aristocracy superior to these, would he not have summoned it to his court?

At San Simeon, an exquisite informality prevailed. It was true that "you never know all your fellow guests, who wander about exchanging vague nods." Yet only the unworldly would fail to be at ease; and "eventually some one greets you." The obligations were few: attendance at the rituals of luncheon, dinner, and the nightly film show in a regal theater. For the rest, "the newcomer is left to his own devices, and the casualness of the day is baffling."

Baffling? Had a crassly regimented world obliterated caprice? Here, whim alone reigned. Pleasure depended upon imagination, nothing more: you simply had to lift the nearest telephone to ask for an automobile, a tennis professional, a drink, a fishing outfit, or a cowboy to ride with. And were there not, at hand, the inexhaustible wonders of the enchanted hill, awaiting exploration? The colonnaded gardens. The outdoor swimming pool large enough to sail a boat on, fed by a fountain resembling the splendid fountains of Michelangelo. The subterranean gymnasium, beneath the tennis courts, with its golden-galleried indoor pool walled and roofed in Venetian glass mosaic. The majestic library. The opulent private suites in which visitors were quartered—"a guest sleeps in Cardinal Richelieu's bed, opens his eyes to gaze upon a Goya, reaches for a Camel in an alabaster box set on an ancient cassone." In their closets, guests found complete wardrobes, anticipating the entire repertory of activities available for their pleasure. One ungrateful criticism was sometimes made by insomniacs, disturbed by the howling of wild beasts under their windows: the royal menagerie was, perhaps, a trifle too close.

Guests were instructed to assemble in the great hall at seven-thirty. In this immense, lofty room, filled like all others with priceless objects of art, they awaited the arrival of the master, while butlers passed among them with cocktails. Sometimes he did not descend from his Gothic study until nine, or later. For he still worked, and he worked hard; the air around him was thick with flying messages. In a remote part of the building, telephones rang incessantly, teletypes chattered, telegraph instruments clicked; a chief secretary and his staff transmitted orders, decisions, policies, gathered news, prepared the master's clip sheets; all day and almost all night people came in and went out. Of this perpetual bustle, guests saw very little. They waited until a secret panel in the wall of the great hall opened, and the master appeared from a carved elevator said to be hung with paintings. He was a tall, powerful man, once slender and erect, now slightly stooped and paunchy. He had a long face like a horse, a thick neck, big clumsy bones. A guest might never, during the course of his stay, be formally presented. But, should an introduction be effected, one noticed that "when he turns to look at you his ice-cold blue eyes bore into your soul."

Presently, the court moved into the vast refectory that was the master's artistic pride. There, seated at long antique tables, they feasted on superb food, served amid priceless silver, ketchup bottles, jams and jellies in great profusion in homely labeled jars. These unlovely containers, like the paper napkins so surprising to the uninitiated, were not a humorous conceit but a sentimental piety: in boyhood, with his father, the master had camped out on this very spot. But the refectory itself sufficiently demonstrated that Hearst, living literally like a king, had been the nation's number one spender, surpassing Mr. Ford with his schoolhouses and Mr. Mellon with his paintings. Its richly carved ceiling came from a North Italian sixteenth-century monastery and was the finest of his vast collection of carved ceilings. The walls of the huge hall were paneled with choir stalls taken from a Spanish cathedral; a fire blazed in an historic, monumental French Gothic fireplace; far above, there hung silken Sienese palio banners softly fluttering from each side of the walls between the high windows. The effect was overpowering. Afterwards, the private theater where movies were shown seemed almost cosy, although it might easily seat two hundred; was hung with an antique, crimson, Italian brocatelle; and was illuminated by *torchères* affixed to huge caryatides, walnut and gold.

After the movies, the court filed back to the great hall. Sometimes, the master tarried with them briefly before ascending to his own quarters. In conversation, he confirmed a notion that had become legendary. Strongly emotional, apparently sincere in his professions, his talk made clear that he was no devotee of the science of ethics, that he was, indeed, peculiarly amoral. What wonder that he was known far and wide for his opinions, not his standards; that his editorial world was a world of sharp focus lacking the light and shadow of profound moral conviction?

Did this lack of moral feeling have any relation to an inflexible rule at San Simeon—that death must never be mentioned in his presence? Did he superstitiously fear what might lie across its threshold? Or, believing that it opened only on extinction, did he resent its finality? Unlike ancient monarchs who chose to inhabit their ostentatious tombs, he could not be comforted by a belief that his accumulations would accompany him. Yet accumulation had always been his mastering passion. It was the sole architect of his incredible empire. It was the real spur to collections of art as stupendous as they were indiscriminate. After filling five lordly establishments, these had once overflowed into a city block of warehouses. Enough still remained to crowd a vaultlike cave under the enchanted hill. And who could say what obscure urgency accounted for his insatiable lust to possess?

Perhaps not even Hearst himself. Certainly not the American people, to whom, for more than fifty years, he had represented many things, from best to worst—and, throughout, had never ceased to be an enigma. During the first decade of the century he was, next to Theodore Roosevelt, the most spectacular and debated figure in the American political arena. On him centered the hopes of the discontented, the underprivileged, the oppressed; and, for a time, his dreaded shadow overhung the White House. At other times, a whirlwind of popular hatred threatened to destroy him. His papers were widely boycotted; in many towns, angry mobs hanged him in effigy. The socialist Upton Sinclair predicted Hearst's election as first Socialist President of the United States; later declared that of nothing in his whole life was he more ashamed than having believed in Hearst. A long line of eminent Americans from Theodore Roosevelt onward denounced

Hearst, generally as an enemy of everything that is nobiest and best in our American tradition. Yet in 1946 the American Legion awarded to him its distinguished service medal, as "an outstanding American" universally known for his "intense patriotism." During the first half of the century, no American in public life evoked more violent oscillations of feelings, more intemperate extremes of judgment. Whatever the "real truth" about Hearst, one fact was undeniable. He continued to challenge the imagination of the American people. It could neither take him, nor let him alone.

Those who tried to explain Hearst—whether for good or for evil—usually started from the premise that he was something unique in American civilization. Was not this a mistake? True, he was exceptionally favored. Great inherited wealth endowed him with almost unlimited opportunity. Granted the possession of creative ambitions, he was in a position to realize them; and he could put his philosophy to the test of actual practice. Early in the century William Graham Sumner, who believed ethics to be purely relative, deplored the moral anarchy which occurred when men's conduct was based on expediency, and ran counter to their genuine convictions. This condition appeared to be exemplified by the great tycoons of Sumner's generation. But what would happen if a belief in expediency became the only genuine conviction which men retained? If, being absolute materialists, they used moral and social ideals merely as instruments to achieve their private aims? Did not Hearst supply the answers to these questions? Even so, he was scarcely unique. He illustrated, on a high stage, on a national scale, the results of a commonly accepted attitude to life. Many Americans had adopted the philosophy of expediency; sincerely believed that whatever "worked" was true, right, and good; wanted nothing more than wealth or power, the two goals exalted by the society in which they lived. Hearst merely got there first, and more spectacularly. He may have been only the most conspicuous of American pragmatists.

Hearst's parents were very unlike in temperament and outlook, and he was strongly influenced by both. His father, George Hearst, had emigrated to California in the gold rush. One of the original sharers in the celebrated Comstock Lode, the elder Hearst went on to acquire interests in gold and copper mines, as well as vast properties in California and Mexico. Typically the robber baron of his time, he soon found, like his colleagues James G. Fair and Leland Stanford, that his enormous holdings made a political career desirable. To further this, he bought the *Examiner*, a San Francisco newspaper, and made himself a power in municipal and state affairs. He died a member of the United States Senate, to which an obedient machine had elevated him for the better protection of his property.

Before accepting wealth and an elderly husband, Hearst's mother had been a schoolteacher. A gentlewoman by birth and breeding, she tried to counteract the father's influence on their son. George Hearst furnished a prime example of hard practicality and ruthless methods, but his wife had a sensitive conscience which asserted the social obligations of great wealth. Resolutely, she attempted to saturate the boy with "culture"; to imbue him with a love of art; to inculcate in him the sentimental idealism which she applied to a wide range of philanthropies. Hearst's temper and methods were to be those of his father. But it was his mother who inspired his early interest in "reform," and who awakened an uneasy respect for culture which later made him secure, for his papers, many of the most distinguished literary talents of the time.

Hearst was sent to a fashionable school in the East. It did not seek to persuade him to stay. He entered Harvard where, according to his contemporary George Santayana, he was little esteemed by the student body. His plebeian origin, unconventional ways, and prodigal extravagance displeased the undergraduate mind, for which a standard was set by Beacon Hill. But Hearst's budding powers as a newspaper owner and manager made him invaluable to the *Lampoon*, which he rescued from financial disaster. The rebuffs administered by social snobbery merely provoked him to greater flagrancy. He was suspended for a time; finally, he was expelled. The bitter contempt which the Hearst press later lavished on Eastern Society, and on academic institutions and their faculties, may well have had its source in his unsatisfying experience at Harvard.

Upon leaving Harvard, Hearst went to New York. There he made a thorough study of the methods and policies which Joseph Pulitzer was using to secure mass circulation for the *World*. Returning to San Francisco, Hearst in 1887 persuaded his father to let him take over the *Examiner*. The Senator gave his consent reluctantly; he had no high opinion of his son's abilities, and he considered publishing the least amusing of ways to lose money. But Hearst's motives, however eccentric they appeared, were eminently practical. He didn't want to go into any business that would take a long, dull preparation. To him the newspaper business seemed to offer more attractions than any other—more immediate attractions, and as many ultimate rewards. So he said shortly afterwards; the statement illuminated his subsequent career. Newspaper publishing was not, for him, either a public service or a platform, except incidentally. It was a business, conducted for private profit. But it was a business which offered to a wilful, unconventional temperament more opportunities than any other to give free rein to personal impulse—and to make money by doing so.

The soundness of this insight Hearst soon demonstrated in San Francisco, with a journalistic pattern that was later to enable him to reach millions of Americans, the country over, every day, and influence public opinion as no other man, except perhaps the President, was able to do. From the very outset, a Hearst paper reflected the psychology and personality of Hearst himself. Its chief permanent purpose was revenue; its only policy was expediency; its views on public affairs, the actions which it urged or campaigned against, were determined, at any given time, by the impulses and objectives which for the moment happened to be controlling Hearst. Flexibility was the dominant characteristic of a Hearst newspaper; but public memory is short, and few noticed, from month to month, how remarkably inconsistent a lively, volatile sheet could be. Whim easily passed for principle.

Hearst took over from Pulitzer, and developed to an extreme perfection of which Pulitzer was never capable, the chief ingredients of yellow journalism. Lurid stories; juicy scandals; provocative, strident headlines; the discovery of a fresh sensation every day: with these he arrested attention, gained readers. When the day's events yielded nothing sensational, Hearst newsmen created the news—dreamed up a sensation or actually produced one. To reach the hearts of the naïve, Hearst incubated the first "sob sister" in journalistic history, and developed a long, able line of successors. To capture the hasty, he fostered the talents of men who were to become America's most powerful cartoonists: Homer Davenport, T. A. Dorgan, Bud Fisher. To woo the literate, he secured features from the most celebrated writers. His golden net snared Mark Twain, Rudyard Kipling, Jack London, Ambrose Bierce, Stephen Crane; later, such crusaders for reform as Henry George, Ida M. Tarbell, Upton Sinclair, Charles Edward Russell. This youth, half playboy, half rabble rouser, and all embryonic tycoon, who, according to Bierce, looked like an unearthly child and spoke in a voice like the fragrance of violets made audible, decided that any paper which he published had, in one respect, to be unique. Its range of contents must be such as to provide something for every category of intelligence. People might praise the paper or damn it; so long as it was capable of raising their temperature, he didn't especially care what they felt. But a Hearst paper must be one which nobody could, if he chose, ignore.

Like Pulitzer, Hearst saw that vigorous intervention in public affairs would attract circulation. He surmised that, to be effective, it ought to combine attack, exposure, and the appeal to principle which is always so persuasive to the righteous. Truculence, scandal, and moral idealism composed a new formula. The brew proved to be as intoxicating as he anticipated. The plain people swallowed it and seethed. Then they rolled up their shirt sleeves and tried to trounce the miscreant. What came to be called "Hearstism" often roughly interfered with the accepted economic and political processes of the nation. It crystallized into a threatening force the blind need and ignorance and resentment of those at the bottom. It stirred the mire, and brought up a plug-ugly.

As time passed, conservatives, capitalists, large-scale employers of labor, the minions of great corporations in Congress and the state legislatures, all began to declare that the Hearst press represented the very dregs of journalism. Was it not preaching the destruction of the established order, the dissolution of the American system? Hearst papers were banned from homes where carriages stood at the door. But their circulations soared, nevertheless. Hearst got the people. He also got—for a time—the reformers, the radical wing of the intellectuals, the conscience ridden. It was these who, later still, became his most violent detractors.

When, at length, the idealists and reformers deserted Hearst, they could not forgive him for their own mistake. They had assumed him to be, like themselves, pure in heart. He wasn't; he had never really pretended to be. It was an ancient story: "the Jews of old were looking for a Messiah, but they pictured him as a king coming on a throne to do what they wanted done." The reformers wanted a Parsifal. When they found that they had a very sullied Lancelot, their indignation boiled over. They protested that Hearst had deluded them. They had merely deceived themselves. Hearst needed no Richard Wagner to show him that a pure idealist may also be a pure fool. It was one of his earliest intuitions.

As a reformer, Hearst always conformed to a pattern of realism which became evident during his first intervention in public affairs. Not long after taking over the *Examiner*, he launched a ferocious attack on the Southern Pacific Railroad. This Huntington-Stanford-Crocker enterprise was the malevolent "octopus" of the Far West. It dominated politics and the economy. It was an outstanding enemy of democracy. It was a major obstacle to the welfare of the plain people. In the end, Hearst's campaign produced valuable results. It brought the railroad up before the Federal government; forced it to pay an ancient debt to the public treasury; reduced its tyrannical power. But an odd, perhaps significant, intermission had occurred in Hearst's attack. Why, having dropped the issue, had he revived it? Some reporters asked old Collis P. Huntington. Sourly, the magnate told them. It was, he said, because "we won't keep him on the payroll." The Southern Pacific had agreed to pay Hearst thirty thousand dollars "in order to enjoy immunity from hostility in the columns of the *Examiner*." The attack had been dropped; when the railroad reneged, Hearst promptly resumed it.

Did this mean, as Representative Johnson of California charged on the floor of Congress, that Hearst was "a common, ordinary, everyday blackmailer—a low highwayman of the newspaper world"? Not necessarily. But it signified other things, more important to the nation, and seldom comprehensible to idealists. It indicated that Hearst, when he went into battle against privilege, was primarily fighting for Hearst. Also, it suggested that Hearst was fighting privilege with the weapons of privilege. A crusader against the plutocracy who adopted the methods of Morgans and Rockefellers and their like—this was a novelty indeed! Many Americans found it perplexing. They preferred their reformers to use only "clean" methods. They really liked their Morgans and Rockefellers to profess only good motives; to uphold Christian morality even when failing to exemplify it. From the very outset, Hearst looked like a moral maverick.

The plain people didn't care. Hearst was fighting against privilege; they were ready to adopt him as their champion. But other good Americans became increasingly troubled, as his crusades progressed, because these were often accompanied by a noise notably unlike the fragrance of violets made audible. For them, Hearst raised an ethical issue. Do good ends justify the use of means that are dubious, if not downright immoral? Studying Hearst after he had become a power in national politics, Lincoln Steffens reported that he seemed "to think that democracy is an end in itself, and that the end justifies the means—his journalism." This, Steffens surmised, meant that "to give us a better government he would make us a worse people." Such, too, was the verdict reached by many Americans sympathetic to the reforms which Hearst's early crusades supported.

Yet was not Hearst a typical product of the system whose other typical products he was so savagely attacking? The important thing about him, as Steffens acknowledged many years later, was that he suffered from no moral illusions; he understood that in the life of society it is economic, rather than moral, forces that count. The American system of free enterprise had made possible the rise to power of Morgans and Rockefellers, by methods often profoundly immoral. And the system also asserted that social welfare is contingent upon unrestricted private profit. Now it appeared that abridgement of the privileges enjoyed by the powerful could be had—at a price. The price was the aggrandizement of Hearst. Would the American people be any better off if the powers of Morgans and Rockefellers were curbed—and seized—by a Hearst? This was the real question which Hearst raised. It was also a question which nobody thought to ask.

From San Francisco, Hearst moved on to New York. His object was to vanquish Pulitzer, and to conquer the East. Senator Hearst, apparently distrusting his son's reckless extravagance, had vested control of his seventeen-million-dollar estate in his widow. Borrowing on his inheritance, Hearst flung millions into his long, historic duel with Pulitzer. He raided the brilliant staff which Pulitzer had assembled: in one day, Hearst captured Morrill Goddard, the "yellow" genius of Pulitzer's Sunday magazine; Pulitzer bought him back; Hearst bought him again, and kept him. Eventually, he acquired Arthur Brisbane, who was to become the most widely read editorial writer in the country. Brisbane had prestige among the intellectuals and reformers. His father, Albert Brisbane, had been one of the earliest American socialists, a member of the celebrated colony at Brook Farm, whose book *The Social Destiny of Man* was admiringly remembered. Arthur Brisbane was a man of many talents, not all of which were praiseworthy. But one was to prove extremely valuable to Hearst; Brisbane's ability to talk politics and philosophy in the language of truckmen. This ability, which became Hearst's principal instrument for influencing public opinion, ultimately made Brisbane a millionaire, a quasi-partner of his employer, and the most highly paid of American journalists, with a reputed annual salary of a quarter of a million dollars. During the forty years of their association, it was often stated that "the Hearst of today is, to a great degree, the product of Mr. Arthur Brisbane." Nothing could have been further from the truth. The ideas were Hearst's. Brisbane was a reputation, a signature: a stooge.

From his duel with Pulitzer, Hearst emerged as the undisputed master of mass journalism. And he had also become a man of power in national politics. In the bitter Presidential campaign of 1896, Hearst supported Bryan against McKinley. He was almost the only newspaper owner of national prominence who took this stand, and it made him the outstanding champion of the common people in their grim rebellion against the money power and big business. He was preaching democracy, government ownership, nationalism. In San Francisco and New York, he was attacking local combines; on the national scene, the great trusts. The savage, brilliant cartoons in which Homer Davenport portrayed Mark Hanna as a corpulent plutocrat covered with dollar marks, McKinley sitting on his knee like a ventriloquist's dummy—these swept the country, fanned class hatred into flame. Was not Hearst the most implacable enemy of the established order? So, indeed, it seemed. Few recalled that Senator Hearst's estate included vast holdings in silver mines. Bryan had declared for the free coinage of silver.

After McKinley had been installed in the White House, Hearst determined to intervene in foreign policy. Conscientious Americans had long been appalled by tales of Spanish misrule and cruelty in Cuba. Capitalists foresaw profit in the economic development of a backward island, should it achieve independence. An insurrection was brewing in Cuba. Should the United States intervene; if necessary, go to war? Opinion over the country was oddly divided. McKinley and Mark Hanna, the accredited spokesmen of big business, were against war. So were men like Mark Twain, William Dean Howells, William James; no friends to unbridled capitalism. Theodore Roosevelt, already a shining symbol of social reform, wanted war. William Graham Sumner, who taught that reform was a delusion, preached against war. In Washington, old Henry Adams, convinced that civilization was rapidly going to hell and that nothing could be done about it, amused himself by devising political strategy for the Cuban revolutionary junta. In this confused atmosphere, Hearst arrived at a very practical deduction. A war would boost newspaper circulation; a war provided the liveliest of issues. Hearst wanted war. He sent the painter Frederick Remington to Cuba for pictures of "a gallant revolution." Remington found no revolution, and so informed him. Hearst's reply told the whole story: "You furnish the pictures and I'll furnish the war."

If Hearst did not actually furnish the war, he did, at least, whip public sentiment into a frenzy that made war inevitable. Hearst newsmen industriously created news designed to inflame hatred against Spain. Girl-martyrs to Spanish lust were invented, and their pitiable stories spread over the land. The fabulous exploits of an imaginary group of American volunteers provided another sensation. An indiscreet private letter of the Spanish Ambassador was filched from the Havana post office; Hearst played it up as the "worst insult to the United States in its history." When war was finally declared, Hearst had the best correspondents in the field; debonair Richard Harding Davis, who became a national hero, and masterly James Creelman.

He pushed the "journalism of action" to unprecedented limits. After Manila had surrendered, it was rumored that a Spanish fleet was setting out for the Philippines by way of the Suez Canal. Hearst promptly chartered a vessel, sent it to the Suez Canal under British colors, and ordered it sunk there should the Spainsh fleet try to pass. That this project violated international law and might have brought on war with Great Britain apparently caused him no qualms. But when the war was over, Hearst had accomplished his aim. He had the largest circulation in the country. Only an old-fashioned publicist like Edwin Lawrence Godkin would predict the death of democracy from the fact that "a blackguard boy with several millions of dollars at his disposal has more influence on the use a great nation may make of its credit, of its army and navy, of its name and traditions, than all the statesmen and philosophers and professors in the country." For was not this the new journalism, freshly minted for the new century?

From the cresting wave of his success, Hearst suddenly sank into ignominy. Renewing his campaign against McKinley as the puppet of monopoly and Wall Street, he carried it to a pitch of virulence that shocked decent folk. What did he mean by publishing a verse which prophesied that a bullet was speeding "to stretch McKinley on his bier"? What did he mean by declaring, editorially, that "if bad intentions and bad men can be got rid of only by killing, then killing must be done"? Was he merely trying to sound the warning that monopoly and contempt for the common people bred anarchy?

When the President was assassinated by a supposed anarchist, Hearst was branded as an accomplice. In many towns, he was hanged or burned in effigy. The Grand Army of the Republic—predecessor of the American Legion which so long afterwards was to honor his patriotism—instituted a boycott of his papers. Theodore Roosevelt, McKinley's successor in the White House, whose career had been enormously advanced by the war which Hearst helped to precipitate, singled him out for opprobrium. In his message to Congress, the new President castigated "those who, on the stump and in the public press, appeal to the dark and evil spirits of malice and greed, envy and sullen hatred." Nobody had to ask whom he meant. Hearst took to working with a revolver beside him.

Yet his circulations continued to mount. Labor was with him; the submerged populations of the great cities; the discontented farmers. And William Jennings Bryan, still their "peerless leader," was with him too. Bryan suggested that he invade Chicago, and when he did so rewarded him with the presidency of the National Association of Democratic Clubs. Organized labor invited him to establish a paper in Los Angeles, a notoriously anti-labor city, and he did. Why not go into politics? He began to organize the Democratic clubs as an instrument for his own political advancement. Making a deal with Charles F. Murphy, the Tammany boss, he had himself elected to Congress. There, however, he could not be kept fettered to his desk, but as often as possible escaped to the outside world. He had seven papers, now; if he made few speeches in Congress, through them he spoke in a masterful way to millions. Already, he was looking to 1904, and the next Presidential election. A political leader, who was to keep the country in a turmoil for a decade, had been born.

The Hearst press now intensified its attack on privilege, monopoly, corporate power, the "plunderbund' of great bankers, the trusts. Hearst's new campaigns spread over a wide area of the nation's economic life. They paved the way for the more accurate and scholarly reports of S. S. McClure's brilliant staff of muckrakers. They also registered substantial practical accomplishment. He had exposed the "embalmed beef" scandal of the recent war; turning again to the beef trust, he attacked its terrorization of competitors, brought lawsuits against the packers, and forced an injunction on them. In the great coal strike, he intervened on behalf of the miners led by John Mitchell, and ultimately secured Federal action against the coal trust. In New York, he succeeded in jailing the president of the ice trust. In Chicago, he associated himself with Clarence Darrow and John Peter Altgeld in their fight for municipal ownership of public utilities and other reforms. And, simultaneously, the advertising columns of the Hearst press were open to manufacturers of poisonous patent medicines, to houses of assignation, to promoters of fraudulent stock schemes; its editorial opinions on matters theatrical—as the journalist Will Irwin soon proved—were nakedly for sale.

Meanwhile, anxiety rose in the citadels of conservatism. Dangerous enough as a publicist, where would political aspiration carry this "millionaire radical"? The Morgans and Rockefellers understood the ominous implications of his political creed. "Combination and organization are necessary steps in industrial progress," Hearst declared. "We are advancing toward a complete organization in which the government will stand at the head and be the trust of trusts. It is ridiculous to attempt to stop this development." But—wasn't this socialism?

To the plain people, the damning label of socialism seemed irrelevant. They agreed with Hearst that "the government of the nation . . . is no longer a government of the people organized for their own betterment. It has degenerated into a corporation of organized monopoly operating . . . for the enrichment of a small predatory class." Certainly it was true, as a contemporary publication alleged, that the Hearst "movement" stood "for every phase of social and economic discontent. It has its tinge of fanaticism. In the minds of many adherents of it, the movement is idealistic and Utopian."

Yet this was nothing new. In the American political arena all reform movements—originating in frustration, and inimical to things-as-they-are—were idealistic, and in some sense utopian. For what was more utopian than the American dream itself, the hope of a truly democratic way of life? The element of novelty in the Hearst movement lay in another quarter: the frame of mind of the people who flocked to it. Here were Americans, millions of them, who had seemingly abandoned the traditional form of American political action. They felt it useless to join with their fellow citizens in dealing with public problems at first hand. They had resolved to look to a single individual to deal with social and political ills. They were ready to delegate responsibility for the content and context of individual life to a kindly paternal government. Was this a merely transient despair? Or was it a permanent disillusion with the democratic method of achieving democratic ideals?

Hearst offered himself to the Democratic convention of 1904 as a candidate for the Presidential nomination. His cause was pleaded by Clarence Darrow, and although he failed to capture the nomination, he secured a sufficient number of votes to establish him as a prospective claimant. In the following year, having broken with Tammany Hall, he ran for mayor of New York City as the candidate of a third party that was little more than his personal machine; yet he enlisted the support of many eminent citizens who saw in him a vigorous foe of corruption, an upright champion of reform. In the election, the Tammany forces resorted to fraud; officially, Hearst was defeated by thirty-five hundred votes. A year later, again as the candidate of his own party, Hearst ran for governor of New York. The eyes of the whole nation were on him; it was clear that, if elected, nothing could stop his nomination for the Presidency in 1908. Charles Evans Hughes, fresh from his meteoric rise to fame as prosecutor of the insurance ring, was drafted to oppose Hearst. President Theodore Roosevelt personally intervened in the whirlwind, frenzied campaign. A rising tide of Hearstism threatened to sweep the state. On election night, the nation anxiously awaited the New York returns. Hearst was defeated— but by less than sixty thousand votes.

While the campaign raged, Hearst had in his possession material which might have won him the governorship of New York, and put him far on the road to the White House. For two years, humble employes of the Standard Oil Company had rifled the files of the corporation by night; brought correspondence to the Hearst offices, where it was photographed; replaced it in the files before morning. The letters were deeply incriminating. Most of them were written by, or addressed to, John D. Archbold, vice-president of Standard Oil, and they proved that certain Senators and Representatives were stipendiaries of the corporation, retained and paid to protect its legislative interests. Hearst began issuing these letters during the Presidential campaign of 1908, and continued their publication over four years. They shocked the country. They caused panic in high quarters. Even President Roosevelt found it necessary to summon Hearst to the White House—he wished to be assured that none of the correspondence contained material that could be interpreted to his discredit. Why had not Hearst released these letters during his campaign? Apparently, because he had political affiliations with some of the individuals involved, and at that time was in no position to expose them. But, after all the material had been published, a less agreeable question was flung at him. Why—with so much authentic and incontrovertible evidence in his possession—had he found it necessary to perpetrate, and play up, five cleverly forged letters? That they were forged, *Collier's* established beyond doubt, thus exposing Hearst in his own most spectacular exposure. But the question was never answered.

The Hearst with whom a later generation of Americans were to become familiar emerged at the outbreak of the First World War. Before the United States joined the Allies, Hearst strongly championed the German cause, defending unrestricted submarine warfare, protesting against the "draining of our food supplies and military supplies to Europe." After the United States entered the conflict, the Hearst press continued to derogate the Allies, and defended the Germans as often as possible. Theodore Roosevelt asserted that Hearst was "doing his best to weaken the effect of our war against Germany." Other spokesmen for the nation's military effort charged him with conveying "the subtle poison of insidiously disloyal utterances," and declared that "his power for evil is immeasurable." A boycott of Hearst papers spread widely. Once again he was hanged and burned in effigy. A Senate investigation established a connection between the Hearst press and German agents in the United States. It also revealed that certain Hearst employees were on the payroll of the German government.

In 1927, the Hearst press tried to precipitate a war with Mexico. In this instance, it was clear that Hearst had his own interests at heart. He owned vast properties in Mexico; immense ranches, valuable mines. And the Mexican government, under President Calles, was putting into effect the policy of expropriating foreign holdings decreed by the revolutionary Constitution. A beginning was being made with the properties of the oil companies. Hearst alleged a Mexican plot against the United States, purportedly involving the bribing of four Senators, two of them being the "insurgents" William E. Borah and George W. Norris. The Senate promptly opened an investigation. Hearst's documents, offered in evidence, proved to be clumsy forgeries. When their fraudulency had been absolutely established, Hearst admitted it as a possibility. Nevertheless, he insisted, "the essential facts contained in the documents were not fabricated"—though these "facts" existed nowhere else. After the investigation closed, Senator Norris contemptuously told the nation that "the Hearst system of newspapers, spreading like a venomous web to all parts of our country, constitutes the sewer system of American journalism."

As the years passed, an increasing number of Americans came to share Norris' opinion. For Hearst's activities swiftly darkened; often had a sinister look. In conjunction with certain leading shipbuilding and steel interests, he subsidized the unsavory William B. Shearer, who helped to wreck the Geneva Disarmament Conference called by President Coolidge. In Chicago, he supported the corrupt administration of William Hale Thompson; and in circulation wars there employed gunmen and gangsters to create a reign of terror. In New York, his political creature was Mayor John F. Hylan, a public servant conspicuous neither for intelligence nor integrity. On the national political scene, he effected alliances with the most reactionary elements in both major parties.

He began to preach a new "Americanism." It supported the ill-reputed American Liberty League, and that dubious patriot, Father Coughlin. It was implacably hostile to organized labor. It extolled Adolf Hitler. Hitler, Hearst declared, would "accomplish a measure of good not only for his own people but for all humanity." He affirmed that Hitler was beginning a struggle which all liberty-loving peoples were bound to follow with understanding and sympathy. Was it not natural, therefore, for the Hearst press to publish widely the literary efforts of Herman Goering? Had not Hearst, somewhat earlier, instructed his editors to "disregard, or cover perfunctorily, subjects which are merely important, but not interesting"? Perhaps Goering, as a journalist, was "interesting" in the way that Hitler, as a political leader, was "good." Surely it was ungenerous of critics to point out that the Nazi propaganda division in Berlin had signed a profitable contract for the Hearst news service; to hint that, in return, Hearst might have been willing to assume the role of authorized disseminator of Nazi propaganda in the United States!

Once, the underprivileged classes of the United States had looked to Hearst as their champion, their political savior. But, by the mid-nineteen thirties, to a nationwide radio audience, Hearst was speaking of the proletariat as "without property of any kind, and without the constructive or executive ability to acquire any." Was this class, "which is the least able successfully to manage its own affairs, the best able to manage the affairs of a nation"? Indeed, did "our competent business men, who have built the wealth of this nation, want to be plundered and driven out of business by a thriftless and shiftless crew of organized incompetents"? As for government by the plain people, what else was it than "government by the least capable and the least conscientious element of the community—government by the mob, government by ignorance and avarice"?

For Hearst, who at the outset of his career had professed himself a Jeffersonian Democrat, was pleading, now, for the rule of a Hamiltonian plutocracy. He intended to be the savior of American capitalism. And it was a role for which he was not unsuited. He had inflated his inherited seventeen millions of dollars to some two hundred and twenty millions. Outside the field of publishing, his properties were stupendous. In the business of publishing, he could be described as a one-man trust. He was estimated to have thirty million readers in America. He owned twenty-nine newspapers in eighteen cities. His Sunday supplement, distributed by other publishers as well as his own papers, covered the entire country. He owned ten magazines, a newspaper syndicate, an international news service. He owned eight radio stations, and he made news films. And what he owned, he owned in person. Like Henry Ford, he had always held his hundreds of millions apart from and above the banks.

Yet it was said of him, at this splendid summit of achievement, that he was an economic anachronism. And this appeared to be true. For, whereas Ford regarded capital as something to be put to work, Hearst had always considered it something to buy things with. Having made his money off the bourgeois world, he treated it as if it came to him by divine right rather than by his own shrewdness. His personal expenses were reputed to run to fifteen million dollars a year. His policy regarding the economic direction of his publishing empire was equally self-indulgent, and absolutely arbitrary. In his whole career, he had sold only one newspaper. "When a Hearst newspaper loses money, the chief may simply toss in some more raw meat in the form of cash. He may change editors, raise hell here and there, but the proposition is never abandoned, no matter how hopeless, so long as it gives him a voice."

In the late nineteen-thirties, rumor predicted the imminent collapse of the Hearst empire. This prediction was premature. The empire did not collapse: there were many creditors, banks and newsprint manufacturers dominating the enterprise who wanted to hold the giant together a while longer. They forced a reorganization, depriving Hearst of financial authority, and assuming it themselves. Six Hearst newspapers were sold or killed. He was divested of a magazine, a news service, six radio stations. Valuable real-estate holdings were put on the market. Large portions of the Hearst art collection were removed from storage and placed on sale in a department store. Gossip asserted that his new financial overlords required drastic economies in his personal expenditures; his allowance was reported as being a paltry five millions a year. But he retained full editorial control of a still vast publishing domain. So he remained a power in the land. To his readers, however, he need no longer seem "almost like a myth." While financiers had been strenuously salvaging the tycoon, artists had been quietly at work on the man. He would not lack immortality of a kind; he had entered the realm of art. William Randolph Hearst, the man, was portrayed, for all who cared to see, in Orson Welles' film, *Citizen Kane*, in Aldous Huxley's novel, *After Many a Summer Dies the Swan*. Neither portrait made him admirable.

What his fellow citizens thought of Hearst was perhaps important in only one respect. Any judgment passed on him was likewise a verdict on the society which had bred, nourished, and prospered him. In judging Hearst, Americans would really be judging themselves. For he was chiefly significant as an illustrative social product, a specimen in whom typical attributes existed in a highly developed form. He was a result of the materialism of American society. He exemplified the consequences of its cult of expediency as an equivalent for morality. He flourished under the authority of its conviction that collective social welfare and a democratic way of life are engendered by an individualistic capitalism, so far as possible exempt from social accountability.

Meanwhile, American philosophers and educators were emphasizing the increasing collectivistic character of American society. Among them, many wished to align education with the broad democratic tendencies in American life. They proposed to expound "those values of the American cultural heritage which would aid in the task of insuring democratic control of the new technology, the new interdependence of life." Against this program, William Randolph Hearst launched one of the most vigorous of all his many crusades. Perhaps, in his reactionary old age, he could scarcely be expected to believe that there existed a genuine need for developing collective responsibility for American well-being. To him, the meeting of this need had the look of communism. To many of his fellow citizens it appeared to be nothing more than the function of democracy.

[3] BLUESTOCKING IN BABYLON

A powerful reaction against yellow journalism from within the press itself appeared, in 1896, to be highly improbable. What seemed altogether likely was the triumph, everywhere, of the methods of Pulitzer and Hearst, however repugnant these might be to conscientious publishers and a conservative public. The old-fashioned press had been made obsolete, overnight. Could circulation be attracted by anything save sensationalism? Although a good many homes, schools and clubs deliberately excluded the *World* and the *Journal* in 1896, they were believed to hold the formula of the future.

But it was in that very year that the first guns in the aggressive war against yellow journalism were heard. To many onlookers, the campaign seemed all but hopeless. Had the onlookers been acquainted with all the facts, they might have accounted the fight lost even before it was begun. For there was no war chest to offset the millions of dollars which Hearst and Pulitzer were pouring into their private contest. There was no immediate prospect of public support. Materially, the campaign was based upon nothing more promising than the union of a bankrupt paper and an insolvent publisher. If, from the outside, the undertaking looked dubious, from the inside it looked worse. It represented the supremacy of gall for a country newspaperman burdened with debts. Such was Adolph S. Ochs' personal opinion of his project to take over the stricken New York *Times*.

On both sides, the union was a marriage of expediency. The stockholders of the paper wished, if possible, to retrieve their investment. Experts had warned them that it would require several millions of dollars to resuscitate the *Times*. The millions were not forthcoming. They accepted Ochs' offer for the paper as a last resort. As his biographer revealed fifty years afterwards, Ochs was taking a desperate gamble in an effort to retrieve his personal fortunes. He owned a successful newspaper in Chattanooga, Tennessee. But he had invested heavily in other enterprises, and the panic of 1893 made these investments worthless. Although it was not known at the time, he was technically insolvent. Faced with the alternatives of retrenchment and possible security, or vast extension of risk and possible total failure, he chose to gamble.

In this, he illustrated a paradox characteristic of American business-men of his generation. They were, in general, intellectual conservatives who, in their personal careers, applied the most speculative radicalism to practical affairs. Ochs was inveterately opposed to all radicalism in the field of ideas. But at the greatest crisis in his professional life, his course could scarcely have been more radical. He was thirty-eight years old. At the age of eleven, he had started in the newspaper business as a carrier. Thereafter, he had worked up, from printer's devil, through all the departments of a small-town paper. At twenty, he borrowed two hundred and fifty dollars to buy the Chattanooga *Times*. He installed himself as publisher with a working capital of twelve dollars and fifty cents. He succeeded in lifting the paper to prosperity and prestige.

Ochs was to duplicate this achievement, on a far more spectacular scale, in New York. As the success of the *Times* was to prove, his strongest assets were a conviction about the public, and a concept of the nature of news. Their value far exceeded his own estimate. On his twenty-fifth anniversary as its publisher, he said that the success of the *Times* was beyond the earlier dreams of those who were its chief beneficiaries. In 1896, with a circulation of about nine thousand, he set his mark at reaching fifty thousand local readers. By 1921, the *Times* had a daily circulation of a third of a million, and a Sunday circulation of more than half a million, with readers throughout the country. In 1946, the daily circulation stood at more than six hundred thousand.

Ochs was convinced that a large portion of the public was composed of intelligent, thoughtful people. Though the rapidly mounting circulation and advertising of the yellow press appeared to prove him wrong, he resolved to abstain from what he later characterized as coarse, vulgar and inane features, muckraking and crusades of every character. The appeal of his paper was to be based on nothing more sensational than fairness, accuracy, and intelligibility. Its object was to give the news, all the news. It would so far as possible or feasible, make impersonal the treatment of news and its interpretation. Since he was directly attacking the yellow press, he tried to sum this up in a motto—"all the news that's fit to print." As he later acknowledged, it was made sport of and ridiculed. But it was destined to become the paper's permanent slogan, thus long surviving its original purpose—and perhaps confusing a generation of readers ignorant of the journalistic conditions which justified its original adoption.

By 1946, even the *Times* was publishing material that, fifty years earlier, it might have rejected as not fit to print. The criterion had yielded to changing mores. But the principle still held. "The fact of an atrocious crime or a deplorable scandal is news. The sordid particulars have sometimes a legitimate news value, but more often their only appeal is to the salacious curiosity." Such was the distinction drawn by Elmer Davis, then a member of the *Times* editorial staff, in 1921. By 1946 many respectable folk might have found it hard to define "salacious curiosity." But the *Times* continued, whenever possible, to ignore "the sordid particulars." It denied any public appetite for the sensational. So, also, it had always refused to satisfy the increasing demand for comic supplements and strips. It still stood on Ochs' contention that the proper content of a newspaper is news.

But the concept of the nature of news held by the *Times* brought it, over the years, to a position of unique eminence. Undoubtedly, news is made up of the significant events of the day; local, national, international. For Ochs, even at the outset, this was merely a starting point. He extended the definition, extraordinarily, both in scope and in depth. This double extension—which had important consequences for American journalism, and for the mind of the American people—was to be his real contribution to the public. It was foreshadowed by three immediate innovations. One was a book review, intended as a literary newspaper, treating newly published books as news—not originally designed as a journal of literary criticism, though destined to become one. A second was a pictorial Sunday magazine, devoted mainly to news of an informative, though not necessarily "spot" character. A third was a weekly financial review. This, in its various different forms, became a detailed survey of worldwide economic, financial, and commercial trends. The policy already implicit in these additions was, in the end, to lead the *Times* to spend literally millions publishing matter that nobody on the staff expected any single purchaser of the paper to read through.

Extension of the scope of the news gradually resulted in the creation of a multiple newspaper, every department of which was technically specialized. Though no public profession was made, it became clear that, for the *Times*, the "news" included all forms of enterprise in which any intelligent person might be supposed to be interested. Thus, for example, the paper greatly increased popular understanding of the phenomenal developments that were taking place in pure and applied science. It reported extensively Marconi's experiments, and his eventual perfection of wireless telegraphy. It contracted for Admiral Peary's account of what was to be his successful dash for the North Pole; it later published the narratives by Amundsen and Scott of their discoveries of the South Pole; long afterwards, it made a similar arrangement with Admiral Byrd covering his voyages to Antarctica. During the years before the First World War, it promoted experimentation in aviation, and gave this new form of transportation large coverage. It reported in considerable detail congresses of scientists and scholars. When, during the Second World War, official announcement was made of the fission of the atom, the *Times* excelled in its scientific accounts of this portent of a new era. What was true of its treatment of science was likewise true of its treatment of other fields. The *Times* was to become the newspaper of record, the one to whose files future historians would refer when it became necessary to settle some obscure point. It came, indeed, to resemble a daily encyclopaedia. It also came—especially after the great expansion of its foreign service during and subsequent to the First World War—to furnish a day-by-day history of the world: political, social, and intellectual.

All this represented extension of the scope of the news. But Ochs likewise extended its depth. He did so by furnishing whatever documentation might assist readers to appraise the major events of the day. This policy was modestly initiated, by publication of a cabled verbatim report of a speech made in London, in 1910, by ex-President Theodore Roosevelt. Roosevelt had just concluded an expedition to Africa, and the speech was important as a declaration of his views on political affairs. After the outbreak of the First World War, the *Times* began publishing, in full, the speeches of the leaders of all European governments. It went on to print the "white papers" of the British and German governments, and such other diplomatic records as were issued by the various nations engaged in the war. It was the only paper in the United States, or in the world, which printed the full text of the draft of the peace treaty. This ran to eight pages of the paper, and was published simultaneously with its publication in the *Congressional Record*. As this policy extended, over the years, the *Times* became a repository of the original documentary records covering most important phases of current history.

Still later, the *Times* extended its concept of the news to include evaluation. By most newspapers, such evaluation was then limited to the expression of editorial opinion in the editorial columns. It was a function later widely taken over by syndicated columnists. The *Times'* approach was somewhat different. Its foreign correspondents, in addition to strictly factual articles, began to supply analytical commentaries on the developments taking place in the countries which they covered. Authorities on various subjects were invited to take temporary assignments when live issues arose in their fields. Ultimately, commentators were added to the permanent staff: specialists in foreign affairs, education, industrial relations and the like; a military and naval analyst, a political observer in Washington. In general, their function was to interpret the meaning of the news rather than to report it.

The meaning of the news is necessarily a matter of opinion. Even specialists and experts are subject to prejudice. And in certain fields— such as national affairs and industrial relations—all interpretation is likely to take a controversial form. When he took over the *Times*, Ochs announced his intention to make its columns "a forum for the consideration of all questions of public importance, and to that end to invite intelligent discussion from all shades of opinion." Twenty-five years later he declared that a newspaper without sympathies or prejudices "would be a nuisance and a plague, an excrescence on the bodies social and politic." The interpretations of the news furnished by the *Times'* analysts sometimes aroused violent disapproval among readers whose prejudices clashed with those of the interpreters. Yet occasionally the analysts were at odds with the editorial policy of their own paper. The *Times*, for example, had no use for Bolshevism as a political and economic gospel. But, for a period before the Second World War, Walter Duranty, its correspondent in Moscow, commented on Russian affairs from a point of view highly favorable to the Soviet Union.

On the whole, however, evaluation of the news and editorial opinion tended to accord. Ochs defined the editorial policy of the *Times* as that of an independent conservative newspaper. What came to be its traditional conservatism was forecast by his own salutatory announcement. This advocated, among other things, "no more government than is absolutely necessary to protect society, maintain individual and vested rights, and assure the free exercise of a sound conscience."

The *Times* frequently represented liberal opinion in its policy with respect to foreign affairs; notably, in its support of the League of Nations, the World Court, and the United Nations. But liberals seldom agreed with its editorial stand on matters of domestic policy. It was steadfastly opposed to all extension of the power of the Federal government, and this fundamental principle dictated an opposition to most programs of long-range social and economic reform. Looking back, in 1921, at the record of the liberal-progressive movement, Elmer Davis phrased the attitude of the *Times* by dismissing it as a "carnival of purity." The paper, he remarked, did not pretend to have a patented cure for industrial ills, nor to know where that cure can be found. As the *Times'* official historian, Davis summed up its attitude to all social reforms as one of conscientious skepticism. Liberals who believed that social reform was bound to originate in the field of economic controversy, were inclined to account for the *Times'* opposition by its concern for the maintenance of "vested rights." Conservatism, in their opinion, could scarcely go further than to find in Thomas Jefferson an exponent of "dilettante radicalism"!

Fifty years after Ochs took it over, the *Times'* editorial attitude to the major social and economic issues confronting the American people remained conservative. Yet it was still true that a great many people who cordially despised the political and economic opinions of its editors felt that they had to buy the paper to get the news. Over the years, the *Times* had impressed its concept of the nature of news on other newspapers. It had likewise impressed this concept on a large and intelligent segment of the American public. It had produced a genuine demand among readers for the comprehensive information, the basic documentary records, and the interpretation of complex or technical subjects, without which nobody could hope to arrive at an understanding of the perplexing world of the mid-twentieth century. In doing this, it had greatly raised the standard of American journalism, it had surely contributed to broadening the outlook of the American people. It had perhaps even become, as Ochs stated in his will, an institution—charged with a high public duty and impressed with a public interest.

In 1904, when the success of the *Times* was assured, the paper erected a building on an island at Forty Second Street and Broadway. The district was then a region of no particular importance or distinction. But by 1913, when—having outgrown its new home—the *Times* moved to another, nearby, the character of the district had been established. Times Square had become the center of New York's garish night life. To many readers there was a pleasant irony in the fact that the most sober, literate, and erudite of American newspapers was—like a bluestocking in Babylon—nightly put to bed in the midst of a perpetual revel.

[4] THE CONSCIENCE OF MAIN STREET

One spring evening in 1895, a considerable crowd of idlers assembled at the railroad station of Emporia, Kansas. An event of importance was about to happen, but they were not aware of it. Habit had collected them. A prime diversion of the little town was to see the two plug trains come in from Kansas City.

Among the travellers discharged by one of the trains was the man who, over the next fifty years, was to make Emporia world famous. William Allen White, a native townsman, was returning after an absence of ten years to take up permanent residence. With three thousand dollars borrowed on his personal notes, he had bought the failing *Emporia Gazette*, an afternoon newspaper with few readers, little equipment, and an unquestioning loyalty to the Republican party. He was twenty-seven, married, paunchy, heavy-jowled, an incurable optimist with respect to everything but his rapidly thinning brown hair; a lover of life; and his attire declared him a dude.

His cash resources, when alighting from the train, totaled one dollar and a quarter. He had a moment's indecision. "Should I lug my heavy baggage uptown to the boarding house where I was expected, and establish a reputation as a frugal, thrifty young publisher, or should I establish my credit in the community by going in a hack?" The hack cost a quarter, and White took the hack. He always remembered the decision, and never regretted it. He was always to feel that a good front is rather to be chosen than great riches. But White's notion of a good front was an unorthodox as many of his other notions. It involved neither duplicity nor pretence. It had little to do with calculation, or the gaining of any personal advantage. To put on a good front, White believed, was to square conduct with the potentially best, rather than the expediently mediocre. He spent most of the rest of his life trying to persuade the American people to adopt this principle.

This singular mission was largely accidental. It was in line with his character, but it was a by-product of his job. The results to which it

led were extraordinary. To the day of his death, in the mid-nineteen-
forties, the circulation of White's newspaper never exceeded eight
thousand copies. Yet its influence was far greater than that of many
a metropolitan daily with hundreds of thousands of readers. On every
momentous issue before the country, its editorial opinion was anxiously
awaited, widely quoted, both at home and abroad. The town of
Emporia—with a population of less than fifteen thousand—became,
because of William Allen White, the most famous small, modern city
in the English-speaking world. Except for President Franklin D.
Roosevelt, White was probably the American interpreter of his time
best known to people in foreign countries who sought an understanding of the United States. In his old age, many of his countrymen accounted him the nation's leading private citizen. Abroad, he seemed
to guarantee the survival and strength of American idealism, sometimes doubtful. Like Emerson and Mark Twain, he attained to a
world view by remaining invincibly provincial. Like Jane Addams, he
rose from sentimental dissatisfactions to a gospel of social ethics. From
time to time he was drafted for tasks of national scope. But to the end
of his days he thought of himself as only a country editor. In sober fact,
he was the embodied, articulate conscience of Main Street.

White soared to national celebrity on the explosive force of an
editorial which, within a very few years, he bitterly repented. During
the stormy presidential campaign of 1896 a street-corner dispute with
some fellow townsmen erupted into "What's the Matter with Kansas?"
—an attack on the Populists which, as White later acknowledged, was
pure vitriol. Widely quoted by the Republican press, it attracted the
attention of Mark Hanna, the Cleveland industrialist who was national
boss of the party and campaign manager for William McKinley.
Aware of its value to his candidate, Hanna flooded the country with
reprints; in his opinion, it did much to bring about the defeat of William Jennings Bryan. So White soon began to figure in high party
councils. And national magazines, welcoming the articles and the
fiction which he began to produce in his leisure hours, prepared an
audience for all his later books. An angry outburst, useful to those
who were bent upon guiding the Republic in the profitable ways of a
ruling plutocracy, thus magically paved the way to White's subsequent
career as a fighting liberal.

Reviewing that career in his old age, White was still puzzled by the
fact that he had been "a superficial young Pharisee, blinder than a bat

to the great forces that were joining issue in our politics, forces that would be in combat for fifty years and more and finally would tear up modern civilization by the roots in devastating wars." It did not occur to him that the election of 1896 turned on the issue of property rights as opposed to human rights. He knew and admired Hamlin Garland, who was stumping the Middle West for the Populists; he knew the Populist leaders—the scholarly Ignatius Donnelly, the erudite "Sockless Jerry" Simpson, and Mary E. Lease, the woman with a voice who took to the highway and was really a great exhorter. But he did not understand that these reformers were trying to use government as an agency of human welfare, or that they were seeking to establish economic as well as political equality, to help the underdog, to cut down some of the privileges that wealth carried by reason of its size and inherent power. To White, in 1896, William Jennings Bryan—the first national leader who had boldly and unashamedly made his cause that of the poor and the oppressed—was an incarnation of demagogy, the apotheosis of riot, destruction, and carnage!

White's conversion was swift, sudden, and complete. It was brought about, over a luncheon table in Washington, by Theodore Roosevelt, then assistant secretary in the Navy Department. White did not dream that anyone, other than fanatics like the Populists, had any question about the divine right of the well-to-do to rule the world. But Roosevelt—hard muscled, hard voiced even when the voice cracked in falsetto, with hard, wriggling jaw muscles, and snapping teeth, even when he cackled in raucous glee—shook his faith in the established order. Roosevelt poured ironical rage on Hanna's reign of privilege, on the whole deep and damnable alliance between business and politics for the good of business, and sounded in White's heart the first trumpet call of the new time that was to be. That call was to take him into the forefront of political and social insurgency; into the long struggle for reform which, initiated by Bryan, was carried forward by Theodore Roosevelt, the elder Robert M. La Follette, Woodrow Wilson, and Franklin D. Roosevelt.

Characteristically, White tried to ascertain the real, rather than the superficial, meaning of the liberal movement. In so doing, he laid the foundation for his immense influence as a journalist. For this effort led him to the discovery of general principles, and equipped him to interpret all particular issues, and specific reforms, in their light. He assumed that his readers were very like himself; and he believed that the American conscience, when confronted by alternative courses in which moral principle was at stake, would find no shelter in evasion. So, although himself deeply immersed in practical politics, White lifted his causes to the plane of ethical justice, and fought for all reform measures as elements of a single sacred crusade. The immediate battle might seem to be no more than a minor local skirmish—but White always saw it, and presented it, in its relation to a great, overarching conflict. The result was that his readers not only had a sense of active participation in history, but were persuaded that the forces making history could be guided by moral principle.

The reform movement began as an attempt to curb rollicking economic lechery and to secure distributive justice. But White saw that, in the large, it was a struggle between democracy and capital. Three years before Charles A. Beard published his startling *An Economic Interpretation of the Constitution*, White anticipated its thesis. In *The Old Order Changeth*, White exposed the fundamental conflict between the Declaration of Independence, with its insistence upon human equality, and the Constitution, which annuls the Declaration by its checks on the majority. Democracy, White asserted, was fighting for the rights of man against the rights of property. But he could not view this battle as one merely between the rich and the poor. For him, it was a struggle in every man's heart between the unselfish and the selfish instincts of his nature for supremacy. The immediate objective of American democracy, he held, was to check our national greed and to make business honest. Yet, was not this the problem of individual self-sacrifice coming from individual good will?

Like Henry Adams, White made steam power the symbol of all technological progress. And, like Adams, he believed that this progress, advancing far more rapidly than society's ability to subordinate it to the general welfare, had generated new conditions in the world, making for greed and oppression and misery in this land of ours. Americans were trying, he said, to socialize steam, to make its results and achievements a part of an equitable existence. Yet, unlike most liberal reformers, White was not deluded into assuming that mere economic or political tinkering with the social order would suffice. "We cannot hope to socialize the forces of steam in our civilization," he declared, "until we control and socialize ourselves."

Although White conceded that the ultimate aim of the reformers was a peaceful revolution, what a later generation would term a "revolution by consent," the blueprints of socialism and communism were equally abhorrent to him. The reformers, he said, were trying to establish all over the civilized world more equitable human relations. America had solved its problem of production of wealth and the great problem of the distribution of wealth challenged the country. "We were trying to distribute the economic surplus of the machine age," he wrote in his old age, "and curiously, we thought that if we took the surplus away from the rich and gave it to the poor, we would be achieving our aims." But he insisted that the contest being waged by the liberals against the oligarchy was not a struggle of classes, not in America; it was a contest in the heart of the common people. To him, Emporia was a microcosm of the United States, and though Emporia had its poor, they were no more proletarian than was he; they were, like himself, of the middle class, the plain people. He was profoundly disturbed by everything in American society that made for class feeling. Noticing the tendency of men of standing and property to line up on the right, he deliberately chose to align himself a little farther to the left than he might have done had he not always remained a private citizen. His object was to persuade "what for want of a better word we will call the under-privileged that some of their well-to-do neighbors have a sense that there is a real problem of adjustment to be worked out under the democratic process now, and in the next decade and generation and in this century."

White was clearly aware of the problem, but he wanted its solution to be achieved within the democratic process. He thought that the emphasis of American politics would largely be on a widespread readjustment of income, and perhaps a readjustment of title in property—not all property, but certain property affected by public use. Under the democratic process, this could only be brought about slowly. But he was convinced that where revolution tries to hasten the process, the friction of compulsory confiscation and the probable bloodshed thereunto appertaining will slow down the march of progress. He wanted to be an influence for the stabilization of the social conflict, which he felt it would take nearly a century to achieve.

It was therefore natural that the movement led by Theodore Roosevelt, culminating in the Progressive revolt of 1912, should win his absolute allegiance. It exercised an appeal transcending the merits of its immediate program: it was not a class movement. As White understood it, it was a middle-class revolt against the injustice of our society, our industrial organization, our economic establishment, our political institutions. But, more than that, it was a protest against the political expression of class feeling. This, for White, constituted its high moral excellence.

In later days, after the First World War, White tried to determine what causes had brought about the failure of the liberal movement. It had sought to make government an agency of human welfare. But the major mistake of its leaders, White surmised, had been to make government the *only* agency of human welfare. Had they not forgotten "that masses who require the stimulation of a just prosperity for their happy well-being must themselves first learn to love justice in their own hearts before they can get much out of prosperity except food and clothes and shelter"?

The liberal movement, he thought, had died in the final defeat of Woodrow Wilson; its revival under the New Deal of President Franklin D. Roosevelt bewildered him. He found the President, whom he had long known, a great puzzle. As the spectacular first term unfolded, White acknowledged that the President had done many fine things— "he has started us down so many roads that long had been blocked by an arrogant plutocracy that I cannot ask perfection and I am glad he came." But he was worried by what he took to be the ultimate objectives of the New Deal. Was not the President aiming at "the same target at which both the fascists and the communists are shooting; that is to say, the socialization of capital, the regimentation of industry and agriculture, and, finally, a more equitable distribution of wealth, a guarantee of a minimum standard of living for all who have worked honestly . . . "? With the last two objectives, White was heartily in accord, and had been since the days of the Progressive revolt. But about the first two he was extremely dubious. Were the American people ready for the revolutionary change, the fundamental break with the American past that would be necessary if this revolution took hold permanently? Past his sixtieth year, he wondered whether the New Deal might not be "socializing the forces of steam" at too rapid a rate. Could government chain its dollars, harness them to the common good, and still retain free men and free institutions? It had never been done before, and White felt that political liberties always go when economic liberty is circumscribed. Yet American democracy had been, for more than a century, a "new order"—and White was willing to grant the possibility that it could do this strange thing—establish a new revolution of free men with their dollars in shackles.

But the outbreak of the Second World War drove him back upon his earlier, middle-of-the-road liberalism. "The militant liberal," he said, "believes in is heart that if he is patient and persistent justice will come far more swiftly than if in rage and temper he strikes out blindly," and he urged the overcoming of injustice through compromise in the orderly parliamentary democratic processes. He acted as an intermediary, on the issue of foreign policy, between the President and Wendell L. Willkie, and Willkie won his loyalty as only Theodore Roosevelt had. Willkie, he thought, was fighting for the old hard way of American life, for a capitalism that stresses opportunity, whereas the President wanted a capitalism that would over-use government as an agency of human welfare and make men soft. His strategic advice to Willkie in 1943 made White's final position explicit: "Tell the people that the extension of government powers into planned economy in time of peace is the denial of liberty inevitably. For the very theory of planning requires that man shall become a wooden figure without will, without individuality, that he shall be, in short, that powerless human sheep, the economic man, a social and political eunuch."

So, in his last years, White declared that the capitalist system must not break down—for, unless it was willing to organize, to sacrifice, to envision its own self-interests in the renewal and revival of civilization, a Second World War would end in failure; a weary, disheartened world would turn to some totalitarian tyranny; and mankind would be regimented in inevitable economic slavery. A liberal, he held, realizes that haste makes waste in a democracy and too much haste brings tyranny; no true liberal believed that he must destroy to build. As he looked into the future through the miasma of war, White was certain only that the duties of a decent victor would be burdens and not tokens of triumph.

Once before, he had seen his own hopes for his country like shifting clouds blown away before the winds of circumstance. But did this matter? Was there not, in the stuff that holds humanity together, some force, some conservation of spiritual energy, that saves the core of every noble hope, and gathers all men's visions some day, some way, into the reality of progress? This might be mysticism, White admitted; but decades earlier he had declared himself an optimist; an idealist. He was of those who know that tomorrow also is a day. He had always felt that coming events must be met, not by a party or a program, but by an attitude of spirit. So in the end he could continue to affirm the faith that had welled up in him during an hour of national shame: that life is worth living, that dreams come true, that man's visions are God's reality. It was, so to speak, his testament as an American.

[5] SAVIOR OF THE SIMPLE-MINDED

Near the end of the First World War, Captain Joseph Medill Patterson of the famous Rainbow Division paid a visit to London. There he talked with Lord Northcliffe, whose tabloid *Daily Mirror* had won a circulation of some eight hundred thousand copies. Would not Americans, likewise, take to the tabloid press? Northcliffe threw out a suggestion. Why not launch a tabloid newspaper in some American city —a paper bright and simple enough to entice the masses?

Late in June, 1919, Patterson brought out the first issue of the *Daily News*—"New York's Picture Newspaper." The American tabloid press was born. In the opinion of many experts, a new era was opening in journalism. Eleven years later, the paper was installed in a ten-million-dollar tower; one of the notable masterpieces of modern business architecture. By 1946, when Patterson died, it had the largest circulation of any newspaper in the world. To meet the Sunday demand, four and one-half million copies of the *Daily News* were printed. This was enough to supply fifty-five percent of the population of New York City. However one disagreed with Patterson's editorial policies, as the *Times* wistfully observed, no one could deny that he was a force for many years in the journalism of this country.

A force, certainly. But what kind of force?

The historian Charles A. Beard, when reviewing the rise of American civilization, considered the tabloid press to be a downward thrust of quantity production in the search for more purchasers, resulting from the extension of the machine system throughout the publishing world. The tabloid press was the lowest of many strikes into the successive strata of general ignorance. It could present to masses previously unreached that part of the day's news which called for no abstract thought or background of knowledge. It added to the "reading public" multitudes "who could not vie with stable boys and kitchen maids in stumbling through giant headlines." Furthermore, "millions who spoke foreign tongues could grasp the illustrations, at least dimly, spell their way through picture captions, and gain some notion, true or false, of events taking place in the world about them."

These things were true, certainly. But they did not exhaust the truth. That the *Daily News* was aimed at the less than fourteen-year-old mind, as the journalist George Seldes asserted, would probably not have been denied by its publisher. Did this justify a deduction that more than half the population of New York City could not, in mentality, vie with stable boys and kitchen maids? If this deduction was true, it indicated a condition of overwhelming social importance. It implied the total failure of public education under democracy.

Patterson was able, as the *Times* acknowledged, to reach many persons who had never before read newspapers regularly. Even by journalists, this was accounted his greatest achievement. It probably was not. For the persons who had never before read newspapers, the semiliterate, and the millions who spoke foreign tongues, did not constitute his entire audience. Any observant New Yorker knew better. The *Daily News* also had a mink-coat public; and it had a dyed-rabbit-coat public too. It was as great a bedside favorite along Park Avenue, in fashionable Sutton Place, in the gilded estate section of Long Island, as in flop houses along the Bowery. But it was likewise read in the literate Bronx, and the bourgeois suburbs. In this sense, tapping as it did all economic levels of American society, the *Daily News* was a significant democratic phenomenon. Whatever it implied as to the prevalence of ignorance and approximate illiteracy, it pointed to something more. It revealed the existence of a psychological common denominator which, obviously, had little relation either to education or economic station. It suggested that more than half the population of the most sophisticated American city was, fundamentally, simpleminded. Patterson's greatest journalistic achievement was to discover this, and to build his tabloid solidly upon what Henry James had described as the immensity of the native accommodation, socially speaking, for the childish life.

Patterson always prided himself on his understanding of "the man in the street." It is said that, while planning for the *Daily News*, he haunted the Bowery; that he was not just an onlooker, but lived among the down-and-outers, ate with them, and panhandled coins. Even long after the success of his paper was assured, he was reported as still liking to pull down his slouch hat, pull up his coat collar, play the workingman, go into the streets, mingle with the common people, and find out what they do and what they want.

The character of the *Daily News,* in its early years, reflected the knowledge acquired on these expeditions. The tabloid told the news, so far as possible, in pictures. The more sensational the pictures, the better. In 1928, for example, Patterson was widely condemned for publishing a photograph which showed Ruth Snyder, a passionate instigator of murder, dying in the electric chair. The picture, by his personal order, had been obtained in violation of prison regulations. Aside from pictures, the paper was filled with lurid stories of sex and crime; comic strips; contests of various kinds for cash prizes. It featured a daily political cartoon, and the editorial page offered brief, colloquial, hard-hitting expressions of Patterson's personal views. "The success of the *Daily News,*" Patterson said, "was built on legs, but when we got enough circulation we draped them."

In later days, when the paper had won a sufficient audience, its character was somewhat modified. The more sensational techniques of yellow journalism were gradually relinquished. Scandal, sex, and crime were still featured; treatment of them was more discreet, and also more insinuating. The gossip of Hollywood, of New York's café society, and of political Washington was exhaustively reported by well-known columnists. There were daily interviews on topical issues with a random sampling of "the people"; and their views were further recorded in a letter column. The most important news stories of the day were reduced to skeletal form, and reported with maximum brevity and simplicity. Thus, whatever could not be graphically told by a picture was condensed and predigested. And the *Daily News* ran more comic strips than any other paper. Patterson's use of them to express his economic and political philosophies was considered an especially interesting experiment.

The *Daily News* was not only Patterson's individual creation from day to day. It was also his pulpit and his platform. Even more importantly, it was a kind of shrine; dedicated to the people of course, but likewise, perhaps, and privately, to his belief in his mission in the world and to his innate, half-repressed, half-satisfied, quest for a full, free life of admirable action and true *noblesse oblige.* The critic Burton Rascoe, who knew Patterson well and long, asserted that he never lost the social conscience which flared up in his stormy youth; that he remained by nature, by action and by conviction democratic and equalitarian; that he was always trying to live up to his principles. But, Rascoe pointed out, Patterson was devoid of all except the most elementary reasoning powers, and his mistakes had been made through the initial errors of assuming that he was thinking when he was merely feeling, and of attempting to apply a logical process to matters of pure instinct and emotion. What wonder, then, that his paper pleased the simple-minded? Was he not one of them?

Patterson's early career sharply illuminated his later achievements as a force in journalism. He was born to great wealth, being the grandson of Joseph Medill, founder of the Chicago *Tribune*, of which his father was general manager. Newspaper publishing thus ran in the family, and Patterson's sister, Mrs. Eleanor Patterson, was later to control the Washington *Times-Herald*, while his cousin, Colonel Robert R. McCormick, was to preside over the *Tribune*. Patterson was educated at Groton and Yale, taking his degree after a year's absence in China to report the Boxer Rebellion. He joined the staff of the *Tribune* at a salary of fifteen dollars a week—but his allowance stood at between ten and twenty thousand dollars a year.

Patterson's youth, his college and post-college years, coincided with the cresting of a wave of liberalism. The crusade for social justice was advancing on many fronts. In magazines like *McClure's*, in newspapers like Pulitzer's *World* and Hearst's *American*, the malign alliance between big business and corrupt politics was being thoroughly ventilated. Socialism was a respectable doctrine, especially appealing to intellectual youth. Active enlistment in one or another movement for reform was general among Americans of sensitive conscience, particularly of the middle class. But there was evidence that it was spreading among the wealthy, likewise. Were there not such notable instances as Joseph W. Fels, the Philadelphia soap manufacturer; Edward A. Filene, the Boston dry-goods merchant; Tom L. Johnson, the former partner of Mark Hanna who, converted to reform by Henry George's *Social Problems* and *Progress and Poverty*, had become mayor of Cleveland and resolutely fought his earlier associates? The movement for reform sprang from conscience. It drew its energy from morality, not from reason. That—as was later to be pointed out by disgruntled reformers like Lincoln Steffens, by scholars like John Erskine and Vernon L. Parrington—was characteristically American, but a fundamental weakness. It made for sentimentality, for romantic enthusiasm, but not for intelligent realism.

Patterson readily confessed that he was no intellectual; had he not had to pay money to tutors to drill into his head information of a remarkably simple character? But he was a young man with a conscience and good intentions—as what American, regardless of economic station, is not, from his own point of view? He took his creed from the prevailing winds of doctrine. The conservatism of the family newspaper with respect to all public issues exasperated him. He thought it reactionary. He was right. At twenty-four as a reform candidate, Patterson was elected to the Illinois legislature. There, he advocated the municipal ownership of street railroads, and on one occasion staged a demonstration so violent that it drove the presiding officer to seek safety in the cloak room. When he was twenty-six, he entered municipal politics, supporting a Democratic candidate for mayor whom the *Tribune* opposed. The Democratic ticket was elected, and Patterson became Commissioner of Public Works. A year later he resigned. Reform, he declared, was impossible under the capitalistic system. He announced that he had become a convert to socialism.

This, naturally, attracted attention. And Patterson, as usual moved by feeling and excellent intentions, proceeded to publish in the *Independent*, a highly reputable magazine, an article titled "Confessions of a Drone," which was to become one of the most celebrated pamphlets of the time. Taking himself as a representative example, he set forth, from the socialist standpoint, the economic parasitism of the "idle rich." "Socialism," he said, "urges the underpaid to unite and insist on receiving the full amount of the wealth they produce." He was widely attacked by what he called "the capitalist press"; its favorite question was why, if he felt as he said he did, he did not give his own wealth to the poor. He retorted to this. There was one good reason why the whole capitalist class did not give away its money and go to work. "It is quite satisfied with its present arrangement of luxury, dominion and idleness. As long as the working class is satisfied with its present arrangement of poverty, obedience and laboriousness, the present arrangement will continue. But whenever the working class wants to discontinue the present arrangement it can do so. It has the great majority."

Two years after publishing this article, Patterson made an even greater sensation with his novel, *A Little Brother of the Rich*. This was —in 1908—an explosive document in "exposure"; a scourging of the moral obliquity, vulgarity and economic corruption of fashionable society; an extolling of the fortitude and nobility of the poor. The capitalist who figures as central character confesses, in the end, that his way of life has been a disastrous failure. "My whole life is a horrible lie, a poisonous blunder, a soul destroyer. Sometimes I catch a vision of the truth, but always I turn away from it quickly, or I couldn't keep on." The heroine, a great actress, spoke for Patterson in saying that her art "is for the people's sakes, to bring them a little more understanding, a little more wisdom and hope and courage."

As a novel, *A Little Brother of the Rich* was inexpert. As a tract for the times, it showed that Patterson, however little his intellectual understanding of social issues, had a perception of their existence and importance. It was as characteristic a product of his feeling, his conscience, and his elementary reasoning powers as the *Daily News* was to be long afterwards. In both novel and newspaper, the same oversimplification of issues was dominant. In both, the same capacity for strong conviction and high feeling was obvious. The novel enjoyed a sensational popular success, running through many editions. But the highbrow critics of the time, and the intellectuals of socialist persuasion, did not praise it. So close a student of Patterson's career as George Seldes was inclined to believe that this snobbery of the literary left lost the radical cause one of the most powerful publishers in America.

In 1910, Patterson's father died. Active management of the Chicago *Tribune* fell into the hands of a deputy of Patterson's mother and her sister, Colonel McCormick's mother. The two young cousins wished to secure control of the paper—and succeeded in doing so by executing a coup with proxies in the best robber-baron tradition. It was widely believed that this seizure of power dated Patterson's conversion to economic and social conservatism. In the early days of the First World War, he went to Europe as a correspondent for the *Tribune*; in 1916, when war with Mexico seemed likely, he served in the army, on the border; when the United States entered the First World War, he went overseas with a commission, participated in five major engagements, was wounded and promoted, and returned to found the *Daily News* at the age of forty.

That Patterson had ceased being a socialist long before he founded his paper, was obvious. But he had not ceased being—in his own way— a liberal. This in time was proved by his staunch, vigorous championship of President Franklin D. Roosevelt, and the economic and social policies of the New Deal in its early phases. His support was given at a time when most other newspaper publishers were savagely opposed. He broke with the President on the issue of the Second World War, and thereafter attacked Roosevelt and all his policies with a venom which often brought down on him a flood of condemnation. Had he been primarily a thinker, rather than a man of feeling, he might have opposed the President's foreign policy, while continuing to support his program of domestic reform; as the more logical New York *Times* supported the foreign policy, and continued to oppose the domestic. But Patterson's only logic sprang from conscience and feeling—and these responded, always, to immediate circumstance. There was little to distinguish his ultra-nationalism from isolationism; after the United States entered the war his paper, with those controlled by his sister and cousin, became generally known as the isolationist "McCormick-Patterson axis." Thus Patterson found himself where he may not have wished to be, and perhaps did not conceive of himself as arriving— among the reactionaries. In the pre-election period of 1936, he had devoted the page opposite his editorial page to arguments from both Democrats and Republicans. In the following year, he named this page the "Economic Battle Page" and devoted it to free discussion of both sides of the labor problem. These acts were one of the most honest things that has happened in American newspaper history. They indicated, along with other evidence in the *Daily News*, a genuine liberalism.

What explained his final emergence as a conservative? Probably neither increasing age, nor increasing wealth. Probably not his violent break with the President, which may have merely furnished the occasion. Men of his generation who had been vigorous liberals in their youth, and who were more intellectual than Patterson had ever been, had likewise taken the same turn because of disillusion with reform: younger men, for example, like Sinclair Lewis and Walter Lippmann; older men, like Jack London, William Allen White, Frederick C. Howe, Ray Stannard Baker. All of them, like Patterson, had endeavored to do something for the people's sakes, to bring them a little more understanding, a little more wisdom and hope and courage. All of them had a conviction of failure. Patterson, to the very end, apparently had no such conviction. His case was special. Being simple-minded, he was either afraid of intelligence, or distrusted it. He thought that conscience, benevolence, and the best intentions were enough. And they were not enough. They were not enough even to keep him from winding up where he did not belong. Not enough even to make him aware of where he stood. They served only to bring him—as he probably did not realize—to confusion.

He was important, not only because he reached a vast audience, but because he expressed it. And the common denominator of American democracy which he represented was dangerously significant as the twentieth century neared its mid-point. The existence, the phenomenal success of Patterson's *Daily News*, of later magazine ventures like the *Reader's Digest* and *Life*, indicated the tragic surrender of the simple-minded. For them, the world had become too complex; the acquiring of information too difficult; the process of thinking too arduous. Theodore Dreiser, so far back as 1911, had remarked this: the very complexity of modern civilization, he said, "wearies and stultifies the moral nature . . . induces a sort of intellectual fatigue . . . Our modern brain-pan does not seem capable as yet of receiving, sorting, and storing the vast army of facts and impressions which present themselves daily."

To this condition such publications as the *Daily News* responded. It tried to reduce information to a visual image. It oversimplified the complex. It provided soluble capsules of opinion which, when swallowed, made not-illiterate people think that they were thinking. And in its comic strips it comforted people of good will with a never-never land where sentiment and simplicity would bring all things right in the end. From a world of extreme insecurity, it offered an escape into the warm and certain safety of adolescence—the "childish life."

Of a well-known liberal who later became a reactionary, the philosopher John Dewey remarked that "he does his thinking in something like a vacuum." Was not this pleasant but unprofitable habit precisely what the *Daily News* encouraged? At least, its enormous circulation suggested that the habit had been deliberately adopted by many Americans—not all of whom were ignorant, or underprivileged, or mentally incapable, or morally callous.

And this, in 1946, did not augur well for the future of American democracy.

CHAPTER IX
"Raising the Tone of Democracy"

[I] GRAND LAMA OF THE MATRONS

In the autumn of 1919, after thirty years of consecration, Edward Bok resigned his editorship of the *Ladies' Home Journal*. Immediately, from all over the nation, the newspapers clamored for his opinions about women. Very rightly. What man knew the American woman as intimately as Bok? His opportunities for knowledge exceeded those of any husband, probably those of any lover. Had he not received nearly one million letters a year from her, upon all conceivable problems, including those of the most confidential nature? Though thirty-five junior editors devoted all their time to allaying her anxieties and improving her mind, it was to Bok himself that the American woman turned in her hours of perplexity or anguish. To her, he was not so much a man as a fountain of wisdom. She had adopted him as her confidant and domestic counsellor; her esthetic arbiter and intellectual leader; above all, her spiritual guide. Certainly no American layman had ever before been charged with so awesome a cure of souls.

This privileged eminence was not without consequences in the less exalted realm of material phenomena. Under Bok's guidance, the *Ladies' Home Journal* had become a national institution such as no other magazine had ever been—a temporal institution. Did anyone doubt that it was indisputably accepted by the public and by business interests alike as the recognized avenue of approach to the intelligent homes of America? The last issue under Bok's personal control did away with doubt. It was oversold with a printed edition of two million copies—a record never before achieved by any other magazine. Moreover, it carried between its covers the amazing total of over one million dollars in advertisements, and so broke another record even more pleasing to Bok. The Grand Lama pretended no indifference to his ecclesiastical revenues. But for them, would he have seen to it that the magazine had not remained an inanimate thing, but had become a vital need in the lives of its readers? He did see to it. And, inevitably, whenever the domestic pinch came, his readers had a ready retort for thrifty husbands or fathers: they did not feel that they could do without it. So Bok left it probably the most valuable and profitable piece of magazine property in the world.

Still, reflecting on his career, Bok felt that he had been paying a high price for his success. During the course of his long sovereignty over feminine America, something had toppled off its pedestal which could never be replaced. This something was not Edward Bok. Humility did not figure among his many exemplary virtues. At the age of thirteen, when poverty forced him to quit school for a job, his Dutch common sense made him appraise the probable rewards of humility—and reject it forever. His later omniscience, which in another man might have been only a difficult adjustment to vocational necessity, was as predictable as a physiological change. Nature, as it were, prepared Edward Bok for the function of pontifying. He accepted this natural destiny as a moral obligation. For thirty years he let no occasion for wisdom—temporal or spiritual—pass unfulfilled. Yet ready as he always was to respond to duty, he flatly refused, when abdicating, to divulge his opinions on the subject of American women. Could the Grand Lama acknowledge that they had reduced him to a state of extreme disillusion?

Immediately after his retirement, Bok wrote his autobiography. The story of his "Americanization" quickly became a minor classic. For it proved that, in the United States, life imitates art and myths are literally true: Bok's career was, in every detail, another fable by Horatio Alger. The book was a masterpiece of self-revelation. It showed how thoroughly Bok had become Americanized—especially in his attitude to women. When, at the age of twenty-six, he assumed his high and delicate office, Edward Bok's instinctive attitude to women was one of avoidance. He did not dislike women. And it could not be said that he liked them. The plain fact was that they had never interested him. He had not the slightest desire, even as an editor, to know them better, or to seek to understand them. Understand them? He was certain that, as a man, he could not, and let it go at that. Indeed, he saw no compelling need to know women; he could employ women for that purpose. Nevertheless, after thirty years of personal contact with his readers through the more intimate departments, he reached two significant conclusions. He knew that women had revealed their worst side to him, and he did not like the picture. And he was sadly aware that his ideal of womanhood had received a severe jolt.

What man but an American could honestly say that women did not "interest" him? Or accept as axiomatic the proposition that his sex was an insurmountable obstacle to understanding them? As an editor Bok's persistent concern was for the best interests of the home. A home was not beyond the understanding of the American male—was this because sex played a relatively minor role on the domestic stage? In any case, Bok felt that he understood a home: he had always lived in one; had struggled to keep it together; and he knew every inch of the hard road that makes for domestic permanence amid adverse financial conditions. So, in his magazine, like many other American men in their lives, it was at the home he aimed rather than the woman in it.

Bok was, however, specifically concerned with one aspect of women; their adaptability to the disposition of the male. Not to the male as lover or companion. To the male as householder, husband, and parent, whose career was staged outside the home. Woman's function was to satisfy him on the domestic margin of his existence. This was a drastic restriction of the interest that women are presumably capable of offering to men—but was it not American? To Bok, at least, a high ideal of womanhood and a low opinion of women did not seem incompatible. Strangely enough, it was as much due to Bok as to any man that the United States ultimately became a "paradise of women." One feature of the paradise which every foreign visitor noted with astonishment was the absence of the male. It was, as Henry James remarked, a society of women fixed in a world of men; but between the sexes there appeared to be an impassable gulf. Bok encouraged no attempts to swim this social Hellespont. As one of the chief architects of paradise, he undertook to conserve the original design. So paradise turned out to be a place where womanhood was venerated. Also where women, amply provided for in a material sense, were left to their own devices by men.

Among other convictions, Bok cherished the belief that he possessed a dual personality. He felt that Edward Bok, editor and publicist, had had and had been, in many respects, a personality apart from his private self. The private Bok often wished to give his feminine audience the best obtainable—not only what they thought they liked, but what he thought they should have. With this, the editorial Edward Bok never had the least patience. "Give the people what they want," was his slogan; "give the people what they ought to have and don't know they want," was the slogan of the private Bok. Once, when the private Bok temporarily dislodged his editorial alter ego, and took over, eighty thousand readers discontinued buying or subscribing to the magazine within six months. On another occasion, the conflict between them was peculiarly exhausting, and resulted in a nervous breakdown. So Bok gradually learned to squelch his private self, and give the successful editor free rein. Was it not the editor to whom two generations of American women looked for guidance?

But the editor's was not a work which fulfilled Bok; which he would have deliberately chosen to express his "real self." Why not? Because of his attitude to women, and because he did not really enjoy maintaining their paradise. There was, indeed, a certain contempt in his explanation. Said Bok: "There are undoubtedly acute problems which concern themselves with the proper ingredients in cooking recipes, the correct stitch in crocheting or knitting, the most desirable and daintiest kinds of lingerie, and the momentous question whether a skirt should escape the ground by six or eight inches. These are vital points in the lives of thousands of women, and their wisest solutions should be given by the best authorities. But is it too much to say that they are hardly of a nature to develop and satisfy the mental and spiritual nature of a man? At least, not for a lifetime!"

Nevertheless, even in his most pessimistic mood, when he felt that he had wasted great talents and misspent a life, Bok could not decry the genuine achievements of his long sovereignty. He could not belittle the wonderfully constructive piece of work carried out by Edward Bok during his editorship. For the record spoke too loudly to minimize its influence and potentiality. He had not limited himself to the gamut that comprised cooking, lingerie, and the subtle metaphysics of skirts. Possibly as much as any man in public life during his time, Bok had succeeded in producing changes in the American mores. And, in certain instances, he had utterly failed to do so. He was proud of his successes, though disposed to take them for granted. Flowing from the decrees of infallible wisdom, were they not to be anticipated? It was his failures that made him brood. They aggrieved him. They gave his "ideal of womanhood" the rude and destructive jolt from which it never recovered. They demonstrated the unsuspected limitations of infallibility—and they left Bok morally indignant as well as permanently puzzled. Defiance of his edicts would have been sinful, even had its motive been intelligible. But when, after profound reflection, one could attribute it only to sheer perversity. . . . Perhaps it made him regret his boast to William Dean Howells: that he appealed to the intelligent American woman rather than the intellectual type—to the sensible female, and not the eccentrics. What wonder that private Bok published a verdict which terrified editor Bok, who termed it a slander on womanhood? It was Rudyard Kipling's affectionate tribute: "The Female of the Species."

Most of Bok's failures could have been foreseen by a man not infallibly wise; at least, not so wise as to be indifferent to women as as women. There was the audacious and absolute dictatorship exercised by Parisian couturiers, often themselves of little taste and scant morals. Bok exposed their "deceit and misrepresentation." He persuaded Sarah Bernhardt to express her horror on seeing American women of refined sensibilities and position dressed in the gowns of the *déclassée* street women of Paris. He engaged the most expert designers in the world of women's dress and commissioned them to create American designs, some of which had their source in the decorative motifs of the American Indians. Obstinately, the American woman ignored them, and continued her immoral traffic with the diabolic Worth and Paquin. She even took a malicious delight in flagrancy. If elevation to paradise reduced her to the status of a squaw, she would behave like an angel—and she would dress like a streetwalker. Bok concluded that she had absolutely no instinct of patriotism. She simply refused to be awakened from her unintelligent submission. Inconceivably, she preferred to be a tool: to be made a fool of. Sadly, after a year of fulmination, the Grand Lama decided to let the matter drop.

Then came the question of aigrettes, the most desired of all the feathered possessions of womankind. Here, at least, he felt himself to be on solid ground. He could appeal directly to the noblest of womanly emotions, and the sacred instinct of motherhood. He published photographs and texts exposing the cruel torture of the mother heron for which the cult of the aigrette was responsible. Confidently, he awaited results. And they came. Shortly after the photographs reached his readers, he discovered that the demand for the feather had more than quadrupled! This time, he decided to punish defiance. Very quietly, he carried his case to the state legislatures, and persuaded men to pass laws which would prevent American women from wearing the hallmark of torture. It was men, not women, who responded to what he had been led to believe was the most sacred instinct in a woman's nature! What wonder that he derived little satisfaction from the character of his victory?

But Bok was dauntless, and in 1914, when America was dance mad, and the character of the dances rapidly grew more and more offensive, he was inspired to take action. The dance, surely, was an art: and wasn't art beauty, and wasn't there something to the effect that beauty and truth are identical? Well, he could see no reason why the people should not dance, if they wanted to, so long as they kept within the bounds of decency. So he secured the services of Vernon and Irene Castle, to introduce, through his magazine, better and more decorous new dances. And the Castles were equal to this missionary opportunity. As "new dances" they did their best to revive the gavotte, the polka, and finally the waltz. Alas, poor Bok! Once again the American woman revealed her pitiable frailty—the public refused to try the new Castle dances, and kept on turkey-trotting and bunny-hugging!

All this was nothing, as compared with the troublesome, insistent problem of suffrage for women. Did he not have to take a stand? Indeed he did, if only because no man sat at a larger gateway to learn the sentiments of numbers of women on any subject. He took a straw vote among a selected list of thosands of his subscribers. He consulted women of every grade of intelligence and in every station in life. And he, who was infallible, graciously deigned to discuss the issue with its eccentric proponents; among them, Susan B. Anthony, Julia Ward Howe, Anna Howard Shaw, and Jane Addams. What did posterity not miss, in lacking the records of these confabulations! Did Mrs. Howe declare, as always, that "women are people"? Bok had the satisfaction of knowing that he kept his own mind open. He was willing to advocate whatever might serve the best interests of the American woman. And, after long, and certainly searching, meditation he announced his fateful decision. He would oppose suffrage; he felt that American women were not yet ready to exercise the privilege intelligently and that their mental attitude was against it.

This conclusion corroborated—if it did not originate in—his secret, personal, lifelong opinions. He was never to believe that women were capable of assuming positions of executive responsibility. Not even on a women's magazine. At the end of his editorial career, when the *Woman's Home Companion*, rival of his own publication, was being brilliantly edited by Miss Gertrude Lane, he asserted that women did not have sufficient experience in the world of business to cope successfully with the material questions of a pivotal editorial position. Despite much contradictory evidence accumulated during the First World War, he remained positive that women would work infinitely better under the direction of a man than of a woman. Obviously, one question continued to exasperate him. Why were women becoming so restless in the lovely insulated paradise which he had worked so hard to create for them? One possibility never occured to him: that insulation might contribute to unrest—that women might resent being set apart; exalted in the aggregate, pampered and patronized in the individual case. Could it be that they were rebelling against the frustrations imposed on them by the determined idealism of the American male?

Bok was made unpleasantly anxious by the growing unrest among American women. He invited Rudyard Kipling—of all odd choices—to discuss it in the magazine, but this project was never carried out. Being a kindly man, Bok never complained that their unrest betrayed a signal ingratitude for all his services to "women in the home." And these were many. Very many.

They had begun early. They were, in fact, inaugurated by his first act in the editorial chair. This bachelor of twenty-six divined the fact that in thousands of cases the American mother was not the confidante of her daughter. He, by means of the magazine, must repair this lamentable lack of American family life. A woman might do so; a woman infallibly wise and understanding, tactful, winning. . . . But where could he find this paragon? Nowhere. So, as "Ruth Ashmore," he wrote two installments for a new department: "Side Talks with Girls." Seven hundred letters arrived within two days of publication. He read the first three. They proved, to his embarrassment but subsequent profit, how far the feminine nature would reveal itself on paper. Bok hastily found a feminine replacement. He went on, in Mrs.

Margaret Bottome's "Heart to Heart Talks," to dispose of the spiritual needs of the mature woman. For the next thirty years, girls and matrons alike were to flock to an inviting human personality, and invoke blessings on Bok. And the magazine quickly became a great clearing-house of information.

It was not long before Bok discovered the widespread unprepared-ness of the average American girl for motherhood, and her desperate ignorance when a new life was given her. Must not this, too, be changed? He set up a department to dispense information about prenatal and postnatal care. Five years later, it was successfully raising babies by mail! But this led to an "unsavory subject." The mere mention of venereal disease was taboo in polite society, and abso-lutely prohibited in every periodical and newspaper of standing. Could the dreadful conspiracy of silence be broken—with due decorum? Fearlessly, in 1906, Bok broke it in his magazine. He lost seventy-five thousand horrified readers before he made the nasty subject publicly debatable, if not a new conversational topic. But he was shortly to earn his reward. There were published, in five volumes, the *Edward Bok Books of Self-Knowledge*. These did not, as one might suppose, expound the Socratic dialectic. They took the question of natural life, and stripped it of its false mystery. And they sold! Who could say that, with innovations like these, Bok was not effecting radical changes in the American mores?

He effected changes in the environment, also. They were quite as radical. Theodore Roosevelt declared that Bok was unique; the only man who had ever changed, for the better, the architecture of an entire nation. Bok had always felt a keen desire to take hold of the small American house and make it architecturally better. In the end, as is the way with desire, it proved insatiable: he was constrained to dalliance with art, decoration, furnishing, landscape gardening. For many years he published small-house plans by the foremost architects of the country. If babies could be raised by mail, why not homes? His plans were so extensively used throughout the United States that the eminent architect Stanford White proclaimed Bok the greatest single force for good in the profession. All of them eliminated the American parlor, which Bok considered a useless room. But so absolute was his authority over the faithful in affairs of this kind that, of the tens of thousands of women who lived in Bok-conceived houses, only one ever commented on its inexplicable absence.

Bok went on to the pictorial presentation of the most carefully furnished homes in America, and to the illustration of good taste and bad taste in furniture. With his customary success: within five years, the physical appearance of domestic furniture in the stores completely changed. The problem of art now lured him, irresistibly. He conceived a systematic plan for improving the pictures on the walls of the American home. A year later, nearly one hundred thousand of the faithful were able to point with pride to such exemplary touchstones of taste as W. L. Taylor's "The Hanging of the Crane" and—inevitably—"Home-Keeping Hearts." But Bok, like other pontiffs, learned as he went; infallibility, though constant, can also be progressive. A younger generation of the faithful fared better. With the introduction of four-color presses, Bok secured permission to reproduce pictures from the greatest American private collections. And he distributed more than seventy million reproductions of celebrated paintings by the "old masters." Then, when he was flushed with triumph, private Bok inconveniently rose to the surface, and ordered reproductions of masterpieces of Chinese painting. Editor Bok pondered them. They might be art, but they wouldn't make much sense to the faithful. They were, definitely, risky. They were not distributed.

Having rebuilt the American home, landscaped it, furnished it, filled it with art, could he rest? Decidedly not. There was the public domain, still untouched by Bok; still, therefore, frightful. Cities. There were disreputably untidy spots disgracing the residential and business quarters. Bok undertook a photographic campaign. When it wound up, a dozen American municipalities were hard at work tidying their blushing faces. The Pullman parlor car, atrociously decorated, unsanitary; a wretched thing of riotously discordant colors, carved and gilded wood, cord portières, tasselled fringes. Another campaign: the Pullman campany issued a cynical rejoinder. But was the company any match for the embattled Bok? It was not. In the end, its officials wisely reorganized their decorative department. From the interior of the car to the landscape viewed from its window was merely a logical progression. Bok tried to do away with unsightly billboards. Advertisers protested; vested interests fought back. He did not accomplish much.

The American woman would have been justified in disliking her paradise had Bok neglected her intellectual life; had he failed to provide appropriate outlets for her intense emotions. But these areas of obligation likewise engaged his beneficent attention. He looked into the women's clubs—and he saw at once that what might prove a wonderful power in the civic life of the nation was being misdirected into gatherings of pseudo-culture. Was this to be tolerated? Bok collected his evidence, and then expressed his opinion of it. But the walls of Jericho did not collapse. Instead, he had a hornets' nest on his hands. This, naturally, increased his determination: he continued his articles of criticism in the magazine, and these, of course, added fuel to the conflagration. Petitions for his removal came in; boycotts of the magazine were instituted by irate clubwomen. Remove him as editor? He was the son-in-law of Cyrus H. K. Curtis, owner of the magazine. As for the boycotts, he met those easily, with the threat of action under the anti-trust law. But, for a time, the prestige of the Grand Lama was in grave jeopardy. Then, as always, he came out with a constructive plan. He advocated less of the cultural, and more of the civic interest. Although for years the clubwomen of America did not forgive Bok, they presently came round to his way of thinking. He could afford to wait for time to heal the wounds of vanity—on both sides. And it did. The General Federation of Women's Clubs gratefully conducted an official department in his magazine.

Meanwhile, was he not, month by month, enriching the mental life of the American woman? He persuaded ex-President Harrison, and, later, Theodore Roosevelt, to explain to her the workings of her government. He brought her the delicious fiction of F. Marion Crawford and Anthony Hope; the humor of John Kendrick Bangs; the always quotable verses of James Whitcomb Riley and Eugene Field; the authoritative social determinations of Mrs. Burton Harrison. He gave her judicious feedings of the more elevated masters; Howells and Mark Twain. He published the epistolary remains of Louisa M. Alcott, the conjugal reminiscences of Mrs. Gladstone, thus admitting her to the world of the great, and showing how very like her own it was. Only once did he go too far. Ignoring the mounting disapproval of his votaries, he persistently dosed them with the products of Rudyard Kipling, whom he thought "the greatest of his day." But at *Puck of Pook's Hill* they rebelled, with a loud wail. Disconsolately, he abandoned this effort to give them "what they ought to have."

One needed only to look at the American woman to appreciate his influence on her existence. During the hour before dinner, for example. Her Bok-designed home was in a Bok-tidied city. Her Bok-raised children were upstairs, quietly imbibing the Bok-explained facts of natural life. In her Bok-furnished living room, hung with Bok-chosen pictures, she had no anxiety about the coming meal; it was being prepared according to directions by Bok. And what was she doing? Very probably, pouring out her vivid, intense Bok-encouraged emotions. Had he not provided her with the music of Sir Arthur Sullivan, Tosti, and Richard Strauss? Had he not hired Madame Blanche Marchesi, teacher of operatic stars, to give a series of vocal lessons to his readers? Had he not, indeed, engaged Josef Hofmann, the eminent pianist, to undertake a regular department in the magazine and a salaried editorship?

What more could the American woman ask? Surely, he had foreseen, and provided for, every contingency arising from a fruitful life for women in the home. Yet feminine unrest continued to rise. More rapidly, now, than ever before. Revolt in paradise? Perhaps; though Bok didn't like to believe it. But the American woman was not only getting out of the home. She was getting out of hand as well. Bok began to wonder "whether the day of the woman's magazine, as we have known it, is not passing." He foresaw a constantly diminishing necessity for the distinctly feminine magazine. There would, of course, always be a field in the essentially feminine pursuits which have no place in the life of a man. But this field would be covered by other kinds of publications. They would supplant the practical portions of the woman's magazine. Then, what would be left? Nothing but the general contents—"equally interesting to men and to women"! In this unexpected conclusion, Bok registered his melancholy perception of change. He could no longer deny its ominous nature—"the interests of women and of men are being brought closer with the years, and it will not be long before they will entirely merge." Paradise was fast becoming obsolete.

In one of the last issues of the *Ladies' Home Journal* before Bok's leavetaking, there appeared four advertisements which listed rouge, among other products. Only one went further, with the decorous assurance that the rouge would be "imperceptible if properly applied." Exactly ten years later, an advertiser was offering lipstick, with the very different appeal that "it's comforting to know that the alluring note of scarlet will stay with you for hours."

The alluring note of scarlet . . . Would not the Grand Lama have denounced it vigorously? To others, it might symbolize the emancipation of the American woman. To him, would it not have shamelessly announced a paradise lost? He was spared any dolor. A characteristic prescience had warned him of the psychological moment to stop. Famous, eminent, wealthy beyond the most ambitious dreams of his youth, he had been able to decide that the Great Adventure of Life was something more than material work, and that the time to go is when the going is good.

So Edward Bok, who cared too deeply about womanhood to really like women, retired to private life. Unselfish service, which had been his profession, became his recreation. He merely went on to continued good works—turning, without regret, to the welfare of birds and the affairs of men.

[2] THE MIRROR OF THE MUCKRAKERS

While Edward Bok was wheedling the American women toward contentment, his contemporary, S. S. McClure, was rousing the public to anger. Month after month, the magazine that bore his name was exposing cankerous evils in government, in the economic structure of society—and asking what the American people proposed to do about them.

As the new century opened, Sam McClure was among the first ten men who were important in the American scene. So judged William Allen White, who accounted him the pioneer of a reform that was to surge onward in American life and run for forty years as the dominant note in our political, social and economic thinking. The journalistic crusade which he invented and led soon spread widely. It furnished a basis, in fact and conviction, for the national effort to achieve social democracy. Long after the crusade had spent its force, its influence lingered in the persistence of that effort. So McClure's effect on the national temper was not only spectacular, but lasting. It was, on his part, deliberate. But it was not wholly inspired by conscience. Those who knew him best unanimously declared McClure to be a genius. None of them suggested that his genius moved in the direction of ethical principle.

Like Bok, McClure was a businessman. He was astute; he always had a keen eye for the main chance; he saw everything big. Neither Bok nor McClure lacked guile; both preferred to call it by other names. After reaching positions of leadership, they professed moral indignation at practices which, in their less distinguished days and on a far inferior scale, they had profitably cultivated. Did this indicate a late flowering of moral sensibility? Possibly. But it was a turn customarily taken by American tycoons under the hot limelight of eminence. Bok and McClure wrote autobiographies, and each attributed his success chiefly to instinct. Neither found it necessary to remark that instinct is morally blind. They were sentimental, and genuinely benevolent. But early privations had given money-making an overwhelming significance. There was no disadvantage in being naturally ambidextrous.

McClure, like Bok, came to the United States as an immigrant; struggled against bitter poverty in childhood; extricated himself by his wits; broke into the field of publishing by founding a newspaper syndicate which quickly prospered. He had managed to put himself through Knox College, in Illinois. Being, even then, "a born salesman, a fast talker, a go-getter," he had earned his education as an itinerant peddler of notions, pots and pans, selling his wares along the rural roads of the Middle West. In later life, proud of his exploits as a peddler, he recounted them very fully to Robert Louis Stevenson. In *The Wrecker*, Stevenson portrayed McClure most engagingly, as Jim Pinkerton. William Dean Howells also made a literary portrait of him, less complimentary than Stevenson's. In *A Hazard of New Fortunes*, he put McClure "like a bug on a pinpoint in the character of Fulkerson." Indeed, McClure puzzled, exasperated, and strongly attracted every important writer with whom he came in contact. Many of them, at one or another stage of a tempestuous association, recorded their vivid feelings about him, under the pleasant illusion of exercising a talent for portraiture. McClure's effect was never neutral.

In his mid-forties at the turn of the century, McClure had already become a kind of one-man literary trust. His newspaper syndicate was flourishing. He had launched, and brought to astounding success, the magazine which bore his name. He had organized a book-publishing firm that was conducted like a compromise between a broker's office and a textile mill. He was planning wonderful new magazines, three or four of them; his projects were usually grandiose. He had a Napoleonic belief in his own star. His projects and his faith sometimes drove his less exuberant associates into nervous breakdowns. Eventually, they resulted in a mass resignation from his enterprises. He was a short, blond man "with a yellow mustache, big sensitive but challenging eyes, a sharp, hard but still ingratiating high voice snapping orders like a top-sergeant, conscious—Heavens, how conscious—of his power and glory, yet concealing his complacency by self-deprecation."

But, surely, he was entitled to a degree of complacency. Was not Mc-Clure, in his own realm, on the way to being a magnate, comparable in stature to Carnegie or Rockefeller in theirs? He, at least, believed so—and his attitude to his product, and the materials which went into it, resembled theirs. Rudyard Kipling once asked him whether he had read *David Harum*; McClure did not grasp the question, but his reply was characteristic: "No. He's dead." His business, as Kipling understood, was dealing in brain futures. Of what use was a dead author to McClure? He was concerned only with what was really alive, timely, interesting, and so every contemporary idea seethed promiscuously in his brain. To do business, he needed good writers; for them, the only critic worth listening to was the publisher—the critic who backed his judgment with his money. His own judgment was made with his solar plexus rather than with his brain; he estimated the value of any piece of writing by the pull it exerted on something inside of him. This was entirely sound. Moreover, McClure realized that he was open-minded, naturally enthusiastic, and not afraid to experiment with a new man. It was certainly true that with talent, he made electrical contact. Lacking any literary scholarship, he had an almost infallible literary divination. Remarkably few of his swans proved to be geese. There was never absent from his calculations the sense that he controlled such an instrument of publicity as had probably never been built before. Whatever he touched had to feed that mill.

Though McClure's motives were those of a businessman, his temperament was that of an artist; it was there that his genius lurked. His imagination was continuously effervescent, inexhaustibly fertile. He did not know how to channel it, or discipline it; but he had the faculty of enlisting those who did. This led him to the brilliant trinity of staff writers—Ida M. Tarbell, Ray Stannard Baker, and Lincoln Steffens—upon whose work the permanent fame of his magazine was chiefly to be based. It led him to choose as his partner John S. Phillips, a college friend who, as McClure acknowledged, "had an orderly and organizing mind—which I had not—and . . . a much wider education." On the magazine, it was said that while McClure had three hundred ideas a minute, Phillips was the only man around the shop who knew which one was not crazy. McClure admitted that he usually lost interest in a scheme as soon as it was started, and had no power of developing a plan and carrying it out to its last detail. At that point, his intractable imagination got the upper hand; the artist in him was forever on the move to the future. But the fires he kindled were brighter than any flames his staff could produce without him.

McClure traveled constantly, to Europe and to all parts of the United States, to see things and men, to listen and to talk. He wanted always to know in which of the happenings in the world people took the keenest interest. It was obvious that ideas were his meat, and he never knew where he got them. He would descend on the office, or write from Europe, enclosing in his letters fat packets of newspaper articles, headings, editorials, usually not cut out but torn out, jagged, scored and underlined, as suggestions for "stupendous new series of articles." Then the staff had to unite and fight against, say five out of seven of his new, world-thrilling, history-making schemes. In their judgment, many of these were merely foolish. Yet they recognized in him the receiver of the ideas of his day. They worked under some natural law of desperation, for McClure's very presence was disruptive. To finish an article before the deadline, they would often take secret refuge in a hotel. This strategy sometimes failed; New York was not large enough to conceal them from McClure; occasionally they had to seek the precarious security of a Washington bedroom to get their work finished. Ellery Sedgwick, who served an apprenticeship to him before becoming editor of the *Atlantic Monthly*, affirmed that there was never, in American business, a brighter talent than McClure's for disorganization. In any week, he could reverse the process described in the Book of Genesis. From order, he managed to bring forth chaos.

Paradoxically, McClure cherished—and enforced on his staff—the ideals of thoroughness and absolute accuracy. It was these ideals which gave authority to the exposures which the public soon identified as "McClure articles." He believed that each of these required the accumulation of knowledge and material enough to make a book. So he invented a production system which, long afterwards, was to be successfully revived by other magazines. He gave his writers adequate time for research, and paid them for their study rather than for the amount of copy they turned in. Thus, Miss Tarbell spent five years on the fifteen articles in which she dealt with the history of the Standard Oil Company; and each article cost the magazine about four thousand dollars.

No editor had ever before spent as liberally. But McClure, as a business-man, foresaw the profits to be made by establishing with the public a conviction that, in his magazine, accuracy was a moral force.

Though he had no gift for writing, McClure likewise set a high standard for the presentation of material. He insisted that articles should not only be clear to any reader of reasonable intelligence, but be interesting. The simplicity of this requirement was deceptive: most typical McClure articles dealt with dry, difficult, and technical sub-jects. They had to be accurate and thorough, but they likewise had to be made vivid; everything turned on the quality of the writing. Mc-Clure would inflame the intelligence of his staff into molten excite-ment, and demand its expression in clear, logical, intelligible, hard-hitting form. His standards produced a new, unique kind of jour-nalism. The exposure articles of Miss Tarbell, Baker, and Steffens were authoritative social studies. They were so invulnerable that only one libel suit was successfully brought against the magazine—and this was based on the inaccuracy of an official state document. But the articles did more than present startling facts. They blazed with what Miss Tar-bell called "righteous indignation." The writers were personally aston-ished, personally ashamed, personally indignant at the conditions they discovered and revealed. They wrote earnestly, with a kind of hortatory fervor. The combination of fact and fervor aroused a demand for re-form that was to outlast the magazine, the writers, and many of the conditions.

In 1903, when these articles began appearing, the American people were prepared for their revelations. For years, the country had been swept by the agitation of soap-box orators, prophets crying in the wilderness, and political campaigns based upon charges of corruption and privilege which everyone believed or suspected had some basis of truth, but which were largely unsubstantiated. The novelty of the ex-posure articles was their production of real evidence, abundant and usually sensational. Month after month, the public eagerly read dis-sertations of ten or twelve thousand words, and clamored for more. Their general drift was very clear. Cumulatively, they led to a single arresting deduction: that a democratic social order might not be capa-ble of surviving the economic and political practices to which it had given birth.

Nobody understood this better than President Theodore Roosevelt, then proclaiming his determination to institute a "square deal." He conferred often with the McClure writers. He used much of the information with which they supplied him in his recommendations to Congress. He acknowledged that he looked to their articles for real help. But after some years, when the crusade had spread to other magazines, he turned against the whole movement. In a speech, he denounced all writers of exposure articles, generically likening them to the man with the muckrake in *Pilgrim's Progress* who would not lift his eyes from the mire; and the disparaging epithet stuck. Undoubtedly, as Lincoln Steffens remarked long afterwards, Roosevelt was an honest man; he could not tell a lie until he had made himself believe it.

The originators of muckraking looked at American society from the same point of vantage as Roosevelt. Their position was squarely middle-of-the-road. To McClure, as a businessman, social radicalism was repugnant. It was no less so to Miss Tarbell, Baker and Steffens, though for quite other reasons. They had a passionate faith in the American way of life, as it was supposed to be. They believed that it could be achieved only under a democratic capitalist system. They were therefore partisans of the established order. It was, indeed, the intensity of their convictions that turned them into reformers; and, almost accidentally, made them seem to be attacking what they were only seeking to defend.

For, like Roosevelt himself, they were deeply troubled by the sense that things had somehow gone amiss. The American way of life as it was supposed to be? It had not been achieved; it was becoming more remote every day. The established order was failing to produce its anticipated results. They feared for the future. Powerful forces seemed bent upon negating democratic institutions, and might eventually destroy them. On the other hand, popular discontent was rising, and despair of social justice might explode in a revolutionary overturn. As patriotic Americans, they did not want to see democracy replaced either by the rule of plutocracy, or by socialism.

It was characteristic of Roosevelt to mistake his vigorous moral feelings for realistic intelligence. So the problem looked simple to him. If he could only identify "the devil in the mess" and vanquish it, everything would magically come right. The real job was to expose bad men and drive them from power. Who were these bad men? Obviously, whoever had last aroused the President's moral indignation; at any moment one could be sure that he had just found the prime mover, the real scapegoat. But this scapegoat was a protean creature. At various times, and in varying circumstances, it turned out to be the "male-factors of great wealth," the trusts, the "guilty labor leaders," the "cor-rupt politicians." The President's passionate invective often proved to be a delusive substitute for the process of thought.

The further they pushed their researches and investigations, the less Miss Tarbell, Baker and Steffens were disposed to agree with him. They knew, perhaps better than he did, the precise degree of guilt that could be fairly attributed to each of his favorite scapegoats; had they not fur-nished him with the evidence? But they realized that none of these were ultimate; behind each of them there lurked another force; the locus of final responsibility was never directly visible. Roosevelt him-self was amazed by this insight, which he would have liked to ap-propriate had his temperament permitted. He recorded his surprise that these fact-minded writers did not regard any of his scapegoats "as ex-ceptional villains but merely as ordinary Americans, who under given conditions are by the mere force of events forced into doing much of which we complain." Could it be, as Miss Tarbell, Baker and Steffens were intimating month after month, that responsibility for the parlous state of affairs rested with the nation as a whole? That the mass of ordinary Americans were by no means innocent of complicity in the conditions against which they were so wrathfully protesting? That failure of the established order was due to no inherent defect in the nature of a democratic society? But that the average citizen was getting exactly what he asked for and that, as Baker acknowledged with hor-ror, the conditions of corruption were deliberately organized—they actually represented the American way of life in many of its most im-portant activities?

Editorially, *McClure's* pointed to "the American contempt for law" —a universal and dangerous trait. Reviewing the contents of a typical issue, which contained one of Miss Tarbell's articles on Standard Oil, one of Baker's series on the labor movement, and one of Steffens' studies of city government, the editorial remarked that these con-stituted "such an arraignment of American character as should make every one of us stop and think." The three articles showed "capitalists, workingmen, politicians, citizens—all breaking the law, or letting it be broken." There was no one left to uphold it; "none but all of us." "We are all doing our worst and making the public pay. The public is the people. We forget that we all are the people; that while each of us in his group can shove off on the rest the bill of today, the debt is only post-poned; the rest are passing it on back to us. We have to pay in the end, every one of us. And in the end the sum total of the debt will be our liberty." More than forty years later, these words still rang true.

But in 1903, this conclusion was novel. And it was a very odd one for the three writers, each of whom had arrived at it independently. For none of them had begun their investigations with any personal desire to make the discoveries which they actually made. None of them had any inclination to "radical ideas"; their only prejudice was in favor of the way of life which tradition had taught them to believe was es-sentially American. There was, perhaps, a certain naïveté in their horror at finding so glaring a discrepancy between democratic assumptions and democratic practice. But their naïveté and horror were shared by a large segment of the American public. Lincoln Steffens found that the most corrupt city bosses, like Israel W. Durham of Philadelphia, and mil-lionaire captains of industry like William Ziegler who bribed and bought legislatures as a matter of course, were genuinely shocked when he confronted them with the real implications of their activities, show ing them how these were invalidating democracy. Even ex-President Grover Cleveland confessed his utter inability to understand that brib-ery and corruption could be done by good men and that it was a proc-ess changing the very nature of our government!

McClure had assigned Miss Tarbell the subject of Standard Oil—the "mother of the trusts"—because the feeling of the common people had a sort of menace in it; they took a threatening attitude toward the trusts, and without much knowledge. What he hoped for was some articles on the business achievements and methods of the Standard Oil—more especially, the great care that had built up their methods of economical handling and distribution. His expectations, as it turned out, were ful-filled. But the results were far from what he anticipated.

Miss Tarbell, a tall, matter-of-fact woman who looked much more like a schoolmistress than an editor, was aptly described by Finley Peter Dunne in the language of Mr. Dooley: "Iderem's a lady but she has the punch!" She had been born in Pennsylvania at about the time oil was discovered there, and her father had been ruined in the early oil wars. One of the first generation of college women, she had not been satis-fied to join women in the home. She became a teacher, went on to an editorial position with the Chautauqua movement, decided to become a biographer and historian, and went to Paris to study at the Sorbonne.

There, by way of a chance article on the paving of Paris streets, Mc-Clure found her, and presently hired her for a staff job. She had already written a life of Napoleon for him, and had followed it with a life of Lincoln which achieved great popular success, when he turned her loose on Standard Oil. A scholar by temperament, and a research historian by training, she soon found that she was embarked not upon a series of articles, but upon the factual history of the greatest of American business enterprises. When Henry H. Rogers of Standard Oil got wind of the project, he sent his friend Mark Twain to offer the corporation's assistance. She accepted it. If there was in her anything of the crusader for social justice, she rigorously suppressed it while gathering materials for, and writing, her history. She was impartial, objective, exhaustive; she discussed with Rogers all the charges made by Standard Oil's enemies and critics; she took to them the official rebuttals offered by Rogers. She mastered the long, complex records of Congressional and state investigations, the testimony of Rockefeller, Archbold, and other Standard Oil officials; she interviewed all surviving parties to thirty years of litigation.

Her series of articles—soon published in two volumes—took the country by storm. For the stark, soberly told history involved the nation as a whole and still involved it at the time of reading. Miss Tarbell was content to let the record speak for itself; she made no attempt to indict Standard Oil. She acknowledged its efficiency, its economy, its magnificent organization, its very considerable achievements. But she likewise showed how all these had been accomplished. The bill to the people included bribery, fraud, coercion; the ruthless elimination of competition by means of espionage, violence, arson, and techniques of financial wrecking; the debauching of railroads, legislatures, public officials. All these "business practices" which a democratic capitalist society had developed could be collectively described as a systematic, relentless criminality. Here, certainly, were capitalists conspiring among themselves, shrewdly, upon legal advice, to break the law so far as it restrained them, and to misuse it to restrain others who were in their way. Here was efficient monopoly of a product in universal use. The people paid—not only in money, but morally—whatever the monopolists saw fit to charge.

Behind the whole structure of "real greatness" was an ordinary American who happened also to be a genius. Rockefeller exemplified all the virtues of which Americans approved. He was thrifty, frugal, hard-working. He was pious, abstemious, and charitable. He was a model of domestic propriety. He was as indifferent to social prestige as he was averse to personal luxury and extravagance. His only passions, so far as anyone knew, were success and money. And, in genuine honesty, he accounted himself a good citizen. Was he? Did he fulfill the concept of good citizenship held by the ordinary American? Standard Oil was more than a great business enterprise. It was one of the real, if unacknowledged, rulers of the nation, and Rockefeller had made it so. Miss Tarbell's honest, accurate account of the genesis of its sovereignty—in which Rockefeller's partner, Rogers, had himself collaborated—invited the American people to assess their complicity.

This same embarrassing invitation was repeated by Lincoln Steffens' remarkable studies of the actual working of municipal and state governments. Soon made available in book form as *The Shame of the Cities* and *The Struggle for Self Government*, they enlisted popular support for the progressive movement in national politics. During the first decade of the century, they furnished the most powerful of all influences for reform. But, in origin, they were as accidental as Miss Tarbell's history. McClure, having hired Steffens to join his staff as managing editor, sent him off to the Middle West to dig up material for the magazine. In Chicago, Steffens learned that Joseph W. Folk, the prosecuting attorney of St. Louis, was unearthing sensational evidence of bribery and corruption in the city's government. He went to St. Louis, interviewed Folk. Folk incredibly asserted that "it is good businessmen that are corrupting our bad politicians; it is good business that causes bad government—in St. Louis." And Steffens soon found himself launched on the series of articles which, proving the truth of this assertion with respect to one after another great American city, shattered the complacency of the American public.

Steffens was a diminutive, wiry man whose rumpled hair, goatee and flowing tie gave him the look of an artist; but whose keen, restless eyes behind their spectacles suggested the scientist. He was a little of both. The son of a wealthy California merchant, Steffens went to college, then on to Europe. He studied psychology with Wundt in Germany, and ethics. He dabbled in music and art. He traveled widely, and continued his studies in Paris. His intention was to become a novelist. On his return to the United States, his father unexpectedly stopped his allowance. Steffens got himself a job as reporter on E. L. Godkin's *Post*. He covered Wall Street, mastering the realities of high finance. He covered the New York police department during the sensational "vice crusade" led by the clergyman Dr. Charles H. Parkhurst; and he learned about the tie-up between the police and the criminal underworld.

Steffens had developed a fascinated interest in men and motives, and his studies in ethics had freed him from the conventional American habit of dividing the human race into the morally good and the morally bad. He met all kinds of people on their own terms: reformers like Parkhurst and Roosevelt; corrupt city bosses like Richard Croker, and their henchmen in the government, like Thomas F. Byrnes, the grafting chief of police; great financiers like J. P. Morgan, eminent captains of industry, corporation lawyers. Flattered by his genuine desire to understand their points of view, they all told him the truth as they saw it. If he was shocked by learning that men like Croker—who frankly acknowledged that he was corrupt—were the paid, accredited agents of respectable men of affairs honored for their public spirit and civic morality, Steffens did not betray it. Like Miss Tarbell, he made a practice of laying all his cards on the table. He made friends with the political bosses and their grafting henchmen. He placed before them the evidence that he had accumulated, gave them an opportunity to disprove or explain it—and never published *all* the discreditable facts that he had gathered. This shrewd precaution kept them in a state of wholesome uncertainty, but it likewise earned their gratitude, and won their confidence.

The facts which Steffens published in *McClure's* were sensational enough to provoke nationwide excitement. And there soon emerged something even more exciting: a social pattern, designed for the express purpose of producing anti-social results. With minor local variations, it occured on a national scale. Steffens' investigations showed that the paper government did not count. The constitutional structure did not correspond with the actual government. Actual government was the function of a party machine, often controlled by a private citizen who, like Croker, worked for his own pocket all the time. Business, always requiring some form of privilege for its expansion or its prosperity, favored this arrangement and sought to maintain it; privilege could be bought from a party boss. So the machine mediated between organized business, official government, the criminal underworld and the grafters. The whole arrangement was highly efficient;

everyone profited; everyone was satisfied. This was obvious from the fact that whenever a "reform" administration was elected, its tenure was brief; it was "bad for business," and the best businessmen saw to it that the old machine was reinstated. Steffens concluded that, since the pattern occurred everywhere in the same form, then this universal evil must be, not an accidental consequence of the wickedness of bad men, but the impersonal effect of natural causes.

Speaking in Los Angeles, to a group of the city's business leaders and other public-spirited citizens, Steffens was asked by the Episcopal bishop how the corrupt "system" had originated. His reply humorously expressed his own diagnosis: "Most people, you know, say it was Adam. But Adam, you remember, he said that it was Eve, the woman, she did it. And Eve said no, no, it wasn't she; it was the serpent. And that's where you clergy have stuck ever since. You blame that serpent, Satan. Now I come and I am trying to show you that it was, it is, the apple."

For the truth that Steffens was trying to drive home to the American people was the truth of their own moral complicity. It was only by their tacit consent that representative government had ceased to represent them. It was clear to him that "business men do not want good government much more than they want a representative democracy, that the people do not like good men and good government, or, let us say, professionally good men in office and unyielding good government. They both prefer 'bad' government." Why? Because nearly every American was in some respect involved by business—and all business, great or small, had a common need of privileges: franchises and special legislation, which required legislative corruption; protective tariffs, interpretations of laws in their special interest or leniency or "protection" in the enforcement of laws, calling for "pulls" with judges, prosecutors, and the police. If there was a devil in the mess that devil was privilege; the remedy was to take down the prizes by wiping out privileges and all hope of privileges—as it were, to destroy the apple.

To do this, Steffens in time came to believe, required nothing less than a fundamental change in American culture: the fault could be traced to the American ideal of success, which set up the temptation of power and riches. Until that change could be wrought, Americans were likely to exist in the atmosphere of a moral paradox, corrupt and contented, busily striving to pervert the institutions of a democratic society to anti-social ends. Was there not, indeed, something wrong in our ends as well as in our beginnings, in what we are after as well as what is after us, in American ideals as well as in American conduct and its causes?

Meanwhile, Ray Stannard Baker had been looking into the relations of labor and capital for *McClure's*, reaching conclusions that reinforced those of Miss Tarbell and Steffens. Baker, born in Michigan and a college graduate, cherished a lifelong desire to write fiction, and occasionally did so. He had been a reporter in Chicago, deeply interested in industrial conditions, when, after the publication of some of his stories, McClure invited him to join the staff of the magazine. A quizzical, scholarly-looking man, Baker was no academic theorist. He soon came to be recognized as the greatest reporter in America. He had the gift of absorbing himself in his subject, no matter what his subject might be. Whereas Miss Tarbell restricted herself, in the main, to subjects in the field of economics, and Steffens dealt almost exclusively with politics, Baker was at home in both provinces, and in many others also. He could write with equal authority about science and philosophy; the recondite iniquities of the railroads; the desperate social situation of the Negro; the effort of the churches to meet the new spiritual unrest. This versatility sprang from the nature of his major interest. Like Henry Adams, he believed life to be a process of "education." He wanted to master the art of living in a crowded world. He found that it was all-inclusive.

Baker began his studies of the relations of labor and capital just when business was beginning to realize that labor organizations had come to stay. A series of prolonged, costly and violent strikes had raised a popular demand for labor and capital to get together. In some instances, Baker found, they had done so: organized labor and organized capital had joined forces and formed what was in effect a complete monopoly in various industries, thus enabling them to prey upon the public. He discovered the social phenomenon which a later generation, far more familiar with it, was to call "labor racketeering"; in that comparatively innocent day, certain large corporations bribed powerful labor leaders, or secretly put them on their payrolls, charging the cost to their customers. This simple formula only took it out of the public. In regions where organized capital and organized labor were at war—as in the mining camps and smelter towns of Colorado— neither obeyed the law; local governments were unable to control the situation, or prevent riots, bloodshed, destruction of valuable property, with the result that a condition of anarchy prevailed. He looked into the city of San Francisco, where organized labor had won control of the political administration; had gained what were said to be the highest wages paid anywhere in America; and, politically, continued to represent the same business, vice, and criminal interests that had always been served by the machines of the two major political parties. Elsewhere, he found labor unions, in their effort to recruit strength, depriving non-union men of "the right to work." He found the new employers' associations seeking to use methods of despotism. All these conditions, Baker argued, were symptoms of a disease which was circulating in the blood of the American people. For the evils were not sporadic. They were deliberately organized and generously financed. They represented the "way of life" which many Americans preferred. He concluded that "if we want self-government—not the name, but the real thing mentioned in the Declaration of Independence and the Constitution, we have got to work at it ourselves."

The import of Baker's articles, like those of his colleagues, challenged the American people. Was it not true that they wanted good government without being willing to contribute anything whatsoever, either in time or in thought; they wanted something for nothing? What was the remedy? Baker thought he knew it: not new mechanisms, or a new system of government, however inciting they appeared to sanguine reformers, but more knowledge, more understanding, more sense of obligation on the part of all the people, more willingness to sacrifice immediate profit to future welfare. But, at the end of his life, reviewing the achievements of the muckraking movement, Baker ruefully acknowledged that "while there have been superficial improvements in forty years in the conditions we reported, the deeper-seated injustices remain, still unpurged. We are still far from the democracy of our vision." Had the process of "education," as a social remedy, failed? He could only reaffirm the profound truth of a quotation from Henrik Ibsen which he had used nearly a half century earlier: "And men still call for special revolutions, for revolutions in politics, in externals. But all that sort of thing is trumpery. It is the human soul that must revolt."

After some years, Miss Tarbell, Baker, Steffens and Phillips, with other key members of McClure's staff, resigned in a body, bought the *American Magazine*, and undertook to conduct it, along the McClure lines, as a co-operative enterprise. They added to their number William

Allen White and, even more importantly, Finley Peter Dunne, the creator of "Mr. Dooley." Dunne, already famous the country over as Dooley, was the most valuable of recruits to muckraking; he offset its earnestness with robust humor. But though he made the American people laugh, he also made them think. The edge of his irony was frighteningly sharp, especially to sacred cows.

Dunne was a native of Chicago, the son of Irish immigrants who had prospered. The environment from which he sprang was bitterly portrayed, in a later generation, by the novelist James T. Farrell; the contrast between Dunne's genial picture of it and Farrell's indicated what marked changes in American life, and in the temper of the American mind, the interval had produced. At seventeen, Dunne became a reporter on a Chicago paper; ten years later he had invented the wise, witty, skeptical character who, for the rest of his life, practically displaced him. People didn't know Dunne; they knew Dooley, and from Dunne they wanted nothing else. Dooley caught the national imagination with his shrewd common sense, his impudent refusal to be awed by pretensions or prestige, his savage hatred of all shams and all forms of hypocrisy. He was a daring creation. America had never been without its cracker-box philosophers. But Martin Dooley came of the socially despised immigrant class, and was proud of it. Worse still, his profession was disreputable; he was a barkeeper. Yet the nation soon found that the most penetrating criticism of its day-by-day life, the most deadly appraisal of its leaders and their policies, were issuing from a fictitious, fly-specked saloon on Archey Road.

Dooley's account of the symposiums held there were eagerly read throughout the country; they often shaped public opinion. They were anxiously followed by all men in public life, who had reason to dread the puncturing barb of Dooley's scorn. Had he not made Andrew Carnegie ridiculous? Had he not swept the American people into laughter at Teddy Roosevelt's exorbitant vanity and egotism, with the result that Roosevelt genially, if nervously, courted his friendship? Dooley's appeal was like a social plumb line. It not only struck the plain people at the bottom but reached to the intellectuals at the top. He was a favorite of such improbable readers as Henry Adams and Henry James. He was, indeed, the only man of letters whom Henry James expressed a wish to meet on his return to the United States. Mrs. Wharton arranged the meeting. It proceeded very like a scene from one of James' later novels. Mr. Dooley floundered helplessly in the heavy seas of James' parentheses; thought that everything he said was splendid; but wanted all the time to tell him, "Just 'pit it right up into Popper's hand." It was a characteristic Dooley reaction.

Dunne was incorrigibly lazy, a hard drinker, given to outbursts of explicit profanity; he had wisdom, but could not apply it to Peter Dunne; he loathed writing, and ran away from it whenever he could. These were not qualities to inspire the admiration of Miss Tarbell who, although she had a punch, was a "lady"; or of the unhumorous Baker and dynamic Steffens. But his spell was irresistible, even to them. And, for all his skepticism, he shared their sanguine view of the American future. He, too, loved his country too well not to feel confident that, granted time and patience, it would solve all its problems wisely; above all, with justice. He had a searching eye for evil, but his vision was of good, and his deepest conviction was that all souls are alike before man as before God.

In the *American*, Dunne continued to whet his irony on the living flesh of native sacred cows: any tycoon befuddled by his own power; any self-appointed savior inflated with his gaseous panaceas; any notable exemplar of hypocrisy and the money motives it concealed. What his colleagues were trying to drive home to the American people in their books, Dunne sometimes could distill in a single pungent sentence: "If ye'd turn on the gas in the darkest heart ye'd find it had a good raison for th' worst things it done, a good varchous raison, like needin' th' money or punishin' th' wicked or tachin' people a lesson to be more careful, or protectin' th' liberties of mankind, or needin' th' money." Better than any of them, he knew the fitful nature of American enthusiasm, to which they were all appealing. He had once likened it to a fire on an ice floe: "It burns bright so long as ye feed it, an' it looks good, but it don't take hold, somehow, on th' ice." But he worked to keep the flame alive. He was, as Dooley said of himself to his friend Hennessey, "a post to hitch ye'er silences to."

Even before the emergence of the *American* as the leading organ of muckraking, the movement launched by S. S. McClure had spread to other publications, and began to engage some notable talents. None looked more picturesque, or proved to be more effective, than Thomas W. Lawson, the Boston stock-market speculator, whose *Frenzied Finance*, published serially in *Everybody's*, became a national sensation. Lawson was a man with many grudges and, as the journalist Charles Edward Russell asserted, no one could tell how much of him was business acumen, how much megalomania, how much love of the spotlight, how much resentment against his business associates, and how much a sincere desire to expose and correct great evils. In whatever proportion, all these figured among his motives, and the heady mixture gave his book an explosive force.

Lawson, the son of a carpenter, had quit school at twelve, found a job in Boston's financial center, and by the age of sixteen, through daring speculation in stocks, had managed to acquire sixty thousand dollars. He lost it in one dazzling plunge, but he had won the formula of his later financial success. He proceeded to make, lose, and again make several fortunes in ways that were legal, legitimate, and perhaps not immoral. It was the heyday of great "promoters"; Lawson had a Napoleonic self-confidence, as well as a touch of Barnum's genius for personal publicity. Conservative financiers deplored his panoplied forays into print, but the public enjoyed them, and he attracted the wide following he required for his schemes. A millionaire by the time he was forty, he was a man of arresting appearance, dark haired, blue eyed, heavy jawed, with the stocky, muscular build of a pugilist and the wardrobe of a fashion plate.

Unlike most self-made millionaires, Lawson affected to despise Society. The sentiment, in Boston, was reciprocated with an amenity which itself was an insult. Never acceptable to the aristocrats of State Street, he was unable to secure membership in the Boston Stock Exchange. But, if Society proposed to exclude him, Lawson saw to it that it should not have the added satisfaction of being able to ignore him. He provided himself with a costly home. He collected glittering paintings. He placed fabulous bets at the races; made widely publicized efforts to acquire an opera box; paid thirty thousand dollars to have a specimen carnation named for his wife. Gentility did not attempt to conceal its amusement at these antics of a commoner. Later, wishing to compete for the right to defend the America's Cup against Sir Thomas Lipton—who greatly resembled him—Lawson built a racing yacht at a cost of some two hundred thousand dollars. The New York Yacht Club promptly excluded him from the preliminary trials; he was not a member. This was a severe social rebuff, and while Lawson made capital of it by insisting on his democratic right to compete for the privilege of representing his country, thus provoking a controversy which made headlines on both sides of the Atlantic, the outcome further aggrieved him. After one unfortunate trial race, he ordered his costly yacht scrapped.

Meanwhile, Lawson had come into close business relations with the group of magnates who dominated the affairs of the Standard Oil Company. Apparently, like the tycoons of State Street, they too disliked Lawson, and perhaps distrusted his unconventional, erratic ways. But they needed him, and were quite ready to use him. They were lone wolves who had discovered the mutual advantages of hunting as a pack; Lawson, never admitted to any pack, had made his isolation into independence, and his independence into a resource. He was to be permitted to run with the Standard Oil pack, but not belong to it. Presumably, as an alliance against all lambs, the arrangement had its profitable uses for everyone concerned. At the turn of the century Lawson developed the most grandiose of his schemes. This was the creation of a super-trust in copper through the consolidation of great Western mining properties engaged in ruthless competitive war among themselves, and collectively in violent strife with labor. For this project, Lawson succeeded in winning the support of H. H. Rogers, his closest associate in the Standard Oil group, and thus—in his view—the support of the corporation and its affiliated interests.

Presently, the Amalgamated Copper Company was launched, with Lawson in command of stock-market operations. It was his job to dispose of the company's securities; his name stood behind the iridescent prospects of fortune devised to captivate the public. The plain people, as he later declared, responded with alacrity; they promptly invested two hundred millions of dollars of their savings. But, in less than five years, Lawson found that he had been thoroughly tricked by his colleagues. He also knew that one hundred millions of dollars were lost, thirty men committed suicide, and twenty previously reputable citizens went to the penitentiary, directly because of Amalgamated. He had unwittingly been made the instrument by which thousands upon thousands of investors in America and Europe had been plundered.

Lawson had already begun denouncing his former associates in newspaper advertisements when *Everybody's* proposed that he write a series of articles, with their editor, John O'Hara Cosgrave, serving as literary collaborator. Lawson's attack by means of advertising was unconventional; but did it amount to anything more than up-to-date strategy in an old-fashioned war? Exposure articles were quite another matter.

Inevitably, they would wash the dirtiest and most private of linen in public. Tradition decreed that, however ferociously titans battled with one another, their collective alliance against the public always remained in force. There were sound practical reasons for the rule of honor among thieves. Plundering might become a useless art if its technical secrets were revealed. Lawson was no more squeamish than his associates, as his record proved—but had he not been treated as a pariah, always pointedly excluded? He resolved to betray the ritual of the guild. He would have the satisfaction of revenge. And he would get it under the best of auspices, as a champion, now, of the plain people from whom he sprang.

Miss Tarbell's history of Standard Oil, in process of publication, had paved the way for his story. Apparently, Lawson saw himself not only as the people's champion, but as their leader in a national crusade against the entrenched power of wealth. His intention, he said, was reform: the whole nation must no longer be taxed, in the stock market, for the benefit of a few bandit magnates. His narrative had one claim to be regarded as unique, and *Everybody's* made the most of it: "for the first time in the history of High Finance we have the High Priest tell it as it happened." Lawson would withhold none of the cold-blooded facts; spare no individual, not even himself. For the inner clique of Standard Oil magnates, Lawson coined the dramatic name, "The System," itself an indictment. As a document in finance, his book professed to explain, and to illustrate abundantly, its methods of operation; to show how it made money by fleecing the public, and how in the process it was enabled to extend its dominion by the constant addition of new provinces. None of the methods which Lawson described was actually new; most of them had been used by Daniel Drew, Commodore Vanderbilt, and Jay Gould. But no writer before Lawson had ever been in a position to expound their interrelation, their contemporary refinements, their twentieth-century efficiency.

Lawson did precisely this. The System, he alleged, was ultimately responsible to nobody, and was powerful enough to circumvent all legal restraints. He outlined its ramifications; its control of the resources of Standard Oil; by means of this, its indirect control over the resources of a great bank; through this, its control over those of three colossal insurance companies. These multiplied resources—actually, the people's money to which, in theory, the System had no legal access—were, he charged, being diverted to its private speculative use; the public's funded savings were being employed to exploit the public, merely to further enrich a very small clique of millionaires. If Lawson's charges were not true, they were obviously libelous. But no legal action was ever brought against Lawson or the magazine.

However, Lawson's story was not only a document in high finance; it was also a picture of one phase of American society. Here were a group of "ordinary Americans" who had risen to positions of vast power and public trust; who in their personal lives, as Lawson acknowledged, were exemplary; who nevertheless, in their economic function as trustees, deliberately used their position to betray the public interest, turning their command of credit to anti-social ends. Here was the American economic order as it looked from the inside: a nightmare of savagery, man returned to the jungle, still fashionably clad and boasting the ordinations and amulets of civilization—a staggering showing. Lawson's book, in its disclosures of reckless viciousness, seemed to show new capacities in the human spirit for the cruel and the avaricious.

The plain people derived two impressions from Lawson's vivid narrative. One was of the unscrupulous use of power by great capitalists. The other had to do with the new age into which they had moved without being aware of it—the age of finance capitalism. In it, the basis of power had shifted from the tangible possession of money and property to the control of credit. Credit was something intangible, and the people suspected that it was created by access to their resources. Whoever possessed absolute control of credit occupied the seat of ultimate sovereignty. And who was this? Obviously, J. P. Morgan the elder. Lincoln Steffens, writing an article on Morgan as "the boss of all the bosses," was merely setting forth what everyone knew. Everyone, as it turned out, but Morgan himself. For Morgan's sense of his own position by no means corresponded with that of the public.

After his article had been published, Steffens, at the Morgan bank one day, was summoned by a junior partner. This man had laid the article on Morgan's desk. Morgan had read it twice, and shaken his head. He professed not to understand it. The junior partner asserted that not only did Morgan have no conviction of absolute power but that as a matter of fact his power was not absolute; it was very limited. And he related an incident to prove this amazing assertion. Morgan "had discovered that he could not make the New York, New Haven and Hartford Railroad, which he controlled, buy its coal from a coal company he controlled, without the consent of 'Diamond Jim' Brady.

He was so enraged that he was going to fight Brady; 'if he did nothing else the rest of his life, he would lick that man.' But he didn't; he accepted him, and the reason was that Brady represented a company in which the officers of the New Haven and other railroads held shares; the company had the exclusive privilege of selling supplies to these railroads."

Two decades later, this clubby, efficient arrangement figured profitably in the operations of tycoons like Al Capone and Dutch Schultz. The American people then learned to describe it, not without admiration, as a racket. In the opening years of the century, however, though legitimate, respectable, and one of the normal economic blessings for which a system of free enterprise could be praised, information about it was very wisely held to be top secret. And why not? It brought a handsome profit to "insiders"; its costs were rightly borne by the investors who were privileged to be represented by them; and they—ignorant alike of the mechanisms and the ethics of finance—could scarcely be expected to appreciate its esoteric beauty. Far better not to trouble the innocent investors with a managerial complexity so obviously beyond their understanding.

This arrangement deeply impressed Steffens. A remarkable development, surely, since the ramifications of its business, influence, and power were so complex that even Morgan dared not touch it! Did it not suggest that the structure of American business was beginning to duplicate that of American politics? In both, apparently, the real bosses—the men who were supposed to exercise absolute power—actually had to yield to the less powerful men whose support they required. Many Americans had come to feel that the boss could not be eliminated from either politics or business; and others were convinced that it would be undesirable to do away with him. They spoke hopefully of finding "honest bosses." But—didn't the very conditions which made the boss necessary likewise operate to prevent him from remaining honest? It was his function to organize the control and distribution of privileges —the basis of prosperity. In discharging his obligation, could he represent anything more than an efficient adjustment of competitive grafts? Steffens surmised that neither the privileged nor the unprivileged, neither the bosses nor the bossed, understood this or meant it.

Perhaps the American people could not be expected to understand what was so transparently clear to a man like Steffens, who was cursed with an inconvenient propensity to philosophizing. But their education was proceeding swiftly. Lawson had announced that he was going to cause a life-insurance blaze that would illuminate the policy holders' world and expose the scoundrels who dwelt there. Life-insurance funds —the savings of the American people—were supposedly a "sacred" trust. Lawson unkindly disclosed that they were being used as the private reserve of great financiers. Pulitzer's *World* took up the charge, and dredged up a mass of evidence that substantiated it. How had these strange practices originated? S. S. McClure, like many another American, was shocked by them. On his staff there was a bright young journalist, a Yale graduate, Burton J. Hendrick. He assigned to him the task of tracing the history of the insurance business. Hendrick's articles, presently published in book form as *The Story of Life Insurance,* informed the public and contributed to bringing about the investigation undertaken by Charles Evans Hughes. Hendrick—who was later to become the historian of the "age of big business"—went on to study the origins of outstanding American fortunes. His researches, and the more exhaustive ones which resulted in a monumental *History of the Great American Fortunes* by the socialist Gustavus Myers, furnished abundant historical precedent for tactics still operative in the twentieth century. Unfortunately, the effect of these excursions into the American past was to tarnish many illustrious reputations. Was not this perhaps unjust? A finicking discrimination in ethics could only have impeded the unselfish labors of those eminent "ordinary Americans" for whom Jay Gould had spoken in protesting that *"We* have had the country rich, *we* have developed the country. . . ."

The eminent Americans resurrected by Hendrick and Myers had long since gone to their eternal reward. But Charles Edward Russell studied some of their exemplary successors who were still alive. He was moved to inquire, not without impertinence, "Where Did You Get It, Gentlemen?" in a series of articles that traced the beneficent activities of William C. Whitney, Charles T. Yerkes, Thomas F. Ryan, and other current models for the emulation of youth—modest men, all of them, yet never so shy or so sated that they refrained from embracing opportunity with tender affection. As Russell pointed out, a salutary lesson was taught by the good works that had brought them, not only honor, but generous increase. Why need any American remain poor? Their ways and gates to wealth, still open to all, were neither strait nor narrow.

Russell likewise undertook an equally disturbing study of the packing industry. His articles, later issued in a book as *The Greatest Trust in the World*, exasperated that conscientious reformer President Theodore Roosevelt. For they stirred up public resentment to a pitch that displeased certain powerful Republican colleagues. Had not William E. Lorimer, the Republican boss of Chicago who was later to be expelled from the Senate, assured the President that the meat packers were conducting their vast enterprises wholly in the public interest? Had not James R. Garfield, son of an earlier President and now Commissioner of Corporations, gone to Chicago, made a formal inquiry, and reported to Roosevelt that Lorimer's contention was sound? Ironically, however, it was Russell's book that furnished the Interstate Commerce Commission with a basis for subsequent action against the packers.

Russell was the son of an Iowa editor who had been one of the founders of the Republican party. Schooled at St. Johnsbury, Vermont, he had found himself in the very "citadel of privilege," a town feudally ruled by a single family of wealthy manufacturers who were not slothful in business, fervent in spirit, serving the Lord. His observations had led him to deduce that in a so-called democracy they were clothed with autocratic power; without mandate from the people they were the government. And he saw there the germs of the old struggle between power and the masses. Returning to Iowa, he had become a single-taxer and a free-trader; he was, still later, to become a socialist. Meanwhile his father, fighting the tyranny of the railroads over the Middle-Western farmer, lost his paper. Russell migrated to New York, worked as a reporter covering the police courts and the slums of the East Side; joined Pulitzer's staff on the World and rose to the position of city editor; later helped William Randolph Hearst to found the Chicago *American*. By inclination a poet and a biographer, Russell had retired from newspaper work to write books when the unwelcome call came to make a study of the packing industry. Though one of the greatest of the muckrakers, he regarded this activity as purely incidental. He was, he said, only "a side-line reformer."

Russell was, however, a passionately earnest man whose conviction of the necessity for democracy had the force of a religious creed, and whose inherited anger toward those who had stripped the Western middle class of its former strength still burned fiercely. And this subject was one made to his hand, for it involved the railroads. Russell knew that the cattle raisers of the country had long writhed under a system by which they were deprived of a normal market and forced to accept whatever prices the packing-house combination might offer. He knew that the growers of fruit and vegetables, and the produce commission merchants, were subject to their lawless exactions, because they owned the refrigerator cars which the railroads "borrowed" for the transportation of perishable foodstuffs. Here, then, was a bandit monopoly which reached into every American home. By collusive arrangement, the packers and the railroads were able to maintain the economic paradox of abundant crops and fabulously high prices, while keeping the Western producers in a condition of helpless debt and vassalage.

In his campaign, Russell was notably assisted by a parallel investigation of the railroads undertaken by Ray Stannard Baker. Among other conditions, Baker exposed their practice of political corruption by means of powerful legislative and Congressional lobbies, and the influence which they exercised over public opinion through a secret publicity agency furnished with millions of dollars for the purpose of buying the press. Baker, keeping to his role of a dispassionate analyst, went to see the great packer Armour—and to his surprise, found that he liked him. For Armour was not a rich idler, wasting his patrimony; he might have enjoyed an eight-hour day, but he didn't. He hadn't wanted to take control of the family enterprise, but it fell out that there was no one else to step in and take charge of its affairs, or to protect the interests of many other people. Baker soon found that the great machine in which Armour was a cog, albeit an important one, drove him as he would never have dared to drive his own workmen. Was not the great magnate a sort of slave to industry, with no union to protect him, a man held in his place on the wheel as firmly as any Polish butcher who knifed hogs in the Armour packing house?

Here was an American riddle. Armour appeared to be genuinely benevolent in intention. Forthrightly, to Baker, he commended competition as the only fair regulator of industry, asserting that the law of supply and demand was the only law that could operate successfully. Yet he was also secretly doing his best to prevent competition and build up monopoly in every business in which he was concerned. Very obviously, he wanted free competition for the people who dealt with him; and he wanted unrestricted power to do away with competition when he dealt with them. Armour was not intellectually dishonest. He was willing to make an implied admission of the evils of the system under which he was thriving. But his defense, like his paradoxical position, was one with which Americans were to become increasingly familiar during the next forty years. Armour merely asserted that even if he should step aside the man who took his place would be forced to play the game just as he did. Armour believed himself to be a good citizen. Like the railroad owners, he and his associates did not scruple to buy legislators, congressmen, and the press. The two systems of corruption worked hand in hand, in a joint conspiracy against the public. Were men like Armour—as Baker felt—victims of conditions imposed by the economic order? Were they—as Russell charged—deliberate, malevolent enemies of the people? Or, perhaps, were they both? Some day, the American people would be forced to decide.

Baker's dispassionate analysis and Russell's angry indictment made the American people resentful, and so exasperated President Theodore Roosevelt. But they did not result in immediate reforms. The agent of reform was a novelist, who stirred up a whirlwind of national fury that overwhelmed a reluctant President and an obdurate Congress. During a bitter strike in Chicago's Packingtown, the socialist magazine *Appeal to Reason* commissioned young Upton Sinclair to go there, live among the workers, and write a novel about their plight. Sinclair was an unhappy man, oppressed by an intolerable injustice in human affairs, convinced that only brotherhood and honesty could solve the world's ills, and already embarked upon an assault against organized society. He had a profound belief in his own literary genius; he wanted to write great poetry and great novels about the American scene. He was achieving prominence in the Socialist Party. He had won brief notoriety in literary circles with *The Journal of Arthur Stirling*, a novel about a writer very like himself. The commission from the *Appeal to Reason* excited him.

Sinclair went to Packingtown, lived for seven weeks among the striking workers, and then wrote his novel. He intended it to portray a representative example of capitalist oppression of the working class. He wrote it in a blistering rage that spared no circumstance of the degradation, the squalor, or the misery which bound the immigrant workers in the slaughterhouses, which made their human prospect hopeless. But it was neither this theme, nor Sinclair's powerful treatment of it, that made *The Jungle* a national sensation. As an incentive to reform, the novel was to have a social effect greater than that of any American work of fiction since *Uncle Tom's Cabin*—yet this effect was neither foreseen, nor planned, by Sinclair. It was produced by a few pages, regarded by Sinclair as merely incidental to the development of his major theme. In those pages, he had furnished gruesome details about meat production: the casual grinding of rats, refuse and even employees into beef products—the generally foul conditions under which the meat was prepared.

Horror, disgust, and fury swept across the country. The gruesome details accomplished what exposures of economic and social injustice, of political corruption, had not succeeded in bringing about. Yet these exposures had not been without effect, for they confronted the American people with a pattern of conduct that menaced their freedom. And even for Sinclair's gruesome details—which deposited certain dubious results of the pattern on every American dining table—the way had been prepared. There had been a long investigation of the "poison trust"; the patent-medicine industry which, in a country of some eighty million people, was doing an annual business valued at approximately fifty-nine millions of dollars. Here, also, there emerged an insidious threat to the daily life and health of the average American. And the threat issued from an alliance of uncontrolled greed with, apparently, uncontrollable power. Samuel Hopkins Adams—later to become widely known as a novelist and biographer—told the whole story in *The Great American Fraud,* and this book, too, caused a sensation.

Adams proved that the nostrums distributed by the "poison trust" were medicinally worthless. Many were only substitutes for intoxicating liquor. Others were massively doped with habit-forming drugs. Still others contained ingredients which, if consumed in sufficient quantity, would cause death. All these nostrums were freely purchasable; one or another was likely to be found in most American homes. Adams proved that, in their advertising contracts, the leading manufacturers bound the newspapers to aid their fight against hostile legislation. He showed that they maintained legislative lobbies in many states. When, as a result of Adams' book, public clamor caused the writing of a regulatory law, the public learned more about the power of the trust. The bill was called up for debate in the Senate. But the power of the trust reached even into that august body. Senator Nelson B. Aldrich—whom many Americans considered the real political boss of the United States—vigorously opposed passage of the regulatory law, which was designed to bring the traffic under Federal control. His argument was one that the American people would hear again and again in the future. Aldrich fought the bill in the name of popular as against "bureaucratic" government.

Could the people, then, look to their government to defend their interests—to protect all of them against exploitation by various small groups of "ordinary Americans" whose prosperity seemingly depended upon the success of conspiracy? Sitting one day in the press gallery of the United States Senate, Charles Edward Russell looked down on well-fed and portly gentlemen, every one of whom, as the reporters knew perfectly well, was there to represent some private (and predatory) interest. Was it not true that "strictly speaking we had no Senate; we had only a chamber of butlers for industrialists and financiers"?

The articles which this question suggested to Russell were written, not by him, but by the novelist David Graham Phillips. It was Phillips' savage series, "The Treason of the Senate," that inspired the President's denunciation of the muckrakers. Roosevelt explained that he wanted to let in light and air but had no desire to let in sewer gas; he professed his abhorrence of slanderous and mendacious attacks upon men in public life and upon men engaged in public work. But the real reason for his anger was one that he did not state. Phillips had struck the most sensitive spot in the anatomy of all "practical politicians"—and was not the President one of them? Had he not genially assured the railroad magnate E. H. Harriman that "we are both practical men?" In the President's sense, Phillips was not a practical man. He was an extreme idealist. He was not of those who are always perfectly content with things as they are and recognize clearly in them the divine command, to oppose which is impiety toward God and treason against the State. He believed in truth. He refused to compromise it.

Phillips was reluctant to undertake the series of articles. Despite the nationwide agitation that it caused, he always considered it the one failure of his career. This was ironical; he would be remembered chiefly for that "failure." He did not live long enough to see its outcome. It proved to be a major influence in producing the Seventeenth Amendment to the Constitution, which provided for the direct election of senators by the people—a radical change which, in the opinion of many Americans, subsequently transformed the Senate, making it a frequent source of progressive social legislation.

Phillips had resigned an editorship on Pulitzer's *World* to devote himself to fiction. A tall, handsome man of forty, his friends all believed that he was destined to become a major novelist. He wanted to produce an American *Comédie Humaine*, and had already found his theme. Was not society being perverted by the madness of much wealth? Was it not to this madness that the old moralities, the old modes of life, that had constituted the bases of a past democracy, were yielding? If any democracy was to survive, the old moralities and modes of living would have to be replaced by new ones, and the effort of society to develop these seemed to Phillips the greatest of contemporary themes. It was for this reason that Mrs. Wharton, in her old age, deplored the oblivion that had overtaken his novels, and insisted that he was among the most significant of modern American writers. But the theme, in one of its aspects, rang out in his series of articles on the Senate.

Phillips prefaced his articles with the Constitutional definition: "Treason against the United States shall consist only in levying war against them, or in adhering to their enemies, giving them aid and comfort." He concentrated on the second half, showing how it was exemplified by senator after senator; men who represented railroads, industrial corporations, owners of mines—all the myriad vested interests of the nation's economic order, but never the interests of the nation's people. He showed the absolute control exercised by Senator Aldrich, Republican boss and majority leader, whose function it was to reconcile competing claims and satisfy all members of the economic and financial constituency. He demonstrated that Aldrich, in matters of practical politics, worked closely with Senator Gorman, leader of the Democratic minority.

To the pictures of business conducted as a conspiracy against the welfare of the people, Phillips added one of government by conspiracy. But, like Baker and Steffens, he pointed to something far more significant than individual corruption. Was not corruption merely a symptom? Was it not the indication of a process, a slow and pervasive decay that was occurring in government precisely as it was occurring in business? Did not this decay have its origin in a moral deterioration to which the entire nation was subject? Phillips surmised that the root of evil was to be found, not in politics or in business, but in the moral outlook of the American people. Indeed, was not their outlook an explicit sanction?

If it was a sanction, what was its effect upon the lives of the less fortunate? Those who still read the American dream as a reality could take comfort from the story of Owen Kildare, a Bowery hoodlum rescued by love, who in manhood made himself a respectable citizen and an educated man, and wrote *My Mamie Rose* to prove that the social regeneration of an outcast remained possible. But other observers were not so sanguine; and one, with a knowledge of the lower depths quite as extensive as Kildare's, disconcertingly reported that misery, too, had developed its own form of conspiracy against the social order.

This was Josiah Flynt, who at the turn of the century serialized in *McClure's The Powers That Prey* and *The World of Graft*, two remarkable studies of the underworld which shocked many decent Americans by making vividly clear the role of a criminal class in the national economy. Flynt was the nephew of the venerated Frances E. Willard, crusader for prohibition and ardent suffragist, whom death had only lately removed from the idolatry of women's clubs and the embattled churchly. There was a remarkable lack of family resemblance between the aunt and nephew. They appealed to quite different audiences.

Flynt had been born in circumstances of relative affluence. His father was editor of a Chicago newspaper, and he might have looked forward to opportunity and privilege as his normal destiny. Instead, in boyhood, he often took to the road as a vagrant. He lived for long periods among the outcasts and hoboes who preyed on the prosperous; he mastered their argot and adopted their manners; he was accepted by them on terms of equality. Intelligent, handsome, obstinately self-willed, he found the temptation to sink into the underworld irresistible. He indulged it whenever it came over him. He was committed to a reformatory as a result of one escapade. Later, he went to college, and to the University of Berlin. In Europe, as in the United States, he lived mainly among the disinherited, and though he sought out Tolstoy, Ibsen, and other famous writers, he found his chosen friends among criminals, tramps, the damned and the lost.

In his books, Flynt reported on their life as they saw it, with a cynicism, a hardness, and an indifference to morality which he deeply shared with them. He was no slummer, and no reformer. He saw that his friends were the inevitable product of a social system—but he had no particular desire to change the system. He was, however, very willing to acquaint society with the cost of its mores. The cost, he asserted, was payable not only in human degradation, but in a perpetual guerilla warfare waged against the social order by those whom it attempted to outlaw. Society, achieving its economic purposes through corruption at the top, should not be surprised, Flynt thought, by finding that it had also succeeded in generating corruption at the bottom.

He reported upon the operations of the criminal class in a number of American cities. He showed the methods by which they carried on their war against organized society. Financiers and industrialists corrupted the lawmakers; criminals in precisely the same way corrupted the police. For money, the police would not only protect their depredations, but often suggest them, and the alliance frequently extended to higher officials and to political bosses. Why should Americans be shocked by learning that those whom they employed to protect their property were profitably conspiring to steal it? Was not that the accepted way of economic life, the process resorted to by the great magnates in dealing with the courts and the legislatures? This undersized, delicate, somewhat effeminate-looking man, who drank to excess, who took drugs, who despised respectability and conventional morality; who astonished his literary friends by an ability to change completely before their eyes merely by shifting his gait, altering the movements of his hands and eyes, and talking rapidly in a strange, unfamiliar language; who was often hard put to extricate himself from the criminal plans of his associates—this maverick had the temerity to declare that the police, not the criminals, were principally responsible for crime. Worse still, he traced the ultimate responsibility to society itself, to the "best people." He reported that the criminals were convinced that society wanted no change, that it would not support reforms. If it believed in reform, why did it tolerate corruption among its police? Why, in fact, did it resort to corruption itself?

This same question was asked by a professional reformer. It was the very point of Judge Ben B. Lindsey's *The Beast*, which soberly recorded some of the more conspicuous achievements of democracy. Lindsey had set up the first juvenile court in the country. Long experience with delinquents had convinced him that crime sprang, not from character, but from economic environment. What determined the environment? Lindsey asserted that it was ruthless private greed, flowering in an irresponsible capitalism. This had produced "the rule of the plutocracy," with its inseparable evils of privilege and corruption. Who were the enemies of society? The delinquents, whom society was cynically willing to have transformed into habitual criminals? The hardened offenders, graduates of penal institutions designed to produce nothing else? Lindsey suggested that the true enemies of society were respected men in public life. Men like the governor of Colorado, who had conferred on great corporations the right of naming members of the state's highest court. Men like the officers of those corporations; seeking special privileges, they did not hesitate to acquire them by subverting justice and flouting the law.

What Lindsey affirmed about the economic basis of crime was corroborated by another reformer. Robert Hunter, a member of the privileged class, had many years of experience as a social worker, and he had become a socialist. In *Poverty*, he made an extended study of the existence to which the rise of an industrial plutocracy had condemned large segments of the American city population. It challenged many comfortable assumptions of the middle class. Was there, indeed, only one offense which democratic capitalism found unforgivable—failure? The trouble with the poor, Hunter suggested, was nothing more than poverty.

As the years passed, the mirror of the muckrakers reflected one after another facet of American society. Probably never before in the nation's history had there developed so swiftly as varied, vigorous, and fearless a criticism of the existing social order. As the movement gathered momentum, the writers abandoned all pretense of mere objective reporting. They became crusaders. They investigated, indicted, prosecuted, passed judgment. Above all, they tried to move the American people to demand social change. And the people began to respond. Whenever a political leader rose to undertake their defense, they rallied to him. To Theodore Roosevelt, campaigning for a second term on the issue of reform. They supported him the more enthusiastically for knowing that he was no visionary—that he had been schooled at the very headquarters of corruption and privilege, in the Republican machine. To Robert M. La Follette, in Wisconsin. To Joseph W. Folk, in Missouri. To Hiram Johnson, in California. Even to William Randolph Hearst, in New York. So pronounced was the trend to "radical" leaders that Roosevelt expressed his concern to his friend Senator Henry Cabot Lodge: "no one can tell how far such discontent will spread"—"there has been during the last six or eight years a great growth of socialist and radical spirit." For Roosevelt—like the originators of muckraking, like Franklin D. Roosevelt three decades later—conceived his mission to be the saving of the democratic capitalist system. Again and again, he warned the great magnates that their obstinate unwillingness to adjust themselves to the new spirit abroad in the land was making it difficult for him to discharge that mission.

The new spirit was a spirit of unrest. Demand for reforms—political, economic, social—became insistent. From the articles and books of the muckrakers, the American people were fitting together, as if it were in a jigsaw puzzle, a kind of total picture. They realized, with dismay, that economic privilege, political corruption, and social injustice were not isolated areas of evil; that they were, in fact, interrelated and interdependent. And this insight made action imperative. For it revealed the appalling extent to which their existence, their environment, and their government had slipped from their control. It convinced them that the democratic way of life was in grave jeopardy; that it must be rescued quickly if it was to be preserved at all.

So the mood of the people swept Theodore Roosevelt's "square deal" beyond the limits which he had set for it. It was, in time, to sweep Roosevelt himself to his platform at Armageddon. Reform was in the air, a menace to any obstructive agencies. Conservatives like Leslie M. Shaw, former Secretary of the Treasury, confessed that they were alarmed by the trend of things in this connection. But wiser men of the same persuasion, like the corporation lawyer Samuel Untermyer, shrewdly detected advantages in the inevitable. One reform, control of the railroads, Untermyer comfortingly reported to his fellows, "saved us from Government ownership of the railroads, as the like Regulation of Industrial Corporations will save us from Socialism." The people didn't want socialism, either—but they may have been a trifle perplexed at finding the representatives of privilege playing on their team. It would be long before they were able to evaluate so novel a tactic. For the moment, they felt that every victory in reform was a spur to further conquests. The tide of popular impatience, of determination to achieve the largest possible measure of social democracy, rose to its crest. Woodrow Wilson was elected to the presidency. And there came the far-reaching changes produced by the "new freedom" of his first term.

In 1906, Edwin E. Slosson, a scholarly and versatile writer, had attempted to appraise the literature of exposure as it would be viewed fifty years later. He predicted that it would be accounted a true intellectual force, a vital element in the creative activities of later years. It was, he asserted, a reality in the mental life of the American people, and it had accomplished a great purpose, for they would be sounder, more sincere, more fearless in right doing because of it.

"The public conscience has been awakened," Slosson said, "and wrong-doers have been stricken with wholesome fear. But henceforth the work of exposing evil must be transformed into a steady-going, constructive effort to prevent it. . . ."

Forty years later, the advice still held good.

[3] EVANGELISTS AND ENTERTAINERS

By the fourth decade of the century, many of the publications famous in the era of Bok and McClure had disappeared. Yet the American people continued to receive both guidance and inspiration from their favorite magazines. The messianic tradition had not lapsed. The plain people were being exhorted to courage, hope, renewed ambition. They were being assured that the age of opportunity had not closed. To the contrary; it stretched, dazzlingly, into the future. The American alchemy that transmuted today's hot idea into tomorrow's cold million still worked. The most incandescent ideas were simple ones, the kind that might occur to anyone. Or nearly anyone. Such was the cheering burden of the "success stories" appearing in the most popular magazines. The formula had become classic.

Certainly the formula had "worked" for two powerful publishers: De Witt Wallace of the *Reader's Digest*, and Henry R. Luce, of *Time*, *Life*, and *Fortune*. Both had started with simple ideas and small capital in the giddy, gaudy nineteen-twenties. Now, both were big business, of a stature and scope probably inconceivable to either Bok or McClure. The *Reader's Digest*, born in a Greenwich Village basement with a shears and paste pot instead of a silver spoon, had eleven million readers. It appeared in English, Spanish, Portuguese, Swedish, Finnish and Arabic. It had an edition in Braille. It was even inscribed on phonograph records. No less inspiring was the saga of the Luce publications. These had sprung from a schoolboy's fanciful notion. One of them, said to reach twenty-two million Americans every week, could claim to be the most widely read periodical in the world. If Wallace and Luce preached the old verities and the old faith, who could say that they were not justified by their personal experience?

The evangelical tone of the *Reader's Digest* presumably was an inherited characteristic. Wallace and his wife, its chief editors, came from families having a strong vocation for the pulpit. A lively idea struck Wallace after the First World War. "We're living in a fast-moving world. People are anxious to get at the nub of matters." Would they not welcome a periodical which, saving them time and effort, kept them abreast of their own dizzying speed? From "leading magazines," Wallace would select articles of "enduring significance." These he would boil down, concentrating their essence. Without advertising, they could be packaged in compact form. A pocket-sized booklet would be portable anywhere. Thus, it would be available during infrequent moments of pause. It could fertilize the marginal total of daily inertia. Under the Wallace plan, Americans, too busy to read what was produced for their pleasure and information, were insured against being uninformed. A very slight effort—easily accomplished while hustling—would make them contemporary with their world. In their pockets or purses reposed the synoptic wisdom of the best minds. They need do very little more than look.

In 1922, the Wallaces sent the first issue of their magazine to fifteen hundred subscribers. One generation earlier, the American reading public had taken in their stride the long, hard dissertations put out every month by McClure. Now, they were being invited to absorb a capsular feast; some thirty pellets, each containing two thousand words or less. When the *Reader's Digest* had attained the prominence of a national institution, captious critics emphasized this difference in intellectual fare. In their view, it indicated a process of mental regression. Almost certainly, they were wrong. Did not the Wallace idea have an honorable ancestry? President Eliot of Harvard, with his "five foot shelf" of indispensable classics, could be reckoned as among its forefathers. So could the *Literary Digest* and *Living Age*, both excerpters of other periodicals, which in their day had been, like aspidistras and pyrographed knicknacks, standard equipment in the parlors of America's most intellectual homes. The desire to obtain a maximum of information with a minimum of effort was nothing new. Nor was it peculiarly American. The most sacred of books attributed it to Adam.

After twenty years of publication, Wallace made two comments on his magazine. It was, he said, dedicated to the effort "to promote a Better America, with capital letters, with a fuller life for all, and with a place for the United States of increasing influence and respect in world affairs." By preference, it treated subjects which "come within the range of interests, experience, and conversation of the average person." In the light of its wide appeal, these statements made the *Digest* seem an approximately accurate register of the mental and spiritual climate in which many Americans were living.

One odd conclusion about that climate was likely to occur to any attentive student of the magazine. It suggested that the average American, although mentally at home in his fast-moving environment, was spiritually adrift in it. His mind lived happily in the present, but his heart apparently yearned for the past. Why else should the *Digest*, most resolutely "inspirational" of all major periodicals, likewise be the most nostalgic in its general tone? Its "success stories," dealing with the technique of getting ahead in the realm of practical affairs, offered stimulating models for emulation. Genially, persuasively, these miniature biographies of the victorious asserted the continuing validity of traditional virtues. Ambition, self-reliance, enterprise, thrift, and hard work were shown to issue in material prosperity and happiness. If this held true, need any American fail, or be discontented? The *Digest* seldom conceded that any ground for unhappiness existed. Yet its articles dealing with what may be called "the art of living" often produced a melancholy impression. From them one inferred that, however armed with the traditional virtues, many Americans were, in fact, neither conspicuously prosperous, nor consciously happy.

For the *Digest* expounded the philosophy of the stiff upper lip. It counseled the discovery of the materials of happiness in resources too often neglected: writing letters, listening to the sound of breakfast eggs frying on the stove, making new acquaintances, cultivating some hobby costing nothing. Most of all, it emphasized the spiritual rewards of material poverty. It affirmed that the happiest people were mostly poverty stricken. It extolled comparative poverty as a way of escape from the laminated multiplicities of modern American life. It declared that genuine values in living are not based on superficial things, on printed paper money or overstuffed upholstery or underslung sedans, but on something deeper, vital, spiritual. The *Digest* did not neglect the gospel of material success, so easily achieved. But it also argued, and forcefully, that spiritual success is the high compensation for material failure.

Did this apparent inconsistency have its source in the circumstances of average American life? Every American craved the satisfactions of a well-gadgetted existence, and praised the merits of a simple one while trying to avoid it. He wanted to believe that the highroad to wealth was still open to all. But the assumption was one which his environment and experience made increasingly dubious. Did he not need to be assured that, remaining poor, he should not feel humiliated; that, lacking the printed paper money, he could be certain of the deeper spiritual gold? A wide gulf stretched between the standards of the society in which he lived, and his personal chances of approximating them. What wonder, then, if his heart rebelled against its "laminated multiplicities"?

Certainly the "better America" projected by the *Digest*, where there would be "a fuller life for all," bore little resemblance to the actual America of the nineteen-forties: largely urban, highly indus-trialized, with an economy dominated by massive concentrations of capital. It looked very much more like the America affectionately re-membered by those who were middle-aged: a land of prosperous small towns, kindly neighbors, independent economic units, and unlimited opportunity for the industrious—where the daily life of the average American had justified his faith that "a man's best assets are his health, a stout heart, confidence in his own integrity." Could that America be recovered, its vanished way of life reinstated? The *Digest*, in making nostalgia a vision, and memory a hope, probably spoke for the dis-contented hearts of a large proportion of its readers. Whatever their economic situation, they could take courage from its confident opti-mism, consolation from its creed of fortitude. And they could agree that "most of us can at best own only a small piece of earth, but the vast skies are ours for a glance."

Like the Wallaces, Henry R. Luce enjoyed the advantage of evan-gelical antecedents. He was born in China, where his parents were Presbyterian missionaries; he may therefore have come naturally by the desire to improve his fellow-men. In any case, the desire arrived early, with an overtone of duty. At school, in the United States, he and his friend Briton Hadden reached the conclusion that most people were not well informed and that something should be done. This pert conceit bore fruit three years after their graduation from Yale, where Luce, among other collegiate honors, acquired the key of Phi Beta Kappa, certifying him as one surpassingly well informed. In 1923, they sent out the first issue of *Time*, the "weekly newsmagazine." Seven years later, Hadden having meanwhile died, Luce launched *Fortune*, a monthly periodical which surveyed the economic and financial aspects of American capitalism. He bought the old humorous weekly, *Life*, in 1936, and completely transformed it. It proved to be so popular in its new guise that, within a decade, one of every six Americans was reading it.

In principle, *Time*, like the *Reader's Digest*, proposed to equilibrate Americans in their fast-moving world. It was afflicted by no nostalgia for the past. Its interest in American yesterdays was slight, and chiefly antiquarian. *Time* spoke up briskly for the immediate. If the tone of the *Digest* was as sweetly simple as an old-fashioned valentine, that of *Time* was as smartly sophisticated as a Broadway revue. Inviting readers to enjoy the play of world events as a comedy, its breezy columns mocked the shibboleths of all moralists, and the pompousness of the earnest. To be informed by *Time* was a little like having the dream of being back in school, and finding the teacher to be Ethel Merman.

Like *Variety*, the magazine of show business, *Time* expressed itself in an institutional idiom. Announced purposes of this innovation: brevity, vividness. Probable reasons: innate skepticism, wish to be distinctive. Principal idiosyncrasies bemusing to old-fashioned readers: a propensity to inverted sentences and baby-talk agglutinations ("radiorator," "cinemoppet"); a Phi Beta Kappruriency converting banal strip-teasers into sinful-sounding ecdysiasts; petulant designations for the eminent ("snaggle-toothed," "bull-tongued," "befuddled"). Deliberately shocking was *Time* in its adolescence, more temperate in maturity. Stereotyped soon became its private jargon; of possible interest only to H. L. Mencken, criticalambaster of the 'twenties, long retired to American philology, serene etymological pursuit of the verb "to goose."

Having mastered its peculiarities and discounted its glibness, readers found *Time* a useful survey. Its blend of hard fact, owlish gossip, humor, and often shrewd analysis, added up to a lively bird's-eye view of world events. Some scholars deplored its assumption that complicated issues could be summarized and disposed of presumably in a few "crystal-clear" sentences. They asserted that this fostered superficiality, rapidly becoming epidemic. Doubtless the contention had merit. Yet who now enjoyed leisure, or possessed technical knowledge, sufficient to insure universal competency? The prodigious expansion of the field of knowledge during the twentieth century, no less than the accelerated tempo of existence, was responsible for cultural agencies which—like the *Reader's Digest* and *Time*—resembled Wordsworth's

. . . Powers
Which of themselves our minds impress;
That we can feed this mind of ours
In a wise passiveness.

If not from *Time*, it could be inferred from *Fortune* and *Life* that Luce was at heart an evangelist. In an article on him, the critic Wolcott Gibbs quoted Luce's conviction that without the aristocratic principle no society can endure. In the United States, Luce believed, the principle persisted "in our fetish of comparative success." It had produced "a plutocracy without any common sense of dignity or obligation." Though money had become increasingly the only measure of success, "we insisted that the rich man was no better than the poor man—and the rich man accepted the verdict." To Luce, the triumph of the mass mind was nowhere more apparent than in the frustration of the upper classes. Though Americans might not be well informed, they had long supposed themselves adequately acquainted with the defects of their "upper classes." It was a novelty to have them presented as appropriate objects for compassion. Had they, indeed, been forcibly deprived of their legitimate opportunity to develop a sense of social obligation? Were they merely helpless victims of an emotional defeat by the democratic dogma?

In *Fortune*, so costly as to be available only to the prosperous, Luce undertook their education. This massive, handsome periodical was addressed, primarily, to tycoons and their immediate subordinates. It surveyed the operations—and sometimes the social results—of a triumphant finance capitalism. The articles in *Fortune* were often as long, and as thoroughly researched, as any McClure dissertation. They appeared to be written with as grave a concern for the national welfare. In its readiness to explore highly controversial issues, *Fortune* was likewise reminiscent of its distinguished predecessor. To students of American affairs, it offered a view, from within, of what naïve observers took to be the national "success story." This inside station sometimes made the view alarming. Under a chilly objective light, reality could look less inviting than the glamorous appearance usually identified with it. This was especially evident when *Fortune*, having analyzed some phase of capitalistic function, went on to appraise its effects in the immediate social situation. Thus, for example, when business first began its determined assault on the Wagner Labor Relations Act, the magazine comprehensively reviewed operations under the law, and the trend of proposed alterations; concluded that the purpose of amendment was to negate the principle of collective bargaining; and took a stand directly opposed to that of its readers. Though in issues of this kind *Fortune* did not hesitate to violate the probable prejudices of plutocrats, it made no appeal to their social conscience. It based its arguments on their self-interest, their vital concern for the security of the established order. It represented conservatism, but it refrained from cant. Apparently, *Fortune* was trying to teach the "upper classes" to substitute a realistic self-criticism for a traditional complacency.

Considered solely as a pictorial weekly, *Life* did not appear to be the vehicle for any evangel. Its conspicuous achievement was to confront a vast audience with the bewildering diversity and complexity of American civilization. Few significant aspects of the current scene eluded ts photographic reporters. True, *Life* ran to gargantuan portions of "cheesecake," and sedulously exploited the "hypermammiferous come-on" of Hollywood starlets and New York models. But its pages were crowded with subjects of greater social value. Its photographs, diagrams, models and charts helped to make comprehensible such scientific developments as electronics and atomic fission. It reported on education, industry, labor, agriculture. It made vigorous studies of the current mores, ranging from the way of life of the plutocracy and the peculiar addictions of the teen-aged to patterns of crime, intolerance, and violence. Nor did it neglect the cultural backwaters of American life: the rites of snake worshippers, or the grim survival of one-room schools in prosperous rural regions. For reflective readers, *Life* constantly suggested questions. It presented a society still in process of solution, a culture still in the making. What was the American citizen thinking about the incredible complex?

To the citizen's thinking, Luce addressed editorials and feature articles which made little concession to mental inertia. The basis of *Life's* gospel could be described as an aggressive conservatism. To the increasingly collectivistic trend of mid-twentieth century liberal thought, it opposed a dogmatic assertion of the necessity for individual liberty. After "a century and a half of steady social reform," it inquired in 1946, "where are we?" Would not altruism fail, "when attempts are made to erect it into a social philosophy"? It declared that the besetting temptation of all democracies is to become "welfare states," at the inevitable cost of restrictions on liberty. Since "no political system offers a perfect answer" to the social problem, should not "the burden of prosperity and better living standards . . . be shifted back to the nation's inventors, engineers and business managers"? For *Life* discounted the theory that government can raise living standards. It opposed all forms of social planning, and was content to leave the problem of welfare to the operations of free enterprise and a free market.

Although these contentions had a familiar ring, *Life* offered an intelligent challenge to American liberals. Denying a prevailing belief that social reform would make self-reform unnecessary, it argued that the liberal's first task in the coming era was to remind men that only good individuals, whether rich or poor, could make a good society. It affirmed that mere external change could not, of itself, bring social justice: the only check upon the individual who has chosen freedom is his own magnanimity. Ethical values do not flow from the mechanisms of economics and politics; they flow only from the hearts of men who believe in something greater than any political or economic system. Basically, *Life* contended that good ends never justify dubious means; especially do humanitarian ends not justify restrictions on liberty. Asserting that a well-ordered community life is indispensable to freedom, it denied that this could be arbitrarily imposed. For democracy to succeed, Americans must become genuinely convinced that faith and morals are independent of politics, more important than politics and essential to political liberty. In appealing to ethics rather than to economic and social tinkering as the prerequisite of a better society, *Life* was possibly applying a wholesome corrective to the drift of popular thought.

Meanwhile, the reader could, if he chose, turn to various types of periodical remarkable for the economy of their demand upon his mental energy. The so-called "comic books," devoted to the adventures of "Superman" and other folk-heroes, reached a far wider audience than the juveniles for whom they were originally designed. And the ominous realities of the atomic age did nothing to diminish the popularity of gaudily dressed pulp magazines specializing in scientific fantasy. Reviewing an anthology of fiction culled from this source, Fletcher Pratt described the stories as "the fairy-tales of our time, with space-ships whizzing across light-years, serums that reduce a man to an atom or step up his I.Q. to 243, and robots that can outthink the Harvard calculator." Mental relaxation was likewise furnished by an increasing number of pocket-digest magazines, with circulations ranging from a quarter of a million to four million copies a month. These were often ridiculed by intellectual readers, who deplored their effect on the nation's culture. But what they actually represented, as a cultural influence, remained a mystery until an enterprising critic undertook to find out.

Analyzing the contents of twenty-one of these periodicals over a considerable length of time, Roger Butterfield reported on the major interests of their readers. He found sex to be outstanding: good lively sex articles were the tidbits most actively sought after by the editors. The ubiquitous "success story" was popular in this field. So were articles about science, especially in its industrial applications. There was a considerable appetite for information about oddities of nature and animal life. The interest in people was peculiar, for articles about "contemporary nonentities" were twice as numerous as those about "contemporary celebrities." To this special public, a woman whose hobby was collecting old potato, flour, or cement bags was twice as stimulating as Senator Taft, or Henry Ford II. Whether this reflected on the readers, or on the celebrities, was not evident. Articles on health, dealing quickly and hopefully with a wide range on bodily ills, and equally optimistic treatises on self-improvement bulked largely. And, in the little digests, the old yellow-journalism staple of immorality still persisted, with stories of alcoholism, drug addicts, prison life, lotteries, wire tapping, vice crusades, swindlers, cheats, liars and short-change artists.

Since a majority of these periodicals could be described as catering to the desire for escape from everyday experience, Butterfield's report of their editorial attitude on current social issues was unexpectedly encouraging. Of the twenty-one which he analyzed, thirteen were liberal, four were definitely the reverse, and the rest had no determinable viewpoint. Still more encouraging was his deduction that Americans who read the pocket magazines were apparently more interested in the state of the world than in any other single subject. The number of pages devoted to this topic offered proof that millions of Americans knew there was a world, and that it was one with their immediate and daily concerns. Perhaps the read-and-run school of journalism was exercising a better influence on the national culture than its disparaging critics supposed.

Part Four

THE FEAST OF REASON
AND THE FLOW OF SOUL

CHAPTER X

All Life Is an Experiment

[I] YANKEE SOCRATES

As the old century was closing, you might have met William James in the streets of Cambridge, on his way to or from Harvard College. A short, middle-aged man—erect, brisk, bearded, intensely masculine —he would have two or three thick volumes and a notebook under one arm, and on his face a look of abstraction that used suddenly to give way to an expression of delighted and friendly curiosity. Sometimes he had forgotten to change the shabby Norfolk jacket in which he worked at home. Or he might still be wearing the ceremonial black coat reluctantly put on for one of those formal occasions which he did his best to avoid. The books, the meditative air, the inattentiveness to costume suggested his professorship. But they were all that did.

His reputation as a psychologist, as a philosopher, was already worldwide. Even he did not foresee the notable work, the greater fame that still lay ahead. About him there lingered an occasional afterglow of Bohemia, mildly visible in the bright stripe of a shirt or the exuberance of a tie. His sense of fun was infectious, but to some disquieting. There were days when he felt "particularly larky," when an old spirit of mischief revived in him; he was then just like a blob of mercury, and relished his success in shocking the stodgy. There were earnest folk who deplored his want of academic dignity. Certain of his students, attached as they invariably were to his person, felt some doubts about the profundity of one who was so very natural. He was amusedly aware that his free and easy and personal way of writing made him an object of loathing to many respectable academic minds. His own lack of enthusiasm for mere respectability was marked, and his admiration for the academic mind rather less than tepid. On a lecture tour, he could perversely wish for the flash of a pistol, a dagger, or a devilish eye, anything to break the unlovely level of ten thousand good people —a crime, murder, rape, elopement, anything would do.

Not infrequently, James felt like a humbug as a professor. He confessed himself one who was unfit to be a philosopher because at bottom he hated philosophy, especially at the beginning of a vacation, with the fragrance of the spruces and sweet ferns all soaking him through with the conviction that it is better to *be* than to define your being. Privately, he held that the collective life of philosophers is little more than an organization of misunderstandings. Were not the paradoxes of their subject somewhat absurd, so trivial and so ponderous at once? And did their pompous speculations amount to anything more than just fancy-work? His former student and junior colleague, George Santayana, suspected that James had never seen a philosopher whom he would have cared to resemble. But James had seen the most eminent ones of his time, and incorrigibly continued to be unlike any. At the back of his mind a rebellious nerve protested that philosophy is a queer thing— at once the most sublime and the most contemptible of human occupations. It was contemptible when you made it a refuge from the teeming and dramatic richness of the concrete world. It might become sublime if you put it to sound use. "The ancients," he said, "did things by doing the business of their own day, not by gaping at their grandfathers' tombs—and the normal man today will do likewise."

Nearly always, William James gave the impression that he regarded nonconformity as the only principle worthy of being conformed to. "Almost any opinion I now have is liable to be changed or even reversed by the experience of tomorrow"—he had ruefully noted this trait at the age of twenty-five. Forty years later, in 1907, he announced it as a kind of obligation, the first step in a method for dealing efficaciously with life. Characteristically, he recommended this method as absolutely the only philosophy with *no* humbug in it. For he had long been impatient with the awful abstract rigmarole in which American philosophers obscured the truth when he put forward his own theory under the forbidding label of "pragmatism." The strange word was, he said, only a new name for some old ways of thinking. But the little book in which he described them pleased him: it was a very unconventional utterance. He would not be surprised, he told his brother Henry, if ten years later it would be rated as "epoch-making." Confident though he was of its eventual prestige, he was unprepared for its immediate meteoric success. It swept across the country; edition after edition was demanded; even "Mr. Dooley" took up pragmatism. When this happened, James gleefully reported that "its fortune's made!" Many who read it must have felt, with Henry James, a wonder at the extent to which, all their lives, they had "unconsciously pragmatized." The book's reception gave William James a unique authority. In him, as only before in Emerson, the American people recognized a philosopher who spoke for their interests, their temper, their native way of sensing life.

His temperament, and many of his personal convictions, fitted James for this national spokesmanship. But he had arrived at these convictions the hard way; and he held others that ran counter to the spirit of the times. His childhood and youth were odd, even for a day when extreme oddity was scarcely remarkable. His father, a son of one of the earliest American millionaires, was an uncompromising individualist who had an addiction to the darker problems of theology. A psychological crisis, destined to be paralleled in William's life, made the elder Henry James a Swedenborgian; but in that faith, as in all else, he remained a steadfast nonconformist. He was a utopian socialist who distrusted all social systems. A passionate democrat, who affirmed—not only humorously—that a crowded horsecar was the nearest approach to heaven on earth, he associated only with the intellectual elite of two continents. A man obsessed by the tragic sense of life, he achieved social celebrity as a great wit and a fanciful humorist. His father's peculiar duality cropped up as one of William's outstanding traits.

In the childhood of William and Henry, the James family moved restlessly to and from Europe, seldom settling anywhere for more than a few months. The boys received a highly irregular education, on principle, acquiring a bent for cosmopolitanism and a facility in many languages. Their health was precarious, and William for many years was the victim of neurasthenia. In their residence abroad, William went in for "experiments"—playing with chemicals, galvanic batteries, marine animals in splashy aquaria, taking curious drugs. Presently, he succumbed to a sudden passion for "giving myself up to art" and, as Henry later noted dryly, "we went home to learn to paint"—a decision typically Jamesian in its eccentricity.

The family settled at Newport, where William and Henry joined John La Farge in the studio of William Morris Hunt. Long afterwards, La Farge said that William had the promise of being a remarkable, perhaps a great painter, but the passion for art petered out as suddenly as it had arisen, and he went to Harvard to study science. In due time, he entered the medical school, but interrupted his course to join his teacher, Alexander Agassiz, on a scientific expedition to Brazil. Later he continued his studies in Germany, returned home to take his degree, and fell into a prolonged melancholia. He suffered a shattering crisis like his father's, from which he emerged by a similar act of faith. He came upon a doctrine of free will put forward by the French philosopher, Renouvier: "the sustaining of a thought *because I choose to* when I might have other thoughts." It was, for him, a revolutionary insight, and it shaped all his future thinking. "My first act of free will," he determined, "shall be to believe in free will." He never thereafter relinquished his will to believe.

He became a teacher of physiology at Harvard. After some years, he deserted physiology for psychology. His great exploratory book on the principles of that science established him as the most eminent authority in the field. But, once the book had been published, he felt that he had exhausted both his interest and his fertility. So he turned to philosophy. All his life he had been looking for a solution that should be not merely tenable as judged by scientific standards, but at the same time propitious enough to live by. In this he reflected the perplexity of his generation; solicited by the new science, confronted by the new industrialism, and deprived of all the old faiths.

The members of James' early circle at Cambridge shared this perplexity. All, like James himself, tried to formulate attitudes to life that would solve it: the lawyer Oliver Wendell Holmes; the historians Henry Adams and John Fiske; the mathematicians Chauncey Wright and Charles S. Peirce; even the budding novelists Howells and Henry James. Some of them saw, in the new civilization that was rising and transforming America, evidence that the individual had a free, active, essentially creative role to play in society; that he had the power to change his environment according to his desire. This was what most Americans wished to believe. But others drew very different deductions. To them, the new scientific doctrines, stemming from Darwin's principle of evolution, suggested that progress was merely an automatic and impersonal process, the expression of a kind of fate or force. They adopted a theory of determinism which left the individual little freedom, and almost no creative function. Was man the master or the creature of his environment? Was he a social agent, or only a hapless social product?

To James, any form of determinism was temperamentally repugnant. Scientific fatalism seemed to him no less deadly than theological predestination; both imprisoned men in an inevitable and foreknown doom, depriving life of any ethical significance. Trained as a scientist, he had no illusions about the finality of any scientific doctrine. His sister Alice said of him that he seemed to be born afresh every morning; this, he felt, was the condition of science, and he wanted it likewise to be the condition of life and society. As a psychologist, he knew better than many of his contemporaries the decisive part which desire and will played in all change—even the most momentous social changes. So it was natural that he should found the whole structure of his philosophy on one very simple fact. The fact was that we cannot live at all without some degree of faith.

Even scientists, he pointed out, were not exempt from this humble groundwork: faith is synonymous with working hypothesis. Every man of science had taken his stand on a sort of dumb conviction that the truth must lie in one direction rather than another, and a sort of preliminary assurance that his notion could be made to work; and had borne his best fruit in trying to make it work. This "dumb conviction" and "preliminary assurance" were, for James, the genuine basis of action. So he could define faith as belief in something concerning which doubt is still theoretically possible. And, since the test of belief is willingness to act, James held that faith is the readiness to act in a cause the prosperous issue of which is not certified in advance.

A risky business, surely. But was it not the method by which human life proceeded? Was it not the way in which men actually did act, with respect to the thousand and one decisions of their daily life, where complete knowledge was lacking, along with positive assurance as to the outcome? James affirmed that in the average man the power to trust, to risk a little beyond the literal evidence, is an essential function. Without it, action would cease. To act on belief is necessary; if the results of action justify the belief, the belief itself becomes true. In such instances, faith creates its own verification. The truths cannot become true until our faith has made them so by the test of experiment.

Scientists, indeed, called the method that of hypothesis and experiment. James, thinking of its application in the daily life of the individual, called it the method of belief based on desire. For, in the absence of complete knowledge, you took your risks in the direction of your desires; you were prompted to try to produce the results you wanted. James held that the thought becomes literally father to the fact, as the wish was father to the thought. If you got the results you hoped for—if your experiment came out—you had not only verified your belief, but you had brought about some form of change in the existing state of affairs. So, said James, driving his point home, "that the course of destiny may be altered by individuals no wise evolutionist ought to doubt."

Progress, or evolution, or living were therefore not automatic processes. Determinism was not operative; spontaneous variations might be produced at any moment. The individual was not a pawn, but an active participant in the game of life. Nothing suggested this more eloquently than the fact that the impulse to take life strivingly is indestructible in the race. Was it not true that in the total game of life we stake our persons all the while? James asserted that success depends upon energy of act; energy depends upon faith that we shall not fail; and this faith in turn on the faith that we are right—which faith thus verifies itself. Of course, there is really no scientific or other method by which men can steer safely between the opposite dangers of believing too little or of believing too much. But, said James, to face such dangers is apparently our duty, and to hit the right channel between them is the measure of our wisdom as men. He saw life, and social progress, as a perpetual experiment. But he did not preach reckless faith. He preached courage weighted with responsibility—the right of the individual to indulge his personal faith at his personal risk.

Was not this right the basic source of American domocracy? A social organism of any sort, James held—and the opinion seemed especially relevant to the democratic system—is what it is because each member proceeds to his own duty with a trust that the other members will simultaneously do theirs. When a desired result is brought about by the co-operation of many independent persons, its existence as a fact is a pure consequence of the precursive faith in one another of those immediately concerned. Without such mutual trust— whether warranted or not by prior evidence—not only is nothing achieved, but nothing is even attempted. You arrive at your democracy by believing in its possibility, having confidence in yourself and your fellows—and setting to work.

Whatever field of life you touched, you came on its dynamism: upon experiment, action, work. Therefore the pragmatist, James insisted, always turns towards concreteness and adequacy, towards facts, towards action and towards power. To him, ideas and beliefs are really rules for action. He asks the practical cash value of any idea, program, or theory. What is its worth in actual use, its results when you set it at work within the stream of your experience? Theories thus become instruments, said James; we make nature over again by their aid. An idea, or a theory, is merely an indication of the ways in which existing realities may be changed. Its truth means nothing other than its power to "work." In fact, James declared "the true" is only the expedient in the way of our thinking, just as "the right" is only the expedient in the way of our behaving.

Expedient? The word outraged old-fashioned moralists. What became of absolute ethical standards, or final truth? They went overboard, James admitted calmly. One could only say that truth and right were whatever is most expedient *now*; expedient in almost any fashion, and, so far as can be determined, in the long run and on the whole. For what meets expediently all the experience in sight won't necessarily meet all farther experience equally satisfactorily. Experience, said James, has ways of boiling over, and making us correct our present formulas. Meanwhile, we have to live today by what truth we can get today, and be ready tomorrow to call it a falsehood. This fundamental relativity—or insecurity, or commitment to risk—is the price we pay for the privilege of living in an unfinished world, in a society essentially plastic, which we help to create by our thinking and action. In point of fact, said James, the use of most of our thinking is to help us to change the world. We are creative in our mental as well as in our active life; we mold our environment; we engender truth, he explained picturesquely, upon reality. What could be more inspiring than the assurance that the world, the society in which we live, stands really malleable, waiting to receive its final touches at our hands?

So the genuine pragmatist, James held, is willing to consider life really dangerous and adventurous. He is willing to live on a scheme of uncertified possibilities which he trusts; willing to pay with his own person, if need be, for the realization of the ideals which he frames. Like Emerson—his father's friend, who had blessed him in his cradle—James asserted for the individual the indefeasible right to be exactly what one is, provided one only be authentic. Nothing to him seemed more wretched than to consent to borrowing traditions and living at second hand. "The weight of the past world here is fatal," he once wrote to his sister from Rome; "one ends by becoming its mere parasite instead of its equivalent." Actually, he inclined to doubt the utility of past wisdom to the present. That wisdom might so easily have become only the dead heart of the living tree; it might have grown stiff with years of veteran service and petrified in men's regard by sheer antiquity. Were not the vital ideals of living men altars to unknown gods? And might not the best life consist at all times in the breaking of rules which have grown too narrow for the actual case? The important thing for each of us—the highest good—is to achieve our proper life. This, James felt, can come about only by help of a moral energy born of the faith that in some way or other we shall succeed in getting it if we try pertinaciously enough.

Here again, James struck the note of uncertainty, risk, change, plasticity. Did not life, as it came, bear the expression of being, or at least of involving, a muddle and struggle, with an "ever not quite" to all our formulas, and novelty and possibility forever leaking in? Certainly he could admit nothing final in any actually given equilibrium of human ideals. It seemed to him that, as our present laws and customs have fought and conquered other past ones, so they will in their turn be overthrown by any newly discovered order which will hush up the complaints that they still give rise to, without producing others louder still. Reformers welcomed James' vision of society as a flux, which seemed to give their efforts genuine legitimacy. They scarcely understood that their pet reforms, if accomplished, might with time become stiff and petrified. James himself thought that society would have to pass toward some newer and better equilibrium, that the distribution of wealth has doubtless slowly got to change. He confessed a utopian belief in the reign of peace and in the gradual advent of some sort of socialistic equilibrium. But even this, should it come, would be neither final nor stable: such changes have always happened, and will happen to the end of time.

Primarily, however, James' concern was for the individual, and especially for those traits in which the individual differed from, rather than resembled, his fellows. Society itself and all social institutions, of whatever grade, were for him secondary and ministerial. They existed to serve man, not to standardize him; their function was "instrumental." So he viewed with suspicion this intensely worldly social system of ours, in which each human interest is organized so collectively and so commercially. There were times when he was less than unqualifiedly respectful of "civilization"—with its herding and branding, licensing and degree giving, authorizing and appointing, and in general regulating by system the lives of human beings.

Society would always be in flux; it would always have to decide through actual experiment by what sort of conduct the maximum of good could be gained and kept in this world; but to the extent that it sacrificed plasticity to organization, it became suspect. System was hostile to the free play of individuality. So James demanded one constant in his flux. He warned his countrymen that they must always preserve the well-known democratic respect for the sacredness of individuality. He urged them to remember that many as are the interests that social systems satisfy, always unsatisfied interests remain over, and among them are interests to which system, as such, does violence whenever it lays its hânds on us. Let Americans guard well their faith in personal freedom and its spontaneities! Let them not forget that the best commonwealth will always be the one that most cherishes the men who represent the residual interests, the one that leaves the largest scope to their peculiarities!

In such warnings as these, James expressed his anxiety about the direction that American life was taking as the twentieth century opened. He welcomed the immense scientific and technological conquests of the industrial age. They proved that environment was malleable, and man essentially creative. They were pregnant with change and with promise. It was only when he came to consider their social effects that James was aware of reservations. He disliked what he saw; he was profoundly dubious about what appeared predictable. The moralist in him, as well as the nonconformist, protested against bigness and greatness in all their forms.

For he felt that the bigger the unit you deal with, the hollower, the more brutal, the more mendacious is the life displayed. He therefore took his stand against all big organizations as such, national ones first and foremost; against all big successes and big results; and in favor of the eternal forces of truth which work in the individual and immediately unsuccessful way, underdogs always, till history comes, after they are long dead, and puts them on the top. In the era of the great trusts, the vast structures of finance capitalism, James looked at these results of "progress" and said that they were not good. The new element of "bigness" in American civilization had bred a national disease: "the exclusive worship of the bitch-goddess Success." On the word success, his countrymen were putting only a squalid cash interpretation. It was resulting in a moral flabbiness, a callousness to abstract justice which James condemned as sinister, incomprehensible blots on American civilization.

Looking at the society of his time, he sometimes thought that the higher heroisms and the old rare flavors were passing out of life. Where now was the American who, like Alexander Agassiz, would proudly announce that he had no time for making money? The "bosom-vices" of twentieth-century America were not redeemed by splendor. They were mean and ignoble. James enumerated them publicly: "they are swindling and adroitness, and the indulgence of swindling and adroitness, and cant, and sympathy with cant—natural fruits of that extraordinary idealization of 'success' in the mere outward sense of 'getting there,' and getting there on as big a scale as we can, which characterizes our present generation." Even the universities guaranteed little but a more educated cleverness in the service of popular idols and vulgar ends. James asserted that our undisciplinables are our proudest product; and eventually he discovered great fields of heroism in the American social landscape. They were, he said, in the daily lives of the laboring classes.

So James did not hesitate to assert that democracy was on its trial, that no one knew how it would stand the ordeal. Was the irremediable destiny of Americans no more than vulgarity enthroned and institutionalized, elbowing everything superior from the highway? There were those who had already begun to draw Uncle Sam with the hog instead of the eagle for his emblem! James could not agree. For democracy was a kind of religion, and we were bound not to admit its failure. The best Americans were still filled with a vision of a democracy stumbling through every error till its institutions glow with justice and its customs shine with beauty. In the long run, he was willing to put his stakes on the "civic genius" of the American people. If this genius failed in vigilance, or atrophied in function, neither laws nor monuments, neither battleships nor public libraries, nor great newspapers nor booming stocks; neither mechanical invention nor civil service examinations could save us. But the genius would not fail. Of this he was confident.

From Europe, he wrote to a colleague that "we must thank God for America; and hold fast to every advantage of our position." Distrustful as he was of bigness, of the worship of mere pecuniary success, James loved his country for her youth, her greenness, her plasticity, innocence, good intentions. He was an inveterate voyager, a hereditary one, and sufficiently a cosmopolitan to feel, from time to time, that life in Europe was preferable to life at home. But these moods were transient. He could never, like Henry, become an expatriate. He had a sense that a man coquetting with too many countries is as bad as a bigamist, and loses his soul altogether. Once abroad, he was impressed by the seamy side of European life: America didn't know the meaning of the word corruption compared with Europe. There forces of corruption were rooted and permanent, while at home the only serious permanent incentive, he thought, was party spirit. Millionaires and syndicates had their immediate cash to pay, he admitted, but they had no intrenched prestige to work with, like the church sentiment, the army sentiment, the aristocracy and royalty sentiment which, in Europe, could be brought to bear in favor of every kind of individual and collective crime—appealing not only to the immediate pocket of the persons to be corrupted, but to the ideals of their imagination as well.

So was it not the moral obligation of American intellectuals, James asked, to work actively to keep our precious birthright of individualism, and freedom from these institutions? He had no special respect for intellectuals as such—there was just man thinking, whether he be greengrocer or metaphysician—but, seemingly, the framing of ideals was a part of their vocation. If their influence on the national life was meager, might not the fault be theirs? Too many of them, he felt, nursed the notion that ideals are self-sufficient and require no actualization to make us content. This, surely, was not "healthy-minded"; it was a kind of resignation and sour grapes. Ideals, James declared forthrightly, ought to aim at the transformation of reality—no less! If, in America, there existed a "treason of the intellectuals," James suspected that it was hatched in an ivory tower.

His own antipathy to ivory towers amounted almost to a phobia. His private bogey, he said, was dessication, the occupational malady of those who stood aloof from the rough turbulence of common life. He enjoyed a world which was unfenced, uncultivated, untidy, and unpredictable, which slipped through every ideal container—and nothing delighted him more than personally to slip through the meshes of decorum or to shy a pebble at constituted authority: the smug authority of Science, for instance, in the form of abstraction, priggishness and sawdust, lording it over all. To him, technicality seemed to spell failure. He made colloquialism a principle, and vivacity a kind of method, in conduct as well as in thought. How else should a man express his deep conviction that something is doing in the universe, and that novelty is real? So, in England, his brother Henry had frequent reason to be shocked. William displayed an imperturbable indifference to social conventions. He didn't care what kind of hat he turned up in at week-end parties. He thought nothing of climbing a ladder to get a peek at G. K. Chesterton over a high garden wall. He failed of a fine fastidiousness in his choice of acquaintances. No man, Henry sighed, could well have cared less for the question, or made less of the consciousness, of dislike. And, at home, pedants found it hard to swallow a scientist and philosopher of worldwide fame who dabbled in hypnotism, frequented mediums, didn't talk like a book, and didn't write like a book, except like one of his own. At the end of one of his lectures on pragmatism at Columbia University, the audience thronged down to the edge of the platform, assailing him with questions. James wound up by sitting on that edge himself, all in his frock coat as he was, his feet hanging down, and, unmindful of his dignity, absorbedly continuing the discussion. What, after all, could you make of a man like that?

His sister Alice thought that William expressed himself and his environment to perfection when he told her that his summer home in the New Hampshire hills had fourteen doors, all opening outwards. The doors of his spirit opened outwards, too, and there were many more than fourteen. He wanted, like his teacher Alexander Agassiz, always to live in the light of the world's concrete fullness, and if novelty did not put in an appearance, he simply went out to look for it. System, convention, officialdom—all categorical refusals to give novelty a hearing—closed the doors on what might be important to the future. James had not only, as he said, a love of sportsmanlike fair play in science, but an abiding suspicion that to no one type of mind is it given to discern the totality of truth. He could not help but feel that

orthodox science was a symbol of arrogance and vulgar success all too
ready to abuse its power by disparaging and crushing innovations
which threatened its authority. The disapproval of academic circles
merely reinforced his temperamental nonconformity, and his chivalry
toward doctrines that were despised by the genteel. He felt, he said,
like a man who must set his back against an open door quickly if he
does not wish to see it closed and locked. The results were sometimes
disconcerting, especially to admirers who lacked his quixotic rashness.
They seldom understood why he risked his personal fame for the
right of others to proceed with working hypotheses which, often
enough, he did not share. He did so repeatedly. It seemed almost as if
he were using his mounting prestige as a kind of bank account, re-
serving it for the heavy drafts of unpopular causes, pledging it to the
service of theories or sects of dubious repute.

One of these hazards, which brought him displeasing notoriety, was
his public support of the Society for Psychical Research, of which in
due time he assumed the presidency. Nothing was more shocking to
the reigning intellectual tastes than the phenomena produced by
spiritualists. To conventional folk, James' association with table rap-
ping, automatic writing, and "materialization" smacked of intellectual
bohemianism, of a fondness for excursions to the scientific underworld.
Could so great a man be deluded by the spurious? Privately, James
retorted with a scriptural quotation: "And base things of the world
and things which are despised hath God chosen, yes, and things which
are not, to bring to naught things that are." He discovered, investigated,
and reported on the Boston medium, Mrs. William J. Piper, who rode
to celebrity on this connection with his fame. For twenty-five years
William James held the door open for spiritualism. As a scientist, a
psychologist, he was never able to claim more for it than that facts
were still lacking to prove "spirit-return." Yet, in the end, though
skilled in the detection of fraud, and skeptical about the evidence
accumulated, he still found himself believing that there was something in it. It was a characteristic illustration of what he called "the
will to believe."

Quite as unselfish, and even more perilous, was James' vigorous
championship of the cause of "mental healers" and "faith healers." He
was disposed to curiosity about all forms of psychotherapy, not only
as a psychologist, but as a lifelong sufferer from attacks of nervous
exhaustion and melancholy. During one of his bouts of enervation, he

offered himself as a patient to a healer, and after a course of treatments recorded that his state of mind was revolutionized. Nevertheless, he declared that he held no brief for the healers, and that his intellect had been unable to assimilate their theories. But when the medical profession of Massachusetts sought passage of a law designed chiefly to prevent Christian Science practitioners from continuing their work, William James was roused to public protest.

In his dual capacity of physician and psychologist, James went to the State House, and spoke against his fellow scientists. It cost him more moral effort, he said, than anything that he had ever done. But he felt that he could face the condemnation of his colleagues much more easily than that of his own conscience. Why should scientists, professing faith in experiment and discovery, seek to stop the really extremely important experiences which these peculiar creatures were rolling up? Speaking as a scientist himself, he asserted that their facts were patent and startling; and anything that interfered with the multiplication of such facts, and with the opportunity of observing and studying them, would be a public calamity.

Such forays as these made James permanently vulnerable to the charge of gullibility. He was, indeed, publicly accused of "mysticism" by his colleague Hugo Munsterberg, whom he had persuaded Harvard to import from Germany to take over the psychological laboratory which he founded. But James had a sound scientific reason for what seemed to be his credulity. He was one of the earliest "functional" psychologists, and one of the first to approach the study of the mind by way of its pathology. His major interest was therefore the twilight region that surrounds the clearly lighted center of experience, fertile in what he described as exceptional mental states. This interest led him to propound two doctrines which appealed strongly to the imagination of the American people, and which left curious traces in the national life.

James readily adopted the theory of the "subliminal," or subconscious, mind, advanced toward the turn of the century. He followed the experimental studies of Sigmund Freud and Carl Jung with eagerness; hoped that Freud and his pupils would push their ideas to their utmost limits, since they couldn't fail to throw light on human nature, but was skeptical of Freud's dream theories and his use of symbolism as a method. Freud's theories implied a kind of determinism, by making the individual's behavior result from obscure mental forces beyond his control; and determinism was a principle which James could not tolerate. He took the contrary view. In a widely reprinted article on "The Energies of Men" James suggested that the "twilight region" was, in reality, a storehouse of unsuspected resources; that there existed incremental powers available to every individual, provided that he could find the key which would release them. The appropriate key, James said, might in every case be a different one; but he enumerated a number of disciplines which in his estimation had furnished impressive evidence of "working" efficaciously. Among them, he included Yoga, New Thought, Christian Science, as examples of a wave of religious activity passing over the American world; and, on a humbler level, he mentioned the current fad called "Fletcherism," a form of rumination and wishful thinking advocated by the popular American "philosopher," Horace Fletcher.

Excitements, ideas, and efforts, James asserted, are what carry us over the dam, and he called attention to the common denominator of these optimistic faiths. All of them negated feelings of fear and inferiority; all of them, on the positive side, operated by the suggestion of power. James explicitly stated that by "power" he meant not only outward work but inner work—the capacity to achieve a higher qualitative level of life. But many of his readers ignored this. The doctrine he advanced was that men the world over possess amounts of resource which only very exceptional individuals push to their extremes of use, and that under appropriate conditions everyone might do so. Did it not give scientific validity to the common American conviction that anything may be accomplished by anybody? For nearly four decades after his death, the sanction of William James was invoked to spread gospels of materialistic mysticism which, if applied perseveringly, would enable their fortunate exponents to sell more goods, radiate "charm," acquire friends and command influence, or rejoice in a satisfying love life.

There was a side of James' teaching which made this perversion of it almost inevitable. As a psychologist, he was persuaded that there is a continuum of cosmic consciousness, against which our individuality builds but accidental fences, and into which our several minds plunge as into a mother-sea or reservoir. To this fixed conclusion, James gave a religious application. It was received enthusiastically by a generation of Americans for whom orthodox dogmas had been discredited by science, and who were therefore disconsolately seeking congenial substitutes for them. Like James himself, they wanted a faith scientifically tenable, and propitious enough to live by. James candidly acknowledged both his predicament and his need. Did there not exist a feeling of unseen reality shared by large numbers of best men in their best moments, responded to by other men in their "deep" moments, good to live by, strength giving? As for himself, James felt no living sense of commerce with a God; he envied those who did. Yet, though lacking the active sense of God, he knew that "there is something in me which makes response when I hear utterances from that quarter made by others. I recognize the deeper voice. Something tells me:—thither lies truth. . . ."

This intuition would have been oddly at variance with his pragmatic reverence for fact, had James not assigned to it the status of a fact like all others. He held that it carried objective significance. It came from an altogether other dimension of existence into which the further limits of our being plunge. That other dimension, he asserted, is the source of most of our ideal impulses, which we find possessing us in a way for which we cannot articulately account. We belong to that dimension, James argued, in a more intimate sense than that in which we belong to the visible world, for we belong in the most intimate sense wherever our ideals belong. Yet the unseen region is not merely ideal. It produces verifiable effects in the everyday world. When we commune with it, James declared, work is actually done upon our finite personality, for we are turned into new men, and consequences in the way of conduct follow in the natural world upon our regenerative change. How, then, could one call unreal the unseen or mystical world? Did it not precipitate an actual inflow of energy in the faith-state and the prayer-state?

How did the transforming inflow of energy take place? James answered this question as a psychologist. He pointed to the phenomenon of "prayerful communion," in which certain kinds of incursion from the subconscious region take part. The subconscious mind is the channel of contact between our finite personality and a wider world of being than that of our everyday consciousness. By holding open the "subliminal door," James affirmed, we can experience union with something larger than ourselves and in that union find peace. Through that door higher energies filter in to increase our vital potential. Were not the practical needs of religion sufficiently met by the belief that beyond each man and in a fashion continuous with him there exists a larger power which is friendly to him and to his ideals?

For James, they were. He could keep more sane and true by pragmatically asserting the fact that the conscious person is continuous with a wider self through which saving experiences come. This was the essence of his religious doctrine. As fact, it was scientifically tenable. As faith, it was sufficiently propitious to live by. It was true, because it "worked." To many Americans—like James, reluctant agnostics—his practical mysticism provided a moral equivalent for the religion of which they felt deprived. Like him, they had a "mystical germ." It was, he said, a very common germ. He might have added that it had always been endemic in America. From the time of Jonathan Edwards to that of Mrs. Eddy there had never been wanting spiritual leaders of a strongly mystical cast. Surprisingly enough, their attraction had usually been most powerful when the nation's energies were being devoted mainly to practical affairs. Emerson had brought to the Western pioneers the gospel that the spiritual principle should be suffered to demonstrate itself to the end. During the gilded age of the robber barons, Mrs. Eddy had gained her swelling tide of converts in the East, the Middle West, and the Far West. Apparently, whenever materialistic incentives dominated the American people, an element of the native conscience rebelled against them. It seemed as if, in a revulsion of sheer disgust, as Margaret Fuller once said, they had to quarrel with all that is, because it is not spiritual enough.

It was therefore quite natural for William James' religious doctrine to emerge from the stupendous prosperity of the new century. To the American people, neither his mysticism nor his practical justification of it seemed novel. These merely gave sophisticated form to inarticulate and dormant popular convictions. James' real innovation consisted in making mysticism scientifically respectable. This had the happy effect of enabling the spiritually adrift to yield to their intuitions without violating their intelligence. As a result, the influence of James' doctrine ultimately reached many Americans who possibly had never heard of James himself. It penetrated the churches of liberal Protestantism. It was felt by adherents of various "social gospels" and "new" sects. And—as James might have been surprised to learn—it fertilized many of the esoteric cults which later sprang up and flourished under the sun of southern California.

But the influence of James' pragmatism was far more extensive and decisive. The doctrine, the point of view, gave a fresh turn to important functions of the nation's life: to politics and social reform; to the law; to public education. The central ideas of pragmatism were taken over by the Progressive movement in politics. Theodore Roosevelt had been one of James' students; and James' thought also affected the thinking of Woodrow Wilson. By 1913, Wilson was declaring that the word "progress" was almost a new one; that the modern idea is to leave the past and to press on to something new. The social planners of the Wilson era, and of President Franklin D. Roosevelt's New Deal, drew their inspiration from James. Pragmatism equipped them with a notion of the instrumental use of social theory; with their sense that society is both plastic and experimental; with their belief in the positive virtue of change; with their identification of the good and the expedient; even with their faith that, through the "welfare state," the maximum of freedom will accrue to the creative individual.

Apart from these channels, however, James' philosophy entered the stream of popular American thought, and in some sense became part of the intellectual equipment of the average citizen. James knew the natural tendency of "satisfying" ideas to filter in; once, he confessed that his personal hopes were centered on "the newer generation." He might have been dismayed by the use to which some of them put his theories. Americans who lacked his stern moral sense, and who worshiped the bitch-goddess Success that he detested, found in his doctrines of expediency and efficacy a sound justification for the principle that you had a right to whatever you could get away with. And James' denial of ethical absolutes, his insistence on relativity, furnished a convenient support for the moral cynicism of the jazz age.

But, in the main, James' teaching strongly reinforced traditional American convictions. As the twentieth century aged, the concept of determinism—economic, political and social—gained in authority, the world over. Many Americans continued to find it repugnant, and vigorously resisted it. The influence of James persisted in their confidence about the future, their faith in the resources and creative function of the individual, their emphasis on action as the end to which everything should contribute. James taught that a man must take his part, believing something, fighting for what he believes, and incurring the risk of being wrong. Many of his countrymen still considered this the best basis on which to conduct their lives, individually and collectively. To a group of Harvard students, James once said: "Believe that life *is* worth living, and your belief will help create the fact."

Americans, on the whole, still lived in the light of that doctrine.

Everything, in the end, depended not upon mechanism, but upon man, and especially upon his exercise of his moral will. Man's "practical control of nature," James pointed out, "accelerates so that no one can trace the limit; one may even fear that the *being* of man may be crushed by his own powers, that his fixed nature as an organism may not prove adequate to stand the strain of the ever increasingly tremendous functions, almost divine creative functions, which his intellect will more and more enable him to wield. He may drown in his wealth like a child in a bath-tub, who has turned on the water and who cannot turn it off." But for Americans in 1946 the vital question, more than ever before, seemed to be the one which James had asked forty years earlier. "Will you join the procession? Will you trust yourself and trust the other agents enough to face the risk?"

[2] THE GREAT DISSENTER

The old chamber of the Supreme Court, in the Capitol, was crowded. It was a small room, semicircular and glass domed. There was a formal elegance about its gray-painted walls, Potomac marble columns and crimson draperies that did not suggest a hall of justice dedicated to the nation's gravest issues. On this December day of 1902, the ceremony of induction was taking place. Tall, lean, erect in his flowing black robe, the new member of the Court recited the solemn oath of office. People thought Mr. Justice Holmes extraordinarily handsome, remarking his soldierly bearing and piercing gray-blue eyes. He had a long head, crested with a mass of whitening gray hair, and he wore a full, drooping moustache that was already white. A striking figure, certainly. He produced an impression of high personal distinction.

He felt that this ceremony was, for him, the opening of a great adventure. In it, he hoped that he might play his part nobly. "To have one's chance to do one's share in shaping the laws of the whole country," he had told his former colleagues, "spreads over one the hush that one used to feel when awaiting the beginning of a battle." He was sixty-one years old, and he counted on some ten years of active service as Associate Justice. But three decades were to pass before his retirement. During that period, he would come to be recognized as the greatest judge in the English-speaking world. To his fellow-citizens, he would seem something more. An elder statesman of unimpeachable moral authority; a mentor who, by translating all vexing problems of the current American way of life into terms of an ethical quest, kept alive in men's hearts that faith which had created their country and preserved it as a union. For his wisdom and faith he was venerated. But for other qualities he was beloved by millions of Americans who never knew him: the jet of his humor and play of his irony; his fortitude and large tolerance; his passionate attachment to liberty. So it seemed singularly appropriate that his ninetieth birthday should be marked by a nationwide broadcast of tribute. By then he had become a pervasive and intimate national possession, so much a part of the American past and present that it was, indeed, hard to think of a future that he would not share.

Oliver Wendell Holmes had sat on the Supreme Court of Massachusetts for twenty years, and had served as its Chief Justice for three, when President Theodore Roosevelt called him to the nation's highest tribunal. "His father's name entitles the son to honor," the President wrote to his friend, Senator Henry Cabot Lodge of Massachusetts, "and if the father had been an utterly unknown man the son would nevertheless now have won the highest honor." Roosevelt thought Holmes "typical of the American character at its best," and praised his "aloofness of mind" and "broad humanity of feeling." He did not mention Holmes' most conspicuous title to honor; his great book, *The Common Law*, already a classic. But, as "a strong point in Judge Holmes' favor," the President noted certain labor decisions which had been "criticized by some of the big railroad men and other members of large corporations." These, surely, indicated where Holmes stood in the contest between predatory capital and the people.

This contest was much on the President's mind, for he had recently embarked upon an offensive against "malefactors of great wealth," and against the trusts. So he wanted, on the Supreme Court, a justice who, "in the higher sense," was a "party man"; who would be "absolutely sane and sound on the great national policies for which we stand in public life." He had concluded that Holmes' "whole mental attitude . . . is such that I should naturally expect him to be in favor of those principles in which I so earnestly believe." Only a year later, he was bitterly regretting the appointment—so bitterly, that he considered excluding Holmes from the White House. During the interval, Roosevelt's first "trust-busting" suit reached the Supreme Court. The government won its case. But Justice Holmes wrote a vigorous dissenting opinion; and three of his colleagues concurred in it. To the President, this seemed little less than treason. As Holmes remarked many years later, he "looked on my dissent as a political departure (or, I suspect, more truly, couldn't forgive anyone who stood in his way)." There were few things for which Theodore Roosevelt was less fitted by temperament and intellectual discipline than gauging the "whole mental attitude" of Justice Holmes.

As a youth of twenty, newly graduated from Harvard, Holmes was swept into the War between the States. He served as an officer for three years, with outstanding gallantry, and was severely wounded in three battles. War, he said at the time, was an organized bore. The young ladies of Beacon Hill chirped about the young hero's peculiar want of patriotism. More than a half-century later, discussing a biography of Lincoln, he said, "I hate to read of those times." He detested the waste and the folly of war; yet he also felt that now, at least, and perhaps as long as man dwells upon the globe, his destiny is battle, and he has to take the chances of war. Though he found it horrible and dull, he also knew that for him its message was divine. War burned into him deeply. He emerged from it old beyond his actual years, with convictions that were to remain unshaken throughout his long life.

The new scientific doctrines of the day merely confirmed a lesson that Holmes had learned in war: the finality of force. "I believe that force, mitigated so far as may be by good manners, is the *ultima ratio*," he said, "and between two groups that want to make inconsistent kinds of world I see no remedy except force." Man, he thought, at present is a predatory animal whose importance in the scheme of things it was foolish to exaggerate. "It seems to me probable that the only cosmic significance of man is that he is part of the cosmos, but that seems to me enough." Yet war had taught him that man has in him that unspeakable somewhat which makes him capable of miracle, able to lift himself by the might of his own soul, unaided, able to face annihilation for a blind belief. So he came to think that man "is born a predestined idealist, for he is born to act. To act is to affirm the worth of an end, and to persist in affirming the worth of an end is to make an ideal." Identifying life with action, Holmes asserted that the final test of men is battle in some form—actual war—the crush of Arctic ice—the fight for mastery in the market or the court. Because life is essentially a struggle, a battle, he could not help but believe that the great problems are questions of here and now.

Mustered out of the army, Holmes returned to Harvard to study law. He always claimed that he rather was shoved than went into the law; at bottom, he hankered for philosophy. So it was as a philosopher that he approached the law, and later expounded it. Emerson, a philosopher, had been the hero of his early years; and at the age of ninety he said that the only firebrand of his youth that burned to him as brightly as ever was Emerson. But even if Holmes had lacked a natural addiction to speculative thinking, he probably would have acquired it by contagion. It was epidemic among the circle of his friends at Harvard. The impact of the new science, the collapse of the old faiths, the swift transformation of the society in which they were living, all conspired to make them take stock of their world and their beliefs. In a very real sense, Chauncey Wright, Charles Peirce, William James, Henry Adams and his younger brother Brooks, were philosophers as much by force of necessity as by choice. With James, his closest friend in those years, Holmes spent long evenings "twisting the tail of the cosmos." The habit persisted to the very end of his life. President Franklin D. Roosevelt, calling on the Justice a few days after his first inauguration, found him reading Plato in his library. Why, the President inquired, did he choose to read Plato? Quietly, the Justice replied: "To improve my mind, Mr. President." Had he not noted, but a few years before: "I always say the chief end of man is to form general propositions—adding that no general proposition is worth a damn"?

What Holmes appropriated from the new science was its technique of doubting, its theory that knowledge begins in skepticism. He wanted, he said, to multiply his skepticisms. Applying this desire to the law, he soon concluded that few of its traditional "general propositions" were genuinely tenable. Was it not obvious that certainty generally is illusion? The great jurists of the past—Story and Kent and Marshall—had appealed, for an ultimate sanction, to "natural law." They had assumed the existence of a fundamental, unchanging code; ethical, and eternally valid. They might have said, with Justice Sutherland, one of Holmes' juniors on the Supreme Court, that "there are certain fundamental social and economic laws which are beyond the power, and certain underlying governmental principles, which are beyond the right of official control, and any attempt to interfere with their operation inevitably ends in confusion, if not disaster." Could it not be affirmed, of these, that though conditions might change, "the principle itself is immutable; once righteous, it is always righteous"? This had been the opinion of the great early American jurists, and they had held that the function of the judge is to use precedent and logic in discovering the application of unchanging law to the conflicts of a changing world.

To none of this could Holmes agree. Its very simplicity had ceased to satisfy men's minds. He was unable to concede the existence of an absolute ethics. Was any system of ethics more than a body of imperfect social generalizations expressed in terms of emotion? It seemed to him that certitude is not the test of certainty, for men had been cocksure of many things that were not so. Men's values and beliefs were largely determined by their early associations. Their experiences thus made certain preferences dogmatic for them; they seldom realized that others might be equally dogmatic about quite different ones. The jurists who believe in natural law, he said, appeared to be in that naïve state of mind that accepts what has been familiar and accepted by them and their neighbors as something that must be accepted by all men everywhere.

Having thus discarded the historic concept of a natural law embodying eternal principles, and superior to the limited wisdom of men, Holmes proceeded to other conclusions equally disquieting to legal traditionalists and social conservatives. He declared flatly that judges make law—in the sense that, at any given time, the law for practical purposes is what the judge proclaims it to be. Being, like other men, subject to the social pressures and demands of their day, judges in making law are always remaking it: what the courts declare to have always been the law is in fact new. Judicial precedents survive in the law long after the use they once served is at an end and the reason for them has been forgotten. If they survive long enough, new reasons more fitted to the time have been found for them, and they gradually receive a new content, and at last a new form. It is revolting, Holmes asserted, to have no better reason for a rule of law than that it was so laid down in the time of Henry IV—especially if the grounds upon which it was laid down have vanished long since, and the rule simply persists from blind imitation of the past. So Holmes denied the binding force of precedent, or tradition, upon the present. He affirmed that the present has a right to govern itself so far as it can; and that it ought always to be remembered that historic continuity with the past is not a duty, it is only a necessity.

In Holmes' view, the law, like other mortal contrivances, is subject to chance and change. It has its roots in history and its justification in expedience, real or supposed. Its substance at any given time pretty nearly corresponds, so far as it goes, with what is then understood to be convenient; but its form and machinery, and the degree to which it is able to work out desired results, depend very much upon its past. For the law is always approaching, but never reaching, consistency. It is forever adopting new principles from life, while retaining old ones from history which have become merely vestigial. In a revolutionary statement, Holmes declared that the life of the law has not been logic; it has been experience. By taking this position, he was applying to law the philosophy of pragmatism, and the application produced radical results. The most significant was Holmes' doctrine that, at any specific moment in history, the basic rules of law are determined by the felt necessities of the time, the prevalent moral and political theories, institutions of public policy, avowed or unconscious, even the prejudices which judges share with their fellow men. The true source of the law's vital juices, he claimed, was seldom acknowledged by judges, and always with an apology. That source was to be found in considerations of what is expedient for the community concerned.

That law is an expression of social expediency was a notion from which traditionalists could be expected to recoil in horror. Holmes had other shocks in store for them. Who shall decide "what is expedient for the community"? All social conservatives, and all who asserted the primacy of property rights, saw their interests menaced by Holmes' answer to this question. It reaffirmed the basic axiom of American democracy; that the will of the majority shall prevail. Holmes stated that the duty of embodying in law the will of the majority—as to what is expedient for the community—rests with the elected representatives of the people in Congress and the state legislatures. He was under no illusion about the probable social and economic drift of popular legislation. All legislation, he acknowledged, favors one class at the expense of another, and none the less when the *bona fide* object is the greatest good of the greatest number, since if the welfare of the living majority is paramount, it can only be on the ground that the majority have the power in their hands. In the United States as elsewhere, he pointed out, legislation is "empirical." It is made a means by which a body, having the power, puts burdens which are disagreeable to them on the shoulders of somebody else. But that this is the case, Holmes declared, is no sufficient condemnation of legislation. The view was scarcely reassuring to the financial magnates whose tightening grip on the economic life of the nation an apprehensive people were seeking to break by the enactment of regulatory laws.

For, while Holmes was serving on the Massachusetts Supreme Court, an economic revolution had imposed finance capitalism on the American social order. Technological advances made large-scale industry possible. Great industry developed mergers and monopolies. Economic concentration brought the control of industry into the hands of bankers, acting in groups which commanded the enormous resources of credit that the new tendency to combination made necessary. In vast areas of enterprise, the "older capitalism" of individual initiative had given way to "corporate collectivism"—the new structure evolved by the new finance capitalism.

The financiers who brought about this change were farseeing. The old capitalism had flourished under laws embodying the economic doctrine of *laissez faire*. They wanted the doctrine to continue to apply to the operations of the new capitalism, even though these operations were producing profound alterations in the nation's social order, as well as in its economic life. Reasserting the doctrine of *laissez faire*, they claimed that economic activity is governed by natural laws of its own, which work out for universal welfare so long as their free play is not impeded by government. Let enterprise continue to remain unfettered and unhampered. Let the government keep its hands off. To secure a maximum freedom from interference for corporate enterprise, the celebrated "due process" clause had been inserted into the Fourteenth Amendment to the Constitution.

Meanwhile, the rapid growth of big business altered the relations of capital and labor. Trade unionism spread over many areas of industry. Combination by capital on a national scale was being matched with similar combination by labor. Capital contended that strong unions abridged the right of freedom of contract, and sought to limit the power of labor by preserving the "open shop." Organized labor relied on the strike as a potent economic weapon in bargaining. Capital attempted to cripple this use of the strike by resorting to judicial injunction. State legislatures, under popular pressure, enacted laws which capital regarded as hostile. Even Congress was persuaded to enact regulatory legislation in the Interstate Commerce Act and the Sherman Act directed against trusts.

In these circumstances, capital could not look, for protection of its privileges, to the elected representatives of the people in the state legislatures and in Congress. But it could look to the final arbiters of legality: the justices of the Supreme Court, who were appointed for life, and were thus beyond the reach of the people's will. Theirs was the power to strike down any restrictive legislation, whether originating in Congress or the legislatures, by declaring it unconstitutional. And so long as they construed the Constitution strictly, as a code which prescribed in detail answers for the social problems of all time, capital could consider its privileges safeguarded.

Capital did not. look to the Supreme Court in vain. One of the Justices, speaking before the American Bar Association in 1893, warned of "the danger which lurks in any radical disturbance of the present social system." Another, speaking before the New York State Bar Association, declared it to be "the unvarying law that the wealth of the community will be in the hands of the few." He protested that any "attempt to give to the many a control over the few" was "a step toward despotism." Were there not many reforms, fathered by social dissidents, which had this as their object? The Justice urged his hearers to oppose all coercive measures directed to making property and its uses subject to the will of the majority. That the Supreme Court was profoundly averse to any progressive social or economic legislation, that it had determined to protect the privileges of capital and confirm the primacy of property rights, became obvious one year later. The Court was required to pass on the constitutionality of an income-tax law. It struck down the law. To a majority of the justices, a tax on incomes signalized nothing less than "the beginning of an assault on capital . . . communism on the march"!

Clearly, the Supreme Court was shaping the laws of the whole country, and the nation's social policy also. It was probably to this decision, and others of a similar import, that Holmes referred in a statement made long afterwards. "When twenty years ago a vague terror went over the earth and the word socialism began to be heard, I thought and still think that fear was translated into doctrines that had no proper place in the Constitution or the common law." And, passing to the psychology of the judiciary, he added: "We too need education in the obvious—to learn to transcend our own convictions and to leave room for much that we hold dear to be done away with short of revolution by the orderly change of law."

By 1902, when Holmes joined the nation's high court, the American people were already deeply involved in an effort to subdue the new structure of "free enterprise," erected by finance capitalism, to the general social welfare. This effort was expressed, and achieved political power, in the Square Deal of President Theodore Roosevelt, the New Freedom of President Woodrow Wilson, and—after Holmes' retirement from the Court—the New Deal of President Franklin D. Roosevelt. In substance, the objects of all three movements were identical: to reconcile modern, complex economic forces to the needs of a popular democracy. During Holmes' thirty years of service, and for long afterwards, the major issue confronting the Supreme Court was that of social control over the economic circumstances of the American people. Legislation enacted in order to effect this control—through extension of government supervision over economic activity; through programs of welfare; through benefits to be secured for the common man—came before the Justices in a steadily rising stream. Did it accord with the organic charter of the Constitution? In rendering their decision on this question, the Justices were not only making law. They were determining whether or not "the present has a right to govern itself so far as it can."

Holmes believed that the decisions of the Supreme Court too frequently translated into law the private philosophy and economic predilections of its members. This was usually the case with respect to debatable and often burning questions of social policy. "It is a misfortune," he observed, "if a judge reads his conscious or unconscious sympathy with one side or the other prematurely into the law, and forgets that what seem to him to be first principles are believed by half his fellow men to be wrong." In one of his most celebrated dissents, he urged that the case was being decided upon an economic theory which a large part of the country did not entertain. The theory in question was that of *laissez faire*, to which Holmes himself subscribed. Nevertheless, he continued, "I strongly believe that my agreement or disagreement has nothing to do with the right of a majority to embody their opinions in law." He went on to elaborate this view in a statement which became classic. A constitution, he declared, "is not intended to embody a particular economic theory, whether of paternalism and the organic relation of the citizen to the state or of *laissez faire*. It is made for people of fundamentally differing views, and the accident of our finding certain opinions natural and familiar or novel and even shocking ought not to conclude our judgment upon the question whether the statutes embodying them conflict with the Constitution of the United States."

Repeatedly, Holmes urged that the Constitution embodied only relatively fundamental rules of right, and must not be perverted to become the partisan of a particular set of ethical or economical opinions. Its provisions, he asserted, were not mathematical formulas, but living institutions. Their significance was vital. It was to be gathered not simply by taking the words and a dictionary, but by considering their origin and the line of their growth. It was enough for the Founding Fathers to realize or to hope that they had created an organism; it had taken a century and had cost their successors much sweat and blood to prove that they created a nation. Cases brought before the Supreme Court on the issue of constitutionality, he insisted, must be considered in the light of our whole experience, and not merely in that of what was said a hundred years ago.

As was perhaps inevitable, Holmes' constitutional views were seldom concurred in by a majority of his colleagues. As a result, he became known as "the great dissenter," not so much because of the frequency of his dissenting opinions, as the nobility with which they stated his social philosophy. The failure of his view to prevail brought about the defeat, by judicial veto, of a wide variety of legislation designed to subject economic power to social responsibility. Much of it foundered on the "due process" clause of the Fourteenth Amendment, specifically extending to the states the prohibition which the Fifth Amendment had laid upon Congress. It had been incorporated in the Constitution purportedly to protect the civil rights of the freed Negroes. But its authors were corporation lawyers, and they had framed it for the additional purpose of protecting corporate enterprise from adverse legislation by the states. In early cases, they had succeeded in winning the assent of the Supreme Court to this purpose. By the time Holmes joined it, a body of precedent had been created under which the Court, almost at its own option, was able to uphold the sanctity of property as against the social aims of the American people.

Holmes protested; vigorously, earnestly, and always. He warned against the dangers of a delusive exactness in the application of the Fourteenth Amendment. Was not such exactness a source of fallacy throughout the law? By calling a business "property," he said, you make it seem like land, and lead up to the conclusion that a statute cannot substantially cut down the advantages of ownership existing before the statute was passed. But business is not property, Holmes declared. It is a course of conduct and like other conduct is subject to substantial modification according to time and circumstances both in itself and in regard to what shall justify doing it a harm. Here, indeed, was a formidable challenge to vested privilege! Were the rights of free enterprise merely relative—subject to popular determinations of what is expedient that changed according to time and circumstance? Holmes went further. "I have not yet adequately expressed the more than anxiety that I feel at the ever increasing scope of the Fourteenth Amendment in cutting down what I believe to be the constitutional rights of the States. As the decisions now stand, I see hardly any limit but the sky to the invalidating of those rights if they happen to strike a majority of this Court as for any reason undesirable. I cannot believe that the Amendment was intended to give us *carte blanche* to embody our economic or moral beliefs in its prohibitions."

In using the Constitution to prevent legislation that sought to rectify obvious inequalities in the distribution of economic power, Holmes contended that the Supreme Court was exceeding its own powers and invalidating the democratic process. "There is nothing I more deprecate," he said in a very significant dissent, "than the use of the Fourteenth Amendment beyond the absolute compulsion of its words to prevent the making of social experiments that an important part of the community desires, in the insulated chambers afforded by the several States, even though the experiments may seem futile or even noxious to me and to those whose judgment I most respect." This admonition, too infrequently heeded by the Court, was dictated by Holmes' genuine liberalism. As he understood, and many of his admirers did not, genuine liberalism is not a program but an attitude of mind; its roots are in the original, classic principle of *laissez faire*, and it extends to the realm of thought the free, competitive exchange which that principle imposes upon the market place. So Holmes felt a moral, as well as an intellectual obligation to sustain the right of others to hold theories which were obnoxious to him.

Personally, he viewed all "social experiments" with extreme skepticism. He supported the right of the American people to undertake them, for he interpreted the Constitution as a dynamic charter for a society conceived as being itself dynamic, and proceeding by the method of trial and error. In a broad sense, he justified social legislation as a pragmatist, by its instrumental utility. It helped in reaching a social end which the governing power of the community had made up its mind that it wanted. It was, so to speak, good if it worked. But as to the wisdom and worth of the ends which such legislation was designed to achieve, and even as to its practical efficacy, Holmes was usually dubious. To his old friend Sir Frederick Pollock, he admitted that he was so skeptical as to our knowledge about the goodness of laws that he had no practical criticism except what the crowd wants. He was, he said, willing to bet that the crowd if it knew more wouldn't want what it does—but he felt that this was immaterial.

Even before his appointment to the Supreme Court, Holmes had concluded that for the rational study of the law the man of the future is the man of statistics and the master of economics. The prediction accurately described his future colleague, Justice Brandeis, but it likewise pointed to an intellectual equipment which Holmes knew that he did not possess. Statistics and economics were outside the orbit of his interests. One of his warmest admirers surmised that his thinking in the field of economics stopped at twenty-five. Such as it was, his economic thinking followed orthodox lines. His hobby, he said, was to consider the stream of products, to omit all talk about ownership and just to consider who eats the wheat, wears the clothes, uses the railroads and lives in the houses. On this basis, he was convinced that the crowd now has substantially all there is, that the luxuries of the few are a drop in the bucket, and that unless you make war on moderate comfort there is no general economic question.

This conviction—steadfastly maintained while the Supreme Court was flooded with cases arising from the presumptively nonexistent "general economic question"—reflected the one facet of Holmes' mind that was incorrigibly naïve. He disliked grubbing in the "ragbag of details." He was always impatient of mere information about transient conditions. He admitted without pride or shame that he never read the newspapers. Justice Brandeis teasingly accused him of talking about improving his mind, but exercising it only on the subjects with which he was already familiar. Brandeis, he confessed, drove a harpoon into his midriff by urging him, in his summer reading, to try something new, study some domain of fact. He proposed that Holmes take up the textile industry of Massachusetts, read all available reports on it, go to Lawrence and get a human notion of how it really is. Holmes pondered the suggestion, then recorded his private comment: "I hate facts. . . . I have little doubt that it would be good for my immortal soul to plunge into them, good also for the performance of my duties, but I shrink from the bore." His intellectual furniture, he said, consisted of an assortment of general propositions which grew fewer and more general as he grew older—and he doubted the validity of any general propositions. "All I mean by truth," he once remarked, "is the road I can't help travelling. What the worth of that *can't help* may be I have no means of knowing. Perhaps the universe, if there is one, has no truth outside of the finiteness of man."

Political and social progressives, inspired by Holmes' championship of the people's right to undertake social experiments, claimed him as a reformer like themselves. But Holmes was not a reformer. He was a social philosopher. Looking at the American scene, the reformers were aroused by what they took to be a climactic struggle between human rights and property rights. Looking at the same social convulsion, Holmes saw only a conflict of forces which he surmised to be inevitable, in the nature of things, and probably, in one or another form, continuous. "I believe," he said, "that the wholesale regeneration which so many now seem to expect, if it can be helped by conscious, coordinated human effort, cannot be affected appreciably by tinkering with the institution of property, but only by taking in hand life, and trying to build a new race. That would be my starting point for an ideal for the law. The notion that with socialized property we should have women free and a piano for everybody seems to me an empty humbug." Nevertheless, seeing how the law had grown, without a break, from barbarism to civilization, Holmes found in what had been done some ground for believing that mankind yet may take its own destiny consciously and intelligently in hand.

As respects the immediate social situation, Holmes was disposed always to test it by a question: What proximate test of excellence can be found except correspondence to the actual equilibrium of forces in the community—that is, conformity to the wishes of the dominant power? All that could be expected from modern improvements in legislation, he held, was that it should easily and quickly, yet not too quickly, modify itself in accordance with the will of the *de facto* supreme power in the community, and that the spread of an educated sympathy should reduce the sacrifice of minorities to a minimum.

This attitude furnished a frame for his view of the bitter contest between capital and labor, which he recognized to be the most important of contemporary social conflicts. Holmes took the position that, under the American system, the doctrine generally had been accepted that free competition is worth more to society than it costs. He was not inclined to underestimate the costs. Among them, he asserted, was the intentional inflicting of temporal damage, including the damage of interference with a man's business, by some means, when the damage is done not for its own sake, but as an instrumentality in reaching the end of victory in the battle of trade. He refused to admit that the policy of allowing free competition—or, as he preferred to term it, free struggle for life—was confined to persons of the same class competing for the same end. It extended to all conflicts of temporal interests in society. So it applied to the conflict between employers and employed.

In modern industrial society, Holmes contended, free competition means combination, an ever-increasing might and scope of combination. Whether beneficial, as he personally believed, or detrimental, the tendency to combination was inevitable, unless the fundamental axioms of society, and even the fundamental conditions of life, are to be changed. Opposition to it was therefore futile; the point was to discover its bearing upon social conflict. "One of the eternal conflicts out of which life is made up is that between the effort of every man to get the most for his services, and that of society, disguised under the name of capital, to get his services for the least possible return. Combination on the one side is potent and powerful. Combination on the other side is the necessary and desirable counterpart, if the battle is to be carried on in a fair and equal way."

On this principle, Holmes sustained the right of labor to organize as effectively as possible, both because it established the equality of position between the parties in which liberty of contract begins, and because unity of organization is necessary to make the contest of labor effectual. He upheld the strike as a lawful instrument in the universal struggle for life; but he also asserted that it was a fallacy to suppose that there is a body of capital of which labor as a whole secures a larger share by that means. He upheld labor's right to institute a "primary boycott" against an employer during a controversy. He argued for the legality of a "secondary boycott" applied to those dealing with the boycotted employer. Later, on the Supreme Court, he sustained a wide variety of labor laws—among them, one which outlawed "yellow dog" contracts forbidding employees to join unions, and others which regulated hours of work and fixed minimum wage scales.

As early as 1894, Holmes remarked humorously that, because of his presumed sympathies with labor, among the respectable there were some who regarded him as a dangerous radical! Had he seen fit to clothe his views in different language, he thought he could have been a pet of the proletariat—whereas they cared nothing for him and some of the others distrusted him. The distrust endured. When, impressed by Holmes' disposition to strengthen the hand of labor in its contest with capital, President Theodore Roosevelt appointed him to the Supreme Court, Holmes reported to Pollock that he found powerful influences against him, because some at least of the money powers thought him dangerous, wherein they were wrong. The money powers were wrong. But so was the President. Roosevelt assumed that Holmes was pro-labor, therefore anti-capital. He anticipated Holmes' favorable decision in a suit to dissolve a railroad merger under the Sherman Act. But to Holmes the Sherman Act was no less repugnant than were anti-labor laws, and for the same reason. He considered it a humbug based upon economic ignorance and incompetence. It rested, he claimed, on the theory that you must compete but you mustn't win. It restricted the process of combination which free competition made inevitable. That the policy of free competition exacted heavy social costs Holmes never denied; he inclined to the belief that it reduced all economic conflict to naked warfare. But wasn't all life a roar of bargain and battle? To conduct the battle "in a fair and equal way" was the best solution; the law should make that solution always possible. For the rest, Holmes had no belief in panaceas and almost none in sudden ruin. He was not interested one way or another in the nostrums then so strenuously urged. But, as his friend Justice Frankfurter pointed out, Holmes denied that the Constitution stereotyped any particular distribution of economic power for all time. Short of revolution, by the orderly change of law, society could alter the scheme as it might see fit. "The law has got to be stated over again," Holmes said, long before his appointment to the Supreme Court, "and I venture to say that in fifty years we shall have it in a form of which no man could have dreamed fifty years ago."

In the aftermath of the First World War, as he passed his eightieth year, Holmes' creed of liberalism received expression in a series of memorable dissents. Exceptionally, for him, they were conceived in indignation and written with passion. It is hard to resist the conclusion that he intended them not so much to make explicit his differences with his colleagues as to challenge and rebuke all his countrymen. They were elicited by a series of cases involving civil liberties; specifically, the right of free speech, and the right to hold opinions condemned by the majority. Revolution had triumphed in Russia. The doctrines of Marx and Lenin were blowing across the Atlantic. Fear had gripped the hearts of many Americans. Intolerance was rising throughout the nation. Wartime espionage laws, not yet revoked, permitted the launching of a witch hunt of "radicals."

It was in this climate of suppression and persecution that the cases reached the Supreme Court. Some involved humble fanatics who, allegedly, had obstructed the war effort by circulating their opinions; these were violently opposed to war. In one case, as Holmes noted, sentences of twenty years imprisonment had been imposed for the publishing of two leaflets that he believed the defendants had as much right to publish as the Government had to publish the Constitution of the United States vainly invoked by them. The punishment, he held, was grossly excessive, unless the defendants were to be made to suffer not for what the indictment alleged but for the creed that they avowed —a creed that Holmes believed to be the creed of ignorance and immaturity when honestly held.

Yet this, Holmes felt, did not go to the heart of the matter. Surely the widest possible opportunity for the free play of intelligence, for the pursuit of truth by trial and error, was an indispensable condition of a free society. The long, slow advance of civilization was the history of a never-ending process of displacement: official truth found to be error, yielding to new and different beliefs; these, in their turn, doomed to give way to others. Intellectual liberty was the highest of social achievements, and the most precarious. It was forever vulnerable to intolerance, to the hysteria of fear. Persecution for the expression of opinion would always occur, since men having no doubt of their premises or power, and wanting a certain result, would attempt to embody their wishes in law, and sweep all opposition away.

"But when men have realized that time has upset many fighting faiths," Holmes wrote, "they may come to believe even more than they believe the very foundations of their own conduct that the ultimate good desired is better reached by free trade in ideas—that the best test of truth is the power of the thought to get itself accepted in the competition of the market, and that truth is the only ground upon which their wishes safely can be carried out. That at any rate is the theory of our Constitution. It is an experiment, as all life is an experiment. Every year if not every day we have to wager our salvation upon some prophecy based upon imperfect knowledge. While that experiment is part of our system I think that we should be eternally vigilant against attempts to check the expression of opinions that we loathe and believe to be fraught with death, unless they so imminently threaten immediate interference with the lawful and pressing purposes of the law that an immediate check is required to save the country."

Ten years later, as Holmes' ninetieth birthday approached, the wave of intolerance had not greatly receded. Rosika Schwimmer, over fifty years of age and an avowed pacifist, had applied for American citizenship. Her application was denied because she refused to promise to bear arms for the United States in a future war. A majority of the Supreme Court held her not to be attached to the principles of the Constitution. Once again, Holmes dissented. Sternly, he asserted that "if there is any principle of the Constitution that more imperatively calls for attachment than any other it is the principle of free thought— not free thought for those who agree with us but freedom for the thought that we hate. I think that we should adhere to that principle with regard to admission into, as well as to life within, this country." Nearly seventy years earlier, hating war, he had not hesitated to bear arms for his country, and the memory colored what he had still to say of citizenship. "And recurring to the opinion that bars this applicant's way, I would suggest that the Quakers have done their share to make the country what it is, that many citizens agree with the applicant's belief and that I had not supposed hitherto that we regretted our inability to expel them because they believe more than some of us do in the teachings of the Sermon on the Mount."

Could he say less, having himself faith in a universe not measured by our fears, a universe that has thought and more than thought inside of it?

Once, he had stated his faith in words which Americans might always remember. "I do not pin my dreams for the future to my country or even to my race. I think it probable that civilization somehow will last as long as I care to look ahead—perhaps with smaller numbers, but perhaps also bred to greatness and splendor by science. I think it not improbable that man, like the grub that prepares a chamber for the winged thing it never has seen but is to be—that man may have cosmic destinies that he does not understand. And so beyond the vision of battling races and an impoverished earth I catch a dreaming glimpse of peace."

[3] SAVONAROLA IN SILK

After the summer of 1916, Americans who followed the proceedings of the Supreme Court grew familiar with a phrase that time and frequency were to make celebrated. It concluded many a report of the Court's decisions, especially in cases involving social legislation and civil liberties. It recorded "Holmes and Brandeis dissenting."

The new Associate Justice was in his sixtieth year; a tall man, slightly stooped, spare and rugged, with a high forehead, deep-set, brooding eyes, and a broad, unsmiling mouth. Louis D. Brandeis had practiced law in Boston for thirty-seven years when President Woodrow Wilson, late in January 1916, sent his appointment to the Senate for confirmation. The appointment was unexpected. It provoked a violent controversy in the press. In the Senate, a bitter contest developed. The Judiciary Committee, during a prolonged investigation, heard many reputable citizens who strongly objected to the President's choice.

A group of Boston men of affairs filed a petition for rejection. Five former presidents of the American Bar Association—among them, ex-President Taft—considered it their painful duty to oppose confirmation. Eminent leaders in political, financial and legal life joined in the protest. So determined and powerful was the opposition that President Wilson took the unprecedented step of intervening. Defending his appointment in a letter to the Judiciary Committee, he dismissed the charges brought against Brandeis as "intrinsically incredible." Brandeis, the President declared, "is a friend of all just men and a lover of the right; and he knows more than how to talk about the right—he knows how to set it forward in the face of his enemies." The President was an excellent judge of this particular form of knowledge, for he too commanded it. He was shortly to be embittered by the discovery that it is not universally held in esteem. Brandeis had found this out long before.

The contest over his appointment was in one respect unique: its real significance, though generally understood, was so far as possible concealed. The charges brought against Brandeis included infringements of legal ethics, unjudical temperament and even chicanery and dishonesty. These were abundantly disproved. They were not the true grounds upon which opposition to his appointment was based. The Supreme Court, as the New York *Times* remarked when the President announced his choice, "by its very nature is the conservator of our institutions"—and Brandeis was "essentially a contender, a striver after changes and reforms."

The nature of the legal work he had undertaken in the public interest; the tenor of his social views, recorded in two books; the fact that on every major economic issue likely to come before the Court he had formed and expressed opinions notably at variance with those held by the representatives of economic power—these were the actual grounds for a concerted effort to prevent Brandeis from joining the Court. In the contest over his appointment, economic power was fighting a decisive and defensive battle against the people's determination to subject it to social control, a determination which they had expressed in electing Woodrow Wilson to the presidency. The battle over Brandeis was an episode of the spectacular national drama in which an old order was having to meet the challenge of an emerging new one.

Progressives and reformers had long held Brandeis in high repute. They honored him as a formidable crusader who possessed an intimate, realistic knowledge of modern economic processes. And they found their own aims expressed in what they called his social philosophy. Brandeis himself asserted that he had no rigid social philosophy; he had been intense on concrete problems of practical justice. But from these concrete problems he drew a body of economic doctrines and social ideals which, in his public legal work and his decisions as a Justice of the Supreme Court, took on the character of guiding principles. He carried over into the field of law the attitude of the pragmatists, the militancy of the muckrakers, and a romantic concept of the American way of life which dated from his childhood.

His parents and their relatives had come to the United States from Bohemia after the abortive democratic revolution of 1848. They were political liberals and, in a sense, political refugees, of Jewish faith, with a long tradition of wealth and culture. To them, democracy, individual liberty, and social justice were not mere phrases. They were genuine realities, and attainable only in the United States. This conviction was the earliest, and probably the strongest, influence on Brandeis' mind.

He never ceased to believe that the old American ideals were still valid for a highly complex industrial society, and that within its framework the democratic way of life could be realized through the application of new knowledge to new conditions.

This belief was also held by the muckrakers. Like them, Brandeis took the position that the evils which he was fighting were not inherent to American capitalist society. They were unnatural outgrowths which could, and should, be pruned away. The industrial monopoly, the tyrannical "money trust," the pyramided corporations over which a few great magnates exercised absolute control, the powerful and irresponsible labor union—to Brandeis, these did not represent normal developments of an efficient capitalism. They were not its natural products, or its logical and appropriate consequences. They were, for him, sinister abuses; largely the result of unwise, man-made, privilege-creating law, which had stimulated tendencies to inequality instead of discouraging them. So Brandeis forthrightly announced that the process of capitalizing free Americans is not an inevitable one. The effort to arrest that process, if possible to throw it into reverse, became the great enterprise of his life.

He was forty years old, one of the most successful corporation lawyers in New England, and already wealthy when he embarked upon it. The best lawyers, he felt, had allowed themselves to become adjuncts of great corporations and had neglected the obligation to use their powers for the protection of the people. Too much was heard of the "corporation lawyer," like himself; too little of the "people's lawyer." He resolved to devote half his time, or more, to serving as a lawyer for the people. He refused to accept fees for undertaking any cause in the public interest; thus, he retained his freedom of opinion and action.

Causes flowed to him. He soon became celebrated locally, then nationally, as the "people's counsel." The nature of the problems with which he was required to deal brought him into conflict with the very class whose interests, in his private practice, he had been retained to defend. So he quickly won the enmity of those in whom economic power was lodged. Had he been content merely to "talk about the right," they might have accounted him only a pious nuisance. But he was content with nothing less than action, or preparation for it. He possessed an expert knowledge of the strategy to which his opponents resorted when seeking to expand their power. He was familiar with the intricacies of corporate finance, the uses of political pressure, the manipulation of credit made possible by free access to the funded savings of the people. He soon mastered the technique of "creating public opinion." Whether in court, or before legislative committees and other public bodies, or in the pages of the national magazines to which he contributed with increasing frequency, he proved himself to be a resourceful antagonist.

His arguments made a deep impression on the plain people. So it did not take long for the masters of economic power—the great financiers and their satellites, whose grip on the nation's economic life he exposed and attacked—to view him as a menace. Bankers like Morgan and his associates, Brandeis charged, controlled the people through the people's own money. They managed to obtain command over the nation's liquid capital; this gave them almost absolute power. The fetters which bound the people, he asserted, were forged from the people's own gold. What were the masters of capital to make of a man who had prospered by playing the game according to rules in force for a half century—and who now insisted that these rules be revoked? What was his secret, sinister purpose? Brandeis talked of "social justice." Social justice, indeed! What about business and profits? What about the rights of free enterprise?

Perhaps perennially, capital interests will fling these questions at advocates of social change. In the first decade of the century, reformers and muckrakers had only one answer to them; a moral one. Brandeis was a novelty. He chose to expound social principle in terms of hard economic and financial facts. As he saw it, the American social situation was being shaped by conditions mainly economic in nature. The forces that were decreasing individual freedom and narrowing the area of individual opportunity had been generated by the process of industrial development. "The old method of distribution and developing of the great resources of the country," he asserted, "is creating a huge privileged class that is endangering liberty. There cannot be liberty without financial independence, and the greatest danger to the people of the United States today is in becoming, as they are gradually more and more, a class of employees." This was the foundation of Brandeis' "social philosophy." In essence, it was a conviction that political democracy depends upon economic democracy; that the national welfare requires preservation of the small business unit and the creation of conditions propitious to the individual enterpriser. Property, he said, must be subject to that control of property which is essential to the enjoyment by every man of a free individual life. And when property is used to interfere with that fundamental freedom of life for which property is only a means, then property must be controlled.

As counsel for the people, and adversary of the masters of capital, Brandeis undertook to prove how property was being used to the detriment of fundamental freedom. In major crusades against monopoly in life insurance and railroad transportation, and in the behalf of the Clayton Anti-Trust Law, he dealt with the purely economic aspects of the issue. He interpreted it as a problem of accelerating financial concentration, leading to the creation of massive corporate units which eventually combine in monopolies. Brandeis hated "bigness" as intensely as did William James, and for much the same reason. His attack on it was sensational. The chief advocates of big business extolled its efficiency. Brandeis proposed to show that its vaunted efficiency was an illusion. By analyzing the actual operations of some of the country's largest corporate enterprises, dominated by Morgan and others popularly regarded as geniuses in the realm of practical affairs, he attempted to prove that bigness, carried beyond a certain point, results in economic inefficiency. He did not hesitate to talk of the "curse of bigness." He argued that it is clear that an organization may be too large for efficiency and economical management as well as too small. Big business, he alleged, had not developed as the result of a genuine industrial or economic necessity. It sprang from the avarice of the great bankers—the "money trust"—who, through promoting combinations, were able to market enormous issues of securities which merely capitalized an inability to compete. The end results of swollen size, Brandeis sought to demonstrate, were diminishing industrial efficiency, rising prices for goods and services, and unreasonable losses to the investing public.

But although Brandeis stressed economic facts, he did not neglect their social implications. Is it not irony, he asked, to talk of equality of opportunity in a country cursed with bigness? The issue could not be justly solved for the American people by looking at it through the spectacles of bonds and stocks. You should study it, he declared, through the spectacles of people's rights and people's interests. When you do that you will realize the extraordinary perils to our institutions which attend the trust; you will realize the danger of letting the people learn that our sacred Constitution protects not only vested rights but vested wrongs. Brandeis asserted that the government must keep order not only physically but socially. It must move steadily toward more resolute control, with the purpose of protecting American citizens from the new oppressions which a subtler civilization had substituted for the old ones of physical force. The new, towering industrial structures were becoming too large to be tolerated by a people who desired to be free. Brandeis thought that the American people would lose their political independence or they would acquire industrial independence. But he asserted that there was no need to amend the Constitution, which had not lost its capacity for expansion to meet new conditions, unless it be interpreted by rigid minds which have no such capacity—the minds of reactionary jurists on the Supreme Court who dealt with the law, not as an expression of the "felt needs of the time," but of eternal righteous principle. Brandeis wanted to work within the frame of historic American institutions. What required amendment was not the Constitution, but men's economic and social ideals.

Since the foundation of all his thinking was economic, Brandeis saw the immediate future in the United States as a continuing and ever-increasing contest between those who have and those who have not. The people had become aware of a profound inconsistency in their present situation: it combined political democracy and industrial absolutism. They were beginning to doubt whether in the long run democracy and absolutism can coexist in the same community; whether there is a justification for the great inequalities in the distribution of wealth. They were beginning to think and their thought would presently result in action. Whether such action would run on lines of evolution or on lines of revolution rested with lawmakers and the judiciary. He predicted that there will come a revolt of the people against the capitalists, unless the aspirations of the people are given some adequate legal expression. He stood out for individualism as against the great uprising of socialism on the one hand and of the accumulation of great fortunes on the other. In the immediate contingency, he put forward two ideas which were destined to exercise considerable influence on the life of the nation. One was the doctrine of "social invention." The other was the theory of the "living law." Both, essentially, were social applications of pragmatism.

By social invention—which he declared was the most insistent need of the times—Brandeis meant the use, under democratic safeguards, of the experimental method in solving those vital problems which were generating social unrest. His own public legal work yielded a number of arresting illustrations which brought the doctrine national celebrity. In the sensational insurance investigation conducted by Charles E. Hughes, Brandeis participated as the representative of a policy-holders' group. His analysis of the high cost, inadequate protection, and unreasonable rate of loss to workers who took out policies in commercial insurance companies suggested the need of an efficient alternative. He devised legislation which permitted savings banks to undertake the writing of insurance, thus providing the workers of Massachusetts with adequate low-cost protection on which they also received high dividends, resulting from notable economies of operation. Brandeis hoped to tie in this popular savings policy with co-operative credit societies which would divert the "people's gold" from the pool of liquid capital available to the money trust, and make it productively serve its actual owners; but this hope was not realized. He resorted to social invention once again when, dealing with the application of major railroads for substantial increases in their freight rates, he announced that they could achieve savings of one million dollars a day by adopting the new formulas of "scientific management" devised by Frederick W. Taylor and other industrial engineers.

The formulas of Taylor and his colleagues were regarded with considerable hostility by organized labor. Brandeis undertook to dispel this hostility by demonstrating that of the profits that were to come from the new scientific management, the people were to have their share. His prestige with labor had been established by his most widely publicized use of social invention—made when he was invited to settle a bitter, paralyzing strike of some seventy thousand cloakmakers in New York City. Among other issues involved was that of the closed shop, on which employers and the union had split, apparently beyond the hope of conciliation. Brandeis invented a compromise, the "preferential union shop," to the experimental adoption of which both parties agreed. He devised a "protocol," or over-all working agreement governing the entire industry, and binding upon the manufacturers and the union. It provided for price committees, shop chairmen, committees on grievances, a board of sanitary control, and a board of arbitration for future disputes over which Brandeis agreed to preside as impartial chairman for the industry. A body of precedents and industrial rules soon developed which, based on justice to both sides, enabled them to adjudicate specific controversies. Of eight thousand disputes that arose in a period of two years, only nine had to be carried up to the board of arbitration for final settlement. For Brandeis, the new setup exemplified the method to be employed in attaining that industrial democracy which should ultimately attend political democracy. It established his thesis that "the problems of a trade should no longer be the problems of the employer alone. The problems of his business, and it is not the employer's business alone, are the problem of all in it. The union cannot shift upon the employer the responsibility for conditions, nor can the employer insist upon determining, according to his will, the conditions which shall exist."

But social invention required a foundation of legal validity in order to achieve genuine efficiency. To provide this, Brandeis put forward his theory of a living law, which he illustrated in a number of notable cases, and later consistently emphasized in his judicial opinions as a member of the Supreme Court. Because the theory revolutionized the practice of constitutional law in the United States, the legal profession came to regard it as Brandeis' most conspicuous achievement. In a sense, the theory sprang from his attempt to make the law approximate Holmes' definition of it as expressing "the felt necessities of the time."

Brandeis asserted that American law had not kept pace with the changes occurring in the fundamental conditions of American life. Clearly, the things needed to protect liberty were radically different from what they were fifty years back, but the law had lagged behind, while our longing shifted from legal justice to social justice. In the divorce of law from life, appeal was made to constitutional provisions in order to stop the natural vent of legislation. Statutes based on new social facts were vetoed by the Supreme Court, which declared such facts immaterial, and based its decisions not on life, but on logic and precedent. Brandeis contended that industrialization of the American economy had invalidated many historic precedents; they were no longer applicable to existing conditions. Though the social sciences took account of the changes produced by industrialization, legal science —the unwritten or judge-made law as distinguished from legislation— was largely deaf and blind.

One disastrous consequence was obvious: the small man needs the protection of the law; but the law becomes the instrument by which he is destroyed. If the law was to be made responsive to the new needs developed by a changing social order, argument and judicial conclusions must be based, not upon ancient abstractions, but upon modern facts. They must be shifted from the barren ground of precedent and logic to the higher ground of social function and social situation. Not preconceived notions and precedents, but the actual economic and social setting from which legislation emerges, should be made the controlling factor in judicial decision.

What Brandeis meant, he first made clear in a celebrated brief which he submitted to the Supreme Court in 1908, in a case contesting the constitutionality of an Oregon state law fixing the maximum working hours of women in industry. Opposing counsel argued that women, like men, were endowed with the fundamental right of free contract, which must not be impaired by limiting their hours of work. Brandeis disposed of this issue in two pages of his brief. He devoted another fifteen to a review of American and foreign legislation respecting working hours. But he based his case upon ninety-five pages devoted to the facts of common knowledge of which the court might take judicial notice. The argument was no more daring an innovation than was the material. For the facts which Brandeis adduced were of a type certainly not within the common knowledge of the Supreme Court. They furnished massive evidence to prove that the female organism suffered under strain, fatigue contributed to chronic ailments and accidents, overwork caused moral laxity, deterioration inevitably made the entire community suffer. His plea was based, not on constitutional precedent, but on the stern issue of preventable human waste. In unanimously upholding the Oregon statute, the Court not only reversed its precedent, but announced that its decision took judicial cognizance of Brandeis' social facts. Later jurists, therefore, agreed with Justice Frankfurter in holding that this brief was epoch making. It opened a new era in the disposition of cases presenting the most important present-day constitutional issues.

Subsequently, Brandeis used the same method in a series of cases which won increasing acceptance for the doctrine that the states have an obligation, as well as a right, to keep order not only physically but socially. One of the most important of these related to another Oregon statute, which fixed minimum wages for women in industry. In his argument, Brandeis attempted to justify his concepts of social invention and living law. "Nothing could be more revolutionary than to close the door to social experimentation. The whole subject of woman's entry into industry is an experiment. And surely the federal Constitution—itself perhaps the greatest of human experiments—does not prohibit such modest attempts as the women's minimum wage act to reconcile the existing industrial system with our striving for social justice and the preservation of the human race."

After he joined the Supreme Court, Brandeis was often associated with Justice Holmes in dissent. Because of this, the American public spoke of them, almost interchangeably, as liberals. Actually, their liberalism was by no means identical. Between them there existed an old, warm friendship. Each admired the other. They shared a common devotion to the ideals of democracy and individual liberty. They saw life as a conflict of forces, and defined the function of government as the production of a just equilibrium. But notwithstanding this basic unity of view, the area of their difference greatly exceeded that of their agreement. Both were aware of this. "I'm afraid Brandeis has the crusading spirit," Holmes once remarked of his junior. "He talks like one of those upward-and-onward fellows." And, after reading one of Brandeis' exhaustive dissenting opinions, decorated with concise footnotes referring to trade reports, to studies of committees, to tables of figures, Holmes noted on the margin: "This afternoon I was walking on the towpath and saw a cardinal. It seemed to me to be the first sign of Spring. By the way, I concur." It was almost as if, to the transient phenomena so meticulously considered by Brandeis, Holmes wished to oppose the assertion of a timeless process. For him, the immediate was temporary; it would give way to something else. For Brandeis, because it molded the shape of things to come, the immediate was of paramount importance.

This distinction made them take different attitudes to social change, which they agreed in considering inevitable. "Generally speaking I agree with you in liking to see social experiments tried," Holmes wrote to Brandeis, "but I do so without enthusiasm because I believe that it is merely shifting the place of pressure and that so long as we have free propagation Malthus is right in his general view." Holmes was skeptical of the wisdom of popular majorities. What he respected was their power: he felt that, wise or not, the proximate test of a good government is that the dominant power has its way. But for Brandeis, this was not enough. He distrusted sheer power. He believed the sense of unrestricted power to be just as demoralizing to one group as to another. Neither our intelligence nor our character, he declared, can long stand the strain of unrestricted power. What, then, should restrict it? Brandeis believed that power should submit to the guidance of factual knowledge. So he asserted that a lawyer, or a judge, or a government official who had not studied economics and sociology was very apt to become a public enemy.

Subject the use of power to the guidance of factual knowledge, Brandeis held, and you transform the right of the dominant power to have its way into a constructive instrument of social progress. Holmes saw social change from the evolutionary point of view, as a result of the struggle between competing forces that were possibly blind. Brandeis was convinced that it could be given conscious direction; thus, all change could become progress. Holmes was content that society should pursue the course of trial and error; privately, he suspected that most trials would turn out to be errors. Brandeis wished to minimize the possibility of error in every trial. Holmes felt required to protect the right of the people to make social experiments. Brandeis, regarding that right as axiomatic, was concerned that the experiments be genuinely effective—that each one should advance the cause of social justice and in some predictable fashion contribute to the democratic way of life.

Unlike Holmes, therefore, Brandeis did not abstain from founding his judicial decisions on his personal theory of a wise public policy. He did not share Holmes' protest against cases being decided upon an economic theory. He wanted cases to be decided upon the basis of social and economic facts; but he assessed the facts in the light of his own social and economic preconceptions. Holmes was willing to uphold the constitutionality of legislation in which he personally disbelieved. Brandeis, on the whole was not—his verdict on it was usually determined by its conformity to his own standards of social justice. The wisdom or reasonableness of proposed legislation, he declared, "can ordinarily be determined only by a consideration of the contemporary conditions, social, industrial and political, of the community to be affected thereby. Resort to such facts is necessary, among other things, in order to appreciate the evils sought to be remedied and the possible effects of the remedy proposed. Nearly all legislation involves a weighing of public needs as against private desires; and likewise a weighing of relative social values. Since government is not an exact science, prevailing public opinion concerning the evils and the remedy is among the important facts deserving consideration; particularly, when the public conviction is both deep-seated and widespread and has been reached after deliberation. What, at any particular time, is the paramount public need is, necessarily, a matter of judgment."

In arriving at final judgment, Brandeis was guided by "social values." Public conviction might express itself, during a time of hysteria, in criminal syndicalism laws, or laws intended to suppress radical agitation; Brandeis would strike them down without a qualm. During a depression, an agricultural community might seek to enact "privileged legislation" for co-operatives; Brandeis would uphold it. So, too, he would uphold the right of a state to deprive capital of recourse to judicial injunction in labor disputes. He would support laws fixing maximum hours of work, setting a minimum wage, establishing a system of social insurance. In a conflict between property rights and human rights, he acknowledged no alternative. He gave judicial consent to any public control of property which might seem requisite to the enjoyment of a free individual life by the small man who so urgently needed the protection of the law.

So, as the publicist Max Lerner certified in 1932, a very large body of American liberal opinion made almost an idol of Mr. Justice Brandeis and acknowledged the leadership of his thought. Liberals applauded his aggressive championship of the common man, helplessly at the mercy of those in whom economic power was vested. They approved his implied conviction that government, functioning through the Supreme Court, could drive a wedge of direction through the flux of economic life and turn it into socially accredited channels. Particularly during the era of President Franklin Roosevelt's New Deal, liberals honored Brandeis for his pioneer efforts to further the creation of a new American social order—a system of socialized and regulated capitalism operating under a welfare state, which it seemed likely that the New Deal would succeed in imposing on the nation.

To liberals, Brandeis came to personify an ideal of progressive economic statecraft. Yet, ironically, the core of his economic thinking was nostalgic rather than prospective, romantic rather than practical. He warned against the oppressive progress of integration in finance and industry, and thought it could be stayed. Through size, corporations were sometimes able to dominate the state; yet there was no need to accept the evils attendant upon the free and unrestricted use of the corporate mechanism as if these evils were the inescapable price of civilized life. Convinced as he was of the economic fallacy of the huge unit, Brandeis never ceased asserting that if we make competition possible, if we create conditions where there could be reasonable competition, these monsters would fall to the ground.

In 1933, when a depression had paralyzed the American economic system, Brandeis—then in his seventy-seventh year—wrote an opinion which summed up his economic and social policy. "There is a widespread belief that the existing unemployment is the result, in large part, of the gross inequality in the distribution of wealth and income which giant corporations have fostered; that by the control which the few have exerted through giant corporations, individual initiative and effort are being paralyzed, creative power impaired, and human happiness lessened: that the true prosperity of our past came not from big business, but through the courage, the energy, and the resourcefulness of small men; that only by reopening to them the opportunities for leadership, can confidence in our future be restored and the existing misery be overcome; and that only through participation by the many in the responsibilities and determinations of business, can Americans secure the moral and intellectual development which is essential to the maintenance of liberty."

That Brandeis, at the time, was speaking for prevailing public opinion was scarcely open to doubt. But there remained a problem which opinion alone could not solve. Under the capitalist system, however modified by social invention, could Americans turn back the economic clock? In the mid-twentieth century could they both preserve their social order, and recapture their former way of life? It was neither his economic scholarship, nor his social vision, that persuaded Brandeis that they could. These, indeed, might have forced him to conclude that they could not. But this conclusion would have been repugnant to his optimism, and to his own practical mind might have invalidated his major efforts. The burden of those efforts rested on a prophecy. So Brandeis made it, in the confident American way. What nourished his faith was something invulnerable to any melancholy assaults by knowledge. It was a profound attachment to old ideals.

[4] A PRAGMATIST LOOKS AT TOMORROW

By the mid-nineteen forties, pragmatism had touched the lives of two generations of Americans. Perhaps never before had a philosophy been applied so hopefully, over so wide an area, to shape the minds of youth to the uses of a greater freedom. If social power and insight were developed in the young, must not society eventually be perfected?

Whether or not they knew it, most Americans born in the twentieth century played some part in this experiment. For it had taken place in the most universal of their institutions. In less than fifty years, pragmatism had transformed the American school.

But the anticipated improvement in society had not begun. And hopefulness had faded. In men's beliefs, as well as in their practical affairs, there was no more widespread sense than that of insecurity. No one was more keenly aware of this than the thinker whose doctrines had inspired a reform of education. For John Dewey, the situation was a challenge, a summons to action. It roused him to undertake what might become the most fruitful enterprise of a long, prolific career. William James had tried to persuade his countrymen to apply a new way of thinking to their personal problems. Holmes and Brandeis, adopting it as a method of resolving social conflicts, had sought to give it an institutional effect in the law. Dewey, looking to the social action of future citizens, had attempted to establish it, by means of the school, not only as a habit of mind, but as a way of collective life. Considering the American social order in his old age, he concluded that the sum of these efforts had been failure. One grim fact attested it. Social instability, he acknowledged, had reached a point that might portend revolution if it went on unchecked.

How had this condition arisen? By what means could it be remedied? What changes were required to make, for the common man, the possibilities of American life commensurate with the possibilities of its material culture? From his seventieth year onward, Dewey wrestled with these questions. Always before, he had addressed students, educators, professional philosophers. Now he began speaking to his fellow-citizens, in a time of crisis, as one of them: and there could be little doubt that he hoped to be heeded by the nation's youth. The American people came to know him as they never had before.

To the great public, the later Dewey was a new figure, emerging from a fame that paradoxically resembled obscurity. Everyone had heard his name. Everyone knew that he was the "father of progressive schools," the innovator who had been summoned on educational missions to China, Mexico, Japan, the Union of South Africa, Soviet Russia. But relatively few laymen had troubled to read the books in which his educational theories were set forth. Fewer still were aware how inadequately the progressive schools of America approximated the ideals he had invented for them. His many philosophical works were virtually unread, except by specialists. Laymen merely knew of their existence and their celebrity. Philosophers conceded their importance, and ruefully complained that they were tough reading. Justice Holmes, whose appetite for technical philosophy survived all incidental difficulties, was compelled to re-read one of Dewey's major works several times before he understood it. In the end, he attributed to it an unequalled feeling of intimacy with the inside of the cosmos. Dewey, he reported with exasperated admiration, spoke as God would have spoken, had God been inarticulate but keenly desirous to tell you how it was.

The later Dewey spoke very differently. A sense of urgency made him simple and eloquent. He drew up a formidable, blistering indictment of the established order, and the way of life which it imposed upon the American people. He castigated the powerful. He explained, again and again, how a needless surrender of their liberties had been wrung from the great majority of his fellow-citizens; how they had been tricked into tacit consent; how they were being induced to perpetuate their servitude. But he also answered the common man's question: where do we go from here? A liberal and a democrat, Dewey spoke as an American whose vision of the national future proposed a new way of life in which its traditional promise might be realized. There was anxiety in his tone; but there was no despair. He still affirmed that we live not in a settled and finished world, but in one which is going on, and where our main task is prospective.

Though his earlier fame had been won in scholastic fields, Dewey had never been a cloistered academician. Even the look of him, as he neared his ninetieth year, suggested how much he had always lived in the thick of things. Erect and compact of figure, with yellowing white hair, a deeply lined, strong-jawed face, a bristling cropped moustache, and quizzical eyes behind his spectacles, his appearance was anything but professorial. For all that it told, he might have been a retired businessman, a physician, or a lawyer; you thought of him as relaxing in slippers with a good thriller, and you were right. He looked like everyone's image of the average middle-class American for whom he spoke, and only the New England twang in his low, husky speech gave him a local origin.

He was born in Vermont, just before the War between the States; spent his early manhood in the Middle West, and in middle age moved on to New York. He had been as deeply involved as Brandeis in the rough and tumble of American life. He knew the industrial world as well as the technological one. He had taken an active part in the labor movement. Like Holmes, he believed that the doctrines which one loathed had a right to be heard, so he was always in the forefront of the battle for civil liberties, as in the Sacco-Vanzetti case, and that of Leon Trotzky. If he had a fetish, it was liberty—and he did not hesitate to rebuke American "liberals" of a younger generation for their inadequacy. Democracy was a fighting faith; instead of acting, they merely talked, and not too wisely. He always said that he was glad to have been born at a time and place where the earlier concepts of liberty and the self-governing community prevailed. They were his central ideals, and his aim, as a social philosopher, was to give them values attainable by an industrial society in which science and technology, being the controlling forces, were likewise the finally significant ones.

A deep-rooted devotion to traditional American ideals linked Dewey to James, Holmes and Brandeis. But the temper of his mind was unlike theirs. A tough Yankee practicality kept him from sharing the purely intellectual skepticism of Holmes; the will-to-believe optimism of James; the romantic, nostalgic faith of Brandeis that the clock could be turned back to restore the conditions of an earlier day. Social conflicts were as obvious to him as to Holmes; he did not think the achievement of a mere equilibrium of forces an adequate solution. With James and Brandeis, he condemned the current worship of the bitch-goddess Success; he did not share their fear of bigness. And unlike any of them, he realized that the old ideals had to be given new meaning appropriate to a new age. Ideals, he said, express possibilities; but they are genuine ideals only in so far as they are possibilities of what is now moving.

In twentieth-century America, the old concepts were obsolete and irrelevant; catchwords for those who proposed to maintain the present state of affairs. Rugged individualism, Dewey said, had become ragged individualism. Any system that could not provide elementary security for millions had no claim to the title of being organized in behalf of liberty and the development of individuals. In the current social order, control was being exercised by the few who have economic power, at the expense of the liberties of the many and at the cost of increasing disorder. To talk about free individuals, equality of opportunity, and the automatic blessings of democracy, was to ignore existing facts; to deal in the kind of social ideas, Dewey said, that were represented by the Liberty League and ex-President Hoover. The old ideals, framed in an age of agrarian economy and physical pioneering, had been relevant to then existing conditions. Since that day, the whole of American life had been transformed. "I see no way," Dewey acknowledged, "to 'restrain' or turn back the industrial revolution and its consequences."

There was no way to do so; nor was there any need. Machinery had opened up undreamed-of reservoirs of power. Science and technology offered vistas of a material environment far superior to the existing one. It was a commonplace that an era of material abundance and material security for all was possible, here and now. What postponed it? Dewey claimed that, although Americans possessed a revolutionary transforming instrument, they had been content to harness it to the dollar rather than to the liberation and enrichment of human life. They were bound by traditional aims and values, confined to a mentality that equated personal gain with social advance. How could they be brought to realize that concrete liberty of opportunity and action depends upon equalization of the political and economic conditions under which individuals are alone free in fact, not in some abstract metaphysical way? Could anyone deny that, under the operations of institutionally established and supported finance capitalism, genuine liberty had all but disappeared in twentieth-century America? The tragic breakdown of democracy, Dewey asserted, was due to the fact that the identification of liberty with the maximum of unrestrained individualistic action in the economic sphere, under the institutions of capitalistic finance, was as fatal to the realization of liberty for all as it was fatal to the realization of equlity. There was no point in blaming science or the machine. The trouble lay in the use that was made of them. The real culprit was the American mind.

The United States, Dewey pointed out, had steadily moved from an earlier pioneer individualism to a condition of dominant corporateness. This movement, in the economic field, was both a cause and a symbol of the tendency to combination in all phases of life. The most socially significant fact of twentieth-century America was that the opportunities, choices, and actions of individuals were being increasingly determined by some form of organized association. Americans were thus conducting their lives in what was essentially a collective civilization. But they were doing their thinking in terms of an individualism derived from a pre-scientific, pre-technological era. Their real aims and ambitions, many of their social institutions and the legal concepts which these embodied, and nearly all their public policy, were obsolete—irrelevant to their actual environment, and therefore without practical efficacy. In consequence, millions of Americans were leading lives that were personally frustrated, economically precarious, and socially sterile. Yet, Dewey declared, nothing was more certain than that this need not be the case.

To the temporal gap between the realities of life and the ideas and purposes with which Americans faced it, Dewey attributed the origin of most contemporary social problems and the utter failure to solve them. The American theory was that man plans and uses machines for his own humane and moral purposes. The American fact was that man was being borne wherever the machine carries him. Most citizens would be horrified to learn that the United States was practicing—and more efficiently than any other country—a rigorous economic determinism.

Yet it actually was. For the corporate or collective patterns of existence were not being made to yield greater benefits to the masses. They were being deliberately used to advance the interests of those who had acquired control of the economic machine, and thus held effective power. Was the new corporateness of life an inherently evil condition? To the contrary, Dewey asserted, it contained the possibility of a more universal welfare, a more genuine democracy, than men had ever known. The causes that generate insecurity for the many no longer spring from nature. They were now to be found in institutions and arrangements that are within deliberate human control. Institutions and arrangements, if defective, are always subject to change. Americans had merely permitted the corporate organization of society to get stuck on the cash level.

They had assented, Dewey showed, to its subordination to an economic individualism of motives and aims. Their contemporary plight was an inevitable result of the notion, sedulously cultivated by the class in power, that the creative capacities of individuals can be evoked and developed only in a struggle for material possessions and material gain. For economic power was reactionary. It had become an organized social institution that resists all further social change that is not in accord with itself, that does not further and support its own interests as at present existing. It controlled the great mechanisms of mass publicity and propaganda—the press, radio, the movies. Its philosophy was the official philosophy of the schools. So it was able to make the American people identify the power and liberty of the individual with ability to achieve economic success—or, to put it in a nutshell, with ability to make money. Yet this was flagrantly contradicted by the facts of experience. The nature of American industry was such that—except as a member of some organized group—the average American had neither power, nor liberty, nor equal opportunity to achieve economic success. The persistance of a horse-and-buggy individualism in a technological, mechanized, corporate age had worked out to the utter undoing of the individual.

So Dewey asserted that Americans, in effect, had been guilty of a great abdication. As a nation, they held an unprecedented command of practical instruments. They possessed a secure technology. Yet the mass of citizens did not ask how these might be used to create a stable equitable society. So far as their social thinking went, they merely continued to glorify the past, and legalize and idealize the *status quo*. Nothing could be accomplished, Dewey declared, unless they learned to think in terms of the age in which they were living.

What did this mean? For one thing, it meant that Americans must reject the prevailing assumption that the present situation is final; that it presents something inherently ultimate and fixed. It was not fixed, except in so far as popular inertia permitted it to remain so. It could be treated as a situation in process; as material to be dealt with in shaping a later outcome. It could be treated as a problem. The problem was not one of economics, but of social relations. For economic determinism was no longer a theory; it was a fact. We are in for some kind of socialism, Dewey declared, call it by whatever name we please, and no matter what it will be called when it is realized. Yet a choice still existed. There were two alternatives. Americans could have a blind, chaotic, and unplanned determinism, issuing from business conducted for pecuniary profit. Or they could have the determination of a socially planned and ordered development. The choice lay between a capitalistic socialism, and one which was both public and democratic. Capitalistic socialism would be administered by a financial oligarchy, purely for its own advantage. Public socialism would be a co-operative way of life. If Americans, faced with these alternatives, preferred the second, there was immediate need for associated thought to take account of the realities of the situation and to frame policies in the social interest.

By associated thought, Dewey meant collective thinking. It had obtained, with respect to public affairs, in the small, self-governing American communities of an earlier day. He believed that it could be revived within the larger associated groupings which united men in the new corporate age. As a pragmatist, he held that ideas are only plans for action; that ideals are only expressions of purpose. If the ideas are to result in effective action, they must be practicable. If the ideals are to have any genuine meaning, they must be capable of being realized. Both ideas and ideals must therefore be framed out of the possibilities of existing conditions, even if these be the conditions that constitute a corporate and industrial age.

Most Americans, Dewey asserted, cherished the belief that the spectacular material achievements of their civilization were primarily due to the operations of a *laissez faire* economics. This, he claimed, was sheer nonsense. Industrialization had not been brought about by capital, or by the free activities of men seeking their own profit as isolated individuals. The true cause of the great release of productive energies was the rise of experimental science and its technological application. The entire modern industrial development was the fruit of technology. Every process involved in the present production and distribution of goods was dependent upon use of results achieved by the collective intelligence of scientists. To speak baldly, Dewey said, it is a plain falsehood that the advances which the defenders of the existing regime point to as justification for its continuance are due to mere individualistic initiative and enterprise. Private enterprise had merely appropriated the fruits of collective, co-operative intelligence. But, having transformed civilization materially, could not science and technology now proceed to transform it socially? Dewey held that they could. They furnished the obvious pattern for collective social thinking; they illustrated corporate intelligence at work.

To effect social change, the new collective thinking must adopt the method of experimental science, and apply its technology to the framing of social purposes and plans for action. Dewey pointed out that science depends, for its development, on the free initiative, invention, and enterprise of individual inquirers. But its authority derives from collective activity, organized co-operatively. An individual scientist, depending upon methods and conclusions that are common property and not privately owned, puts forward a new theory. It may contradict prevailing beliefs. It is tested experimentally, and openly, by other scientists who work collectively. If it is confirmed by this co-operative test, it is generally adopted, and passes into the common fund of scientific knowledge. It is in this fashion that science produces agreement, and unity of belief. The method of science, Dewey suggested, closely paralleled the form of collective thinking which Americans had originally practiced in their self-governing communities. It was a genuinely democratic method. It preserved individual initiative and enterprise; and it subjected their fruits to the test of trial, and a collective consensus of judgment.

What would be the results of applying this method to social action? All policies and proposals would be treated as working hypotheses, to be tested; not as programs to be adhered to and executed. They would be subject to constant, flexible revision in the light of their consequences when experimentally put in action. Genuine discoveries would be made. Advances and improvements of technique would follow. General adoption would be determined by efficiency of results. Agreement and unity of belief would thus be produced—instead of the perpetual conflict of purposes now obtaining. There would always be differences of opinion as to the relative merits of alternative proposals. But these would be reconciled by a collective verdict. Thus, social beliefs formed in the absence of real evidence would be reduced, and their influence diminished. More importantly, obsolete beliefs could no longer—as now—be frozen into absolute standards and eternal truths. The present policy of irresponsible social drift would be replaced by a democratic policy of social direction. The *status quo* would no longer be glorified, legalized, and considered final.

In any case, Dewey predicted, the existing social situation could not long be maintained. For it proclaimed the virtual bankruptcy and moribund state of a regime of individual initiative and enterprise conducted for private gain and subject to no control by recognized, collective authority. If the inevitability of change seemed assured, how would Americans prefer that it be brought about? Within thirty years they had seen three European regimes rise to power on programs that effected social change by violent overthrow of existing institutions. The consequences scarcely recommended the method of revolution. In the United States, Dewey declared, tradition and national character favored change by democratic and peaceful methods. There was still time, though obviously not too much, in which to put the method of organized and collective intelligence to use. Essentially, it was the method not only of science, but of democratic liberalism. Yet liberalism had hitherto failed. It held that the ultimate place of economic organization in human life is to assure the secure basis for an ordered expression of individual capacity and for the satisfaction of the needs of man in non-economic directions. But, while overwhelming evidence to the contrary piled up, it continued to assume that this ideal could be realized under the existing economic system. Liberalism had failed to adopt the scientific method, which, as Dewey acidly remarked, "is not just messing around nor doing a little of this and a little of that in the hope that things will improve."

So liberalism would have to renovate itself. Its new objective, necessarily, was to bring about drastic instead of piecemeal social changes. It must resolve that, instead of using social power to ameliorate the evil consequences of the existing system, it would use social power to change the system. It must repudiate its former support of the prevailing order; its old reliance upon economic tinkering, compromise, and minor "reforms." The failures of the Square Deal, the New Freedom and the New Deal sufficiently demonstrated their inadequacy. The cause of liberalism would be lost for a considerable period, Dewey predicted, if it is not prepared to go further and socialize the forces of production, now at hand, so that the liberty of individuals will be supported by the very structure of economic organization. The goal was co-operative, democratic socialism; the method, peaceful revolution by democratic process.

Dewey did not minimize the resistance to be anticipated from concentrated and organized property interests. They exercised a coercive power greater than that of the political state. He warned that the reactionaries are in possession of force, in not only the army and police, but in the press and the schools. Possessing force, they disguise its existence and its use with idealistic phrases like "free enterprise," "individual initiative," "liberty." A century ago, these phrases identified emancipating ideas. Now, Dewey asserted, they have been appropriated by reactionaries as instruments with which to delude the plain people, to forestall social change, to defend and retain their own power. Would the American people, once aroused to their situation and intent upon change, be victimized by slogans? Dewey thought not, and hoped not. But he offered one bit of radical advice. Should the reactionaries determine to oppose social change with the use of massed force, let all liberals remember that the method of intelligence does not commit it to unqualified pacifism!

What would be the place of the common man in this movement of collective thinking and collective action? About this, Dewey was dogmatic. No effort to make over the institutional scheme of things could succeed without the active participation of the common man. Individuality is the capacity for active response to conditions as they present themselves, in an effort to remake them according to a deliberately chosen possibility. The common man had this capacity in his personal life and used it. But he had been deprived of the possibility of putting it to social use by the economic system under which he existed. If the object of social change was his liberation, it could be achieved only to the degree that he participated in winning it. His contribution was indispensable. For, as Dewey insisted, in the absence of an articulate voice on the part of the masses, the best do not and cannot remain the best, the wise cease to be wise.

To Dewey, as he approached his ninetieth year, it seemed inconceivable that Americans living in the tradition of Jefferson and Lincoln would long permit the present defeat of democracy to continue. He felt confident that they would never weaken and give up, without a whole-hearted effort to make democracy a living reality. The machine age, he said, is a challenge to generate new conceptions of the ideal and the spiritual. Its problem is so to perfect its machinery that it may become a means for life, not its despotic master. The foundation of democracy remains what it always has been; faith in the capacities of human nature; faith in human intelligence and in the power of pooled and co-operative experience. Not faith that these are final. Faith that, if given a chance, they will grow and be able to generate the knowledge and wisdom required to guide collective action. "By accepting the corporate and industrial world in which we live," he declared, "and by thus fulfilling the pre-condition for interaction with it, we, who are also parts of the moving present, create ourselves as we create an unknown future."

CHAPTER XI

The Mourners Go about the Streets

[I] THE PENSIVE TRINITY

Of a late afternoon, walking westward from the Capitol, Justice Holmes sometimes fell in with an old friend. He had known Henry Adams since their youth, and in Washington they were near neighbors, but nowadays they saw little of one another. Whenever they met in the street, Holmes carried away the impression that Adams could be delightful. Yet he could seldom bring himself to call at Adams' house. A visit usually left Holmes weary, somewhat exasperated. For Adams had another side, which obscured his distinction, great ability, and genuine kindliness. At home, one was likely to find him posing to himself as the old cardinal, and in his favorite role he would turn everything to dust and ashes.

The fatiguing habit, as Holmes well knew, was a family trait. It cropped out in Henry's older brother, Charles Francis, and in their younger brother, Brooks. Holmes had a fondness for Brooks, enjoyed his companionship, thought him diverting. He had come to accept the position of a crank. He was full of pessimistic notions. But he could tell you history with inimitable vividness not unmixed with enhancing profanity. Holmes had always found Brooks more suggestive than almost anyone—usually with propositions which Holmes did not believe. Nevertheless, after lifelong intimacy, he couldn't quite make up his mind about Brooks; couldn't formulate him with confidence of justice. Why, with their extraordinary talents, did the Adams brothers turn all life to ashes?

It was a favorite question in polite Washington—the diplomatic, senatorial, cabinet set—during the decade before the First World War. Henry Adams had long been a fixture there; so long, that he sometimes alluded to himself as a *monument historique*, and humorously wondered that the government did not take charge of his repairs. Charles Francis was relatively a newcomer, having lately bought a huge house on Massachusetts Avenue. Henry's senior by three years, Charles Francis was past seventy, and was enjoying a second social blooming. Henry looked with marvel at Charles' delight in entertaining, and going about. Charles, he remarked with some asperity, "endures bores to an extent that seems to be suicidal to me." But Charles was the most genial of the brothers, though he reproached himself for being self-conscious and socially awkward, a victim of the hereditary Adams manner, and liked to quote James Russell Lowell's remark that "the Adamses have a genius for saying even a gracious thing in an ungracious way!" Certainly Charles was, socially, less squeamish than Brooks who, with his wife, frequently came to stay with Henry, but always rather tried to avoid his lighter social circle. Brooks had turned sixty, and made his residence in the old house at Quincy where the second President and his son, the sixth, had bitterly brooded over the ingratitude of their countrymen, the failure of their political careers, and the rapidly deteriorating nation.

That Charles displayed a capacity to endure bores was in no way surprising. Business had inured him to their society; he had spent more of his life than he cared to remember among a coarse, realistic, bargaining crowd. Now, having run great risks, having more than once narrowly averted financial shipwreck, he had finally emerged, as he said, not ruined. It was hard to tell whether he was more delighted by being quit of business, or by being quit of Boston. Boston had never really liked any Adams, nor had any Adams ever felt at home in Boston. But Charles, who had always resided there or nearby, had loathed it from childhood. It was no more than a big village development, he declared; an eddy in the great world current, into which no fresh outside life ever flowed. Ten generations of colonials and provincials had produced a senseless, frivolous society, oddly conventional and cramped. One could look forward to nothing more exhilarating than an annual exchange of dinners with what might be called a very good society stock company, stagnant and stationary, a world unto itself. Charles Adams felt that he had tried Boston socially on all sides: he had summered it and wintered it, tried it drunk and tried it sober; and, drunk or sober, there was nothing in it—save Boston! How should Henry understand his pleasure in Washington— Henry, who had abruptly fled Boston thirty years before him? In Washington, there was a varied and amusing society, with people coming from all parts of the country, and from foreign lands. And there were ideas in the air.

These were what Charles Adams wanted, in the calm, prosperous sunset of his age, to allay that intellectual restlessness which had tormented him from youth. For many years he had turned, whenever possible, to the writing of history, and he hoped now to continue with it. Meanwhile, however, he had undertaken another task. This was to prepare an autobiographical sketch for the guidance of some unknown writer who, presumably, would compose a brief memoir after his death. So he was being forced to review, and to assess, his career. Did the sum total come to achievement, or to failure—for a man who, in boyhood, understood that as a grandson of John Quincy Adams he was not quite as other boys?

Charles Adams admitted that his opportunity had been infinite. No man could ask for better chances. In a literary way, financially, politically, he might have been anything he wished, had the possibility of being it only been in him. The capacity, he felt, not the occasion, had been wanting. As ability went, his had been considerable; never first rate, he surmised, but more than respectable. Yet, taken as a whole, his life had not been the success that it ought to have been.

Even his historical writings, which meant more to him than anything else, fell short of his standard. He judged them, as he judged himself and his times, unsparingly, and almost without illusion. Creditable, in a way, they constituted a record in which it was not possible for a man to take any considerable or real satisfaction; for it was a record of dissipation and of quantity rather than one of quality and concentration. Was not that dispersal of energy, so true of every other activity in which he had engaged, the symptom of his failure? If he had his life to live over again, he thought he would like only to accumulate one of those vast fortunes of the present day rising up into the tens and scores of millions—what is vulgarly known as "money to burn." Not for himself, since he had made enough money for his needs; he would give the surplus millions to Harvard University. But he had been offered ample and frequent opportunity to realize even this ambition. Why, then, had he failed—and so variously?

The question prompted him to consider the swiftly changing social order in which he had lived. Obviously, he had not come to appropriate terms with it. Could this be because he was naturally inclined to be otherwise-minded and a bit iconoclastic? He was strongly individual; he had never been able to see things, and take things, quite in the usual and average way. His opinions were apt to differ sharply from those of the majority of his fellow-citizens. There was, for instance, the democratic dogma. Charles Adams believed in the equality of men before the law; but social equality, whether for man or child, was, for him, altogether another thing. In his childhood, at least, social equality hadn't been forced upon him, and he was grateful. He did not now associate with the laborers employed on his summer estate at Lincoln, in Massachusetts. Such association would have proved disagreeable to both parties. They were divided by insurmountable differences in customs, language, habits and conventionalities. Why pretend to faith in a dogma to which it was impossible to give practical effect in action?

As for political democracy, Charles Adams had decided reservations about the way it actually worked. In his view, public opinion and patience were the best possible agents for successfully solving industrial, social and economical problems. He had had considerable experience with all three. He concluded that an enlightened public opinion, based on facts elicited by a fair-minded public investigation, ought to constitute the court of final appeal. But, as Americans practiced democracy, appeal was taken only to the desire of the man in the street to get things done and, as he imagined, once and for all disposed of. The result was a growing tendency to excessive legislation in which the supposed popular will was crystallized and penalized. Unlike Justice Holmes, Charles Adams saw no merit in this tendency. So he had always failed to be in sympathy with the sturdy champions of the "Dear Peepul." Were they not merely the contemporary equivalents of the old-time courtier, the sycophant and parasite of the Tudor and Stuart periods? Only the identity of the sovereign had changed; and, as between the divine right of kings and the divine right of the "peepul," what was there to choose?

Charles Adams thought he knew how the government of a republic ought to be conducted. An illustration was not wanting. For twenty years, he and his older brother John had managed the affairs of the ancestral town of Quincy, doing this out of pure public spirit. And what was the result? "The town-meetings were reduced from a mob to a model; the finances were straightened out; the school system was reorganized and made famous; the Public Library building was erected and endowed; a system of Parks was devised and developed; and, finally, Quincy was actually freed from debt." Such were the benefits accruing to the people when their government was in the hands of a responsible, unselfish, and farsighted oligarchy. At bottom, Charles Adams no more believed in political democracy than did his great-grandfather, the second President.

The second President had based his hopes, in great measure, upon the propertied class. To Charles Adams, who had spent most of his active years in intimate association with the magnates of the new finance capitalism, such hopes seemed ludicrous. Unlike his brothers, Henry and Brooks, who had merely observed the process of social change, he had directly participated in it. Like all the Adamses, he set out to be a lawyer, a profession for which he quickly realized that he had no aptitude. He took part in the campaign to elect Abraham Lincoln, and briefly dallied with the project of a political career. Then came the War between the States, and his father's appointment as Minister to England. Henry went to England as his father's secretary, and Brooks, a mere boy, accompanied them. Charles Adams took the field as an officer. He rose to the rank of colonel, and received his discharge with the brevet rank of brigadier general. At the end of the war, he found himself once again at the foot of the ladder. As Henry put it, the generation between 1865 and 1895 was already mortgaged to the railways, and none of them saw this more clearly than Charles Adams, who fixed on the railroad system as the most developing force and largest field of the day, and determined to attach himself to it. He began to study the problems of railroad expansion and regulation, and to write about them. He collaborated with Henry in a masterly exposure of the scandalous operations of Jay Gould and Jim Fisk. Then, finally, he managed somehow to catch on to the railroad interest by devising the first state regulatory commission, and securing an appointment to it.

Thereafter, for a quarter of a century, Charles Adams was at the very vortex of capitalistic expansion. He became president of the Union Pacific system. He served the bankers of State Street, with whom the house of Adams had always been at war. As whole-heartedly as he was able, he fought for a place at the great barbecue. He was, as Henry astutely noted, a man of action, with strong love of power. But he was also an Adams, a puritan with a strong sense of rectitude. So he sighed with relief when Jay Gould, gaining possession of the Union Pacific and remembering Charles Adams' exposure of the Erie scandals, dismissed him like a lackey. He had wanted to ally himself with the dominant forces of his generation; those forces were industrial and financial; he had throughout dealt with large affairs and several times made decided successes. Had not his plans miscarried, these would have been outstanding, and he knew that he would have been reputed one of the ablest men of his time. The lover of power lamented a dangerous mental activity that had compromised his ambition and deflected his energies. But the puritan, the man of rectitude, could not resist a conviction that his successes, such as they were, added up to failure. And, although he did not explicitly acknowledge it, the failure was a moral one. "I should have settled myself systematically down on the development of my aptitude—the art of literary expression," he reflected bitterly.

An old man, brooding on the sordid and cynical materialism to which he had offered sacrifices for so long, Charles Adams felt only contempt for the social order which he had helped to establish. He had no illusions about the new rulers of America, the financial and industrial overlords in whom property and power were now concentrating. Business success, mere money-getting, he asserted, had its source in a rather low instinct. "I have known," he said, "and known tolerably well, a good many 'successful' men—'big' financially—men famous during the last half century; and a less interesting crowd I do not care to encounter. Not one that I have ever known would I care to meet again, either in this world or the next; nor is one of them associated in my mind with the idea of humor, thought or refinement. A set of mere money-getters and traders, they were essentially unattractive and uninteresting." What would be the fate of a nation dominated by such men? Charles Adams ventured no predictions. But of the new forces released in his time, he had long since had a surfeit—and the surfeit superinduced disgust. The pursuit of power had terminated in a blind alley. The prizes for which his contemporaries lusted, crumbled to dust in his hands.

Those prizes had been relinquished very early by his brother Henry. That Charles was a man of action, Henry said, almost compelled him to become a man of contemplation, a writer and a critic. He was the most worldly, subtle, and sensitive of all the Adamses. He was also the most complex, and perhaps for that reason the least capable of any enduring satisfaction. As an aging man, he came to suspect that his complexity had proved his undoing. If he had failed, was it not because of a profound discord between his spirit and his mind? Life, as he neared its end, took on the look of an unsolvable dilemma.

Like all his line, Henry Adams was a rationalist. What could be more obvious than that all problems must yield to intelligence? The series of revolutionary scientific discoveries that were made during his youth seemed to answer that question forever. His generation pledged their minds to science, and so did he. Darwinism was their evangel. In the doctrine of evolution, they found a form of religious hope; a promise of ultimate perfection. Henry wished for nothing better, but could not commit himself so far, for he liked to think himself a pure skeptic. He took refuge in the conviction that he did not really care whether truth was, or was not, true; indeed, that he did not really care that it should be proved true, unless the process was new and amusing. The conviction played him false. Too late, he discovered that he cared more about ultimate truth than about anything else in life, and that he had chosen what, for him, was the wrong road to it.

However tentatively, he followed the road of science. He hoped that it would lead him to a law applicable to the rapidly accelerating complexity of civilization. If such a law were discovered, it would introduce into complexity the elements of order, unity, and meaning. It would also serve as a formula for social progress. But as he grew older, the trend of scientific discovery appeared to be betraying his hope. Science withdrew its promise of progress, from the simple to the complex, toward some ultimate perfection. The picture of human destiny that it was painting gradually became darker and darker. No longer did science assert that man is capable of capturing and controlling the forces of nature. To the contrary, it implied that man is their captive, no more than a feeble atom or molecule at the mercy of a probably infinite mechanism. Science, the greatest achievement of man's intelligence, seemed bent upon proving that his existence is meaningless, and his hope of progress an illusion. Reading the science of his time, Adams concluded that complexity might only be a prelude to chaos; that civilization was progressing only toward its doom.

As a rationalist, Henry Adams should have found this conclusion as acceptable as any other. He tried to persuade himself that he did. But the fact that nothing has meaning, and that life is lunacy was a fact which he could not stomach. It was spiritually intolerable. His resistance to it surprised him; he had never reckoned with the spirit. The friend whom he admired most, the artist John La Farge, had pursued truth by another road, and had found it in a quite different form. Whereas Adams could only work intellectually, La Farge worked purely intuitively. To La Farge's imaginative insight, life revealed itself directly as having order, unity and meaning. La Farge took Adams to Chartres, and Adams, who had once taught medieval history, had an unexpected revelation. For the first time, he became aware that in the thirteenth century, when man had held the highest idea of himself as a unit in a unified universe, all men understood life precisely as La Farge understood it now, and had lived accordingly.

Adams began to steep himself in medieval art, architecture, poetry, philosophy. They disclosed to him a civilization that had declared the possibility of perfection, that had said of life that Faith alone supports it, and that, if Faith fails, Heaven is lost. Had he not chosen the wrong road to truth? Was not La Farge right in saying that he reasoned too much, trusted too exclusively to intelligence? Perhaps; but it was now too late to retrace his steps. His spirit protested that the truth of science was sterile. But in his heart he knew that he could not embrace the truth attainable by faith.

In his stately house overlooking Lafayette Square, Henry Adams was composing two books which he thought of as history, but which would become a kind of elegy. By comparing the society of the thirteenth century with that of the America of his time, he was trying to show how man had been defeated by the illusion of progress, and his symbol of that defeat was himself. Was he no more than a grotesque wraith, cynical to excess, indifferent to man and incredulous to God? Deeply convinced of his own frustration, and deeply anguished, this was the façade which he wished to present to the world.

He was a squat, dumpy man whose large, almost completely bald head seemed too big for his body, stunted by a childhood illness. Like his brothers, he had the high Adams forehead, heavy eyebrows, and prominent nose. He wore a trim gray moustache; a trim, pointed beard. He dressed formally, fastidiously, with great elegance. Resenting his dwarfed stature, he sometimes affected a strut. It gave him the momentary illusion of physical adequacy. He had even cultivated bad manners, he said, to compensate for his sense of inferiority. He was likely to be unexpectedly brusque at times, but this was a defense against shyness; everyone who knew him testified to his charm. Those who met him for the first time were likely to think him queer to the last degree; cynical, vindictive; and be shocked by his frivolity. The children whom he adored, and whose visits he encouraged, knew better; a secret panel in his library concealed a cupboard which he kept filled with playthings for them. His crony, John Hay, commissioned the sculptor Augustus Saint Gaudens to make a medallion of Henry's head. It showed him with the body of a porcupine and the wings of an angel. This was the notion of him that his intimates cherished.

For many years, now, he had maintained a rather ostentatious retirement. He said that he was stone coffin dead, a long-established ghost. He consented to visit only one or another of six houses. All Washington knew the reason for this eccentricity, and in a remote part of Rock Creek Cemetery, Saint Gaudens' masterpiece—the inscrutable, hooded female figure commonly and wrongly called "Grief" —commemorated it. One Sunday morning long before, when his house was building, Henry Adams went for a walk. He returned to find his wife dead, a suicide by poison. Thereafter, he was a changed man. He had known disappointment; he would never again escape the obsession of overwhelming, irremediable defeat.

A man of thirty, Henry Adams had returned from England, after the War between the States, convinced that the great principle of democracy was still capable of rewarding a conscientious servant. Henry asked nothing better than to become one, to follow the tradition of public service which his family had carried on for three generations. They had always had their hands on the lever of power; Henry and his brothers, conscious that they would like to control power in some form, recognized that their form of power was tied to politics or literature. In London, in daily intimate contact with the highest affairs of state, Henry had begun "to dream the sensation of wielding unmeasured power. The sense came, like vertigo, for an instant, and passed, leaving the brain a little dazed, doubtful, shy." Could he not attain to power in politics by way of the press?

He hoped to serve President Grant, in the exciting days that would succeed prolonged civil strife. The new industrialism, the new technology, the new railroads indicated how large a role science would play in the future America; and through science democracy would rise to a new pinnacle of moral achievement. Then came the Grant administration, steeped in corruption, which outraged every rule of ordinary decency. Henry felt that the world cared little for decency, that it merely wanted a system that would work, and men who could work it. The spectacle disabused him forever of the hope of a career in public service. It also undermined his romantic faith in democracy. He was convinced, as his brother Brooks said long afterwards, that the United States would never develop the intellectual energy to raise itself to that advanced level of intelligence which had been accepted as a moral certainty by Washington, by his own grandfather, and by most of his grandfather's contemporaries.

He went to teach medieval history at Harvard, and remained there, as he thought unprofitably, for seven years. He took over the editorship of the *North American Review*, conducted it successfully, but presently tired of the burden and invited Henry Cabot Lodge, one of his students, to share it. Meanwhile, he married Marian Hooper, called "Clover" by her friends. He was, he confessed, absurdly in love. What held him, he said, was her intelligence and sympathy; and, indeed, Henry James, who had long admired her, described her "intellectual grace" as superior to that of any European woman. She was fond of society and amusement; had a very active and quick mind; read German, Latin, and a little Greek; possessed a ready sense of humor, and was a sparkling conversationalist. There was in Clover Hooper a certain vein of personality which approached eccentricity, and Henry found it very attractive. "She rules me," he said, "as only American women rule men, and I cower before her."

Socially speaking, the match was supposed to be unexceptionable, for Clover belonged to a sort of clan, as all Bostonians do. Her father was a wealthy retired physician, and her maternal grandfather, William Sturgis, a merchant who had controlled more than half the China trade. Clover had enough money to be quite independent; and, as Henry's maternal grandfather, Peter Chardon Brooks, had been one of the earliest American millionaires, there was a sufficient flow of money from both sides to assure an agreeable existence. The young couple spent a year abroad, returned to Boston, took a house in Back Bay. And very soon, Henry became bored with the society of Boston and Cambridge, where several score of the most intelligent, charming people in America united to make a social desert that would have starved a polar bear.

The young Adamses moved to Washington. It was, Henry said, the only place in his native land where society amused him, or where life offered variety. In Washington, he could fancy that he was being of use in the world; he knew that he and his wife were occupying niches that ought to be filled. His own niche fitted him admirably: as far as he had a function in life, it was as stable-companion to statesmen, whether they liked it or not. Statesmen was not the accurate word, but it was the polite one, and Henry's polished irony sometimes took the form of courtesy. He had, by now, found his true vocation as a man of letters, a historian, and was gathering materials for his political history of the administrations of Jefferson and Madison. Long afterwards, he confessed that "if he worked at all, it was for social consideration, and social pleasure was his pay. . . . Artists have done it from the beginning of time, and will do it after time has expired, since they cannot help themselves, and they find their return in the pride of their social superiority as they feel it. Society commonly abets them and encourages their attitude of contempt." In a similar spirit, he advised Lodge to take up literature as a profession, for anyone who had the ability could enthrone himself as a species of literary lion with ease and thus be assured of social dignity, European reputation, and a foreign mission to close. But Lodge, instead, chose to become a part of the Republican political machine.

Washington society, certainly unknowingly, nourished Henry's sense of social superiority, and furnished ample materials to justify his later attitude of contempt. The young Adamses, he soon reported, were very near most of the powerful people, either as enemies or as friends. It began to look as if, one day, he might exercise—however indirectly—the power which he still longed to control. The Adams circle was the most amusing in the capital, unique for good talk about politics, science, literature and art that ran far into the night, and Henry thought that their little dinners of six and eight were as pleasant as any he ever sat at, even in London. The nucleus of this circle was the inseparable "Five of Hearts." It was made up of the Adamses, the incandescent Clarence King, who had in him something of the Greek —a touch of Alcibiades or Alexander—and the John Hays. All were worldly, witty, political minded; collectors of art and gossip and people; and the three men shared both a talent and a taste for writing. Hay, short and bearded like Adams, had married the daughter of a Cleveland millionaire, and was now leading the carefree existence of a man of wealth. He had already had a varied career as author, newspaper editor, and diplomat. He was active in the councils of the Republican party, for he cherished political ambitions. Later, he would be appointed Ambassador to England, and subsequently Secretary of State.

While Henry worked at his history, Hay was engaged in collaborating with John Nicolay on a biography of President Lincoln, whom they had served as secretaries. But these major tasks did not exhaust Hay's literary ambitions, or Adams'. Partly for the amusement of the Five of Hearts, both wrote novels, which they read aloud to the five over Mrs. Adams' tea table. The books were soon published anonymously and, as social criticism, both caused considerable stir. Hay's *The Bread-Winners* stated the case for the established order. It was a vigorous defense of the sanctity of property rights, threatened by the rising "dangerous classes" of organized labor. An attack on the vested rights of private property, Hay declared, was nothing less than an attack on civilization itself; for property was the tangible form assumed by civilization, and therefore could yield to no social purposes whatever, however idealistic these might purport to be. The morality of acquisition, and the immorality of economic failure, was Hay's central theme, and he handled it with all the ethical enthusiasm to be expected of a poor but intensely ambitious man who had married a fortune. Like Andrew Carnegie a few years later, Hay invited the discontented industrial workers of the country to accept the enlightened leadership of the educated—and propertied—class, and to desert the "radical" leadership springing up within its own.

Hay asserted his love for democracy, and his profound faith in it; and, despite his economic and social views, his emotions about democracy were probably sincere. Adams, intellectualist as always, and far more rigorous in his thinking, could no longer make so absolute a profession of faith. His little novel, *Democracy*, purported to satirize the political corruption and social vulgarity that obtained in the Washington of President Garfield. But, actually, it served as the repository of his growing doubts and waning hopes.

Two characters—among the many which the reading public promptly identified, with its usual relish for scandal—spoke for the two sides of Henry Adams' divided nature. Like him, Mrs. Lightfoot Lee was eager for power and ambitious to reform flagrant social abuses; like him, too, she was ultimately disillusioned by the spectacle of democracy at work. Representative Glover, an idealist from Massachusetts concerned with civil-service reform, expressed Henry's attenuated beliefs. Glover "saw himself pinned to the wall, and he turned at bay with almost the energy of despair" when Mrs. Lee asked him whether he believed democracy the best form of government, and universal suffrage a success.

"Democracy," Glover burst out, as Henry himself might have, "asserts the fact that the masses are now raised to a higher intelligence than formerly. All our civilization aims at this mark. We want to do what we can to help it. I myself want to see the result. I grant it is an experiment, but it is the only direction society can take that is worth taking; the only conception of its duty large enough to satisfy its instincts; the only result that is worth an effort or a risk. Every other step is backward, and I do not want to repeat the past. I am glad to see society grapple with issues in which no one can afford to be neutral." But, Mrs. Lee persisted—and this was the question which the other half of Henry's nature wanted answered—what if the experiment fails, and society destroys itself with universal suffrage, corruption, and communism? Such as it was, the believer in Henry had an answer. One must have faith, "not perhaps in the old dogmas, but the new ones . . . faith in science; faith in the survival of the fittest." One must be true to one's times. If the hope of one's times was realized, one should be prepared to assume leadership. If the hope was defeated, one must die bravely in the ranks.

The suicide of Clover Adams extinguished this flickering faith. Henry now found the present positively repulsive, and the past alone real. "As long as I could make life work," he said, "I stood by it, and swore by it as though it was my god, as indeed it was." Thenceforward, he enlisted under the banners of death, not life. He brought his history to a conclusion, paid for its publication, and left it to its fate with ostentatious indifference. With it, he ceased writing for publication; his later books were privately printed in small editions, for distribution among his friends.

For two decades, as opportunity offered, he wandered restlessly about the world. With John La Farge to Japan; to the islands of the South Seas, the East Indies, and Ceylon; to the cathedral cities of

France. With Clarence King, to Cuba and the adjacent islands. To Mexico with Senator Cameron and his wife, and again alone. To Russia, and Normandy and Brittany with the Lodges. To Egypt and Asia Minor, Constantinople and Greece, Italy, Scandinavia, Central Europe. And, more and more frequently, to the parts of France where there remained the architectural glories of that golden age of which the sum is an emotion—clear and strong as love and much clearer than logic whose charm lies in its unstable balance. He would have liked to live in the bright day that had ended with the death of Queen Blanche and of all good things about the year 1250. He would have liked to belong to a believing community whose ideals he could worship. Quincy, in his childhood, had been such a community. . . . almost.

Always, through the years, Henry Adams returned to the house in Washington that he had built for Clover. He and John Hay had bought a large corner plot at Sixteenth and H Streets. Henry Hobson Richardson, Henry's Harvard classmate and America's foremost architect, designed for them adjoining, communicating homes in the rather heavy, New England Romanesque style that he was carrying across the country. Henry's noontime breakfasts were celebrated, with covers laid for six and nobody invited. Intimates merely announced their intention of coming, and a duty rested upon them to bring anyone whom Henry might find interesting. So all the most famous, amusing, or creative people who passed through the capital found their way to Henry's sunny library looking out to the White House across Lafayette Square.

It was a large room, overflowing with books, furnished with deep, leather-upholstered chairs and sofas that had been built to Henry's measure, and were therefore extremely low. A huge carved fireplace, of sea-green Mexican onyx shot with crimson, dominated the room, and there was always a fire on the hearth. The walls were hung with rare Italian-Renaissance drawings; there was a beautiful Turner landscape, and a curious painting by William Blake of Nebuchadnezzar crawling on all fours and eating grass. Masses of flowers stood on the tables. Choice bibelots, the Kwannons, the bronzes and porcelains that he had brought from the Orient were disposed on the tops of bookcases. To some, the room had a "Boston look," and this was an opinion which the host did not relish. But a more perceptive woman friend recorded that it had a mellow patina left by the much good talk it had harbored.

For Henry still rejoiced in good talk, though nowadays he made it a rule to discuss serious things lightly, and light things seriously, and to reduce both, whenever possible, to paradox. "The only thing I wanted in life," he wrote humorously to a friend, "was to be made a cardinal, and in Rome I sounded delicately the pontifical ocean to ascertain the bearings of my hat." So, as Justice Holmes remarked, it was as a cardinal that he posed. A cardinal of the eighteenth century, a political prince of the church temporal, worldly and cynical, avid for gossip and intrigue, luxury loving, but of lenten counsel uttered with a wry smile. He was a dedicated recluse who liked nothing more than to preside over reunions of what he termed an idle, useless and wasteful set. He was dead, but gay as a rabbit. He enjoyed a reputation for preternatural wisdom, and this pleased him. After all, as he told a friend, "you know that our role in life has always been to be wiser than anyone else and the consciousness of that is the only reward we are likely to get from it."

A "stable-companion to statesmen"? So his life had worked out. The American public thought of his companions as statesmen; but Henry, as a later generation was to learn, did not. Hay, next door, was Secretary of State; Lodge was Senator from Massachusetts; there was Senator Don Cameron, unscrupulous millionaire boss of the corrupt Pennsylvania Republican machine. Theodore Roosevelt, Lodge's student at Harvard and now his chum, was wielding the "big stick" in the White House. Adams adored Hay, and worshiped the wives of all his intimates, for no woman had ever driven him wrong; no man had ever driven him right. For the rest, as he told his brother Charles, "we were educated politically, and, as far as I can see, the world has made little or no gain politically. We have no dividends and no profit from our investment. Reform proved a total loss, and abstract morality went into bankruptcy with the Church. All our ideals turned out to be relative."

The foreign policy of the United States was sometimes being made under his roof, by Hay and Lodge and Roosevelt, but his neighbor, the President, was a terrible bore, owing to his absorption in cheap politics, and suffered from the insanity of an *idée fixe* to a degree hardly credible to a sane mind. Of Lodge he could say little more than that "the true type of successful cant, which rests on no belief at all, is Cabot, who grabs everything and talks pure rot to order." Mrs. Lightfoot Lee wanted to see with her own eyes the action of primary forces; to touch with her own hand the massive machinery of society; to measure with her own mind the capacity of the motive power. She was bent upon getting to the heart of the great American mystery of democracy and government. Henry had succeeded where she failed, and the success was an education that taught him what no puritan, no idealist, could find happiness in knowing. "I am fairly tired—bored beyond endurance—by the world we live in and its ideals," he told John Hay, years earlier, "and am ready to say so, not violently, but kindly, as one rubs salt into the back of a flogged sailor as though one loved him." The intention had crystallized, the mood had deepened, and he was now confiding to Mrs. Cameron that "my book is coming on rapidly and will announce the immediate dissolution of the world. My brother Brooks grumbles because I won't make it quicker. . . ."

Brooks Adams was probably privileged to grumble at Henry, however affectionately. For he had profoundly influenced Henry's thinking. In England, as a youthful Darwinist, Henry knew that by rights he should have been also a Marxist, but some narrow trait of the New England nature seemed to blight socialism, and he tried in vain to make himself a convert. Two decades later, when he wrote his great nine-volume history, he regarded politics as the primary force responsible for social change; he held that the nature of society was determined by a political process. Then, after the final volumes of his history were in print, Brooks abruptly undermined this theory. Brooks forced him to recognize that the American society of his time—the "banker's paradise" which they both detested—was the product of an economic process, not a political one. Brooks compelled him to reckon with the principle of economic determinism.

There was a marked similarity in their temperaments. Indeed, Henry felt that they were too much alike, and agreed too well in all their ideas. "I have known you for sixty odd years," he wrote Brooks in his old age, "and since you were a baby I've never known you when you weren't making yourself miserable over the failings of the universe. It has been your amusement, and a very good one. I always say that no one can afford to pose as an optimist, short of an income of a hundred thousand a year. Up to fifty thousand, the pose of pessimism is the only dignified one, just as it is after sixty years old." But this was slightly malicious for Brooks, more earnest and more rebellious than Henry, found scant amusement in pessimism. He took it hard. The future of civilization was something about which he cared very deeply. To Henry, in his sardonic old age, the crumbling of worlds seemed always fun.

Brooks graduated from Harvard while Henry was teaching there, and went on to study law. His father took him, as secretary, to the Geneva conference which arbitrated the claims of the United States against England arising from the War between the States. Afterwards, Brooks established himself as a lawyer in Boston, but soon abandoned this profession to become a writer of history like his brothers. At the age of forty he married a sister of Mrs. Lodge, and they set off on travels that ranged as widely as Henry's. Eventually they settled in the old house at Quincy, and there Brooks began a revolutionary book, ultimately to be published as *The Law of Civilization and Decay*. He was thus engaged when the panic of 1893 broke over the nation, threatening his financial ruin and that of his brothers. Henry, on holiday in Europe, was urgently summoned to Quincy.

During long, hot summer nights, while waiting for their fortunes to mend, Brooks and Henry sat late in the study that had been used by two Presidents, and discussed the ideas which were shaping Brooks' book. Like Henry, Brooks had inherited a faith in the democratic dogma, as he had inherited a pew in the Quincy church. Now, that faith was shattered; he had come to look on man, in the light of the evidence of unnumbered centuries, as a pure automaton, who is moved along the paths of least resistance by forces over which he has no control. His study of world history had convinced him that the strongest human passions are fear and greed. So he concluded that so much and no more might be expected from a pure democracy as might be expected from any automaton so actuated. His book, surveying the course of history from ancient Rome to the rise of modern capitalism, offered little comfort to anyone inclined to identify evolution and progress. For Brooks showed that the movement toward ever-increasing complexity and centralization was accompanied by a decline in the quality of human intelligence, an impoverishment of the spirit, an atrophy of creative imagination, and the death of those superior values which ought to be the fruit of a civilized life.

History, as Brooks interpreted it, was a series of recurrent cycles in each of which there occurred a conflict between the creative and acquisitive instincts. In this conflict, the acquisitive instinct always triumphed; but its victory presaged the inevitable collapse of the civilization it had produced. The modern cycle, Brooks asserted, began with the collapse of the Roman Empire, when a dispersed population was a prey to fear. Fear bred superstition, from which, in turn, religion was born. In the Middle Ages, when religion was the centralizing force, three types dominated society. The priest, the warrior, and the artist were all imaginatively creative, as the shrine and castle and cathedral remained to prove. Then the acquisitive instinct took over. The usurer and trader rose to power. The priest was expropriated; the warrior became a mercenary in the police of the money lenders; the artist a mere servant of the altars of wealth. Imagination was at a discount; the man of greed, the capitalist, aided by the natural science which he endowed, seized social control.

As centralization proceeded swiftly to complexity, industrial capitalism gave way to finance capitalism. The banker, now dominant, used gold and credit as instruments of oppression, manipulating them to his own advantage, bringing into existence a huge debtor class of proletarians doomed to servitude. In his lust for power and greed for profits, the banker irresponsibly prospered or depressed producers in alternate booms and panics. But the effect of increasingly intense economic competition was one of progressive social degradation. Centralization and concentration necessarily reached a climax. At that point, energy, instead of accumulating, began to diminish. Brooks asserted that in the high stages of centralization, where unrestricted economic competition prevails, this loss of energy is manifested by a gradual dissipation of capital, which, at last, ends in disintegration. There might occur a period of illusory equilibrium. But it would soon terminate in disastrous wars, in mere exhaustion, or in the revolt of the enslaved proletariat—any of which might produce the collapse of civilization and a return to primitive barbarism.

Such was Brooks' view of history, and Henry, reading it as the banker-made, gruelling depression of 1893 spread over the nation, acknowledged its soundness. But he advised Brooks not to print it. Brooks, he said, was monkeying with a dynamo, and would never be forgiven by the "gold-bugs," the bankers and their political henchmen. For, as the hot summer evenings wore away "amidst an excitement verging on revolution," the relevance of Brooks' theory to the immediate situation in the United States became obvious. The nation was about to be plunged into a convulsive political struggle between the creditor and debtor classes, and its outcome would be conclusive for the future.

Brooks, in his book, showed that the whole course of past history negated the comfortable assumption of the bankers, capitalists, and Republican party that limitless "progress" would result from their victory. That victory, he implied, would merely establish, once and for all, their rule over American society through control of the political state. Democracy would cease to exist, though its forms might be maintained. The tyranny of the money-power would be absolute. "The aristocracy which wields this autocratic power is beyond attack," Brooks prophesied, stating the probable future in the present tense, "for it is defended by a wage-earning police, by the side of which the legions were a toy—a police so formidable that, for the first time in history, revolt is hopeless and is not attempted. The only question which preoccupies the ruling class is whether it is cheaper to coerce or to bribe." And if the conflict between capitalists and people resulted in victory for the people, he foresaw no millennium and no utopia. The optimistic assumptions of the socialists struck him as no less delusive than those of the capitalists. The victory of the proletariat would not usher in collectivism, but anarchy.

As to this, Henry disagreed. He thought anarchy very far off, and insisted—though liking socialism no more than capitalism—that the only possible political party must stand on a well-defined platform of State Socialism, since nothing else could reflect the social movement. But Brooks' ideas impressed him deeply, and revolutionized his thinking. "Were we on the edge of a new and last great centralization," he asked, "or of a first great movement of disintegration? There are facts on both sides; but my conclusion rather is—and this is what satiates my instinct for life—that our so-called civilization has shown its movement, even at the center, arrested. It has failed to concentrate further. Its next effort may succeed, but it is more likely to be one of disintegration, with Russia for the eccentric on one side and America on the other. . . ." And, with the triumph of the bankers in 1893, he saw the United States finally imprisoned in a capitalistic system which, if it were to be run at all, must be run by capital and capitalistic methods, with the inevitable result that unless the usurers developed some new force, which would concentrate society in a miraculous way, disintegration must go on. It was scarcely any wonder that Mrs. Brooks Adams, asked for a title for her husband's book, whimsically suggested "The Path to Hell: A Story Book." Brooks liked the title, but thought that it promised too much. How could he assure his readers that he would show them anything so good as a path to Hell?

In later years, Brooks Adams examined the results achieved, in the United States, by that process of capitalistic concentration which he and Henry alike regarded as the prelude to social collapse. The governing capitalist class, he said, had reached the acme of its popularity and power about 1875; thereafter, resistance to its methods began to take shape in restrictive legislation. American capitalists, he declared, appear to have been evolved under the stress of an environment which demanded excessive specialization in the direction of a genius adapted to money-making under highly complex industrial conditions. This extreme specialization had developed a new social principle: the capitalist conceives sovereign powers to be for sale. Brooks furnished an eloquent illustration. Control of the national highways was a sovereign power; railroads were, in effect, national highways; these had been seized by capitalists, who treated them as ordinary chattels, to be administered for the profit of the owner exclusively, and denounced all attempts to hold the capitalists socially accountable as an infringement of their constitutional rights. Could capital continue to assume the position of an irresponsible sovereign, living in a sphere beyond the domain of law, without inviting the fate which has awaited all sovereigns who have denied or abused their trust? Brooks Adams was convinced that it could not.

Labor, like capital advancing toward monopolistic concentration, was already protesting against the irresponsible sovereignty of the capitalist class. It was, Brooks held, preparing to levy actual war against society, and might shatter the social system in its effort to reduce the power of capital. Yet the mind of the American capitalist was too specialized to comprehend a social relation beyond the narrow circle of his private interests. "He is not responsible, for he is not a trustee for the public. If he be restrained by legislation, that legislation is in his eye an oppression and an outrage, to be annulled or eluded by any means which will not lead to the penitentiary. . . . Thus, of necessity, he precipitates a conflict, instead of establishing an adjustment. He is, therefore, in essence, a revolutionist without being aware of it." Faced with the prospect of being held socially accountable, of being compelled to accept a position of equality before the law, the American capitalist was refusing to compromise while compromise was still possible. He was seeking to retain his right to purchase extralegal privileges.

The capitalist ruling class, Brooks asserted, had retained its immunities and its privileges through its control of the courts, particularly the Supreme Court, which exercised not only a judicial function, but a political one, by acting as a censor of legislation. The American capitalist therefore regarded the constitutional form of government which exists in the United States, as a convenient method of obtaining his own way against the majority. Buttressed by the courts, he had thus far been able to perpetuate his rule. But Brooks Adams surmised that his stupidity would prove his own undoing. Dependent upon law enforcement for his protection as well as his power, he was, of all men, the most cynically contemptuous of the law, and of all citizens the most lawless. "He appears to assume that the law will always be enforced, when he has need of it, by some special personnel whose duty lies that way, while he may evade the law, when convenient, or bring it into contempt, with impunity. The capitalist seems incapable of feeling his responsibility, as a member of the governing class, in this respect, and that he is bound to uphold the law, no matter what the law may be, in order that others may do the like."

Meanwhile, as the twentieth century advanced, it became clear that the American people had determined to impose the will of the majority upon the judiciary, and if this effort succeeded, the last bulwark of capitalist rule would be levelled. Brooks Adams felt that the social order could then survive only if there emerged a high order of generalizing mind, capable of grasping, and effectively controlling, a multitude of complex relations. In any age, such minds would be rare. But they were scarcely to be hoped for in the United States, where capitalist rule had raised educational standards only in science and mechanics, and through its cult of the narrowly specialized mind had brought about an ominous decline of administrative intelligence. So Brooks Adams predicted that unless capital could, in the immediate future, generate an intellectual energy, beyond the sphere of its specialized calling, very much in excess of any intellectual energy of which it had hitherto given promise, and unless it could besides rise to an appreciation of diverse social conditions, as well as to a level of political sagacity, far higher than it had attained in recent years, its relative power in the community must decline. With that decline, social disintegration would intensify. And the end of social disintegration would be, in the United States, precisely what it had always been everywhere else—a revolution, with a redistribution of property, the rise of a new favored class, and a fresh beginning from a lower level of civilization.

Henry, too, felt that if civilization were not to perish, the next generation would require a new social mind. Since history was first recorded, every generation in turn had toiled with agony to attain and apply power, while betraying alarm and horror at the power they succeeded in creating. Now, thought itself was being whirled about in the vortex of infinite forces. "Power leapt from every atom, and enough of it to supply the stellar universe showed itself running to waste at every pore of matter. Man could no longer hold it off. Forces grasped his wrists and flung him about as though he had hold of a live wire or a runaway automobile. . . ." But the human mind, Henry surmised, must have nearly reached the limits of its expansion. So far as he could see, the new American—the child of incalculable coal power, chemical power, electric power, and radiating energy, as well as of new forces as yet undetermined—must be a sort of god compared with any former creation of nature. And that the new American would really resemble some sort of god, Henry Adams profoundly disbelieved.

So society, he concluded, must therefore incur disaster. Civilization would be wrecked by the march of science, by the multiverse of forces with which it was beyond the capacity of man's present social intelligence to cope. For twentieth-century men were like monkeys monkeying with a loaded shell. They neither knew nor cared where their practically infinite energies came from, or would carry them. Thus society was actually laying its head under the axe, and inviting the blow. A thinking individual had only one choice left: to join those who preferred to perish with society, or those who were willing to help its destruction. Facing what he believed to be the imminent dissolution of his world, Henry Adams asserted that he saw nothing in the present society worth preserving, and nothing that was worth substituting for the present.

With the outbreak of the First World War, and the subsequent revolution in Russia, it seemed to Henry and to Brooks that their prophecies were being realized. To Brooks, as the war ended, as the peace was being made, it appeared that there must be a still more bitter struggle within a generation—at furthest. He drew an ironical implied comparison between President Wilson and Moses, the proto-type of all modern scientific optimists who anticipate perfection. Moses based the social system which he tried to organize, not on observed facts, but on *a priori* theories evolved out of his own mind, and he met with the failure that all men of a visionary cast of mind must meet with, when he sought to realize his visions. Brooks was now certain that the system of industrial, capitalistic civilization was near-ing its end; that it had attained its ultimate stages, and would pres-ently dissolve in chaos. "Democracy in America," he said, "has con-spicuously and decisively failed, in the collective administration of the common public property. Granting this much, it becomes simply a question of relative inefficiency, or degradation of type, culminating in the exhaustion of resources by waste; unless the democratic man can supernaturally raise himself to some level more nearly approach-ing perfection than that on which he stands." For, to Brooks as to Henry, nothing was more self-evident than that the democratic man cannot change himself from a competitive to a noncompetitive ani-mal by talking about it, or by pretending to be able to become other than he is—the victim of infinite conflicting forces. To deserve the name of civilization, society must be an embodiment of order, or must at least tend toward a social equilibrum. And Brooks Adams, like Henry, could not at the end of his life resist a conviction that the universe, far from being an expression of law and an embodiment of order, is a chaos which admits of reaching no equilibrium, and with which man is doomed eternally and hopelessly to contend.

[2] THE HORIZONS OF DESPAIR

Brooks Adams once remarked to Justice Holmes that philosophers are hired by the comfortable class to prove that everything is all right. He might have cited one of their contemporaries. The ex-ample, though not quite accurate, would have been suggestive. Wil-liam Graham Sumner was certainly not a Pangloss. But, as a social philosopher, he spoke for the comfortable class of the Gilded Age. He advocated a theory of life which many Americans were acting on; and perhaps they wished to be told, authoritatively, that it was the true one.

For nearly forty years Sumner had a personal and very powerful effect on the social outlook of Americans. He produced it with his lectures at Yale, his books, his constant flow of articles in newspapers and popular magazines, the controversies which he touched off and then happily entered with a bludgeon. But, like the Adams brothers, he wrote his most enduring book when past his sixtieth year; and its significance was not generally recognized for more than a decade. By that time, Sumner was dead, but his book, *Folkways*, carried his influence forward to later generations. His was one of the minds that continued to challenge young Americans of the nineteen-forties.

Sumner's later students, at the turn of the century, used to say that he looked like an old lion. He was a tough, truculent realist, stern and forbidding in manner, and the impact of his mind resembled that of a sledge hammer. He had, they said, an iron voice; he growled his lectures rather than spoke them. There was no mistaking his quality when you saw him—a bald, ruddy-faced man with a powerful body, a bulldog jaw, cold eyes, a mouth set in grim disdain, always fastidiously groomed in an old-fashioned style. Few of his students suspected that he had served as an Episcopal clergyman before coming to Yale, back in the distant eighteen-seventies, to fill the newly created professorship of political and social science. It probably would have shocked them to learn that he had never formally renounced his priesthood. For he was the first, and possibly the most savage, of all debunkers. "I have never discarded beliefs deliberately," he told an associate in his old age. "I left them in the drawer, and, after a while, when I opened it, there was nothing there at all." In that same drawer, with his faith in God, Sumner later packed away his faith in man.

Like the new capitalist rulers of America who were his contemporaries, Sumner was a self-made man, and he applied to scholarship the insatiable acquisitiveness, the propensity to daring raids, the unremitting industry that they applied to the making of millions by gathering up railroads, or oil refineries, or iron foundries. His temperament was that of his times, and both shaped his philosophy. His parents had emigrated from Lancashire; only the ambition and frugality of his father, a railroad mechanic, enabled Sumner to secure a college education. As a student at Yale Sumner was an outstandingly brilliant classicist. He formed a friendship with William C. Whitney, his rival for scholastic honors, and Whitney advanced him enough money to hire a substitute for military service in the War between the States, and to spend three years in Europe studying theology. For some time after his return, he taught at Yale. He associated himself with certain alumni who, observing the successful reforms instituted at Harvard by President Eliot, were urging that Yale adapt itself to the conditions of worldly success in a new era. Sumner left Yale for New York, where he was ordained, and presently he secured a parish in the fashionable suburb of Morristown, New Jersey. There the invitation to a professorship reached him.

Apparently, he was not reluctant to abandon the pulpit for the platform. Certainly he was delighted that his new province had been little explored. He turned first to economics, later to sociology; he was a pioneer in both fields, and since both were highly controversial he found in them congenial opportunities to show his mettle as a fighter. Belligerence was the characteristic quality of his writing; but as a disciple of Darwin, a follower of Herbert Spencer, he forced himself to respect the methods of science and make use of them. Always a prodigiously hard worker, in his later years, when he was devoting himself to anthropology and ethnology and ranging over the cultures of the world, Sumner set himself to master a new language every summer, lest any important material elude his grasp. When he died, the results, reduced to carded notes, filled fifty-two receptacles each holding some three thousand cards. But for the fact that he was a philosopher, not a plutocrat, they might have been securities in strongboxes.

Sumner joined the Yale faculty two years after Henry Adams joined that of Harvard. Both rejected participation in the major enterprises of their time for study of the changing society that surrounded them. Adams viewed it with patrician distaste; Sumner, at first, with warm approval. The era of America's new rulers had already opened. From the White House, President Grant offered his benediction to the "captains of industry"—the masters of railroads, oil, beef, iron, coal. The Congress was eager to serve them—as it proved, at a price. On Nob Hill in San Francisco, along lower Fifth Avenue in New York and Bellevue Avenue in Newport, ornate monuments to victory were rising, soon to be stuffed with the fantasies of upholsterers and the immense, gilt-framed literalisms of foreign painters. Desolate and disease-ridden slums were spreading in the larger cities. There was an angry unrest evident among the workers; there would shortly occur a strike of unprecedented violence, paralyzing the nation's trade, and broken only by the army. Industrialization was proceeding swiftly. Consolidation was to follow. Sumner, still studying American society, would live to see the industrial capitalist displaced by the financier—like his friend Whitney, who was a friend of Adams also, and who accumulated forty millions of dollars in less than a decade. He would likewise live to see, and condemn with unsparing ridicule, a cresting wave of popular discontent that finally broke in a crusade for social justice.

This was the society that an economist and sociologist had to interpret. Sumner was a man of few prepossessions, but he had a profound belief in the old American dream that the self-reliant, independent citizen, though he started from scratch, could make his way to the top by frugality, skill, and enterprise. The fundamental guarantee of democracy was opportunity. As one who had risen from humble circumstances, Sumner had faith in democracy. Looking at the new industrial society, he saw it in terms of opportunity, and thought it good. But he was vowed to science, and the business of a scientist was to discard illusions, to arrive at truth by investigating reality. Sumner surmised that democracy was not the result of an ideal formulated by the Founding Fathers. Every ideal, he thought, is a phantasm, formed by giving up one's hold on reality and taking a flight into the realm of fiction. Did not the principle of evolution hold true for society, as for organic life? What, then, had precipitated the rise of democracy? Sumner concluded that the political and social structure of the state had been determined exclusively by the operation of economic forces. Ideals, aspirations, preferences, conscious intention played no part in it. Men could not by merely thinking things call them into being. Economic forces, acting on the interests of men, and through them on human nature, made or broke institutions. The wisest statesman, the most successful man of affairs, merely went along with these forces, like a chip on the current. Whether he liked it or not, man lived in a deterministic world. His area of liberty was confined to a choice between adapting himself to conditions as he found them, or refusing to adapt.

Sumner thought he saw, in the swift industrialization that was transforming America, the greatest economic and social revolution that had ever taken place. How absurd to interpret it from the point of view of ethics, of what ought to be! The real obligation of a scientist was to investigate what actually was happening, and discover both why it was inevitable and what adaptations it required. So Sumner, a censorious puritan, made a valiant attempt to exclude all moral judgments from his thinking. He would be objective; he would base his theories squarely upon reality—upon the facts as they were shaping up.

This decision, inevitably, made him the preacher of an economic and social gospel that the times wished to hear, if for no other reason than that it justified the way things were actually going. By rejecting moral judgment, Sumner produced one very odd result. He soothed the consciences of many Americans who occasionally suspected that their practices, however successful, failed to square with the morality they professed. He became the apostle of *laissez faire*, the foremost champion of rugged individualism and triumphant capitalism. Nature, he asserted, had ordained the chances and conditions of life on earth once for all. The case could not be reopened; no revision of the laws of human life was possible. "This is a world," he declared, "in which the rule is, 'Root, hog, or die,' and it is also a world in which 'the longest pole knocks down the most persimmons.'" Capital, in the form of wealth or private property, is power over nature. It is also, unquestionably, the most invincible of all the interests of men.

Capital, Sumner argued, alone makes a civilized society possible, and serves to maintain it on a kind of platform elevated above primitive life and barbarism. Human welfare therefore requires that capital, or wealth, be augmented by every means possible. Nothing must be permitted to impede the process of its accumulation. The process is carried on by individuals whose incentive is their self-interest, and who obey a fundamental law of life—competition. Did this mean that life is a chaos of warfare and ruthless competition? Not so, said Sumner. There is such a thing as "antagonistic co-operation"; men sink their minor antagonisms of interest and combine to their mutual advantage, in order to satisfy a major interest which they hold in common. Antagonistic co-operation is organization. Economically, it is the most productive form of enterprise.

No limit should be set to enterprise, Sumner held. Arbitrary restrictions of any kind will merely operate to discourage initiative, and thus defeat the primary social aim of accumulating capital. Government, therefore, must adopt a hands-off policy, remain neutral

as between competitive interests, and assume only the function of preserving order and maintaining civil liberty. Civil liberty, Sumner
asserted, is the condition in which each man is guaranteed the use
of all his powers exclusively for his own welfare. Society, he declared, must do no more for any man than insure that he should be
left free to do the most for himself that he can, and should be guaranteed the exclusive enjoyment of all that he does. Society had no right
to regulate his enterprises, limit his gains, or determine his use of
them. The increasing concentration of wealth was not only inevitable,
but beneficial; it exemplified the highest possible degree of economic
organization, and therefore the most profitable one. Millionaires, said
Sumner, are a product of natural selection, acting on the whole body
of men to pick out those who can meet the requirement of certain
work to be done. In this respect they were just like great statesmen,
or scientific men, or military men; and it was only because they were
the naturally selected agents of society that wealth aggregated in
their hands. That the captains of industry owed their opportunities
to society, Sumner did not deny. But he pointed out that society owed
its increasing wealth, and advancing civilization, largely to them.

To Americans who hoped to achieve wealth by emulating the
methods of the captains of industry—the Vanderbilts, Carnegies,
Goulds, Stanfords—Sumner's doctrines furnished a scientific sanction. They were adapting themselves to the prevailing economic forces
of industrialization, combination, corporate control. Did anyone dare
to suggest that the expanding American economy obeyed no law
but that of the jungle? Sumner invited their attention to Darwin.
The American economy clearly exemplified the law of evolution.
It exhibited the competitive struggle which results in the survival of
the fittest. It displayed the operation of evolution at a high stage of
complexity, and foreshadowed a still greater complexity for the future.
Americans would have to adjust to the present and the future, not
strive to change them. For the sentimental, and the conscience-ridden,
Sumner had a stern warning: men interfere with the operations of
natural law at their peril. "The truth is," he thundered, "that the
social order is fixed by laws of nature precisely analogous to those
of the physical order. The most that man can do is by ignorance and
self-conceit to mar the operation of social laws."

Meanwhile, discontent was rising in the land. The social consequences of industrialization were being bitterly protested. What had

become of traditional American equality, of the fundamental rights of man? Sumner dismissed the notion of equality, whether economic or social, as pure illusion. Inequality, he affirmed, was an inescapable condition of life, and on the whole a beneficial one. Economic inequality resulted from the competition for wealth. Competition tested and developed men's powers, and the more intense it became, the better the powers it would develop. Social inequality was the effect of an identical process of natural selection. These processes were the system of nature. Men could amend the system in one way only. "We can take the rewards from those who have done better and give them to those who have done worse. We shall thus lessen the inequalities. We shall favor the survival of the unfittest, and we shall accomplish this by destroying liberty. Let it be understood that we cannot get outside this alternative: liberty, inequality, survival of the fittest; non-liberty, equality, survival of the unfittest. The former carries society forward and favors all its best members; the latter carries society downwards and favors all its worst members."

To the tender-minded who spoke of fundamental human rights, Sumner retorted with the thesis that man possesses only one: the right to maintain himself, if he can, in a world of incessant struggle and peril. The doctrine of natural rights set forth in the Declaration was sheer fantasy. Such rights as exist, he asserted, are those which force has created in the long course of human history. "If a thing has been done and is established by force (that is, no force can reverse it), it is right in the only sense we know, and rights will follow from it which are not vitiated at all by the force in it. There would be no security at all for rights if this were not so." The original act of force might have wrought flagrant injustices, and these might have become the source of many others over the years till the aggregate of injustice appeared to be intolerable. But the original act could not be revoked; its rights stood as established; the present condition, whatever its nature, had the sanction of law, and only force could alter it. Did this thesis do violence to ethics, to traditional concepts of democracy? Sumner had a pungent answer. "Every age is befooled by the notions which are in fashion in it," he said. "Our age is befooled by 'democracy.'"

Looking at democracy, as the years passed, Sumner became apprehensive about its future. It would have to meet two grave dangers, both of which originated in the mounting antagonism of those-who-have and those-who-have-not. The latter, being in the numerical majority, possessed effective political power. He surmised that they would use it to make the government an instrument for improving their situation—as he saw it, to plunder the successful and wealthy. Already, reformers and humanitarians—he denounced them, scornfully, as crackpots and meddlers—were proposing schemes for the alleviation of economic hardship, and social injustice, by government action. All such schemes rested on the assumption that social evolution is amenable to social control. Sumner declared this to be nonsense. If these misguided demagogues had their way—and they were being abetted by labor leaders, clergymen, and certain segments of the press—democracy would be construed as a system of favoring a new privileged class of the many and the poor. To develop into a sound working system, Sumner urged, democracy must oppose a cold resistance to any claims for favor on the ground of poverty and hardship. Once such claims were admitted as valid, the way was paved for socialism. They involved a renunciation of liberty, as he saw it, and he deplored a growing tendency among Americans to want somebody to come and help them to be free. Men had always failed of freedom, he said, not because they had been enslaved, but because the price of liberty was too high and too great for them. Rather than pay the price, they preferred servitude, and they got it.

Sumner also feared that government might be captured by the wealthy. He disliked the prospect of rule by a plutocracy as much as that of rule by the poor. Plutocracy was the use of capital politically rather than industrially. And the captains of industry were, undeniably, purchasing privileges. They were seeking to operate upon the market by means of legislation, artificial monopoly, a protective tariff, the creation of special advantages. As plutocrats, they, too, were plunderers. The modern industrial system furnished them a magnificent field, one usually far more profitable than that of legitimate industrial enterprise. Was the political machinery of democracy adequate to restrain them? He doubted it. The machinery offered too many opportunities for manipulation and corrupt abuse. The danger could be averted only by minimizing, so far as possible, the relations of government to industry. As long as such relations obtained, every industrial interest would be forced, by the profit motive, to employ plutocratic methods. Capital, Sumner asserted, should be excluded from all interest in government action, and thrown upon the laws of the market. Industry should be as widely separated from the state as the church was. There would then remain only what he termed that power of capital which is rooted in the industrial and social order, which nothing can set aside or overcome.

Paternalism or plutocracy appeared to be the alternatives before the American people, and Sumner began to wonder whether democracy could any longer be considered the end product of social evolution. More and more he came to doubt the possibility of any equilibrium under the American system. The outlook was for increasing class antagonism, and eventual class war. "It is the tendency of all social burdens," he concluded, "to crush out the middle class, and to force the society into an organization of only two classes, one at each social extreme." The real victim would be the man who had watched his own investments, made his own machinery safe, attended to his own plumbing, and educated his own children. A man like Sumner's father, or Sumner himself, and the sociologist found a name for him. The victim was "the forgotten man," a phrase that was to be used, long after Sumner's death, by an American President who believed, as he did not, that the fortunes of the American people were amenable to social control.

As the nineteenth century waned, Sumner quietly relinquished his faith in democracy, in progress as the concomitant of evolution, and in man. With a proud and powerful plutocracy on one side, and a hungry proletariat on the other, could democracy find resources anywhere for controlling the elements of human greed and passion? Obviously not. The old social war which again and again had retarded civilization was not over. Democracy had settled nothing. As a political form, it had merely set loose all the old evils in new guises. The robbery of a merchant by a robber baron, the robbery of an investor by a railroad wrecker, and the robbery of a capitalist by a collectivist were all identical. In the impending conflict, democracy could only stand aloof, and let nature take its course. The outlook, as Sumner saw it, was dark indeed: "but that a democracy can solve the antagonisms in the newest order of things, can adjust the rights of the contending interests by a series of 'ethical' decisions, or that it can, by siding with one party, give it a victory over the other, and thereby found a stable social order, it is folly to believe."

Sumner had reached pessimism, as Henry Adams had; and, like Adams, he turned to the writing of a book which was to have a profound effect on the thinking of later generations. He called *Folkways* a treatise; but it was, in fact, a kind of tragic epic. Its subject was the evolution of society; its theme, the immutable force of determinism which coerces man's action, strangles his liberty, and mocks his aspirations. Sumner set it forth in a study of the significance and operation of custom, or determined conduct, in social evolution. And he wove into it his appraisal of American democracy, of American society, and of their probable future, as he saw these in the light of studies that had carried him back to the very fountainhead of history.

Man, he said, did not begin by thinking, but by acting. Instinct prompted ways of meeting needs. Experiment resulted either in success and satisfaction, or failure and pain. Between these lay the channel of subsequent effort. Over time, selection occurred. The ways of action which worked best in meeting the conditions of life were automatically adopted. Habit in the individual became custom in the group. Such customs were folkways, which fulfilled with some degree of success the needs defined by the four great motives of human action: hunger, sex passion, vanity, and fear of the supernatural. The folkways were not creations of intelligence. They resembled products of natural forces which men unconsciously set in operation. From them, however, arose all concepts of right, morality, truth, life policy, and world philosophy.

When folkways came to include the judgment that they promoted the welfare of the group, they became coercive. At this stage, Sumner called them mores. The mores, he said, are those ways of doing things which are current in a society to satisfy needs and desires, together with the faiths, notions, codes, and standards of welfare which inhere in them. They pervade and control the group ways of thinking in all the exigencies of life. They exercise a decisive force on all action. Conscious thought is their worst enemy, because their expediency often depends on the assumption that they will have general acceptance and currency independent of it. They are the regulators of individual and group conduct. Behind the mores lies the power of the ruling class, and the inertia of the masses; both are essentially conservative. Mores change only as life conditions change. Sometimes they make for progress, sometimes for retrogression.

The individual can do almost nothing to alter the social drift of his times. His narrow area of liberty consists in the ability to propose variations in the mores which society may ultimately accept.

But changes will be adopted only if they have reference to interests of which society has already become conscious, and if they express convictions about those interests already dormant in the group mind. Thus, in a sense, even the trivial liberty of the individual is also subject to determinism. All that Sumner could say was that this condition should not "discourage our reason and conscience from their play on the situation, if we are content to know that their function must be humble."

Humble, indeed! The ability of reason and science to improve life in the present, or to shape the future, was almost negligible. They existed on sufferance. Their knowledge could have no application unless, in some fortunate moment, it accorded with a blind force expressed in customs that, in the main, were purely irrational. At no time would men ever be able to make their social environment, or even the conditions of their existence, realize the possibilities that were within the grasp of their intelligence. Life would always lag behind the mind, and the mind's highest conquests might easily be lost. The spirit of man was permanently imprisoned; it could beat against the walls if it would, and perhaps with luck tunnel its way out, but only to be trapped and again incarcerated.

Science itself, being conditioned by the mores, was suspect, as Sumner relentlessly demonstrated. Evolution, he said, is now accepted as a final fact, and a philosophy of nature is derived from it. Yet, to all but a very few, the philosophy has no guarantee except that is is current. All accept it because all accept it, and for no other reason. Is it a final fact—or merely a phase of thought sanctioned by the present mores? Yet from the implications of this devastating conclusion, Sumner himself recoiled. It was, he thought, intolerable; and we should live as if it were not true. "The only security," he said, "is the constant practice of critical thinking. We ought never to accept fantastic notions of any kind; we ought to pursue all propositions until we find out their connection with reality. That is the fashion of thinking which we call scientific in the deepest and broadest sense of the word." But this, as Sumner's book established, was at best a fragile and melancholy security, almost inevitably fated to prove an illusion. In *Folkways* he shut and locked the door to hope that William James, in *Pragmatism*, almost simultaneously declared to be flung wide open as never before.

Sumner's book explicitly denied the central doctrines of American democratic faith. Long afterwards, it exercised a revolutionary influence, undermining ancient national traditions and inherited attitudes. But in the first decade of the new century political liberalism appeared destined to usher in an era of social justice. The climate of the mind was hopeful. Americans still believed in the freedom and creative potency of the individual. They continued to define evolution as progress toward an ultimate perfection. They were convinced that the democratic system, and the way of life that it made possible, assured the realization in society of those ideals which the nation had always cherished. These beliefs gave Americans a sense of optimism; they illuminated the road ahead; they pointed to the positive moral objectives toward which society must advance. Sumner rejected every one of them.

Democracy, he said, had two aspects; that of ideal, and that of actual conduct in life. Ideals were mere phantasms, destitute of foundation in fact, for the realization of which there existed no correct process. " 'Democracy,' " he asserted, "is not treated as a parallel word to aristocracy, theocracy, autocracy, etc., but as a Power from some outside origin, which brings into human affairs an inspiration and energy of its own." It was a sacred word like "Americanism" or "The People," protected from any realistic evaluation; a token coin chiefly valuable to the ruling class, who could use it as an instrument for achieving their own purposes. "Who dare say that he is not 'American'? Who dare repudiate what is declared to be 'Americanism'?" Sumner asked, sardonically. "If there is any document of Americanism, it is the Declaration of Independence. Those who have Americanism especially in charge have repudiated the doctrine that 'governments derive their just powers from the consent of the governed,' because it stood in the way of what they wanted to do. They denounce those who cling to the doctrine as un-American. Then we see what Americanism and patriotism are. They are the duty laid upon us all to applaud, follow, and obey whatever a ruling clique of newspapers and politicians chooses to say or wants to do."

Democracy was in the mores, and the mores, Sumner asserted, can make anything right and prevent the condemnation of anything. But, as a way of life, and even as a political system, he considered it to be in its final phases. It was, like all other modern mores, a product of the play of economic forces that had begun centuries earlier: the discovery and colonization of new continents, the immense increase of movable capital, the advance of industry under scientific development. "All our popular faiths, hopes, enjoyments and powers are due to these great changes in the conditions of life. The new status makes us believe in all kinds of rosy doctrines about human welfare, and about the struggle for existence and the competition of life; it also gives us all our contempt for old-fashioned kings and nobles, creates democracies, and brings forth new social classes and gives them power. For the time being things are so turned about that numbers are a source of power. Men are in demand, and an increase in their number increases their value." But, said Sumner, the existing status is temporary and the conditions in it are evanescent. "When the earth is underpopulated and there is an economic demand for men, democracy is inevitable. That state of things cannot be permanent. Therefore democracy cannot last. It contains no absolute and 'eternal' truth."

If democracy as an ideal was merely a myth, and as a way of life was in its decline, what would be the American future? The drift in the mores of twentieth-century America, Sumner affirmed, was toward state regulation, militarism, imperialism, toward petting and flattering the proletariat, toward whatever appeared to be altruistic and humanitarian. As respects these tendencies, what American could get out of his group prejudices? He might as well attempt to get out of gravity or the pressure of the atmosphere. Could Americans determine their own future? Could any one of them form judgments not by his ruling interest or conviction, but by the supposed impact of demographic data on an empty brain? Americans of the twentieth century had no grounds for confidence in the ruling tendencies of their times. These were only temporary phases in the endless shifting of ethical doctrine and philosophical generalization. All that Sumner could foresee was a blind effort, by the application of social policy, to subject society to another set of arbitrary interferences, dictated by a new set of dogmatic prepossessions that would only be a continuation of old methods and errors.

But the rigorous intellectual honesty which led to these conclusions did not compel Sumner to find them pleasing. The doughty old warrior was not happy with them. The theory that ethics are purely relative to time and place, that good and evil have no reality apart from the local decrees of irrational custom, would be congenial to an iconoclastic later generation. But could it inspire enthusiasm in a man who had once found intellectual security in the old democratic faith, based on eternal moral law? Life, as the operation of sheer blind force in a world of fate, was an anguishing spectacle.

American society had carried into practice the economic and social gospel that Sumner preached. Observing it in the opening decade of the twentieth century, he saw only moral anarchy, and the puritan in him found this revolting. "We live in a war of two antagonistic philosophies: the ethical policy taught in the books and the schools, and the success policy," he acknowledged bitterly. In politics, finance, industry, he saw the man-who-can-do-things elevated to a social hero whose success overrode all other considerations. And where that code was adopted it called for false conventions and untruthful character. It debauched society. Any morality, he reflected, is better than moral anarchy. Yet moral anarchy was the inevitable result of the worship of success, the doctrine of the primacy of wealth, the philosophy of *laissez faire*. And who had done more to evangelize this cult among Americans than Sumner himself?

There was no comfort in the inexorable logic of disbelief. Not even if one determined to cling to the hope that scientific thinking is possible and eternally valid, though science itself might turn out to be merely a "phantasm," an illusion. To Sumner, the future portended only disaster. "I have lived," he told an associate shortly before his death, "through the best period of this country's history. The next generations are going to see war and social calamities. I am glad I don't have to live on into them."

In the early eighteen-eighties, Sumner found among his graduate students a rugged, skeptical, contentious young man who gave the impression of being far older than his actual age. Thorstein Veblen was the child of Norwegian immigrants who had taken up a homestead in Minnesota, had tamed the unbroken prairie, had succeeded in maintaining themselves at the cost of unremitting struggle and deprivation. In later years, with his long hair, sweeping moustache, and imperial, he would have the look of an artist, a musician perhaps, but he would never lose the earthy rudeness which distressed his teachers and classmates. Sumner considered him a man of very settled and sturdy character and great industry. Others recognized these merits, but were nevertheless intimidated.

Veblen was miserably poor. He ignored niceties of attire. He had a deep distrust of effete ways, of luxury, of the ostentatious sophistication which he met with in the prosperous Eastern states where capital had aggregated. These so-called civilized folk who lived so prodigally —they did not work, as he understood work. They produced nothing. Their livelihood was derived from control of wealth, from management of capital. They were ruthlessly exploitative. It was they who, by means of the banks and railroads that they owned, kept the farmers of the Middle West in perpetual debt, condemning them to a kind of peonage.

Veblen had grown up in the center of that ferment of radical social and economic ideas which was sweeping the rural Middle West, and would lead, in time, to an embittered revolt of the farmers. Suspicion of the conspicuously wasteful ways of wealthy city folk was natural in a farm boy. In Veblen, because of the grinding poverty of his childhood, it was almost instinctive. And it bred resentment; in him there smouldered the moral anger of his people. The distrust and the resentment expressed themselves obliquely, in a defiant contempt. Veblen was not a man to rub the wrong way. He had sharpened the weapon of a deadly wit. He had a gift for irony. He could turn on a withering sarcasm. He had an aptitude for the satirical exposure of cant and sham. He was always ready to resort to these talents under provocation, and usually he found the provocation.

This made people fear and respect him, even admire him in a grudging fashion, but it did not command their affection. He had an accurate sense of the caliber and quality of his intelligence, and he was intellectually arrogant, perhaps as a compensation for being socially uneasy. In later years, his arrogance increased in direct proportion to the fear, suspicion, and dislike that his personality stirred up in his associates. For nearly a decade after receiving his doctorate from Yale, he was unable to secure a teaching post commensurate with his abilities. Almost his whole life was spent unhappily. He moved restlessly from one university to another, detesting the routine of teaching; everywhere, as he felt, underpaid and refused the recognition that was due him. Even his growing fame displeased him, for it flourished in the wrong quarter. His books became a fashion among the "intelligentsia," the literary radicals. Veblen despised the radicals.

But it was no accident that Veblen gained an immediate prestige in literary, rather than academic, circles. The talents which made him a disturbing personality operated also to make him a distinguished writer; and William Dean Howells, reviewing his first book, praised it as much for its art as for its ideas. Did a theorist in the field of economics have any business making use of literary airs and graces? Certainly not. It was the function of textbooks and scholarly treatises to be sound, not enjoyable. Dryness and dullness were virtues to be cultivated, and Veblen's perversity in rejecting them exasperated the guild of professionals. Did it not indicate dilettantism, even frivolity? Unfortunately, his books displayed a formidable erudition, and no one could deny the originality of his ideas. Those ideas were destuctive of complacency. Still worse, they undermined the official "science" of economics. Clearly, Veblen was all too likely to become a disruptive influence; it was a misfortune that his books steadily made their way among laymen. The college of economic cardinals ignored him when they could, depreciated him when they could not.

Nevertheless, he came to exercise a powerful effect on the thinking of Americans; and, like Sumner, he continued to challenge his countrymen long after his death. His youthful ambition was to become a philosopher and, in a sense, he treated economics as a province of philosophy, but with the methods of modern science. Nearly fifty years after its publication his first, possibly his greatest, book, *The Theory of the Leisure Class*, had attained the rank of a classic. A classic in American literature; a source of ideas which formed part of the general intellectual heritage; a source of phrases which, having become part of the colloquial idiom, retained their vitality as fighting terms. For this book, launched with misgivings and largely at his own cost by an obscure teacher, remained one of the most merciless criticisms of the American social order ever made by an American writer.

Sumner was the only man for whom Veblen expressed a deep unqualified admiration, though his teacher's economic views were repugnant to him, and their embodiment in the social order became the ground for his attack on it. The Sumner who influenced him was the man who eventually wrote *Folkways*, who even in Veblen's student days had already turned to anthropology, ethnology, and history for light on the process of social evolution. Veblen, also an explorer, followed in his wake, but arrived at a very different destination. He likewise shared with Sumner, possibly even caught from him, the propensity to debunking which they both converted into an intellectual method. There was, however, a sharp contrast in their ways of using it. Sumner, the votary of elegance who believed that a man should always dress for dinner, put on overalls and attacked illusions with a pickax and sledge hammer. To Veblen, cultivated elegance was itself an illusion, and one that aroused in him the hot contempt of a son of the soil. But for the purpose of destroying it, he chose a delicate rapier, and conducted his attack with the fastidious grace of an aristocrat engaged in a duel.

Veblen's book, preceding Sumner's by seven years, also professed to be a treatise. He called it an economic study in the evolution of institutions, but his major interest was the mores of American society. Sumner, projecting the doom of a world civilization, produced a work of epic proportions, tragic in tone. Veblen, foreshadowing the inevitable disintegration of an industrially complex and professedly democratic order, wrote in the tone of classical comedy. His central theme was essentially moral, not economic. What he showed was the corrupting—even the depraving and debauching—of a whole society by its ruling class, through the pervasive influence of their ideals and their way of life. Its final collapse, he implied, would take the form of economic ruin. But the genuine source of that collapse would be moral obliquity and social decay. Veblen's delinquent heroes were the new rulers of America, the aristocrats of capitalism. His comedy was a comedy of manners.

Veblen adopted as his standard of judgment one which he asserted to be that of dispassionate common sense. In order to be at peace with himself, "the common man must be able to see in any and all human effort and human enjoyment an enhancement of life and well-being on the whole." To possess merit, a society must be such as to promote the general welfare. It must "approve itself under the test of impersonal usefulness—usefulness as seen from the point of view of the generically human." For there is deeply ingrained in the race, Veblen argued, a strong sense of purpose—an instinct of workmanship, as it were—which finds futility distasteful and condemns waste. The ways in which this instinct has attempted to achieve satisfaction have, in the end, brought it perilously close to defeat. Veblen saw the American capitalistic order as a climax in its frustration.

American society, he contended, preserved the institutions, the hierarchy, and the standards of a barbaric stage of civilization, and would ultimately be destroyed by them if it did not discard them. On the barbaric level of life, aggressive predatory exploit is regarded as the only appropriate occupation of the superior individual, the hero. Useful employment carries with it the stigma of unworthiness, of personal inferiority, and is therefore considered irksome. As civilization advances, two classes develop. The leisure class, held in honor, is dedicated to exploit. The disesteemed class—whether slaves, or socially submerged—is charged with productive labor. The instinct of workmanship is not only frustrated, but begins to be perverted.

This situation, Veblen charged, is perpetuated in the highly industrialized, theoretically democratic, civilization of the United States, with paradoxical results. Wealth and ownership have become the goal of competitive effort, but predatory exploit remains for the capitalist, as for the barbarian, the only road to achievement and honor. Productive labor—industrial employment, the wage-gaining occupations and services—carries with it the connotation of drudgery. The stigma of inadequate prowess attaches to those who engage in it. The American superior individual, or hero, is the financial freebooter. The American disesteemed inferior, or social failure, is the workingman. Both, however, retain the instinct for workmanship, and the distaste for futility. The dominant incentive of the capitalist is the invidious distinction attaching to wealth. Society sets a constantly advancing standard of financial prowess, or pecuniary reputability. It intensifies the competitive struggle to reach the standard by visiting with a sharper disapproval all evidence of shortcoming in point of pecuniary success. So the capitalist must constantly extend his conquests, even though these may long since have ceased to have any genuine economic justification. His situation resembles that of the barbarian hero who, after the tribe has attained conditions of stability, must nevertheless continue exploits that have become unnecessary. In both instances, these have only a ritual significance. They constitute claims to veneration. They are, socially, the more honorable for being so obviously superfluous.

The great capitalists and their dependents form the American leisure class. Veblen, analyzing its mores at the end of the Gilded Age, in the full-blown splendor of Newport and Fifth Avenue, used them to illustrate the paradoxical results of a social process. The single standard of wealth thoroughly perverts the instinct for workmanship. The so-called civilized satisfactions available to it among members of the leisure class are precisely those which, in its normal function, it rejects as abhorrent. To establish their status in the eyes of the world, members of that class must conspicuously abstain from all useful occupations. They must therefore restrict themselves to activities which are significantly trivial, unmistakably irrelevant to life, or positively harmful. For these will display most impressively the fact that their expenditure of time is flagrantly unproductive. From the society columns of the time, Veblen was able to compile an extraordinary series of illustrations on which to exercise his talent for satire.

Simultaneously with time-wasting activities, the economically fortunate, in order to advertise their status, must cultivate a conspicuous consumption of goods and services—or, as Veblen also termed it, a conspicuous waste. For if the wealth that they command is not ostentatiously displayed, how will the world know that they possess it; and if they do not outdo their rivals, wherefore shall they be honored? The American hero must demonstrate his ability to sustain large pecuniary damage without impairing his superior opulence. Hence, the cult of competitive luxury, of prodigal disbursements for conspicuously wasteful expenditure of time and substance and effort. This cult registers the operation of an economic law.

This law produces the need for a multiplicity of residences, yachts, equipages; costly banquets and balls; rapid changes of fashion; retinues of attendants, many of whom serve no useful purpose and therefore vicariously exhibit the leisure of their masters. All these contribute to a demonstration that the economically fortunate are, indeed, the elect, since they are so majestically superior to any vulgar need. The social destiny of the leisure class is to celebrate superfluity and exemplify waste. In them, the instinct for workmanship becomes its absolute opposite—a compulsion to futility. But, since they personify the current standard of achievement and success, and also constitute the effective ruling class, their ideals and ways are emulated, so far as possible, by the middle class, and finally come to affect the masses. Thus the philosophy of keeping up with the Joneses permeates the whole American social order. The dominant traits of the leisure class —the archaic, psychologically recessive traits of ferocity, self-seeking, clannishness, disingenuousness, a free resort to force and fraud, usually appearing in more sophisticated disguises—are thus socially perpetuated. The American social order, Veblen held, notably failed to justify itself as enhancing life and well-being. It denied that purpose, and defeated it.

Essentially, Veblen's criticism of the social order was that its major institutions had become obsolete; that their persistence, in spite of irrelevance to contemporary conditions, effectually blocked all social progress. But he recognized that there was reviving, among workers in the large industrial cities, an attitude of moral indignation at conspicuous waste and the futile life. He thought he saw a renascence of the instinct for workmanship, and with it a growing admiration for the kind of character which makes for peace, good will, and economic efficiency, rather than a life of self-seeking, force, fraud, and mastery. The probable social conflict, he thought, might take its rise from the antagonism of obsolete institutions and new circumstances; of classes respectively representing the past and the future.

In his first book Veblen also suggested an identical antagonism in the economic order, and his later books were chiefly devoted to developing its various implications. The principal defect of the American capitalist economy, he asserted, was a profound conflict of purposes that might well bring it to ruin. The economy expressed two opposed interests: the making of goods, and the making of profits. Modern industrial development had created a new class of technicians, whom he described as engineers. Their responsibility was the production of goods. Technically, they controlled an industrial power capable of effecting a material revolution in American life. But they could not employ this power to its full capacity. They were not masters of production. They were the servants of finance capitalists in whom ownership of industry was vested. Their masters, ignorant of the technical side of industry, dictated its business policy. Policy was determined, not with the object of making more goods, but with the object of making more money. Since profits were often increased by slowing production, or bringing it to a full stop, the capitalists irresponsibly set in motion the "business cycle" of alternating prosperity and depression, as their advantage dictated, and without regard to social or economic consequences.

Veblen considered the capitalists, or businessmen, to be anachronistic survivals of a pre-scientific, pre-industrial era. They were, he said, parasites on the economic process of production; their coercive power impeded social progress. The engineers, in his view, represented the contemporary era and the future. The economy, for him, became the theater of a dramatic conflict arising from the antagonism of the new and the old; production and profit; social progress and social stagnation. He furnished no blueprint for the resolution of this conflict. But he suggested the possibility of eliminating, from the American economy, its characteristic capitalist features; the business interest and the profit motive. He described a potential planned economy administered, solely for increased production, by industrial technicians, or engineers. Shortly after Veblen's death, and at the outset of the Great Depression, this idea was elaborated in the program of a movement called "Technocracy," under the leadership of Howard Scott. The program achieved wide publicity, but the movement soon collapsed. The impotence of an eminent engineer in the White House did not argue persuasively for the adoption of Veblen's plan.

But Veblen's ideas, and Sumner's, carried weight with later critics of the American scene. The doctrine of economic determinism which they had adopted was subsequently applied by Charles A. Beard to the economic interpretation of American history. Another historian, James Harvey Robinson, skillfully carried on Veblen's analysis of the American social order, and Sumner's dissection of traditional American faiths. Their influence was also evident in the work of a still younger critic, Thurman W. Arnold, professor of law at Yale and Assistant Attorney General in the administration of President Franklin D. Roosevelt. During the Great Depression, Arnold produced witty analyses of the symbols of American government, and the folklore of American capitalism. He undertook to examine the myths that have accreted to democratic institutions and capitalistic agencies. He suggested that they furnished Americans with a body of fiction which reconciled them to an unsatisfactory environment. The popularity of these books reflected the mood of disillusion of the moment. But a decade later, as the nineteen-forties were closing, it seemed that disillusion had not waned. The literary reputations of the Adams brothers, of Sumner and Veblen, were steadily advancing. The appeal of deterministic philosophies appeared to be increasing. Perhaps Americans were facing, more critically than ever before, a widening gap between their traditional ideals, and the actual realities of their social order.

CHAPTER XII

The Mysticism of the Middle Classes

[I] THE UNITY OF GOOD

On a June day in 1906, some twenty thousand pilgrims thronged into the city of Boston. They came to attend the dedication of a new temple; a vast, splendid white building with a dome that rose higher than Bunker Hill Monument. Crowds began milling around it at dawn. The doors were opened an hour later. At seven-thirty, the first of six services commenced. The last did not conclude until after night-fall. All day, the great chimes rang out hymns, while congregations of worshipers entered and departed, five thousand people at a time. On a subsequent evening, there was a service at which men and women from cities all over the world testified to miraculous cures wrought by their faith.

The American press ran long accounts of the temple and its dedica-tion. In most reports, there was an undertone of amazement; in many, a touch of awe. The building had cost two million dollars, had been fully paid for before completion. Congregations in New York had raised, in that city, edifices almost equally magnificent and costly. In all, the faith numbered nearly seven hundred churches. Did this not suggest that, at the very least, several hundred thousand Americans subscribed to its strange tenets? "There is no life, truth, intelligence nor substance in matter. All is infinite Mind and its infinite mani-festation, for God is All-in-all." If these words meant anything, they denied the reality of the material world, the world described by science and familiar to daily experience. In the twentieth century, was it possible that Americans accepted them as literally true? The press speculated, wonderingly. But the white cathedral of a new faith was an eloquent answer. It declared that a mystical view of life was gaining converts throughout the land.

Was there a deep-rooted tendency to mysticism in the American spirit? As the century advanced, the discoveries of science accelerated. In physics, revolutionary theories invalidated all old concepts of the structure of the universe. But many Americans demanded a truth that was ultimate and absolute; beyond any truth attainable by science. They sought it in what William James described as an "altogether other dimension of existence." Occult philosophies, native and foreign, flourished as never before. Some Oriental faiths exercised a wide appeal. In the larger cities, Vedanta and Baha'i prospered. Rosicrucianism, Theosophy, Yoga won adherents. There were churches of Divine Science, Religious Science, the Science of Mind, and even The Truth. At meetings of the Anthroposophical Society and the Biosophicum, earnest folk pursued the liberation of the "spiritual intelligence in man." There were thriving centers of New Thought and Unity. And evangelists who emphasized the supernatural and miraculous elements of Christianity effected spectacular mass conversions. On another plane, but no less indicative of a propensity to mysticism, the "sciences" of numerology and astrology enjoyed great prestige. Some Americans made a *mystique* of psychoanalysis. Others made one of communism.

Thus, forty years after its dedication, the Mother Church of Christian Science no longer aroused either wonder or speculation. It had come to resemble a shrine of orthodoxy; a repository of conservative tradition; a link with the remote, highly reputable past. In retrospect Mrs. Mary Baker Eddy, the founder of the religion, seemed remarkable for the ways in which she had anticipated the future. She was not recognized, in 1906, as a forerunner. Yet, like her contemporary Mrs. Julia Ward Howe, Mrs. Eddy had been a harbinger of social change; and the change was already well advanced. In a sense, both could be reckoned as announcing a generation of women—Miss Jane Addams was the most famous—who were bent upon transforming their environment and improving society. But while Mrs. Howe prefigured the American woman's domination of this world, Mrs. Eddy portended her annexation of the next. Mrs. Eddy was a woman of many extraordinary achievements. Certainly not the least of these was to point forward to the diminishing spiritual authority of the American male, and the increasing assumption by women of command over the nation's spiritual life.

Mrs. Eddy did not attend the ceremonies at her Mother Church, and her failure to do so presently resulted in tribulations. For many years she had been living, in virtual seclusion, at Concord, New Hampshire. She was seldom visible even to the hierarchy of her church, though she continued to exercise a remote, autocratic control over all its affairs. Her only excursions into the world took the form of brief drives in a closed carriage. She was eighty-five years old. Her hearing was impaired, her memory no longer always reliable. Though mentally as vigorous as ever when at her best, she was physically feeble. She had always been vain, and vanity still ran strong in her. She did not wish to be seen by her followers, or by the world.

The tenets of Christian Science, which promised humanity deliverance from suffering, made disclosure of its founder's infirmities almost impossible. And Mrs. Eddy was not only feeble; at times, she suffered from an acutely painful malady. This was kept secret from all but her immediate household. For indiscreet questioners, there was an official answer. Mrs. Eddy had retired from the world in order to devote herself to systematic meditation. "All that I ask of the world is time, time to assimilate myself to God." So she had told a reporter, the year before. "I would take all the world to my heart if that were possible," she said, "but I can only ask my friends to look away from my personality and fix their eyes on truth."

The world, never recklessly friendly to Mrs. Eddy, ignored this plea. For some time, dark rumors about her had been circulating. She had died, and a double was replacing her in her carriage. She was mentally incompetent, the helpless victim of conspirators who were stripping her of her wealth. She had been stricken by a fatal disease, and was sinking to death. These rumors whipped up public curiosity. It had already been excited by her absence from the triumphant dedication, by descriptions of the splendors of the Mother Church, by exaggerated reports of the rapid growth and numerical strength of Christian Science. Ever since her distant girlhood, Mrs. Eddy had craved personal publicity, had sought it with every means at her disposal. Now she shrank from it. Had she not already provided for the public's claims?

For Mrs. Eddy had never doubted that her evangel would become a world religion. Fifteen years earlier, she foresaw that posterity would require a suitable account of its genesis and its founder. Who, other than herself, could assume the obligation of providing it? It was an obligation; and, in one respect, peculiarly insistent. There existed a situation not unfamiliar in the lives of earlier apostles. Certain aspects of Mrs. Eddy's mortal career plainly misrepresented her immortal spirit. Others seemed incompatible with her predestined spiritual eminence in the illusory mortal world. Even to Mrs. Eddy. But—was this seeming not an instance of error? Men talked glibly of facts, of the literal truth about this and that. Were facts any less illusory than the context of shifting appearances in which they occurred? Why, then, pretend that they represented truth, or were related to it?

In composing her account, Mrs. Eddy rejected many illusory facts in behalf of higher truths. Some critics—they were usually spokesmen for quite different systems of metaphysics—later attributed this substitution to vanity, and an incorrigibly romantic temperament. Long in circulation, her account was almost the only authoritative source of information about her. Presently, it was to be charged with flagrant inaccuracy. Those who brought the charge were skeptics, and personally hostile. The voluminous material with which they substantiated it made Mrs. Eddy's predicament very clear. She had wanted to justify the reverence in which her mortal personality was held by her following. According to her own evangel, her mortal personality was unreal, an imperfect shadow of being. But could she acknowledge the degree of its imperfection? Would not such an admission shake the faith of her adherents, tarnish the luster of her evangel? Apparently, she was unable to solve this dilemma. She therefore tried to create a canonical legend. Was it because her personal faith had faltered that she succeeded only in producing a minor masterpiece of fiction?

While the ceremonies of dedication were in progress, a series of ordeals were being prepared for Mrs. Eddy. Responsive to rumor and public curiosity, Joseph Pulitzer's *World* determined to investigate her actual condition. Certain curious transfers of her personal property were uncovered. Intimidated by the threat of unfavorable publicity, she consented to receive reporters during an attack of her malady. They saw an emaciated, rouged old woman, with black-pencilled eyebrows, whose thinning white hair was padded out with false "switches." She was obviously in great pain, and extremely feeble. The *World* broke a sensational story. Mrs. Eddy was dying. Control of her person, her church and her fortune had been seized by an ambitious and criminal clique.

In order to capitalize on this feat of yellow journalism, the *World* proceeded to finance a lawsuit. Technically, it was brought in Mrs. Eddy's behalf by her alleged "next friends." These were her son and granddaughter, a nephew, and an adopted son with whom she had broken off relations. The ostensible purpose of the suit was to gain control of Mrs. Eddy's fortune, and conserve it for the heirs to whom she had determined not to bequeath it. But the *World* also had an ulterior motive. It hoped to establish Mrs. Eddy's mental incompetence. And, even more sensationally, it wished to establish, through a judicial verdict, that her evangel was based upon an insane delusion. Some months later, Mrs. Eddy was subjected to prolonged examination by deputies appointed by the court. She had meanwhile recuperated, and her responses to questions made it clear that her mind was unimpaired. The examiners were especially impressed by her account of her method of choosing investments: this unworldly mystic was as shrewd about practical affairs as that almost equally legendary eccentric, Mrs. Hetty Green! When they had concluded their examination and were about to depart, Mrs. Eddy recalled them. Though the court had excluded the issue of her evangel, she wished to give an account of it. She did. After a year of sensational publicity, the *World's* project collapsed.

Meanwhile, there had been an attack from another quarter. Mark Twain, long hostile to Christian Science and to Mrs. Eddy, brought out a book which subjected certain of her claims to stinging ridicule. There was, in Mrs. Eddy, an Amazonian pugnacity which denunciation always drew to the surface. She was never at a loss to take care of herself in any row. But ridicule left her exposed and defenseless; thought she had plenty of punch and passion, she had no humor whatever. Ridicule usually came from the intellectuals, and was the more intolerable for that reason. For Mrs. Eddy had an exaggerated respect for the approval of the erudite, possibly because it was so conspicuously lacking. Mark Twain's sardonic jibes at her *Science and Health* spoke, in a way, for the intellectual class, and were bound to infuriate her. Doubtless she took scant comfort from one aspect of the situation that was not barren of compliment. To have merited a book, however objectionable, from America's most distinguished man of letters was evidence that Mrs. Eddy was important, if not precisely illustrious.

But, as if these tribulations were not sufficient, Mrs. Eddy was presently to suffer another. The editors of *McClure's*, then at the apex of its muckraking fame, had decided to "expose" her. They were publishing a biography which also related a history of the Christian Science movement. It was supported by abundant documentation, and many affidavits. After serialization in the magazine, it was issued in book form. So prejudicial was it considered by Mrs. Eddy and the hierarchy of her church, that a way was found to have it withdrawn from circulation. But this expedient was futile, and probably unnecessary as well. The disclosures made by *McClure's* remained accessible to later investigators, and were often repeated over the years. As a subject of controversy, they kept Mrs. Eddy before the public long after her death. They undermined the legend she had created for posterity. They also set scholars to ferreting out the possible human sources of doctrines which she declared to be divinely inspired. But they failed to halt the march of Mrs. Eddy's evangel, or the growth of her church.

At the age of eighty-five, she not only survived these ordeals, but went on to meet others. Her ability to override calamity compelled admiration. Was not hers a success story in the classic American pattern? What magnate of the rags-to-riches school had overcome more obstacles, risen above more misfortunes, achieved a more spectacular victory by unaided, incessant struggle? There was even some touch of greatness in her defiant assertion of the unreality of a world that had done its best to defeat her; that would continue to pursue her with afflictions to the very end. The most damaging facts accumulated by her detractors only served to illustrate how dire had been the odds against her. The drab story which she wished to repudiate might have had a power greater than that of any legend she could invent.

Obscurity, poverty, a lack of formal education entered into her story. So did sickness, and a lifelong nervous instability that was plainly psychopathic. All during her life, Mrs. Eddy could exercise an extraordinary personal magnetism whenever she chose. But its effect was often canceled by her incapacity to sustain personal relationships. Her career was a chaos of quarrels, defections, lawsuits, irresponsible slanders, excommunications; these made her the victim of panic fear, and delusions of persecution. In middle age, usually penniless and always frustrated, she was desperately wandering from lodging to lodging. Past her fiftieth year, and precariously settled in the manufacturing town of Lynn, she gathered a handful of disciples among the factory hands, and began systematically preaching her gospel. She was nearing sixty before, with borrowed money, she was able to print the first edition of her book. Could anyone have detected in this thwarted, eccentric, contentious seeress the astonishing organizing gifts—akin to those of a Morgan or Carnegie—which Mrs. Eddy so improbably began to display as she approached the ripe age of threescore and ten? Indeed, would anyone have dared to predict that, within thirty years of its inauspicious birth, her evangel would spread over the nation, and even across the sea?

Yet there had seldom appeared in the United States a gospel more attractive to its time. For, as many understood it, the new religion not only offered a remission of afflictions—sickness, poverty, personal misfortune, unhappiness—but held out the assurance of a more abundant life. And the gilded age, though one of aggressive materialism, was also an age of anxious conscience, "reform," determination to achieve a better life. Long before pragmatism expressed it for them, Americans had a conviction that ideals were sound and true if they worked. Miss Addams was the kind of an idealist they understood. Was not Hull House—that social laboratory for the world—a concrete proof of the practical value of her theories? Judging the efficacy of Mrs. Eddy's gospel by its works, they were not put off by its inherent mysticism. Even Mark Twain, implacably hostile as he was, testified to his knowledge of its remarkable cures. For many Americans, less prejudiced but no less practical, Mrs. Eddy's evangel had a strong appeal. To them, it implied the existence of latent powers, previously unknown and untapped, which everyone possessed, could harness and put to work. Furthermore, did it not seem to prove that, by professing the unreality of the material world, they would be able to live in it more prosperously, happily, and fully? Why strain at a paradox? The camel, not the gnat, was the prize. Besides, they were sometimes guiltily aware of an excessive devotion to material values. Conscience might be appeased by the declaration that these, like the world that gave rise to them, were pure illusion.

Mrs. Eddy always repudiated this interpretation of her gospel. The gospel had been born of her sickness, and it included the therapy by which she had been healed. But in what did the therapy consist? Again and again, she asserted that it was a total spiritual regeneration. "Learn this, O mortal, and earnestly seek the spiritual status of man, which is outside of all material selfhood." What, she might have inquired, was the theme of *Science and Health*, if not a quest for conscious union with Principle, with Godhead? The quest was true prayer, "the desire of the heart." And she insisted that "if spiritual sense always guided men, there would grow out of ecstatic moments a higher experience and a better life with more devout self-abnegation and purity." In her youth, Emerson had asserted his conviction that the currents of the Universal Being—the Over-Soul—flowed through him. He had declared himself to be "part or parcel of God." This sense of transcendant union, this perception of identity with the eternal and good, were what Mrs. Eddy meant by the spiritual status of man. It should be man's objective. Not as a means to worldly ends. As an end in itself and the only genuine one.

This doctrine, which affirmed reality rather than denied it, expressed Mrs. Eddy at her best. It was the fruit of her time of desperation. Then, an outcast in the material world, she had sometimes been visited with an intense consciousness of God. So strong had been her sense of God as the ultimate truth of man's being, that it turned all earthly goods to ashes. The experience gleamed darkly in the first edition of her book, lighting its obscurities with flashes of ecstasy. The book brought Bronson Alcott to Lynn, to seek out the unknown sybil. He returned to Concord and spoke of her, as he said, with something akin to wonder and sweet surprise, to a group at Emerson's house, one Sunday evening. Emerson had already heard of the seeress and her book; Mrs. Emerson expressed a wish to meet her. The others listened, without disloyal criticism, to Alcott's account of her.

Did Emerson and Mrs. Eddy ever meet? She once described a secret visit to him, some months before his death, undertaken for the purpose of healing him. He was, she said, as far from accepting Christian Science as a man could be who was a strict moralist. She thought Alcott far in advance of him. As soon as she got into the deep recesses of Emerson's thoughts, she saw that his case was quite hopeless. His mind was failing, then, and he knew it. Replying to one of her questions, he affirmed his belief in the powers of God above all other causation. But he protested that it would be profane to believe that God either could, or wanted to, prevent this result of old age. So what could Mrs. Eddy do?

If the ecstatic seeress and the tranquil sage had received the same revelation, the languages in which they expressed it were strikingly unlike. Mrs. Eddy was always to have a way of her own with words. The meaning of meanings was as immaterial to her as it was later to be to Miss Gertrude Stein. She liked nothing better than to strip words of their accepted connotations and equip them with new ones, and this whimsical pleasure often led to startling results. Adultery, for example, might only signify adulteration of the truth; and belief was error. An equivalent originality characterized her more mystical passages. It was no wonder that Bronson Alcott, equally orphic in his utterance, recognized a kindred spirit. But an increasingly prosaic age was impatient of cryptic gospels. It asked for blunt, unequivocal statement.

When Mrs. Eddy was not being sibylline, she liked to be a genteel Victorian lady. So she finally resolved to capitulate to the disparaging comments of well-bred folk. This decision involved sacrificing the apocalyptic to the refined. A retired Unitarian clergyman was invited to revise *Science and Health*. Dr. James Henry Wiggin was an urbane skeptic who had little taste for Christian Science, but he favored a straightforward prose style. He did not revise; he rewrote. He planed away as much as possible of Mrs. Eddy's exuberant rhetoric, and eliminated, so far as he could, all traces of her visionary ecstasy. As a result of his efforts, Mrs. Eddy no longer spoke like an oracle. To posterity, she sounded more like an argumentative schoolmistress.

Nevertheless, in time, she spoke to the world. And, beyond the seas, she seemed to speak authentically for America. Despite all editing, did she not prove that the great continent, so prodigally endowed with natural resources, could breed its peculiar version of Saint Teresa? Europeans were more likely to ask this than were Americans. For, in general, Americans no longer considered mysticism a mystery. They were inclined to take it in their stride as an aid to efficiency, and many of them hastened to acquire the latest model creed with the latest model car. Mrs. Eddy, already middle-aged when Lincoln entered the White House, had the air of a quaint survivor from the long-vanished past. She seemed to belong to that almost forgotten era when, in isolated New England hamlets, there lived local visionaries who deduced an entire universe from the farms, the church, the store and smithy and millpond that made up their world.

But, representing the historic past, Mrs. Eddy also anticipated the disturbed future. Was there not, in her lurid preoccupation with the problem of evil, a hint of the personal disillusion that was to overtake many Americans, making them view life as a dubious experiment rather than as a challenging opportunity? Mrs. Eddy's theories about evil were the least pleasing elements of her gospel, and they seemed to contradict her genuine vision. But who could say that the vision of later generations of Americans was not equally clouded by fear that the malign in life outweighed the good?

Mrs. Eddy lived in an era that had pledged its faith to reform, to change in external conditions as the means to a better life. Americans oscillated between two notions of how best to achieve the better life. Sometimes they asserted that society cannot be improved unless human nature is changed. At other times, they believed that a change in human nature cannot be brought about without first transforming the social environment in such fashion as to give human nature a chance. In an age dedicated to reform, Mrs. Eddy proclaimed the inadequacy of all purely external change. The better life, she insisted, could be achieved only through a regeneration of the spirit. Against her were arrayed not only the reformers, like Miss Addams, but the liberal clergy, who were seeking to make religion a social gospel. But, by the nineteen-forties, reformers had become less optimistic, and the liberal movement in American religion had come under heavy attack. Religious leaders like Monsignor Fulton Sheen and Dr. Reinhold Niebuhr were once again asserting, as Mrs. Eddy had asserted so long before, that social action is not enough; that the good life will come only when men find themselves at one with God.

None of this would have astonished Mrs. Eddy. In the vast, vague patchwork of her prophecy, she had left room for any far-off divine event that might occur. At the end of her life, she wanted to withdraw from the world, renew her earlier vision; and the world would not let her alone. She never set foot in the Mother Church that had been erected to her glory, perhaps never even saw it. A few months before her death, she asked to be driven into Boston from the suburban mansion to which she had recently moved. Her carriage passed along the Fenway, to afford her a view of the great building. One of her attendants noted that she was overcome with exhaustion. She did not seem to realize where she was. In the flood of tribulations that vexed her last years, did she succeed, as she hoped, in assimilating herself to God? Nobody could say. But the last words she ever wrote, tremblingly scrawled on a slip of paper, expressed a certainty that many Americans of a later day were to envy. The words were: "God is my Life."

[2] HOPE FOR A MIRACLE

For many years, the New Thought movement stimulated Mrs. Eddy to some of her most picturesque denunciations. She condemned it as a perverse and dangerous plagiarism of her own evangel. On the other hand, its founder, Julius A. Dresser, publicly accused her of having plagiarized the doctrines of Phineas Parkhurst Quimby, on which he based New Thought. Quimby was a mental healer of considerable renown in New England, who practiced in Portland, Maine, until the end of the War between the States. Dresser and Mrs. Eddy had been fellow-patients at his clinic, and both had testified to miraculous cures. Dresser remained a loyal disciple, while Mrs. Eddy, absorbing Quimby's theories, inconveniently lost their originator somewhere on the higher levels of her metaphysics. With their thundering recriminations, Dresser and Mrs. Eddy kept the supernatural in continuous upheaval. From this contest in salvation, the quality of mercy was notably absent. But both movements thrived on a prelatical feud. New Thought made its way among the American people almost as rapidly and contagiously as Christian Science.

New Thought, like Christian Science, established itself initially as a form of therapy. Later, it became a secular revelation which contributed to the unofficial American religion of success. It purported to endow converts with "knowledge of the Inward Presence *as power*," and light the way to a "dynamic experience beyond mere meditation and worship." Mere, indeed! Many Americans were still striving to practice them, sometimes in extremely original forms. If already obsolete, to what superior exercises had they yielded? To the pre-chromium era, New Thought brought formulas that were strictly functional. It dealt with specific needs. It promised that the life made concrete through concentration will begin at once to take effect. Was there not a correspondence "between inward need and outward supply"? There most certainly was. Some disagreement developed as to the nature of the laws governing this correspondence. Orthodox apostles defined them as spiritual, preaching "service" and unselfishness as the methods of making potential supply concrete. The newer school postulated mental laws, knowledge of which enabled the convert to dominate circumstance, and they advocated a more single-minded dedication to the elevated experience of prosperity. Both schools affirmed the existence of a boundless source upon which to draw, and agreed that the neophyte could test his progress by the degree to which his results exemplified the fundamental "law of abundance."

Cheerfulness and inexhaustible confidence saturated the dogmas of this new creed. Did this indicate that a growing insecurity, an increasing anxiety and doubt, were beginning to corrode the lives of the plain people? Many Americans hopefully undertook the effort to achieve that dynamic experience in which, a higher activity once received, it may be directed according to need. In meeting halls across the country, they valiantly sought to ascend into an immaterial realm, assimilating power and wisdom without regard to time. Power, in any case. Wisdom sometimes had the look of a shabby consolation prize. At home, they pondered the counsel of Ralph Waldo Trine, who celebrated the esoteric delights of being in tune with the Infinite. Over the years, they bought three million copies of the ebullient gospels of Orison Swett Marden.

Marden harnessed the Infinite to the national vocation of merchandising. He assured the nation that the currents of knowledge, wealth and success are as certain and fixed as the tides of the sea. There was, apparently, a tacit understanding that all tides are incoming; Marden never recognized the existence of an ebb. At the end of a long inspiring career, he summed up his teaching in a message proof against skepticism. The law of prosperity, he declared, is just as definite as the law of gravitation; just as unerring as the principles of mathematics. "It is a mental law. Only by thinking abundance can you realize the abundant prosperous life that is your birthright." When not thinking abundance, the ambitious experimented with subtle thought-waves and vibrations of consciousness. These impalpable forces were no longer occult. They were accurate, and extraordinarily efficient. They could overwhelm the recalcitrance of any customer, irresistibly compel him to sign on the dotted line. It was gratifying to know that this result demonstrated the operation of mental law, not the less reputable power of high-pressure salesmanship. According to the later school of New Thought, failure to make a sale was evidence only of technical bungling; the law was infallible. None of the succeeding apostles ventured to assert, with the movement's earlier evangelists, that salesman, prospect, and goods were alike destitute of real existence.

Times could not be bad for adepts in New Thought. They had only to practice their simple disciplines, and invoke the infinite abundance at their command. They "controlled" their thoughts. They concentrated for an hour daily, actively "visualizing" the success, wealth, and power to which they aspired—obviously only because these bore witness to the attainment of a higher life. Will power could be applied to the receipt of a definite sum of money on a given date; to the negotiation of an advantageous contract at a pre-established time. These possibilities recommended New Thought to Hollywood, where it appeared to "work" especially well, and converts were numerous among the early film colony.

There, during her altruistic cultural mission, Mrs. Elinor Glyn one day sat in her costly hotel suite, unaware that she was about to take the road to apostasy. Long converted to New Thought—which had brought her easy wealth, success, notoriety, even perpetual youth—Mrs. Glyn was devotedly concentrating. She was demanding of the Absolute the immediate delivery of a set of alluring pink chiffon underclothes, seen in a shop window, but priced too high. Apparently, in this instance, the Absolute failed to respond. Subsequent jaundiced reflection, after leaving Hollywood, persuaded Mrs. Glyn that New Thought exacted an extreme penalty for its benefactions. Did it not require the sacrifice of all superior qualities of the soul? Amongst the millionaires of America, were there not many Fausts who had made a bargain with Evil; in Hollywood were there not many Marguerites all too eager for an opulence contrived by black magic? To Mrs. Glyn, her pristine faith now undermined, New Thought, and the other "semi-occult pseudo-religions" which pervaded America, came to represent a deeply sinister element in the nation's life.

Regrettably, Mrs. Eddy did not live to see the rise of Hollywood, a metropolis of illusion that dedicated its nonexistence to the spawning of mirages. For, very appropriately, it was on the periphery of Hollywood that the growing power of women over American spiritual life achieved one of its most impressive demonstrations. During two decades, from her huge Angelus Temple, Mrs. Aimee Semple McPherson —Sister Aimee, "the world's most pulchritudinous evangelist"—implied the possibility of an eventual monopoly in salvation.

The web of enchantment which she cast over a segment of the public was vividly colorful, but it proved also to possess more substantial attributes. It was, so to speak, armor-plated, and its impregnability enabled Sister Aimee to bring about, in the minds of her followers, a revolutionary revision of opinion. They were Fundamentalists; orthodox in religious belief, aggressive conservatives in matters of morals, staunch supporters of the conventional. It was Sister Aimee's remarkable achievement to convince them that a vocation for saving souls does not make personal sanctity indispensable. From what appeared to promise a reluctant but inevitable martyrdom, she was able to retrieve a miracle wrought upon the mores.

Penniless, with two children, Sister Aimee arrived in Los Angeles in 1917, having driven across the continent in a battered jalopy. For the extravagant saga that was to constitute her future, the past had furnished an odd, but not inappropriate preparation. Aimee's mother, a member of the Salvation Army, had married a Canadian farmer. Sister Aimee was born on the farm. In a rural high school, the theory of evolution shook her Fundamentalist faith, but Robert Semple, a handsome Holy Ghoster revivalist, restored its equilibrium. Not illogically, she married him. They were sent to China as missionaries, and he died there. With the assistance of humble, friendly preachers of the faith, she returned to the United States; undertook the vocation of a traveling revivalist after having contracted and dissolved a second marriage. The special creation of man had been the doctrinal basis of her conversion, but man himself was obviously her special, personal problem.

Five years after her unpromising arrival in Los Angeles, Sister Aimee opened Angelus Temple, the tabernacle of her "Four Square Gospel." A squat building, resembling a wedge of white cake, it held fifty-three hundred people, and was filled at every service. Its powerful radio station carried to remote listeners the impassioned sermons of Sister Aimee, the music of a large, white-robed choir, a great organ, a band, an orchestra, and assorted soloists, vocal and instrumental. Sister Aimee, clad in flowing white draperies, carrying an enormous sheaf of roses against her bosom, would slowly move down a ramp while colored lights played on her, until, at the front of the platform, she faced her congregation, her "people" as she called them—the anonymous, devout, conforming, hard-working thousands over whose monotonous lives her blonde, imperious beauty trailed an orgiastic excitement. It need not be resisted; this was God-intoxication. Her uplifted hand could bring them to their feet, make them weep, sing for joy, shout hallelujahs.

No Hollywood studio commanded the services of a showman as expert as Sister Aimee, who sometimes unexpectedly produced an "illustrated sermon," making her entrance, for example, on a motorcycle with blazing headlights and shrieking siren, in the uniform of a traffic cop, to dramatize a dire warning: "Stop! You're speeding to ruin!" Bedlam broke loose at these spectacular, redemptive exhortations. "The secret of success in evangelism," Sister Aimee held, "is to hide your own personality behind the Christ you are preaching, that the world will see no one save Jesus." For that reason, she said, she always tried to be as unostentatious and inconspicuous as possible.

She had theories, too, about her mission. From the day of its dedication, the doors of her temple were never closed, its lights never extinguished. Prayers were conducted, without intermission, in two hour shifts. Volunteers staffed the social services, free employment agency, parole committee, Lonely Club, music department, publishing organization, the Bible school that held sessions day and night. Yet all these varied forth-putting endeavors were, for Sister Aimee, secondary. It was her mission to fill the void, and satisfy the hungry soul, of a lost world. And this, she knew, was not to be done by preaching an historic Christ, a Christ of yesteryear rather than the Christ of the vital, throbbing present.

One gospel alone would meet her needs, and the needs of her "people"—"a Christ who still delivers from sin, heals the sick, strikes off the shackles of dope, breaks down the gates of brass, saws asunder the bars of iron Satan has made, and leads His people to freedom and victory!" This gospel would pack any building in the world and bring multitudes to their feet with radiant faces and uplifted hands, singing the praises of the Lord. Did not her every service prove it? And when she gave the "altar call"—summoning sinners to step out, come down the aisles, publicly declare themselves on the Lord's side—did they not sweep down like a human flood, hundreds, even thousands? Emotionalism? Only the cynical would use this word. For here were people kneeling in surrender to the Lord who, but a few hours earlier, had been headed for destruction on the scintillating primrose pathway! Surely this work would abide when the heavens and the earth had passed away.

Sometimes, her own powers frightened her. Even before the building of Angelus Temple, she had won nationwide celebrity as a "miracle woman," a faith healer. There had been a meeting in the public park of San Diego, to which thirty thousand came: the crippled, the blind, the desperately ailing. And hour after hour, as they passed across her platform in chairs, litters, wheelbarrows, or staggering on their feet, she had laid her hands on them and prayed. There was no lack of miraculous cures. But the mystery, the force that was unpredictable and uncontrollable, alarmed her; so far as possible, she gave up healing.

Yet there seemed to be nothing that she could not do. Fashionably attired, furred, jeweled, every inch a woman of the world, she went forth to view the enemy at first hand, study the methods of Satan in the dance halls and illicit night clubs of the large cities. In Chicago, she spent an interested evening at Bert Kelly's Stables, then added to its popularity by denouncing it as the trap door to hell. In New York, with reporters in attendance, she made a tour of the principal hot spots. Texas Guinan commanded her public to "give this little girl a great big hand." These expeditions, making the headlines, caused her people no dismay. "I believe that there is such faith in Angelus Temple and loyalty to its pastor," she said at one time, "that if an angel from Heaven were to come down and say, 'Sister is not a child of God,' they would not believe it!" And this, too, was frightening. For she surmised that it was not her Four Square Gospel that filled Angelus Temple, and won conversions to the Lord. It was not even Sister Aimee. It was Aimee Semple McPherson, a masterful clerical actress who, if Sister Aimee's gospel was true, was herself speeding to ruin.

One afternoon in May, 1926, Sister Aimee, with her secretary, drove out to a beach where it was her custom to go swimming. She changed into a bathing suit, sat in her tent writing some notes for a sermon, and sent her secretary on an errand. Then she rose, walked down to the shore, and struck out into the Pacific. Nobody saw her again. By nightfall, newspapers over the country were carrying the story of her disappearance, under banner headlines. In Angelus Temple, to an hysterical throng, Aimee's mother announced her death: "She is with Jesus—pray for her!" They did; two thousand moaning, sobbing men and women who kept an all-night vigil. On the following Sunday, five thousand went to the beach, to sing and pray and weep: to await Sister Aimee, who would arise from the waves, and walk upon the waters.

But the press, not given to mysticism, had begun a relentless investigation; a search into facts. Angelus Temple was not only a tabernacle of the Lord. It was a flourishing business enterprise, the private property of Sister Aimee and her mother, who managed its financial affairs. These were not negligible; good-will offerings alone had exceeded a million dollars. There were rumors that mother and daughter had wrangled over money matters. And, presently, there was another rumor. Its subject was a former radio operator at the Temple, a married man, separated from his wife. Sister Aimee had shown a marked interest in him. This was not universally attributed to redemptive zeal. By a strange coincidence, he, too, had disappeared. He reappeared briefly; was immediately lost to view. Hysteria mounted among the people, while the press exploited a sensation. One month after Sister Aimee had vanished, a "memorial service" brought eleven thousand worshipers to the Temple—that shrine without a light. Three days later, Sister Aimee telephoned from a hospital in Douglas, Arizona.

To the world, she told a dramatic story. She had been abducted, drugged, transported to a shack in the Mexican desert. There, held for ransom, she had been subjected to torture. By luck making her escape, she had wandered about the desert, leaving the imprint of her French heels in the burning sand. But, within a day, all this was proved to be pure fantasy. Nevertheless, she asserted it to be true. On her return to Los Angeles, she was greeted by the largest and wildest crowds the city had ever seen. A procession two miles long accompanied her to her home. She took to the radio, and to the Temple platform, to defend her story against the attack of skeptics. She swore to it before a grand jury, which refused to indict her unknown alleged abductors. Then, by a series of mischances, the sordid, pathetic truth came out. She had intended to disappear forever with her lover—hoping by doing so to save, for her people, their faith in her. But her notoriety made this easy escape impossible. So she spent ten idyllic days in an isolated bungalow with him. Then, fearful of discovery, they set out on uneasy wanderings. Finally she had resolved to return, and had invented a legend to account for her absence.

When sufficient information had been accumulated, Sister Aimee was arrested and charged with perjury. Preliminary hearings brought out a mass of unsavory evidence which delighted the cynical. Over the air, and from her Temple, Sister Aimee defended herself. She refuted nothing, denied everything, demanded unquestioning belief. The forces of Satan were conspiring to destroy her; through her, to destroy Christianity itself. Ultimately, though she received no vindication, the case against her was dropped. But was she not a child of

God? The faith of her people was steadfast. Unworldly, devout, morally squeamish, they nevertheless refused to be dismayed, whatever the evidence against her, by proof that Sister Aimee could violate the moral code under which they lived—the code she went on preaching. And she was to try their faith again and again. For her life now proceeded from one sensational scandal to another; and each seemed more discreditable than the one before.

Yet the Temple still drew its thousands, and Sister Aimee continued to make her extraordinary mass conversions. In these, she had long since surpassed her only contemporary rival—William A. Sunday, the former baseball star who for thirty years had been calling sinners to "hit the sawdust trail." It was thought that Sinclair Lewis, in his vitriolic *Elmer Gantry*, had portrayed them both. If this was true, Sister survived his attack. And she also survived the rapid decline of old-fashioned evangelism that followed. After all, why not? Had she not once explained her function to reporters? "I bring spiritual consolation to the middle classes," she told them, "leaving those above to themselves, and those below to the Salvation Army."

Sophisticated Americans, who had a bowing acquaintance with modern science, regarded with supercilious distaste the peculiar forms taken by faith among some of their countrymen. They had been moved to laughter, but also to shame, by the absurd "monkey trial" in Tennessee. Incredible that, in twentieth-century America, the concept of science itself could be brought to the bar of judgment and outlawed! Yet, undeniably, a large segment of the population remained medieval-minded. There were those for whom William Jennings Bryan spoke, and Billy Sunday, and Sister Aimee. There were folk in rural Pennsylvania who existed in perpetual terror of a "hex." In remote Virginia valleys, there were those whose worship required the cherishing of poisonous snakes. Strange cultural backwaters still existed in the world's most advanced and literate civilization, where even the poor had their cars and their radios. Sophisticated Americans found it perplexing that so many of their countrymen continued to live in a world of dark, primitive superstition. In the circumstances, it was somewhat ironical that the most superstitious and medieval of all cults should make its first conquests among the affluent and worldly-wise.

For, in New York City, a new seeress had risen to celebrity, and her cult was destined to play as large a role in the nation's life as that of any latter-day apostle. Her earliest converts were made among the upper classes, but her fame soon spread to the great public. By the mid-nineteen-twenties, an article in a popular magazine, describing her activities but not revealing her identity, attracted some twelve thousand requests for her name and address. By then, she had won legal sanction for her cult, which initially was not only illegal but socially disreputable. Such were her powers and her prestige that she succeeded in having it judicially declared an exact science. As to this, the agreement of scientists in other fields was by no means unanimous. A considerable number of them unkindly persisted in calling it humbug.

In the later years of her career, Miss Evangeline Adams did not suggest the seeress. She had the look of an exceptionally successful businesswoman. She was both. Stout, strong jawed, brisk in her manner, highly efficient in her occult rituals, she gave an impression of extreme practicality. She had long since achieved her ambition to become the best-known astrologer in America. She had already cast the horoscopes of nearly one hundred thousand Americans, many of them very prominent, and nearly all of them prosperous; for her fees were not low. Her mail was stupendous; her telephone was incessantly busy; the stars, she declared ruefully, must help her find more hours of the day and night.

All this represented material achievement, success as the world understood it. But Miss Adams' view of life was mystical. When she discussed what she was pleased to call the oldest of sciences, she managed to make it also seem a metaphysical system. Perhaps it would have been natural in a Bostonian to make a philosophy out of any form of calculation. But Miss Adams, in her youth, had enjoyed somewhat special advantages. She had been brought up within the influence of Miss Elizabeth Stuart Phelps and Mrs. Harriet Beecher Stowe, authoresses who, in their day, had been regarded as holding very advanced views about the supernatural. And the supernatural, though it was Miss Adams' domain, was also her dilemma. In casting her horoscopes, she tacitly acknowledged that destiny was mathematically predictable. Man's life is governed by the unchangeable movement of the planets. The stars, she asserted, make no mistake; they are prophets of almost unbelievable farsightedness. Yet, in Miss Adams, there was a protesting Yankee strain. She rebelled against so inexorable a determinism, as her ancestors had rebelled against the theological doctrine of predestination.

Though there could be no appeal from the Infinite and Inevitable, she succeeded—like William Graham Sumner—in establishing a narrow area of liberty for individual reason and conscience. Man was free, she said, to co-operate with the planets that ruled his destiny. And it was her function to show him how. The horoscope was a problem in mathematics, but its interpretation was an exercise in philosophy. Miss Adams was not only a seeress. She was a spiritual director. "I strive," she said, "by showing God's pattern as I see it in the horoscope and interpreting God's law as I have seen it in my experience, to open the eyes to truth." She did it by the clock, every half hour, every afternoon.

If her attitude to her profession was mystical, that of her clientele was even more so. For most of them, quite obviously, were seeking divination of the future rather than instruction in the appropriate use of free will. And belief in the infallibility of divination could rest only upon pure faith. Yet among her clients, she numbered the elder J. Pierpont Morgan, who had little reputation for credulity, and whose official relations with the supernatural were conducted in the decorous, nonmystical precincts of St. George's in Stuyvesant Square. Miss Adams not only read his horoscope many times; she furnished him with a regular monthly service explaining the changing position of the planets and their probable effect on politics, business, and the stock market. His initial attitude was one of curiosity tinged with suspicion, but this melted away at their first meeting, and in the end the great colossus of finance invited Miss Adams to join him on his yacht in the Orient, for several months of scientific investigation of the occult in those parts of the world where its practice reaches back into prehistoric time. If Morgan—the dominant power in the American economy—did not disdain to make use of divination in working out his projects, what wonder that Miss Adams' clientele also included society women, financiers, farmers' wives, mothers with wayward children, lovers of all ages, presidential candidates, publishers, actors, opera singers, even ministers, priests and rabbis?

By her own account, the problems brought to Miss Adams' mathematical confessional were as varied as the professions of her clients. But she noticed one very significant fact. Most people came to her because, as she put it, they had been temporarily thrown off their spiritual center and cut off from their subconscious selves. They were at odds with their environment; they were victims of the tensions and pressures of modern American life; they wanted a way out of their troubles, a kind of insurance against fate. During thirty years, in addition to her personal consultations, Miss Adams had received thousands of letters. And all of them pleaded for help.

Almost certainly, this indicated not only a growing dissatisfaction with life, but an increasing conviction that the individual could no longer master circumstances, and must therefore invoke the aid of occult forces the existence of which modern science explicitly denied. And the implications of modern science were becoming less and less reassuring. The old sense that the universe was orderly, and ran according to law, was rapidly being made obsolete. What the new physics postulated was a universe pervaded by indeterminism; as one writer described it, a universe without hitching posts. A new principle of uncertainty appeared to be the only certainty that science was now able to affirm. Whether or not they read the findings of the scientists, many Americans began to feel that the old props that had supported their view of life were crumbling. Insecurity had come to be the dominant element of their experience. Instability seemed to be the most striking characteristic of their world. Some shared the pessimism of Dr. Reinhold Niebuhr, who in 1932 predicted that "the middle-class paradise which we built on this continent, and which reached its zenith no later than 1929, will be in decay before the half-century mark is rounded."

Meanwhile, if the confidence of Americans in their environment was diminishing, their faith in themselves, as rational beings capable of controlling it, had also been seriously crippled. The theories of the new psychology had gained a wide circulation. Their import was that man led a life scarcely recognizable as rational. His so-called intelligence, his conscious mind, possessed no mastery. It was a casual lodger in its own house, always under threat of eviction, and usually subject to the dictates of the turbid subconscious. The result of this dismal news was to give immense prestige to the various disciplines of psychoanalysis. Among the affluent, to be analyzed soon became a vogue. It was perhaps significant that many undertook analysis in the same spirit in which they resorted to astrology, or adopted mystical faiths. For the mental life of man now seemed no less a theater of occult forces than his material life, or the life called spiritual. And if it was the part of wisdom to co-operate with the planets in their courses, and to attune oneself to the Infinite, might it not also be wise to come to terms with a trauma?

By the decade of the nineteen-forties, there was abundant evidence that many Americans, suffering from a sense of inadequacy to an environment which they conceived to be unfavorable, if not actively hostile, were turning eagerly to any self-appointed saviors who promised them relief. A social worker and psychologist, Mrs. Lee R. Steiner, after twelve years of investigation, published a report on a large number of the popular spiritual comfort stations. Newspapers offered the syndicated "advice columns" of feminine fountains of wisdom. They also printed daily astrological indications. There were radio oracles who dispensed psychological static. There were graphologists, numerologists, spiritualists. The apostles of homemade cults did an excellent business in what looked like philosophical batik. Beauticians gave courses which implied a promise of psychotherapeutic effects. Professors of public speaking indicated that their subject provided a complete renovation of life. There were many others. And, in addition, there existed a vast body of literature that made explicit the principles of self-transformation—for a mere two dollars and fifty cents you could, for example, become well known to thousands, even millions. All this suggested, in America, a national pageant of troubled souls, endlessly seeking—perpetually hoping for a miracle, confident that miracles were still possible. It was a striking symptom of the mysticism of the middle classes.

In Boston, at the Chardon Street Chapel, a convention was being held. "Madmen, madwomen, men with beards, Dunkers, Muggletonians, Come-outers, Groaners, Agrarians, Seventh-Day Baptists, Quakers, Abolitionists, Calvinists, Unitarians, and Philosophers,— all came successfully to the top, and seized their moment, if not their hour, wherein to chide, or pray, or preach, or protest." For this was a convention of Friends of Universal Reform. The year was 1840, and Ralph Waldo Emerson, with a curiosity about adventures in salvation, attended. The proceedings were, to be sure, rather odd. But they expressed the life and aspirations of the moment. They were modern America.

A century later, they still seemed contemporary.

CONCLUSION

At the End of an Era

THE YEAR 1946 drew to a close, apprehensively. Under the clamor of American life one sensed a tense quiet, like the ominous stillness that presages storm. The plain people were plainly anxious. Pessimism about the state of the world, about the future, stained daily existence. If catastrophe impended, what could anyone do to avert it? The individual felt powerless. A mood of fatalism spread across the land.

Like a canker, disbelief was corroding hope. Never before in its history had the nation been so prosperous. But the people surmised that prosperity would be brief, and high quarters gloomily anticipated the wreck of the gravy train. Having emerged victoriously from a second World War, the United States was the most powerful of nations. But predictions were not lacking that another and more terrible war was inevitable—and, if power could not prevent it, what was the value of power? The machinery of international peace had been set up; a fragile chalice for the world's confidence. On Manhattan Island, towers not yet raised would contain men's last chance to make civilization endure. Were faith and will and skill equal to this challenge? Americans understood its awful gravity. Were they certain that it could be met?

Of one thing, at least, they were sure. An era had ended. In harnessing the basic power of the universe to a bomb, science had abruptly opened a new one. During the old era, men's ingenuity had far outrun their wisdom. If, now, their wisdom could not surpass their ingenuity, and quickly, the new era might be brief indeed. Forty years earlier, a theorist of science—his name then virtually unknown to laymen—had devised an equation for the possible conversion of mass into energy. It was this equation that had engendered the new era. It profoundly altered the nature of the world as men knew it. It had unceremoniously blown humanity into a new habitat. The theorist was aware that often in evolutionary processes a species must adapt to new conditions if it is not to perish. In 1946, he contrived a formula for survival. It was as rigorous as his pregnant equation.

Albert Einstein spoke to Americans in a simple, practical way. If mankind was to survive and move to higher levels, he said, it was obvious that a new kind of thinking had become essential. Science had spawned a danger greater than any that humanity had ever conquered. But the real problem was neither atomic power, nor its mechanisms. The problem was in the minds and hearts of men. Its solution depended upon the ability of men—specifically, of Americans —to change their minds and hearts. For America's temporary possession of the secret of atomic fission laid upon her the tremendous responsibility of leading humanity's effort to surmount the crisis. "When we are clear in heart and mind—only then shall we find courage to surmount the fear that haunts the world."

In these words, Einstein declared the inadequacy of all mechanisms. Nothing less than a new orientation, spiritual and mental, would suffice. And it would have to originate among the American people; soon, while there was still time.

Time alone would prove whether Einstein's formula was as fateful as his equation. But to Americans born within the previous half century, only its terrible urgency was novel. Its meaning had long been familiar. For this meaning was, so to speak, the central theme of the living culture which had nourished the minds and hearts of the American people for fifty years. Almost to the exclusion of any other, it had preoccupied the major creative writers. It had insistently haunted philosophers, social theorists, spiritual leaders, crusaders for reforms, the most conscientious journalists; even the inventors of trivial compensatory creeds. On whatever level one explored the vital culture of the United States during the period from 1896 to 1946, one was likely to find it recording an increasing disillusion. It condemned what actually existed. It affirmed something very different: what ought to be.

It was the culture of an uneasy conscience, and an ideal dissatisfaction. Though its temper ran the gamut from buoyant optimism to sterile pessimism, the extremes were less significant than they appeared to be. In nearly every respect save one, optimists and pessimists agreed. The main issue that divided them was the possibility of change. Optimists asserted that men possess the ability to change themselves and their environment. Pessimists denied this. But both protested against things-as-they-are, and the grounds of their discontent were usually the same.

Thus, American culture represented, in effect, an indictment of the society from which it sprang. This was its most familiar feature, but not its most important one. On its highest level, American culture rose above indictment. It arraigned society, but it also made a vision articulate, and proposed an ideal. It spoke not only for the conscience of the American people, but for their dreams and hopes and aspirations. Indeed, these supplied the only standards of reference upon which its indictment was based. Through American culture there ran the implicit premise that what ought to be, could be. Even pessimists, denying the possibility of change, tacitly accepted the criterion of what ought to be, and used it to discredit the existing state of affairs. Notwithstanding a tone of increasing disenchantment and intensifying censure, American culture seldom relinquished the assumption that men can transform their experience and their environment to accord with their desire. It was probably unique in affirming the ultimate reality of ideals, and the relative, plastic, transient nature of the actual.

Was not this the real source of a disillusion that, over the years, became its most conspicious feature? As early as 1896, there was evident a breach between two sets of standards; those by which American culture judged American society, and those which governed American life as it was actually being lived. As time passed, this breach steadily grew wider. By 1946, the relation between the two sets of standards resembled absolute polarity. For the standards of culture, rooted in dreams and desires, had remained almost fixed. Those of life had drawn further and further away. Culture continued to express what the American people acknowledged to be their genuine aspirations. What wonder that its verdict on American life took the form of a thundering denunciation?

The issue between culture and society was clear. Culture resolutely held to an ethical concept of life. But life itself, in the main, was conducted as a materialistic process. Culture asserted that all mechanisms exist to serve spiritual ends; that so far as they fail to do so, they are being misused. The social order, the economic structure, and even the state are instrumental devices; their object is to produce a wider freedom and more universal welfare in which men may achieve the good life. And the good life is that which completely fulfills the spirit. Why, culture asked, had Americans been betrayed into identifying means with ends? Why had they so complacently sacrificed the needs of the spirit to the uses of purely material progress? Why had they rejected the life of values for the life of mere things? Why had they harnessed their superb transforming instruments to the dollar, instead of to the liberation and enrichment of existence?

By 1946, many Americans had made two discoveries. Their personal experience had confirmed the teaching of their culture. And their consciences assented to the verdict passed by culture on the national life. Had they been guilty of a great abdication? Had they needlessly surrendered the dream of a good life for the illusion of material success?

The national income was estimated at one hundred and seventy-seven billions of dollars. But half of the nation's families, in the time of its greatest prosperity, were living on less than twenty-four hundred dollars a year. A report furnished to the United States Senate indicated that the American economy was dominated by some two hundred gigantic corporations. Of these, ninety-eight were controlled by three families and five financial groups.

"What is the real meaning of this increase in concentration?" Senator James E. Murray inquired. "In my opinion, it lies basically in the fact that concentration is the forerunner of collectivism. It is a fact that every industrialized nation which has become highly concentrated has succumbed to one form or another of collectivism. What right have we to assume that we can automatically escape this historical trend?" Senator Murray went on to utter a warning that had become familiar over fifty years. "If we believe that our system of free enterprise should be preserved, if we believe that the American economy should be the expression of a free society, then we cannot stand idly by and watch the march of monopoly to power. We cannot risk the consequences—for in this struggle, if we are too little and too late, there will be no second chance."

Was the system of free enterprise, so loudly advertised, a sorry illusion, like the goal of material success? Was the free society of America slowly perishing? If the feeling and thought of the American people had darkened, was it not because they were doubtful that they could annul their surrender? Disillusion, with them, had its source in the conviction that they had somehow failed. Their ingenuity had contrived the most efficient transforming instruments that the world had ever known. But their wisdom had not been adequate to the task of making these instruments socially productive; still less, to that of making them serve predominately spiritual ends. Many Americans felt that they were the slaves, not the masters, of their instruments, and knew that this was true failure. Could the failure now be obliterated, or was it already too late? Some Americans—relatively, they were few in number, though noisy in effect—had drifted into an acceptance of determinism. Preaching a revolutionary utopia, they were nevertheless the most pessimistic of all. For, to them, democracy was merely a delusion, and their gospel made the possibility of a free society a lie.

Faith in progress as a benign process had seriously diminished. Fifty years earlier, perhaps with irresponsible optimism, most Americans had assumed that the familiar benefits would continue to accumulate automatically; that American things were bound to ascend to unprecedented magnificence; that progress was as inevitable as gravitation. In 1931, an American summarized the attitude to progress that, fifteen years later, would be held by most of his countrymen. "Perhaps our most progressive step," he declared, "will be the discovery that we have not made so much progress as the clatter of the times would suggest. Certainly there is today a wider and more intelligent recognition of the shortcomings of our civilization than at any previous period in this country, and that is a big step toward something better. . . . We shall go over our economic machine and redesign it, not for the purpose of making something different than what we have, but to make the present machine do what we said it could do." This was not the opinion of a social radical. It was that of Henry Ford, who, more than any other American, had been responsible for the extreme acceleration of progress during the half century.

Did Americans, who had experienced greater progress than any nation in the world, now believe that progress itself, if defined exclusively in material terms, is a myth? If so, surely there was hope for the change of mind and heart that Albert Einstein so eloquently demanded; that the American people, in their current disenchantment, seemed so impatiently to await.

And there *was* hope, even though disenchantment prevailed at the end of the era. Always before, Americans had drawn courage from their culture, and incentive from their experience. The old faiths, for the moment, were inarticulate. But disenchantment was the most persuasive symptom of their survival, for to be disenchanted is to care greatly about the still unrealized ideal. So one felt, under the mood of the time, the pulse of traditional American faiths: faith in the individual, in justice and liberty, in the future; faith in the potential, rather than the actual, as to human nature, society and environment; faith in life itself and its ultimate, intrinsic goodness. Lacking these, would Americans care enough about what ought to be to deplore their actual situation?

They had succumbed to disillusion often before, for the disparity between what is and what ought to be always aggrieved them. Even the most optimistic of all Americans had known his moments of despair. "Society has played out its last stake; it is checkmated. Young men have no hope. Adults stand like day-laborers idle in the streets. None calleth us to labor. The old wear no crown of warm life on their grey hairs. The present generation is bankrupt of principles and hope, as of property. I see that man is not what man should be. He is a treadle of a wheel. He is the tassel at the apron-string of society. He is a money-chest. He is the servant of his belly. This is the causal bankruptcy, this the cruel oppression, that the ideal should serve the actual, that the head should serve the feet. . . ." So wrote Ralph Waldo Emerson in 1837, anticipating the mood of his countrymen more than a century later.

But the mood was itself a challenge, and the challenge could be met—again, as in the past. For one thing every American knew in his heart, though a philosopher had recorded it with wonder. "To be an American," George Santayana had told people across the Atlantic, "is of itself almost a moral condition, an education, and a career."

Bibliography

ADAMS, BROOKS: *America's Economic Supremacy*, The Macmillan Co., 1900. *The Emancipation of Massachusetts: The Dream and the Reality* (Revised and enlarged edition, with a new preface), Houghton, Mifflin Co., 1919. *The Law of Civilization and Decay* (with an introduction by Charles A. Beard), Alfred A. Knopf, 1943. *The Theory of Social Revolutions*, The Macmillan Co., 1913

ADAMS, CHARLES FRANCIS: *Charles Francis Adams 1835–1915: An Autobiography* (with a memorial address by Henry Cabot Lodge), Houghton, Mifflin Co., 1916

ADAMS, EVANGELINE: *The Bowl of Heaven*, Dodd, Mead & Co., 1926

ADAMS, HENRY: *A Cycle of Adams Letters 1861–1865* (edited by Worthington Chauncey Ford) (2 vols), Houghton, Mifflin Co., 1920. *The Degradation of the Democratic Dogma* (with an introduction by Brooks Adams), The Macmillan Co., 1919. *Democracy: An American Novel* (published anonymously), Henry Holt & Co., 1880. *The Education of Henry Adams,* Houghton, Mifflin Co., 1918. *Esther: A Novel* (published under the pseudonym Frances Snow Compton), Henry Holt & Co., 1884. *Henry Adams and His Friends: A Collection of His Unpublished Letters* (compiled, with a biographical introduction, by Harold Dean Cater), Houghton, Mifflin Co., 1947. *History of the United States of America During the First Administration of James Madison* (2 vols), Charles Scribner's Sons, 1890. *History of the United States of America During the First Administration of Thomas Jefferson* (2 vols), Charles Scribner's Sons, 1889. *History of the United States of America During the Second Administration of Thomas Jefferson* (2 vols),

Charles Scribner's Sons, 1890. *History of the United States During the Second Administration of James Madison* (3 vols), Charles Scribner's Sons, 1891. *John Randolph* (American Statesmen Series), Houghton, Mifflin Co., 1882. *The Letters of Henry Adams* (edited by Worthington Chauncey Ford) (2 vols), Houghton, Mifflin Co., 1930–38. *Letters to a Niece, and Prayer to the Virgin of Chartres* with *A Niece's Memories*, by Mabel La Farge, Houghton, Mifflin Co., 1920. *The Life of Albert Gallatin*, J. B. Lippincott, 1879. *The Life of George Cabot Lodge*, Houghton, Mifflin Co., 1911. *Mont-Saint-Michel and Chartres*, Houghton, Mifflin Co., 1913.

ADAMS, HENRY
See also under
   Adams, James Truslow

ADAMS, JAMES TRUSLOW: *The Adams Family*, Little, Brown & Co., 1930. *Henry Adams*, A. & C. Boni, 1933.

ADAMS, MARIAN HOOPER: *The Letters of Mrs. Henry Adams: 1865–1883* (edited by Ward Thoron), Little, Brown & Co., 1936

ADAMS, SAMUEL HOPKINS: *A. Woollcott, His Life and His World*, Reynal & Hitchcock, 1945. *The Great American Fraud*, P. F. Collier & Co., 1905

ADDAMS, JANE: *Twenty Years at Hull House*, The Macmillan Co., 1910. *The Second Twenty Years at Hull House*, The Macmillan Co., 1930

ALLEN, FREDERICK LEWIS: *Only Yesterday*, Harper & Bros., 1931. *Since Yesterday*, Harper & Bros., 1940

ANDERSON, MAXWELL: *Both Your Houses*, Samuel S. French, 1937. *High-Tor*, Dodd, Mead & Co., 1937. *Saturday's Children*, Longmans, Green & Co., 1927. *Winterset*, Dodd, Mead & Co., 1935

ANDERSON, MAXWELL, AND HICKERSON HAROLD: *Gods of the Lightning*, Longmans, Green & Co., 1928

ANDERSON, MAXWELL, AND STALLINGS, LAURENCE: *What Price Glory?*, Harcourt, Brace & Co., 1926

ANDERSON, SHERWOOD: *Hello Towns!*, Horace Liveright, Inc., 1929. *Horses and Men*, B. W. Huebsch, Inc., 1923. *Many Marriages*, B. W. Huebsch, Inc., 1923. *Marching Men*, B. W. Huebsch, 1917. *Memoirs*, Harcourt, Brace & Co., 1942. *Poor White*, B. W. Huebsch, Inc., 1920. *A Story Teller's Story*, B. W. Huebsch, Inc., 1924. *The Triumph of the Egg*, B. W. Huebsch, 1921. *Winesburg, Ohio*, B. W. Huebsch, 1919.

ANDERSON, SHERWOOD
See also under
   Chase, Cleveland B.

ARCHER, WILLIAM: *America Today*, Charles Scribner's Sons, 1899

ARNOLD, THURMAN W.: *The Folklore of Capitalism*, Yale University Press, 1937

AUSTIN, MARY: *Earth Horizon: Autobiography*, Houghton, Mifflin Co., 1932

BAINBRIDGE, JOHN: *Little Wonder: or The Reader's Digest and How It Grew*, Reynal & Hitchcock, 1946

BAKER, RAY STANNARD: *American Chronicle*, Charles Scribner's Sons, 1945

BARRY, PHILIP: *The Animal Kingdom*, Samuel French, 1932. *Here Come the Clowns*, Coward, McCann, 1939. *Holiday*, Samuel French, 1929. *Hotel Universe*, Samuel French, 1930. *Paris Bound*, Samuel French, 1929. *The Philadelphia Story*, Coward, McCann, 1939. *Tomorrow and Tomorrow*, Samuel French, 1931. *White Wings*, Boni and Liveright, 1927. *Without Love*, Coward, McCann, 1943

BARTON, BRUCE: *The Man Nobody Knows: A Discovery of the Real Jesus*, The Bobbs-Merrill Co., 1925

BATES, ERNEST SUTHERLAND, AND DITTEMORE, JOHN T.: *Mary Baker Eddy: The Truth and the Tradition*, Alfred A. Knopf, 1932

BAUDELAIRE, CHARLES
See under Symons, Arthur

BEARD, CHARLES A. AND BEARD, MARY R.: *America in Midpassage*, The

Macmillan Co., 1939. *The American Spirit,* The Macmillan Co., 1942. *The Rise of American Civilization,* The Macmillan Co., 1927

BEER, THOMAS: *The Mauve Decade,* Alfred A. Knopf, 1926. *Stephen Crane: A Study in American Letters* (with an introduction by Joseph Conrad), Alfred A. Knopf, 1923

BEHRMAN, S. N.: *Biography,* Farrar & Rinehart, 1933. *Brief Moment,* Farrar and Rinehart, 1931. *End of Summer,* Random House, 1936. *Meteor,* Brentano's, 1930. *No Time for Comedy,* Random House, 1939. *Rain From Heaven,* Random House, 1943. *The Second Man,* Doubleday, Page & Co., 1927. *The Talley Method,* Random House, 1941. *Wine of Choice,* Random House, 1938

BENNETT, ARNOLD: *Your United States,* Harper & Bros., 1912

BENT, SILAS: *Justice Oliver Wendell Holmes,* The Vanguard Press, 1932

BIDDLE, FRANCIS: *Mr. Justice Holmes,* Charles Scribner's Sons, 1942

BIGELOW, POULTNEY: *Seventy Summers,* Longmans, Green and Co., 1925

BLATCH, HARRIOTT STANTON, AND LUTZ, ALMA: *Challenging Years,* G. P. Putnam's Sons, 1940

BOK, EDWARD: *The Americanization of Edward Bok: The Autobiography of a Dutch Boy Fifty Years After,* Charles Scribner's Sons, 1921. *Twice Thirty: Some Short and Simple Annals of the Road,* Charles Scribner's Sons, 1925. *Perhaps I Am,* Charles Scribner's Sons, 1928

BOURGET, PAUL: *Outre-Mer,* A. Lemerre, 1895

BOWEN, CATHERINE DRINKER: *Yankee From Olympus: Mr. Justice Holmes and His Family,* Little, Brown & Co., 1944

BRADFORD, GAMALIEL: *American Portraits: 1875-1900,* Houghton, Mifflin Co., 1922

BRANDEIS, LOUIS D.: *Business—A Profession* (with a Foreword by Ernest Poole) Small, Maynard & Co., 1914.

The Curse of Bigness (edited by Osmond K. Fraenkel), The Viking Press, 1934. *Other People's Money, and How the Bankers Use It* (Preface by Norman Hapgood), Frederick A. Stokes Co., 1914. *The Social and Economic Views of Mr. Justice Brandeis* (edited by Alfred Lief: foreword by Charles A. Beard), The Vanguard Press, 1930

BRANDEIS, LOUIS D.
See also under
  Frankfurter, Felix
  Lief, Alfred
  Mason, Alpheus Thomas

BRIGHT, JOHN: *Hizzoner Big Bill Thompson,* Jonathan Cape and Harrison Smith, 1930

BROOKS, VAN WYCK: *The Flowering of New England,* E. P. Dutton & Co., 1936. *New England: Indian Summer,* E. P. Dutton & Co., 1940. *The Ordeal of Mark Twain,* E. P. Dutton & Co., 1920. *The Pilgrimage of Henry James,* E. P. Dutton & Co., 1925

BRUNNER, EDMUND DE S. AND KOLB, J. H.: *Rural Social Trends,* The McGraw-Hill Co., 1933

CANBY, HENRY SEIDEL: *The Age of Confidence: Life in the 'Nineties,* Farrar & Rinehart, 1934

CARLSON, OLIVER: *Brisbane: A Candid Biography,* Stackpole Sons, 1937

CARLSON, OLIVER AND BATES, ERNEST SUTHERLAND: *Hearst, Lord of San Simeon,* The Viking Press, 1936

CARNEGIE, ANDREW: *Autobiography,* Houghton, Mifflin Co., 1920. *Triumphant Democracy: Fifty Years of the Republic,* Charles Scribner's Sons, 1886

CARTER, MORRIS: *Isabella Stewart Gardner and Fenway Court,* Houghton, Mifflin Co., 1925

CATHER, WILLA S.: *Lucy Gayheart,* Alfred A. Knopf, 1935. *My Antonia,* Houghton, Mifflin Co., 1918. *My Mortal Enemy,* Alfred A. Knopf, 1936. *Obscure Destinies,* Alfred A. Knopf, 1932. *One of Ours,* Alfred A. Knopf, 1922. *O, Pioneers!,* Houghton, Mifflin Co., 1913. *The Professor's House*, Alfred A. Knopf, 1925. *The Song of the Lark*, Houghton, Mifflin Co., 1915. *Youth and the Bright Medusa*, Alfred A. Knopf, 1920

CATHER, WILLA S.
See also under
Rapin, René

CATT, CARRIE CHAPMAN AND SHULER, NETTIE ROGERS: *Woman Suffrage and Politics*, Charles Scribner's Sons, 1923

CHANLER, MRS. WINTHROP: *Autumn in the Valley*, Little, Brown & Co., 1936. *Roman Spring*, Little, Brown & Co., 1934

CHAPMAN, JOHN JAY: *Memories and Milestones*, Moffat, Yard & Co., 1935

CHASE, CLEVELAND B.: *Sherwood Anderson*, Robert M. McBride & Co., 1927

CLARK, BARRETT H.: *Eugene O'Neill*, Robert M. McBride & Co., 1926

CLEMENS, SAMUEL LANGHORNE
See under Twain, Mark

CLEMENS, CLARA: *My Father Mark Twain*, Harper and Bros., 1931

CLEMENS, CYRIL: *My Cousin Mark Twain*, Rodale Press, 1939

CLEMENT, LILLIAN SYMES AND CLEMENT, TRAVERS: *Rebel America*, Harper & Bros., 1934

CLEWS, HENRY: *Fifty Years in Wall Street*, Irving Publishing Co., 1908

CLOUGH, FRANK C.: *William Allen White of Emporia*, Whittlesey House, 1941

CLURMAN, HAROLD: *The Fervent Years*, Alfred A. Knopf, 1945

COHN, DAVID L.: *The Good Old Days: A History of American Morals and Manners as Seen Through the Sears, Roebuck Catalogues, 1905 to the Present* (introduction by Sinclair Lewis), Simon and Schuster, 1940

COLBY, NATHALIE SEDGWICK: *Remembering*, Little, Brown & Co., 1938

CONWELL, RUSSELL H.: *Acres of Diamonds*, Harper & Bros., 1915

COOKE, DELMAR GROSS: *William Dean Howells: A Critical Study*, E. P. Dutton & Co., 1922

COREY, ARTHUR: *Christian Science Class Instruction*, The Parallon Press, 1945

CORTISSOZ, ROYAL: *John La Farge: A Memoir and a Study*, Houghton, Mifflin Co., 1911. *Life of Whitelaw Reid* (2 vols), Charles Scribner's Sons, 1921

CRANE, STEPHEN: *The Work of Stephen Crane* (edited by Wilson Follett) (12 vols), Alfred A. Knopf, 1925-6

CREELMAN, JAMES: *On the Great Highway*, Lathrop Publishing Co., 1901

CROLY, HERBERT: *The Promise of American Life*, The Macmillan Co., 1909

CURTI, MERLE: *The Growth of American Thought*, Harper & Bros., 1943

DAKIN, EDWIN FRANDEN: *Mrs. Eddy: The Biography of a Virginal Mind*, Charles Scribner's Sons, 1929

DARROW, CLARENCE: *The Story of My Life*, Charles Scribner's Sons, 1932

DAVIS, ELMER: *History of the New York Times: 1851-1921*, The New York Times, 1921

DAVIS, ROBERT H. AND MAURICE, ARTHUR B.: *The Caliph of Bagdad*, D. Appleton & Co., 1931

DECIES, ELIZABETH, LADY: See, Lehr, Elizabeth Drexel

DESTI, MARY: *The Untold Story: The Life of Isadora Duncan*, H. Liveright, 1929

DEWEY, JOHN: *Democracy and Education*, The Macmillan Co., 1916. *Education Today* (edited and with a foreword by Joseph Ratner), G. P. Putnam's Sons, 1940. *Experience and Nature*, Open Court Publishing Co., 1925. *Individualism Old and New*, Minton, Balch and Co., 1930. *Liberalism and Social Action*, G. P. Putnam's Sons, 1935. *Philosophy and Civilization*, Minton, Balch & Co., 1931. *Problems of Men*, Philosophical Library, 1946. *The Public and Its Problems*, Henry Holt & Co., 1927. *The Quest for Certainty*, Minton, Balch & Co., 1929. *School and Soci-*

ety, University of Chicago Press, 1909

DEWEY, JOHN AND DEWEY, EVELYN: *Schools of Tomorrow,* E. P. Dutton and Co., 1915

DEWEY, JOHN
See also under
Hook, Sidney
National Committee for the Celebration of the 70th birthday of John Dewey

DE VOTO, BERNARD: *Mark Twain at Work,* Harvard University Press, 1942. *Mark Twain's America,* Little, Brown & Co., 1932

DICTIONARY OF AMERICAN BIOGRAPHY: 21 volumes, Charles Scribner's Sons, 1928–37

DORFMAN, JOSEPH: *Thorstein Veblen and His America,* The Viking Press, 1934

DORR, RHETA CHILDE: *What Eight Million Women Want,* Small, Maynard & Co., 1910

DRAPER, MURIEL: *Music at Midnight,* Harper & Bros., 1929

DREISER, THEODORE: *A Book About Myself,* Boni & Liveright, Inc., 1922. *The Bulwark,* Doubleday & Co., Inc., 1946. *Chains,* Boni and Liveright, 1927. *Dawn,* Horace Liveright, Inc., 1931. *The Financier,* Harper & Bros., 1912. *Free and Other Stories,* Boni & Liveright, 1918. *A Gallery of Women* (2 vols), Horace Liveright, 1929. *The "Genius,"* John Lane Co., 1915. *Jennie Gerhardt,* Harper & Bros., 1911. *The Titan,* John Lane Co., 1914. *Twelve Men,* Boni & Liveright, 1919. *Sister Carrie,* Boni & Liveright, 1925

DRESSER, HORATIO W.: *A History of the New Thought Movement,* Thomas Y. Crowell Co., 1919. (Editor): *The Quimby Manuscripts,* Thomas Y. Crowell Co., 1921. *Spiritual Health and Healing,* Thomas Y. Crowell Co., 1922

DUMESNIL, MAURICE: *An Amazing Journey,* I. Washburn, 1932

DUNCAN, IRMA AND MACDOUGALL, AL-

LAN ROSS: *Isadora Duncan's Russian Days,* Covici-Friede, 1929

DUNCAN, ISADORA: *My Life,* Boni and Liveright, 1927

DUNCAN, ISADORA
See also under
Desti, Mary
Dumesnil, Maurice
Duncan, Irma
Kinel, Lola

DUPEE, F. W.: *The Question of Henry James: A Collection of Critical Essays,* Henry Holt & Co., 1945

EDDY, MARY BAKER G.: *Retrospection and Introspection,* Allison V. Stewart, 1908 (first published in 1891). *Science and Health With Key to the Scriptures,* Allison V. Stewart, 1913. *Science and Health,* in the first edition of 1875, has been photographically reproduced. It was read, in this form, for the present book. *The Unity of Good and Unreality of Evil,* published by the author, 1891.

EDDY, MARY BAKER
See also under
Bates, Ernest Sutherland and Dittemore, John T.
Dakin, Edwin Franden
Haushalter, Walter M.
Milmine, Georgine
Wilbur, Sybil

EINSTEIN, IZZY: *Prohibition Agent No. 1* (introduction by Stanley Walker), Frederick A. Stokes & Co., 1932

ELLIOTT, MAUD HOWE: *This Was My Newport,* Mythology Co., 1944. *Uncle Sam Ward and His Circle,* The Macmillan Co., 1938

ELLIOTT, MAUD HOWE
See also under
Richards, Laura E.

ELLIS, WILLIAM J.: *"Billy" Sunday: The Man and His Message,* no publisher listed: copyrighted, L. T. Myers, 1914

"Entertaining a Nation: The Career of Long Branch," American Guide Series, n. d.

ERNST, MORRIS L.: *The First Freedom,* The Macmillan Co., 1946

ERSKINE, JOHN: *The Influence of Women and Its Cure*, The Bobbs-Merrill Co., 1936

FARRELL, JAMES T.: *A World I Never Made*, The Vanguard Press, 1936. *Father and Son*, The Vanguard Press, 1940. *The League of Frightened Philistines*, The Vanguard Press, 1945. *My Days of Anger*, The Vanguard Press, 1943. *No Star Is Lost*, The Vanguard Press, 1938. *A Note on Literary Criticism*, The Vanguard Press, 1936. *Studs Lonigan: A Trilogy*, The Modern Library, 1938

FAULKNER, HAROLD UNDERWOOD: *The Quest for Social Justice, 1898–1914*, The Macmillan Co., 1931

FAULKNER, WILLIAM: *The Portable Faulkner* (edited with an introduction by Malcolm Cowley) The Viking Press, 1946. *Absalom, Absalom!*, Random House, 1936. *The Hamlet*, Random House, 1940. *Sanctuary*, Cape & Smith, 1931. *These Thirteen*, Cape & Smith, 1931

FELS, MARY: *Joseph Fels: His Life Work*, B. W. Huebsch, 1916

FERBER, EDNA: *A Peculiar Treasure*, Doubleday, Doran, 1939

FILLER, LOUIS: *Crusaders for American Liberalism*, Harcourt, Brace & Co., 1939

FIRKINS, OSCAR W.: *William Dean Howells*, Harvard University Press, 1924

FITCH, CLYDE: *Plays* (Four Volumes), (edited with an introduction by Montrose J. Moses and Virginia Gerson) Little, Brown & Co., 1915.

FITCH, CLYDE
See also under Moses, Montrose J.

FITZGERALD, F. SCOTT: *The Portable F. Scott Fitzgerald* (selected by Dorothy Parker; introduction by John O'Hara) The Viking Press, 1945. *The Crack-up* (edited by Edmund Wilson), New Directions Press. n.d. (1945). *The Last Tycoon: An Unfinished Novel*, Charles Scribner's Sons, 1941. *This Side of Paradise*, Charles Scribner's Sons, 1920

FLEXNER, ELEANOR: *American Playwrights: 1918–1938*, Simon and Schuster, 1938

FLYNT, JOSIAH: *My Life* (introduction by Arthur Symons), Outing Publishing Co., 1908. *The World of Graft*, McClure, Phillips & Co., 1901

FLYNT, JOSIAH AND HODDER, A.: *The Powers That Prey*, McClure, Phillips & Co., 1900

FOWLER, GENE: *The Great Mouthpiece: A Life Story of William J. Fallon*, Covici-Friede, 1931

FRANKFURTER, FELIX: (editor) *Mr. Justice Brandeis*, Yale University Press, 1932. *Mr. Justice Holmes and the Supreme Court*, Harvard University Press, 1938

GABRIEL, RALPH HENRY: *The Course of American Democratic Thought: An Intellectual History Since 1815*, The Ronald Press Co., 1940

GIBBS, WOLCOTT: *Bed of Neuroses*, Dodd, Mead and Co., 1937

GILMAN, CHARLOTTE PERKINS: *The Living of Charlotte Perkins Gilman: An Autobiography*, D. Appleton-Century Co., 1935

GLYN, ELINOR: *Romantic Adventure* (Autobiography), E. P. Dutton & Co., Inc., 1937

GOLDMAN, EMMA: *Living My Life*, Alfred A. Knopf, 1931

GOLDWATER, ROBERT AND TREVES, MARCO: *Artists on Art*, Pantheon Books, Inc., 1945

GRANT, ROBERT: *Fourscore: An Autobiography*, Houghton Mifflin Co., 1934

GRATTAN, C. HARTLEY: *The Three Jameses*, Longmans, Green and Co., 1932

HAPGOOD, HUTCHINS: *A Victorian in the Modern World*, Harcourt, Brace & Co., 1939

HAPGOOD, NORMAN: *The Changing Years*, Farrar & Rinehart, 1930

HAPGOOD, NORMAN AND MOSKOWITZ, HENRY: *Up From the City Streets: Alfred E. Smith*, Harcourt, Brace & Co., 1927

HARLAND, MARION (MRS. M. V. TER-HUNE): *Talks Upon Practical Subjects,* The Warner Brothers Co., 1895

HARRIMAN, MRS. J. BORDEN: *From Pinafores to Politics,* Henry Holt & Co., 1923

HARRISON, MRS. BURTON (CONSTANCE CARY HARRISON): *Recollections Grave & Gay,* Charles Scribner's Sons, 1911. *The Well Bred Girl in Society,* Curtis Publishing Co., 1898

HAUSHALTER, WALTER M.: *Mrs. Eddy Purloins From Hegel,* A. A. Beauchamp, 1936

HAY, JOHN: *The Breadwinners: A Social Study* (published anonymously), Harper and Bros., 1905 (copyrighted 1883)

HEMINGWAY, ERNEST: *For Whom the Bell Tolls,* Charles Scribner's Sons, 1940. *In Our Time,* Boni & Liveright, 1925. *Men Without Women,* Charles Scribner's Sons, 1927. *The Sun Also Rises,* Charles Scribner's Sons, 1926. *To Have & Have Not,* Charles Scribner's Sons, 1937

HENDRICK, BURTON J. *The Story of Life Insurance,* McClure, Phillips & Co., 1907. *The Age of Big Business* (Chronicles of America, vol 39) Yale University Press, 1919

HENRY, O: *Cabbages and Kings,* McClure, Phillips & Co., 1904. *The Four Million,* McClure, Phillips & Co., 1906. *The Gentle Grafter,* The McClure Co., 1908. *Heart of the West,* The McClure Co., 1907. *Options,* Harper & Bros., 1909. *Roads of Destiny,* Doubleday, Page & Co., 1909. *Rolling Stones,* Doubleday, Page & Co., 1912. *Sixes and Sevens,* Doubleday, Page & Co., 1911. *Strictly Business,* Review of Reviews Co., 1913. *The Trimmed Lamp,* McClure, Phillips & Co., 1907. *The Voice of the City,* The McClure Co., 1908. *Whirligigs,* Doubleday, Page & Co., 1910

HENRY, O.
See also under
Davis, Robert H. and Maurice, Arthur B.

Jennings, Al
Smith, C. Alphonso

HINSHAW, DAVID: *A Man From Kansas: The Story of William Allen White,* G. P. Putnam's Sons, 1945

HOLMES, OLIVER WENDELL: *Justice Oliver Wendell Holmes, His Book Notices & Uncollected Letters and Papers* (edited by Harry Clair Shriver), Central Book Co., 1936. *Collected Legal Papers of Oliver Wendell Holmes* (edited by Harold J. Laski), Harcourt, Brace & Co., 1920. *The Common Law,* Little, Brown & Co., 1881. *The Dissenting Opinions of Mr. Justice Holmes* (arranged with introductory notes by Alfred Lief), The Vanguard Press, 1929. *The Holmes-Pollock Letters* (edited by Mark De Wolfe Howe) (2 vols) Harvard University Press, 1941. *Representative Opinions of Mr. Justice Holmes* (arranged with introductory notes by Alfred Lief), The Vanguard Press, 1931. *Speeches,* Little, Brown & Co., 1913.

HOLMES, OLIVER WENDELL
See also under
Bent, Silas
Biddle, Francis
Bowen, Catherine Drinker
Frankfurter, Felix

HOLT, HENRY: *Garrulities of an Octogenarian Editor,* Houghton, Mifflin Co., 1923

HOOK, SIDNEY: *John Dewey: An Intellectual Portrait,* The John Day Co., 1939

HOWARD, SIDNEY: *Alien Corn,* Charles Scribner's Sons, 1933. *The Ghost of Yankee Doodle,* Charles Scribner's Sons, 1938. *Half Gods,* Charles Scribner's Sons, 1930. *Lucky Sam McCarver,* Charles Scribner's Sons, 1926. *Ned McCobb's Daughter,* Charles Scribner's Sons, 1926. *The Silver Cord,* Charles Scribner's Sons, 1927. *They Knew What They Wanted,* Doubleday, Page & Co., 1925

HOWARD, SIDNEY AND DE KRUIF, PAUL:

Yellow Jack, Harcourt, Brace & Co., 1934

Howe, Frederick C.: *The Confessions of a Reformer,* Charles Scribner's Sons, 1925

Howells, Mildred: *Life in Letters of William Dean Howells* (2 vols), Doubleday, Doran & Co., 1928

Howells, William Dean: *Between the Dark and the Daylight: Romances,* Harper & Bros., 1907. *Bride Roses: A Scene,* Houghton, Mifflin Co., 1900. *Certain Delightful English Towns: With Glimpses of the Pleasant Country Between,* Harper & Bros., 1906. *The Daughter of the Storage, and Other Things in Prose and Verse,* Harper & Bros., 1916. *The Day of Their Wedding,* Harper & Bros., 1896. *Familiar Spanish Travels,* Harper & Bros., 1913. *Fennel and Rue: A Novel,* Harper & Bros., 1908. *The Flight of Pony Baker: a Boy's Town Story,* Harper & Bros., 1902. *Heroines of Fiction* (2 vols), Harper & Bros., 1901. *Hither and Thither in Germany,* Harper & Bros., 1920. *Imaginary Interviews,* Harper & Bros., 1910. *Impressions and Experiences,* Harper & Bros., 1896. *An Indian Giver: A Comedy,* Houghton, Mifflin Co., 1900. *The Kentons: A Novel,* Harper & Bros., 1902. *The Landlord at Lion's Head,* Harper & Bros., 1897. *The Leatherwood God,* The Century Co., 1916. *Letters Home,* Harper & Bros., 1903. *Literary Friends and Acquaintances: A Personal Retrospect of American Authorship,* Harper & Bros., 1900. *Literature and Life: Studies,* Harper & Bros., 1902. *London Films,* Harper & Bros., 1905. *Miss Bellard's Inspiration,* Harper & Bros., 1905. *The Mother and the Father: Dramatic Passages,* Harper & Bros., 1909. *Mrs. Farrell: A Novel* (with an introduction by Mildred Howells), Harper & Bros., 1921. *My Mark Twain: Reminiscences and Criticisms,* Harper & Bros., 1910. *New Leaf Mills: A Chronicle,* Harper & Bros., 1913. *An Open-Eyed Conspiracy: an Idyl of Saratoga,* Harper & Bros., 1897. *A Pair of Patient Lovers,* Harper & Bros., 1901. *A Parting and a Meeting: Story,* Harper & Bros., 1896. *Parting Friends: A Farce,* Harper & Bros., 1911. *A Previous Engagement: Comedy,* Harper & Bros., 1897. *Questionable Shapes,* Harper & Bros., 1903. *Ragged Lady: A Novel,* Harper & Bros., 1899. *Roman Holidays, and Others,* Harper & Bros., 1908. *Room Forty-five: A Farce,* Houghton, Mifflin Co., 1900. *The Seen and Unseen at Stratford-On-Avon: A Fantasy,* Harper & Bros., 1914. *Their Silver Wedding Journey* (2 vols) Harper & Bros., 1899. *Seven English Cities,* Harper & Bros., 1909. *The Smoking Car: A Farce,* Houghton, Mifflin Co., 1900. *The Son of Royal Langbrith: A Novel,* Harper & Bros., 1904. *The Story of a Play: A Novel,* Harper & Bros., 1898. *Through the Eye of the Needle: A Romance with an Introduction,* Harper & Bros., 1907. *The Vacation of the Kelwyns,* Harper & Bros., 1920. *Years of My Youth,* Harper & Bros., 1916. *A Traveller from Altruria,* Harper & Bros., 1894

Howells, William Dean
See also under
    Cooke, Delmar Gross
    Firkins, Oscar W.
    Howells, Mildred

Hunter, Robert: *Poverty,* The Macmillan Co., 1904

Huxley, Aldous: *After Many a Summer Dies the Swan,* Harper & Bros., 1939

Ireland, Alleyne: *Joseph Pulitzer: Reminiscences of a Secretary,* Mitchell Kennerley, 1914

Irwin, Will: *The Making of a Reporter,* G. P. Putnam's Sons, 1942

James, Alice: *Alice James: Her Brothers, Her Journal* (edited, with an introduction, by Anna Robeson Burr), Dodd, Mead and Co., 1934.

JAMES, HENRY: *The Ambassadors,* Harper & Bros., 1903. *The American Scene,* Chapman and Hall, London, 1907. Harper & Bros., 1907. (Reissued with additional material, and introduction by W. H. Auden), Charles Scribner's Sons, 1946. *The Art of the Novel* (critical prefaces, with an introduction by Richard P. Blackmur), Charles Scribner's Sons, 1934. *The Awkward Age,* Harper & Bros., 1899. *The Better Sort,* Charles Scribner's Sons, 1903. *The Bostonians,* The Macmillan Co., 1886. *Embarrassments,* The Macmillan Co., 1896. *English Hours,* Houghton, Mifflin Co., 1905. *The Finer Grain,* Charles Scribner's Sons, 1910. *The Golden Bowl,* Charles Scribner's Sons, 1904. *In the Cage,* Herbert S. Stone, 1898. *Italian Hours,* Houghton, Mifflin Co., 1909. *The Letters of Henry James* (selected and edited by Percy Lubbock) (2 vols), Charles Scribner's Sons, 1920. *The Middle Years,* Charles Scribner's Sons, 1917. *Notes of a Son and Brother,* Charles Scribner's Sons, 1914. *Notes on Novelists,* Charles Scribner's Sons, 1914. *The Novels and Tales of Henry James* (The New York Edition) (24 volumes), Charles Scribner's Sons, 1908–1909. *The Other House,* The Macmillan Co., 1896. *The Outcry,* Charles Scribner's Sons, 1911. *The Question of Our Speech: The Lesson of Balzac,* Houghton, Mifflin Co., 1905. *The Sacred Fount,* Charles Scribner's Sons, 1901. *A Small Boy and Others,* Charles Scribner's Sons, 1913. *The Soft Side,* The Macmillan Co., 1900. *The Spoils of Poynton,* Houghton, Mifflin Co., 1897. *The Two Magics,* The Macmillan Co., 1898. *Washington Square,* Harper & Bros., 1881. *What Maisie Knew,* Herbert S. Stone, 1897. *William Wetmore Story and His Friends* (2 vols), Houghton, Mifflin Co., 1903. *The Wings of the Dove,* Charles Scribner's Sons, 1902

JAMES, HENRY
See also under
Brooks, Van Wyck
Dupee, F. W.
Grattan, C. Hartley
Matthiessen, F. O.
West, Rebecca

JAMES, WILLIAM: *The Letters of William James* (edited by his son, Henry James) (2 vols), The Atlantic Monthly Press, 1920. *Memories & Studies,* Longmans, Green & Co., 1911. *On Vital Reserves,* Henry Holt & Co., 1911. *Pragmatism: A New Name for Some Old Ways of Thinking,* Longmans, Green & Co., 1907. *The Principles of Psychology* (2 vols), Henry Holt & Co., 1890. *The Varieties of Religious Experience,* Longmans, Green & Co., 1902. *The Will to Believe: and Other Essays in Popular Philosophy,* Longmans, Green & Co., 1897

JAMES, WILLIAM
See also under
Perry, Ralph Barton

JENNINGS, AL: *Through the Shadows with O. Henry,* The H. K. Fly Co., 1921

JOHNSON, GERALD W.: *An Honorable Titan: A Biographical Study of Adolph S. Ochs,* Harper & Bros., 1946

JOHNSON, TOM L.: *My Story* (edited by Elizabeth J. Hauser), B. W. Huebsch, 1911

JONES, MARY HARRIS: *The Autobiography of "Mother" Jones* (introduction by Clarence Darrow), Charles H. Kerr & Co., 1935

JOSEPHSON, MATTHEW: *The Robber Barons,* Harcourt, Brace & Co., 1934

KARDINER, ABRAM: *The Psychological Frontiers of Society* (with the collaboration of Ralph Linton, Cora Du Bois, and James West), Columbia University Press, 1945

KAUFMAN, GEORGE S.: *The Butter and Egg Man,* Boni and Liveright, 1926

KAUFMAN, GEORGE S. AND CONNELLY, MARC: *Beggar on Horseback,* Boni and Liveright, 1924. *Dulcy,* G. P.

Putnam's Sons, 1921. *To the Ladies,* Samuel French, 1923

KAUFMAN, GEORGE S. AND FERBER, EDNA: *Dinner at Eight,* Doubleday, Doran and Co., 1932. *The Royal Family,* Doubleday, Doran and Co., 1928

KAUFMAN, GEORGE S. AND HART, MOSS: *The American Way,* Random House, 1939. *The Man Who Came to Dinner,* Random House, 1939. *Merrily We Roll Along,* Random House, 1934. *Once in a Lifetime,* Samuel French, 1933. *You Can't Take It With You,* Farrar and Rinehart, 1937.

KAUFMAN, GEORGE S. AND RYSKIND, MORRIE: *Of Thee I Sing,* Alfred A. Knopf, 1933

KELLER, A. C.: *Reminiscences of William Graham Sumner,* Yale University Press, 1933

KELLY, FLORENCE FINCH: *Flowing Stream,* E. P. Dutton & Co., 1939

KELLY, GEORGE: *Behold the Bridegroom,* Little, Brown & Co., 1928. *Craig's Wife,* Little, Brown & Co., 1926. *Daisy Mayme,* Little, Brown & Co., 1927. *The Show-Off,* Samuel S. French, 1924. *The Torchbearers,* Samuel S. French, 1924

KILDARE, OWEN: *My Mamie Rose: The Story of My Regeneration,* The Baker and Taylor Co., 1903

KINEL, LOLA: *This Is My Affair,* Little, Brown & Co., 1937

KOLODIN, IRVING: *The Metropolitan Opera: 1883–1935,* Oxford University Press, 1936

KRUTCH, JOSEPH WOOD: *The American Drama Since 1918,* Random House, 1939

LAWSON, THOMAS W.: *Frenzied Finance: Vol. I, The Crime of the Amalgamated,* The Ridgway-Thayer Co., 1905. *Friday the Thirteenth,* Doubleday, Page & Co., 1907

LAWTON, MARY: *A Lifetime with Mark Twain: the Memories of Katy Leary,* Harcourt, Brace & Co., 1925

LEARNED, ELLIN CRAVEN (MRS. FRANK LEARNED): *The Etiquette of New York Today,* F. A. Stokes & Co., 1906

LEHR, ELIZABETH DREXEL (ELIZABETH, LADY DECIES): *"King" Lehr and the Gilded Age,* J. B. Lippincott Co., 1935. *Turn of the World,* J. B. Lippincott Co., 1937

LEWIS, SINCLAIR: *Arrowsmith,* Harcourt, Brace & Co., 1925. *Babbitt,* Harcourt, Brace & Co., 1922. *Cass Timberlane,* Random House, Inc., 1945. *Dodsworth,* Harcourt, Brace & Co., 1929. *Elmer Gantry,* Harcourt, Brace & Co., 1927. *The Innocents,* Harper & Bros., 1917. *The Job,* Harper & Bros., 1917. *Main Street,* Harcourt, Brace & Co., 1920. *Our Mr. Wrenn,* Harper & Bros., 1914. *The Prodigal Parents,* Doubleday, Doran & Co., 1938

LEWIS, SINCLAIR
See also under
  Van Doren, Carl

LIEF, ALFRED: *Brandeis—The Personal History of an American Ideal,* Stackpole Sons, 1936

LINDSEY, BEN B.: *The Dangerous Life* (edited by Rube Borough), Horace Liveright, Inc., 1931

LINDSEY, BEN B. AND EVANS, WAINWRIGHT: *The Companionate Marriage,* Boni and Liveright, 1927. *The Revolt of Modern Youth,* Boni and Liveright, 1925

LINDSEY, BEN B. AND O'HIGGINS, HARVEY: *The Beast,* Doubleday, Page & Co., 1910

LODGE, HENRY CABOT: *Early Memories,* Charles Scribner's Sons, 1913

LONDON, CHARMIAN: *The Book of Jack London* (2 vols), The Century Co., 1921

LONDON, JACK: *The Call of the Wild,* The Macmillan Co., 1903. *The Iron Heel,* The Macmillan Co., 1908. *John Barleycorn,* The Century Co., 1913. *Martin Eden,* The Macmillan Co., 1909. *The People of the Abyss,* The Macmillan Co., 1903. *Revolution,* The Macmillan Co., 1910. *The Road,* The Macmillan Co., 1907. *The Sea Wolf,* The Macmillan Co., 1904. *The*

Son of the Wolf, Houghton, Mifflin Co., 1900. *War of the Classes,* The Macmillan Co., 1905

LONDON, JACK AND STRUNSKY, ANNA: *The Kempton-Wace Letters,* The Macmillan Co., 1903

LONDON, JACK
See also under
London, Charmian
London, Joan
Stone, Irving

LONDON, JOAN: *Jack London and His Times: An Unconventional Biography,* Doubleday, Doran & Co., 1939

LUNDBERG, FERDINAND: *Imperial Hearst: A Social Biography* (with a preface by Charles A. Beard), Equinox Co-operative Press, 1936

LYND, ROBERT S. AND LYND, HELEN MERRELL: *Middletown,* Harcourt, Brace & Co., 1929. *Middletown in Transition,* Harcourt, Brace & Co., 1937

MCALLISTER, WARD: *Society as I Have Found It,* Cassell Publishing Co., 1890

MCCLURE, S. S.: *My Autobiography,* Frederick A. Stokes & Co., 1914

MCKENZIE, R. D.: *The Metropolitan Community,* The McGraw-Hill Co., 1933

MCPHERSON, AIMEE SEMPLE: *In the Service of the King: The Story of My Life,* Boni and Liveright, 1927

MCPHERSON, AIMEE SEMPLE
See also under
Mavity, Nancy Barr

MANTLE, BURNS: *American Playwrights of Today,* Dodd, Mead & Co., 1929

MARBURY, ELISABETH: *My Crystal Ball: Reminiscences,* Boni and Liveright, 1924

MARCOSSON, ISAAC F. AND FROHMAN, DANIEL: *Charles Frohman: Manager and Man,* Harper & Bros., 1916

MARDEN, ORISON SWETT: *Character: The Grandest Thing in the World,* T. Y. Crowell & Co., 1899. *Every Man a King: Or Might in Mind Mastery,* T. Y. Crowell & Co., 1906. *Getting On,* T. Y. Crowell & Co., 1910. *The Miracle of Right Thought,* T. Y. Crowell & Co., 1910. *The Optimistic Life,* T. Y. Crowell & Co., 1907. *Pushing to the Front: Or Success Under Difficulties,* The Houghton, Mifflin Co., 1894

MARTIN, FREDERICK TOWNSEND: *The Passing of the Idle Rich,* Doubleday, Page & Co., 1912

MASON, ALPHEUS THOMAS: *Brandeis: A Free Man's Life,* Viking Press, 1946. *Brandeis: Lawyer & Judge in the Modern State,* Princeton University Press, 1933. *The Brandeis Way,* Princeton University Press, 1938

MATTHIESSEN, F. O.: *Henry James: The Major Phase,* Oxford University Press, 1944

MAVITY, NANCY BARR: *Sister Aimee,* Doubleday, Doran & Co., 1931

MERZ, CHARLES: *The Dry Decade,* Doubleday, Doran, 1931

MENCKEN, H. L.: *The American Language,* Alfred A. Knopf, 1936. *Heathen Days: 1890–1936,* Alfred A. Knopf, 1943. *Prejudices* (Series 1–6), Alfred A. Knopf, 1919–27

MILLER, HENRY WISE: *All of Our Lives,* Coward, McCann, 1945

MILMINE, GEORGINE: *The Life of Mary Baker G. Eddy and the History of Christian Science,* Doubleday, Page & Co., 1909
This book, withdrawn from circulation, was founded on articles by the same author in McClure's Magazine—Vol 28–29 (1907) and Vol 30 (1908); in which form it was consulted by the present writer.

MOSES, MONTROSE J., AND GERSON, VIRGINIA: *Clyde Fitch and His Letters,* Little, Brown & Co., 1924

MYERS, GUSTAVUS: *History of the Great American Fortunes,* Charles H. Kerr & Co., 1910

National Committee for the Celebration of the Seventieth Birthday of John Dewey: *John Dewey: The Man and His Philosophy,* Harvard University Press, 1930

O'CONNOR, HARVEY: *The Astors,* Alfred A. Knopf, 1941

ODETS, CLIFFORD: *Golden Boy*, Random House, 1937. *Night Music*, Random House, 1940. *Paradise Lost*, Random House, 1936. *Rocket to the Moon*, Random House, 1939. *Three plays*: *Awake and Sing, Waiting For Lefty*, and *Till the Day I Die*, Covici-Friede, 1935

OGDEN, ROLLO: *Life & Letters of E. L. Godkin*, The Macmillan Co., 1907

OLDER, MRS. FREMONT: *William Randolph Hearst, American* (with a foreword by Fremont Older), D. Appleton-Century Co., 1936

O'NEILL, EUGENE: *Ah, Wilderness!*, Random House, 1933. *Desire Under the Elms; The Hairy Ape; Welded*, Boni and Liveright, 1925. *Dynamo*, Horace Liveright, 1927. *The Great God Brown, The Fountain, The Moon of the Caribbees, and Other Plays*, Boni and Liveright, Inc., 1926. *Marco Millions*, Boni and Liveright, Inc., 1927. *Mourning Becomes Electra: A Trilogy*, Horace Liveright, Inc., 1931. *Strange Interlude*, Boni and Liveright, 1928

O'NEILL, EUGENE
See also under
Clark, Barrett H.

PAINE, ALBERT BIGELOW: *Mark Twain: A Biography* (3 vols), Harper & Bros., 1912

PARRINGTON, VERNON D.: *Main Currents in American Thought*, Harcourt, Brace & Co., 1930

PASLEY, FRED D.: *Al Capone: The Biography of a Self-Made Man*, Ives-Washburn, 1930

PATTERSON, JOSEPH MEDILL: *A Little Brother of the Rich*, The Reilly and Britton Co., 1908

PERRY, RALPH BARTON: *The Thought and Character of William James* (2 vols), Little, Brown & Co., 1935

PORTER, WILLIAM SYDNEY
See under Henry, O.

PRINGLE, HENRY F.: *Theodore Roosevelt*, Harcourt, Brace & Co., 1931

PUTNAM, EMILY JAMES: *The Lady*, Sturgis and Walton, 1010

QUINN, ARTHUR HOBSON: *A History of the American Drama from the Civil War to the Present Day*, F. S. Crofts & Co., 1937

RAPIN, RENÉ: *Willa S. Cather*, Robert M. McBride, 1930

RASCOE, BURTON: *Before I Forget*, Doubleday, Doran Co., 1937

RICHARDS, LAURA E. AND ELLIOTT, MAUD HOWE: *Julia Ward Howe: 1819–1910*, Houghton, Mifflin Co., 1915

RILEY, WOODBRIDGE: *American Thought from Puritanism to Pragmatism*, Henry Holt & Co., 1915

ROOSEVELT, ELEANOR: *This Is My Story*, Harper & Bros., 1937

ROOSEVELT, THEODORE: *Autobiography*, The Macmillan Co., 1913. *Selections From the Correspondence of Theodore Roosevelt and Henry Cabot Lodge*, Charles Scribner's Sons, 1925

ROOT, GRACE: *Women and Repeal: the Story of the Women's Organization for National Prohibition Reform*, Harper & Bros., 1934

RUSSELL, CHARLES EDWARD: *Bare Hands and Stone Walls*, Charles Scribner's Sons, 1933. *The Greatest Trust in the World*, B. W. Dodge & Co., 1908. *Lawless Wealth*, B. W. Dodge & Co., 1908

SAINT GAUDENS, AUGUSTUS: *The Reminiscences of Augustus Saint Gaudens* (edited and amplified by Homer Saint Gaudens) (2 vols), Century Co., 1913

SANGER, MARGARET: *An Autobiography*, W. W. Norton & Co., 1938. *My Fight for Birth Control*, Farrar & Rinehart, 1931

SANTAYANA, GEORGE: *Character and Opinion in the United States: With Reminiscences of William James and Josiah Royce and Academic Life in America*, Charles Scribner's Sons, 1920. *The Genteel Tradition at Bay*, Charles Scribner's Sons, 1931. *The Last Puritan: A Memoir in the Form of a Novel*, Charles Scribner's Sons, 1936. *The Life of Reason* (5 vols), Charles Scribner's Sons, 1905. *The*

Middle Span, Charles Scribner's Sons, 1945. *Persons and Places: The Background of My Life,* Charles Scribner's Sons, 1944

SEITZ, DON C.: *Joseph Pulitzer: His Life and Letters,* Simon & Schuster, 1924

SEDGWICK, ELLERY: *The Happy Profession,* Little, Brown & Co., 1946

SELDES, GEORGE: *Freedom of the Press,* The Bobbs-Merrill Co., 1935. *Lords of the Press,* Julian Messner, Inc., 1938

SINCLAIR, UPTON: *The Jungle,* Doubleday, Page & Co., 1906

SLOSSON, PRESTON W.: *The Great Crusade and After: 1914–28,* The Macmillan Co., 1930

SMITH, C. ALPHONSO: *O. Henry Biography,* Doubleday, Page & Co., 1916

SMYTH, HENRY D.: *Atomic Energy for Military Purposes,* Princeton University Press, 1945

STARR, HARRIS E.: *William Graham Sumner,* Henry Holt & Co., 1925

STEFFENS, LINCOLN: *The Autobiography of Lincoln Steffens* (2 vols), Harcourt, Brace & Co., 1931. *Letters* (edited with an introduction and notes by Ella Winter and Granville Hicks, with a memorandum by Carl Sandburg), Harcourt, Brace & Co., 1938. *Lincoln Steffens Speaking,* Harcourt, Brace & Co., 1936. *The Shame of the Cities,* McClure, Phillips & Co., 1904. *The Struggle for Self-Government,* McClure, Phillips & Co., 1906

STEINBECK, JOHN: *The Grapes of Wrath,* Viking Press, 1939. *In Dubious Battle,* Covici-Friede, 1936. *Of Mice and Men,* Covici-Friede, 1937

STEINER, LEE R.: *Where Do People Take Their Troubles?,* Houghton, Mifflin Co., 1945

STONE, IRVING: *Clarence Darrow for the Defence,* Doubleday, Doran, 1941. *Sailor on Horseback: The Biography of Jack London,* Houghton, Mifflin Co., 1938

SULLIVAN, MARK: *The Education of an American,* Doubleday, D ran & Co., 1938. *Our Times: The United States 1900–1925,* Charles Scribner's Sons, 1926–35

SUMNER, WILLIAM GRAHAM: *The Challenge of Facts and Other Essays* (edited by A. G. Keller), Yale University Press, 1914. *Earth Hunger and Other Essays* (edited by A. G. Keller), Yale University Press, 1913. *Folkways: A Study of the Sociological Importance of Usages, Manners, Customs, Mores and Morals,* Ginn & Co., 1906. *What Social Classes Owe to Each Other,* Harper & Bros., 1883

SUMNER, WILLIAM GRAHAM AND KELLER, ALBERT GALLOWAY: *The Science of Society* (2 vols), Yale University Press, 1927

SUMNER, WILLIAM GRAHAM
See also under
Keller, Albert Galloway
Starr, Harris E.

SYMONS, ARTHUR: (translator), *The Letters of Baudelaire,* Albert & Charles Boni, 1927

TARBELL, IDA M.: *All in the Day's Work,* The Macmillan Co., 1939. *The History of Standard Oil* (2 vols), McClure, Phillips & Co., 1904

THAYER, WILLIAM ROSCOE: *The Life and Letters of John Hay* (2 vols), Houghton, Mifflin Co., 1915

THOMPSON, CRAIG AND RAYMOND, ALLEN: *Gang Rule in New York,* The Dial Press, 1940

TRINE, RALPH WALDO: *In Tune With the Infinite: or Fullness of Peace, Power and Plenty,* Thomas Y. Crowell, 1897

TWAIN, MARK: *Captain Stormfield's Visit to Heaven,* Harper & Bros., 1907. *Christian Science,* Harper & Bros., 1907. *Following the Equator,* American Publishing Co., 1897. *How to Tell a Story, and Other Essays,* Harper & Bros., 1897. *Personal Recollections of Joan of Arc* (2 vols), Harper & Bros., 1899. *Mark Twain, Business Man* (edited by Samuel Charles Webster), Little, Brown & Co., 1946. *Mark Twain in Eruption* (edited and with an introduction by Bernard De Voto), Harper & Bros., 1940. *Mark Twain's Letters* (Arranged with Comment by Albert Bigelow Paine) (2 vols), Harper & Bros., 1917. *Mark Twain's Notebook*: (Prepared for Publication with Comment by Albert Bigelow Paine), Harper & Bros., 1935. *The Autobiography of Mark Twain* (With an Introduction by Albert Bigelow Paine) (2 vols), Harper & Bros., 1924. *The Man That Corrupted Hadleyburg, and Other Stories and Essays*, Harper & Bros., 1900. *The Mysterious Stranger*, Harper & Bros., 1922. *The $30,000 Bequest and Other Stories*, Harper & Bros., 1906. *What Is Man?, and Other Essays*, Harper & Bros., 1917

TWAIN, MARK
See also under
    Brooks, Van Wyck
    Clemens, Clara
    Clemens, Cyril
    De Voto, Bernard
    Lawton, Mary
    Paine, Albert Bigelow

VAN DOREN, CARL AND TAYLOR, HARVEY: *Sinclair Lewis: A Biographical Sketch*, Doubleday, Doran & Co., Inc., 1933

VAN DRUTEN, JOHN, AND MORRIS, LLOYD: *The Damask Cheek*, Random House, 1943

VAN DRUTEN, JOHN: *I Remember Mama*, Harcourt, Brace and Co., 1945. *Old Acquaintance*, Random House, 1941. *There's Always Juliet*, Samuel French, 1932. *The Voice of the Turtle*, Random House, 1944

VAN RENSSELAER, MRS. JOHN KING: *Newport, Our Social Capital*, J. B. Lippincott Co., 1905.

VAN RENSSELAER, MRS. JOHN KING, AND VAN DE WATER, FREDERICK F.: *The Social Ladder*, Henry Holt & Co., 1924

VEBLEN, THORSTEIN: *Absentee Ownership and Business Enterprise in Recent Times: The Case of America*, B. W. Huebsch, Inc., 1923. *The En-gineers and the Price System*, The Viking Press, 1933. *Essays in Our Changing Order* (edited by Leon Ardzrooni), The Viking Press, 1934. *The Place of Science in Modern Civilization and Other Essays*, B. W. Huebsch, 1919. *The Theory of Business Enterprise*, Charles Scribner's Sons, 1915. *The Theory of the Leisure Class*, The Macmillan Co., 1899

VEBLEN, THORSTEIN
See also under
    Dorfman, Joseph

VILLARD, OSWALD GARRISON: *Fighting Years*, Harcourt, Brace & Co., 1939. *Prophets True and False*, Alfred A. Knopf, 1928

WALD, LILLIAN D.: *The House on Henry Street*, Henry Holt & Co., 1913

WEBSTER, SAMUEL CHARLES: *Mark Twain, Business Man*, Little, Brown & Co., 1946

WECTER, DIXON: *The Saga of American Society*, Charles Scribner's Sons, 1937

WELLS, H. G.: *The Future in America*, Harper & Bros., 1906

WEST, JAMES: *Plainville, U.S.A.*, Columbia University Press, 1945

WEST, REBECCA: *Henry James*, Henry Holt & Co., 1916

WHARTON, EDITH: *A Backward Glance*, Appleton-Century Co., 1934. *The Custom of the Country*, Charles Scribner's Sons, 1913. *The Decoration of Houses*, Charles Scribner's Sons, 1897. *The House of Mirth*, Charles Scribner's Sons, 1905

WHITE, WILLIAM ALLEN: *The Autobiography of William Allen White*, The Macmillan Co., 1946. *A Certain Rich Man*, The Macmillan Co., 1909. *The Changing West*, The Macmillan Co., 1939. *In Our Town*, The Macmillan Co., 1906. *In the Heart of a Fool*, The Macmillan Co., 1918. *Masks In a Pageant*, The Macmillan Co., 1928. *The Old Order Changeth*, The Macmillan Co., 1910. *A Puritan in Babylon*, The Macmillan Co., 1938

WHITE, WILLIAM ALLEN
See also under
  Clough, Frank C.
  Hinshaw, David
WHITLOCK, BRAND: *Forty Years of It*, D. Appleton & Co., 1914. *Letters and Journal* (edited with a biographical introduction by Allan Nevins; with an introduction by Newton D. Baker), D. Appleton-Century Co., 1936
WILBUR, SYBIL: *The Life of Mary Baker Eddy*, Concord Publishing Co., 1908
WILLEBRANDT, MABEL WALKER: *The Inside of Prohibition*, The Bobbs-Merrill Co., 1929

WINKLER, JOHN K.: *William Randolph Hearst: An American Phenomenon*, Simon and Schuster, 1928
WISH, HARVEY: *Contemporary America: The National Scene Since 1900*, Harper & Bros., 1945
"Women at Work." *New York Career Tours: 1939* (articles by Ida M. Tarbell, Dorothy Canfield Fisher, Inez Haynes Irwin, Mary R. Beard, Margaret Culkin Banning)
WOOD, MARY I.: *The History of the General Federation of Women's Clubs*. Historical Dept., General Federation of Women's Clubs, 1912
WYLIE, PHILIP: *Generation of Vipers*, Farrar and Rinehart, 1944

INDEX

Acres of Diamonds, 126

Adams, Brooks, 7, 30, 50, 177, 342, 379, 380, 383, 388, 394–399, 400, 401, 421

Adams, Charles Francis, 379–384, 393, 421

Adams, Evangeline, 440–442

Adams, Franklin P., 185

Adams, Henry, xxiii, xxiv, 7, 22, 23, 25, 52, 99, 237, 255, 292, 324, 342, 379–381, 383–401, 403, 404, 409, 421

Adams, Mrs. Henry (*see* Hooper, Marian)

Adams, John, 382

Adams, Maude, xxi, 172, 175

Adams, Samuel Hopkins, 303

Addams, Jane, 34, 36–42, 44, 46, 47, 49, 56, 59, 113, 124, 127, 162, 253, 272, 423, 428, 431

After Many a Summer Dies the Swan, 245

Agassiz, Alexander, 324, 330, 332

Ainslee's Magazine, 112

Alcott, Bronson, 38, 429, 430

Alcott, Louisa May, 276

Aldrich, Nelson B., 303, 304

Alger, Horatio, 99, 117, 268

Allen, Viola, 172

Altgeld, John Peter, 162, 240

Amalgamated Copper Co., 295

American Academy of Arts and Letters, 130

American Institute of Architecture, 27

American Mercury, The, 142, 143

American Journal of Folklore, 30

American Magazine, The, 291, 293

American Way, The, 187

Anderson, Maxwell, 189, 195–199

Anderson, Sherwood, 145–148

Animal Kingdom, The, 207

Anna Christie, 181

Anthony, Susan B., 27, 28, 272

Appeal to Reason, 302

Archbold, John D., 241, 286

Armour, Jonathan Ogden, 301, 302

Arnold, Thurman W., 166, 421

Astor, William, 4

Astor, Mrs. William, 11–13, 19, 27, 29, 31, 66, 67, 71

Atherton, Gertrude, 69

Atlantic Monthly, The, 84, 106, 281

Austin, Mary, 115

Awake and Sing, 201–203

Babbitt, Irving, 137

Baer, George, 41

Baker, George F., xvi

Baker, George Pierce, 178, 190, 206, 209

Baker, Ray Stannard, 7, 107, 265, 280, 282, 283, 284, 290, 291, 293, 301, 302, 305

Bancroft, George, 5

Bangs, John Kendrick, 276

Banning, Margaret Culkin, 51

Barnum, Gertrude, 39

Barnum, Phineas Taylor, xx, 294

Barrett, Lawrence, xxi
Barrie, James M., xxiii
Barry, Philip, 205–209
Barrymore, Ethel, 173
Barrymore, John, 96
Barton, Bruce, 70
Beard, Charles A., 50, 255, 259, 421
Beard, Mary R., 51
Beast, The, 307
Beggar on Horseback, 187, 189
Behold the Bridegroom, 195
Behrman, Samuel Nathaniel, 205, 206, 208, 209, 210, 211
Belasco, David, 76
Belmont, Mrs. August, 4, 5, 15, 16
Belmont, Mrs. O. H. P., 27, 28
Bennett, Arnold, 64, 65
Berenson, Bernhard, 25
Berkman, Alexander, 46
Bernhardt, Sarah, 271
Beyond the Horizon, 181
Bierce, Ambrose, 233
Bigelow, Sturgis, 23
Bingham, Amelia, 173
Biography, 210
Black Oxen, 69
Blatch, Harriott Stanton, 27
Bloodgood, Clara, 173
Bok, Edward, xviii, 267–278, 279, 310
Booth, Edwin, xxi
Borah, William E., 242
Boston Cooking School Cook Book, The, xxiii
Boston Woman's Rescue League, xviii
Both Your Houses, 199
Bourget, Paul, 8
Brady, James Buchanan ("Diamond Jim"), 19, 297, 298
Brandeis, Louis Dembitz, 350, 356–368, 369, 371
Bread-Winners, The, 390
Brisbane, Albert, 236
Brisbane, Arthur, 220, 236, 237
Broun, Heywood, 185
Bryan, William Jennings, xxiii, 6, 35, 158, 224, 237, 239, 253, 254, 439
Bulwark, The, 129
Burnett, Frances Hodgson, xxiii
Burns, Lucy, 27
Butterfield, Roger, 318

Byrd, Richard, 249
Byrnes, Thomas F., 288

Cabell, James Branch, 136
Caldwell, Erskine, 159, 160
Calvé, Emma, xxi
Calkins, Earnest Elmo, 137
Cameron, James Donald, 392, 393
Canfield, Dorothy, 48
Capone, Al, 65, 66, 67, 298
Carnegie, Andrew, xvi, xxv, 46, 99, 101, 119, 280, 292, 390
Carter, Hodding, 158
Castellane, Comte Boni de, xix
Castle, Irene, 272
Castle, Vernon, 272
Cather, Willa, 130–133
Catt, Carrie Chapman, 50
Century, The, 108
Chamberlain, John, 165
Chaplin, Charles, xxv
Chattanooga Times, The, 247
Chesterton, Gilbert K., 332
Chicago American, The, 300
Chicago Tribune, The, 262, 263, 264
Citizen Kane, 245
Clark, William Andrews, 100
Clemens, Samuel L. (Mark Twain), 98–101, 103, 105, 109, 129, 138, 209, 233, 237, 253, 276, 286, 426, 428
Cleveland, Grover, xviii, 223, 285
Clews, Henry, 30
Cohn, Fannia M., 43, 49
Collier's Weekly, 20, 242
Common Law, The, 340
Commons, John R., 35
Comstock, Anthony, 54
Comstock Lode, 6, 231
Congressional Record, 249
Conrad, Joseph, 111
Conwell, Russell Herman, 126, 128
Coolidge, Calvin, 70, 138, 154, 243
Cosgrave, John O'Hara, 295
Cosmopolitan, The, 32
Coughlin, Charles (Father), 243
Count of Monte Cristo, The, xxi, 177, 178
Cowley, Malcolm, 162
Craig, Gordon, 59, 60
Craig's Wife, 193, 194
Crane, Stephen, xxii, 54, 107–110, 233

Crane, Walter, 16
Crawford, F. Marion, 276
Creelman, James, 238
Croker, Richard, 288
Cromwell, William Nelson, 223
Croly, Herbert, 136
Crothers, Rachel, 205
Cummings, E. E., 68
Curtis, Cyrus H. K., 276
Czolgosz, Leon, 46

Daily Mirror, The, 259
Daisy Mayme, 195
Damask Cheek, The, 212
Damnation of Theron Ware, The,
    xxiii
Damrosch, Walter, 57
Darrow, Clarence, 41, 43, 158, 162, 163,
    240, 241
Davenport, Homer, 233, 237
David Harum, 280
Davidson, Thomas, 219
Davis, "Dixie," 77, 79, 80
Davis, Elmer, 248, 250
Davis, Richard Harding, 238
Debs, Eugene V., 35, 119
Decker, Sarah Platt, 33
Democracy, 390
Desire Under the Elms, 183
Deuel, Joseph M., 20
Dewey, John, 41, 266, 369–378
Dewey, Thomas E., 74
De Wolfe, Elsie (Lady Mendl), 21, 22,
    173
Diamond, "Legs," 78
Dickinson, Emily, 109
Diggs, Anna L., 43
Dinner at Eight, 188
Dockstader, Lew, xxi
Donnelly, Ignatius, 254
"Mr. Dooley" (*see* Dunne, Finley
    Peter)
Dorgan, T. A., 233
Dorr, Rheta Childe, 33, 34
Dos Passos, John, 68
Dreiser, Paul (Paul Dresser), 121–123
Dreiser, Theodore, 54, 108, 121–131,
    226, 266
Dresser, Julius A., 432
Dresser, Paul (*see* Dreiser, Paul)
Drew, Daniel, 296

Drew, John, xxi, 172
Drexel, Mrs. John, 16
van Druten, John, 205, 206, 212, 213
Dulcy, 187
Duncan, Isadora, 14, 57–63
Dunne, Finley Peter ("Mr. Dooley"),
    285, 292, 293, 323
Duran, Carolus, 13
Duranty, Walter, 250
Durham, Israel W., 285
"Dutch Schultz" (*see* Flegenheimer,
    Arthur)

Eames, Emma, xxi
*Economic Interpretation of the Consti-
    tution, An,* 255
Eddy, Mary Baker, 337, 423–431, 432,
    434
Edison, Thomas A., xx
*Edward Bok Books of Self-Knowledge,
    The,* 274
Einstein, Albert, 445, 449
Einstein, Izzy, 70, 71
Eliot, Charles W., 70, 403
Elliott, Maxine, xxi, 21, 172
Elmer Gantry, 439
Ely, Richard T., 35
Emerson, Ralph Waldo, 38, 201, 253,
    328, 342, 429, 443, 449
Emperor Jones, The, 181
Emporia Gazette, The, 252–259
Enormous Room, The, 68
Equitable Life Assurance Society, 17,
    222
Erskine, John, 52, 53, 262
Essenine, Sergei Alexandreivitch, 61, 62
Evans, "Honeyboy," xxi
Everybody's, 293, 295, 296

*Fads and Fancies of Representative
    Americans,* 19
Fair, James Graham, 6, 231
Fallon, William J., 76, 77
Farley, James A., 80
Farmer, Fannie Merritt, xxiii
Farrell, James T., 162–166, 204, 292
Faulkner, William, 160–162
Fay, Larry, 72, 74, 83
Faversham, William, xxi, 172
Fels, Joseph W., 262
Ferber, Edna, 184, 188

Field, Eugene, 276
Field, Marshall, 72
Filene, Edward A., 262
Financier, The, 127
Fish, Stuyvesant, 13
Fish, Mrs. Stuyvesant, 16, 18, 19, 21, 71, 73
Fisher, Bud, 233
Fisk, James, 65, 383
Fiske, John, 324
Fitch, Clyde, 30, 172–177, 182
Fitzgerald, F. Scott, 30, 56, 68, 149–153
Flegenheimer, Arthur ("Dutch Schultz"), 64–83, 298
Fletcher, Horace, 335
Flexner, Eleanor, 205
Flynn, Edward J., 77
Flynn, Elizabeth Gurley, 44
Flynt, Josiah, 306, 307
Folk, Joseph W., 287, 308
Folkways, 402, 410, 411, 416
Ford, Henry, xx, 36, 134, 136, 147, 229, 244, 448
Forbes, Kathryn, 213
Fortune, 310, 313, 315, 316
Frankfurter, Felix, 353, 364
Frederic, Harold, xxiii
Frenzied Finance, 293
Freud, Sigmund, 128, 192, 334
Frohman, Charles, 173
Fuller, Henry B., 106
Fuller, Margaret, 23, 45

Gardner, Mrs. John L., 22–25
Garfield, James A., 390
Garfield, James R., 300
Garland, Hamlin, 107, 109, 254
Garnett, Edward, 107
Geisha, The, xv
General Federation of Women's Clubs, 32, 33, 276
Generation of Vipers, 53
George, Henry, 233, 262
Gershwin, George, 69, 187
Ghost of Yankee Doodle, The, 191
Gibbs, Wolcott, 315
Gilder, Richard Watson, 108
Gillette, William, xxi
Gilman, Charlotte Perkins, 32
Girl With the Green Eyes, The, 173
Glaspell, Susan, 177

Glyn, Elinor, 97, 98, 434
Goddard, Morrill, 220, 236
Godkin, Edwin Lawrence, 238, 287
God's Little Acre, 160
Gods of the Lightening, 196, 197, 198
Goering, Herman, 243
Golden Bowl, The, 89
Golden Boy, 202, 204
Goldman, Emma, 44–47, 113
Gompers, Samuel, 43, 44
Goodwin, Nat, 173
Gorki, Maxim, 54
Gould, Jay, xix, 66, 67, 68, 100, 101, 128, 219, 296, 299, 383, 384
Grant, Ulysses S., 387, 388, 403
Grapes of Wrath, The, 169, 170
Great American Fraud, The, 303
Greatest Trust in the World, The, 300
Great God Brown, The, 181
Great God Success, The, 226
Guggenheim, Simon, 10
Guinan, Mary Louise Cecilia ("Texas" Guinan), 66, 71–74, 76, 83, 437

Harper's Magazine, 109
Harper's Weekly, 102
Hearst, George, 231, 232, 236, 237
Hearst, William Randolph, 110, 217, 218, 219, 220, 221, 224, 227–246, 300, 308
Held, Anna, 83
Hemingway, Ernest, 69, 154–156
Hendrick, Burton J., 299
Here Come the Clowns, 208
Hickerson, Harold, 197
High Tor, 199
Hines, James J., 66, 77, 79, 80, 81, 83
History of the Great American Fortunes, 299
Hitler, Adolf, 243
Hackett, James K., xxi
Hadden, Briton, 313
Hale, Edward Everett, 4
Hanna, Mark, 253, 254, 262
Harding, Warren G., 68, 70, 75
Harland, Marion, 51
Harriman, Mrs. Borden, 29, 30, 51
Harriman, Edward Henry, 222, 223, 304
Harriman, Mary, 28
Harrison, Benjamin, 276

Harrison, Mrs. Burton, 55, 276
Harvard Lampoon, The, 232
Harvey, Colonel George, 102
Hay, John, 387, 389, 390, 392, 393, 394
Hays, Will H., 66
Hazard of New Fortunes, A, 279
Hofmann, Josef, 277
Holiday, 207
Holmes, Oliver Wendell, Jr., 23, 324, 339–356, 363, 365, 366, 369, 370, 371, 379, 382, 393, 401
Hooper, Marian ("Clover") (Mrs. Henry Adams), 388, 390, 391, 392
Hoover, Herbert, 53, 70, 187, 372
Hoover, J. Edgar, 84
Hope, Anthony, 276
Hotel Universe, 207, 208
House of Mirth, The, 10, 54
Howard, Sidney, 189–192, 195
Howe, Frederick C., 265
Howe, Julia Ward, 3, 4, 5, 6, 13, 28, 66, 272, 423
Howe, Samuel Gridley, 4
Howells, William Dean, xv, xxiv, xxv, 52, 54, 90, 101–107, 109, 127, 134, 175, 208, 237, 271, 276, 279, 324, 416
Hubbard, Elbert, 108
Hughes, Charles Evans, 17, 222, 223, 241, 299, 362
Huneker, James, 175, 176
Hunt, Richard Morris, 5, 11, 21, 27, 28
Hunt, William Morris, 324
Hunter, Robert, 308
Huntington, Collis P., 235
Huxley, Aldous, 245
Hyde, James Hazen, 17, 18
Hylan, John F., 243

Ibsen, Henrik, 306
Independent, The, 263
Influence of Women and Its Cure, The, 52
Ireland, Alleyne, 225
I Remember Mama, 213
Iron Heel, The, 118
Irwin, Inez Haynes, 50
Irwin, Will, 240

James, Alice, 325, 332
James, Henry, xxiv, 5, 6, 11, 14, 15, 23, 30, 38, 45, 52, 58, 89–96, 103, 105, 106, 107, 127, 143, 151, 204, 208, 209, 210, 260, 269, 292, 293, 323, 324, 331, 332, 388
James, William, 22, 23, 41, 90, 114, 219, 237, 321–339, 342, 360, 371, 411, 423
Jefferson, Joseph, xxi
Jennings, Al, 111, 112, 114
Jewett, Sarah Orne, 130
Johnson, Hiram, 308
Johnson, Tom L., 262
Jones, Howard Mumford, 130
Jones, Mary Harris ("Mother" Jones), 29, 42, 43, 44
Jones, Mrs. Pembroke, 16
Journal of Arthur Stirling, The, 302
Joyous Season, The, 207
Jung, Carl, 334
Jungle, The, 302
Jurgen, 136

Kardiner, Abram, xxv
Kaufman, George S., 185–189
Kavanaugh, Mrs. George Washington, 83
Kelcey, Herbert, 172
Kelley, Florence, 39, 49
Kelly, Florence Finch, 48
Kelly, George, 189, 192–195
Kelly, Walter, 192
Kentons, The, 105
Kildare, Owen, 306
King, Clarence, 389, 392
Kipling, Rudyard, 233, 271, 273, 276, 280
Krutch, Joseph Wood, 186, 205
Ku Klux Klan, 137, 158

Ladies' Home Journal, The, xviii, 267–278
Lady of Quality, A, xxiii
La Farge, John, 324, 386, 391
La Follette, Robert M., 254, 308
Landis, Kenesaw Mountain, 66
Lane, Gertrude, 273
Langley, Samuel P., xx
Langtry, Lily, 173
Lardner, Ringgold Wilmer (Ring), 152
Lathrop, Julia C., 39
Law of Civilization and Decay, The 395

Lawrence, D. H., 69
Lawson, Thomas W., 293, 294, 295, 296, 297, 299
Learned, Mrs. Frank, 55
Lease, Mary E., 43, 109, 254
Lehr, Harry, 18, 19
Lerner, Max, 367
Lewis, Austin, 120
Lewis, Sinclair, 73, 95, 105, 134–142, 144, 156, 187, 265, 439
Life, 84, 144, 266, 310, 314, 315, 316, 317
Lilienthal, Otto, xxi
Lindsay, Vachel, 39
Lindsey, Ben B., 56, 307, 308
Lippmann, Walter, 136, 148, 265
Lipton, Sir Thomas, 294
Literary Digest, The, 136, 311
Little Brother of the Rich, A, 263, 264
Living Age, 311
Lodge, Henry Cabot, 308, 340, 388, 389, 393, 394
Long, Huey P., 159
"Lohengrin" (*see* Singer, Paris)
London, Jack, 108, 115–121, 135, 233, 265
Longworth, Alice Roosevelt, 29
Lorimer, William E., 300
Lowell, James Russell, 23, 380
Lowell, Josephine, 39
Luce, Henry R., 310, 313, 315, 316
Lucky Sam McCarver, 191
Lynd, Helen Merrell, xxv
Lynd, Robert S., xxv

McAllister, Ward, 13, 21
McClure, Samuel Sidney, 48, 130, 239, 278–286, 287, 290, 291, 293, 299, 310, 311, 315
McClure's Magazine, 107, 108, 130, 262, 284, 288, 290, 306, 427
McCormick, Robert R., 262, 265
McFadden, Bernarr, 69
McKinley, William, xxiii, 46, 237, 238, 239, 253
McPherson, Aimee Semple, 434–439
MacMonnies, Frederick, 54
Madden, Owney, 78
Maggie: A Girl of the Streets, 54, 108
Main Street, 134–137
Mann, Col. William, 19, 20

Man Nobody Knows, The, 70
Mansfield, Richard, 173
Man Who Came to Dinner, The, 188
Marbury, Elisabeth, 21, 22
Marchesi, Blanche, 277
Marco Millions, 181
Marconi, Guglielmo, Marquis, 249
Marden, Orison Swett, 128, 433
Marx, Karl, 201, 203, 204, 354
Merington, Marguerite, 174
Marlowe, Julia, xxi, 173
Masters, Edgar Lee, 39
Matthews, Brander, 106
Martin, Mrs. Bradley, 16, 17
Maxwell, Elsa, 18
Meteor, 210
Medill, Joseph, 262
Melba, Nellie, xxi
Mellon, Andrew, 229
Mencken, Henry Louis, 137, 142, 143, 144, 314
Mendl, Lady (*see* De Wolfe, Elsie)
Merman, Ethel, 314
Merrily We Roll Along, 189
Middletown, xxv, 141
Middletown in Transition, xxv, 141
Millay, Edna St. Vincent, 69
Miller, Alice Duer, 31, 184
Miller, Henry, 172
Mills, Mrs. Ogden, 12
Mitchell, John, 34, 35, 240
Mitchell, Langdon, 30, 92
Modjeska, Helena, xxi, 173
"Monkey Trial," 158, 439
More, Paul Elmer, 137
Morgan, Anne, 28
Morgan, John Pierpont, 65, 67, 128, 218, 222, 223, 227, 288, 297, 298, 359, 360, 441
"Mother" Jones (*see* Jones, Mary Harris)
Mott, Lucretia, 27
Mourning Becomes Electra, 183
Munsterberg, Hugo, 334
Murphy, Charles F., 79, 222, 239
Murray, James E., 447
Mutual Life Insurance Co., 222
Myers, Francis John, 84
Myers, Gustavus, 299
My Mamie Rose, 306

Nathan, George Jean, 143
Nation, Carrie, 53
National Woman's Trade Union
    League, 49
Nicolay, John, 390
Niebuhr, Reinhold, 431, 442
Nestor, Agnes, 43, 49, 50
Nethersole, Olga, 54
New York American, The, 262
New York Daily News, The, 259–266
New York Journal, The, 217, 246
New York Life Insurance Co., 222
New York Post, The, 287
New York Times, The, 72, 73, 83, 198,
    246–251, 259, 260, 265, 357
New York World, The, 195, 217–227,
    232, 246, 262, 299, 304, 425, 426
Nichols, Charles Wilbur de Lyon, 12
Niesen, Gertrude, 6
Night Music, 202, 204
Nordica, Lillian, xxi
Norris, George W., 242, 243
Norris, Frank, 108, 125
North American Revue, The, 102, 388
Northcliffe, Alfred Charles William
    Harmsworth, Lord, 259
Norton, Charles Eliot, 25, 54, 212
No Time For Comedy, 211

Ochs, Adolph S., 246–251
Odets, Clifford, 200–204, 206
Oelrichs, Tessie, 6
Of Thee I Sing, 187
O. Henry (*see* Porter, William Sydney)
Old Acquaintance, 212
Old Order Changeth, The, 255
O'Neill, Eugene, 177–183
O'Neill, James, xxi, 177, 178
One of Ours, 132
Owen, Russell, 159

Paget, Sir Almeric, xix
Paderewski, Ignace, xxi, 21, 23
Pankhurst, Christabel, 27
Paradise Lost, 202
Parkhurst, Charles H., 109, 288
Paris Bound, 207
Parker, Henry Taylor, 206
Parrington, Vernon L., 262
Parsons, Elsie Clews, 30
Patterson, Eleanor, 262

Patterson, Joseph Medill, 259–266
Patton, Simon N., 35, 41
Paul, Alice, 27
Peary, Admiral Robert Edwin, 249
Peirce, Charles S., 324, 342
Perkins, Frances, 51
Perkins, George W., 222
Perry, Matthew Calbraith, 4
Perry, Oliver Hazard, 4
Phelps, Elizabeth Stuart, xxiii, 440
Phelps, William Lyon, 173
Phillips, David Graham, 226, 304
Phillips, John S., 280, 291, 305
Piper, Mrs. William J., 333
Political Equality League, 27
Pollock, Sir Frederick, 350, 353
Porter, William Sydney (O. Henry),
    111–115, 128
Pound, Ezra, 154
Poverty, 308
Powers That Prey, The, 306
Pragmatism, 411
Pratt, Fletcher, 317
Preston, Harriet Waters, 106
Progress and Poverty, 262
Puck of Pook's Hill, 276
Pulitzer, Joseph, 217–227, 232, 233, 234,
    237, 246, 299, 300, 425
Putnam, Emily James, 49

Queen of Sin, The, 69
Quimby, Phineas Parkhurst, 432

Rain From Heaven, 211
Rascoe, Burton, 261, 262
Red Badge of Courage, The, xxii, 110
Reader's Digest, The, 266, 310–314
Reed, John, 114
Reszke, Jean de, xxi
Rehan, Ada, xxi
Réjane, Gabrielle, 17
Remington, Frederick, 238
Richardson, Henry Hobson, 392
Riley, James Whitcomb, 276
Rip Van Winkle, xxi
Robin Hood, xv
Robinson, Douglas, 223
Robinson, James Harvey, 421
Rockefeller, John D., xvi, 78, 99, 101,
    128, 280, 286, 287
Rocket to the Moon, 202

Rogers, Henry H., 101, 286, 287, 295
Rohde, Ruth Bryan, 51
Roosevelt, Eleanor, 28, 29, 51, 84
Roosevelt, Franklin Delano, 28, 30, 51, 79, 80, 157, 169, 199, 253, 254, 257, 264, 265, 308, 338, 342, 347, 367, 421
Roosevelt, Theodore, 17, 21, 29, 30, 35, 40, 55, 90, 100, 114, 127, 222, 223, 230, 237, 239, 241, 242, 249, 254, 256, 258, 274, 276, 282, 283, 284, 288, 292, 300, 302, 304, 308, 309, 338, 340, 341, 347, 353, 393
Rothstein, Arnold, 66, 67, 75, 76
Royce, Josiah, 23
Russell, Charles Edward, 233, 293, 299, 300, 301, 302, 304
Russell, Lillian, xvii, xviii, xxi, 19
Ryan, Thomas Fortune, 221, 223, 299

Sacco-Vanzetti Case, 158, 197, 198, 371
Saint Gaudens, Augustus, 387
St. Louis Post-Dispatch, The, 219, 226
San Francisco Examiner, The, 232, 235
Sanger, Margaret, 55
Santayana, George, 23, 24, 232, 322, 449
Sargent, John Singer, 25, 26, 176, 182
Saturday Evening Post, The, 136
Saturday Review of Literature, The, 84
Saturday's Children, 196
Schurz, Carl, 219
Schneiderman, Rose, 43, 49
Schwimmer, Rosika, 355
Science and Health, 426, 429, 430
Scopes, John Thomas, 158, 159
Scott, Clement, 174
Scott, Howard, 421
Scottsboro Trials, 158
Scudder, Vida D., 35
Second Man, The, 209, 210
Sedgwick, Ellery, 281
Seitz, Don C., 226
Seldes, George, 260, 264
Semple, Robert, 435
Sentimental Tommy, xxiii
Shame of the Cities, The, 287
Shannon, Effie, 172
Shaw, Anna Howard, 50, 272
Shaw, Leslie M., 309
Shearer, William B., 243
Sheen, Fulton J., 431
Sheppard, Morris, 53

Sherwood, Mrs. John, 55
Show-Off, The, 193
Silver Cord, The, 192
Simpson, Jerry ("Sockless Jerry"), 254
Sinclair, Upton, 135, 230, 233, 302, 303
Singer, Paris ("Lohengrin"), 60, 63
Singular Life, A, xxiii
Sister Carrie, 54, 125
Slosson, Edwin E., 309, 310
Smith, F. Hopkinson, xxiii
Smithsonian Institution, xx
Snyder, Ruth, 261
Social Destiny of Man, The, 236
Social Problems, 262
Soule, George, 136
Sousa, John Philip, xx
Stallings, Lawrence, 195
Standard Oil Company, 159, 241, 281, 284, 285, 286, 295, 296
Stanford, Leland, 231
Stanton, Elizabeth Cady, 27, 28
Starr, Ellen Gates, 39
Steffens, Lincoln, 236, 262, 280, 282, 283, 284, 285, 287, 288, 289, 290, 291, 293, 297, 298, 305
Stein, Gertrude, 154, 430
Steinbeck, John, 167–171, 204
Steiner, Mrs. Lee R., 443
Stevenson, Robert Louis, 279
Stillman, James, 66
Story of Life Insurance, The, 299
Stowe, Harriet Beecher, 440
Strange Interlude, 182
Strauss, Richard, 277
Struggle For Self-Government, 287
Studs Lonigan, 164
Sumner, William Graham, 41, 128, 231, 237, 401–414, 416, 417, 421, 441
Sun Also Rises, The, 69
Sunday, William A. (Billy), 137, 439

Taft, Charles P., 223
Taft, William Howard, 100, 224, 356
Talks Upon Practical Subjects, xviii
Tarbell, Ida M., 37, 38, 48, 50, 233, 280, 281, 282, 283, 284, 285, 287, 288, 290, 291, 293, 296
Taylor, Frederick W., 362
Taylor, William Ladd, 275
Terhune, Mrs. Marion Harland, xviii
Terry, Ellen, 59

"Texas" Guinan (*see* Guinan, Mary Louise Cecilia)
"Thanatopsis Literary and Inside Straight Club," 31, 184
Theory of the Leisure Class, The, 416
There's Always Juliet, 212
They Knew What They Wanted, 190
This Side of Paradise, 69, 150
Thompson, Dorothy, 51
Thompson, William Hale, 243
Three Soldiers, 68
Three Weeks, 98
Through The Eye of The Needle, 105
Tilden, Samuel J., 219
Time, 310, 313, 314, 315
Titan, The, 128
Tobacco Road, 159
Tolstoy, Leo, 37, 104, 306
Tom Grogan, xxiii
Tomorrow and Tomorrow, 207
Torchbearers, The, 192
To the Ladies, 187
Town Topics, 19, 20
Traveller From Altruria, A, 105
Trilling, Lionel, 205
Trine, Ralph Waldo, 433
Trotzky, Leon, 371
True Stories, 69
Twain, Mark (*see* Clemens, Samuel L.)

Untermyer, Samuel, 309

Valentino, Rudolph, 70
Vanderbilt, Consuelo, xix
Vanderbilt, Cornelius (Commodore), 66, 296
Vanderbilt, Mrs. Cornelius, 83
Vanderbilt, Frederick, 28
Vanderbilt, William H., 67
Van Rensselaer, Mrs. Schuyler, 24
Variety, 314
Veblen, Thorstein, 35, 414–421
Virginius, xxi
Voice of the Turtle, The, 212

Waiting for Lefty, 200
Wald, Lillian D., 39, 49
Wallace, DeWitt, 310, 311, 313
Ward, Samuel, 66

Washington Times-Herald, The, 262
Welles, Orson, 245
Wells, Herbert George, 54, 136
Wescott, Glenway, 150
Whalen, Grover, 70
Wharton, Edith, 9, 10, 14, 30, 54, 71, 126, 151, 212, 292, 305
Wharton, Edward, 9
What Price Glory?, 195
Whistler, James A. McN., 18
White, Stanford, 5, 17, 21, 274
White, William Allen, 252–259, 265, 278, 291, 292
Whitman, Mrs. Henry, 22
Whitney, Gertrude Vanderbilt, 30
Whitney, William C., xix, 221, 222, 299, 402, 404
Wiggin, James Henry, 430
Wilcox, Ella Wheeler, 32
Wilde, Oscar, 18
Willard, Frances E., 306
Willebrandt, Mabel Walker, 53
Willkie, Wendell L., 258
Wilson, Edmund, 155
Wilson, Woodrow, 29, 50, 68, 102, 136, 254, 257, 309, 338, 347, 356, 357, 401
Winesburg, Ohio, 145
Winterset, 198
Wish, Harvey, 222
Woman Rebel, The, 55
Woman's Home Companion, The, 273
Women Who Give, 69
Woollcott, Alexander, 18, 185, 188
World of Graft, The, 306
Wrecker, The, 279
Wright, Chauncey, 324, 342
Wright, Orville, xxi
Wright, Wilbur, xxi
Wylie, Philip, 53

Yale, Frankie, 67
Yellow Jack, 191
Yerkes, Charles T., 127, 128, 299
You Can't Take It With You, 187
You Have Seen Their Faces, 159

Ziegler, William, 285
Zorn, Andreas, 25

HARPER COLOPHON BOOKS

CN/1   **ART OF LOVING**
    Fromm $1.25
CN/2   **OUT OF OUR PAST**
    Degler $2.45
CN/3   **EXCELLENCE**
    Gardner $1.45
CN/5   **NEW POLITICS**
    Stillman & Pfaff $1.35
CN/6   **HISTORY OF ENGLAND**
    Woodward $1.35
CN/7   **DOORS OF PERCEPTION**
    Huxley $1.45
CN/8   **VIENNA TO VERSAILLES**
    Seaman $1.35
CN/10   **PROPER STUDY OF MANKIND**
    Chase $1.85
CN/11   **PROTRACTED CONFLICT**
    Strausz-Hupé $1.50
CN/12   **SPANISH CIVIL WAR**
    Thomas $2.95
CN/13   **SALINGER**
    Grunwald $1.75
CN/14   **FRENCH NATION**
    Brogan $1.85
CN/16   **VOICE OF LATIN AMERICA**
    Benton $1.60
CN/17   **STRUGGLE FOR EUROPE**
    Wilmot $2.95
CN/18   **AFRICAN WITCH**
    Cary $1.75
CN/21   **WESTERN PHILOSOPHERS**
    Tomlin $1.95
CN/22   **ORIENTAL PHILOSOPHERS**
    Tomlin $1.95
CN/23   **VICTORIAN PEOPLE**
    Briggs $1.85
CN/24   **VILLAGE IN VAUCLUSE**
    Wylie $2.25
CN/25   **INTERPRETATION OF MUSIC**
    Dart $1.35
CN/26   **GOD THAT FAILED**
    Crossman $1.60
CN/29   **DEMOCRATIC PROSPECT**
    Frankel $1.45
CN/30   **ENTERPRISING AMERICANS**
    Chamberlain $1.75
CN/31   **RETURN OF HYMAN KAPLAN**
    Rosten $1.35
CN/32   **AGES OF MAN**
    Rylands $1.95
CN/33   **ITALIAN ART, LIFE**
    Wall $1.75
CN/34   **MIND OF MAN**
    Bromberg $1.95
CN/35   **ORDEAL OF CHANGE**
    Hoffer $1.35
CN/36   **FREEDOM IN WESTERN WORLD**
    Muller $2.45
CN/37   **THE IMAGE**
    Boorstin $1.75
CN/38   **IMAGES OF TRUTH**
    Westcott $1.75
CN/39   **ERA OF EXCESS**
    Sinclair $2.45
CN/40   **ROOSEVELT I KNEW**
    Perkins $1.95
CN/41   **LONG XMAS DINNER**
    Wilder $.95
CN/42   **OUR TOWN**
    Wilder $.95
CN/43   **RELIGIONS OF MAN**
    Smith $1.95
CN/44   **SOC. STUDIES AMER. SCHOOLS**
    Mayer $1.45

CN/45   **DISSONANT VOICES IN SOV. LIT.**
    Blake & Hayward $1.95
CN/46   **MAN IN WHITE HOUSE**
    Binkley $1.75
CN/47   **PRINCESS CASAMASSIMA**
    James $1.95
CN/48   **ENORMOUS RADIO**
    Cheever $1.60
CN/49   **POLITICS OF HYSTERIA**
    Stillman & Pfaff $1.60
CN/50   **INTRO. TO MUSICAL HISTORY**
    Westrup $1.35
CN/51   **TALK IN VANDALIA**
    Lyford $1.25
CN/52   **ELIZABETHANS & AMERICA**
    Rowse $1.50
CN/53   **STAMMERING CENTURY**
    Seldes $2.45
CN/54   **SELF-RENEWAL**
    Gardner $1.35
CN/55   **SPANISH TEMPER**
    Pritchett $1.75
CN/56   **DIARY NORTH & SOUTH**
    Russell $1.75
CN/57   **MONEY TO GROW ON**
    Chase $1.35
CN/58   **CONGRESS**
    Clark $1.75
CN/59   **COPPER TOWN**
    Powdermaker $2.45
CN/60   **WHAT IS LITERATURE**
    Sartre $1.75
CN/61   **AMERICAN CITIES**
    Green $1.75
CN/62   **AMER. ENCOUNTERS JAPAN**
    Neumann $1.95
CN/63   **LANDMARKS OF TOMORROW**
    Drucker $1.75
CN/64   **SOUL OF CHINA**
    de Riencourt $1.75
CN/65   **THREE INTELLECTUALS**
    Joll $1.60
CN/66   **LITERATURE & WESTERN MAN**
    Priestley $2.75
CN/67   **MEANING OF 20th CENTURY**
    Boulding $1.45
CN/68   **GRASS ROOTS**
    Martin $1.25
CN/69   **LIFE OF LENIN**
    Fischer $2.95
CN/70   **GREENWICH VILLAGE**
    Ware $2.95
CN/71   **NOVEL IN RUSSIA**
    Gifford $1.45
CN/72   **POSTSCRIPT TO YESTERDAY**
    Morris $2.45
CN/73   **DEV. OF POLITICAL THEORY**
    Vereker $1.45
CN/74   **FUTURE OF AMER. POLITICS**
    Lubell $1.75
CN/75   **WHITE AND BLACK**
    Lubell $1.60
CN/76   **ANATOMY OF BRITAIN**
    Sampson $2.95
CN/77   **AMERICAN LEVIATHAN**
    Nichols $1.95
CN/78   **SPANISH TAPESTRY**
    Kenny $1.75
CN/79   **GRANT, LEE, LINCOLN**
    McWhiney $1.25
CN/80   **LOTUS AND ROBOT**
    Koestler $1.75

DATE DUE

APR 24 '69			
MAY 13			
GAYLORD			PRINTED IN U.S.A.